The Keys *to* *the* Kingdom

The Keys *to* the Kingdom

THE RISE OF MICHAEL EISNER AND THE FALL OF EVERYBODY ELSE

With a New Epilogue

Kim Masters

HarperBusiness
An Imprint of HarperCollinsPublishers

HarperCollins books may be purchased for educational, business, or sales promotional use. For information please write: Special Markets Department, HarperCollins Publishers Inc., 10 East 53rd Street, New York, NY 10022.

A hardcover edition of this book was published in 2000 by William Morrow. First HarperBusiness edition published in 2001.

Designed by Fritz Metsch

Library of Congress Cataloging-in-Publication Data

Masters, Kim.
    The keys to the kingdom : the rise of Michael Eisner and the fall of everybody else : with a new epilogue / Kim Masters.
        p. cm.
    Originally published: New York : W. Morrow, c2000.
    Includes bibliographical references and index.
    ISBN 0-06-662109-7
        1. Eisner, Michael, 1942- 2. Chief executive officers—United States—Biography. 3. Walt Disney Company—History. I. Title.

PN1998.3.E36 M37 2001
384'.8'092—dc21
[B]

2001024562

01 02 03 04 05 BP 10 9 8 7 6 5 4 3 2 1

For Delia

CONTENTS

The Keys *to* the Kingdom

PROLOGUE

O N   A   S U N N Y April afternoon, Michael Eisner emerged from the Team Disney building, passing beneath monumental statues of the seven dwarfs who appeared to be holding up the roof. He crossed the green, manicured studio campus. The Burbank lot where the Walt Disney Company had its headquarters often seemed to be an idyllic place, with a Mickey Mouse topiary and signs outside the soundstages playfully admonishing, "No lookie-loos!" But today there was turmoil in the Magic Kingdom. Eisner—Disney's tall, boyish-looking chairman and chief executive—was on his way to the equivalent of a state funeral. Nearly five thousand people had gathered to memorialize Frank Wells, the company's dashing president and chief operating officer. It seemed impossible to believe that Wells—so charming and full of life—was suddenly gone. But Eisner had gotten the shocking news on Easter Sunday: Wells had been killed in a helicopter crash while on a ski trip in the mountains of Nevada.

The overflow crowd packed a cavernous soundstage and a separate room where television monitors draped with black bunting were lined up to show the services. Joining Eisner on this solemn occasion was all the Disney brass. Roy Disney, Walt's nephew and the vice-chairman of the company, had flown in from his home in Ireland. The diminutive Jeffrey Katzenberg, Disney's studio chairman and Eisner's colleague for the better part of twenty years, was there, as were all the other division heads and general counsel Sanford Litvack.

Hollywood stardom was out in force. Warren Beatty, who had quarreled with Wells many years earlier over the making of *Heaven Can Wait*, arrived with his wife, Annette Bening. Gregory Peck, Steven Spielberg, and Quincy Jones were in the crowd. So was the suited power structure of the town: Michael Ovitz, the head of the formidable Creative Artists Agency, and his rival, Jeff Berg, the chilly top man at International Creative Management. The studio gentry was there in the form of MCA chairman Lew Wasserman, Hollywood's aging "godfather," and his number-two man, Sid Sheinberg. Music mogul David Geffen came, as did Warner cochairmen Bob Daly and Terry Semel. Dozens of people from the other parts of Wells's life were present, too—politicians, environmentalists, adventurers.

Eisner still had not fully absorbed the horrifying news. When he rose to speak, he suddenly felt the despair that had not hit him in the flurry of activity following the news of the accident. His voice breaking with emotion, Eisner addressed the crowd. "I spoke more often with Frank than with any other single person over the last ten years," he said. "Over those ten years we never had a fight, never had a misunderstanding, never had as much as a disagreement. I was never angry with him—until last Sunday. And I was angry at Frank because he was not around to help me deal with this difficult situation. . . . I miss him terribly."

Eisner had indeed suffered a serious loss. At a striking six feet four inches, the sixty-year-old Wells was an icon in the entertainment industry— an attractive, craggy, educated, and wealthy man. He and Eisner had engineered one of the most dazzling corporate turnarounds in history. "We're going to ride that mouse into the ground," Wells had told his friend documentary filmmaker Mike Hoover when he had taken the job at Disney in 1984—and he had been as good as his word. Disney had awakened from its slumbers and smashed its own earnings records quarter after quarter.

At the memorial service, Clint Eastwood—who had been on the ill-fated ski trip—spoke about his long friendship with Wells. They had known each other since the days when Wells was a young lawyer and remained close when he became a top executive at Warner. Eastwood recalled settling the terms of the deal to make *Dirty Harry* with a tennis match. Warner chief Bob Daly compared Wells with Clark Kent, "a tall unassuming man with glasses, but Superman underneath." Robert Redford, who shared with Wells a passionate interest in protecting the environment, also spoke. Carrying skis onstage, Wells's twenty-eight-year-old son Briant asked the crowd to sing a rendition of "Hey, Jude"—a song that his father had been singing on the slopes on the day of the accident that claimed his life.

Many were brought to tears by a short video celebrating Wells's adventurous life. There was Wells skiing and taking a spill. Wells in full scuba gear, floating in a tank at Disney World, with Eisner calling through the glass, "Frank, you know there are sharks in there!" (In a cloud of bubbles,

Wells replied through his mask, "That's not part of my deal!") There was a gag reel, made for a corporate event, showing Eisner shoving a cream pie in Wells's face. Next came a moving photo montage of Wells as a boy, Wells with his own children, and Wells during a daring 1981 attempt to become the first man to climb the tallest mountain on each continent. (Despite a lack of experience or skill, he nearly succeeded.)

In 1984, Wells had teamed up with Eisner to run the then-flagging Disney. Most entertainment types who knew Wells thought his modesty was illuminated when he relinquished the chance to be chairman so that Eisner could take the role. Few understood that Wells, the businessman, knew he couldn't save Disney without a creative partner. And his first choice, the ambitious and talented Michael Eisner, had refused to share the number-one spot.

But some who worked with Wells thought he believed, with some justification, that he was the one who kept Disney aloft, in part by keeping Eisner—frequently impulsive, often duplicitous—in check. "Frank was actually the moral compass," says Pete Clark, a veteran Disney executive in charge of partnerships with outside companies. "He was the Jiminy Cricket."

Certainly Wells kept things on a more even keel than Eisner could have. Hadn't he played a key role in getting financing for Disney's movies? And wasn't Wells the one who soothed the Imagineers—the high-strung designers who created the theme park attractions—many of whom lacked confidence in Eisner? These were only some of the internal relationships that Wells had to smooth over, and he had done it brilliantly. Most important, Wells had just finished bailing Eisner out of the gravest crisis of all—a disaster that Eisner had walked into with considerable arrogance and now feared could cost him his job—the sinkhole known as Euro Disney.

The Disney Orchestra played "Climb Every Mountain." The choir from the First African Methodist Episcopal Church sang. Yet even as Wells was being laid to rest, the entertainment industry was asking questions about Disney's future. There were ripples of fear throughout the company. In the quirky Imagineering division, some employees who were leery of Eisner believed they had lost their godfather. Outsiders, too, who had turned to Wells to mediate their disputes with Eisner worried about what would come next. Those closest to the company were not nearly as sanguine as the Wall Street analysts who contended that Eisner had become a seasoned leader and that Disney would not suffer for the loss of Wells.

How would Eisner replace the man who had helped him build Disney from a foundering $2 billion company to a $23 billion juggernaut over the previous decade? Eisner had moved quickly to stop speculation. The Monday after Wells's death, he had decided to hold the regular staff meeting. There, he announced that he was taking over the title of president. The message was intended to soothe anxious shareholders. But to one man, there was nothing soothing about it.

Jeffrey Katzenberg, the aggressive forty-three-year-old chairman of the Disney studios, was in shock. He had been stunned at the Monday staff meeting when Eisner handed out copies of a press release announcing that Eisner would assume Wells's responsibilities. Not even a year earlier, as the two had strolled the streets of Aspen, Katzenberg had exacted what he took to be a promise that the job would be his if something were to happen to Wells. Now Wells was unexpectedly out of the way—not in the manner that Katzenberg would have wished, of course—and Eisner had announced this transition without even offering Katzenberg the courtesy of a discussion beforehand.

Later, the two men met for their usual Monday night dinner at Locanda Veneta, a dimly lit Italian trattoria on Third Street in a wedge of Los Angeles between West Hollywood and Beverly Hills. They talked business while Katzenberg waited for Eisner to address the elephant in the room. He never did. Whether through failure of nerve or some unaccustomed reticence, Katzenberg didn't broach the matter, either.

After an unusually restless night, Katzenberg went into the office the next morning and demanded a lunch with Eisner. In a private dining room, with portraits of Walt and the elder Roy bearing silent witness to the building storm, Katzenberg demanded an explanation. "You had promised it to me," he said. "I don't understand what you're doing. I don't understand why you said nothing to me at dinner. I don't understand why, after eighteen years, you wouldn't first talk to me. If you don't want to do what was promised, I'm leaving."

But rather than offering the apology Katzenberg was so anxious to hear, Eisner was livid. He regarded Katzenberg's decision to press for Wells's job as an ultimatum—and a poorly timed one at that. By the time they parted, they had agreed that Katzenberg should move on from the job he had held for the previous decade.

But both men realized this would be a wrenching divorce. They had worked together with great success for nearly a decade at Paramount Pictures before they turned Disney into the envy of the entertainment world. Katzenberg had been as single-mindedly devoted to his job as any boss could wish—at Disney, he had done everything short of growing round black ears. Most important, he had played an instrumental role in revitalizing the studio's breathtakingly profitable animation division—the engine that drove vast sales of video and merchandise and lured visitors to new attractions at the theme parks.

The day after their dinner, Eisner and Katzenberg agreed to step back from the precipice. There would be a moratorium on discussions about Katzenberg's future until emotion over Wells's death had subsided. When the two men reached that agreement, Wells had still not been buried. But his funeral would be long over—months would pass—and the tensions between Eisner and Katzenberg would continue to build. Before it was over, the battle would be costly in every sense of the word—far more so to Eisner, in the end, than to his seemingly weaker rival.

KATZENBERG WASN'T THE only man whose ambitions were inflamed by the opportunities that arose in the wake of Wells's death. The tragic accident that claimed Wells's life set off a series of events that would sweep through the film industry like a scythe, cutting down the pillars of Hollywood's power structure as it went. The struggle between Eisner and Katzenberg would lead to the creation of DreamWorks, a bold attempt to launch Hollywood's first new studio in decades. The advent of DreamWorks would exacerbate a power struggle at Universal Studios, and within three years Lew Wasserman—the eighty-one-year-old industry godfather who had presided there for decades—would be ousted, along with his second-in-command, Sid Sheinberg.

And that in turn would open the door for Michael Ovitz to leave the mighty agency he had cofounded. Overnight, Creative Artists Agency was no longer a force that controlled much of Hollywood's day-to-day business and brokered the industry's biggest deals. And Ovitz, routinely called the most powerful man in Hollywood, would fall—unceremoniously fired after fourteen miserably unsuccessful months at Disney trying to fill the place once occupied by Frank Wells. It was one of the most stunning reversals of fortune anyone in the industry could remember.

The death of Wells had "a tremendous effect" on the entertainment industry, muses former Warner cochairman Bob Daly. If Wells had lived, he speculates, Katzenberg would have stayed at Disney, Wasserman and Sheinberg might have kept control of Universal, and Ovitz might even still be at CAA. "And the irony, after all these things," he says, "is that Frank Wells's job is still open."

And Michael Eisner, brilliant and ruthless, rules Disney, and rules alone.

1

POOR LITTLE RICH BOY

IT MUST HAVE been difficult, even frightening, for a poor little rich boy whose parents wanted so much for him and demanded so much from him. But a boy who had a lively imagination yet a very short attention span did not necessarily possess the qualities that ensure a brilliant academic career. And in fact, Michael Dammann Eisner had to get used to trying hard without always succeeding. The son of a wealthy New York family, he had grown up on Park Avenue, spending weekends in wealthy Bedford Hills at his maternal grandparents' estate.

The Eisners were wealthy but not extravagant, and Michael was inculcated with a sense of thrift bordering on cheapness. His mother constantly admonished him to turn out lights when he left a room. If the family went to dinner and Michael wanted a shrimp cocktail that wasn't included in the prix fixe menu, his father complained that this indulgence was "ridiculous and unnecessary." Early on, Eisner was taught to believe that money was to be taken very seriously. The message that his father drilled into his head was that "you do not spend capital."

For the first three years of Michael's life, his father, Lester, was away flying transport planes in the Second World War. Being the only boy (he had one older sister), Eisner was his mother's young prince and he learned that by being "clever and playful and likable" he could almost always have his way. To the young boy, Lester's return seemed a change for the worse. It wasn't a happy dynamic. A longtime Eisner associate says that his father was weak and vacillating with his wife, but self-righteous and overbearing with others, including his children. Relentlessly dissatisfied with them, Lester insisted that they call him by his first name. In his mother, Maggie, Michael had a powerful ally. Complain as Lester might, Maggie saw to it that her boy got to savor his à la carte shrimp cocktail.

Eisner says his father was popular, charming, and funny — but also recalls that his best friend, John Angelo, was "terrified of him." An avid sportsman, Lester was highly competitive and demanded much of his children. When he took them galloping on cross-country rides every weekend, he hardly noticed that they were scared to death. Both children learned to hate and fear riding.

Michael's sister, Margot, liked to figure-skate. Lester pushed her hard and she became a capable little technician, laboring at her performances with such grim determination that she failed to win over the judges in competitions. Her brother knew better how to have his way. "Smile," he told her. "Play the game." It was a natural gift for Michael, but for Margot, it was not.

Michael attended the exclusive Allen-Stevenson School on East Seventy-eighth Street, a school known for its children's orchestra. (Eisner played glockenspiel.) He set out each morning dressed in a blue uniform with a blue cap. He was relatively happy there, not because of a love of learning, but because he was one of the best athletes in the relatively small school and got to be quarterback of the football team from the fourth through eighth grades. He found that he liked calling the plays. Academically, he never really distinguished himself—much to the unconcealed disappointment of his father. "I wanted to please him, and it was nearly impossible," Eisner said later. The anxious and protective Maggie did her best for her son, even forging his homework for him when he fell behind.

Eisner portrays himself as an insatiably curious child whose father begged for relief from his incessant questions. He also saw himself as having had a fairly adventuresome youth. " 'Give me a subway station and I will go,' was my motto as I traveled to Yankee Stadium, to the Polo Grounds, to Madison Square Garden, and to the World's Fair," he later remembered. Certainly, a genuine and enthusiastic curiosity was one of Eisner's most engaging traits. Even so, the disciplined attention needed to shine in school eluded him.

Lester was also perennially dissatisfied with Michael's standards of conduct. Lester held himself out as a rigidly moral man, but even as a child, Michael had learned to "play the angles," as a boarding-school housemaster put it in a letter to his parents. Michael may not have been an academic star, but surely he learned some interesting lessons—maneuvering between a constantly discontented, stiff-necked father and an iron-willed mother who helped him cheat at his schoolwork. At some point, clearly, he concluded that his father's standards could not be met—and he didn't intend to try.

Later, Michael would see something of his father, with his strong professions of morality, in Frank Wells. If he saw hypocrisy in either man, Eisner never said so. But the similarity was such that Michael would acknowledge that Wells served as "a governor" to him when he was "tempted to push the boundaries just a little too far."

⚮

AT DINNER IN the family home, young Michael was expected to wear a tie and jacket. Similarly attired, he was dispatched to classes at the Viola Wolff dancing school with white-gloved little girls. His parents took him to concerts and Broadway shows starting at a tender age. A Picasso, *The Bull-fight*, lent by an art-collector friend, hung on his bedroom wall. Television was restricted to an hour a day—and that only after two hours of reading. Michael broke the rule when his parents went out and gradually absorbed a dream of a humbler, happier life, informed by sitcoms of the fifties—*The Adventures of Ozzie and Harriet* and *Father Knows Best*. When his father returned home and found the television still warm, Michael faced his fury for trying to pull off the deception.

Of course, Eisner was a rich boy in Manhattan (and a Jew—if a highly assimilated one who enjoyed his share of unkosher shrimp). His life had little in common with the middle-class, middle Americans portrayed on television. But the Eisners were hardly living as extravagantly as the family's circumstances would have allowed. "Michael had a privileged but not in-dulged upper-middle-class urban upbringing," says childhood friend Susan Baerwald. "It was not a lot of rich kids running around with expensive toys. Nobody had fancy cars or trappings of wealth."

Summer vacations were spent near Lake Dunmore, Vermont, at Camp Keewaydin, the country's second oldest boys' camp but not an especially fashionable (or especially Jewish) establishment. "We lived in tents and had very poor facilities," remembers one alumnus who had Eisner as a camp counselor in the early sixties. "There were bad fields and a pockmarked tennis court." The camp was a place of simple, old-fashioned virtues. HELP THE OTHER FELLOW, read a banner hanging in the dining hall. The em-phasis was on canoe trips and hiking; campers were required to earn cer-tificates of achievement in various areas to ensure that they had a well-rounded experience. Despite its lackluster appointments, Terry Eakin—a Keewaydin camper roughly of Eisner's vintage—remembers the place as "idyllic" and unchanging, as if in a time warp.

"Keewaydin is not one of those Jewish camps," says Baerwald, who later
sent her own children to Keewaydin along with the Eisner children. "It's
not in Maine, it doesn't have speedboating, there's nothing modern. There's
no electricity in the tents. It's woodsy. It's a funky old camp with wooden
canoes."

Camp Keewaydin, which has been around since 1910, had a couple of
other well-known alumni: author John McPhee and Senator Jay Rockefeller
of West Virginia. Lester Eisner also had camped and worked there as a
counselor. Alfred Hare, the beloved camp leader for decades, went by the
nickname "Waboos," a leftover from his own childhood summers at Keewaydin. He remembers a very young Michael showing up with his father
for a weekend visit. Before the child was even registered, Hare says, his
father had signed him on for a Saturday-night boxing match.

The camp was packed with traditions. Campers were organized according to age in "wigwams." There was "the Great Auk"—a night when the
counselors short-sheeted beds and played other pranks. Eisner seems to have
been a truly happy camper. Hare remembers him as "mild-mannered and
congenial," hardly someone who seemed destined to become the "s.o.b."
businessman Hare would later hear about. Eisner was a pretty good athlete
who was probably a better tennis player than his childhood friend John
Angelo, but who consistently choked in matches. He also was an enthusiastic and inventive participant in the regular Friday Night Frolics, where
the different wigwams presented skits.

Even at that youthful age, Eisner remembers that Angelo noticed a quality in him that would define him forever. "You have a way of taking charge
that makes people want to follow even though they aren't always sure why,"
Angelo told his friend. It was true. Eisner had learned early at his mother's
knee to be "clever and likable and playful" and he knew how to use those
qualities to draw people to him.

Camp Keewaydin appears to have commanded more of Eisner's loyalty
than any other institution in his life. He sent his own sons there, far from
home in Los Angeles, and as recently as 1998, he was chairman of a campaign to raise funds to expand the property. He and his friends John Angelo
and Susan Baerwald would enjoy parents' weekend, when they would sneak
pizza into their rooms at the Middlebury Inn, take their kids to the A&W
root beer stand, and go canoeing.

As a young teen, Eisner also spent time at the Jersey shore, where John
Angelo's family had a home in a community called Elberon. A well-to-do

set of regulars belonged to the same beach club. Susan Baerwald, who lived in the ocean community all year long, remembers Eisner as preppie and somewhat shy. Michael's mother, Maggie, made a more indelible impression on Baerwald. "Maggie was a very strong woman, very self-assured," she remembers. "She was Jewish, but not *very* Jewish. German-Jewish—very American and successful. She was a presence.... I liked Maggie but you were a little bit afraid of her." Her fierce watchfulness, her adoration of and anxiety for her son, made itself felt even to Eisner's young friends.

∞

EISNER'S GREAT-GRANDFATHER, Sigmund, arrived in New Jersey from Bohemia in the 1880s with an immigrant's empty pockets. In the next several years he built a uniform business from a two-sewing-machine operation into the largest manufacturer of military uniforms in the country. Winning a contract with the federal government, Sigmund outfitted the Rough Riders, including Colonel Theodore Roosevelt. He was also exclusive supplier to the Boy Scouts of America, starting when the organization was founded in 1910.

He married Bertha Weiss, whose family had helped settle the town of Red Bank, New Jersey. In 1906, Sigmund paid $6,000 for a three-story, sixteen-room nineteenth-century stucco house with a sunroom overlooking the North Shrewsbury River. Even at the time the price was reported by a local paper to be "ridiculously cheap." Sigmund became a much-loved philanthropist, extensively involved in civic and Jewish activities. Among his many contributions, he donated $50,000 toward the Zionist cause.

The Eisners appear to have been a happy couple. On their silver anniversary in 1911, they threw a party for two hundred, some of whom arrived in special Pullman coaches from New York. The guests strolled through a house bedecked with roses and dined on beef, squab, duckling, and turkey. The Eisners renewed their vows before a rabbi, with Sigmund wearing the same gloves he had worn twenty-five years earlier.

The marriage produced four boys, all of whom went to work at some time for the family business. Sigmund was not destined to live a long life. In 1925, at sixty-six, he succumbed to what a local paper described as "an affection of the heart" and a stroke. The entire town of Red Bank shuttered its shops for an hour on the Thursday of his funeral. Flags were flown at half-mast. As his body lay in his home, thousands stood on the lawn outside. Rabbi Stephen Wise, who presided at the services, praised Sigmund's pride in his Judaism and his lifelong commitment to his faith. Five cars loaded with flowers followed his casket to the cemetery.

His estate was estimated at $12 million. In his will, he remembered not just local synagogues but Christian churches of every denomination, including those attended by members of the African-American community. He also left money to every police officer and fireman in the town. Eventually, his sons donated the family house to the town of Red Bank for use as a library. Sigmund's sons kept up their father's philanthropic tradition in the town, and after they all died, the Eisner family continued to donate money to Red Bank until 1997, when the family foundation was dissolved with one final gift of $500,000.

∽

ALL THE EISNER boys had been offered first-rate educations. Three attended Harvard, including Michael's grandfather. J. Lester Eisner spent time in the National Guard following the First World War and called himself "Colonel Eisner." Like his father, Sigmund, he was active in civic and government activities, including a number of state and local commissions created to deal with the Great Depression. During the Second World War, he became head of the American Red Cross in England. He was a member of the Harvard Club, the Army and Navy Club in Washington, the American Club in London, and several yacht clubs.

The Colonel's eldest son, Lester Jr., was only ten years old when his mother, Marguerite, died; he and his two younger brothers were brought up mostly by servants while their father spent evenings dining at '21' in Manhattan. The doubly abandoned Lester Jr. kept up the family's standards by attending Princeton and Harvard Law School. But perhaps his greatest achievement was marrying a formidable wife, Margaret Dammann.

Maggie also came from an extraordinary family. Her father, Milton Dammann, had worked his way from shoeshine boy to president of the American Safety Razor Company. He was also a lawyer with a practice in Manhattan. Like many such successful men, he never lost his anxiety about money—even after he had an apartment at 300 Park Avenue and a seventy-four-acre estate in Bedford Hills, north of Manhattan, with a domestic staff of fifteen. Milton's wife, Reta Weil, came from a rich Southern family but shared her husband's concern about money. When she was in town, she refused into her old age to take a taxi when the bus would do.

Patrick Hart, whose father was superintendent of the Dammann estate,

Cedar Knoll, suggests that Maggie's later insistence on turning off the lights came from her parents. Though the Harts lived in a separate superintendent's house, he says, "We'd have to be careful, too, not to keep the lights on because they could see it from the big house." (On the other hand, Hart says, the Dammanns were generous when his father died in 1945. Patrick was only sixteen years old, but the Dammanns bought the family a home in the area, and his mother remained fast friends with Reta Dammann.)

Michael remembers that his grandfather was chauffeur-driven to work in a station wagon, but Hart says the Dammann family was driven in Cadillacs except during the Second World War. According to Michael, Milton would even go out of his way to save a twenty-five-cent toll on the Triborough Bridge. (Hart says he never witnessed that but finds it credible.)

The Dammann estate had horses, a few cows, poultry, and ducks. There was a pond where the children could swim and a grass tennis court that Patrick had to groom on Sunday mornings. Milton was "a strong person who commanded respect," Hart remembers. Once, young Patrick told the very Republican Dammann that his father had voted for Roosevelt. "My father almost killed me for that," he says.

As a boy, Patrick attended the wedding of Margaret Dammann and Lester Eisner. Massive tents were erected on the lawn near the big wood-frame house. The young "Miss Margaret," as Hart knew her, and her groom made an exceptionally handsome couple. But there was a definite sense that Maggie could have done better. "He was the one who was talked about," Hart says. "He was not looked up to." By the time that vows were exchanged, the Eisner family business was headed toward decline. And despite his Princeton and Harvard degrees, Lester Jr. lacked his father's savoir faire. Even to Hart, it seemed obvious that Maggie was the stronger of the two. "Poor Lester never called any shots," he remembers.

During summer months, Maggie and Lester lived in the chauffeur's cottage — rooms above the three-car garage. Patrick drove little Michael and Margot to their riding lessons. To Patrick, they seemed like run-of-the-mill little kids. But young Michael remembers being so frightened by his grandfather that when Milton took him on a tour of his razor factory, Michael wet his pants — twice.

Meanwhile, Lester set about confirming everyone's worst suspicions. It is unclear why he didn't put his law degree to use, but instead, he started to dabble. He invested in a doomed Ecuadoran airline and then worked unhappily as a soap salesman for his intimidating father-in-law. His next move was to produce sports-and-vacation trade shows—an interlude that his young son, Michael, found vastly entertaining. But Lester lost that business, too, and even as a teenager, Michael wondered why his father had bungled matters so badly. Lester then turned to the public sector. He was a Republican who held several positions with the state and federal government.

Meanwhile, Lester told Michael that Lester's uncles had mismanaged the family uniform business—particularly his uncle Monroe. (When Monroe died in 1973, however, his obituary in the *Red Bank Register* said that his "success in business was parallel to his philanthropy.") Whoever deserved the blame, the Eisner family business was shuttered in the mid-1950s. Lester told his son so many cautionary tales about his great-uncles' supposed arrogance and overconfidence that Eisner developed a lifelong fear of taking success for granted. The lesson that loss might be imminent was so deeply inculcated that Eisner always obsessively anticipated doom even when he had become wealthy and powerful in his own right.

∽

EISNER'S PARENTS MAY have been content to send him to an unpretentious summer camp, but their ambitions were not so modest when it came to college. The plan called for Princeton and then law school—presumably Harvard, which was the alma mater of his father, grandfather, and two of his great-uncles.

Margaret and Lester packed fourteen-year-old Michael off to Lawrenceville, an expensive and elite boarding school that was supposed to feed bright young men to Princeton. Founded in 1810, Lawrenceville boasted a grassy commons, tennis courts, and a golf course. It was also homogeneous in terms of color, gender, and for the most part, ethnicity. Eisner remembers getting his first bitter taste of anti-Semitism when another boy called him a "kike." In a school that required attendance in chapel, Eisner learned what it meant "to be ethnic, going to a school where when you leave the room you can feel that they're talking about you." Even though he had received no religious training as a child, the other boys teased him about temple and bar mitzvahs.

Eisner also experienced a ten-inch growth spurt and found that suddenly he was a gangly teenager who had lost much of his skill as an athlete. Academically, he struggled, too (and reverted to the less-than-honest methods followed when his mother helped him cheat on his homework). It must have been a lonely, painful time for him. Lawrenceville students saw their parents at Thanksgiving, Christmas, Easter, and during four weekends throughout the school year. Given Eisner's lackluster report cards and the negative letters from his housemaster about the boy's predilection for short-cuts, he undoubtedly was berated by Lester. He yearned to go to a less demanding public school.

Young Eisner sampled from Lawrenceville's extensive menu of activities, serving on the school paper one year and the yearbook another. He joined the Periwig drama club but missed out on his only chance to play a major role in *The Caine Mutiny* when he was sidelined by a serious case of spinal meningitis.

By November 1959, it was clear that Eisner was not bound for Princeton. And Eisner was determined not to follow in his father's footsteps at another high-pressure, all-male institution. He talked about going to college in Cal-ifornia, but his father objected. It was too far and the travel expenses would run too high. One can only imagine his parents' feelings when their only son secretly applied to Denison, a sixteen-hundred-student liberal-arts col-lege in Granville, Ohio. To Eisner, however, Denison represented an es-cape to a simpler America—the wholesome place he had glimpsed on television. Eisner enrolled as a premed student but quickly realized that he was out of his element in the demanding science classes. He changed his major in his junior year to English. If there was poetry in Eisner's soul, this was when it tried to express itself.

One day Eisner approached William Brasmer, a professor in the drama department, and asked to have a play that he had written produced. He did not get a warm reception. "I just didn't think it was a good play," says Brasmer, now retired. But Eisner wasn't to be turned away. Brasmer handed it over to a more junior professor, Dick Smith, and the play was presented. "Mike Eisner kept on my back and he complained about the fact that we weren't setting the play right," Brasmer remembers. "And he demanded that we get six open caskets. He got 'em. I had to go out and get 'em for him. I thought it was preposterous."

In rehearsals, Eisner sometimes disagreed with drama professor Dick Smith. "Michael would have a very clear idea about how he wanted a scene and Dick would say, 'No. It won't play,'" says Barbara Eberhardt, who starred in some of Eisner's productions. "And Michael would sometimes sound like he was agreeing but he would always have his way."

Despite Eisner's powers of persuasion—especially impressive since he wasn't even a drama major—Brasmer says he was "just a minor cog of the wheels around here." Nonetheless, Eisner seemed to appear at various times all over campus—and then he would vanish again. "He wanted to know what was happening all over the campus," Brasmer says. "He was like a snoop. He would go to classes where he wasn't registered." Brasmer concluded that Eisner made these explorations "to feed his own imagination, to feed his own knowledge about things."

One of Eisner's more ambitious theatrical efforts was entitled *To Stop a River* (originally called *To Metastasize a River*, until Eisner figured out that the word was usually linked with cancer). Alan Shevlo, who as a freshman performed in the play, says the heroine is kicked out of school for fooling around with boys. She then returns home to "a very unhappy mother-father relationship," he says. The father (played by Shevlo) runs a bar, and in the family, "everybody is fighting with everybody," he remembers. Meanwhile, the daughter had started a relationship with a young man whom she met on the train home. The young man arrives unannounced at the bar when the daughter happens to be away, and winds up sleeping with her mother. When the mother realizes what has happened, she commits suicide.

Shevlo's character tells his daughter, "Every day your mother was alive was a living hell for me because she was not satisfied with anything. . . . In a way, I envy your mother. I've been getting kicked in the face all my life but I never thought I'd live to see you do it."

How much these themes of marital discord and betrayal were drawn from Eisner's experience at home is open for speculation. Shevlo says that Eisner came to rehearsals and listened quietly. Eventually, the drama teacher told the students that the play was too talky and instructed them to read the first line of every speech and delete the rest. The play had a short run and was well received by a local paper. A reviewer wrote that it created a "river of enthusiasm and popularity," though "at times [it] lacked the continuity necessary to make the mission apparent."

Later in life, Eisner liked to say that he wrote his plays in hopes of attracting the young woman who starred in them, Barbara Eberhardt. But Eberhardt, who now teaches in Maine, says Eisner was a friend—someone she never regarded as a potential boyfriend and who didn't seem to have any romantic interest in her. The two were serious about Eisner's writing efforts and planned to remain partners after graduation. "I think he had aspirations to be a playwright and I was going to be his star," she remembers.

Eisner had escaped the rigors of Lawrenceville, but Eberhardt knew him as a "serious" young man. "I wouldn't call him a party person at all and Denison could be a party school," she says. "He was very low key and private. I don't think many people — even his frat brothers — knew that much about him."

Al Bonney, who played the feckless boyfriend in *To Stop a River*, was a member of Eisner's frat, Delta Upsilon, and shares Eberhardt's appraisal. "We were a well-respected group of young men, socially active and acceptable, but we were not the jocks and we were not the rich pretty boys," Bonney says. Eisner had a car and Bonney rode along with him to New York on school holidays. But he didn't get particularly close to Eisner. "He wasn't a loner," Bonney says, "but he was private. . . . We drank together. We did stuff together. Did I know him real well? No."

Eberhardt felt that Eisner had a more spontaneous, less controlled side but kept it under tight rein. "Maybe that was from his parents," she says. "He learned to toe the mark." It may also have been that Eisner, following his experience at Lawrenceville, wanted nothing more than to blend in. There was only a handful of Jewish students at Denison, but they weren't singled out for teasing, and Eisner appreciated that.

Eberhardt got to know the Eisner family and visited the farmhouse that Maggie and Lester had bought in Vermont. Like many others, she came away impressed by Michael's mother. "His mother was a very strong woman," she says. "She was the matriarch. I always experienced her as very warm and generous but watchful. . . . She always appeared to be taller than Lester, but I'm not sure if that's true. She had large bones. Very smiling, but those eyes — whoa. She was alert and a watcher."

Eberhardt also remembers that Eisner seemed self-conscious about attending Denison in the first place. "There was always a sense that this was not the most prestigious place to go," she says. But even if he couldn't fulfill his parents' hopes for a Princeton education, he could try to make them proud of his achievements. "He had certain standards for himself — whether it was an expectation of how a scene would work or to be president of his fraternity," Eberhardt says. "He was a very determined person. . . . He was competitive and controlling and needed to be the one who was on top, or knew exactly what was going on."

Eisner later said he made valuable connections at Denison — not with fellow students, but with the country. In nearby Columbus, Eisner went to his first drive-in movie. Such experiences, he said, were "the reason I'm comfortable in America."

AFTER HIS JUNIOR year, Eisner had gotten a summer job as a page at
NBC through his family's connections with Robert Sarnoff. Conducting
tours of the studio and ushering audiences to their seats, Eisner was not
immediately mesmerized by the world of television. The next summer, after
he graduated, he sailed to Paris, hoping to live the life of a bohemian
playwright. The experiment lasted just weeks. "There were a lot of Americans in Paris who were hiding their American Express checks under their
mattresses and going around acting real poor," he said later.

Eisner returned to New York in the fall of 1964 and, with his mother's
help, found his first apartment (a one-bedroom, fifth-floor walk-up on Sixty-
fourth Street). He went though a difficult job search, sitting through an
array of fruitless interviews arranged by his parents. He made a stab at
finding an agent to represent him as a playwright. Finally, in November,
he was hired as a logging clerk at NBC, tediously recording what commercials were broadcast. Restless, he took a second job doing weekend traffic
reports for WNBC Radio.

Three months later, he moved on to a somewhat more elevated position
at CBS. Eisner worked as a commercial coordinator, screening and scheduling advertisements that would run during children's Saturday-morning
programming. Eventually, he was transferred to the game-show division.
Rising television executive Fred Silverman, who ran CBS's daytime schedule, remembers Eisner as "this big gangly kid with program ideas" — a young
man with "a very aggressive personality."

Once, Eisner managed to get a meeting with Silverman, and tried to
pitch him on a game-show idea called *Bet Your Bottom Dollar*. Silverman
showed him a couple of game shows in the works. One was *Hollywood
Squares* and the other was called *The Face Is Familiar*. "What do you think
of these two shows?" Silverman asked. As Silverman remembers the incident, Eisner picked *Hollywood Squares*. "I ultimately picked *Face Is Familiar* and *Hollywood Squares* went to NBC, where it became an enormous
hit for many years," Silverman recalls. "Had I listened to Michael, it would
have saved me a lot of grief." Eisner, on the other hand, remembers the
story differently. He says Silverman only allowed him to listen to the audio
of the shows and that he was unable to make a choice. Either way, the
interview produced no results for Eisner.

While Eisner tried to climb the ladder, his friend John Angelo had attended St. Lawrence College in upstate New York. He became engaged to an undergraduate named Judy Hart. Eisner began to date and then became engaged to Judy's good friend Jane Breckenridge. They were married in 1967.

In his own biography, Eisner addresses the fact that Jane's parents had probably never even known anyone Jewish before him, but says it was "never an issue" for them. But he doesn't say what Lester and Maggie might have thought about the union. A longtime Eisner friend says that Jane's not being Jewish would hardly have bothered the assimilated Eisner family. "There are a lot of people who aren't thrilled to be Jewish," this friend says. "They were probably thrilled that [Jane] wasn't Jewish." On the other hand, they seemed to withhold their approval in at least one respect. Another Eisner associate says he confided only one thing about his family's response to his marriage: "His parents," that person says, "didn't think she was beautiful enough."

2

ENTER THE DRAGON

HAVING DESPAIRED OF advancement at CBS, Eisner wrote dozens of letters in his quest for a new job. With Jane's help, he sent résumés to television stations and movie studios but received more than seventy-five rejection letters. In the fall of 1966, he finally got a call from ABC. His résumé had been plucked from the pile by a young assistant named Barry Diller. Thus began the complicated relationship between Eisner and Diller—the love, the hate, the competition. Both men were young and at the time ABC was barely an also-ran, struggling to keep up with its far bigger rivals.

Diller had come to ABC through Leonard Goldberg, the head of programming at the network. In 1966, Goldberg was dating a vivacious actress named Marlo Thomas. She was the sitcom star of *That Girl*. "You must meet my agent," she told Goldberg. "He's just out of the mailroom. He's the lowest agent at William Morris, but he's sensational."

One evening, Thomas gave a party at her Hollywood Hills home and in walked her agent, the twenty-four-year-old Barry Diller—already bearing himself with a leonine sense of self-possession. Goldberg, curious to test the mettle of the young man who had so impressed his girlfriend, picked a fight with him. He launched into an attack on the William Morris Agency's practice of "packaging" television shows. If a network wanted to make a show using a star or writer represented by William Morris, the agency not only took 10 percent of the talent's remuneration but demanded that the network fork over 10 percent of the license fee that it paid for rights to air the show. Goldberg thought this was simply a rip-off. "What does your agency do [for this money]?" Goldberg demanded. "What is the service you provide?"

Diller tried to defend the practice, but Goldberg was convinced that his heart wasn't in it. "He was very, very smart, he was very articulate, and

although I sensed that he didn't believe [in] it, he defended
worked there," Goldberg says. "And I liked all those three thi

Born in San Francisco in February 1942, Diller had been rais
erly Hills. His father was a real estate developer who built thousands
houses in Southern California. "He is a noisy man, hypercritical, and he
loves to argue," Diller told one interviewer in 1984. "From a very early age,
I loved to incite him and then do battle. It drove my mother crazy." Diller
never lost the impulse to bait those around him.

The Diller clan apparently was a chilly one, the type of family that didn't
assemble for holidays. And the marriage of Diller's parents apparently hit
some ice floes. His mother, Reva, filed for divorce in September 1949, when
Barry was seven years old, citing "extreme cruelty." His father disputed her
contention in court papers and ultimately she remained in the marriage.
Barry's older brother, Donald, was a wayward youth, scrapping with the law
and battling a heroin addiction starting at age seventeen. (By the time Barry
assumed the top job at Paramount, his brother was in Tehachapi State
Prison for selling drugs. About a year later, he was found murdered in a
cheap motel outside San Diego. Barry paid $555.94 for the funeral expenses
and never asked police about the status of their investigation.)

Barry was also rebellious, though less of an outlaw. He rejects the notion
that he was a loner in school but also concedes that he wasn't especially
popular. "I was *compelling*," he says of himself. "People noticed me."

In high school, Diller's nickname was "the old man." Terry Melcher, a
classmate, says Diller did, in fact, stand out from the crowd. "He did seem
in many ways to be twenty years older than the rest of us," Melcher says.
"It turns out he was." Melcher remembers meeting Diller on a rainy day
for an outing. "I had on jeans and a T-shirt and tennis shoes. Diller appears
with rubber galoshes over his shoes. When's the last time you saw anything
like that? He had a raincoat, a rain hat, and an umbrella. It was very—
mature." Diller also hated rock music and cigarettes, so Melcher sometimes
made sure that his car was smoky and the radio was blaring when he picked
Diller up for school.

Melcher says Diller was also very attentive to parents—including
Melcher's mother, who was Doris Day. "If there were four or five kids at
my house and my mother and dad came home from the studio, the other
kids would say, 'Hi, Mrs. Melcher. Hi, Mr. Melcher.' Barry would say, 'Oh,
Mrs. Melcher! I just saw your new movie and it's a triumph! You looked
so beautiful!' He got started early." Diller was far more aware than other

kids of "whose names were connected to high places in the entertainment world," Melcher says.

A Beverly Hills High School yearbook from 1959 shows a deceptively affable-looking Diller, a smiling young man with a hairline eager to recede, sitting cross-legged on the floor as a member of the school newspaper staff. He was also on the varsity football team, which was shellacked throughout that season. But Diller was hardly the all-American boy he appeared to be. He started at UCLA but dropped out after only four months at the age of nineteen.

At that point Diller's ideas about a career in show business started to gel. He had been a childhood friend of Marlo Thomas and he started pestering her famous father, Danny Thomas, to help him get into the William Morris training program. Thomas was a huge client of the agency and he got Diller an interview. For once, the young man missed his mark: he didn't get an offer. "I began to drive Danny crazy," Diller said. "I remember calling him at the Sands in Las Vegas, between shows. I could tell he wasn't listening. Finally I said to him loudly, 'Listen to me. Please call. Here's the name. Please call tomorrow.'" He did, and this time Diller was hired the next day.

Diller started, like many others with an appetite for a corner office, in the mailroom. The year was 1961. Trainees were encouraged to read correspondence, deals, and memos, and Diller immersed himself in the material. He borrowed files on clients from Sophie Tucker to Elvis Presley and mastered their contents. By 1964, he was promoted to junior agent, but by then he had concluded that "There was nothing left to learn."

Despite Diller's sense that he had absorbed all the wisdom that could be gleaned from the agency, he wasn't that quick to jump when Leonard Goldberg tried to hire him as his assistant at ABC. Diller was comfortable on his home turf and the new job required a move to Manhattan. "He said, 'I want to be an agent,'" Goldberg remembers. "And I think I probably said, 'Nobody *wants* to be an agent. That can't be your goal in life.' I finally took him to an ornate pizza parlor on La Cienega Boulevard and convinced him."

Notwithstanding his lowly title, being Goldberg's assistant meant exercising considerable clout. Goldberg assigned Diller the task of reorganizing the programming department as well as myriad other duties. Diller wrote down Goldberg's orders on a card that he carried in his pocket, and once an entry was on the list, Goldberg found that he never had to worry about that matter again. "Barry could get it done," Goldberg remembers. "I could say, 'A station in Kansas has a problem,' and once he wrote it on his card, I could forget it. I never had to ask how he did it. Barry got it done. He's a closer."

Martin Starger, who became the number-two man in programming several months after Diller arrived, also thought Diller was a sort of corporate Terminator. "If you asked him to do something, it was done," he says. "You never knew how it was accomplished—what walls he walked through and what bodies laid behind him. But it was done. . . . People would call me and say, 'Christ's sake—what's with this Barry Diller? The guy comes in here like he's Bill Paley.' He would not go in bashfully and say, 'I happen to be the lowest man on the totem pole. I'm going to ask you a favor.' That was not his style."

"He was nothing—except you could see he was a genius," says Dick Zimbert, then a business-affairs executive at the network. "He was just a dynamo, an absolutely brilliant analytical mind. So many Hollywooders can be very bright and can go through the minutiae, but Barry has the ability to get to the essence, to see people's motives, to create a conflict and get the truth out of that conflict being discussed. If I walked in and said, 'It's seven o'clock,' he'd say, 'It's eight o'clock.' That was how he worked."

Goldberg was delighted with his new protégé, but Diller quickly became restless. One night, the two went out to dinner and Diller complained that he was unhappy. "Everyone calls me your secretary," he said. "They laugh at me."

Goldberg leaned forward. "I assure you," he said, "within a short time no one will laugh at Barry Diller."

∽

EISNER FIRST MET Diller without realizing it. He had gotten a call from ABC and thought he was going to an interview with Leonard Goldberg. This seemed like a piece of luck. Eisner had found that his future brother-in-law, Norman Freedman, had grown up in the same Brooklyn apartment building as Goldberg. Before his meeting at the network, Eisner lapped up all the information he could, hoping to charm his prospective boss. When he arrived at ABC, Eisner's first thought was that the head of programming had a very expensive-looking suit and a surprisingly small office. A no-nonsense interview began and Eisner tried to work his boyish charm: "The Knicks have a great team this year," he offered.

The effect was not what Eisner had hoped. Unbeknownst to Eisner, he was talking not to Goldberg but to Goldberg's young assistant, Diller, whose interest in such banter was limited at best. Still, the twenty-four-year-old Eisner made a sufficiently favorable impression. Goldberg gave him a job as the assistant to Ted Fetter, who was in charge of specials.

At a glance, Michael Eisner and Barry Diller had little in common. Everything about their affect and style was opposite. Diller had exchanged his old high-school nickname—"the old man"—for a variation: associates at ABC now called him "the ice man." Eisner, on the other hand, was ebullient and charming. "Michael was a little scattered," Goldberg says. "As opposed to Barry's very precise mind, Michael's mind was a little more circular." In meetings, Eisner literally bounced out of his chair.

And while Diller presented a razor-sharp appearance in immaculate starched white shirts and suits, Eisner was something of a slob. "The tie was always a little askew. Something always was a little bit wrong—a slight element of disarray," says Brandon Stoddard, who worked with Eisner at ABC.

"Every time I see Michael, his hair is all messed up," Goldberg complained to Diller at one point. With typical bluntness, Diller asked Eisner about the problem and reported back to Goldberg that Eisner came to work on a motor scooter and his hair was blown about by the wind. "Maybe he should wear a helmet," Goldberg griped. Diller explained that if he wore a helmet, his hair would be mashed down. This was odd dialogue for Diller, whose own hair was a fading memory. "Just figure it out," Goldberg ordered.

If Diller had been a mannish boy, Eisner was a boyish man. Inwardly, however, Diller and Eisner shared a titanium toughness. The difference was that Diller was more confrontational and direct—he attacked from the front. Eisner was friendly and attacked from the rear. "Michael was hard in a much different way," recalls Zimbert. "He had more warmth. He would say, 'Can you do this?' and if you said, 'I can't,' or 'It won't work,' it would be a discussion. With Barry, he'd say, 'I'm telling you to do it.' Right away, there was a hostility. . . . Barry made it really hard. Michael made it fun." Still, Eisner was as effective as Diller at getting his way. "Michael was not a beater-upper—he was a manipulator," Zimbert says. While Diller left bruises, Eisner tried not to leave fingerprints at all.

AS HE ROSE in the ranks, the young Michael Eisner was the anti-Diller. "Instead of sitting there like a sphinx, he would react," remembers Brandon Stoddard. How compelling was Eisner's charm? As Stoddard puts it, "He could make Barry laugh."

While Diller used other people's ideas for target practice, Eisner spewed his own suggestions like a fountain. "Michael would come in with ten ideas a day and seven of them would be absurd, like, 'Let's turn the building upside down so the thirty-seventh floor will be the first floor.' But three of them would be sensational," says his former boss, Martin Starger.

In 1966, before ABC created an entertainment division on the West Coast, programming executives occupied offices in New York at the network's new headquarters on the Avenue of the Americas. There Diller and Eisner became competitors in the freewheeling atmosphere that allowed those who were capable to succeed. "Nobody cared what I did as long as we were successful and responsible, as long as we didn't do junk," Eisner remembered later. In a typically off-center analogy, he continued: "We were all in a fish tank, but there was nobody above saying, 'This fish, that fish.' So the strongest fish dominated, the most creative."

Within a year Eisner was promoted to a manager of talent and specials. "I realized within a couple of weeks that I really had somebody very extraordinary in the brain department," remembers Gary Pudney, who had taken over the specials department and became Eisner's second boss at ABC. "He was using words I had never heard." Pudney found that he had a hardworking underling—though Eisner was outspoken with his opinions and showed absolutely no fear of authority figures. Once, Pudney remembers, "I barked at him and he took me on. He said, 'Don't talk to me like that. You have no right to talk to me like that.' " Pudney was more careful to regulate his tone after that.

Even at that lowly level, Eisner made an impression on ABC chairman Leonard Goldenson. "He used to say to me, 'How's the Eisner boy doing?' " Pudney recalls. Pudney had no idea that "the Eisner boy" was from a privileged background. Having seen him riding to work on his motorbike, he thought, "Poor thing. Can't afford to take a cab." And then, there was his disheveled appearance—the subject of constant comment by other ABC executives as well. Pudney remembers: "They always came to me and said, 'Do something about him. Fluff him up.' "

Eisner's appearance didn't encourage Pudney to accept his dinner invitations. "I put off socializing with him for over a year," he says. "I thought, 'What is this going to be?' I kept seeing myself going to a sixth-floor walk-up in Greenwich Village." Finally Pudney yielded. By now, Eisner had moved from his one-bedroom apartment into a house that he had helped renovate. "I went to this brownstone on East Eighty-first, between Lexington and Third—this elegant, wonderful brownstone full of beautiful antiques," Pudney remembers.

Though Eisner's parents may have been unimpressed, Pudney was astonished by the poise of Eisner's wife, Jane. "She was so attractive and had flowing red hair—then—and I remember one of the first things I said to her was, 'You look like Rita Hayworth.' . . . Michael just worshiped her. He loved it that I thought she looked like Rita Hayworth." Among Jane's many virtues, in Pudney's view, was that she "never got in the way" while Eisner put in extraordinary hours at work.

A former Eisner employee says the marriage seemed to be "a partnership about his career," but adds, "I think she had a hard time. She wanted Michael to have all these wonderful [professional] things, but she also wanted a family life." In later years, when their children's school activities were involved, she insisted that he attend parent-teacher meetings. Eisner managed to put in enough time as a parent to impress his friend Susan Baerwald, who sees him as "always concerned about being there" for his children. But he also liked to work hard.

Before the children came, it was common for Eisner to begin the day at 8:30 A.M. and to stop at one or two o'clock in the morning. As always, Eisner was "full of zeal," Pudney says. "I never had to ask him to do anything. He was willing to go anywhere, anytime, anyplace to pursue the deal. Then I discovered when I had him around talent, they really liked him."

Even then, in the tumult of the late sixties, Eisner wasn't concerned about creating art or making socially important television. He had only a marginal interest in establishing his intellectual bona fides or showing off his taste. He wanted the kind of success that Wall Street understood. Pudney remembers that Eisner was attracted to programming with broad popular appeal—programming that would work for a company like Disney. "It was entertainment for the masses. Masses. Masses would translate to ratings," Pudney says.

And early on, he remembers, Eisner saw a way to achieve the kind of synergy that studios have been talking about ever since. ABC had constructed an aquatic park outside San Francisco called Marine World and

Eisner volunteered to take on a special that was set there. "Somehow he got Bing Crosby—don't ask me how—to host the show," Pudney says. Eisner booked the pop group the Young Rascals and got an unknown to direct the show. It was his first hint that paying top dollar for name talent wasn't always essential. "And Leonard Goldenson loved that show," Pudney remembers. "So the Eisner boy did real good. They began to take notice in the company."

Eisner moved up like a rocket. In 1968, the ad agency Foote Cone & Belding tried to hire him. He recommended a colleague at ABC, who took the job. Eisner slid into the vacant position at the network, becoming a director of prime-time development.

As Eisner ascended, the competition between him and Diller intensified. Starger remembers the two jousting for attention as they watched each other warily. "Each knew what the other made and what the other's office size was," he says. Naturally there was friction between these two bright, ambitious young men. "They had shouting matches with each other but they got along in a strange way," Starger remembers. "They were both combatants, but combatants get along. I think they respected each other's intelligence."

"Michael was always in Barry's face—fearless," Pudney remembers. "Barry could absolutely melt and wilt someone. Michael just didn't care." Eisner was used to being berated by his father. And when it came to formal education he knew he had an edge over Diller, who had barely been to college. Eisner mentioned once that he liked Edith Wharton's gloomy novel *Ethan Frome,* and realized that Diller had no idea what he was talking about. A few days later, he caught Diller leaving the office with an armload of Wharton books.

Starger observed that whatever their stylistic differences, Diller and Eisner had one thing in common: "Neither of them came from a poor background. Barry came from Beverly Hills; his father was in the real estate business. Michael was from New York and Park Avenue. He lived in a brownstone, which he kept very quiet. No one knew that. So they were fiercely competitive, but money per se—money in the sense of what they earned—was never a major issue. It was what they made compared to the other."

Starger bonded with Diller during walks to work through midtown Manhattan. He and his wife at the time would take off with Michael and Jane to spend sporty weekends on Eisner's family property in Vermont. "I was not much of a rider. I almost killed myself a few times," Starger says. "Michael would say—and this is very much Michael—'Get on this horse. It's been in the family for years—it's not a problem.' And the horse would take off." Eisner also gave Starger a rough introduction to skiing. "I guess that's how he was taught by his father—a dive-into-the-deep-end-of-the-pool kind of thing," Starger says.

∞

WHILE EISNER MOVED from job to job in the programming department, Diller had begun to flex his muscles in a bigger arena. One of his earliest assignments was acquiring films to air on the network. This was big business and Diller, still in his mid-twenties, was thrust directly into negotiations with moguls like Lew Wasserman of MCA (then Universal's parent company) and Charles Bluhdorn of Gulf + Western (the parent of Paramount). Though Diller would later say that this was "a remarkable load to put on a kid," he was actually as tough as his adversaries. "He met the titans of the day," Goldberg says. "Who else at his age could have been in one-on-one meetings with the giants of the entertainment industry?"

On some occasions, Goldberg walked by Diller's compact office and heard voices raised in anger. "[Barry] would say, 'Charlie, if you're going to continue to yell, the meeting will be over,'" Goldberg remembers. "The truth was these guys loved dealing with Barry and they'd come out beaming like he was their son. They only respected strength and he could give it back." Goldberg thought Diller had an aura of sophistication that eluded and impressed some of the less polished power brokers of the time. Charlie Bluhdorn, an Austrian immigrant who was considered something of a bottom-feeder in his quest for undervalued assets, seemed to find this quality especially appealing.

Another executive who also observed Diller's endless dickering remembers: "Bluhdorn could spend four thousand hours discussing a gnat's tail." Diller was willing to battle long after others would have dropped from fatigue. "I could see that Charlie Bluhdorn was falling in love with Barry Diller," that executive says.

In the mid-sixties, ABC was struggling in third place, while CBS dominated with shows such as *The Red Skelton Show* and *The Jackie Gleason Show*. ABC had significantly fewer affiliated stations across the country than its competitors and lacked any presence at all in some cities. For the 1966–67 and the 1967–68 seasons, the network had only two of the top twenty shows on the air: *Bewitched* and *The Lawrence Welk Show*. Groping for something to prop up the sagging prime-time programming, ABC decided to gamble on something new: a weekly ninety-minute made-for-television movie would air from eight-thirty to ten, leaving the ten-to-eleven slot free for variety shows, which were popular then.

In Hollywood, wars have been waged over who deserves credit for any given hit. And *Movie of the Week* became such a stunning success that naturally various people laid claim to it. In articles in *TV Guide*, the *Los Angeles Times*, *Newsweek*, and elsewhere, Diller is routinely described as the man who launched the *Movie of the Week*. But though Diller shaped *Movie of the Week*, he did not invent it.

Programming chief Goldberg and his then-deputy Martin Starger both remember that they came up with the idea at an after-hours meeting. But a television producer named Roy Huggins, who created the concept for *The Fugitive* television series and later *The Rockford Files*, maintains that he originated the idea for a *Movie of the Week* while working at Universal. He pitched it around Hollywood without success. CBS and NBC also passed. But in March 1968, *Variety* printed a story laying out Huggins's idea of creating a series titled *Movie of the Week*.

According to Huggins, that article prompted Goldberg to ask Huggins to present the idea to ABC. Huggins agreed. "Barry Diller sat for almost the entire meeting leaning forward, elbows on his knees, hands clenched under his chin, his eyes never leaving my face," Huggins recalled later. Diller asked why ABC should buy a concept that NBC and CBS had rejected. Instead of sealing a deal, Huggins says, he heard nothing. In May 1968, however, ABC announced that it was launching *Movie of the Week*. Huggins says he called Goldberg in a rage. "How can you do that?" he demanded. "I brought you this concept."

"We're going to do twenty-six of these and we think it's too much for any one producer, but we would like you to do a lot of them," Goldberg replied—according to Huggins. "How many would you like to do?"

"Twenty-six," Huggins said.

ABC offered him eight, instead. And Huggins says he came to regret that he didn't accept Goldberg's offer. But decades later, Huggins still says that Diller falsely positioned himself as the creator of the *Movie of the Week*—a development he refers to as "the first lap of Barry Diller's Marvelous Marathon."

"Barry Diller took credit for it," Huggins complains. "The luckiest thing that ever happened to Barry Diller was *Movie of the Week*. It paved the road."

Diller disputes Huggins's entire account. "The concept of doing the movie for television on a weekly basis has no father that I know of—any absolute original claimant does not exist. Certainly [it's] not Roy Huggins," he says. "The concept we adopted was hatched with Len Goldberg, Marty Starger, and myself." But he acknowledges: "It certainly wasn't my idea. What I will claim mightily is the concept of what it was going to be, its financing, its extremely complex underpinnings . . . and every inch of its creative birth happened in my office and in Jerry Isenberg's office, who worked for me."

Goldberg also does not remember events as Huggins describes them. But Starger says "it could very well be" that Huggins had a movie-of-the-week concept, though he doesn't remember attending a presentation about it. In his memoir, however, former ABC chairman Leonard Goldenson says Huggins originated the concept. But he adds, "Len Goldberg, Marty Starger and Barry Diller took Huggins's idea and jump-started ABC's television network with their efforts."

When ABC couldn't get a studio to make the films on its terms, Diller boldly persuaded the network to announce that it would make a couple on its own. At the same time the network made a deal with television producer Aaron Spelling to produce a number of the films. At the time the future powerhouse producer of soapy programming from *Charlie's Angels* to *Melrose Place* was just "a guy with an office," Starger says. Eventually, the *Movie of the Week* helped transform Spelling into a formidable power who virtually controlled ABC. Meanwhile, he helped ABC win control over its made-for-television movies. The studios began to fall into line—asking to make at least some of the films, on ABC's terms. "The phone started ringing off the hook," Goldberg remembers. "The studios started calling and saying, 'Where are ours?' "

Diller took charge of the *Movie of the Week*, exerting a level of control that shattered precedent in the television world. "Barry set the rules, Barry controlled the casting," remembers Zimbert. "He ran it. He didn't wander onto the set to meet girls or guys. It was business." With particular relish, Diller also took charge of advertising, which previously had reported to the head of the network rather than to the programming chiefs. This taught Diller an important lesson: it helps to sell something that can be summarized in a thirty-second television spot.

But Diller never confined himself to high-concept commercial programming. Among the pictures produced for ABC was the classic *Brian's Song*, the story of terminally ill pro football player Brian Piccolo (played by James Caan) and his friendship with Gayle Sayers (Billy Dee Williams). It won an Emmy for Best Film in 1971. *That Certain Summer*, with Martin Sheen and Hal Holbrook, was one of the first films dealing with homosexuality to be broadcast in the U.S.; it won a Golden Globe and Directors Guild Award in 1972. "Barry would force something that had meaning onto the schedule," Zimbert says. "It might not have ratings but it was Barry Diller doing what was right."

Another project nurtured by Diller was *Love Among the Ruins*, a film that brought Laurence Olivier and Katharine Hepburn together in a television project. Legendary as the two stars were, the project was a tough sell because of their advanced ages. But Diller "worked and worked and it was his vision to make that movie," says Brandon Stoddard, a new Diller employee at the time. Diller gave Stoddard a lot of responsibility from the start, ordering him to represent ABC at a meeting with legendary director George Cukor. "I said, 'Barry, I can't. It's George Cukor. I just [got] here. I don't know where the men's room is.' And he said, 'Oh, you can handle it. It's no problem.' It was kind of typical—push me into the pool. And I went there. I had been in movie development for maybe five days, and I had a meeting with Katharine Hepburn and George Cukor about this script. I mean—I didn't say a lot."

Despite his willingness to take risks, Diller showed discipline in financial matters. He stuck to a $350,000 budget for early *Movie of the Week*s. The movies were such successes that by 1973 the network was programming three nights of ninety-minute films. These films helped keep ABC competitive through the mid-seventies.

The next huge innovation for ABC was the miniseries—another groundbreaking concept frequently credited to Diller. In fact, Starger came up with the idea, based on watching similar programming on British television. His proposal for "Novels for Television" was quickly embraced by top ABC management, and Diller was put in charge. The first miniseries, *QBVII*, was based on a Leon Uris novel about a slander trial in England. Diller knew the story—which involved the Holocaust and castration—was challenging material for television. But the project was a smash and Diller chose the second miniseries, *Rich Man, Poor Man*, "simply because I thought it was a good, good read."

Years later, Diller would fully appreciate the freewheeling atmosphere
that permitted him to exercise so much authority as such a young man.
"The wonderful thing about ABC was that it allowed people like Michael
Eisner, me—and an endless list of others—to take all the responsibility we
wanted," Diller said. "We could make almost any decision."

As Brandon Stoddard had already discovered, Diller was both the best
and worst boss imaginable. He didn't merely delegate authority, he rammed
it down people's throats. If they couldn't handle it, they were gone. And
despite his earlier humiliation at being taken for a secretary, he was not
sympathetic to underlings. "Diller would never talk to anybody—especially
lowly secretaries and assistants," says a woman who worked as an assistant
during this era. "He used to throw pencils at his secretaries."

Executives felt his wrath, too. "I think I was taller when I started working
for him," Stoddard says wryly. And Diller wasn't much more communicative
with Stoddard than he was with his secretaries. "Barry used to come in at
the end of the day and he'd say, 'Everything all right?' And I would have
tried to see him seven times and was totally unable to, because he was busy.
I think he used those words—'Everything all right?'—like, 'Good night,'
but I would take advantage [to get] relatively quick answers to my desperate
problems."

Stoddard was "madly trying to learn" and Diller was a tough tutor. "Barry
is a very hard boss. Very demanding and contrarian in many ways," Stoddard
says. "But once you kind of understood that, things got better. . . . He would
be frustrating at times because I'd show him a promo that I had worked on
and he'd look at it and say, 'Boring,' and then turn and walk out of the
room. And I'd run after him and say, 'What did you mean by that? What
part?' And he'd say, 'It's boring,' and then continue to walk." Ungently,
Diller made Stoddard think for himself. "He kept just pushing decisions
down on me—he was a really fine executive that way—he forced me to
make recommendations and fight for what I believed in."

Some outsiders who had to deal with Diller also found him hard to
handle. Frank Yablans, who became president of Paramount in 1971, knew
Diller because the studio sold films to ABC. Abrasive in his own right,
Yablans says he never really liked Diller. (Diller contends that he and Ya-
blans had "an extremely good relationship" at this time—especially because
Diller was on such good terms with Yablans's boss, Charlie Bluhdorn.)

At one point Diller became ill and complained bitterly that Yablans
didn't show any particular concern. Yablans says he went to considerable

trouble to send Diller the biggest gift he could think of: a live baby elephant. (One source says there was a rude note attached, but Yablans denies it.) Diller says he saw this gesture as "a friendly joke," but Yablans remembers Diller calling to complain. Yablans then followed up by sending a baby pig (so that Diller wouldn't be lonely, he says). Diller complained again. This time, Yablans sent him a coffin. Diller doesn't recall this exact progression of events but says he and Yablans exchanged "a series of gifts over a period of months as the kind of silly things that executives would waste their time on — but entirely with no dark vein."

While many wilted under Diller's gaze, those who could cope with his scathing style sometimes developed a deep affection for him. Zimbert forged a bond with him in the summer of 1970, when ABC moved both executives to the West Coast. For a time they stayed at the Bel-Air hotel. "My kids never forgot, he was so nice to them," Zimbert says. "He was a wonderful human being. The fact that he was a son of a bitch to work for never really bothered me."

∾

IN THE SUMMER of 1969, Eisner had become director of feature films and program development. For the first time he had to report directly to Diller, who was head of prime-time programming as well as *Movie of the Week*. Eisner was upset that Diller had become his superior and considered quitting. But his bosses persuaded him to stay.

But the following year, Leonard Goldberg left the top programming job and Marty Starger took over. Eisner was named his executive assistant, which put Eisner on a more equal footing with Diller. Even today Starger seems amazed that he survived being boss to Diller and Eisner. "Imagine having the two of them, side by side, and they're working for you," he says.

Starger soon sent Diller to the West Coast — in part, according to Eisner, "because Barry was difficult to manage and Marty wanted some breathing room." No doubt, Eisner was glad to have Diller out of Manhattan. Diller had his offices on Sunset Boulevard done in a cool minimalist style, with white oak floors and white rugs. There was a patio and Diller had an extra-long cord attached to his phone so he could sit outside while he vented at his adversaries and underlings. Diller's rise to head of prime-time programming had been based largely on the strength of his success with *Movie of the Week*, and his attention still continued to be engaged primarily by these made-for-television films and miniseries.

In 1971, Eisner became head of children's and daytime programming. ABC was in last place in daytime, and even though his new job was not as prestigious as a position in prime time, Eisner saw some advantages. Not only was he overseeing a major profit center for the studio, but he had an opportunity to garner more attention for himself. The network was already performing poorly in daytime, so he concluded, "The risks were minimal."

"Barry built a new area," says Zimbert. "Michael took a disaster area— daytime—and suddenly there was this tall, gangly, kind of goofy guy who brought tremendous energy and focus."

"He had very good instincts and he has confidence in those instincts and that is a very rare quality," says Stoddard—who respected Eisner without especially liking him. To some degree, Eisner was swimming upstream in this division, Stoddard says. "He had to stand up in affiliate meetings and talk about what would happen with *General Hospital* or *All My Children,* and the audience was mostly guys [who ran small television stations] who could care less."

Eisner also turned around children's programming at ABC. At the time, Stoddard recalls, the networks were facing one of their periodic bouts with parents over the lack of quality children's shows. Eisner held a workshop and invited teachers, parents, and opinion leaders—even the other networks, which declined to participate. ABC's award-winning *Afterschool Specials* emerged from this meeting. Eisner also took up a suggestion to air *Schoolhouse Rock,* short animated films that "cost a bloody fortune," as Stoddard remembers, but were well-produced educational features. In a more commercial vein, Eisner put an animated series based on the Jackson Five on the air.

Over at CBS, Fred Silverman noticed Eisner's innovations and still praises them in a somewhat backhanded manner. "To his credit, if he saw that *Scooby Doo* was working on CBS, the next season there would be a show that looked an awful lot like *Scooby Doo,* only it would be a ghost dog," he says. "He had a very commercial sense. The first area where he really excelled was the Saturday-morning kid's stuff. It just happened to use a lot of the ideas and basic concepts that originally started at CBS."

Eisner had yet another area of responsibility: game shows. At one point he and Jane flew to Los Angeles to attend what turned out to be an unexciting run-through of a program that was being pitched to the network. From the pack of William Morris agents who were present, one young man emerged and introduced himself as Mike Ovitz. When Eisner returned to his hotel, Ovitz phoned him there. "I was just wondering how you liked the show," he asked. Eisner hadn't much liked it but told Ovitz that his wife had loved it. In fact, he had been annoyed by the call and was even more irritated the next day when, on returning to New York, he found that Ovitz had sent Jane two dozen roses. "Glad you loved our show," read the card. "Thanks for the help." Eisner called to complain that Ovitz's attempt to enlist his wife's support was inappropriate. Ovitz apologized and took the opportunity to make some jokes that Eisner found disarming. Beneath his annoyance, he said later, he was impressed by Ovitz's nerve as a salesman.

∽

IN 1973, ABC moved Michael Eisner to the West Coast as vice-president for prime-time programming. Despite Diller's success with *Movie of the Week*, ABC's regular prime-time programming was weak. The fall schedule for the 1973–74 season included soon-to-be forgotten new shows like *Toma*. ABC scrambled to line up new shows to plug into its weekly grid. The joke in the industry was that no one could find kidnapped heiress Patty Hearst because she was on ABC at eight o'clock on Friday night.

"Barry never liked series programming," says Fred Pierce, who became president of ABC Television in 1974. "Series programming is about having likable characters. It's about relationships. Movies are more about specific ideas."

Diller says that he was only beginning to get the hang of his job. "I screw everything up before I get it right," he says. But he did not dally at ABC much longer. Gulf + Western chairman Charlie Bluhdorn wanted him to come to Paramount and initially suggested that he could be an executive vice-president, reporting to Frank Yablans. When he made that proposal over dinner one night, Diller replied, "I'd sooner work for the waiter." Finally Bluhdorn said, "I'll give you my job at Paramount — chairman."

Martin Davis, then a no-nonsense Gulf + Western executive working closely with Bluhdorn, later remembered the impression Diller had made. "We clearly were infatuated with him," he said. "Was I enthusiastic? Absolutely. We were super-impressed with Barry, and on talent, we weren't wrong."

But this was a dark day for Yablans — the man who had sent Diller the elephant, the pig, and the coffin. Though he had taken a hand in bringing such films as *Love Story* and *The Godfather* to the studio, Yablans had fallen from Bluhdorn's favor. Many industry observers say Yablans had simply failed to show Bluhdorn sufficient respect. Yablans was noted for mimicking Bluhdorn's Austrian accent, which made his boss livid. A September 1974 article in *New York* magazine, in which Yablans likened himself to Cecil B. DeMille, Jack Warner, L. B. Mayer, and Harry Cohn, was widely perceived as fatal. That account maintained that Yablans had "managed to beat [Bluhdorn] back to a largely supervisory role."

But Diller says Bluhdorn was reacting to a far more serious problem than a wounded ego. "People didn't understand Bluhdorn well because he was so theatrical," he says. "Bluhdorn did not want to 'slap' Frank Yablans because of the *New York* magazine story. Frank Yablans was simply spinning out of control—truly out of control. . . . An executive of a corporation simply could not maintain his position in these out-of-control ways. It had been going on for more than a year."

Bluhdorn called ABC chairman Leonard Goldenson to ask the network to release Diller from his contract. Goldenson conferred with his top executives and concluded that he had better give in. If he didn't, he reasoned, Diller would become an unhappy and problematic employee. As head of a studio, Diller might at least give ABC first crack at promising television shows that Paramount had in the works. Diller was released and took the chairman's title. He was thirty-two years old.

Robert Evans, the head of production under Yablans, had enjoyed his own long and emotional relationship with Bluhdorn while the studio made such enormous hits as *Love Story* and *The Godfather*. When Diller came aboard, the two sat down. "Congratulations, Barry," Evans said. "I'm going to enjoy working together."

"Let's get something straight," Diller replied. "We're not working together. You're working for me." Evans's career as an executive was over; it was time to become an independent producer.

Yablans says Bluhdorn tried to keep him working alongside Diller, talking about the "impossible dream" of assembling the ideal team of disparate executives to run the studio. The impossible dream was one of Bluhdorn's favorite themes, and as an immigrant who was running an enormous conglomerate, he certainly had savored the realization of many impossible dreams. But Yablans says that for him, remaining at the studio seemed like "an impossible nightmare." Diller concurred. Before long, Diller had the place to himself.

3

HAPPY DAYS

WHILE DILLER ASCENDED a steep learning curve in his new job at Paramount, Eisner was enjoying a honeymoon during which he got to run ABC's prime-time programming. By now Eisner lived at 1357 Belfast Drive, just above Sunset Strip. He and Jane entertained often; one friend said Jane was the first woman she knew who had two dishwashers in her kitchen. The Eisners were close friends with Neil and Marsha Diamond, though when that marriage split up, only the relationship between the wives survived.

At the office, Eisner maintained an erratic schedule. He often canceled appointments as more important meetings took precedence. Young agents like Mike Ovitz used to loiter outside his office because they couldn't get their calls returned. Ovitz even gave one of Eisner's secretaries a bottle of perfume to win her favor.

Despite his capacity for switching course, Eisner didn't like being labeled as erratic. "The word 'mercurial' came up in the office," remembers Lee Wedemeyer, who became Eisner's secretary at ABC. "He looked at me and said, 'I am *not* mercurial.' That was a word he did not want used to describe him. Because he was."

Eisner conducted business behind a round glass table that served as his desk. "We must have had to clean it fifty times a day," one of his assistants remembers with a sigh. The furniture was contemporary—black leather couches and chairs.

Martin Starger, who had been Diller and Eisner's boss, left ABC soon after Diller's departure—eased out by Fred Pierce, the recently named president of ABC Television. Like Starger, Pierce was impressed by Eisner's "boyish enthusiasm," and he also quickly saw that Eisner had "mile-a-minute ideas, many of which were not usable." For some months, Eisner worked directly with Pierce on the prime-time schedule. Together they rushed six shows into production for the midseason schedule beginning in January 1975. Three of these—*Baretta*, *Barney Miller*, and the extraordinarily violent *S.W.A.T.*—became morale-boosting hits.

One night around Christmas, just weeks before these shows were to debut, Pierce ran into Fred Silverman at the '21' Club in New York. Silverman had risen to head of programming at CBS, which was riding very high with *The Mary Tyler Moore Show*, *M*A*S*H*, *All in the Family*, and *Hawaii Five-O*. But Pierce knew that Silverman was feeling underappreciated and he made his move. In May, ABC announced that Silverman would become president of ABC's programming division.

Chain-smoking and obese, Silverman was not an especially pretty picture at the time. One assistant remembers that during meetings at his beach house, he would hold up an empty pack of Marlboros and bellow for more. She stayed in his good graces by learning to make a good martini. At three P.M., another associate remembers, Silverman always checked his watch, announced that it was cocktail hour in New York, and started drinking. But Silverman was the most brilliant television executive of the time. For ABC, hiring him was a stunning coup.

For Eisner, it was not welcome news to have the man who had been head of daytime programming at CBS when he had been a lowly commercial coordinator slide into a job that Eisner was already doing. Though ABC was having a bad season, Eisner had started to engineer a comeback and that must have made Silverman's arrival much harder to take. "He probably had a right to feel that way," Pierce concedes. But considering the severity of the network's problems, he says, "I felt it was worth the risk of recruiting Fred Silverman." Eisner made a stab at getting a new job, but finding no eager buyer, made his peace with the situation.

Despite the handful of hits that Eisner and Pierce had put on the schedule, Silverman was hardly excited by what he found at the network. "Barry left ABC in ashes," he says. "It was absolutely terrible. . . . There were a lot of shows with the letter K—*Kolchak*, *Kodiak*, *Nakia*—it was really a disastrous year. So the timing was very fortuitous for him, that he got the offer to go over to Paramount."

Diller says he doesn't really deserve blame for the "K" shows and says Starger was responsible for them. He acknowledges, however, that Silverman is "correct enough," that "ABC was a wreck." He continues: "I think if I had stayed I would have pulled it out of the fire. Maybe I wouldn't have. I'm not defensive about it. Had I stayed, I would have had a lot to do."

∽

FRED SILVERMAN SOON became the beneficiary of a project that Eisner had developed a couple of years earlier. Eisner had been stranded at Newark Airport during a snowstorm with his wife, his three-month-old son, and Tom Miller, the head of development for Paramount. Eisner suggested that he and Miller use the time to think of new ideas for programming. "What was your favorite show?" Eisner asked.

"*Father Knows Best,*" Miller replied without hesitation.

"I liked *Mama,*" Eisner said. That series had been based on a warmhearted 1948 film about a Scandinavian family in San Francisco.

Eisner wrote a four-page paper based on this brainstorming session called "New Family in Town." Miller suggested that Garry Marshall, an established television writer and producer with *The Odd Couple* series under his belt, would have the perfect sensibility for the program. Marshall liked the concept but made a few modifications. "They talked about a sweet, sentimental show like *Mama,*" he says. "I vaguely remembered it. It seemed to be about a Norwegian family with a lot of people named Lars." Marshall suggested setting the show in the Bronx—his home turf. The network rejected that idea (it was considered "too ethnic"). Eisner proposed making it more Midwestern, and since Miller was from Milwaukee, the program was set there.

Marshall had another idea. "The fifties are back," he told Miller. Miller liked the idea of setting the show in an earlier era and called Eisner. "I love the fifties!" Eisner exclaimed.

"I'm glad you do because you're the one who has to tell us to go to script," Miller replied.

Marshall wrote a script that was everything Miller had wanted. When Eisner read it, he called to say that he loved it, too. "Let me give you the go-ahead," he told Miller. "Let me call you right back." But when he called again, Miller could hear the disappointment in his voice. The network didn't want to pay for a pilot.

Eisner tried another approach. Paramount was making *Love, American Style* for ABC and Eisner said the network could pay an extra $100,000 to make *New Family in Town,* now retitled *Happy Days,* as an episode. *Love,*

American Style presented a series of unrelated stories each week so the *New Family in Town* pilot would fit right in.

"What's it going to be, *Love in the Happy Days*?" Miller asked. But Eisner was hoping that his bosses would like the episode so much that they would approve the series and never even air it on *Love, American Style*.

Meanwhile, Miller got in touch with Ronnie Howard, who had been the child star of the long-running *Andy Griffith Show*. "Ron had just gotten his driver's license," Miller remembers. "He was so proud. He said, 'I just started in cinema school and that's what I really want to do.'" But he liked the script and agreed to take the part of Richie Cunningham. The episode was shot and a test audience loved it. As Miller waited outside an executive screening room, Eisner once again tried to convince his superiors to make the show into a series. He emerged with a long face.

"They thought it was wonderful and charming but they just felt it was a little too soft," he said. "Look, you have no idea how much I love this show. Damn it, I know we're right."

But Eisner and Miller were defeated. Several months later, Miller got a call from an upcoming filmmaker named George Lucas, who asked if he could look at some footage of Ron Howard as a fifties teen to see whether he was right for an upcoming film. Based on the television performance, Lucas cast Howard in *American Graffiti*, which became, in turn, one of the top-grossing films of 1973. "Thank God, George Lucas is a genius and he made a wonderful film," Marshall says. "At the same time *Grease* was coming out on Broadway." Now the fifties were indeed back. Miller called Eisner to remind him about *Happy Days*. With the Zeitgeist turning his way and his own star on the rise, Eisner finally got a green light for the show. "Don't get scared but I'm prepared to put this on in five weeks," he said. "Let's meet."

"So fast he's moving?" Marshall asked when Miller told him the news.

"They don't have hits," Miller replied.

Inspired by *American Graffiti*, Eisner told Marshall, "I love that movie! We need a gang!"

Marshall didn't like the idea of blatantly ripping off *American Graffiti*. "We'll have one guy and he'll give you the illusion that there's a gang," he said. Miller came up with an actor named Henry Winkler. Even Winkler thought he was wrong for the part. "This is my Fonzie?" Marshall asked Miller after Winkler left the audition. But Miller convinced him to give Winkler a try.

Happy Days debuted in the middle of 1974 as a midseason replacement facing the stiff competition of two top-rated shows: *Maude* and *Adam-12*. "Michael went crazy. The minute we got any footage at all, he started making promos, promos, promos," Miller remembers. "I was actually embarrassed. . . . He was so completely obsessed that this was going to work — he insisted that the American public tune in against two of the top five shows."

Happy Days wasn't an instant hit. "Fred Silverman seemed to understand that shows evolve — they're not really created," Marshall says. Soon, however, it began to catch on. Winkler's finger-snapping gang of one — the Fonz — was the show's most popular character. The series rose to number one in the country, where it stayed for several years. Even today it still plays in syndication, continuing to throw off cash. It also begat other top-rated spinoff series: *Laverne & Shirley* and *Mork & Mindy*.

"The only thing I felt bad about was that everybody thought *Happy Days* was a ripoff of *American Graffiti*," says Miller, who felt that he had graciously sent the unaired pilot of *Happy Days* to Lucas as a favor. "I saw Lucas on a talk show and he was asked, 'How does it feel to be ripped off?' And he said, 'What are you going to do?' And I thought, 'You know the real story.'"

Happy Days is just the sort of commercial fare that Eisner always enjoyed — a show hardly substantial enough to be analyzed. Marshall told Eisner that he always identified with Ron Howard's fresh-faced character, Richie Cunningham — the innocent and somewhat introspective youth. Eisner responded that he identified not with the thoughtful Richie or the cool Fonz, but with Potsie — a character distinguished mostly by a lack of distinction. Pleasant-looking, not too bright, the character, even Marshall concedes, never developed much of an identity. The idea that Eisner found something sympathetic in the unformed Potsie was puzzling. "I didn't quite get it," Marshall says. "Potsie was the friend who got taken along. The Potsies are part of the group, they're not leaders." Maybe, he concluded, Eisner saw himself as a friend of the "centers," rather than being part of the center himself.

But another former colleague from the years at ABC suggests that Eisner's offhanded remark about this *Happy Days* character reveals Eisner's own lack of a center. To that executive, Eisner seemed as undefined as the sitcom character with whom he identified — always ambivalent and hard to pin down. "Part of Michael, in addition to the good stuff and the talent, is a chameleon capacity," he says. "He can be whatever he needs to be at any moment. I've seen him adjust in seconds to whatever person is around him."

Others who worked closely with Eisner early in his career also say they don't quite know who he is. After knowing Eisner for some thirty years, Pudney acknowledges that he's not even certain who Eisner's friends are. Another longtime acquaintance says he finds Eisner "opaque." Eisner has even kept a physical distance in the often touchy-feely entertainment world. "You don't see him kissing people," Pudney observes. "He shakes hands and he kind of backs off."

Lee Wedemeyer, Eisner's secretary at ABC and subsequently at Paramount, says Eisner wasn't even comfortable shaking hands—partly because of hypochondria. When he broke a finger playing basketball, she reflected that he was probably glad to have an excuse for avoiding contact. She noticed Eisner's aloofness on other occasions. Once he sent her a note and signed it "L—Michael." It wasn't lost on Wedemeyer that he "almost let himself say, 'love,' " but didn't. She pointed it out to ABC executive Bob Boyette. "Bob and I got together and took it to him and said, 'Finish the word,' " she remembers. "He would not. And he didn't think it was funny."

❧

EISNER LEARNED THE limits of courage early on, when he ran afoul of Aaron Spelling. ABC owed a debt of gratitude to Spelling, who had played an important role in the network's efforts to launch *Movie of the Week*. Spelling continued to provide ABC with major hit shows—his *Mod Squad* was a staple for four years—and in exchange, he won increasingly favorable deals from the network. He became dominant to the point that the industry joked that ABC stood for "Aaron's Broadcasting Company."

In the mid-seventies, Spelling had a guarantee that the network would pick up at least one pilot a year. He discussed a number of proposals with Eisner, who didn't like any of them. Eisner instructed his staff to tell Spelling that ABC would pay his fee but would pass on a pilot for the year. This was hardly the sort of respect that Spelling was used to commanding.

"We were having a hard time with Michael," remembers Leonard Goldberg, the former ABC executive who had become Spelling's partner. "This was, I guess, Michael's first real 'I'm the boss' kind of stuff. . . . He was very up-front. He wouldn't hide behind anybody. He was never afraid." But apparently Eisner didn't grasp the scope of Spelling's influence. Goldberg says he and Spelling angrily asked themselves, "Who the fuck is he?"

Spelling knew how to deal with punks. He complained to his attorney, Bill Hayes, a dashing silver-haired figure who had served as a fighter pilot during the Second World War. He was at the epicenter of the old-boy network and was as connected as it was possible to be in a business composed of intertwined relationships. Among his friends was Elton Rule, the president of ABC. Hayes explained to Rule that Michael Eisner was causing problems and might need to look for employment elsewhere.

Hayes told this story to another client, a young producer named Larry Gordon. Gordon had started his career as Aaron Spelling's assistant and subsequently became head of production at American International Pictures, a low-budget movie factory that was then the home of B-movie king Roger Corman. Gordon had befriended Eisner when Eisner had relocated to the West Coast. "Your friend Michael Eisner is in trouble," Hayes told Gordon. He hadn't just annoyed Spelling—others were complaining, too. But Spelling was the one who counted. Gordon told Hayes to hold off while he talked to Eisner. Gordon quickly warned his friend to switch his tack with Spelling because he was about to be fired.

Eisner reversed course and picked up the disputed show: *Starsky and Hutch*. Later, Silverman would pluck *Charlie's Angels* from Eisner's trash heap. Ironically, those were among the hit shows that helped establish Eisner's reputation.

Later, Eisner told Spelling's partner, Goldberg, that he had been tipped off about Spelling's ire. "Until he told me, I thought he was genuinely enthusiastic about our next three shows," Goldberg says. In time, Eisner became adept at shifting blame when he wanted a project killed. "He's usually pretty positive," Pierce says. "That's an art—that art of not saying no."

Another associate at the time remembers watching Eisner phone a writer and tell him, "I read the script. It's fabulous!" But Eisner never addressed the question of whether the network would actually buy it. "I thought it was brilliant," this associate says. "The writer was thrilled but still didn't know if the script would get picked up." Getting to watch Eisner make such a call was a relatively rare treat, this individual remembers. "Normally, he didn't want anyone to see him in action."

∞

ALTHOUGH EISNER SOMETIMES created the illusion that someone else was pulling his strings, he always liked to have his way. "He was in charge of the West Coast and by and large I let him do his thing, I didn't interfere," says Silverman, who ran programming from New York. "He was very sensitive about that."

Silverman may not have thought much of ABC's schedule, but he had an eye for talent. He was particularly impressed that Pierce and Eisner—who, as he sees it, were left to mop up Diller's mess in prime-time programming—"really did a masterful job working together to create some shows and establish some building blocks for the network." Among those shows were *Happy Days*, *Welcome Back, Kotter*, and of course *Starsky and Hutch*. Silverman says he appreciated Eisner's talent so much that he "just bent over backward to make sure he was happy." Within six months of Silverman's arrival, ABC was in first place. The critics were unimpressed with ABC's crassly commercial, youth-oriented programming, but the public loved it.

Silverman also liked the strong staff that Eisner had assembled. In 1974, for example, he hired a young woman named Marcy Carsey as a program executive in comedy. She would prove to be a formidable talent in commercial television, later producing hits including *The Cosby Show*, *Roseanne*, and *3rd Rock from the Sun*. During her job interview, Carsey mentioned that she was three months pregnant and would resume her discussions with the network after she had her baby. "Why would we wait until after you have the baby?" Eisner asked.

Carsey, who knew that the television industry was not especially receptive to women—let alone pregnant ones—replied diplomatically that she thought people would be more comfortable with her after the baby was born. "I'm having a baby, too," Eisner said. "Is this a factor? Why are we talking about this?" Carsey was amazed and grateful that Eisner was willing to hire her knowing that she was expecting a child. Later, Eisner allowed her to bring her baby to work and hold meetings with her child in a bassinet in her office. It was part of an informal but hardworking atmosphere that Eisner encouraged. He held working lunches in the office so frequently that, by one account, his monthly bill once ran to $12,000.

Eisner was not so openhanded with Lee Wedemeyer when he asked her to work for him as his secretary. "In five minutes, we knew this was good," she remembers, describing their immediate rapport. "Michael really wanted me to go to work for him. . . . He needed a classy front and I provided that." But Wedemeyer had already been offered the chance to go to Europe on a four-week working trip for someone else. She asked Eisner if he would wait four weeks for her to start. "As much as he wanted me, he said he couldn't wait a month," she says. "It was interesting to me that he was willing not to have it unless he could have it on his terms. That's Michael." Wedemeyer gave up the trip in favor of the job.

Wedemeyer, who worked for Eisner for several years, says her stint at ABC was the best part of her career, even though she later made more money and acquired more power. Carsey also remembers those years fondly.

"Michael is by far the best executive I ever worked for," Carsey says. "With great courage and a sense of humor, Michael would stand up in front of his bosses at the scheduling board and give his rationale for the schedule he was pushing." Eisner would say, "Either it's going to work or it isn't. If it doesn't, get some other jerk to do this." If he was caught unprepared in a meeting, he took a brief run at his subject before saying, "I don't know what I'm talking about." The effect, she says, was "hugely disarming."

Eisner didn't handle conflict with explosions or confrontations. Once, she remembers, Eisner and a group of his staffers were meeting with Silverman when an executive named Andy Siegel disagreed with one of Eisner's points. Eisner was startled, Carsey says, because he had met with his executives beforehand and had not heard a word of dissent. After the meeting, Eisner started to pace as he reproached Siegel for the ambush. "I have to explain to you why that drives me crazy," he said. Carsey found this a rather low-key response to an issue that might have sent other bosses into a rage. "He was begging Andy to please understand," she says. "It was not polished, it was not corporate, it was not a boss talking to an employee."

Carsey noticed another trait that Garry Marshall also had observed: the sense that Eisner saw himself as an outsider who ultimately stood alone. "Michael taught me that my job wasn't about making friends and influencing people," Carsey says. "It didn't have anything to do with anything except getting a couple of hits a year. . . . He didn't care whether the ideas came from the elevator operator or if they came from going to the right parties." Carsey finds nothing surprising in the idea that Eisner shunned social relationships with colleagues. "Why would you have friends in this town?" she asks. She was more impressed that Eisner often went to Vermont to be with his family.

Though they were not close, Eisner once spontaneously dropped everything to accompany her while she looked at a house she was hoping to buy.
"Michael, it's forty-five minutes away," she said.

But Eisner was always fascinated by buildings. "Let me go with you,"
he urged.

He hopped into her old Honda and offered his usual cornucopia of ideas
about the property. "Michael and I were never friends," Carsey says. "He
was just curious and impulsive."

At first, Carsey was worried that she had been assigned a bunch of bad
shows that would fail. "If they all get canceled, do I get fired?" she asked
Eisner.

"No," he replied. "By then, it'll be somebody else's fault."

Carsey plucked a pilot called *The Life and Times of Captain Barney
Miller* out of the reject pile and asked permission to develop it. The show
debuted in mid-1975 and ran for eight seasons. But if the show had failed,
Carsey says, Eisner would not have reproached her. "I could talk him into
something and he would never, ever come to us later and say, 'I told you
it wouldn't work.' He allowed us to fail. He'd say, 'Give me at least one hit
a year. I don't care how you get there. I don't care if you show me five
pilots that are so horrendous that you have to leave the room, if the sixth
one is great.'"

Despite having the courage of his own convictions that Carsey, Goldberg, and others observed, Eisner also had a characteristic pessimism. Not
only was he "always a bit of a hypochondriac," Pierce remembers, but he
always seemed to anticipate a professional disaster of some sort. "Even today
he operates as if failure is always around the corner," says Pierce. "I think
that's what drives him."

But at ABC in 1976, failure was nowhere in sight. A taped memo that
Eisner made for his boss, Silverman, in July 1976 illustrates the wealth of
commercial material that ABC was creating for viewers for the fall — and
the myriad problems with script, casting, and star personalities that came
with the hit shows. Eisner began by discussing movies: among Brandon
Stoddard's projects was a made-for-television project called *The Love Boat*,
and Eisner said the network was "totally prepared" to make a sequel or a
regular series if the first movie was a big hit. Stoddard was reviewing a script
for another proposed Aaron Spelling–Leonard Goldberg picture called *Fantasy Island*.

And there were high hopes for a nearly completed Spelling-Goldberg picture called *Little Ladies of the Night*. "Brandon tells me that NBC is not only panickly interested as to when we are going to air the movie but exactly how far we went with the teenage prostitution," Eisner said. ABC went far enough to earn the picture one of the highest ratings for any made-for-television movie.

Filming had been completed on *Twenty-one Hours at Munich*, a movie about the terrorist attack at the 1972 Olympics. "One thing that we discussed here . . . because the heat on this whole Israeli terrorism story is so immense — is to make sure that we have *Twenty-one Hours at Munich* early enough to take advantage of that," Eisner told Silverman.

Eisner addressed a number of complaints on the taped message to Silverman: The New York office was interfering too much with decisions that should be made in Los Angeles and needed to be brushed back. "Otherwise, we will kill ourselves," he said in a brief, semihumorous but pointed warning. Another Spelling project in the works — a film named *The Boy in the Plastic Bubble* — needed script work and a cast. Eisner wanted a teenage actor named Gary Frank from the series *Family*. If not, he said, "one of the kids from *Kotter* is a possibility, Robbie Benson is a possibility." The kid from ABC's hit series *Welcome Back, Kotter* — John Travolta — got the part.

The seminal miniseries *Roots*, based on Alex Haley's book, was also in the middle of shooting. The only disappointment, Eisner told his boss, was actor John Amos as the central character, the mature Kunta Kinte. Amos is "strong, powerful, and not a good enough actor to match the rest of the people in the cast, but that won't be a problem 'cause we'll cut around him and so forth," Eisner assured Silverman. Others appearing in the miniseries included LeVar Burton, Ed Asner, Cicely Tyson, Lorne Green, Ben Vereen, Leslie Uggams, Chuck Conners, Louis Gossett Jr., Sandy Duncan, and O. J. Simpson. "So that's a pretty good cast," Eisner said. The same group, he joked, would also put in a guest appearance on an upcoming episode of *The Streets of San Francisco*.

Eisner also used the memo to provide a night-by-night update on ABC's regular series. *The Six Million Dollar Man* — the Lee Majors show about a bionic man with superhuman powers — was in its third season and Eisner said an October episode would feature a guest appearance by Farrah Fawcett, the lavishly maned former model who was red-hot in the new series *Charlie's Angels*. "Farrah is a little flat 'cause she's not the greatest actress in the world, but it's going to be an excellent episode with flashy holographics — whatever those are," Eisner reported.

Eisner also fretted about *Baretta*, a Roy Huggins series starring Robert
Blake as a streetwise cop who lived with a cockatoo named Fred. Blake had
started running the show "in his kind of insane way," Eisner said, and was
now said to be "an inch from cracking." Eisner had also been told that
Blake — who had a problem with substance abuse at this time — "looks
drawn and sullen and strange and noncommunicative and very, very weird."
The show was behind schedule. "They've got to catch up," Eisner said.
"He's letting the producers take over and he's running scared. I don't know
what's going to happen. . . . We're exercising as much control as possible
without putting Blake away." Blake later said he was doing what was necessary to maintain the show's quality. It lasted for one more season.

Whatever his initial misgivings, Eisner now said he was thrilled with
Charlie's Angels. "Whenever the girls are on-screen, the screen lights up
and they are beautiful and sexy and in character," he said. *Welcome Back,
Kotter* was rolling along and *The Streets of San Francisco* was in good shape.
Carsey's pet project was having problems with the actor who played a popular character named Fish. "*Barney Miller* is not quite as smooth as it
should be but it never has been," Eisner said. "Abe Vigoda did not show
up and he has been put on suspension. . . . We cannot fold to Abe Vigoda —
it's that simple."

Happy Days was going along well and Eisner tried to emphasize the
positive about the new spinoff, *Laverne & Shirley*. Penny Marshall and
Cindy Williams were getting a good grip on their characters. "The one
problem we have — and I've had calls from Cindy's agent — is that she's very
unhappy that Penny has all the jokes and all the scenes and all the relatives
and that she's sitting there as the straight man and it's the Penny Marshall
show," Eisner said. This had been a scenario that Williams had feared from
the start, since Garry Marshall — Penny's brother — was producing the show.
At the time, Eisner noted, Williams was in the hospital suffering from pneumonia — an illness that may have been "emotionally caused" in part because
she was so upset after filming the first episode. Eisner said he would try to
get Marshall to beef up Williams's role. It was a dispute he could not settle.

∽

BY THE TIME Eisner recorded that memo in the summer of 1976, his
relationship with Silverman had started to deteriorate. Eisner knew that
Silverman would get all the credit for turning ABC around and he knew
that he wasn't going to advance as long as Silverman was in place. Network

president Fred Pierce, who had been trying to make these two strong personalities complement each other for the previous year, found that he couldn't keep Eisner happy. "Fred [Silverman] was a pretty tough taskmaster and would call at all hours," Pierce says. "At that point Eisner had begun to say, 'I think I've had enough.' "

"Once in a while Michael wanted to get home earlier, wanted not to go over the same thing eight times," Carsey remembers. "Michael had a style that was very efficient, brisk, and energetic. Fred [Silverman] was more obsessive about time spent at work, the details — every aspect of every show. Michael was always the first to want to say, 'Fred, it's all going to be here tomorrow morning. I have a wife and kids at home.' " Once, she remembers, Eisner abruptly stood during a meeting and declared, "Fred, I can't do this anymore. I have to go."

In a similar vein, Eisner's assistant, Lee Wedemeyer, recalls: "Fred needed no sleep, so he would call people at two in the morning because he was up and he was working." When Silverman wanted Eisner to linger at the office, she remembers, Eisner said, "I'm going home or I'm going to have a divorce."

Silverman doesn't remember any friction with Eisner. "We agreed about almost everything," he says. "If we were wrong, we were really wrong together. We put a show on the air called *Mr. T and Tina* with Pat Morita — it was a really bad show. We both went in thinking it was going to be terrific. At least we were wrong together. I can't think of something he wanted to do that I said no to."

Carsey says Eisner wasn't just annoyed by Silverman's compulsive attention to detail. He also felt that Pierce never appreciated his successes. "Pierce never appreciated any of us," she says. "Pierce operated out of a fatal flaw in his thinking. He believed it was all luck."

Feeling harassed and undervalued, Eisner was ready to move on. And there was more. He was being courted by David Geffen, who was then briefly vice-chairman of the Warner studio, to run Warner's television division. At the time Geffen was close to Marlo Thomas, Diller's childhood friend. According to Geffen, Thomas let Diller know that Geffen was courting his old rival. Diller moved aggressively to hire Eisner to head television at Paramount.

Geffen and Diller were longtime friends but deeply competitive. "Barry didn't want Michael [but] he couldn't stand the idea of Michael coming to work for me," Geffen says. Diller disputes this, though he acknowledges that he knew Geffen had talked with Eisner. "I knew he would never take the job," Diller says. "He wouldn't want to be head of a television division."

Diller called Eisner, who had scarcely heard from his former boss except when Diller wanted a favor. "I hear you've really matured as an executive," Diller said now. "You even return your calls." With such honeyed words, Diller began to woo Eisner.

But Eisner hesitated. A friend urged him not to take the Paramount job if it were just to run television. "You want to be in the movie business," the friend urged. "You don't like working for Barry anyway." Diller had to sweeten the pot: instead of just television, Diller offered Eisner the title of president and chief operating officer of the whole studio.

Naturally, Eisner was now all but desperate to get out of his contract at ABC. Pierce refused. "He kept *schreiing* to Silverman, who kept coming to me. Fred wanted to let him out," Pierce remembers wryly. Silverman recalls that he pleaded with Pierce to release Eisner because he realized that it was hopeless to try to keep him. And Silverman says that when Eisner told him, "Barry offered me this job," he looked at Eisner and replied, "I knew I should have had him killed." He tried to convince Eisner to stay, without success. "It was endless," Silverman says. "It was just every day. He wouldn't take no for an answer. Finally we weren't getting any work done."

Eventually, Silverman went to Pierce. "You've got to let him out of his contract," he said. "Life is too short to have to go through this. He's miserable and we're getting 10 percent of what we should out of him." Pierce gave in and Eisner departed to work alongside his old rival at Paramount.

4

REVERSAL OF FORTUNE

BARRY DILLER HAD not been having an easy time of it. When he had arrived at Paramount Pictures in October 1974, in fact, Diller was widely viewed as a joke—little more than Charlie Bluhdorn's revenge on Frank Yablans. "Two or three months after I arrived at Paramount, there was a story in *People* magazine about me failing upward based upon the ABC season to date," Diller says. "That was just the beginning of my baptism for the next couple of years of pain."

It takes time to effect change at a studio—at least eighteen months before a new chief can pack his projects into the pipeline. And Diller had no background in film; he was looked down upon in the studio world as a television guy. He acknowledges that getting his bearings in the film world "took longer than I expected." A colleague still remembers Diller sighing, "Every day I come to work and I am humbled by the chaos of the previous day."

When he left ABC, Diller hired business-affairs executive Richard Zimbert as well as Dick Sylbert, a distinguished production designer who had never worked as an executive. After a few months Diller added David Picker, a veteran of United Artists who had made a mark by launching the James Bond franchise. Diller had hoped that Picker would supply the kind of film-business seasoning that he lacked. But the studio was cold as ice. In 1976, Paramount had the lowest earnings of any of the six major film companies.

Diller remembers that the other executives at the studio were "more than skeptical" about him (although anyone who displayed that attitude openly didn't work there long). "The first two years were a nightmare," Diller says. "More than the first two years—but the first two years were very, very difficult. We were changing the nature of how these companies worked and we certainly failed before we succeeded."

Though Diller's background in television was considered a handicap in the film community, he thinks it ultimately helped him succeed. "My history was in television. I was not nailed down to the movie business. . . . I could not be corrupted by its history," Diller says. And if the movie world regarded him with disdain, he returned the sentiment in full. "I was so scorned," he remembers. "I had nobody paying much attention or arguing very much from wisdom or knowledge against me that I had very much respect for." There were a few whose talent impressed Diller sufficiently that he paid attention to them: Francis Coppola, Warren Beatty, Katharine Hepburn. And, he adds with uncharacteristic vulnerability, "They were the only people who were really nice to me."

The film industry had been in a severe slump. Most of the major studios had moved away from their campuslike lots, and Paramount's management was comfortably ensconced in offices on Canon Drive in Beverly Hills— walking distance from the restaurants where they liked to eat their lunch. The Paramount lot, a few miles to the east on then-unfashionable Melrose Avenue, was virtually shut down and half of it was owned by an Italian firm. With *Godfather II* poised for release shortly after his arrival at Paramount, Diller found himself musing to director Francis Coppola that he had finally gotten to the movie business in a top-level job but didn't really feel the part. "Here I am in the middle of Beverly Hills," he said.

"Why don't you revive the lot?" Coppola asked.

Diller was immediately struck by the idea. "Could we do it?" he said. "Would people come here? Could we make an environment out of it?" After mulling it over, Diller presented the idea to his staff: "I came in and I said, 'Guess what? We're going home. We're going back to Paramount. We're getting out of this building.' And they all thought I was nuts." But Diller began to push the Italian owners off the lot. "I made their lives miserable for a year or two," he says. He also asked production chief Sylbert, the former art director, for advice on what colors to paint the buildings and gates. Eventually, Paramount became green and campuslike—the "environment" that Diller had envisioned.

∽

AS DILLER STRUGGLED to find his footing, there was one dominant influence on his life: the charming, rapacious, manipulative, and infuriating Charlie Bluhdorn. "It was this pressure cooker of Bluhdorn that made me much stronger, because my relationship with Charlie was a constant battle,"

Diller says. "It was excellent for me because it forced me to be strong when I didn't feel like it. It forced me to defend my world and do the things I wanted to do."

Diller's deeply conflicted emotions about Bluhdorn suffuse his recollections. "Charlie was a tempestuous, argumentative, emotional, shrewd, out of control—though never really—personality who would use any tactic, fair or unfair, to get his point across," he says with affection tinged with bitterness. Bluhdorn had hired Diller with the sense that in this young man, he had met as contrary and clever a combatant as he could hope to find, and Diller did not disappoint. Such intense and paternalistic relationships were not uncommon in an industry dominated by patriarchs—especially ones whose own sons do not fulfill their expectations.

"I was Charlie's impossible dream," Diller says. "Here Charlie Bluhdorn took a thirty-two-year-old person who was a middle executive of ABC and one day made him the chairman and chief executive of a movie company. That was insane and unheard of." During Diller's bumpy first two years, the dream seemed impossible indeed. Bluhdorn fretted constantly about Paramount's poor performance.

"Out of seven movie companies, we're the last place that anyone wants to come," Bluhdorn complained. "No one wants to deal with us."

"I like it that way better," Diller replied in his usual contrarian manner.

"You're out of your mind," Bluhdorn retorted. "Why would you like that way better?"

"Because my feeling is that most of the 'good' stuff, the highly prized [material] that you get first is usually terrible. I'm much better, frankly, not having to waste my time dealing with all these big producers and movie stars. We can develop the material we like."

"You're going to bankrupt us!" Bluhdorn exclaimed.

In virtually every way, Diller says, the travails of dealing with Bluhdorn sharpened his skills. "He was totally undisciplined—no sense of organization, which made me have a sense of organization," Diller says. "I was dealing with somebody who would totally disrespect [organization] and that only made me erect the walls higher. He was much more competitive than me and it made me more competitive in response."

One of Bluhdorn's exasperating traits, Diller recalls, was making up ideas for movies. "Charlie had the worst ideas known to man in the movie business," Diller remembers with a chuckle. "He liked actually making up stories. We never made any of those things he made up into movies. I would say, 'What are you doing making up an idea for a movie? I don't make up ideas for movies. Nobody who does the work we do makes up ideas.' . . . To Charlie, the only thing that was worth anything was doing the impossible."

Bluhdorn didn't confine himself to pitching stories. He was deeply involved in the studio's business, for better or worse. "Everyone else failed who tried to talk Francis Coppola into doing *Godfather II*," Diller says. "Bluhdorn did it. It was impossible. Unfortunately [years later, in 1983] . . . I watched Bluhdorn talk [John] Travolta into doing the sequel to *Saturday Night Fever*, and really, if his career had not been completely dead, it was buried on the heels of this movie."

By the summer of 1976, Paramount's performance was still so bad that Diller offered to quit. "I think we're doing good work but the results are so terrible that probably around the first of the year, I think I should leave," he told Bluhdorn. Paramount had suffered through *Won Ton Ton, The Dog Who Saved Hollywood*—a failed satire of Hollywood before the talkies—and a batch of other barkers like *Lifeguard*, *Face to Face*, and *Lipstick*. Bluhdorn seemed ready to agree if things didn't turn around.

The summer had brought the studio one sleeper hit based on a script Diller had bought three weeks into his tenure on Sylbert's recommendation. *The Bad News Bears* starred Walter Matthau as a beer-swilling coach of a kids' baseball team and featured Tatum O'Neal, who had stolen America's heart in *Paper Moon*. The movie grossed $32 million. But otherwise, Paramount's results were awful. Into this discouraging environment stepped the thirty-four-year-old Eisner, another upstart from television with no experience in film. "I was desperate for company," Diller later told a reporter. "I hated everyone in the movie business."

Hiring Eisner—his former rival—was an emotionally nuanced choice for Diller, who certainly must have appreciated the scope of Eisner's ambition. But he didn't want to let Eisner go to work for Geffen, and he certainly needed help. Even now, decades later, Diller betrays ambivalence about the decision to bring his former colleague at ABC to the studio. Rather than praise Eisner as a gifted executive or a brilliant creative mind, Diller portrays Eisner as a prod to his own talent. Asked why he hired Eisner, Diller replies, "Michael stimulated me."

Once Eisner agreed to come to Paramount, he and his assistant, Lee Wedemeyer, walked all over the lot. "We were kids with a new toy," Wedemeyer says. At one point she explored the upper level of the administration building—not yet transformed by Diller—and found an "old, dank" series of offices with cobwebs in every corner. But the space had potential. Eisner's wife, Jane, helped him decorate it, again in contemporary style with another glass-topped desk—larger and oblong this time—and chic off-white Jim Hicks carpeting. Eisner also had a device that let him close his door without crossing the room. Here he often worked through lunch, feasting on cream-cheese-and-jelly sandwiches and a mixture of tea with orange and lemon juice that he called "Jewish iced tea."

Leonard Goldberg, the man who had been Diller's and Eisner's first boss at ABC, saw Eisner a few weeks after he started at Paramount in November 1974 at a meeting about making a sequel to *The Bad News Bears*. As Goldberg arrived in the crowded conference room, Eisner stopped him at the door. "Why did you bring all these people?" he asked.

"They're your people," Goldberg replied.

"I don't know who they are," Eisner confessed.

As the meeting progressed, Goldberg could see that Eisner, like Diller, was getting hazed by those who didn't consider television a worthy apprenticeship for a career in film. But none of this seemed to faze Eisner. It was around Christmas and there wasn't even a script for the *Bad News Bears* sequel, which Eisner was determined to see released in the summer. One Paramount executive declared that the picture couldn't possibly be ready in time if there wasn't even a script yet.

"We'll sit here and think of a story," Eisner said.

"This isn't television," the Paramount executive responded with a sneer. "We can't legislate creativity."

"Maybe it ought to be," Eisner returned. By the time the meeting broke, a story had been outlined. The picture was in the theaters by June 2. And Eisner had taken his first steps down a maverick path in the movie business. Rather than waiting for writers and producers to pitch projects, why not come up with ideas at the studio? That's what Eisner had done at ABC— hadn't he come up with the inspiration for *Happy Days?*—and that's what he would demand of his staff at the studio. Diller and Eisner were going to take control of Paramount's destiny and provide an adrenaline jolt to the entertainment industry. Whether having executives ride herd so closely on the creative process would ultimately lead to better moviemaking, of course, was an entirely different matter.

AS EISNER UNPACKED his boxes at Paramount, he found that one of his festering problems at ABC had followed him to his new job. Cindy Williams, who played Shirley to Penny Marshall's Laverne on the new Paramount-produced hit television series, had grown so unhappy that she had walked off the show. The situation had already degenerated to the point where Williams had asked her manager, Pat McQueeney, to use a stopwatch to time her minutes on-screen and compare them with Marshall's. Each star also began jealously demanding whatever the other was getting: Williams asked for a bathtub in her trailer; Marshall got one, too. Marshall wanted a chauffeur; Williams followed suit. At story conferences, the stars would glance at a script and then one or the other threw it against a wall.

"She has been like a foreign being to me," Penny Marshall said of her costar in an interview. "We were pushed together." As far as she was concerned, Williams was "a baby and a pain."

"I was disappointed," Williams countered. "And I kept telling them I was disappointed and they didn't hear me. So one day, with my knees knocking, and shaking all over, I slithered off the lot and came home. Honestly, I thought they might arrest me." After Williams walked off, McQueeney told the *Los Angeles Times* that her client had been guaranteed roughly as much time on-screen as her costar. The day the story appeared in the newspaper, McQueeney's phone rang at 6:30 A.M. It was Michael Eisner, whose job it was to keep the production going.

"What are you doing to me my first day on the lot?" he asked.

"If you have a script where Cindy has more than three lines, I'll buy you dinner," McQueeney replied.

To Garry Marshall, the show had already turned into a "nightmare." His *Happy Days* cast had always gotten along, but the *Laverne & Shirley* group was either "communally depressed" or "cranky, like a kindergarten class that had missed nap time." He could only conclude that the stars were miserable to deal with because they were unhappy with their lives. Now, according to McQueeney, Penny was so livid at McQueeney's comments that she stormed into Williams's dressing room and threw things around. Rather than take on Marshall—who was, after all, the sister of the show's creator—the producers banned McQueeney from the set. And they finally got Eisner to exile her from the Paramount lot altogether. "Michael did it," McQueeney remembers. Eisner was not going to tackle Garry Marshall over this one. "He shrugged his shoulders and said, 'You're right. But I'm dealing with an eight-hundred-pound gorilla here.'"

∽

EVEN BEFORE EISNER came to the studio, it was clear that Diller was dissatisfied with production executive David Picker. Casual in jeans and open shirts, Picker didn't fit in with Diller at all. "David Picker's philosophy was to pick filmmakers and leave them alone," Diller says. "My philosophy, coming from television, was you never leave anyone alone." Picker was eighteen months into a two-year contract when Diller had told him that Eisner had been hired. And Eisner made it painfully apparent that he was not interested in sharing power. Picker was quickly cut out of the loop as Eisner borrowed a technique from his boss that Diller called "firing by process"—simply setting up a structure that excluded the unwanted employee. When Picker's contract expired, he moved on.

To Richard Sylbert, art had gone out the window as commerce strolled through the door in the person of Michael Eisner. Sylbert had been the production designer on such classic films as *The Manchurian Candidate*, *The Pawnbroker*, *Who's Afraid of Virginia Woolf?*, and *The Graduate*. He saw little prospect of making great movies on Eisner's watch. "Michael Eisner is a machine," he says years later. "He's a sausage-making machine. He invents something to go between commercials. What it is, he doesn't care. . . . There is no such thing as a Michael Eisner idea. It's an oxymoron."

Sylbert attended a series of meetings with Eisner that left him altogether dispirited. "I remember him sitting at the head of the table insisting that people manufacture something," he says. Finally Sylbert went to Eisner's office for yet another meeting. "I'd already been bad-mouthing him anyway," Sylbert says. "He pitched [an idea]. He said, 'It's a space movie—*Romeo and Juliet* in space.' Some strange, stupid idea. And I said, 'You're making the knockwurst *Tristan and Isolde*?' He said, 'Why do you say things like that?' I said, 'Because I think it.' " Very soon, Sylbert was also excised from the ranks.

Despite the hard luck that Diller had been having at the box office, Eisner did not find the studio's cupboards bare. Instead, as Eisner devoted himself to reading his own projects, Paramount's fortunes took a stunning turn. October 1977 brought a glimmer of light in the form of *Looking for Mr. Goodbar*, a dark story about a seemingly straitlaced schoolteacher (Diane Keaton) seeking thrills in New York singles bars. Sylbert had been the one who had proposed buying the rights to Judith Rossner's best-selling novel. "It wasn't a huge success," Diller remembers, "but it was a real movie.

It was different from movies that were being offered then and that kind of said, 'We're not total imbeciles.' "

In December, Paramount opened a big holiday gift. Before he had left, Picker had forged a relationship with producer Robert Stigwood, who had shown him a *New York* magazine article called "Tribal Rites of the New Saturday Night," a story about a young man from Brooklyn who got his release every weekend in the local disco. (It became known later that the story was partly fiction.) Picker had immediately bought the rights.

Eisner had arrived at the studio just as shooting was about to begin. The picture got off to a rough start when director John Avildsen, red-hot off *Rocky*, was fired after clashing with the producers. One of the issues, according to Avildsen, was his inability to cast the female lead. "I didn't see any sense hiring someone I didn't think was terrific, but they thought I was dragging my feet," Avildsen says. "I remember Michael calling me before I got fired, sort of reassuring me that everything was going to be okay. . . . Shortly after that, I got fired." He was replaced by John Badham, a director who had primarily worked in television.

The female lead went to a little-remembered actress named Karen Lynn Gorney. The main character would be portrayed by the kid from *Welcome Back, Kotter* whom Eisner had cast by default in ABC's *Boy in the Plastic Bubble* movie. Now John Travolta strutted across the floor with his open-collared shirt and tight pants and launched himself as a megastar. When it opened in December 1977, *Saturday Night Fever* spawned Travolta look-alike contests and dance competitions across the country. The soundtrack, packed with Bee Gees tunes, racked up record-breaking sales and won five Grammys.

Diller had been certain the picture would be a hit and opening night in New York justified his confidence. "There were lines around the block and the pressure in front of the theater was exciting and crazy and that was the first experience I had with that," he remembers. The picture, which grossed $94 million in the U.S., ranked right behind *The Godfather* on the list of Paramount's all-time moneymakers. It was the industry's third biggest hit of 1977 behind the twin killers, *Star Wars* and *Close Encounters of the Third Kind*. After the picture sat in the number-one spot for several weeks, Bluhdorn had Tiffany's make up a copy of *Variety*'s box-office listings in silver as a gift for Diller. Across the bottom, inscribed in Bluhdorn's scrawl, it read, "We're on the way. Your friend, Charlie." Such praise was touching to Diller, who twenty years later still has the plaque on his wall, albeit in the bathroom.

After *Saturday Night Fever*, Paramount spit out a couple more commercial losers, including the controversial but flaccid *Pretty Baby*, with Brooke Shields as a child prostitute. There was also one of Eisner's first choices as studio chief: *American Hot Wax*, a nostalgic look back at fifties disc jockey Alan Freed. It included appearances by Chuck Berry and Jerry Lee Lewis (as well as early sightings of Fran Drescher and Jay Leno). Eisner loved the film so much that he said he watched it a dozen times, but the *American Graffiti* crowd didn't show up. Nonetheless, producer Art Linson remembers that Eisner never wavered. "When he liked something, he liked it regardless of what anyone else thought," Linson says. "He certainly wasn't afraid of his convictions."

Eisner had inherited many more projects from David Picker and there was one in particular that Diller and Eisner anticipated with dread. The film was based on the long-running Broadway show *Grease*, set in a high school during the fifties. Picker had hated it so much that he walked out in the first act. But Allan Carr, a portly and flamboyant producer, convinced him that a movie based on this featherweight musical would work. John Travolta was cast as the male lead.

"Barry Diller never liked the movie, bad-mouthed the movie, and I think would have canceled it," Carr remembered in an interview some months before his death in 1999. "But *Saturday Night Fever* was such a hit and John Travolta was so hot that he went along." Eisner didn't seem particularly interested in the project, either. "We had pleasant dealings with Michael Eisner but very little [contact]," Carr said.

In fact, Diller was appalled. "One night, Michael Eisner and I screened the rough cut of *Grease* and went, 'Oh, my God, they are going to murder us. We are going to have success in launching a superstar and then drowning one.' It was just horrendous," he says.

But aside from that, Diller's and Carr's accounts diverge. Carr said he faced an uphill battle to get the film respectably launched. His only ally was Frank Mancuso, the distribution chief, who promised Carr that he would look after the picture, making sure it was booked in decent theaters and that it had a good advertising campaign. Meanwhile, Carr said, Diller and Eisner were afraid to let theater owners preview the movie for fear they wouldn't book it. The same concern led them to do a test screening for a recruited audience in Hawaii just a few weeks before *Grease* was to open, hoping they could keep the results quiet. The studio even put fake labels on the film cans before they put them on the plane so no one would know that the film was being screened. *Grease* was spirited to Hawaii under the name *Goin' South*, a bawdy western starring and directed by Jack Nicholson that Paramount was to release in October.

According to Diller, the response in Honolulu was only fair, but Carr said the Honolulu audience adored the film. "It just swept the island," Carr said. He maintained that the positive reaction woke up Diller and Eisner, who summoned Carr to hear suggestions for improvements in the film over brunch at the Royal Hawaiian. By then, Carr said, he was no longer interested in hearing opinions from the Paramount suits. "I said to myself, 'This is all silliness. There's nothing to do.' I excused myself and went looking for a house. I thought, 'I'm going to be very, very rich.' . . . I put a hold on a mansion, and in June, the picture opened and I bought it."

But Diller says the studio reworked the film over Carr's objections. "We spent a good deal of money reshooting, agonizing, driving ourselves crazy," he says. "But [Carr] was more right than we were." Director Randal Kleiser confirms that. Eisner insisted on adding a scene to explain a confrontation between two of the key characters. "I did my best to make it work but it was like a sore thumb," Kleiser says. "He agreed." The scene disappeared.

Grease was a plotless bit of piffle, but between Olivia Newton-John's warbling and Travolta's shimmy, it became a phenomenon. It eclipsed not only *Saturday Night Fever* but *The Godfather* to become Paramount's all-time box-office champ, grossing $96.3 million. *Saturday Night Fever* had hip, urban appeal but *Grease* had the earning power of a film that plays to the heartland. The soundtrack sold twenty-five million copies. If the Paramount brass didn't get its appeal before, they got it now. (Or did they? A few years later they attempted *Grease 2*, without Travolta or costar Olivia Newton-John, hoping that the title alone would draw the crowds. It didn't. The picture grossed a paltry $6.5 million, and the studio wound up $9 million in the hole.)

Carr enjoyed his mansion in Hawaii for years to come, but he never felt that the studio showed much gratitude for the dog that turned out to be such a box-office champion. From Diller and Eisner, he said, he got "no thank-you, no acknowledgment."

Carr wasn't the only one feeling neglected. David Picker had put *Looking for Mr. Goodbar*, *Saturday Night Fever*, and *Grease* into production and yet Michael Eisner acted as if he'd invented them. That feeling intensified as Paramount continued to rack up hits that had been developed while Eisner was still at ABC. In June 1978, the studio followed *Grease* with another winner, *Heaven Can Wait*. The film, a remake of the delightful 1941 film *Here Comes Mr. Jordan*, originated at Warner Brothers. But its star, Warren Beatty, had quarreled with Warner over a number of issues, including his insistence that the studio pay Cary Grant $2 million for a supporting role. Finally Beatty and top Warner executive Frank Wells got to a point of mutual antagonism. The discussion descended to pettiness: As Beatty recalls, Wells refused to foot the bill for a watercooler in Beatty's office. "He said, 'We don't pay for watercoolers,'" Beatty recalls. "I said, 'Give me a day to take this picture somewhere else, and if I can't, I'll do whatever you want.'"

Beatty took the film to Paramount, where his friend Diller allowed him to make a soup-to-nuts Warren Beatty creation. The star produced it, acted in it, shared screenwriting credit with Elaine May, and split the directing chores with Buck Henry. A charming remake, *Heaven Can Wait* had Beatty as a good-hearted football hero who dies before his time and must return to earth in the body of a hard-hearted financier. The picture went on to be nominated for nine Academy Awards and won one. *Heaven Can Wait* was the perfect blend of box-office success and prestige, grossing $82 million.

But Paramount's summer wasn't over yet. It still had *Up in Smoke*, a raunchy homage to illegal substances starring Cheech Marin and Tommy Chong in their big-screen debut. This, too, was a Picker project; he had tried to get this film made for nearly ten years, convinced that comics Cheech and Chong were "the Abbott and Costello of the dope generation." Picker felt that the script was almost irrelevant, that Cheech and Chong would draw a following. Once again, Diller and Eisner weren't convinced. Before the film opened, distribution chief Frank Mancuso called Picker to ask for his ideas on selling it. "Nobody here thinks this picture can do any business," he said. Picker suggested that he find a market where Cheech and Chong records had been hits and start there. Mancuso's plan was to open the film in Texas, where Cheech and Chong were popular, and then broaden it to a national run. The strategy worked and the picture, which cost a couple of million to make, grossed $44 million.

Picker, like so many deposed Hollywood executives before and after, watched in dismay as the slate he had assembled—*Looking for Mr. Goodbar, Saturday Night Fever, Grease, Heaven Can Wait,* and *Up in Smoke*—

propelled Paramount to the number-one spot in Hollywood, with no acknowledgment of his contribution. Michael Eisner seemed to be taking the victory lap that belonged to Picker. In the middle of the summer, the *Los Angeles Times* published an article about the studio's "astonishing success story" without a mention of Picker's name. Instead, it featured Eisner ruminating about the fickle nature of success. As if he wished to keep away the evil eye, Eisner declared, "If you have a successful movie, the wisest thing you can do is think of it as a failure, forget it and move on." It was the type of disclaimer that would become characteristic of Eisner, but at the same time his pride was manifest. "We didn't have a failure," he proclaimed.

Aside from the unappreciated *American Hot Wax*, Eisner had made his contribution to Paramount's dazzling 1978 lineup: on July 19, the studio released *Foul Play*, a screwball romp that teamed Goldie Hawn with Chevy Chase in his debut as a leading man. Eisner had quickly assembled the elements for the project to beef up the summer roster, little knowing at the time that the studio would become a veritable cornucopia of hits. The picture grossed $45 million.

There was more to provoke Picker. Paramount's official biography of Eisner proclaimed that "Mr. Eisner and his team of creative and marketing experts created the strongest group of releases in movie industry history. *Saturday Night Fever, Grease, Foul Play* and *Heaven Can Wait* are among the productions that led to Paramount's number-one position." *Vanity Fair* published an adulatory profile of Eisner, listing *Saturday Night Fever, Grease,* and *Heaven Can Wait* as movies that Eisner "personally can take credit for." It's true that Eisner had shepherded some of these films, but he hadn't put them into production. Finally Picker became so irate that he wrote to Diller asking him to set the record straight. Diller responded that someday he would try to correct the history books.

Twenty years later, Diller seems prepared to make a gesture in that direction. "Picker did *Goodbar, Saturday Night Fever, Up in Smoke,* et cetera, et cetera," he says. "[And] Picker was very angry. Because what happened was that David never got the credit for most of those films."

Eisner was hardly the first to grab credit, of course, and at the time he needed all the help he could get. "When Michael came in, the entire town was buzzing about how stupid he was," remembers one producer who worked on the lot. "He was trying to do a movie and he met with Richard Lester, the director. And he said, 'You know what I want? Who did those

Beatles movies?' And the guy who did them was Richard Lester, and he said, 'Michael, I did them.' Michael said, 'Oh—you know what I mean, then.' Everyone in town talked about that."

The town also laughed when prominent agent Jeff Berg convinced Eisner to buy a script that had been floating for some weeks without attracting much interest. "The first week or two after Eisner was in the office, Jeff Berg told him, 'Oh, I've got this great script, Michael, but I've got to have your answer in twenty-four hours.' And he bought it," remembers a producer then on the lot. "And everyone said, 'What a fool!' " Soon enough, Eisner found out the truth and called Berg to complain that he had been taken. Berg says he offered to excuse him from the deal. But Eisner stayed in. He hoped to get John Travolta for the lead, but at the last minute Travolta dropped out. The studio settled instead for Richard Gere in the role of a male prostitute.

American Gigolo not only launched Gere's career, but it grossed $23 million at the box office. The town may have laughed at first, but Eisner got to laugh last.

∽

IN THOSE DAYS, Barry Diller muses, the culture of Hollywood was different: "There was no publicity about [the studio's performance]. There were no press reports about box-office results on Monday mornings." But he remembers his satisfaction one afternoon during a lunch at Ma Maison with Marvin Josephson, who was then head of International Famous Agency. Diller was reviewing the studio's upcoming films and he told Josephson that all of the movies were going to be in profit no matter what happened. Josephson's jaw dropped. "What are you talking about—in profit?" he asked.

"We have been selling movies to television and tax-sheltering them," Diller explained. "The entire cost [of the films] plus the marketing cost of the next year is paid for."

"That's impossible."

"Well," Diller said, with deep satisfaction, "it's true."

Just a few months earlier, Paramount's fortunes had been sinking. Now life was sweet for Diller, so recently maligned as a know-nothing from television. Though he couldn't have known precisely what the next year's budget demands would be (a film could easily get more expensive than anticipated), he was claiming to have pulled off a financial coup that would be the envy of any other studio. Other film companies used tax-shelter and television deals but didn't come close to covering 100 percent of their costs. (An executive who worked for Diller at the time says he was exaggerating to some degree but confirms that Paramount pulled off impressive feats in financing.) Diller was enjoying himself at last.

"I wasn't leaving," he says. "You couldn't have gotten me out of there with a crowbar."

5

SQUIRT

AMONG CHARLIE BLUHDORN'S favorite movie ideas was a historic fiction that involved an encounter between Adolf Hitler and Sitting Bull. That project was never made. But he was also enthusiastic about a more promising notion: making a movie based on the television series *Star Trek*.

Diller emphatically states, however, that the *Star Trek* idea did not originate with Bluhdorn. "The credit for *Star Trek* goes to Arthur Barron, Paramount's chief financial officer," he says, and adds, as if to answer some unarticulated challenge, "That's the truth. I don't give a fuck what Mr. Eisner or anyone else says." Diller's vehemence is surprising considering that no one had said Eisner took credit for *Star Trek*. Perhaps the simple truth is that Barron originated the idea and Bluhdorn liked it.

In July 1968, the struggling *Star Trek* television series was about to begin its third season when NBC dealt it a deathblow by moving it from a high-profile Monday-night slot to make room for the popular variety show *Laugh-In*. Consigned to a Friday-night graveyard, the series stumbled along until December, when NBC finally pulled the plug.

The series creator, Gene Roddenberry, had packed up and moved off the Paramount lot after NBC bumped the show from its Monday-night berth. Meanwhile, the studio sold the seventy-nine *Star Trek* episodes for reruns. In syndication, the show began to air five nights a week in small- and medium-sized markets. And then, in one of the more famous examples of the capriciousness of public taste that bedevils the entertainment industry, it caught fire. The defunct *Star Trek* was a hit, and the more the shows were repeated, the more fans seemed to love them.

Paramount soon started asking Roddenberry to bring the show back, either as a made-for-television movie or a low-budget feature film. He held off until 1974. The studio hired him to work on a script for a film that would cost no more than $3 million. Some months later, when William Shatner (also known as Captain Kirk) was on the Paramount lot starring in a television series called *Barbary Coast*, he dropped by the former *Star Trek* soundstages. He found them empty and strewn with trash. Then he heard the sound of typing coming from Roddenberry's old office. When he went to investigate, he was shocked to see Roddenberry pounding at the keyboard with an unfiltered Camel cigarette hanging from his mouth. "Hey, Gene!" he called out. "Didn't anybody tell you? We got canceled!"

Shatner concluded that "Gene had finally lost his mind." But it was the executives at Paramount who were going to be driven insane—especially a young, ambitious newcomer named Jeffrey Katzenberg, upon whose slender shoulders the responsibility for this venture would fall.

⌇

JEFFREY KATZENBERG GREW up at 1125 Park Avenue in New York, just a short stroll from Michael Eisner's home at 1085 Park Avenue. His father was a stockbroker and the family was well-to-do, although not nearly in the league of the Eisners.

Katzenberg doesn't know if he was ever really a child. At age six or seven, he asked for a piece of rope for Christmas. "As a joke we bought him a hank of laundry line," his mother, Anne, said later. "He felt every other present, left the other presents alone, unwrapped the rope, and played with it all day. He always knew exactly what he wanted."

"I'm the kid who had a lemonade stand, who shoveled snow off the sidewalks on Park Avenue," he says. He wasn't particularly interested in buying things with the money he earned, he says. But his pleasure lay in the "hustle," the sense of getting things done.

When he was fourteen years old, Katzenberg found the prospect of another summer at Camp Kennebec in Maine especially unappealing after he took a fall and hurt his knee while playing tennis. "I was going to end up limping around the camp for the entire summer," he remembers. Instead, Katzenberg got up an illegal card game. The stakes were each player's weekly candy allowance. When a junior counselor caught the boys, Katzenberg claimed that the camp director had given him special permission to play cards. It was pure fiction.

"Everybody was so terrified by the director of the camp—campers and counselors alike—that I couldn't imagine this new, junior counselor would ever ask him whether that was true," Katzenberg says. But the kid asked.

Katzenberg was told that as punishment, he had to stand by the flagpole. He refused. "That was why I got kicked out of camp," he says. "It escalated. It got to be this ego thing."

So young Katzenberg found himself with time on his hands. He heard that some kids were volunteering for John Lindsay's mayoral campaign. "I had no idea what Lindsay's politics were," he said later. "But it was a better camp than the one I got thrown out of."

Katzenberg immediately brought his energy to this latest pursuit and started organizing little armies of teenage volunteers to distribute campaign flyers by day and stuff envelopes by night. Lindsay's aides started noticing this ubiquitous kid who seemed to want to know everything; they gave him the nickname "Squirt."

"He would go from office to office and listen in on meetings for hours and hours," says Sid Davidoff, then a Lindsay aide. Even the mayor recalled: "If you needed six cups of coffee at three in the morning, Squirt could get them."

"He was sort of like a weasel; he was everywhere," says Richard Aurelio, who became deputy mayor in Lindsay's second administration. "You had the feeling he was absorbing it all—how people govern, how people operate. . . . Normally, someone of his age—we would have said, 'Get lost.' But over time it became uncomfortable if he wasn't there. It was, 'Jeff is loyal, he won't betray us, and we might need something.' "

Work agreed with Katzenberg; school didn't. It is easy to imagine that Katzenberg, small in stature, might find it a struggle to fit in with other children, but he says that was never the case. At the same time he concedes that he always gravitated toward the adult world. "He was a very weird kid," says producer Craig Baumgarten, who worked for Lindsay at the time. "He had no adolescence at all. He went from ten to twenty-three in one leap."

Katzenberg was still in his teens during the late sixties—a crackling time in the city—and Lindsay's team was credited with reaching out to tinderbox urban areas—neighborhoods that were going up in flames in other cities around the country—and minimizing the unrest. Davidoff remembers the fire commissioner telling him that Katzenberg kept a scanner by his bed so he could turn up at major fires. "I think Jeff just wanted to be part of the city," he says. "If it was a happening, a meeting, an event, Jeff was there."

If Katzenberg wasn't much of a student at the exclusive Fieldston School, he was a superstar when it came to carrying out Lindsay administration chores. Loyal and efficient, he was entrusted with all sorts of tasks—

including handling large sums of cash. "Standards have changed dramatically," Aurelio says. "In those days, it was very traditional to pay workers to go to the polls and be poll watchers—and pay them in cash." Katzenberg also accepted cash campaign contributions. He was trusted implicitly, and such was the mayor's gratitude that on Katzenberg's twenty-first birthday, he issued an edict: the nickname "Squirt" was never to be used again.

Aurelio had his own reasons to be grateful to Katzenberg. One night, he was having dinner with staff at the Old Homestead, a downtown steak house, when he got word that his daughter, who was recovering from a horseback-riding accident at Mount Sinai Hospital, had taken a sudden turn for the worse. "I said, 'My God, Jodie is in a coma,' and Jeff said, 'I'll drive you to the hospital,'" Aurelio remembers. "We picked up my wife en route." The enterprising young Katzenberg kept a siren in his car. "He just went through red lights and got us to the hospital in incredible time," Aurelio says. "I got to the hospital just before she died and he made it possible. He stayed with us all that night."

For days, Katzenberg stuck by Aurelio's side. "I don't know how we would have gone through the funeral without him," Aurelio says. "He handled the cars, made sure the right people were taken care of. He took over. My wife and I were in no condition to deal with it. Every morning when I woke up, the doorman would say, 'Jeff Katzenberg is waiting downstairs if you need him.'"

Aurelio, who still hears from Katzenberg regularly more than twenty-five years later, says he'll never forget how he felt that night when he received the news about his child. "There were other people around but I knew that Jeff was the one who would take me to the hospital," he says. "It's obvious that I love the guy."

∽

KATZENBERG SAYS HIS parents fretted as it became clear that he was not going to start college. "I don't want to say it didn't scare them," he acknowledges. But Katzenberg thinks his parents saw him as "a little bit like a wild stallion" that had to have wide boundaries. And given the upheaval of the times, they recognized that what was happening to their son wasn't all bad. "This is the Vietnam War," he says. "The college campuses are shutting down. This is the dawning of the drug age and free love. I was a student during that time and I actually found myself in a very structured and nurturing environment in which these [Lindsay administration] people took an interest in me."

Katzenberg doesn't say so, but according to a close friend, he didn't have the happiest of relationships with his parents. His father, in particular, was competitive with his son, says this longtime Katzenberg associate. It is not surprising, therefore, that Katzenberg perceives his relationship with a number of Lindsay aides as the first in a series of mentoring relationships with older men that have continued throughout his life — including his stint with Michael Eisner and culminating with music mogul David Geffen. He views these men as a series of "older brothers." He describes such relationships in nurturing terms. Rather than compete with his mentors, he seemed simply to want their approval and love. Men like Davidoff "took me in," he says, or "took me under their wing."

At the same time he seems to believe that these mentors have a proprietary right to inflict torment. "David Geffen is very protective and God forbid anyone would ever say anything bad about me, let alone try to hurt me," Katzenberg says. "There is no one other than my wife who would come more to my defense than David would. But he loves to beat the crap out of me — trying to make me better, bigger, and smarter."

In the years when Katzenberg would normally have been going to college, his mentors moved him from job to job in the Lindsay administration. He was a traveling gofer, moving from one agency to the next, from consumer products to real estate to investigations, learning what he could about city government and getting to know "every corner of the five boroughs of New York."

By the time he was eighteen years old, Katzenberg was living in a brownstone at 151 West Eighty-eighth Street, between Columbus and Amsterdam avenues. The house was known as Gracie Mansion West because the roommates included Davidoff, the number-three man in city government and Lindsay's political adviser, and Ted Gross, the flamboyant commissioner of youth services, who made a dramatic appearance in red trousers, fur coat, and floppy cap. Lindsay aide Craig Baumgarten also lived in the house.

All four were single or in the process of becoming single and the brownstone was "essentially a frat house [and] a bachelor's paradise," Baumgarten says. Gross had a black chow chow, Davidoff had a white Samoyed, and Baumgarten had an English sheepdog. Only Katzenberg was without a pet.

Dozens of women came through each week — Katzenberg says Gross was particularly voracious and "was with three women a day, every day, 365 days a year." When it came to women, Katzenberg again was the odd man out. "They had them and I thought about them," he jokes. But his attention seemed absorbed by work. When Katzenberg and Davidoff left the office late at night, they'd head off to a midnight double feature. "We never seemed to sleep, as I look back at it," Davidoff says. "We both loved the movies." But Katzenberg says he didn't especially love film—he mostly sat waiting for his beeper to go off.

Katzenberg had become an increasingly skillful and aggressive card-player, and New York's political establishment—commissioners of various city departments—came to the brownstone for high-powered card games. "Jeff was a terrific poker player," Aurelio says. "He was just difficult to read. He bluffed well. Conservative poker players fold if the first couple of cards are not good, but not Jeff. He loved the action. Most of the time he won."

In this pleasant environment, no one asked a lot of questions when stereos and other high-end electronic equipment materialized in the house compliments of Gross. "Gross was stealing left and right and we all kind of knew it and we all kind of looked the other way," Baumgarten says.

"I'm not sure I actually put two and two together," Katzenberg says. "There did come a time when Sid said, 'This is not kosher.'"

The state of New York did not avert its gaze, however. In 1973—a year after the roommates in the brownstone had split up—Gross was indicted and charged with accepting $41,400 in kickbacks from contractors. He pleaded guilty to taking a bribe and served sixteen months of a three-year prison term. "They tried to squeeze him into turning in the higher-ups," Baumgarten remembers. "I always say the difference between Watergate and Lindsaygate is that John Dean talked and Ted Gross didn't."

In 1976, the forty-four-year-old Gross was found murdered, execution-style, in Brooklyn—slumped in the driver's seat of a four-door Citroën se-dan. His female companion survived the attack. The killer was Kenneth Gilmore, the twenty-one-year-old night manager of a bowling alley. Gilmore worked for James Mosley Jr., the alleged bagman in the kickback scheme that had sent Gross to prison. At trial, it also emerged that Gross and Gil-more had been involved in drug trafficking.

"It was very hard because Ted was truly one of the most fun people that I've ever been around in my life," Katzenberg says. "He was the kind of person who could take the most depressed and down-on-his-luck person and fill them with a sense of going for it. . . . This is a man who had a joy for life. I loved Teddy."

∽

THE MEETING TOOK place in a hotel room somewhere in Wisconsin early in John Lindsay's 1972 campaign for the presidency. A wealthy New York businessman, David Buntzman, had flown in to meet with the candidate. He brought an envelope stuffed with cash. It wasn't illegal, in those pre-Watergate days, to make such undisclosed contributions. And it wasn't necessary for Lindsay even to brush his fingertips across the envelope. Instead, the money went straight into the hands of the only campaign aide who was present — Jeffrey Katzenberg.

Katzenberg was an advance man at a time when various suppliers of services to a presidential campaign — car rental agencies and hotels — demanded to be paid in cash up front. "The companies stopped giving credit because the losers never paid," Katzenberg remembers. "Somebody [from the campaign] needed to have cash all the time. Tens of thousands of dollars. Everybody knew me, trusted me. I came from a well-to-do family. . . . Cash would come from New York to me and I would dole it out. I paid rent, I paid bills. I was the cash machine and there were times that I had almost $100,000 in that briefcase."

But Lindsay's presidential campaign went nowhere and his time in political office ended in 1973. That year Governor Nelson Rockefeller appointed a special prosecutor, Maurice Nadjari, to investigate possible wrongdoing in city government. "He investigated everybody — me, Jeff, quite a lot of people," Aurelio says. "This was a typical prosecutor who went awry."

That hotel room in Wisconsin was of particular interest to Nadjari. The Lindsay administration had given the Buntzman family a lease to operate the Bronx Terminal Market near Yankee Stadium. Davidoff says the Buntzmans got the land because "no one else wanted it. . . . It was at the time an armpit of New York City and they were willing to put in the money, take it over, and do it."

But then the Yankees insisted that the city make improvements to Yankee Stadium — including the addition of a parking structure. "Buntzman had the land and now the city needed it," Katzenberg says. "They're buying the land and he kills them on the deal. He gets an incredible windfall relative to what he paid."

And of course, Buntzman was the contributor who had flown to Wisconsin to hand over an undisclosed sum of cash to Lindsay. It appeared to be a sweetheart deal and Katzenberg was in the middle of it. "The only person in the room who's a witness to this is little Jeffrey and he went after me with both barrels," Katzenberg says. "This guy was having people show up at my house at three or four o'clock in the morning with subpoenas. I was harassed beyond belief."

It lasted for three years, and before it was over, Katzenberg had moved on to a job at Paramount. Even though Nadjari ultimately came up empty, the episode led to a lasting perception that Katzenberg, in his youth, was a "bagman" for the Lindsay administration.

∽

IF JOHN LINDSAY had been presidential material, one can only imagine what might have come next for Katzenberg, who had acted as treasurer in the 1972 campaign. But when the bid failed, the administration disbanded. The lease was up on the brownstone, so Davidoff and Katzenberg moved into an apartment at East Seventy-third Street and Second Avenue. Davidoff and Aurelio opened Jimmy's, a restaurant on the original site of the legendary Toots Shor's sports bar and next to the famous restaurant '21.'

Jimmy's was a hit. There was a round bar on the main floor and an Off-Off Broadway show upstairs featuring stars like Betty Buckley. A nightclub downstairs featured Nixon mimic David Frye (Davidoff had been on the notorious Nixon enemies list) and future shock jock Don Imus, who held forth about the restaurant's operators being former Lindsay "bagmen." Several jazz legends—Maynard Ferguson, Stan Getz, and Buddy Rich among them—recorded live albums in the same space. "It was quite the place to be seen and to find out what was going on," Davidoff remembers. "I used to say there were more judges made in my bathroom than in any other place than city hall."

Katzenberg worked at everything, functioning as a savvy maître d' or washing glasses behind the bar. The older men worried about his education and pushed him to go to college at night. Katzenberg tried it but quickly quit. "No question, I didn't get a classic education, but it's not as though I was uninterested," he says. "Many of the things one would learn in college, I went and learned in the streets of New York. I'm not trained in classical literature, but I think I've acquired a pretty good command of English. I got it but in an unconventional way."

When it became clear that college was out of the picture, Katzenberg's friends nagged him to get a real job. They enlisted the help of Davidoff's friends the Margolies brothers. Abe and Robbie were suppliers to Zales Jewelry and avid gamblers; Robbie was "one of the great card counters in blackjack," as Davidoff recalls. They ran a casino in St. Martin in the Caribbean where Katzenberg was sent to study their business from the ground up.

"I suggested he'd make a good croupier," Aurelio says. "We encouraged him to go down [to St. Martin] and study it and to do it as a career. . . . We knew he was interested in more than being a maître d' or a restaurant manager." Meanwhile, Davidoff was trying to get gambling legalized in New York so he could start a club. He figured that Katzenberg, having learned his trade in St. Martin, could run it.

Despite its popularity, Jimmy's always lost money. "I overestimated my ability to run a business," Davidoff laments. "A lot of people who worked for me opened their own restaurants afterward. You wonder how they could." After hours, Katzenberg and Davidoff spent hours in their apartment practicing counting cards at blackjack. A Margolies brothers' associate (whose métier allegedly had been fixing college basketball games) provided Katzenberg with a training kit, which he has kept for all these years. "Jeff was really good at it," Davidoff marvels. "He's got a computer mind."

It was a perfect Katzenberg arrangement: high-stakes gambling with an element of control. With $10,000 from the Margolies brothers in his pocket, Katzenberg set out for Freeport. The brothers agreed to split Katzenberg's winnings with him. "For wise guys, what was quite wonderful about them is they said they would stake me for six months or $250,000, whichever came first," Katzenberg says. "They allowed me the fantasy and dream of doing this insanely bizarre thing. As much as they were wise guys, I liked them. I'm sure they were into a thousand things that were completely horrible, but they have codes. . . . Their handshake was six months. They did not want me to make a career as a professional gambler."

Katzenberg strolled into a casino in midafternoon and promptly won $25,000. That was enough for one day and he decided it was time to go home. But that was not a popular decision with the casino management. Katzenberg pretended to have an attack of stomach flu to justify his exit. He traveled to Las Vegas, Puerto Rico, Paradise Island. He couldn't stay anywhere long. As soon as the house figured out what he was up to, he was no longer welcome. On one such excursion, Davidoff accompanied Katzenberg to Paradise Island. As they played blackjack, a couple of casino employees approached and asked them to move on. They sat down at the roulette table. "I had come up with a system on roulette," Davidoff explains. But management suggested that what they really needed to do was leave on the next plane. They obliged.

Naturally, Katzenberg was obsessed with making his $250,000 goal. He went to Vegas with about $200,000. He was closing in. But the house was wise to him, roped off his table, and started cutting the deck higher to make it more difficult to count the cards. Katzenberg started losing until finally his money was gone.

Even though he was cleaned out, the casino planned to put Katzenberg's picture in a book of card counters and other unwelcome types. The Margolies brothers intervened on his behalf. They contacted Benny Binion, owner of Horseshoe, and Ash Resnick, the manager of Caesars Palace, then the two premier clubs in the town. Katzenberg agreed to quit gambling to keep his photo out of the book.

It was time for a change. The lease on the apartment was running out. Davidoff was getting married and moving to Queens. Katzenberg had suddenly paired up with Marilyn Siegel, a young woman—a few years older than Katzenberg—who had been a popular undergraduate at the University of Bridgeport in Connecticut and was now a schoolteacher in the Bronx.

She had met Katzenberg through her boyfriend, Donny Evans, who was an assistant to the mayor and hosted a regular Sunday-night poker game. Evans hadn't noticed any sparks between the two when he was dating Siegel, though Katzenberg often tagged along with them to dinners or the movies. In fact, Katzenberg seemed like "a young kid"—hardly a rival at all.

But sometime after Evans and Siegel split, Katzenberg stepped in. Marilyn was so used to hearing him called "Squirt" that she wasn't sure who Jeffrey Katzenberg was when he called her one night. She went to dinner with him "to see how the kid turned out." She apparently concluded that he had turned out well enough. The two quickly became engaged, to the surprise of Evans and others who thought of Siegel as an older woman and Katzenberg as a workaholic kid devoid of romantic interests. But the two forged a lasting partnership that would endure even though Katzenberg continued to devote almost every waking hour to work.

"Jeff decided that Marilyn was going to be whatever she was going to be to him," Davidoff remembers. "Knowing Jeff, he probably said, 'This is the girl I want to marry,' and that was it." This type of intimate information, he adds, was not fodder for discussion despite the closeness between the two.

∽

KATZENBERG'S ANXIOUS GODFATHERS had another idea—they introduced him to some Hollywood types. One was independent film producer David Picker—not yet an executive at Paramount—whose wife had worked in the Lindsay administration. After Picker's wife called to make a reservation for dinner at Jimmy's, Davidoff and Aurelio made sure Katzenberg was there. He also met Marvin Josephson, then head of International Famous Agency. In the wake of his gambling career, Katzenberg decided to become a Hollywood agent. He went to work for Josephson.

It was 1973 and the Arab-Israeli War broke out. Josephson decided to sponsor an ambitious rally for Israel, hooking up the twenty-five biggest arenas in the country by satellite and having stars like Barbra Streisand perform. The whole thing needed to be mobilized fast and Katzenberg was assigned the job. He was in his element—organizing at breakneck speed—when the war ended. The benefit never happened, but Josephson and Katzenberg were rewarded with a VIP trip to Israel. Katzenberg was escorted to some of the scenes where fighting had taken place. He was overwhelmed by the experience. When he returned, life at the agency seemed dull.

Picker, the producer, invited him and Marilyn to Miami for the Christmas holidays. They stayed at the Fontainebleau hotel and amused themselves playing tennis with Dustin Hoffman and Paul Anka. One afternoon, Katzenberg was sitting courtside with Anka when the singer suggested that Katzenberg could be his agent.

"You know, I don't think I should be your agent," Katzenberg said. "I don't know anything about how to book or manage your career. I could devote twenty hours a day, seven days a week to you with a lot of enthusiasm but your agent can do in ten minutes what it'll take me twenty hours to get done. I shouldn't be your agent and I shouldn't be anybody's agent."

As he had talked, Katzenberg realized that being a great agent wouldn't be much fun. When he rejoined Picker, he said, "I'm quitting." He went back to New York and did precisely that.

6

THE GOLDEN RETRIEVER

K ATZENBERG STARTED WORKING as David Picker's $125-per-week gofer. He was dispatched to Africa to help scout locations for a film called *Dangerfield Safari* (the picture was never made). Then he found himself traveling to Miami with Dustin Hoffman during the making of *Lenny*, director Bob Fosse's film about ill-fated comedian Lenny Bruce. He had entered a world of jets, limousines, and yachts. "My mouth never closed," Katzenberg remembers.

Katzenberg was enjoying himself immensely when one day Picker called and asked, "Do you know who Barry Diller is? . . . He's a great guy, very smart and looking for an assistant. I think it would be a fantastic opportunity for you."

"I'm having a great time here!" Katzenberg protested. But in what Katzenberg later described as "the most selfless act that anybody professionally has done for me," Picker insisted that he make the trip to Los Angeles to meet this prospective employer.

Diller had taken the helm at Paramount and was commuting between the New York and Beverly Hills offices, where he met with Katzenberg. Katzenberg wasn't that interested in the job, so he had decided on the plane to be aggressive in the interview — a frightening prospect considering Katzenberg's usual level of intensity. Unless this was the greatest job in the world, he didn't want it.

As Katzenberg recalls the meeting, Diller asked a few pro forma questions and dismissed him with a thank-you. At this point, Katzenberg says, he interjected, "Excuse me. I have a few questions. What exactly is this job? If it involves your laundry and your dry cleaning, I'm really not interested." He still remembers Diller flushing in response.

Diller, however, doesn't remember the encounter that way at all. "We had a brief interview and I was impressed with him," he says. "He certainly wasn't arrogant . . . but smart and alert and willing and full of beans—the good ones, not the confrontational ones." Katzenberg was convinced that he'd never get the job, but the next day, Picker called to say he was in. "I think he saw a lot of himself in you," Picker said.

On his first day, Katzenberg sat down at his desk at the Gulf + Western offices in New York when suddenly he heard the harsh buzzing of Diller's intercom. Katzenberg nearly jumped out of his chair; later he would say that buzzer felt like an electrode wired to his ass. When he went to the boss's office, Diller pushed a thick stack of papers across the desk and said, "Tell me what you think."

This was the manuscript of the Judith Rossner novel *Looking for Mr. Goodbar*. Katzenberg labored through it and returned to Diller. "I have no idea how you make this into a movie," Katzenberg said. "It was all told from inside her mind."

"That's not your job," Diller responded. "That's what a filmmaker will do. Do you think it's a good story to make into a movie?"

Katzenberg tried again. "I imagine women will be really interested," he said.

"How would you know?" Diller snapped. "You're not a woman, are you?"

Katzenberg looked down at his crotch, then back at Diller. "Not that I know of."

"Your job is to go out and find ideas that interest you, that you love—not like—that you love sufficiently to put your career on the line, to have a level of passion to want to make something and to have the courage of your convictions. There is no way you will ever know what a housewife in Kansas or a businessman in Chicago wants to see. Your job is to find things that interest you. Then what you do is you say, 'Yes.' You close your eyes, cross your fingers, and pray that there are millions of other people who feel the same way you do. Anytime you presume what someone else will like, you will lose."

With that, the Hollywood education of Jeffrey Katzenberg began in earnest.

∽

ABOUT THREE MONTHS into his job, Katzenberg made a mistake that aroused Diller's ire to a level Katzenberg hadn't previously seen. Diller phoned him and unleashed a barrage of high-volume rage without letting Katzenberg speak a word in his own defense. At the end, Diller slammed down the phone. Katzenberg says he stood up and marched into Diller's office, barging past the secretary, who protested that Diller was on the phone. He planted both hands on Diller's immaculate glass desk. Outraged at the intrusion, Diller glared at him with what seemed like unalloyed hatred.

"I just want to tell you one thing," the diminutive Katzenberg declared with all the dignity he could muster. "This is the first time and the last time that you will ever talk to me that way while I work for you. If you do not want me here, I will leave. If you ever do this again, either start with 'You're fired' or end with 'You're fired.' Because if you ever do this again, that will be the last conversation we ever have. Let's file this under 'getting to know each other.' "

And according to Katzenberg, Diller never spoke to him in that tone again. While he screamed at Eisner and everyone else on his staff, Katzenberg enjoyed immunity. As for Diller, he doesn't remember the conversation. "It's not my recollection but it's not against my recollection," he says. "There's no question that I thought Jeffrey was more than worth it."

Despite Katzenberg's tales of his youthful cockiness, he also craved the approval of his bosses and worked tirelessly to get it. To some, his zeal to get ahead seem reminiscent of Sammy Glick, the amoral subject of Budd Schulberg's novel *What Makes Sammy Run?* As Diller's assistant, he had special responsibility for decorating and overseeing Gulf + Western's guest house on the company's extensive property in the Dominican Republic. Bluhdorn was especially pleased with the results. "Jeffrey's job, when I met him, was to outfit that house with the powerboat and water skis and floats for the pool," remembers one prominent producer. "He was into it."

Meanwhile Gulf + Western, Paramount's parent company, was having its own problems with the law. The company's top management was under investigation by the Securities and Exchange Commission for allegedly misappropriating funds. If Katzenberg was worried that his legal problems from his days with the Lindsay administration would get him into trouble with Charlie Bluhdorn, he soon found that the effect was quite the opposite. "He completely related to me," Katzenberg says. "In his mind, he was also being harassed and persecuted."

When Diller invited Bluhdorn to Los Angeles, Katzenberg's job was to remain glued to his side, ensuring that he had nothing but fun. And when

Diller wanted to throw a last-minute surprise thirtieth birthday party for his lady friend, Diane von Furstenberg, Katzenberg put together a bash at a chic Chinese restaurant at Third Avenue and Sixty-fourth with two hundred guests, from Mick Jagger to Henry Kissinger. (Diller also marked the occasion by presenting von Furstenberg with thirty diamonds in a Band-Aid box. Katzenberg was responsible for getting the diamonds, which he did with the assistance of his old gambling friends, the Margolies brothers.)

From the start, Katzenberg never did his job by half measures. Martin Starger, who had been Diller's boss at Paramount, remembers that Diller invited him to use the Dominican Republic house for a vacation and promised to have his assistant make the arrangements. Minutes later, Katzenberg was on the phone from New York, asking about Starger's flight plans. When Starger arrived at LaGuardia Airport to make his connection, he was greeted by Katzenberg, wearing a dark suit even though it was a Sunday afternoon.

"He takes me from one plane to another," Starger remembers. "I said, 'You came all the way from Manhattan to make sure I get from one plane to another?' He asked what I like to drink, all that stuff. I get there, and walk into the house and the phone rings—I swear not two minutes after I walk into the house—and I hear, 'Mr. Katzenberg on the line.' . . . It was unbelievable. I mean, the guy knew what room I was going into from three thousand miles away. 'I understand you went skeet shooting. Did you enjoy it?' He was the most efficient young man I had ever seen—other than Barry."

But perhaps because Katzenberg was such a clever assistant, it wasn't long before Diller concluded that the arrangement wasn't working. "He had alienated a lot of people in the first six months or so, which is what happens when you're an assistant and you're young," Diller says. "I couldn't have him be my assistant anymore because it wasn't healthy. The assistant has no role of his own. He's using the authority of the person he works for, and the people who deal with him are not dealing with him in any way other than relative to the person he works for. I felt that it was a rotten luxury for an executive to have an assistant because it makes his life easier and everybody else's life miserable."

In 1977, Diller decided to reassign his protégé. "I thought enough of him to get him a real day job," he continues. "I threw him into the marketing department to get his bearings and he didn't disappoint me. . . . That was the end of assistants for me."

∽

KATZENBERG DIDN'T DALLY in the marketing department for long. While there, he met Michael Eisner—the new head of the studio—and was charmed by his self-deprecating humor and boyish enthusiasm. He also befriended a rising young production executive in Los Angeles named Don Simpson—a particular favorite of Eisner's. Though the straitlaced Katzenberg seemed to have little in common with the hard-partying, profane Simpson, this would hardly be the first time that Katzenberg had enjoyed a friendship with someone who may have operated outside the law (and between hookers and drugs, Simpson broke his share). From Teddy Gross to the Margolies brothers to Simpson, Katzenberg showed no objection to associating with rather colorful characters. He and Simpson started swapping information about goings-on at the studio. In the annals of networking, the Simpson-Katzenberg combination must have been truly formidable. Both men were tireless in their information gathering and both could focus their considerable energies with laserlike intensity.

Katzenberg and his wife were about to buy an apartment in New York when the studio asked him to move to Los Angeles. He was recruited to work on a bold project that Diller was attempting to launch. It was to be called the Paramount Television Service—a fourth network. The notion of taking on the Big Three seemed as hopeless then as it did a decade later, when Diller would try again at Fox. A producer who worked on the lot remembers: "Everybody in the world said Barry was crazy, there can never be a fourth network, it will never happen."

Diller's plan was to attack the programming problem with his strong suit—made-for-television movies—and a new *Star Trek* series. By then, Paramount had been working on the low-budget *Star Trek* movie for a couple of years. Diller had passed on Roddenberry's concept—a dark and controversial riff on the nature of God. The studio had recruited a number of science-fiction writers, including Harlan Ellison, but couldn't come up with a story. A clutch of directors—Spielberg, Lucas, and Coppola—had passed on the project. Paramount was ready to give up on the feature-film idea.

In June 1977, Diller and Eisner announced the fourth network and the new *Star Trek* series to the press. The series would be launched with a two-hour *Star Trek* made-for-television film. With a budget of $3.2 million, this was going to be the most expensive television movie ever made. At twenty-six, Katzenberg was named head of programming for the new web. He didn't have a clue what he was doing but Eisner seemed to have confidence in him. "He would believe in somebody," Katzenberg says. "If you were a talented carpenter, he would think you could be a brain surgeon."

Early on, Don Simpson warned Katzenberg to steer clear of the project. "*Star Trek* is a nighttime freight train," he said. "It's bearing down on you at two hundred miles per hour. Get off the fucking track!" But Katzenberg was a terrier and the prospect of pleasing his bosses by tackling an impossible project was irresistible. Perversely, he would test himself by quitting smoking as the project was going into production. "The single most stressful moment of my life," he explained later. "I knew if I could stop smoking then, I could stop forever." He also bought a Porsche—the same car that Simpson drove. But Katzenberg's was automatic, and to Simpson and his wild bachelor friends, Katzenberg was missing the point.

Paramount had become leery of Roddenberry, who was combative in sticking to a vision that Diller had rejected. The studio hired two producers to work with and discipline him. Soon Roddenberry was waging war over the script. Clearly, the producers would never be able to start the film and then get episodes for the regular series under way in time to launch the fourth network. As it turned out, they didn't have to. Bluhdorn lost confidence in the project and the fourth network died before it made its debut.

That left Jeffrey Katzenberg with nothing but a partially developed script for a two-hour *Star Trek* pilot. He was transferred to film production and told to make the pilot into a feature film. *Star Wars* and *Close Encounters* had gobbled up a fortune at the box office while Paramount, which should have had the edge on the final frontier, wrestled with a fractious group of producers without success. "Jesus Christ, this could have been us!" Eisner had reportedly exclaimed as *Close Encounters* opened to critical raves and massive grosses. Katzenberg was given a relatively modest $8 million budget and told to get this problem solved.

But in the wake of *Star Wars* and *Close Encounters*—which he screened repeatedly—Roddenberry was convinced he needed a lot more than $8 million for special effects or he'd be laughed out of the theaters. Katzenberg went to Eisner and came back with an extra $10 million. With the budget growing, Eisner and Katzenberg courted director Robert Wise, whose credits included *West Side Story* and *The Sound of Music*, as well as *The Day the Earth Stood Still* and *The Andromeda Strain*. Promising that they wanted to make a "top-notch picture," Eisner and Katzenberg told Wise that they thought he would probably be able to bring in the film for less than $18 million.

Wise had never been especially drawn to Star Trek, but his wife and father-in-law were big fans. When Wise brought home the script they read it voraciously—and then recoiled in horror as they realized that the beloved character of Mr. Spock didn't appear in the film. Wise told Eisner and Katzenberg that Spock was a necessary element. At first, says an executive close to these discussions, Eisner didn't see the point: "Michael would say, 'Who gives a fuck what this guy with the ears does?' He would tell Robert Wise, 'Just make the movie!' Who could understand why anyone cared about Star Trek? We would watch the TV episodes—they were the dumbest thing you ever saw."

Nonetheless, the studio decided to include Spock, if possible. Spock had gotten several times more fan mail than all the other characters combined when the series was on the air. But there were a few problems with bringing Spock back. Leonard Nimoy, who played the character, despised Gene Roddenberry, who had engaged him and then abruptly dropped him from another television project without explanation. And Nimoy was suing Paramount for using his likeness in all manner of Star Trek books, T-shirts, and assorted paraphernalia. He had so little inclination to return in a Star Trek movie that when his agent called to discuss the idea, he retorted, "If you ever call me again about Star Trek, you're fired!"

At the time Nimoy was in New York, appearing in a theatrical production of Equus. One afternoon, Katzenberg called and introduced himself. "I'd like to come to New York. I'd like to see you in your play," he said. Nimoy was flattered that Katzenberg would fly all the way to Manhattan and sit through his play just to make contact with him. It seemed to Nimoy that "he genuinely wanted to be helpful."

Two days later, Katzenberg was backstage, pressing Nimoy to join him for a cup of coffee. They talked for a couple of hours at the Backstage Deli and met three more times in the next two days. Katzenberg spent hours listening to Nimoy's grievances about Roddenberry and his fight with the studio. Finally Katzenberg asked whether Nimoy had seen the script for the movie. "No," he said. "I'd prefer not knowing anything about this particular project." Katzenberg said it wouldn't be a problem for Nimoy to work for Paramount even with the suit pending. "I just can't do that. I'm sorry," Nimoy said.

Katzenberg returned to Los Angeles, and within a few days, Paramount contacted Nimoy offering to settle his lawsuit—and asking him to read the script for the *Star Trek* movie. Within a couple of weeks, the court case was resolved; that day, Nimoy received a check from the studio at five P.M. and a copy of the script at six P.M. By seven P.M., the studio called to set up a meeting. Katzenberg had achieved his objective. His career as Paramount's "golden retriever" was well under way.

∞

STAR TREK'S TROUBLES —and Katzenberg's travails—were hardly over. Nimoy hated Roddenberry's ideas. (He realized, however, that if he dropped out, he'd be answering questions for years to come about being the only holdout in the *Star Trek* movie: "How could I answer those questions? 'I didn't like the script'? 'I hated Gene'? 'I was angry at the studio'? I would be carrying that negative shit around with me for the next five years at least.") Nimoy resolved to supply the creative conscience that the studio might lack. He figured, not unreasonably, that the studio was probably just trying to grab its share of post–*Star Wars* sci-fi profits.

Meanwhile, William Shatner was dieting and jogging, trying to get back into Captain Kirk's body suit. Roddenberry was making no progress on the script. Finally Eisner stepped in to help Katzenberg bully Roddenberry into collaborating with a writer named Harold Livingston, who had worked on the film earlier but left in disgust at Roddenberry's refusal to yield any creative control. By now, Livingston despised Roddenberry. "Gene," he once said to him, "you wouldn't know a good story if it was tattooed on the end of your prick." But for a lot of money, and with the understanding that he alone would control the script, he agreed to return.

Livingston sent a chunk of revised material to Eisner and Katzenberg. It wasn't long before Livingston got a call from an incensed Eisner, who demanded, "What is this shit?" They quickly figured out that Roddenberry had intercepted Livingston's work and substituted his own. Similar battles continued throughout the production; even as shooting progressed, Roddenberry and Livingston would send competing revisions to the befuddled cast.

Wise began rebuilding sets that had been constructed for the television show. Paramount footed the bill for the face-lift, all the while paying the cast to wait for a script. The project fell ten weeks behind schedule without a single inch of footage shot. Eisner and Katzenberg ordered Wise to start the cameras rolling. "The script still wasn't in any kind of shape, so we had to start rewriting and shooting all at the same time," Wise remembered later. "It was a hell of a way to make a picture."

The only thing that seemed clear was that the *Enterprise* crew was being joined by a bald beauty, model Persis Khambatta, who provided a love interest for a young commander who had assumed control of the *Enterprise* while Kirk was absent. But without a finished script, shooting quickly bogged down. At one point Livingston quit—for the third time—and Nimoy and Shatner put their heads together to rewrite the material. Nimoy found the third act particularly problematic. "Kirk and Spock were just basically standing around on that fucking bridge [of the *Enterprise*] . . . for pages and pages," Nimoy said later. The director was so discouraged that he suggested shutting down production altogether.

Instead, Nimoy and Shatner came up with a rewrite that Wise immediately embraced. The problem was getting Roddenberry to go along. When they all met, it was obvious that Roddenberry was displeased. But unbeknownst to Nimoy, Katzenberg had already decided how to deal with Roddenberry. After Livingston had quit for the third time, Katzenberg's office had called and invited him to a seven P.M. meeting at his office. When he arrived, Katzenberg's secretary thrust a large glass of Beefeater gin (Livingston's drink of choice) into his hand and seated him in Katzenberg's office. As she left, he heard the lock turn. "This is really strange," Livingston reflected. "I'm locked into the fucking office."

There he sat for the next thirty minutes. By the time Katzenberg turned up, Livingston was pretty well crocked. "You are not getting out of this office until you agree to come back and work on this picture," Katzenberg told him. Addled though he was, Livingston could see that Katzenberg was desperate. "I used the opportunity to soak him for a big raise," he remembered. Katzenberg then broke the news to Roddenberry that Livingston was in charge.

Nimoy and Shatner were left with uneasy feelings. "We'd won our battle, but in the process, we watched Gene Roddenberry get steamrollered," Shatner recalled later. "There was no victory celebration."

❧

ALL THIS TIME, Katzenberg was under tremendous pressure from the studio to get the picture on track. At one point, according to sources who worked on the lot then, he either quit or was fired and spent a couple of days at home before production chief Don Simpson got Eisner to summon him back. But no matter what Katzenberg did, the project resisted order. Three months into shooting, the ending still hadn't been written. The cast was so punchy with exhaustion that the production actually lost an entire day because everyone was seized with giggling fits. Lieutenant Uhura's first line that day, "Captain, the alien has expelled a large object and it's headed in our direction," struck the cast as hilarious. But Nimoy fretted that none of the humor was on the screen.

Principal photography was completed after Thanksgiving 1978, but in the ensuing months, Wise got bogged down with special effects. The release date was December 1979 and he had to scramble to make the date. This was the studio's first experience with a big special-effects movie. "We didn't know what those things were," Diller says. "Bob Wise was a lovely man, but he didn't know, either." The studio poured $11 million into effects, Diller remembers, "and none of it worked." By now, the studio had spent a stunning $45 million on the picture (the average cost of a movie at the time was less than $10 million). It looked like the film was going to be a disaster.

But Paramount had a cushion. The studio had gotten theater owners to guarantee payments of at least $35 million, as long as the picture was in movie houses by December 7. As Wise rushed to finish, the bad buzz grew louder. "Once the theater owners realized that we pulled this scam off on them, none of them liked it," Diller says. "They were all trying to get out of it and we wouldn't let them out of it and we knew, of course, that if we didn't open this picture on December 7, the guarantees would evaporate. . . . The movie was horrible and we were scared to death."

"We delivered it about one minute before it was due in the theaters," Katzenberg says. To get the prints distributed, the studio had to go to charter planes. On opening day, Diller was so relieved that he rewarded Katzenberg with a bonus — several thousand dollars in pennies. (Diller and Eisner remember that the bonus was sent to Katzenberg's house, but Katzenberg recalls being called into Diller's office.) Diller was expressing his relief that the studio was getting out of a terrible mess — but Eisner, who was still unhappy about the whole ordeal, insisted on adding an element of sarcasm.

A couple of days earlier, Shatner had attended the gala premiere in Washington. He found the movie "deathly slow" and concluded that the Star Trek experience had finally ended. "That'll never happen again," he reflected.

To everyone's surprise, audiences jammed the theaters, making the picture into an $82 million hit. Katzenberg, whom Diller still describes as "the little bird dog on the movie," had survived and even triumphed. "Jeffrey spent two and a half years in *Star Trek* hell," remembers Tom Pollock, then a high-powered attorney who represented the young executive. "His career was hanging in the balance. I remember the pain he was in." But *Star Trek*, with its many sequels and television spinoffs, became Paramount's biggest franchise, a property worth hundreds of millions of dollars.

∞

IF AN IMPOSSIBLE dream can be realized, Charlie Bluhdorn had done it with the team that he had assembled at Paramount. Barry Diller, Michael Eisner, Don Simpson, and Jeffrey Katzenberg had been joined by Dawn Steel, a marketing executive who early in her career had come up with a successful gimmick—marketing designer toilet paper—and then had gotten into trouble with Gucci for copyright infringement. Eventually, she landed a job in Paramount's marketing department. Her job was to get toy makers and other merchandisers interested in *Star Trek* products. Faced with the problem of selling manufacturers on a picture that was hopelessly behind schedule and still didn't exist, Steel invited the T-shirt and lunch-box makers to the largest theater on the lot, where she screened a multi-media presentation and managed to "beam" the crew of the *Enterprise*, one by one, onto the stage. Unbeknownst to Steel, Eisner and Simpson had slipped in to watch.

The show was a smash, and the next day in the studio coffee shop, Eisner called across the room, "Dawn, I want to see you in my office tomorrow at eleven." Steel was nearly as petrified of Eisner as she was of Diller and feared that she had done something wrong. When she arrived, Eisner asked, "Okay, what do you want to do with your life?"

"Well, Michael, television could be very—"

"Forget what you want to do," he interrupted. "This is what I've done. Get *Star Trek* finished up. Then you're vice-president of production in features. Congratulations."

"I don't know anything about movies."

"Neither does anybody else. Good-bye, good luck, and break a leg!"

Don Simpson immediately called to claim credit for her promotion. While Steel went into cold sweats about her upcoming responsibilities, she continued to press the *Star Trek* marketing. She landed two huge accounts, getting McDonald's and Coca-Cola interested in the picture. Since Shatner and Nimoy wouldn't allow their images to be used, she came up with the idea of putting the Klingons from the movie in commercials eating Big Macs and drinking Cokes. She flew to New York to show the commercials to Diller, and when he saw the Klingons gobbling two of America's biggest brand names, he laughed. Steel was thrilled. She had never seen him laugh before.

∽

AFTER ALL THEY'D been through, Eisner and Katzenberg balked when Bluhdorn urged them to take a run at a *Star Trek* sequel. Harve Bennett—a television producer who knew Diller and Eisner from his work on *The Six Million Dollar Man*, *Mod Squad*, and the television miniseries *Rich Man, Poor Man*—was summoned to a meeting with Diller and Eisner and found himself face-to-face with the legendary Bluhdorn. The Gulf + Western chairman asked him what he thought of the first *Star Trek* film. "Well, I think it was really boring," he replied.

Bluhdorn turned to Eisner and barked, "You see, by you, a bald woman is sexy!" Then he turned back to Bennett. "Can you make a better picture?" he asked.

"Well, you know, yeah, I could make it less boring—yes, I could," Bennett replied.

"Could you make it for less than forty-five fucking million dollars?"

"Oh boy, where I come from, we could make five movies for that."

"Do it," Bluhdorn decreed.

At first, Paramount maintained that the second *Star Trek* would be a television movie. Bennett says this was a ploy to keep costs down. But Nimoy was dismayed—more convinced than ever that the studio was looking for a cheap killing. "You know, it seemed the thinking behind the film wasn't, 'Let's make a *Star Trek* film and do it right this time,' but more like . . . 'Let's do it on the cheap. We might do less box office but it won't matter, we'll do this thing so inexpensively that we'll still make money.' . . . They had no creative idea," he says.

Bennett lured Nimoy back into the film by convincing him to play Spock's death scene. "I thought, 'It's obviously going to be a much less opulent picture. . . . Maybe I'll go out in a blaze of glory,' " Nimoy says. But after a test screening, it became clear that the audience couldn't accept Spock's death. "What we don't have here is resurrection," Eisner said at a meeting following the screening. "We have the death scene, we have Good

Friday, but we don't have Easter morning." The studio added a few days of reshoots to leave the door ajar for Spock to participate in future sequels. The film's director, Nick Meyer, was so upset about the changes that he declined to work on the revisions.

The studio tested the picture again and the audience roared with applause when it ended. For Bennett, this was "one of the most joyful events of my life." He walked into the alley behind the theater, where he saw Eisner. Ready for the slap on the back that he felt he deserved, Bennett asked, "What'd ya think?" To his surprise, Eisner was fixated on a special-effects sequence in which a dead cave suddenly becomes lush and overgrown. "That matte shot is terrible," he said, referring to the effects work. "You've got to fix that thing or it will ruin the picture."

Bennett knew that Industrial Light and Magic—George Lucas's special-effects house—was having trouble with the sequence, but even so he couldn't believe that was Eisner's only comment. He stamped his foot and said, "Goddamnit, what about the picture!?"

"Oh," Eisner replied. "The picture's great!"

Star Trek II: The Wrath of Khan, which ended up costing nearly $19 million, had the biggest weekend opening of all time, and its $79 million gross nearly matched the first movie. The studio netted more than $25 million in pure profit. But the film's director, Nick Meyer, still smarting over the studio's refusal to kill Spock, recorded an answering-machine message that said, "Hello, this is Michael Eisner. In order to make up for the rather shabby way that Paramount Pictures treated Nick Meyer throughout the production of *Star Trek II: The Wrath of Khan*, I'm gonna be answering his phone from now on. So please leave your name, live long, and prosper." To Meyer's horror one night, he came home and heard Eisner's voice on his machine. "Nick, this is Mike ... uh ... I think this is funny but [distribution chief] Frank Mancuso didn't."

Bennett had received a more felicitous call from Charlie Bluhdorn. "I'm in my airplane. I'm somewhere over the Dominican Republic," Bluhdorn yelled. "I just saw *Star Trek II*. Congratulations! It's great! It's gonna be a big hit! And listen, kid, we're gonna make a lotta movies together. Bye!"

Shortly thereafter, Bennett says, his phone rang again. "Did you just talk to Charlie Bluhdorn?" Eisner asked. "I don't want you talking to Charlie Bluhdorn! You've got to go through me."

"Michael—he called me from his airplane," Bennett said.

"Wait—he called you?"

"Yeah."

Eisner backed off.

Before *Star Trek II* was even in theaters, the studio had decided to go ahead with the third installment. Still concerned by the ineffective matte shot in the second film, Eisner called Bennett. "I've been thinking about it and we should not have any matte shots in *Star Trek III*," he said. "Why risk it?"

"I don't want to be condescending," Bennett remembers replying, "but if you're saying you can't have a matte shot, you're saying we can't have a special effect." The two terms were synonymous, so obviously it was impossible to make a *Star Trek* movie without a matte shot. But after a couple more conversations with Eisner, Bennett realized that he could not get Eisner to abandon his idea that matte shots were trouble. He told his staff that instead of writing "ILM matte" in the script, he would use the words "effects shot—ILM elements." Later, he says, Eisner congratulated him for making the film without a matte shot.

Within six weeks, the script was written. Bennett was summoned to Eisner's office, along with Katzenberg, to hear Eisner's comments. That hadn't happened on the second *Star Trek*, so Bennett was curious what Eisner would have to say. "This is going to be a great movie," Eisner said. Then, starting on the first page, he offered his critique. Within a couple of minutes, Bennett says, he realized that what Eisner had read was an earlier draft.

"This is the wrong script," he said. "I agree with you, but all these changes have been made."

"Who gave me this script?" Eisner asked, looking pointedly at Katzenberg. "I was up from twelve to one reading this script."

"I don't know what to tell you," Bennett said.

"If I spent an hour of my time reading this script, I'm going to give you my notes," Eisner continued. Bennett realized that Eisner was determined to go ahead and, for the next forty-five minutes, listened to notes on a script that had already been revised. Bennett says this display of obstinacy didn't do much to endear Eisner to him. "In a way, it's kind of the same thing as the matte-shot fixation," he says. "It was, 'This is the way it's going to be. This is the way I see it.' It wasn't personal. It was regal."

7

THE KILLER DILLERS

IT WAS A big day for Michael Eisner. The year was 1980 and George Lucas, white-hot after *Stars Wars* and *The Empire Strikes Back*, was coming to Eisner's office at Paramount to seal a deal. For Eisner, getting Lucas was the fulfillment of a dream—even if the terms were so back-breaking that no one else would accept them.

A couple of years earlier, Lucas and his friend Steven Spielberg were vacationing in Hawaii as Lucas nervously awaited the opening of *Star Wars*. Lucas feared that the film would be a disaster, and when he found out that it was burning up the box office, "he was suddenly laughing again," Spielberg remembered. In that brightened mood, he told Spielberg that he wanted to make "a series of archaeology films." Spielberg responded that he wanted to "bring a serial to life," and with that, a collaboration was born. Lucas outlined a story with Phil Kaufman (who later directed *The Right Stuff*), and Lawrence Kasdan (who had cowritten *The Empire Strikes Back*) produced a script.

While it would be hard to imagine a more tantalizing team than Lucas and Spielberg, *Raiders of the Lost Ark* wasn't that easy to sell at the time. Since their enthusiastic chats in Hawaii, Spielberg had taken a bit of a spill with his overbudget bomb, *1941*. He was still the director of *Jaws*, one of the prototypical blockbusters, and *Close Encounters of the Third Kind*. But there was some doubt that the budget of this new project was realistic— and now there was concern about whether Spielberg could keep control. Lucas also had gone way over budget with his latest project, *The Empire Strikes Back*.

And then there was the deal itself. Lucas's terms were astounding. His attorney, Tom Pollock, and Lucasfilm president Charlie Webber had come up with a contract that gave the filmmaker a very high fee as well as extraordinary autonomy and ownership of rights associated with the film. Lucas was to own 50 percent of the film and had control of every expenditure, every theater booked—everything from posters to sequels to a possible television spinoff. Paramount was to assume all the risk of making the film and then give up a hefty share of the revenues before it recouped its costs. "I have to say, for that day, it was outrageous," Pollock acknowledges now. The Lucas team had sent the proposal to the major studios and almost all of them instantly passed. Even Universal's Sid Sheinberg, who was Spielberg's mentor, declared the deal to be so absurd that the studio wouldn't even attempt a counteroffer. But at Warner, Ted Ashley told his colleague Frank Wells to get the project.

One man who especially disliked the deal was Barry Diller. But Eisner had wanted this picture for a long time and he was willing to fight. A year earlier, he had invited Lucas and Webber to a catered lunch in his office just to request that Paramount be considered for this project. "Nobody else called us ahead of time like that," says Webber. "I was very impressed." Meanwhile, Lucas had quarreled with Twentieth Century Fox—the studio that released the *Star Wars* trilogy—during the making of *The Empire Strikes Back*. The picture had gone quickly and dramatically over budget, prompting Lucas's bank to pull a multimillion-dollar loan. Webber asked Fox for help and was stunned when the studio played hardball with the filmmaker. "I've got you and I'm going to squeeze you," chairman Dennis Stanfill told Webber, as Webber recalls the conversation.

"You just lost *Raiders*," the offended Webber declared. *The Empire Strikes Back* was finished with a loan from another bank.

At Paramount, Eisner had to convince Diller that *Raiders* was worth the risk. It was a fight that he would take to the mat. "Barry would tell Michael how stupid he was and how his ideas were insane, and it was like water off a duck's back," remembers Katzenberg. "Michael was relentless. He never took it personally. He'd say, 'You don't know what you're talking about! This is why this is going to work!' That was the strength of the relationship."

Despite Eisner's enthusiasm, Diller considered the Lucas deal to be crazy. (Ironically, the studio would fare much worse with his pet project at the time, *Reds*—Warren Beatty's epic about journalist John Reed and the Russian Revolution.) But Eisner was impervious to Diller's objections. One producer, then a Paramount executive, says he witnessed a particularly heated confrontation as Diller balked at making a deal. "Michael defended the property and essentially said, 'Well, how can I run this company if I can't make the movies I want?'" With that, this former executive recalls,

Eisner stormed out of Diller's office and did not return to work for four days. Diller says this incident never happened.

But Eisner's passion prevailed; he got the go-ahead to start a negotiation. Now his only worry was Warner and Frank Wells. Pollock, who negotiated with both on Lucas's behalf, remembers their contrasting styles. "Michael was like a large, enthusiastic dog who leaps up on you and says, 'Let's do this!' " he says. "Frank as a negotiator was reserved and gentlemanly, always very friendly and straightforward."

Lucas's team, Pollock and Webber, met with Ted Ashley and Frank Wells first. The terms of the deal were so burdensome that Ashley and Wells consulted with Warner Communications Inc. chairman Steve Ross by phone as they negotiated. And they nearly made the deal. But with Wells still tussling over a few points, Webber made an agreement-in-principle with Paramount. Much as it hurt Eisner to break precedent, he was willing to do it, Pollock says. The negotiation came down to a simple distinction, as Pollock says: "Frank was making a deal. Michael was making a movie."

Eisner hammered out deal points "line by line, comma by comma, point by point," according to Paramount business-affairs executive Dick Zimbert (who had followed Diller to the studio from ABC). Then Eisner would report to Diller, who would do the math and discover that it was "terrifying." In meetings with Zimbert, Webber started to feel his position erode. "You could clearly see that he was instructed to take back everything that was given," Webber remembers. "I said to Dick, 'This is not going in the right direction.' I called Barry or Michael and said, 'Let's part friends. You're not honoring what you said you would do.' " Finally, Paramount gave in and the deal was done.

All the Paramount brass assembled for the formal signing of the contract. Pollock remembers that even Charlie Bluhdorn appeared on this occasion. So did Diller. "You're sure you want to make this deal, Michael?" he asked pointedly. "This is going to be a great movie, right? We really have to do this, right?" It was vintage Diller—positioning himself close to the project but not near enough to catch the flak if it blew up. "If a picture didn't work at all or was clearly below par, Barry had a remarkable way of distancing himself," says one executive who worked with him closely. "It was sort of Teflon. 'I didn't read that script. How did that picture get made?' " And if there was ever a picture on which it might be worth laying this kind of groundwork early, *Raiders* was it.

Diller wasn't the only one who had trouble digesting the agreement.

The deal was like a shot that reverberated through Hollywood. When he heard that it was done, Sid Sheinberg stepped out of his office at MCA and bellowed, "Michael Eisner just made a deal that's going to destroy this business!" At Warner, Frank Wells placed a call to Dick Zimbert. "How could you do this?" he demanded. Like Sheinberg, Wells thought the deal was not only bad for Paramount but for the industry.

On many levels, he may have been right. The studio was yielding too much power, too much profit, to talent. Films were going to cost more to make and market. They were going to have to earn more to justify their costs. And studios would become more and more reluctant to take risks on off-center, interesting projects, pouring their resources into staggeringly expensive "event" pictures that were star- or effects-driven, formulaic, and—notwithstanding a lot of "action"—often rather dull.

The great irony was that Eisner—a man who personified the studios' appetite for control and who made a fetish of economy—was a catalyst of this transformation. But Eisner had his eyes on the one prize that mattered to him: profit. He would play by the rules or break them, depending on his instincts. While his choices weren't always winners, he came about as close as anyone ever got in the unpredictable game that is the entertainment business.

⁓

SHOOTING ON *RAIDERS of the Lost Ark* went smoothly after Spielberg got over one major disappointment. He wanted the little-known Tom Selleck to be Indiana Jones—and Selleck jumped at the chance. But he couldn't get out of a commitment to start a drama on CBS called *Magnum P.I.* Instead, Lucas suggested Harrison Ford, who had left behind part-time carpentry some years earlier to take a role in Lucas's first hit, *American Graffiti*. From there, he became Han Solo in *Star Wars*.

Eisner feared that *Raiders* couldn't stay within its budget of about $20 million. "Michael said, 'The first ten pages are going to cost $20 million!'" remembers Frank Marshall, who produced the film for Lucas. "That was the introduction with the rolling rock. But George is the king of movie magic and thought of a way to do it for about ten bucks." Spielberg was also eager to prove that he could get a film done efficiently in the wake of *1941*.

Lucas's deal ensured Spielberg that he would not have to suffer interference from the notoriously meddlesome Paramount executives. The director delivered *Raiders* on time and just about on budget. Marketing was a little more difficult: "Nobody could figure out what the teaser trailer should be because no one knew what *Raiders of the Lost Ark* meant," producer Marshall says. As the film's opening drew near, Diller continued to position himself. In a newspaper interview, he fretted out loud about the deal—embracing and disowning the picture simultaneously. "Lucas has almost everything edged his way and has a very big payoff if the film succeeds," he complained. "But you can't read a script and love it as much as we love this script and not try to find a way to do this film. But would I allow it to be done today? . . . Absolutely not!"

The film didn't have a huge opening in June 1981 but it had staying power. Many critics adored it (Roger Ebert called it "an out-of-body experience"). Diller had been concerned because the picture needed to gross $40 million before Paramount could make a profit. It grossed $242 million—and created one of the most valuable franchises that Paramount has ever had—worth nearly a billion dollars just at the box office. *Raiders* also received eight Oscar nominations, including Best Picture and Best Director (it won four, all in technical categories, plus a special achievement award for sound editing).

The balance of power in the industry may have shifted, but Eisner had created a moneymaking machine of awesome power. "The *Raiders* series, as outrageous as the deal was, turned out to be one of the most profitable things that team ever did for Paramount," Pollock says. "Michael Eisner— no one else—Michael Eisner brought the thing in and made it happen."

✍

BY 1980, PARAMOUNT had established the disparate but exceptional executive team that would become legendary in the industry. Outwardly, it was an oddly assorted group. Diller was as sleek as ever in handmade white cotton shirts and impeccable suits in varying shades of beige. The perennially rumpled Eisner was in corduroys or dark suits that were best described as "loosely tailored." Wild man Don Simpson affected a biker jacket and motorcycle boots; Katzenberg was preppie in Lacoste shirts and slacks; Steel was a great fan of the pointedly professional but not unsexy Armani jacket. The team at Paramount did not look like a cohesive group, and considering the drive and intensity contained on the one lot, it was astonishing that there wasn't actual bloodshed.

"No matter what the chemistry was, those were incredible years to be making movies or television at that studio," says *Star Trek* producer Harve Bennett. "Within the chaos, there was order. Barry was king. Michael brought this incredible flashing energy and Barry would take from that."

The executives who worked for these two men lived with a sense of exhilaration combined with dread. "We were all intimidated by the collective power of Michael Eisner and Barry Diller," Dawn Steel later remembered. "We would see them in the commissary or the parking lot and we'd be panting like dogs, like, 'Oh, please just recognize me.' " To her, working at the studio almost seemed like being in boot camp. If she managed to get Simpson's attention at all, he might occasionally reward her by saying, "Watch it, you're inching toward significance." When she became enraptured with a script called *Flashdance*—a Cinderella story about a steel welder who wants to be a ballerina—she had to threaten to quit to get him to pay any attention to her at all.

Despite his troubles on the original *Star Trek* movie, Katzenberg also rose quickly. His responsibilities expanded to acquiring films to put into Paramount's distribution pipeline. In April 1979, he watched a screening of *Meatballs*, a low-budget picture starring Bill Murray, known until then as a comic on *Saturday Night Live*. Three other studios bid for the picture, but Katzenberg convinced the director, Ivan Reitman, to let him show the film to the Gulf + Western brass in New York. Diller, Eisner, distribution chief Frank Mancuso, and marketing executive Gordon Weaver watched and agreed at once that Paramount should buy it. The picture, which had cost about $1.5 million, was a sleeper hit that grossed $43 million—at the time the most profitable "pickup" ever. It was a big break for Murray and director Ivan Reitman.

But when Reitman was making his next deal for a film called *Stripes*, Paramount drove a hard bargain. Michael Ovitz, the up-and-coming agent who represented Reitman and Murray, stepped out of the office when Diller and Eisner started playing hardball and placed a call on a pay phone to Frank Price, then head of Columbia Pictures. Price snapped up the deal, which brought him *Stripes* and Reitman's next project, the blockbusting *Ghostbusters*.

From the start, the Diller regime at Paramount tried to keep things cheap, spending only when absolutely necessary, as with *Raiders of the Lost Ark*. Thrift and control were two watchwords at the studio. The studio's game was "to break the agents' hold on Hollywood," as Steel said later. Diller and Eisner didn't want to take packages of scripts, actors, and directors from agencies like Ovitz's up-and-coming Creative Artists Agency. Eisner would circumvent an agent to go directly to talent whenever he could. "Michael was enormously effective in dealing with talent," remembers Zimbert. "He had an ability to talk directly to talent—ignoring the agents or the lawyers—and make them feel they wanted to do a project."

Cheapness came naturally to Eisner. "It becomes almost a challenge for me not to pay the ridiculous prices that get paid in this town," he said at the time.

Eisner was often accused of stifling creativity with his cheapness, but those who offered such criticism simply failed to appreciate what he was about. To Eisner, the film business was a business. It wasn't about making *Reds*—that was Diller's province. Sure, every so often Eisner would deviate from relentless commercialism to pursue a more literary passion. He talked forever about making a film adaptation of his favorite Edith Wharton novel, *Ethan Frome*, with Robert Redford. But normally, Eisner was more interested in popcorn than Oscars.

Eisner's fascination with *Ethan Frome* became clarified for one colleague years later at a seminar at a Disney corporate retreat. Participants were asked to write down a moment or book or movie that had shaped their lives. Eisner wrote *Ethan Frome*, and when his colleague asked why, he replied, "It's like my relationship with my mother." Those who knew Eisner only as a child of privilege might have been surprised by this comment, because Wharton paints a relentlessly grim portrait of a repressed New England man whose dreams are stymied by an embittered older woman.

In the novel, it is Frome's wife, rather than his mother, whose only pleasure "was to inflict pain" on her husband. (Given the Oedipal issues raised in Eisner's college play—in which a character sleeps with his would-be lover's mother—Eisner's identification with Ethan Frome might make interesting fodder for Freudian analysis.) Eisner's former secretary, Lee Wedemeyer, doesn't find Eisner's comment about the novel to be surprising. She says Eisner's staff used to refer to his mother as "the barracuda."

"You could see that she was a very tough woman and he was cowed by her," Wedemeyer recalls. "Whatever she wanted, Michael saw to it that she got." Often, Jane Eisner told Wedemeyer that Michael's father was an influence, but Wedemeyer felt certain that his mother counted much more. Either way, Eisner's parents still held considerable sway in his life. "I said to Jane one night, 'Michael needs a business manager,' " Wedemeyer says. "And she said, 'His father would never approve of that.' You took care of those things yourself."

∽

EVEN AT ABC, Eisner had always liked easily grasped ideas with strong marketing hooks. "He's an absolute genius about what the public is going to be interested in," says producer Craig Baumgarten, then a production executive at Paramount.

So when his old friend Susan Baerwald, by then a script reader at United Artists, told him about a project called *Airplane!*, Eisner got ahold of it and agreed that the writers—who had no experience behind a camera—could direct it. Jim Abrahams and the two Zucker brothers, Jim and Jerry, had been members of an improv troupe from Milwaukee. Simpson, Katzenberg, and Baumgarten thought Eisner was out of his mind. But Eisner protected his downside; the directors had to work for scale and the budget was a mere $6 million. Eisner also went along with the writers' desire to assemble an off-center cast that included Robert Stack and Lloyd Bridges, but he vetoed their idea to use a prop plane instead of a jet. When Eisner's executive team went to a screening on the lot, they agreed that perhaps the picture wasn't an outright disaster. But Eisner was enthralled. "This is the greatest! This is a hit!" Rolling their eyes, the three junior executives took bets on how much the picture would gross. The high guess was $16 million. This time, Eisner's faith in talent was justified. The film grossed $84 million. All the more profit considering that it cost $6 million. A perfect Eisner slam dunk.

(Baerwald, who had told Eisner about the script and was a family friend, had half-jokingly asked for a point—or 1 percent of the profit. For a long time nothing happened. "It rankled me when it was so successful," she acknowledges. "But eventually, he gave me two tickets around the world." Baerwald had kids and couldn't afford to pay the taxes on the tickets, so she had to cash them in.)

Sometimes, of course, Eisner's penchant for cheap popular entertainment led him astray. When he saw a production of *Hello, Dolly!* with Pearl Bailey in the lead, he figured Paramount could get a quick, low-cost show by dusting off old scripts from *The Odd Couple* series and reshooting them with an all-black cast. The only problem, in writer-producer Garry Marshall's view, was that "the new series was based on greed." It quickly became apparent that "words written for two square New York Jewish men in their forties just didn't sound right coming out of the mouths of two hip thirty-year-old African-American men."

The project died, but Eisner's impulse to manufacture entertainment without having to put up with a lot of creative blather didn't. "Barry is filet mignon and Michael is cheeseburger," Don Simpson used to say. Producer Larry Gordon — Eisner's longtime friend — referred to them as "the shit and the chic." Eisner seemed self-conscious about these tags, which he thought were too simplistic. He had, after all, been an enthusiastic backer of the well-received 1980 film *The Elephant Man*, the tale of disfigured nineteenth-century Briton John Merrick. Privately blaming Diller for promoting the perception of filet versus cheeseburger, Eisner often invoked his knowledge of literature to offset it. He told a reporter that he became interested in the idea for *Footloose* because of *The Scarlet Letter* and another Nathaniel Hawthorne story called "The Maypole of Merrymount." While delivering this piece of information, Eisner was shrewd enough to mock himself. "My wife . . . told me if I ever talked about any connection to Hawthorne, I was a schmuck," he confided.

Though his commercial instincts often were formidable, Eisner wasn't always on target, as the short-lived *New Odd Couple* series illustrates. When Garry Marshall suggested basing a show on an alien played by the unknown Robin Williams in a *Happy Days* guest appearance, Eisner didn't get it. "That's not a show, it's an actor," he said. Of course, *Mork & Mindy* turned out to be a runaway hit.

In movies, too, Eisner's judgments were hit-and-miss. One weekend, two scripts came in — *Coast to Coast*, with Dyan Cannon attached to the project, and *Private Benjamin* with Goldie Hawn. Eisner picked *Coast to Coast* — a weak road comedy about a debt-strapped trucker — and *Private Benjamin*, which turned out to be a major hit, wound up at Warner.

When production executive Richard Fischoff pitched a movie called *The Big Chill*, both Eisner and Katzenberg passed on the story of seven college friends who come together after the suicide of one of their classmates. "I don't think the kind of friendship or self-analysis that the movie is about were part of Michael's or Jeffrey's life experience," Fischoff says. Fischoff took the picture to Columbia, and in 1983, it became a well-received hit, grossing $56 million. Such are the caprices of the film business, of course, that any executive, no matter how successful, has similar stories to tell. For example, the team at Warner that picked up *Private Benjamin* later let *Home Alone* go to Fox.

∞

WITH THEIR CONTRASTING styles, Diller and Eisner fought like animals. But their differences proved complementary. "Any meeting that Barry and Michael were in, you could sell tickets to," remembers Rich Frank, former television chief at Paramount. "It was unbelievable how they would scream and yell and fight with each other. And they could walk away and there was no residual negativity from the meeting." One low-level staffer, who went on to become an extremely successful producer, used to watch from his window on Friday afternoons as the two emerged from the Paramount administration building and invariably started to quarrel. He was so mesmerized by the angry, sweaty gesticulations that he brought a long-lens camera to the office to photograph the spectacle. (He kept the pictures for his private collection.)

"All the arguments are the same to me," remembers Zimbert, an executive who witnessed many. "One of the major difficulties in a studio is the timing problem. You've got to get hundreds of elements together at one time to start the camera rolling. And Barry, with this convince-me attitude, would make Michael crazy. Michael would sweat with an enormous effort to pull these pieces together. And Barry would start: 'Why does [that writer] get credit? Why does he get gross after breakeven?' Legitimate business questions, but tension would rise and they would yell."

Once, junior executives David Kirkpatrick and Ricardo Mestres were going to accompany Eisner and Simpson to New York to make a presentation to Bluhdorn about the studio's activities. Both were excited, because this was to be their first big meeting in Bluhdorn's presence. They meticulously put together their materials. But in a meeting that dragged on for more than four hours, their part of the agenda was never discussed. Instead, Diller and Eisner — with Simpson pitching in — shrieked at each other about whether Olivia Newton-John should do a cameo in a planned sequel to *Grease*. "All our good work went by the wayside because of the volatility and their wanting to get into the fray," Kirkpatrick laments. As for Bluhdorn, he appeared briefly in the middle of the meeting and said, "I think I would like that boy from *Stripes* and that girl from *Private Benjamin* to do a movie together." With that, he left. The Bill Murray–Goldie Hawn pairing never happened. Neither did the cameo in *Grease 2*.

Dick Sylbert remembers hearing that Eisner and Diller had quarreled after the Oscar ceremony in 1982. Having gotten his fill of life as an executive, Sylbert had returned to production design and had received an Oscar nomination for his work on *Reds*. This project was Diller's baby—complex, sophisticated, and not commercial. It hadn't made any money but it had claimed a Best Director award for Beatty, as well as nods for cinematography and best supporting actress. But Sylbert had lost out in the production-design category to another Paramount film—Eisner's own darling, the wildly commercial *Raiders of the Lost Ark*. Sylbert remembers that Diller asked Eisner how he had voted in the production-design category. "He said he voted for *Raiders*. And Barry said, 'You asshole! We've made millions on that picture. Don't you realize we could have used some help?' "

Diller claims that his fights with Eisner were simply part of the studio's modus operandi. "It was Michael and me, me and everyone," he says. "We had a system of advocacy which produced endless argument, almost every day." It was a Darwinian approach: only the strongest ideas were supposed to survive. When Eisner railroaded through *Raiders of the Lost Ark*, that was supposed to represent the best fruits of Diller's Socratic approach to moviemaking.

In one sense, of course, Diller and Eisner had no argument at all. Both wanted hits, which meant making profitable mass entertainment. But as time went on, studios increasingly favored the safe formula over the gamble. In the contest between *Reds* and *Raiders of the Lost Ark*, commerce prevailed over art. "*Reds* was the end of something," says the film's director, Warren Beatty. "Whatever [Paramount] was, it was a pretty goddamn good training ground for what the movies became. It became about mass release, which changed the content. Everybody has been on that train ever since. But I don't know if that train has done a lot for movies."

∞

DESPITE ITS INTERNAL friction, Paramount's golden team continued to make films that succeeded commercially or artistically during the early eighties: *Airplane!*, *Raiders of the Lost Ark*, *Ordinary People*, *The Elephant Man*, and *Reds* were among those that would be remembered. But the studio also had some notorious losers, such as the big-budget *Popeye* and *Ragtime*. Other pictures died with less fanfare. *Mommie Dearest*, starring Faye Dunaway as Joan Crawford, dropped more than $4 million; *Part-*

ners, a Ryan O'Neal vehicle about a cop pretending to be gay in an undercover investigation, lost $6 million; and the ill-fated *Grease 2* lost nearly $9 million.

It was inevitable with this exceptionally ambitious group that everyone would strain to get ahead. Eisner was frustrated, says an executive who worked for him, because it seemed to him that Diller tried — not very successfully — to cut him out of the loop to Bluhdorn. Diller denies that he tried to cut Eisner out. "I was never insecure about my relationship with Bluhdorn," Diller says. "Almost without exception, I was very happy for Michael Eisner and Charlie Bluhdorn to talk. And Michael was very careful. . . . Once, when I was in Europe at the Royale Hotel in Deauville, Bluhdorn tried — unsuccessfully — to get Michael to overrule something I had said. It was very painful because I was on a holiday and I had to spend ten hours or so fixing it." Otherwise, he doesn't remember Eisner attempting to end-run him.

Eisner also chafed because he wanted greater control over marketing and distribution, which was headquartered in New York even though in theory it reported to him. The head of that operation, Frank Mancuso, persistently kept open his own line of communications with Bluhdorn, calling to deliver box-office results. Bluhdorn was happy to needle his lieutenants by playing them off against each other. And Mancuso had a strong ally in Martin Davis, a powerful Bluhdorn lieutenant who had risen to executive vice-president.

One day in 1981, Eisner called executives Ricardo Mestres and David Kirkpatrick to his office and asked them to tape him as he gave a stream-of-consciousness analysis of the film business — what kind of movies to make, what kind of directors to hire. It was the foundation for a memo that Eisner wanted to write on the state of the business. The subtext of the memo, in the view of one of Eisner's staff, was that marketing and distribution should be moved to Los Angeles. Indeed, Eisner made that proposal in his memo, but if expanding his empire was Eisner's purpose, he didn't succeed.

The memo, however, reveals Eisner's constant anxiety about complacency leading to failure. A January 1982 draft reads, "Decisions are often made for the wrong reasons when things are going well. Success tends to make you forget what made you successful. Just when you least suspect it, the fatal turnover shifts the game, and the other team scores the winning point." Eisner warned that Paramount, which had been the number-one or -two studio over the preceding five years, should consider itself in last place. "We should never become bogged down in the vulnerable stagnation of success."

It wasn't so much a fear of failure itself; Eisner wrote "failure is necessary" and "fear of failure will always stifle bold steps and leave the executive only mediocre." It was not so much a fear of failure that worried him but the failure to fear. Failure teaches important lessons, he added. For example, Paramount passed on *Private Benjamin* because of problems with the story. "What we did not see was the larger conceptual picture of 'Goldie Hawn Meets the Army,' which was key to the success of the movie. From this experience, we had the insight to look beyond the seemingly unworkable deal on *Raiders of the Lost Ark* and understand the potential of a larger creative concept." With this somewhat self-promoting example, Eisner concluded that failure is "central to education." In essence, gambling was necessary, but constant vigilance also was essential.

Nonetheless, Eisner warned, it was imperative to "avoid the big mistake." The big mistake came when "a substantial, unprotected investment is made for the wrong reasons in a movie that does not have a reason for being" and it could be "the downfall of a company." Paramount avoided disaster with *Reds*, he said, because it had a strong concept, a commercially proven director, and an acclaimed cast. Finally, and perhaps most important, "these inherent strengths were coupled with some financial protections that limited our risk." Still, Eisner said, "In the case of *Reds*, the extremely high production budget may prove to make the project not worthy of the risk."

Eisner argued that it was also important to have an eclectic mix of movies. "[We] believe the American public is almost by nature promiscuous," Eisner wrote. "A man's head will turn at a woman strutting down the street, even if she is less attractive than his steady partner." Accordingly, management must include people with diverse tastes.

The perfect executive, Eisner continued, is "a 'golden retriever' with good taste." That combination is rare, he continued, so a creative team needs to have a mix of people who search out material and those who can evaluate its commercial potential. Top management could assess the material if the "retrievers" in middle management sought out ideas for movies from books, magazine articles, and other sources.

And commercial potential, in Eisner's view, was all that mattered. He stated his own goal in succinct terms. "We have no obligation to make history," he wrote. "We have no obligation to make art. We have no obligation to make a statement. To make money is our only objective."

If a film happened to win an Oscar, so much the better. "To make money," Eisner said, "it might be important to win the Academy Award, for it might mean another ten million dollars at the box office." Of course, since Eisner was an executive in a public company, his views in this regard were proper and hardly unique. But the attack on *Reds* and other Academy Award hopefuls could clearly be seen as a swipe at Diller. It was plain that unlike some other executives, Eisner had never been the wide-eyed kid who fell in love with the movies. To him, the bottom line was the bottom line.

8

HIGH CONCEPT

RATHER THAN ADDRESSING the tensions at Paramount, Bluhdorn did what he could to exacerbate them. Eisner would later maintain that he and Diller were too smart to allow Bluhdorn to manipulate them into going after each other, but in reality, relationships at the studio were fraught with tension. One underling who was bucking for a promotion to the head of a department remembers telling Eisner, "I want a number-one job." Eisner replied, "So do I."

In this environment, there was also bickering over credit—not just between Eisner and Diller but among all the upper-level executives at the studio. The jockeying to lay claim to the studio's hits became so pronounced that a joke took hold among employees that Paramount needed an "executive credit arbitration committee," modeled on the Writers Guild committee that assigns credit for screenwriting.

Diller also had Eisner carry out some unpleasant tasks that might seem to fall more into his province. For example, Diller had forced Eisner to drop the hatchet when Beatty was running behind schedule and over budget on *Reds*. "I remember Barry just saying to Michael, 'You tell Warren that *Reds* is finished. They come home Friday. He can put it together with what he's got,' " says a former Paramount executive.

Naturally this type of confrontation was unpleasant to Eisner; like many high-ranking Hollywood executives, he was far more inclined to say yes when he meant no. It was not uncommon for Eisner to respond to a pitch with wild enthusiasm and apparently to approve it. Then he'd call Zimbert or Simpson or some other lieutenant and bark, "You make a deal with those people, I'll kill you." Simpson used to call this ploy "the elastic go."

Eisner fancied himself as protecting his staff from Diller's tirades, playing "something of a mother's role . . . protecting the children from a brilliant and powerful but difficult and demanding father—much as my mother had done in our family." But apparently the "children" didn't feel as if they were cloaked by a mother's love.

Once, Eisner approved a project called *Thief* that was to be directed by Michael Mann and produced by Jerry Bruckheimer. Both Simpson and Katzenberg badly wanted to make the film, but the next day, Eisner said it was off. Katzenberg was deeply humiliated when he had to tell the film-makers that the project was canceled. (United Artists eventually made the movie.) Generally, Eisner transmitted bad news through Dick Zimbert, the business-affairs executive. Eisner seemed to cultivate the view that he was impulsive, and Zimbert capitalized on that when he called to deliver bad news. "I know it's stupid, but you know, Michael is crazy," he'd say.

Leonard Nimoy was to get a taste of Eisner's technique in 1983 when he wanted to direct *The Search for Spock*, the third installment of the *Star Trek* series. He was extremely nervous when he met with Eisner to propose the idea—after all, this was now a valuable franchise, the picture had a $15 million budget, and Nimoy had never directed a film before. To his vast relief, Eisner seemed overjoyed. "Great idea!" he said. "Mancuso will love it. Marketing with love it!" To Nimoy, he seemed sincere. "It all came in a nice selling package," he says. "It was being made on the basis of potential promotion sizzle."

Nimoy left the meeting and heard nothing for six weeks. Expecting to make a deal, he found that the business-affairs staff wouldn't even return his agent's calls. Finally he called Eisner. "What's going on?" he asked. "Weeks ago, we had this great meeting and now I can't even get anyone to answer the phone."

"There's a problem," Eisner said. "I just don't feel comfortable hiring a guy to direct a *Star Trek* feature when that guy hates *Star Trek* so much he insisted on being killed off just to get out. It really bothers me that you insisted they put that in your contract."

Nimoy was astonished. There was no such provision in his contract. He suspected that Gene Roddenberry, still lurking unhappily in the wings, had tried to poison the deal for him. "My contract is in a file in the building you're in," he told Eisner. "Why don't you have someone bring it to you?"

The next day, Nimoy and Eisner met and Nimoy made an impassioned presentation. The gist of his argument was that Eisner had two problems—he needed Spock and he needed a director—and Nimoy could solve both. Finally he closed in for the kill. "You and I are having a very important meeting here," he told Eisner. "This might be the last time we ever speak to each other. We're either going to start working together on something fresh or we're literally down to the final moments of our relationship." Nimoy was wise to play rough. He got his way.

Despite his complaints that he was "getting a lot of hovering" from Bennett, who had returned as producer, Nimoy pulled the film together successfully. When he flew to New York for a test screening, he felt confident as he waited with the Paramount executives for the audience to fill out cards giving their reaction. As the group huddled in an office in the Gulf + Western building, Nimoy overheard Eisner talking about him. "Michael was standing right behind me," Nimoy remembers. "I heard him say, 'He told me he was going to direct the picture or I could go fuck myself.' Which was not accurate. I said, 'Michael, that's not true.' He turned back and said, 'He was a perfect gentleman. But in essence, that's what he told me.' "

Nimoy had won in perhaps the only possible way to win with the Paramount crowd—by playing a very tough game. Not for nothing did the town say that Paramount would green-light a picture and then dare you to make it. *Star Trek III*, which opened in June 1984, grossed $77 million—a great number for the third installment—and Nimoy went on to direct the fourth.

Sue Mengers, the leading talent agent of the day, once commented on the degree of difficulty of doing business with Eisner. "I find Eisner the toughest person I negotiate with, and I don't mean that as a compliment," she told a reporter. "He simply must win." But whenever she was reduced to rage, she added, Eisner would disarm her by saying "something funny or charming or self-deprecating."

Eisner had another weapon in his arsenal. Don Simpson used to say that Eisner had "an optional memory." One case in point was a movie that Eisner wanted to make based on the harrowing true story of a rugby team that was forced to feed on its dead when their plane crashed in the Andes. Eisner fought hard for the picture but Diller thought it would be too expensive and opposed it. Eisner got his way and the studio set about building a dormitory in Portillo, Chile, to house the crew. But the director, an unknown named Tony Scott, told Eisner that the picture had taken too long to get under way. It was late in the season and the snow would melt before he could finish shooting. When the picture was canceled, Eisner turned on Baumgarten, claiming he had never authorized the expenditure of $400,000 to build the dormitory.

"Michael, I can't get forty cents approved at this company without your signature," Baumgarten protested. After that Eisner's underlings agreed that no one—not even Simpson—would go into Eisner's office alone. "You always had a chaperon so there would be a witness," one remembers.

Eisner gave them other reasons to believe that he could be duplicitous. When MGM chief David Begelman wanted to make *Buddy Buddy*, a Jack Lemmon–Walter Matthau picture, Eisner told his troops that Paramount would make sure the project never happened. "We're going to lie," he said, according to one executive who was present. "We're going to tell them we want it and then we're going to bury it."

"He didn't want it," that executive explains. "But he wanted to make sure MGM didn't get it so he wouldn't be embarrassed if it was successful." In this case, Eisner's plan was thwarted and MGM made the picture. But he won anyway: it bombed.

∽

EISNER HAD A way of saying yes when he meant no. This sometimes put his staffers in embarrassing predicaments. And his trick of bypassing agents to talk directly to talent seemed counterproductive because it alienated a segment of the industry that could be helpful in delivering clients and material. In notes that he scribbled to himself in March 1980, Katzenberg complained, "Agents don't want to come to [Paramount]. . . . No effort to turn around—disaster level now. Double dealing/indecisive/call clients direct going behind their backs."

Young executives were under relentless pressure to make contacts and deliver ideas, directors, actors. Meanwhile, Eisner shot down ideas without seeming to consider them. "No team spirit," Katzenberg wrote. "Atmosphere is too competitive/Everyone tries to position." Katzenberg did not think his boss, Simpson, was much of an ally: "Don—No longer strong counterbalance/totally capitulated—decide to accept and support. No longer stands up for projects—I've seen Don turn totally around just because he doesn't have energy to take on so many fights."

But Katzenberg's harshest words were reserved for Eisner. "First instinct is negative/Approach is to confuse + stall," he wrote. "Deal making is unequivocally a destructive process. . . . Refuses to take anyone seriously— everyone has an angle and everyone is out to screw him. . . . His world is the whole universe/there is no room for other opinions/no consideration for other points of view/no other perspective than own. . . . Totally shoots from hip and then tries to create his own set of facts to support (Alive). . . .We don't romance, hold hands, build relationships—hit + run/No answers, no understanding. . . . He is out of control—has burned more bridges including best friends."

Eisner's former secretary, Lee Wedemeyer, says she "didn't see that part" of Eisner but acknowledges that she looked the other way. "I always thought Michael was the smartest man I knew and so quick on his feet," she says. "Later, people told me he's smart and quick on his feet but his word means nothing. . . . I didn't want to see it, but that's the rap on him." And she acknowledges that she saw Katzenberg's struggles. "Jeffrey had to fight so hard—and he didn't win—to get Michael's respect."

As other Katzenberg memos reveal, he discussed his growing frustrations with Simpson—or tried to. "You let M.D.E. get away with his shit—your job is to deal with him on behalf of your staff," Katzenberg wrote at one point. "Watch M.D.E. turn you around on story, ideas . . . you think he's better—bullshit." With some prescience, perhaps, he also wrote: "Writing on wall—follow M.D.E. and end casualty or start doing what is right. . . . Fool if you don't see it coming."

Katzenberg's assertion that Simpson didn't stand up to Eisner must have been particularly galling to Simpson, who always carried himself with a swagger that suggested fearlessness in battle. He was a brilliant, tortured, complicated man who had escaped from what was, by his angry and often-embellished accounts, a bleak childhood in a blue-collar enclave of Anchorage, Alaska. He was amusing and offensive, abusive and yet capable of bursts of great generosity.

Simpson, who was burly, almost short, with a look that reminded screen-writer and novelist John Gregory Dunne of "a carved Eskimo totem," had his first job in marketing at Warner. But he realized that he wanted to work on the movies rather than sell them. Shacking up with his friend Jerry Bruckheimer, whom he had met at a screening of *The Harder They Come*, Simpson set about partying hard while simultaneously educating himself in the movie business. He started hanging out at Schwabs Drugstore and swiping film books from the Larry Edmunds Bookshop, returning them after he read them. "I lived with Truffaut and Hitchcock," Simpson remembered later. "I had this big bed and there'd be books stacked all over the floor. Bruckheimer used to joke that he only knew when I was going to get laid when there would be a path through my books."

Eventually, Simpson's friend, aspiring producer Steve Tisch, got him an

interview at Paramount. He borrowed a sport coat and snagged a job working for Dick Sylbert, then briefly Paramount's chief of production. Within
two years, Simpson had Sylbert's job. "In my time, he hadn't enough money
to buy too much coke," Sylbert says. "He was an executive." But as he rose
through the ranks at Paramount, Simpson found that drugs became ever
more affordable—and irresistible.

When Eisner arrived at the studio, Simpson was quick to adjust. Sylbert
and Simpson had been working on a small, sweet, and eventually well-
reviewed film called *Citizen's Band*. The picture was an early effort from
director Jonathan Demme, who would later direct *The Silence of the Lambs*
and *Philadelphia*. Eisner arrived in the midst of the production and Sylbert
left the studio soon after. Sometime later, Sylbert ran into Demme, who
told him, "Remember how Don used to watch all the dailies and how he
loved the picture? The day you left, Michael Eisner looked at that movie
and said, 'What is this piece of shit?' And Don Simpson looked at me as if
I had made a nightmare."

Eisner made Simpson his head of production when a confidant urged
him to act quickly before Diller had a chance to install his own man in
the job. Simpson became an integral part of Paramount's box-office magic
and ascended steadily. "Don was very helpful to Michael," remembers
Wedemeyer. "There were a lot of things about moviemaking that Michael
didn't know and Don could fill him in." He was as hands-on as Eisner and
Diller might have wished, with a strong sense of story. "Don was the best
at recognizing a movie moment when he saw one," said producer Larry
Mark, then a junior executive. "He knew when a movie needed one, he
knew how to get to one." Simpson had his executives churn out voluminous
notes on scripts and wrote some of the most incisive ones himself. In Katzenberg's estimation, "he really was without peer when it came to working
with material and being able to pinpoint the things that made a script work."

As Simpson later acknowledged, he was part of a management team that
did not make things easy on talent. "Paramount [tried] to make your movie
for you," he said. "When I was in the job, I was not a nice person. I never
lied or cheated but I did run roughshod over people."

And many critics didn't think Simpson's style—which he continued to
practice when he and Jerry Bruckheimer became one of Hollywood's most
successful producing partnerships—was especially good for the movies.
John Gregory Dunne felt that working with Simpson was "simply taking
dictation," transforming the writer into an expensive stenographer. Film

writer Peter Biskind said many other writers thought Simpson's methods "inaugurated an era of decline, when executives would convince themselves that they knew best." But from the standpoint of commerce, Simpson's methods often worked exceptionally well.

If writers sometimes felt that Simpson was tough on them, executives suffered more. David Kirkpatrick remembers working so hard at one point that he hadn't returned home in three days. "I complained to Don Simpson and said, 'I haven't showered, I haven't slept.' I broke into tears in Don's office and he said, 'Go home. We'll work it out.' Monday I came in and my office had been moved. There was a note saying where to find the new office. I went in and they had put in a foldout bed and a shower so I could take care of my necessities right there."

Simpson worked hard, too, but his habits became increasingly erratic. One Paramount executive at the time remembers him showing up at a company retreat late, wearing a T-shirt emblazoned with the words "Maui Wowie," cheeseburger in hand. "Sorry," he apologized. "I got pulled over doing a hundred and twenty in my Porsche."

Another junior executive at the time remembers that Simpson regularly showed up for work at eleven in the morning—more than four full hours after Katzenberg pulled in—and would leave at four in the afternoon. At one point, he says, he didn't see Simpson at all for a couple of weeks. "Don's style was different," that executive says. "He'd work all weekend, stay up all night, call us at four-thirty A.M. with script notes. Jeffrey was in at six-thirty A.M., and he would go for [a working] dinner at eight."

One member of a producing team that worked with Paramount remembers getting involved in a project in which a writer turned in a dark, unworkable script. To the producers' surprise, however, Simpson declared with glittering eyes that he loved the material. They were panicked at the prospect of trying to make the film. But the next day, Eisner called them to a meeting in his office along with Simpson. "A terrible injustice has been done to you," he said as Simpson sat with his head hanging down. "I have read this abomination. I want to apologize."

"He went on and on about how Don fucked up," one of the producers remembers. "In front of us. This was punishment. As we got up, he walked down to the end of the table, dropped the script in front of Don, and said, 'We have to talk.'"

By the early eighties, it had become increasingly apparent that Simpson was not keeping up the pace. He had always prided himself on being able to press his luck in his private life without jeopardizing his work. Even in his high-school yearbook, he had bequeathed to underclassmen "my ability to 'walk on the wild side' while still maintaining a reputation that's 'above reproach.'" But at thirty-seven years old, he was losing his ability to sustain the game. His life became a series of peaks and valleys: productive periods where he was fit and coherent followed by protracted binges of mind-boggling drug abuse, weight gain, and professional disintegration.

The summer of 1982 was a deep valley for Simpson and the studio was slumping, too. Paramount's parent, Gulf + Western, had just reported a 53 percent drop in profits for its third quarter, and its Leisure Time Group, which included the studio, was among the operations that were responsible for the decline. There was some hope for one of Bluhdorn's favorite projects, *An Officer and a Gentleman* with Debra Winger and Richard Gere, which was set to open at the end of July. But there was bad buzz about a clutch of other projects in the works, including *White Dog*, Eisner's pet project about a dog trained to hate blacks, as well as a picture named *Young Lust* and *Jekyll and Hyde . . . Together Again*. Eisner had told Simpson that *An Officer and a Gentleman* was "a little romantic movie [but] *White Dog* is *Jaws*." He was wrong. *An Officer and a Gentleman* was a smash, netting the studio more than $50 million in profit, but the others, in fact, lost millions.

Paramount had suffered through a string of flops, partly because of Eisner's insistence on rushing seven films into production before an anticipated directors' strike in 1981. "The scripts were ridiculous and Don took the hit for a lot of them," Steel said later. When *Grease 2* was in the works, Eisner saw a cut and asked for changes. Simpson didn't follow up, and when the film premiered in May 1982 at the Cinerama Dome in Hollywood, Eisner realized that his directions had not been carried out. Simpson, who attended the event with his date—one of Richard Pryor's former wives—and Paramount executive Craig Baumgarten, was boasting that he had single-handedly saved the picture by reworking it. "He said he'd been working around the clock, which was code," Baumgarten remembers. "He'd been working twenty-four hours, but he'd been getting loaded, too."

The premiere was a disaster and Eisner was furious that his instructions had been ignored. (The picture was such a flop that Paramount did not exercise an option to make another picture with its female star, a then-unknown Michelle Pfeiffer. "Very few people could figure out that she was going to be a star from that," Baumgarten says.)

Soon afterward, sources close to the situation say Eisner and Diller took

Simpson to lunch hoping to persuade him to clean up. But Simpson was in terrible shape and Diller and Eisner decided they could do no more. Simpson had to be fired. Eisner's longtime mentor, producer Larry Gordon, pleaded for Simpson to get a face- and possibly life-saving production deal. Eisner agreed. In *Variety*, Simpson's departure was portrayed as a voluntary decision to become a producer and rid himself of "administrative details." Simpson told the *Los Angeles Herald Examiner* that he had been sick of his job for five years. "Before I'm 40, I want to make pictures of my own — and I want to get rich," he said. He would do both.

Eisner wasn't sure, at first, who would replace Simpson, but he knew he had to act before Diller got involved. "At that time, Michael didn't like [Katzenberg]," says a source close to Eisner. "Jeffrey was really Barry's guy. He was an arrogant little prick. . . . He wanted the job desperately, of course." With Gordon urging him on, Eisner gave the job of production chief to Katzenberg, who may have been Diller's guy but not as much as some other candidates might have been.

∞

AND AT AGE thirty-one, Katzenberg — a married man who boasted that he had never ingested an illegal substance in his life — was essentially the anti-Simpson. "Jeffrey was incredibly disciplined, incredibly driven, very organized and methodical," says Richard Fischoff, who was hired as a creative executive shortly before Simpson's demise at the studio. In June, Katzenberg was named president of production. "I trained him," Simpson told the media.

The biggest rap against Katzenberg was that he had never demonstrated any particular brand of taste or creative instinct. "The thing about Jeffrey that plagued him his whole life is that smart as Jeffrey is, Jeffrey isn't a guy who can feel it," says Baumgarten. "Jeffrey will go to a record store, buy the top-ten albums, and listen to them. But he doesn't love 'em." Another former colleague puts it more harshly. "Jeffrey was always the plodder," he says. Yet another remembers urging Katzenberg to hire a bright young animator at Disney named Tim Burton. "Talk to me when he's established," Katzenberg said.

But Katzenberg tried to tackle the creative part of the process through the combined powers of his will and his brain. And no doubt Eisner saw him as a perfect, relentless "retriever" and planned to supply the "gut" himself when it came to picking movies. Not only would he provide the

gut but—to whatever degree it was needed—the intellect. It didn't help
Katzenberg to admit in a meeting that he had never read *The Scarlet Letter*
when Eisner mused that he'd like to do a movie version. Katzenberg was
unvarnished, all right, but he was willing.

The other widely held criticism of Katzenberg was that he was only too
willing—happy to execute Eisner's mandate to control the filmmaking process and keep down costs. When headstrong director John Milius hired a
composer without consulting the studio, Katzenberg refused to let the man
score the film. Milius vowed never to work with Katzenberg again. "He's a
wonderful human being if he agrees with you," Milius said later, "but he
has no ethical conscience and sees that as a virtue." If Katzenberg was
exceptionally aggressive, Eisner undoubtedly admired the quality. He and
Katzenberg cheerfully kept up an enemies list; a former Paramount executive remembers Eisner sticking his head in Katzenberg's office occasionally
to ask, "So-and-so called. Do we hate him? Is this guy dead to us?"

While Katzenberg was flexing Eisner's muscle, Simpson teamed up with
his roommate, Jerry Bruckheimer, to produce *Flashdance*—the picture that
Dawn Steel had championed so passionately when Simpson had been head
of production. *Flashdance* was an ugly duckling, destined to be a megahit
that would spawn epic battles over who deserved the credit. But when
Flashdance was nearing its opening, the studio failed to realize what it had.
There was a small screening with a test audience on the lot, mostly teens,
and when it was over, the film executives walked back toward the administration building.

The audience seemed to enjoy the film, but as seasoned executives
know, success with a test audience that is invited to see a movie for free
does not necessarily translate into filmgoers making the trek to theaters and
shelling out their own money for tickets. Nonetheless, one low-level executive thought the picture had really hit home with the audience. "I really
loved it," he ventured. The reaction was icy. "I got, 'What the fuck do
you know?'" he remembers. "Everybody bashed the movie other than
Mancuso."

"To show you just how much Paramount believed in the movie, they
sold off 25 percent of it to a private investment firm as a hedge against
losses—a few weeks before it opened," Steel said later. "They wanted to
cover themselves in case it bombed." With a budget of $7 million, it grossed
more than $90 million domestically, produced a smash record, and inspired
a ripped, off-the-shoulder T-shirt craze that every young woman with aspi-

rations to cool would wear that summer. Simpson launched himself into one of the most successful film-producing careers in industry history.

∽

ANYONE WHO EXPECTED life at Paramount to get easier after Simpson left was doomed to bitter disappointment. Katzenberg's work habits became legendary in the community: the Monday-morning calls to dozens of agents, the back-to-back breakfast meetings, the if-you-don't-come-in-Saturday, don't-bother-showing-up-Sunday work ethic that would be emulated by ambitious young suits throughout the industry. Ricardo Mestres took to the routine like a fish to water. "I thought this was what the rest of the industry was like," he said later. "But the rest of the world was the opposite—they'd wait for the phone to ring and field offers. Jeffrey made everybody nervous. Nobody worked the hours or covered the territory that Jeffrey seemed to."

David Kirkpatrick remembers "looking out the window and seeing Jeffrey put his hands on our car hoods to see if they were warm or cold at five in the morning. . . . We worked twenty-hour days, but it was thrilling to be a part of it. You were at the center of it all and the [bosses] didn't mind unmasking their feelings for all to see. That was exciting to a young pisher."

But there was a downside, too. Kirkpatrick recalls being at the studio on Christmas Eve, trying to recut *It Came from Hollywood*. He complained that it was a holiday. "So we'll order some turkey sandwiches," Katzenberg replied.

Another executive says Katzenberg taught him to fight for his convictions, to make his deadlines, to impose discipline on himself that was rare in Hollywood. But he also realized his life was being ruined after he told Katzenberg he was going to New York to spend Christmas with his wife's family. Though Katzenberg seemed unperturbed at first, he called the young man into his office a few days later and handed him a stack of scripts. "I want you to go to the Gulf + Western building on Christmas Day and fax me notes on these," Katzenberg said. He did as he was told and spent several hours in Katzenberg's immaculate white-on-white New York office. He missed Christmas dinner, and when he arrived at his in-laws', he found his wife with tears in her eyes. "If you want to hang on to your marriage," his brother-in-law admonished, "you'd better get out of Paramount." It wasn't long before he did exactly that. "I realized I had totally, totally lost my soul to this place," he said later.

∽

WHEN SIMPSON WAS fired, producer Larry Gordon and his young protégé, Joel Silver, were already working on a Paramount film called *48 Hrs*. The script, which was about a cop who teams up with a con to catch the bad guys, had kicked around Hollywood for a few years under Gordon's wing. Gordon was a salty little man who frequently boasted that he had gotten tough being raised as "the only Jew in Mississippi." He was also the man who had warned Eisner, years earlier at ABC, that he had incurred Aaron Spelling's displeasure and might lose his job. Since then, he had become Eisner's constant adviser.

He and Eisner were friends and their wives were close as well; in 1978, Jane Eisner and Margie Gordon had even conceived a television series together about two working mothers and their children sharing a household. They pitched the idea to Marcy Carsey, Eisner's protégée at ABC, who advised them to get a professional writer and then raised eyebrows in the industry by giving the two novices a deal and agreeing that the network would pay for script rewrites. Bill Persky, a veteran television writer-producer who was among those who came and went, said he signed on because he was represented by the same agency as the two ladies—Creative Artists Agency, the rising boutique that had been formed by Michael Ovitz and his partners.

After going through many revisions, the Eisner-Gordon collaboration, *A New Kind of Family*, beat the odds by winning a slot on Sunday evenings as the lead-in to *Mork & Mindy*. The show died a quick death and the two women gave up the television business.

Of course, the husbands were doing business together, too. Gordon had set up shop at Paramount when he teamed up with the studio to produce a short-lived television show called *Dog and Cat* for ABC. (The police drama featured a young Kim Basinger.) Gordon already had a deal ensuring that the show would get on the air, so it was something of a favor when he brought it to Paramount. Eisner gave his friend especially nice offices that had belonged to Jerry Lewis and then to producer Ross Hunter, who had meticulously decorated it with wood paneling and marble detailing.

In its original incarnation, *48 Hrs*. was Gordon's idea. The concept was to team a cop and a con—both white. He paid Roger Spottiswoode out of his own pocket to write the script. Gordon tried to set it up with Clint Eastwood as the convict, but Eastwood passed. Next it went to United Artists with Sylvester Stallone as the convict and Gene Hackman as the cop. The studio—poised to release *Rocky II*—reneged on the deal because of doubts about Stallone's star power. Another version was meant for Burt Reynolds and Richard Pryor, who had some interest in working together. But Gordon couldn't get Pryor and Reynolds to commit.

The project finally got on track when Gordon walked into Eisner's office while the studio chief was fighting with an agent over a deal involving Nick Nolte. Paramount had an option to make a movie with Nolte that was about to expire. Eisner wanted to lock Nolte into a project before he went off to do another film, taking a $750,000 fee with him. When he hung up, he turned to Gordon and asked if he had anything that might be good. Gordon said he did. "Could it be in theaters in December?" Eisner asked. He figured Paramount could use an action film to complement the studio's 1982 Christmas comedy, *Airplane 2*. Gordon said it could. Walter Hill was attached as director; all they needed was a black actor to play the buddy. Having conceived of the role for Pryor, it seemed natural to look for another African-American to take the part.

By this time, Pryor—with hits like *Silver Streak* and *Stir Crazy* to his credit—was too hot to play second fiddle to Nolte, so the producers went after Bill Cosby, who passed. They tried Gregory Hines but he was locked into a stage show, *Sophisticated Ladies*. Finally someone—and many have claimed credit—suggested a young comic from *Saturday Night Live* named Eddie Murphy. Hill, the director, says the idea came from Murphy's agent at the time, Hildy Gottlieb—who happened to be Hill's girlfriend and later became his wife. Another former executive says the idea began with Larry Wilson, who later wrote *Beetlejuice*.

Don Simpson, then still head of production, was enthusiastic about Murphy, as was Gordon's young protégé, Joel Silver. Silver was an intense, portly, curly-haired young showman-in-the-making who made it his business to know everything there was to know about Hollywood and pop culture. *48 Hrs.* would be his first producing credit.

No one expected the studio to go for Murphy because he was only a television comic. But Eisner looked at tapes of Murphy—he wasn't familiar with his work—and quickly agreed to hire him. By now, the studio needed to move quickly if it wanted the picture in theaters for Christmas.

Hill was a little nervous about using Murphy because the comic lacked acting experience. "Eddie didn't always concentrate," Hill says. "I remember saying to Nick, 'This is going to be a tough movie on you because this guy is a terrific talent but he's not a trained actor. This is like working with a kid or a dog. You've got to be great in every take because the one take where he's great, we're going to print.' "

48 Hrs. was a new blend of gritty action and humor. Eisner expected it to be much more broadly comedic than Hill intended. One source close to the production says Eisner repeatedly asked, "Did you put them in chicken suits yet?" This was a reference to an especially marketable movie moment—perfect for television ads—in *Stir Crazy*, Pryor's 1981 hit with Gene Wilder. "Michael was always very suspicious about me shorting the humor of the movie and leaning on the action part," Hill says.

Hill and Eisner weren't particularly fond of each other; they had clashed repeatedly when Hill had directed *The Warriors*—notably when Eisner forced Hill to keep some dialogue that Hill wanted to excise. "It was the only time I was ever ordered to do something or be fired," Hill remembers. (Later, Pauline Kael gave the film a positive review but criticized the dialogue. Hill circled that observation and sent the review to Eisner but got no response.) "The reason [Eisner] is the most successful film executive since—I don't know—the Second World War, is that he's got two advantages," Hill says. "One, he actually believes in his own taste. And second, he doesn't care what you think about him."

Now Hill was again resisting Eisner, making a harder-edged film than the studio chief envisioned. Knowing about Eisner's concerns, Katzenberg looked at dailies as soon as he took over from Simpson. He started to panic. He called Gordon and asked to meet with him and Hill about Murphy. "We're having trouble with dailies," Katzenberg said. "He's not funny."

According to Hill, Silver had been the first to recognize Murphy's potential as a movie star. In a story that Silver has told to associates for years since, he maintains that he was in New York tending to his dying mother when Katzenberg called to say that Murphy had to be replaced.

Silver maintains that Katzenberg made him go directly from the cemetery to Newark Airport—the beginning of an enmity between him and Katzenberg that would last for years. It should be noted that Silver was so driven himself, according to costumer Marilyn Vance, that Gordon had to force him to get on a plane to go home in the first place. But Silver believed that Katzenberg callously forced him to return—a claim Katzenberg emphatically denies. Indeed, Silver was not high on the totem pole—Gordon was the man responsible for handling this fight and Silver's presence wasn't required. (This is especially true because Eisner disliked Silver and didn't want him attending meetings at all.) But Silver was clearly passionate about the project and felt compelled to get to Los Angeles at once.

Hill—working in a swirl of rumors that the film was about to be shut down—cut together some scenes for Eisner and Katzenberg, hoping they would see that his approach was working. Tension was high when Gordon and Silver showed the footage in a screening room on the lot and awaited Eisner's reaction.

"Have you seen the black guy in *Airplane 2*?" Katzenberg asked, referring to Clint Smith, a friend of Murphy's who was then filming the sequel to Paramount's hit. Clearly he was suggesting that Smith was funnier than Murphy. Gordon was annoyed that he had been called into the meeting at all and bristled at the idea of reshooting Murphy's scenes. "Who would we replace [Eddie] with?" he demanded. "It's ridiculous. You guys are crazy." Hill wanted to know how the studio expected him to reshoot all the footage with a new actor and still stay on time and on budget. The conversation soon heated to a point where no one wanted to continue the discussion.

It became obvious that replacing Murphy wouldn't offer any easy answers, so, at Eisner's insistence, the producers provided him with an acting coach. "That was all just kind of papering things over," Hill says. "Eddie didn't pay attention to him, nor was there reason to." But according to Vance, the costume designer, much of Murphy's dialogue had to be rerecorded after the film was finished because he didn't have his pace through much of the shoot.

Eisner and Katzenberg weren't done. From the start, Don Simpson remembered years later, "Michael chopped [Gordon] on budgets—he ground him." This was astonishing to Simpson because Gordon and Eisner were friends. The relationship with Gordon seemed to be Eisner's most genuine bond in the industry. But he wasn't going to change the rules because of that. "It was endless," Simpson said. "I'd say, 'What are you doing? He's your friend!' And he'd say, 'This is how business is done.'"

The pressure to cut costs didn't diminish as filming progressed. "Every day, it was something," Hill says. "Paramount in those days was a very unpleasant place to work. That was their style." Hill was convinced that Eisner's friendship with Gordon seemed to make things worse. "I think Larry felt that being Michael's friend put him on a much higher crucible than anyone else—that Michael was determined that he would not be taken advantage of. No special favor was ever going to be given."

Gordon and Silver used a band called the Bus Boys to perform a song

called "The Boys Are Back in Town" for a scene in a black club. They
spent a good portion of their music budget to have the song recorded in a
studio—a process that would enhance the sound and the performance.
Later, the plan was to make a studio recording of a country-and-western
band for a parallel scene in a white bar. Katzenberg wouldn't hear of it.
"You used up your budget on the other version," he said. "Do it with a
jukebox."

Silver tried to explain that the point of the scene was to have Murphy
create a disturbance by throwing a glass, causing the entire room to stop in
its tracks—including the band. That element was crucial to the atmo-
spherics, underscoring the incongruity of the one black man in the ocean
of white faces. "Have someone pull the plug out of the jukebox," Katzenberg suggested.

"Why would someone pull the plug on the jukebox?" Silver demanded.

Gordon and Silver managed to get a live band to record in a studio,
but Hill says some other element had to be cut to keep the film on budget. As the filming neared completion, however, it was becoming apparent that the picture was starting to gel. After the bar scene was filmed,
Hill turned to Silver and said, "I think we're rich." Still, Silver felt the
studio—which was expecting a lot from *Airplane 2: The Sequel*, opening
soon after *48 Hrs.* in December 1982—did not do justice to the film,
booking it in inferior theaters and only grudgingly showing it to the media to generate publicity for it.

A test screening in Long Beach showed that *48 Hrs.* was likely to far
outperform the *Airplane* movie. Paramount offered Murphy the role in a
project it was developing then called *Black and White* and sent him a check
for a million dollars. The deal turned out to be a tremendous bargain for
the studio. Murphy was teamed with Dan Aykroyd and the film was released
in 1983 under the title *Trading Places*. The picture—which involved a poor
street hustler changing places with a wealthy commodities trader—was a
smash. Murphy would go on to make a string of hugely successful films for
Paramount, including the *Beverly Hills Cop* series.

Silver and Gordon could console themselves, however, with the success
of *48 Hrs.* It grossed $82 million, and by the end of its run, the studio would
net more than $22.3 million in pure profit. With its combination of menace
and violence with big laughs, *48 Hrs.* became the model for a series of huge
successes from *Die Hard*, which Gordon and Silver later produced for Fox,
to the *Lethal Weapon* series, which Silver subsequently produced for War-

ner. Meanwhile, Eisner's favored project, *Airplane 2*, managed to clear only a $4 million profit.

∽

DESPITE LARRY GORDON'S success with *48 Hrs.*, his relationship with Eisner was doomed. Gordon's next project was a film called *Streets of Fire*, the tale of a rocker kidnapped by a biker gang. The screenwriter was Walter Hill, who, after his experience on *48 Hrs.*, was fed up with Paramount. Besides, Universal was offering more money for *Streets of Fire*. Gordon was worried about how Eisner would react when he heard the project was going elsewhere, but the choice was Hill's. Sure enough, when the deal went to Universal, Eisner was livid. He felt that he should have gotten the project because both Hill and Gordon had offices on the Paramount lot. Actually, Gordon's overall deal with Paramount was only for television and the studio had already decided not to renew it. But Eisner was so angry about losing *Streets of Fire* that he barely spoke to Gordon.

Gordon was also setting up *Brewster's Millions*, the second remake of the 1935 British film about a man who has a month to spend a million dollars. Gordon decided he would like to direct. Eisner agreed, but only if the budget did not exceed a certain number. Gordon resisted this provision and got Universal to make him a better offer. With Eisner out of town, Katzenberg called and asked Gordon to tell him whether Paramount was getting the film. Gordon, who later said that Katzenberg explicitly said Paramount would not object if the movie was made elsewhere, said he would make the deal at Universal.

That weekend, when Eisner found out what had happened, he thought Gordon had used Paramount's offer as a prod in his negotiation at Universal. He and Gordon had an explosive argument and Eisner vowed to throw him off the lot. As far as Eisner was concerned, Gordon had betrayed him. On Monday morning, a studio employee showed up and asked Gordon's staff to leave. "I'm going to have a truck pick up all your stuff and I'll take it wherever you want," the employee said.

Gordon asked the man, "Are you telling me if I refuse you're going to come in and take my furniture from underneath me?" He vowed to defend his turf with a baseball bat if anyone touched his belongings.

Incredulous that his longtime friend — a man he had helped and counseled in numerous ways over the years — would treat him so coldly, Gordon called his lawyer. The lawyer phoned business-affairs executive Dick Zimbert and demanded a ninety-day notice period. Zimbert said he could not override Eisner. With extraordinary boldness, Gordon had his lawyer obtain a court order preventing Paramount from evicting him. The studio retaliated by banning Gordon from the commissary. The next day, Gordon made a point of having lunch there and tipped the maître d' to seat him near Eisner.

Neither *Streets of Fire* nor *Brewster's Millions* (which Gordon ultimately decided not to direct) performed well. But that didn't mollify Eisner. "They didn't speak for years," Don Simpson remembered later. "Their wives were in business together. Their kids were on the same baseball team." Eisner hid when Gordon came to pick up his children at Eisner's house and even passed Gordon at school meetings without so much as a nod. Later, Eisner had a script written about the episode, though it was never made. Gordon used to joke that Eisner would cast Robert Redford to play himself and Jack Palance or some other bad-guy character actor to play Gordon.

"Michael would have close relationships with very few men," Wedemeyer says. "They often ended badly." It would be years before Gordon and Eisner would reconcile.

Wedemeyer's relationship with Eisner ended badly, too. Wedemeyer eventually was promoted to talent relations but was hurt when Eisner informed her that as part of an effort to reduce the number of people reporting to him, she would have to answer to a new boss—obviously lower on the totem pole than Eisner. She promptly resigned. Eisner refused to accept her resignation, but she insisted. When the head of marketing, Gordon Weaver, offered her a job in his department, Eisner wouldn't allow it. If she didn't work where he wanted her, she wasn't going to work for the company at all. Eisner always seemed to be anticipating a betrayal. When it came—or when he thought it did—the rupture was always painful and dramatic.

∽

EISNER DIDN'T SINGLE out Gordon when it came to grinding down budgets. He was constantly on the lookout for ways to save and no one was immune. James L. Brooks was a television genius who had created *The Mary Tyler Moore Show* with his partner, Allan Burns, and followed with *Taxi*, an exceptional series about misfits in a garage that launched the careers of Danny DeVito, Christopher Lloyd, Andy Kaufman, Marilu Henner, and Tony Danza. He had also written *Starting Over*, a modestly successful film starring Burt Reynolds and Jill Clayburgh. Now Brooks wanted to try his hand at directing for the big screen. His choice was a Larry McMurtry novel called *Terms of Endearment*, the story of a mother's relationship with her doomed daughter.

Given the daughter's fate, *Terms of Endearment* wasn't the sort of project that warms a studio chief's heart. "They always thought, 'No, no . . . cancer—she dies of cancer,' " explains producer Lawrence Mark, then an executive at the studio. Diller and Eisner figured the picture could never outperform one of their earlier grim but well-received efforts, *Ordinary People*, which meant that it couldn't possibly gross more than $50 million. So even though they were willing to give Brooks a shot, they weren't happy about giving him the $11 million budget he wanted, though that was roughly the average cost of a film at the time.

Jeff Berg, Brooks's agent at International Creative Management, thought Eisner owed Brooks some benefit of the doubt. After all, Paramount had lured Brooks to the studio with a promise that he could make feature films. Brooks had kept up his end of the deal by creating *Taxi*, a series that was going to make the studio a lot of money. Paramount could afford to let Brooks make a picture that wasn't exceptionally expensive. But the studio refused to finance the project and Berg tried to set it up elsewhere without success. Finally MTM, the production company founded by Mary Tyler Moore and her then husband, Grant Tinker, offered to invest a million dollars in the film. Paramount agreed to ante up $8.5 million, although Eisner made it clear that he still wasn't overjoyed at the prospect of making this movie. To keep to the budget—$1.5 million less than originally forecast—a very tight shooting schedule was set.

Brooks had a spectacular cast—Shirley MacLaine and Debra Winger, with Jack Nicholson as the degenerate former astronaut living next door. (Originally, the Winger role was going to be played by Sissy Spacek. Burt Reynolds, who was going to make a run at serious acting by abandoning his lifts and his toupee, was going to play the astronaut. At the eleventh hour, he opted to do *The Man Who Loved Women*. After trying to interest Clint Eastwood, the studio turned to Nicholson.) Jeff Daniels, John Lithgow, and Danny DeVito also appeared in the film.

Despite the dream cast, the production quickly turned into a nightmare. As a first-time and nervous director, Brooks took the unusual step of shooting the movie in sequence and it wasn't the most efficient approach. He started shooting in Houston, where he insisted on spending a lot of time in rehearsal on fully dressed sets. Even before shooting began, Brooks was falling behind on a schedule that was too tight in the first place.

To make matters worse, Debra Winger engaged in a lot of erratic behavior, possibly because she was ingesting too much cocaine. (When the production moved to Lincoln, Nebraska, where Winger met future beau, then-governor Bob Kerrey, the producers checked her into detox for several days.) She also had developed an abiding hostility toward her on-screen mother, Shirley MacLaine. One day, the two sat side by side looking at screen tests of Winger wearing various outfits. Winger appeared on the screen in a red dress which she was to wear early in the film. "Isn't that cute!" MacLaine said, and reached over to touch her costar's arm. Unfortunately, she missed. "You grabbed my tit!" Winger shrieked, and to the amazement of others in the room, she punched MacLaine. Alarmed crew members had to pull Winger off her costar.

Winger then set out to bait MacLaine in every way she could, simultaneously campaigning to have her fired. "I don't know how I can possibly act with her," she told Brooks. "We have different styles." She also complained to Brooks about her love life and other woes. "Debra would spend hours crying in Jim's office," remembers one member of the crew. "I cannot tell you what a one-woman movie-stopper she became." When MacLaine had to do a scene in bed with Nicholson, Winger crept under the sheets and licked her leg. At one point Winger let on that she had gotten to see some footage of the film before MacLaine. Infuriated by the endless taunting, MacLaine ran to her car and tried to make an escape. But time was short and Brooks couldn't afford to have MacLaine go AWOL. Coproducer Penny Finkelman Cox threw herself on the hood of the car to stop MacLaine from leaving.

It didn't take long for Paramount to panic over the pace of the production. Soon after filming started, Eisner flew to Houston to take a look at this disaster in the making. He was whisked into a screening room and viewed some footage, hastily cut together for his visit. He saw an opening sequence, in which Shirley MacLaine wakes her baby in a panic over whether the child is still breathing, as well as a sequence that had been shot that day (which discreetly showed Winger performing oral sex on her husband). Brooks and his associates waited anxiously for Eisner's reaction. "We were hoping for a miracle to get the studio off our backs," says a member of the crew. In this case, the miracle came. Eisner could see that Brooks just might be making an extraordinary film and gave him a bit more breathing room.

But not much. Katzenberg was given the job of enforcer, relentlessly hammering on Brooks to hurry up. "We would work from five or six in the morning until we lost the light and then Jim would get on the phone with Jeff in his trailer and sometimes we wouldn't get to dailies until eleven P.M.," remembers a Brooks associate. "We would wait while there was yelling every night. Katzenberg was yelling so loud that I could hear his voice over the phone." The debilitating arguments over time and money continued as the studio constantly threatened to shut down the movie if Brooks didn't speed things along, while he declared that he was going to quit anyway. "It was not a fair fight," said one Brooks colleague. "Jeffrey does a fair fight and Jim's smarter than that. Jim was outboxing him."

One of Brooks's goals was to get the money he needed to shoot scenes of Winger meeting her friend Patsy's circle of New York acquaintances on location in Manhattan. There was a key sequence when Winger asked why she wasn't supposed to talk about her illness, and Brooks was determined to get it exactly right. "I made the movie for that scene!" he told colleagues. Katzenberg told him that New York was out unless he could catch up on the shooting schedule.

Brooks finally got four days in New York—barely enough to get his scenes shot. And the studio made it clear that every day had to count. The Memorial Day weekend was coming up and the studio had no intention of paying for the cast and crew to work overtime on a holiday weekend. But when the cast got to New York, Winger wouldn't come out of her room at the Plaza Hotel. She had a large pimple and didn't want to be seen.

Brooks and Winger had barely been speaking since the production had moved to Lincoln. But her agent, Rick Nicita of CAA, could not get her to emerge. Finally Brooks went to the hotel, praying for the wit or inspiration that would persuade her to open the door. As he approached the room, he still had no idea what to say. Finally he knocked.

"What do you want?" Winger asked through the locked door.

"Let me in," Brooks pleaded. The inspiration came. "I have to pee," he said.

Still, she refused to leave her room. An entire scene showing Winger having lunch with the women at a restaurant was shot around her absence. Only the next day did she show up to perform her lines.

Even though early screenings of the film didn't go well, Brooks reworked the picture and transformed it into a major hit. Paramount's projections were shattered when the picture scored $108 million at the box office. The picture was nominated for eleven Academy Awards and won five, including Best Picture, Best Director, Best Actress (for MacLaine, who beat the also-nominated Winger), Best Supporting Actor (Nicholson), and Best Screenplay Based on Material from Another Medium. Critics loved it. Ironically, *Newsweek*'s David Ansen noted that in her performance as Emma, Winger was "the mortar that holds all the parts together." The movie business is indeed one of illusions.

9

DEATH OF A MOGUL

C HARLIE BLUHDORN COULDN'T even die without stirring controversy. When the end came on February 19, 1983, the official story was that the fifty-six-year-old Bluhdorn had suffered a massive heart attack. There were subsequently various rumors about his physical whereabouts when he died. The official story was that he was stricken on his jet while returning from a trip to the Dominican Republic. In fact, he had died at Casa Grande.

The news came as a shock, but it shouldn't have. Bluhdorn was suffering from leukemia—a fact that a major public company clearly should have reported to the Securities and Exchange Commission. But if the federal government was right, this wasn't the first time Bluhdorn had violated federal securities laws.

His successor was Martin Davis, a fifty-six-year-old Gulf + Western veteran who leapfrogged over other high-level executives to take the helm. Davis's tenure at Paramount dated back to 1958. His first task at the studio, in his own unminced words, was to "reorganize or be the hatchet man" in the advertising and sales department. He was well suited for the role. In the mid-1960s, Davis was a key player in fending off a hostile takeover of the studio. He assembled a committee of friendly shareholders; as head of that committee, Davis picked a theater owner from Boston named Sumner Redstone.

By 1965, Davis was Paramount's chief operating officer and an assistant to the president. His next move was to broker a marriage with Bluhdorn's Gulf + Western—a conglomerate involved in auto parts and zinc. Bluhdorn was thrilled with the purchase of Paramount and show business quickly became his first love. "Charlie liked Hollywood and women," Davis said in an interview before his death in 1999. "Nothing wrong with that." Another studio veteran put it more bluntly. "Paramount," he said, "was the biggest purchase for pussy in the history of America to that time."

Davis wasn't the type to fritter away time in Hollywood. Instead, he made himself useful to Bluhdorn in many ways. He managed the acquisition of Consolidated Cigar Corp. and eventually moved into the corporate side of the business. In October 1981, he helped Bluhdorn resolve a bruising five-year battle with the Securities and Exchange Commission, which had filed a suit charging the company and Bluhdorn personally with wide-ranging "fraudulent courses of conduct."

In essence, the suit alleged that Bluhdorn had used Gulf + Western as a personal cookie jar. He was accused of improperly spending company funds on planes and limousines for purposes unrelated to business. He also allegedly had obtained personal loans from banks that hoped to do business with Gulf + Western. He was said to have used the company's pension fund to make inappropriate investments in businesses in which he had an interest. And Bluhdorn was accused of unilaterally investing $64 million of the company's money in sugar futures in the Dominican Republic without disclosing the transaction.

In the settlement, the government didn't require Bluhdorn to make any restitution of funds. Gulf + Western agreed to improve its corporate housekeeping but Bluhdorn neither admitted nor denied the charges. Davis, who said that Bluhdorn was devastated by the investigation, insisted that Bluhdorn did not deliberately break the law. "If he was short of anything, it was common sense but not integrity," he said.

Davis said Bluhdorn's battles—with the SEC and his leukemia—changed him. He started to spend several days a week in the Dominican Republic, with direct lines to the company's Manhattan headquarters installed. He started "running things by phone." But Davis said he was unaware that Bluhdorn had cancer. Others say Bluhdorn was apparently ill—after all, he had taken to wearing a wig in an attempt to conceal the hair loss caused by chemotherapy. But his sickness was never addressed.

After Bluhdorn died, his widow, Yvette, backed Davis as his successor. Barry Diller allied himself with Davis, who had promised not to make changes at the studio. With Davis taking the top job, *Variety* declared, "there no longer can be any question about possible dilution of Diller's authority, either by political ploy within Paramount or on the upper reaches of G+W." The report was diametrically wrong.

"It was a terrible mistake of mine," Diller says now about his role in supporting Davis. After the board resolved that no one should take Bluhdorn's title or his office, Davis did both. Davis also turned on Yvette Bluhdorn, taking away the company limousine, yanking support for a Bluhdorn-founded arts center in the Dominican Republic, and canceling other benefits.

Such measures, according to Davis, were necessary to salvage Gulf + Western, which had become a debt-laden and irrational collection of assets. He said he waited a respectful six months before taking Bluhdorn's title and his office, but then it was time to get on with business. "We were letting go of a lot of people," he said. "We were trying to cut down and then build ourselves up. To do that, you do not win a popularity contest. We cut out the airplanes and we cut out a lot of the limousines—not just for [Yvette Bluhdorn]."

Davis acknowledged that his relationship with Diller quickly soured. "When I restructured the company, he could not have the same relationship with me that he had with Bluhdorn," Davis said. "That was emotion-driven and with me, as well as I knew him, it was all business. I had thirteen other division chiefs. He was only one."

At first, however, Diller seemed to be on the rise. Soon after Bluhdorn's death, in March 1983, Davis promoted him to chief of a newly formed Entertainment and Communications Group, giving him responsibility for Simon & Schuster, the New York Knicks, Madison Square Garden, and the Sega video-game division. The effect on Diller's relationship with Eisner was not salutary. Eisner hoped this would give him more control of the studio, but he was disappointed. "Michael thought I was moving away from Paramount," Diller says. "I had no intention of moving away from Paramount. . . . That pissed him off." Eisner said later that at this time "a chill set in" between him and Diller.

But Diller's added responsibility did not bring with it the autonomy that he thought he had been promised. Martin Davis could be stubborn to the point of irrationality—a trait that became more apparent as he assumed the helm at Gulf + Western. "I became a control freak, which I clearly admit," he later acknowledged. And in the case of Paramount Pictures, he was bent on instituting a new management style. About two months after Bluhdorn's death, Davis told Diller that he had always disliked Eisner and suggested that Diller fire him. Diller declined. "I didn't know Marty Davis—I didn't know his methodology," he says. "That was the way he weakened people—

to go after their number-two man. For at least six months, I fought against Marty Davis trying to get him not to do this. And I was unshakable. I never told this to Michael Eisner because I thought it was my job to deal with this. I didn't want to drive him out of the company." Davis, he says, "used Michael Eisner to break me—not that I understood what he was doing, because I didn't."

Davis denied that he was out to "break" Diller; instead, he blamed Diller for allowing his attack on Eisner to continue. "Any feuds and alleged feuds that Michael and I have had should never have happened," Davis said. "I didn't know him and he didn't know me. . . . Barry was very protective. You never saw any of the others in the organization unless he deemed it necessary."

Despite Diller's insistence that he came to Eisner's defense, Eisner became convinced that Diller was not his advocate. He even suspected that Diller might be undermining him with Davis. Diller says Eisner simply "was not in possession of the facts." But his relationship with Eisner started to fray. "I so resented being in this position that in addition to blaming Marty Davis, I blamed Michael Eisner," he says.

In March 1984, *Terms of Endearment* picked up its five Oscars. And Diller, as Davis resentfully remembered it, was "building up a great image." Several stories in the press heaped praise on Diller and his management team. Davis's jealousy was not the only problem: the studio's very success was undermining it from within. The long-simmering tension between Diller and Eisner was now at full boil, arousing Eisner's natural tendency to anticipate betrayal. "When you're failing, all the brothers were brave and the sisters were virtuous," says one executive who was there at the time. "When we all got rich and successful, there was a lot more fucking each other over."

Davis had another bone to pick with Diller and Eisner. Both received hefty bonuses every year—and they were splitting more than half of the bonus pool for the entire studio. (Eisner had tapped into the bonus pool in 1982, when he had renewed his contract at Paramount. At the time he was being courted by Bill Paley to run CBS, and holding the advantage, he convinced Bluhdorn to loan him enough money to buy his dream house in Bel Air as well as a share in the bonus pool.) In fiscal 1984, Diller's take was 31 percent while Eisner got 26 percent. And Diller and Eisner were each pulling down seven-figure salaries (Davis made far less). "I wanted that changed," Davis said. "People say I was jealous that they were making more

than me. Nonsense. Whatever Barry wanted, he generally got from Bluhdorn. Not from me. At some point you have to decide. Do you want to be
held hostage? . . . Barry is not going to work for anybody. You either give
him his candy or you throw him out."

∞

IT IS COMMON in Hollywood for a significant realignment in the power
structure to be preceded by a single piece of journalism that serves as a
catalyst. This had been the case when Bluhdorn unceremoniously ejected
Frank Yablans from his perch at Paramount. It happened again in July 1984
when *New York* magazine published a story by Tony Schwartz called "Hollywood's Hottest Stars." Diller and Eisner were pictured on the cover of the
magazine, both looking exceptionally genial.

The article chronicled Paramount's success and described the executive
team's bare-knuckle management style as the "chemistry of confrontation."
By now, Paramount's management team had been in place for eight years,
far longer than any other studio's top team. In Hollywood terms, Paramount
was a dynasty. It had been among the three most profitable studios for each
of the preceding six years. "By nearly any standard other than popularity,"
Schwartz wrote, "Paramount is the leading studio in Hollywood."

Though Schwartz got Diller to acknowledge that argument was a daily
staple at Paramount, he did not write about a conflict that arose, according
to Don Simpson, over Diller's desire to cut Eisner out of the *New York*
article altogether. Jeffrey Katzenberg concurs. "This is when Barry and Michael started to go at each other," he said. "Barry started the article and
Michael found out about it halfway through. He had a shit fit."

Simpson said Eisner simply disregarded Diller's orders to stay away from
Schwartz. "He said, 'Fuck Barry Diller,' " Simpson said. "He talked to the
press and you know what Barry did? Nothing. Michael Eisner played poker
with Barry Diller and won." Diller denies ever having instructed Eisner to
stay away from Schwartz, and Eisner says he doesn't recall the incident.
(Some years later, Eisner would call on Schwartz to coauthor Eisner's autobiography.)

After a dinner, Diller took the reporter to a theater to see how audiences
were responding to *Indiana Jones and the Temple of Doom*, which was
Eisner's project. Eisner wasn't about to let Diller grandstand over it, so he
and his wife had gotten there first. The next day, Schwartz got a call from
an unnamed source who told him that Diller's excursion was a ploy. "He

never goes to check audiences," the caller said. But Eisner often did. "He's a maniac," the caller exclaimed. "He went to two more theaters after he left you. Eisner's your man."

When Schwartz's article hit the newsstands, it was obvious even to a casual reader that a spin competition had taken place. The article provided a memorable snapshot of the executives who made up Paramount's storied management team. Diller and Eisner were wealthy and successful men. The article said Diller was pulling down $2.5 million a year, Eisner a bit less. (The figure eclipsed Davis's earnings of $584,699.) Diller was single, as always, and moved in chic circles. Calvin Klein and Diane von Furstenberg were among his best friends. Eisner had been married for seventeen years and didn't socialize with celebrities.

The competition between Diller and Eisner remained keen. "Having each other's approval means a lot to both of them, and I'm not sure either one is happy about that," the astute director James L. Brooks told Schwartz.

Katzenberg was described in an unattributed quote as "a golden retriever [who knows] what's going on with every producer, agent, lawyer, director and star in town." To his chagrin, this nickname would stick to Katzenberg forever. The article also raised what was becoming a persistent question about Katzenberg's taste: was he all organization but no instinct?

Perhaps the most ironic statement in the entire article was a quote from an unnamed producer. "Paramount's great strength," he said, "is that their executives know they'll be there tomorrow."

∽

MARTIN DAVIS WAS possibly one of the most unpleasant bosses in the annals of business; a former employee once described him as a man with "a tiny, cruel heart." He was a no-nonsense corporation man who had once, according to legend, told an unhappy executive to come to his office early one morning to discuss his grievances and then left the hapless employee waiting hour after hour for an appointment that never happened. The story holds that Davis finally breezed by at the end of the day with the parting words "That's to remind you who's boss."

Davis maintained that such tales were fictitious.

If Diller and Eisner had hoped that the *New York* magazine article would impress or intimidate Davis, they were wrong. "That was a stupid story," he remembered. At the time he reportedly started complaining to associates that Diller and Eisner were "overrated and overpaid." Davis denied that he made that remark, but said the *New York* article was a slap at the rest of the company because it failed to acknowledge the contributions of others—especially Frank Mancuso, the marketing and distribution chief who still operated, despite Eisner's best efforts, from his base in New York.

By now, Eisner and Katzenberg were completely convinced that despite his gentlemanly demeanor, Mancuso was doing everything in his power to undermine them. Those on the production side even called Mancuso "the Sicilian." But a buttoned-down businessman like Davis found Mancuso's low-key approach far more palatable than the unpredictable and emotional style of the West Coast executives. And Davis believed that Mancuso's skill in marketing was more valuable to Gulf + Western than whatever instinct Diller and Eisner brought to picking the movies. Davis had been especially irked by a quote from Eisner in the *New York* article: "It's great to have good marketing and I think we have the best, but you don't need it to sell *E.T.* and it won't help if you're selling *The Pirate Movie*. This is a business based on twelve decisions a year. They are very important. Nothing else is close." Mancuso had taken offense, too. He circled the quote and sent it to Diller, Eisner, and Katzenberg with a sarcastic note.

As the relationships degenerated, Davis was supposed to be in contract discussions with Diller, Eisner, and Katzenberg. Their deals expired almost simultaneously in September 1984. Months earlier, Davis had a few conversations with Diller but neither side pressed for resolution. Diller suggested that Davis start with the junior man and told Katzenberg to fly to New York. When Katzenberg arrived, the negotiation began on a sour note. "I have people in Hollywood who tell me you're Sammy Glick," Davis intoned, alluding to the grasping character from the famed Budd Schulberg novel. He berated Katzenberg for being gossipy and for lacking creativity. He accused Katzenberg of conspiring with Diller, Eisner, and Mancuso to go to the board and have him thrown out. At this, Katzenberg says, he started to laugh.

"What are you laughing about?" Davis demanded.

"Marty, we can't decide what time the sun's coming up," Katzenberg replied. "If you think the four of us can get together to do something about you, you don't understand."

But despite his sarcasm, Katzenberg was horrified by Davis's attack. He also observed that during the entire discussion, Davis gazed coldly out of his office window. "He never took his eyes off New Jersey," Katzenberg says. The meeting ended inconclusively and Katzenberg went to Diller's office to report to his bosses. Though Eisner would later say he was shocked when he heard what Davis had said to Katzenberg, Katzenberg remembers events differently. As he recalls it, Diller insisted on getting Eisner on the phone before Katzenberg could say a word. When Eisner came on the line, Diller looked at Katzenberg and said, "Well?"

"You assholes set me up!" Katzenberg burst forth.

As he remembers the episode, Diller and Eisner burst into laughter.

The superficial camaraderie of the moment did nothing to dispel Eisner's distrust of Diller. "Barry's taking care of Barry," he told Katzenberg. And even in his junior position, Katzenberg could read the silence whenever he asked Diller for reassurances about the future. Diller would tell him, "Hang in there. It'll all be okay." But he never told Katzenberg what he wanted to hear: "You'll always have a place with me."

Eisner had started to cast about for his next position. He had called Roy Disney to ask whether there might be a job for him at the then-faltering studio. Disney was in the midst of a takeover battle, however, and the outcome was uncertain. Eisner's preferred option was to start his own film company with $375 million in financing from his old friends at ABC. "I'm talking to Leonard Goldenson and Fred Pierce," he told Katzenberg. "I think ABC will put up the money." Eisner and Katzenberg started working out a business plan and registered their company's proposed name: Hollywood Pictures.

For Diller, the escape route amounted to changing a single consonant, from Martin Davis to Marvin Davis. He started negotiating with the latter Davis, the outsized oilman, about taking charge of Twentieth Century Fox. Meanwhile, the Davis who ran Gulf + Western was pressuring Diller to promote Mancuso. Rather than report to Eisner, he would report to Diller. Katzenberg would then report to Mancuso as well as to Eisner. Finally Diller called Katzenberg into his office and handed him a press release announcing the change. Katzenberg was infuriated, but Diller tried to reassure him that business would still be conducted as usual.

Martin Davis arrived in Los Angeles on Tuesday, September 4, 1984. He had some inconclusive discussions with Diller about his contract and then met uncomfortably with Eisner. When Davis reiterated his complaint that Diller and Eisner were being paid too much, Eisner responded, "I think you're being paid too little." The conversation went nowhere. Next, Davis met with Katzenberg and took a different tack. Perhaps he sensed that Katzenberg could be the last of the Diller dynasty who might consider remaining at Paramount. Davis apologized for his earlier diatribe. "I relied on third parties, who did a very effective job of downgrading you," he said. "I realize I was misled. I withdraw the negative things I said. I think you have a superb future."

The following Friday, Davis again met with Eisner. By now, Eisner was emboldened; he was certain that Disney was about to offer him a new job and he told Marty Davis that he was in demand. Davis was indifferent. Later that afternoon, Eisner learned that he had spoken too soon. But it was too late.

That night, top Paramount executives gathered for a dinner in Davis's honor at Diller's Coldwater Canyon house. A couple of weeks earlier, the *New York Times* had published another adulatory profile, headlined BARRY DILLER'S LATEST STARRING ROLE, in which Diller was praised for presiding over "perhaps the best-run, most stable and most consistently successful movie company in Hollywood." The article detailed Diller's exceptional skills at picking and marketing films and concluded that he was "brilliant, very hard-working and a tough negotiator." Still, it was obvious that however successfully Diller had run the studio—and however effectively he had romanced the publications that spoke most directly to Wall Street—Davis was going to mow him down.

Against the backdrop of all the simmering hostilities, the dinner party was not exactly a pleasant event. "It was the most tense social engagement that I've ever been at," marvels one of the executives who attended. Katzenberg remembers the evening as "genuinely terrible. Just pain." The awkwardness wasn't eased when Davis made a point of singing the praises of his absent favorite, Frank Mancuso.

The following Monday, September 10, Diller announced that he was leaving to become chairman and chief executive at Twentieth Century Fox. Davis was indifferent. "I said, 'Fine. Good-bye,' " he remembered.

But Eisner was stunned by the way Diller made his announcement. "Michael didn't know," says a former Paramount executive. "I think Michael felt completely betrayed because Michael had been assured by Barry that he'd be defended." Even though Eisner had not relied on those assurances, he was angry and upset that Diller had frozen him out.

Diller maintains that he had told Eisner a month earlier that he was in talks about going to Fox and even asked Eisner to join him. At the time Eisner had other irons in the fire and clearly must have been hoping, finally, to step out of Diller's shadow—whether at Paramount, Disney, his own new company, or someplace else. Regardless, Eisner clearly thought that Diller should have told him by the night of his party that his departure was imminent. As it was, Eisner was in the dark. Diller says he held back because he had not quite made up his mind. "I was 98 percent gone—99¾ percent," he asserts. "I had not signed a deal with Fox. I did not sign until Sunday."

The next Tuesday, Davis called Eisner at home. By now, it was about six P.M. in Los Angeles. Davis asked Eisner to fly to New York at once. Eisner stalled. "I can't come tonight," he said. "It's my son's first day of school tomorrow." Davis said he should come the next day. "Are you going to ask me to report to Mancuso?" Eisner asked. If so, he didn't see the point in making the trip. Davis said nothing had been decided.

Diller says he implored Eisner to stay home: "I said, 'Don't go to New York. Marty Davis is going to repudiate you.' And Michael didn't trust me. And he thought I was probably manipulating him to get him to go to Fox with me. . . . Marty Davis lied to him and I begged him not to go."

By happenstance, Eisner's former boss at ABC, Fred Silverman, was at a meeting in Eisner's office at this time and witnessed some of these discussions with Diller. Both men were very nervous, he recalls. "They talked about [Davis] like he was Vlad the Impaler," he says. "I found that kind of interesting because these two are not exactly pussycats."

Tuesday afternoon, Eisner and Katzenberg flew to New York—and they flew commercial. They spent the flight talking about their hope that Davis would breach Eisner's contract, which required Paramount to offer Eisner the top job if Diller left. If Davis passed Eisner over, Gulf + Western would have to pay Eisner to go away.

Rich Frank, president of Paramount's television division, had also been summoned to New York. He flew separately and found that he had arrived at the Gulf + Western building first. It was late at night when he was ushered into Davis's office. To his shock, Davis peremptorily told Frank that the top job at the studio was going to Mancuso. "Michael's a child," Davis said contemptuously. "If I put blocks on the floor, Michael would sit down and play with them."

"Then get all the blocks you can," Frank said, "and let him play."

Frank told Davis that he was about to commit a blunder that would become textbook material at the Harvard business school. Just as Frank was leaving, Eisner and Katzenberg arrived. They were put into separate offices and told to wait while Davis conducted successive meetings.

Eisner went into Davis's office just after midnight. According to Davis, Eisner "fought like hell" for the job. Eisner does not remember waging any battle at all. Both agree that Davis asked Eisner if he would report to Mancuso, and Eisner said no. When the meeting ended, Davis did not sound as resolute as he had been when he spoke to Rich Frank. "I'll have to sleep on it," he told Eisner. Then Katzenberg had his turn. Davis once again expressed his view that Eisner was simply an overgrown child but repeated that no decision had been reached about the top job. He asked Katzenberg for a commitment to stay after his contract expired. Katzenberg said he couldn't give him an answer on the spot.

Later, Eisner and Katzenberg commiserated at the Brasserie, an all-night restaurant, and then Eisner went to the Mayfair Regent. Katzenberg preferred the Regency. By now it was the wee hours of the morning. On his way to his hotel, Katzenberg picked up an early edition of the *Wall Street Journal*. There it was in black and white: the *Journal* was reporting that unnamed Gulf + Western executives had disclosed that Frank Mancuso would be named Diller's successor that day. Davis was quoted criticizing the studio's performance.

Katzenberg called Eisner's room frantically to tell him the news. It was an exceptionally cold way for Davis to let Eisner know that he had reached a decision. Davis always maintained that the *Journal* simply made a lucky guess. "Was it a good bet?" he said. "I wouldn't deny it."

Eisner called Diller at home in Los Angeles. "I said, 'Sorry to tell you, I told you so,'" Diller says. "He was devastated. He was publicly repudiated."

Eisner may have been upset but he was hardly incapacitated. He maintained that his contract guaranteed him the right to be considered for the top job if it became vacant. Now Eisner argued that Davis had never really given him that opportunity. Before he had even met with Davis, the *Journal* had the story that Eisner was out of the running. Eisner had brought along a copy of his contract and a letter drafted by his lawyer, Irwin Russell, that he could use if events played out this way. It pointed out the breach and demanded that the studio forgive certain loans—such as the $1.25 million that Eisner had borrowed for his house in Bel Air—and make payments that were due to him. Eisner sat in Davis's office and refused to leave until he was given a cashier's check for the full amount—$1.55 million.

He got it. That afternoon, he and Katzenberg strolled together to the Chemical Bank and promptly deposited the money. (Davis contended that he never actually breached Eisner's deal. "His contract had expired," he said. "[But] he did have money due him.") Despite all the signals that Davis was more than willing to let Eisner go, Eisner felt deeply betrayed. He was so anxious that he insisted that the Chemical Bank deposit the money, as cash, at once.

Eisner issued a statement that mentioned neither Davis nor Gulf + Western: "The untimely death of Charles Bluhdorn . . . and this week's resignation of Barry Diller, chairman of Paramount Pictures, marked a period in my life to move on. I will always be indebted to both men."

Katzenberg returned to Los Angeles while Eisner remained in New York to talk to Arthur Krim, one of the founding partners of Orion Pictures. Orion was one of Hollywood's most artistically successful studios—it was home to Woody Allen and had produced Oscar winners like *Amadeus*— but the company always struggled financially. Aware of the troubles at Paramount, Krim wondered whether Eisner might want to make a deal and bring some of his commercial know-how to the studio. Despite Davis's low opinion of him, Eisner was a hot property.

Diller says he also asked Eisner to join him at Fox. And according to Diller, Eisner agreed to take the job and even negotiated a contract. But Eisner must have figured that he would be an apparent afterthought at Fox. Diller's move had already made a splash, with plenty of publicity trumpeting his deal as the richest in the history of the business. Eisner was not prepared to go meekly to work for Barry Diller again.

In Hollywood, speculation continued to swirl around Eisner's next move. Rumors had surfaced that he had been approached about working for Disney. He denied those reports. "I don't even know where Disney is," he said at one point. And it could have been true. Disney was such a nonentity among the studios that there was little reason to visit its faded Burbank lot.

But as it happened, Eisner knew exactly where Disney was because he had been to the lot in Burbank more than once in the previous couple of years to talk about a job—running the studio or even the whole company. Those earlier talks had not borne fruit. But times had changed, and now, even as Eisner denied knowing where Disney was, he was hoping that he would be moving into a very nice office there in the near future.

∽

WHEREVER EISNER AND Katzenberg landed, one thing was clear: the dynasty at Paramount was over; the dream team that made it all happen was about to scatter and the effects would be far-reaching. Top management was changing at Fox, Paramount, and Disney. The death of Charlie Bluhdorn had set into motion a chain of events that would transform the face of Hollywood and refashion the entertainment that America and the world watched.

At the age of forty-one, Diller was off to Fox, where he would eventually defy skeptics by launching the fourth television network. The man with the highbrow tastes would help bring the world *Married with Children* and *Beverly Hills 90210,* as well as the hit animated series *The Simpsons.* Those who worked for him, the so-called Killer Dillers, would do well, too—at least for a time. Dawn Steel would become one of the first women to run a studio when she took over Columbia Pictures in 1987. Later, she would become a producer. But she died at fifty-one from a brain tumor.

Don Simpson, in partnership with Jerry Bruckheimer, would become one of the most successful producers of his day and create a string of megahits—*Flashdance, Top Gun,* the *Beverly Hills Cop* series, and *Crimson Tide.* The films grossed more than a billion dollars even as they advanced the noisy, high-concept approach to filmmaking that had worked so well at Paramount. But success would not satisfy Simpson. He continued his life of excess, gaining and losing dramatic amounts of weight, undergoing repeated plastic surgeries, patronizing prostitutes, and ingesting mind-bending quantities of drugs.

As for Michael Eisner and Jeffrey Katzenberg and about twenty-eight other Paramount employees—they were soon to determine the precise location of the Walt Disney Company. There they would engineer one of the most dazzling corporate turnarounds in the history of business.

10

RISKY BUSINESS

A ROUND 6:30 A.M., Frank Wells drove his blue Mercedes four blocks from his house in Beverly Hills to pick up his jogging partner, Stanley Gold. It was January 1984, and Wells, who had served many years at Warner Brothers, had just finished a sabbatical that he had spent mountain climbing. Now he was back home in Los Angeles, acting as a consultant to Warner. In other words, he didn't really have a day job.

He and Gold went to the UCLA track, where the two men jogged for a mile. Then, while Gold circled, Wells ran up and down the stairs to strengthen his legs. Finally the two returned to Gold's house for breakfast.

This was their routine on many mornings. They had much to discuss. Gold was an attorney who had once practiced law at Wells's old law firm, Gang, Tyre, Rudin & Brown. But they weren't reminiscing; they were hatching an audacious plan to take over Walt Disney Productions. Disney was a quirky place that shunned innovation. Its managers seemed to be so conscious of the value of the Disney brand name that they actually were afraid to exploit it. The film studio no longer ranked among the Hollywood majors. It was becoming apparent that the whole of the company was worth less than the sum of its parts. Even as Gold and Wells spoke, Disney was beginning to leave a trail of pungent blood in the water. Soon the sharks would be converging.

∞

STANLEY GOLD, A short man with a tendency to portliness, was outspoken and sometimes obnoxious. He was also smart. His star client was Roy E. Disney. Though Roy looked like Walt, he was not the son but the nephew. Roy's father, Roy O. Disney, had feuded bitterly with his brother, and as a result, Walt Disney Productions was split for many years between

"Walt" men and "Roy" men. But when Walt succumbed to cancer in 1966, Roy O. Disney became chairman. In those days, the younger Roy made nature films for the company.

After the elder Roy Disney died in 1971, his son became increasingly discontented with Disney management. He was convinced that too much focus was put on real estate and not enough on the film studio, which he believed was the company's soul. Indeed, following the 1969 hit *The Love Bug*, Disney suffered through sixteen long years without a single live-action success. And the company's signature animation division had not offered much to boast about, either.

But Disney's management, headed by chairman and chief executive E. Cardon Walker, was not especially interested in the younger Roy's opinions. Walker was a "Walt" man, and as the story went, Walt once told Walker that young Roy would "never amount to anything." Roy was dismissed as "the idiot nephew." When he tried to establish his own production deal at the studio, Walker turned him down. In March 1977, Roy resigned from his position as vice-president of the company. But he held on to his board seat.

Despite his complaints, Roy wasn't especially interested in business matters. In 1974, he had handed over his own affairs to Stanley Gold, who had served him well: his net worth had doubled to about $200 million. Roy's diversified holdings included cattle ranches and radio stations as well as 1.1 million shares in Walt Disney Productions. But now Disney was adrift. In January 1984, Gold advised Roy that the value of his stake in the company had declined from about $80 million to $50 million in the past year.

Roy had to make a choice, Gold said. Either take a run at unseating Disney's management or sell. The risks involved in attacking management were obvious. "You and I are going to be described as a know-nothing producer and a shyster lawyer," Gold warned. But Roy was ready to enter the fray. Gold increased Roy's stake in Disney to 4.7 percent—just below the level that would have required him to report his holdings to the public. He also had lunch at Wells's house, and asked Wells whether he wanted to be part of a run at Disney. If things worked out, Gold said, there might be a job for Wells in it.

∽

IT WASN'T AS if Disney's management was invulnerable to cruel characterizations. The chief executive, Ron Miller, was Walt's son-in-law—a good-looking former football player. Miller was not a particularly assertive fellow but he had recognized that the film division needed revitalization. When he was president of the company, he had tried to make some films with adult appeal while maintaining his vow that wholesome Disney would never make an R-rated movie on his watch. Disney was so conservative that he still faced considerable resistance from within. As it turned out, Miller's efforts failed. The most visible of his miscalculations was 1982's *Tron*, a $21 million science-fiction adventure about a programmer who gets caught inside his own video game. The film bombed resoundingly.

The same year, Walker retired after presiding over the opening of Tokyo Disneyland. The new theme park was a missed opportunity because Disney didn't own it. It belonged to the Oriental Land Company, a Japanese railroad and real estate concern. Disney licensed its name and characters and received only 10 percent of admissions and 5 percent of food and merchandise sales. Disney made millions but missed out on many more millions.

With Walker's exit, Miller was promoted to chief executive officer—a decision that didn't sit especially well with several board members who lacked faith in his experience and abilities. The company tried to bolster Miller by naming a strong new chairman: Ray Watson, a board member who had been an important adviser on the just-opened Epcot Center. Before long, Watson was essentially running the company.

By now, Disney was grossing more than $1 billion a year. But Watson was astonished to find that the company was so out of sync with the times that it lacked even a business plan. The company's health was failing. In fiscal 1982, net income dropped 18 percent. The following year, profit fell from $100 million to $93 million. The studio wasn't helping. In 1983, Disney's film division released only three movies and lost $33.4 million (including more than $28 million that went toward starting the Disney Channel). A year earlier, Miller had approached Michael Eisner about running the film division, but when Eisner asked to run theme parks as well as the studio, Miller had passed.

Instead, he hired Richard Berger, a former Fox executive, to launch a new film label, Touchstone. The idea was to release more adult-oriented fare without risking the sterling Disney brand name. But Berger turned out to be too Hollywood for Disney—executives at the company were annoyed when he admonished them to "go to the movies more often" and horrified that he had an automatic door-closer, just like Eisner's. He didn't get along with Miller, either.

Eisner had talked to Disney again early in 1983—around the time of

Bluhdorn's death. This time, he met with outgoing chairman Card Walker. He had trimmed his sails a bit; now he was willing to start as president with a primary responsibility for film and television. He could take over the rest of the company later, he must have reasoned. Walker seemed receptive to giving Eisner the studio job, at first, but after the meeting, Eisner became convinced that Walker saw him as a typical shallow Hollywood executive, "slick, self-promoting, and obsessed with power and status." Eisner sensed that Walker would always look down on him. He called Ron Miller and said he wasn't taking the job, which was just as well because Walker had already concluded that Eisner was wrong for Disney.

In March 1984, Touchstone opened Disney's first hit movie in years. *Splash*, starring Tom Hanks and Daryl Hannah, was a mildly racy tale about a romance between man and mermaid. The director was young Ron Howard, who had not allowed the success of *Happy Days* to deter him from his dream of becoming a filmmaker. But *Splash* was too little, too late. Wall Street had taken note of Disney's falling earnings and the company was ripe for a takeover.

∞

BORN IN MARCH 1932, Frank Wells came from a prominent Mormon family that traced its presence in North America to the days before the American Revolution. (Thomas Wells was the colonial governor of Connecticut.) Frank's great-grandfather, Daniel Wells, was a polygamous Mormon leader who had six wives and fathered thirty-six children. Among them was Heber Wells, Frank's grandfather, a brilliant conversationalist and a talented stage actor in his youth. Heber was elected Utah's first governor in 1896. From his forebears, Frank Wells would inherit a taste for politics, a reverence for the environment, and a hearty appetite for women.

Frank's father was a career naval officer who raised his family on military bases in California and on the East Coast. Tall and rangy, Frank looked more athletic than he was. He had played water polo and basketball as a young man but his real gifts were academic. He had left Pomona College in Southern California with a summa cum laude degree, a Phi Beta Kappa key, and a Rhodes scholarship.

At Pomona, Wells had an audacious dream of being the first to scale Mount Everest. His entire climbing experience had been a relatively easy trip to the top of Mount Whitney in the Sierra Nevada, but that didn't perturb him. Then one day in 1953, a frat brother told him that "some guy

named Hillary" had beaten him to Everest. That led Wells to consider
another plan. He could be the first to scale the highest mountain on each
continent. Before he had a chance to attempt such an undertaking, he was
off to Oxford.

Having arrived with shining academic credentials, Frank wasn't ready to
immure himself in an ivory tower. He and his schoolmate, a Dartmouth
graduate named Vince Jones, hatched a plan to fly their own plane from
London to South Africa. Later, Wells said they made the trip during spring
break, but Jones says they really took off during an independent study period
when their fellow students were cloistered with their books. "If you're an
American and you're not in class, you're on vacation," Jones says. "We
didn't study a bit."

Jones had three hundred hours of flight time under his belt. "I've got
my pilot's license so we'll pool our money, buy a cheap plane, and fly from
here to Cape Town and back," he suggested. They took out a loan against
their scholarships and bought themselves an Auster Aristocrat three-seater
for $600. They named it the *African Queen.*

Wells was in charge of obtaining visas and landing permits. The two
added an auxiliary fuel tank to extend the plane's limited range, but they
still needed to make stops in dozens of countries or principalities. Later,
Wells would say that the night before the two departed, Jones handed him
a book on navigation. "There's one more thing you'll have to be in charge
of because I haven't had time to learn how," Jones said—or so went Wells's
recollection. Wells stayed up all night frantically studying the book and
finished only after they were airborne. But Jones dismisses this account.
They were well prepared, he remembers, but Wells liked to create a certain
aura of impulsiveness. "Frank thought being spontaneous, somewhat scat-
terbrained, and adventuresome beyond good judgment was some sort of
sign of—not manhood, but being noteworthy," Jones says.

The two young men made their way into North Africa. In a memoir,
Wells recalled seeing Kilimanjaro's snowy peak through the plane window
and making an on-the-spot decision to stop. "Let's climb it," Wells remembered saying to Jones. But again, Jones says they had planned to attempt
Kilimanjaro all along.

The climb up Kilimanjaro took six days, and by the last leg, the adventure must have seemed less than splendid. Wells and Jones had chosen a
comparatively easy route and Jones, an asthma sufferer, was striding along.
But, plagued with altitude sickness, Wells doubled over and threw up every

ten minutes or so. "I was amazed he made it," Jones says. "That was just sheer determination. He was just miserable and yet he had a goal." Wells's nausea didn't detract from the thrill of reaching the summit. It was a feeling he would remember for years.

The two resumed their adventure, stopping to visit Nairobi. A classmate at Oxford was the son of the governor of Kenya, who invited them to accompany a hunting party to the Serengeti Plain. When they arrived, the guides wanted to be sure the two young Americans could shoot a gun. They set up targets on enormous anthills, eight or nine feet tall, and asked them to fire away. "Frank thought he was going to be great because he was in the ROTC at Pomona," Jones remembers. But after a couple of tries, it was clear that neither Jones nor Wells could hit the broad side of an anthill. "You could just see the perspiration on the guide's brow," Jones says. "They made us practice for a couple of days."

Both became proficient enough to gun down some wildebeests. The next challenge was getting the trophies home. With all their baggage, they feared their plane would be too heavy to get off the runway at Arusha, south of Nairobi. They considered dumping their long-range fuel tank but then decided to attempt a takeoff fully loaded. They got airborne, but as they passed over a small range of mountains, they were caught in a downdraft. Jones knew the plane was going to crash.

"We survived, thanks to Vince's quick-mindedness in cutting the switches and finding a field to crash in," Wells remembered years later. On this, they concur. "It was a masterpiece," Jones says. But even though he landed so the wheels would run in the direction of the furrows plowed into the ground, Jones soon discovered that the furrows changed course midfield. The plane bounced into ruts cutting across its path and flipped. Wells and Jones escaped with barely a scratch but the plane was wrecked.

Wells remembered hitching a ride back to England on a military transport. But Jones says they actually caught a flight chartered by a construction company in a plane filled with rowdy workers. The flight attendants, anxious to stay as far from the men as possible, made Wells and Jones earn their passage by serving drinks.

Back at Oxford, Jones remembers, Wells decided to pull a prank by disassembling a professor's car and rebuilding it in his office. To Jones, Wells seemed less caught up in the joy of the stunt than in spinning his legend at Oxford. Wells was mulling a future that might include politics — hardly surprising, given his ancestry. He liked the idea of doing "harmless things that would set him apart," Jones says. But in this case, he almost went too far.

"Apparently the tutor was not the least bit amused," Jones says. "Frank came very close to getting thrown out of the university." Though Wells later recounted his trip to Africa to many audiences, he didn't talk about the failed stunt.

∞

WELLS LEFT OXFORD in 1955 with a master's degree in law, did a stint in the army, and then went to law school at Stanford University, where he made law review and was in the Order of the Coif. He flourished as an attorney at Gang, Tyre, Rudin & Brown, with a client list that grew to include James Garner and Clint Eastwood.

One of his first major trials in 1960 involved Garner, who says he was introduced to Wells by senior partner Martin Gang. Garner claimed Warner Brothers had breached his contract by laying him off from his series, *Maverick*. Warner dropped him ostensibly because of a slowdown in production caused by a writers' strike. But Garner felt that the studio, which didn't offer him any other work, was paying him back for being a chronic complainer. "They could have used me for anything—opening delicatessens if they wanted to," he says. "They were angry at me because I was vocal if I didn't like what they were doing. A year earlier I had gotten an ulcer and the doctor said, 'Jim, you can't hold things in.' So I didn't."

When the case went to court, Wells had to face the notoriously tough mogul Jack Warner, who was called as a witness. But Wells was unintimidated. "He was very smooth—you didn't see any of the novice in him," Garner recalls. "He reminded me of Jimmy Stewart in court. He was tall and thin and he had this bearing—you just knew he was the good guy."

According to Garner, Martin Gang advised Wells to ask Warner whether the studio had the money to pay Garner during the strike. "Jack Warner said, 'Of course I had money. That's all I had was money. We couldn't get writers.' And the judge looked at him like, 'You mean, nasty old man.' . . . We won the suit. We got Jack Warner on the stand and that's where they lost it."

Another Wells client was Richard Sylbert, the distinguished production designer who later became an executive at Paramount working for Diller. In the mid-1960s, Sylbert consulted Wells about a pending divorce. "I had a house on Fire Island I had bought for $20,000," Sylbert remembers. "My three boys and wife loved the house." He was willing to give them the house but Wells urged him not to do it. "This discussion went on for months," Sylbert says. "He kept saying, 'Don't do it.' This is the difference between Frank and me. Frank was tough. But you didn't know it until you ran across these things. . . . He was a really hard man." While Sylbert was in Paris producing *What's New, Pussycat?*, he decided to ignore Wells's advice. Frustrated, Wells sent him a terse letter. It said simply, "Schmuck."

"Twenty years later my ex-wife sold that house for $800,000," Sylbert laments. "Frank knew that would happen."

Wells also represented and befriended a quirky producer named John Calley, who was tapped by Warner chairman Ted Ashley to run production at the studio in the late sixties. Thinking that Wells would make "an astonishing executive," Calley offered him a job as head of business affairs. Wells hesitated. This was 1969, years before attorneys routinely stepped into executive jobs at entertainment companies. "We talked about it a lot," Calley says. "It was terrifying for him but he was ambitious."

Wells took the job and soon found that he loved being an executive in the entertainment industry. If ever there was a risky business—a business that demanded spontaneity—this was it. Wells enjoyed the exercise of authority, the feel of making executive decisions and dispatching the troops to carry them out.

The era of the original movie moguls was ending in Hollywood as Wells arrived at Warner. A new generation of executives—men like Barry Diller and Michael Eisner—would soon bring enormous changes to the industry. But before this new guard was ushered in, the executive team of Ashley, Calley, and Wells made deals that transformed Warner into a powerhouse. While much of Hollywood was suffering through a slump in the early seventies, Warner's slate brought the studio that elusive mix of profit and prestige with films like *Klute, Billy Jack, A Clockwork Orange, Deliverance*, and *What's Up, Doc?* The stars had not yet discovered that they had the clout to demand shares in the profits and the studio's pictures, on average, cost less than $2.5 million. The Ashley team was minting money.

"Frank Wells had the best negotiating style in the world," remembers Tom Pollock, then an attorney building a formidable client list that would eventually include George Lucas, Oliver Stone, Ron Howard, and many other top executives and filmmakers. "He'd lay out the deal and he'd say, 'You're going to ask for this. We're going to offer this. Here's where we're going to end up. What do you say?' It avoided a lot of rigmarole."

Of course, it wasn't always quite so simple. In 1970, Wells was faced with a project that was foundering. Warner had developed a script about a tough-cop character for Frank Sinatra. But just as the movie was ready to roll, Sinatra withdrew. Wells called his former legal client, Clint Eastwood. The two negotiated but reached an impasse over one arcane provision that the star demanded. With Eastwood ready to break the deal, he visited Wells at his Beverly Hills home.

Wells had a tennis court in his yard—or, strictly speaking, half a tennis court. When Wells had decided to build a court, he found that his property wasn't quite deep enough. He persuaded a neighbor to put half the court in his yard. Spotting this palpable example of Wells's negotiating skill, Eastwood proposed a match. If he won, he would prevail on some minor deal points; otherwise, Wells could set the terms. Eastwood won and became *Dirty Harry*. Not only was the film a major hit, but Eastwood became a fixture at Warner, earning the studio hundreds of millions of dollars (as well as four Academy Awards for *Unforgiven*, his grim and unconventional 1992 western).

By 1973, Wells had become president of the studio. While Calley's tastes were eclectic, Wells was more a businessman than a connoisseur of film. Calley recalls sitting with Wells while they watched a rough cut of British producer David Puttnam's film *Chariots of Fire*. Both men were riveted by the story of the rivalry between two British runners—a Scottish missionary and a Jewish student at Cambridge—who competed in the 1924 Olympics. As the film wound to its moving conclusion, Wells was weeping. But pragmatism dominated—this was artsy fare, not blockbuster material. Through his tears, he turned to Calley and said, "You want to release this? . . . Who would want to see it?" Fox eventually released the picture after the Ladd Company, which had a deal there, agreed to acquire it. It grossed a strong $59 million and won the Oscar for Best Picture.

As Warner soared, its top executives prospered. Steve Ross, the legendary chairman of the studio's parent, Warner Communications Inc., had instituted a system of bonuses so lavish that they elevated his key men above their peers at rival studios and sometimes even above Ross himself. Calley recalls that Wells balked at accepting these outsized offerings. "He thought it was inappropriate," Calley says. "I had to threaten him to get him to take the same [amounts] that we did."

Wells was even disdainful of that most coveted and closely watched symbol of power in Hollywood: the reserved parking space. He had the names of the company's top executives painted out of the circular driveway in front of the studio's low-slung main building. It wasn't a particularly meaningful move because only the top men were allowed to park in the area anyway. One day, he drove onto the lot to find that a spot had been repainted to read "Reserved for Frank Wells." Wells went inside to complain that his instructions had been ignored. In fact, Steve Ross was playing a prank. While Wells was in the building, Ross had the sign quickly painted over again. Ross then accused Wells of being so obsessed with the issue that he had imagined the "reserved" sign. Wells got the joke—but still refused to paint the names on the driveway.

Wells rebelled against the corporate hierarchy so relentlessly that Ross dubbed him "the company socialist." But in fact, he was deeply ambivalent about the perks of power. Wells was a bundle of contradictions, but the complexity of his character went largely unnoticed in Hollywood, where denizens like to grab onto outsized stories and archetypal personalities.

Most saw Wells as an unpretentious and plainly honest man who didn't crave the power and luxuries that he in fact relished. But others believed he was capable of pride and hypocrisy. "He had the most charming combination of genuine humility and genuine arrogance of any man I've ever met," says Herbert Allen, the industry's most prominent investment banker. Another close associate from the Warner days remembers that Wells "hated for people to think he was rich," even while making millions. In some ways, says this executive, "he was tortured" by his own contradictions.

Though men like Calley admired Wells's sense of modesty, others thought it seemed somewhat studied. Vince Jones, his Oxford schoolmate, says Wells "felt it was classier to be overmodest." Wells's sense of integrity was complicated, too. Steve Ross once observed that Wells believed he was "100 percent right on everything and . . . 100 percent honest." Obviously, Ross knew that the truth was more complex. Another high-level Warner executive who worked with Wells closely shared that appraisal. "He was very diabolical in many ways," that executive says. "He was not a religious man but acted like one. He would act righteous and proper, and then people would feel, 'Where did that deal come from?' "

Wells applied his peculiar brand of humility to personal matters as well as business dealings. In 1992, he decided to install a waterfall on his Malibu property. A dedicated environmentalist, Wells knew that using water this way was frivolous in arid Los Angeles; on the other hand, he was a wealthy man and he wanted his waterfall. He decided to balance the scales by making a contribution to support nearby Pepperdine University's water conservation efforts.

No doubt, Wells enjoyed the fruits of his labors. Longtime friend and business associate Roland Betts remembers that on ski trips, Wells always hired an instructor—but not because he wanted lessons. "The instructor would say, 'Okay, what do you want to work on today?' " Betts remembers affectionately. "And he just wanted to cut the line."

∞

IN 1975, ASHLEY and Calley both astonished Hollywood by retiring from Warner, leaving Wells as the top man. But Wells couldn't come close to replicating the success of Ashley and Calley. "It was a lot for Frank to do," says Terry Semel, then head of distribution. "He had basically been responsible for the business side of the company. This was a big leap." The studio quickly reshuffled its talent. In less than a year, Ashley and Calley were lured back and music mogul David Geffen was brought in as vice-chairman. Wells kept the president's title.

Things still weren't working well. Geffen and Ashley clashed and Geffen left after less than a year. By 1980, Ashley—who confided to his colleagues that he was having personal problems—said he was leaving again, and this time for good. In a particularly shrewd piece of corporate recruiting, Warner hired Bob Daly from CBS to be chairman of the studio. Wells was now awkwardly situated and before Daly was fully engaged in his job, Wells said he wanted to take a sabbatical for a year to pursue an old dream.

Wells had been increasingly distracted by a personal project. He hadn't done much mountaineering since his nausea-inducing visit to Kilimanjaro, but Wells had never forgotten his plan to climb the tallest mountain on each continent. He had mentioned this idea to his friend Clint Eastwood, who introduced him to a man named Jack Wheeler, a self-styled professional adventurer who had helped Eastwood scout locations in the Arctic for an upcoming film, *Firefox*.

Wheeler was slightly acquainted with Dick Bass, another successful businessman and ambitious amateur mountain climber who, at age fifty-one, was only slightly older than Wells. Bass had recently climbed Mount McKinley, the tallest peak in North America. One afternoon in July 1981, Wheeler called Bass to ask if he would give Wells a few tips. "He wants to climb the highest mountain on each continent," Wheeler explained.

Bass was stunned. He already wanted to try the seven summits himself.

No one had ever done it. Faced with pressing business problems, he had put the idea aside. Now he saw his chance. Wells was a man of means who could share the costs of a seven-summits expedition, which in Bass's estimate might reach $650,000.

With oil interests in Texas and coal interests in Alaska, Bass was such a zestful talker that some called him "largemouth Bass." His passion and obsession was the Snowbird Ski Resort, which he had spent years developing in Utah. Despite his devotion, Bass complained that projects like Snowbird took so much labor that he sometimes felt as though he were "on a treadmill in a dark tunnel." Mountain climbing presented a clear goal that depended primarily on his own physical skill and stamina.

But when it came to experience, he didn't have much more than Wells. To make the seven-summits dream come true, Bass and Wells would have to climb Aconcagua in South America, Everest in Asia, McKinley in North America, Kilimanjaro in Africa, Elbrus in Europe, Vinson in the Antarctic, and Kosciusko in Australia. They seemed unlikely candidates to set a record: they didn't even rate as decent amateurs. "I was a total novice as a climber and a klutz to boot," Wells acknowledged later.

Bass flew to Los Angeles for a lunch meeting in Wells's private dining room on the Warner lot. To his dismay, Wells was determined to do all the talking. Standing as Bass sat at the table, Wells delivered a twenty-minute monologue before abruptly seating himself and devouring his lunch. Wells wanted to attempt Elbrus in the Soviet Union first, offering to have Jack Valenti, the motion-picture industry's silver-haired man in Washington, contact the Soviet ambassador about arranging a permit. Wells seemed a bit full of himself but he had cash, energy, and ideas. Bass agreed to a partnership.

With only weeks before the two men were to meet in Europe for the Elbrus climb, Wells had to hurry to get in shape and learn something about mountain climbing. He sought advice from Rick Ridgeway, a climber whom he met through Wheeler. The two tried to climb Sespe Gorge, a rock cliff north of Los Angeles. They took a route considered easy to moderate, but before he was halfway up, Wells was in trouble and wanted to quit. Ridgeway urged him on, telling him that Tom Brokaw had recently "zoomed" to the top on his first climb. Wells redoubled his efforts. When he finally made it, he had "sewing-machine leg"—a climber's term for limbs that vibrate rapidly from exhaustion.

Ridgeway walked away thinking that Wells had "absolutely no natural ability as a climber." And he sensed that Wells had no grasp of the danger that lay ahead, that he had "no real idea what it was like up there in what climbers call the death zone." But Ridgeway continued to assist Wells.

When Bass and Wells attempted a practice run on Elbrus, an 18,510-foot challenge, Wells quickly fell behind. Their Russian guides were openly contemptuous. As Bass reached the summit, Wells collapsed in an abandoned hut hundreds of vertical feet below and would have died right there without the guides' prodding. Nonetheless, he was determined to pursue the seven summits. His wife, Luanne, was distressed that he would expose himself to such danger, leaving her at home with two teenagers. Undeterred, Wells told Bass that they should try to cram the seven summits into one year because they would find it difficult to stay in top condition if they took longer. They decided to go for it in 1983.

On a family vacation in Hawaii a few weeks after his Elbrus adventure, Wells tried a hike up Mauna Loa, a 13,680-foot mountain on the Big Island. He stumbled and plunged headlong into the jagged lava rock. With his hand over his face as it gushed blood, Wells had to drive for an hour to get medical attention. The gash required fifteen stitches. But Wells pressed ahead, joining Bass in a practice run at Mount Rainier. Meanwhile, they made plans to try Everest with a team that was attempting to carve an untried route. It was a bold plan considering that Wells had yet to reach a peak. And he fared no better on Rainier. Once again, Wells fell behind as Bass reached his goal.

Wells was convinced that he simply needed more practice. He and Bass turned next to Aconcagua in Argentina. It was January 1982, two months before they were to start a three-month expedition to Everest. At this point, with the seven-summits project taking up an increasing amount of his time and energy, Wells went to Daly and asked for a leave from Warner. But Daly told Wells that if he wanted to go for a year, he would have to be replaced.

A few months shy of his fiftieth birthday, Wells quit his job. He was as successful as any reasonable man could hope to be: he had a beautiful wife, two handsome teenage sons, a home in Beverly Hills, a house at Malibu, condominiums in Vail and Sun Valley, and a glamorous job as cochairman of Warner. But he wanted more and he was willing to risk his own life and the happiness of his loved ones to get it.

∽

UNFORTUNATELY, WHAT WELLS had in determination he lacked in competence. As Wells and a new team of mountain climbers took a pass at Aconcagua—at 22,835 feet, the highest peak in the Western Hemisphere—one of his companions took note of this trait. Seattle attorney Jim Wickwire wrote in his diary: "He seems almost incapable of taking care of himself, and Bass has to look after him when we don't." Once again Wells fell behind and failed to summit; Bass looked on in dismay as Wells ignored advice on how to correct his technique. Wells seemed to pose a risk to himself and the others. Still, the team went forward with plans to try Everest.

It was a disaster. Within a few weeks, Wells had lost more than thirty pounds. He had developed pneumonia and was ordered to rest in camp. "I guess I have to be honest and say it's a relief," he wrote home. "[If] I leave feeling I have done my share of the work, and the team is successful, I will be completely fulfilled." He allowed excerpts from this letter to be published in *Variety*. Wells may have been gone, but that didn't mean he wanted the industry to forget him. A setback for Wells turned into a tragedy when one member of the team—seasoned climber Marty Hoey—fell to her death. Foul weather ended the attempt.

So far, all these climbs had been a prelude to the official launch of the seven-summits effort. Before Wells set off, he had dinner with Michael Eisner. The two men scarcely knew each other but they had met on the slopes of Vail. Characteristically, Eisner grilled Wells on the arcana of mountain climbing, asking about everything from how he relieved himself in subzero temperatures to how he coped with altitude sickness. Eisner was amazed when Wells acknowledged how poorly prepared he was. Wells, he concluded, was a dangerously reckless man.

On New Year's Day 1983, Wells sat in his breakfast room at his Beverly Hills home and signed an updated will. His wife wanted his affairs to be in order. Luanne had assumed power of attorney and shouldered the burden of the family's financial affairs. She was preparing herself to be a widow. As he left, she was weeping.

Her worst fears were nearly fulfilled on the first climb. As Wells struggled up Aconcagua in Argentina, he fell and slid to the very edge of a cliff. This time, the danger was obvious even to him. His first question was whether anyone had recorded the tumble on film. "I don't want to have almost died for nothing," he explained. Still, he forged ahead. To Bass's exasperation, Wells still expected others to watch out for him. "Frank, you've got to learn to bring your own things," Bass told him as Wells borrowed a packet of energy powder. "I swear, you'll go to your grave still not knowing how to care for yourself." But on his second try at Aconcagua, Wells made it to the top. Leaning on his ax, almost unable to speak, he called back: "You mean this is it?"

The expedition returned to Everest. Bass set out first but turned back because of bad weather. Wells was next. "The team begged me not to try it because of my lack of experience, my weak condition at high altitude, and a deserved reputation for losing my footing at the wrong time," Wells said later. "Understandably, none of the team would go with me. So I took two Sherpas, and with oxygen, I reached the famous South Call, 26,200 feet above sea level." Only a day's climb from the top, Wells could taste success. "I'd be the oldest person in history to make it and making the seven summits would be practically assured," he said.

When the weather took a turn for the worse, Wells bribed the two Sherpas with a year's wages to stay with him. But supplies and oxygen soon ran low and Wells was forced to turn back. Bass made one more run at the summit but the persistent bad weather foiled him, too. Undaunted, the two made plans to return after they had gotten a few of the other summits under their belts.

Wells and Bass went on to conquer McKinley, Kilimanjaro, and then Elbrus, where they strode to the finish in lockstep, reciting Rudyard Kipling's "Gunga Din." Their next stop would be Vinson—a logistically challenging trip to the Antarctic. Meanwhile, they were planning another attempt at Everest. But this time, Luanne drew the line. As far as she was concerned, Wells had all but abandoned his wife and sons. "I'm not saying you can't go," she told him. "But . . . if you go back to Everest again and are lucky enough to get home alive, I won't be here." Wells decided to settle for six summits.

Vinson was a mere six hundred miles from the South Pole and, in Wells's words, "two thousand miles from anything that could possibly be called civilization." In some ways, it was the toughest outing of all. The mountain had been climbed only twice before. Wells was incensed that the American military was actively discouraging would-be climbers from making the attempt. He worked the phones for a week to find a plane to make the journey and for six weeks to get special casualty insurance from Lloyd's of London. He took three trips to persuade the Chilean government to do a parachute fuel drop halfway down the Antarctic Peninsula. His hard work paid off when he made it through the climb, frostbitten and vomiting.

The trip was notable for another reason: it was the first time that Wells had actually "cooked." He really just heated some leftovers during a layover on his way home, but he considered it a feat. He was so excited that he told Luanne about the marvelous "microwave thing" that he had used. "Darling, we've got to get one," he said.

"Frank," she replied, "we've had one for twelve years."

Wells and Bass had an easy stroll up Mount Kosciusko in Australia, marking the sixth of the seven summits. Wells kept his promise to Luanne. Bass was left to conquer Everest alone, and at fifty-three, he became the first person to climb the seven summits. He and Wells later wrote a book about their adventures (coauthored by Rick Ridgeway), but Wells's part in the seven-summits attempt ended as he and Bass stood atop Kosciusko, reflecting on their achievements. "I just hope one thing," Bass told Wells.

"What's that?" Wells asked.

"I just hope, now that this is over, you're able to go home and find yourself a job."

11

THE EIGHTH SUMMIT

WITH THE SEVEN-summits adventure behind him, Wells threw himself into Stanley Gold's plot to take over Disney. It was starting to look as though he might not wind up in the unemployment line after all. In fact, Wells was already thinking about recruiting talent to help him when and if he got in the door at Disney. "Whatever else you do, get Michael Eisner," Wells told Gold. Wells and Eisner were not friends, but Eisner was a hot talent and Wells undoubtedly knew that things had started to unravel at Paramount in the wake of Bluhdorn's death.

In early 1984, however, personnel matters were not the first priority. In February, Gold and Wells had gone to New York to line up a team of investment bankers and lawyers as they explored potential lines of attack. Roy Disney, who had been attending the company's annual meeting in Florida, flew up to join them. In a late-night meeting over a room-service dinner at the Ritz-Carlton, Gold and Wells pointed out to Roy that he had a looming conflict of interest. If he intended to launch a serious fight, Roy would have to resign from Disney's board of directors.

On March 9, the day that *Splash* opened, Roy sent Ray Watson a terse letter of resignation. He offered no explanation for his departure. Since Roy had hardly uttered a complaint about the company in recent years, Watson was stunned. He phoned repeatedly, and finally wrote, to see whether things could be worked out. Roy never responded.

The very day that Roy's resignation was made public, corporate raider Saul Steinberg started buying shares in Disney. The dominoes had been given the nudge that would topple them. By the end of the month, it was apparent that Steinberg was a potential hostile buyer. Sid Sheinberg, president of MCA/Universal, gave Ron Miller a sympathy call. What a pity it would be, he said, if Disney were snapped up so cheaply. He asked if there was anything MCA could do. Unbeknownst to Miller, Sheinberg also covered his bases by calling Roy Disney. Maybe MCA would find an opportunity there, in the event that Roy went on the attack.

Those discussions came to nothing. But it was clear that Disney's managers had to act. Anyone who acquired the company would not only throw them out but possibly break up the company and sell it off in pieces. Disney started looking into a defense. Watson turned to the Bass brothers of Texas to help fend off Steinberg.

Bass Brothers Enterprises was a $4 billion conglomerate that had its origins in oil and gas leases. In some circles, the Basses were considered to be just as predatory as Steinberg. But Sid Bass, the eldest of the four Bass brothers, was determined to convince Watson that he was more than a quick-buck kind of guy. In fact, the Bass brothers had held significant stakes in companies like Church's Fried Chicken and Prime Computer for years. Over lunch at the Carlyle Hotel in New York, Watson came to believe that the Basses might answer his problems.

On June 6, 1984, Disney and the Bass brothers got into bed together when Disney agreed to buy Arvida, a Bass-owned Florida development company, for $200 million in stock. The idea was to bring in a friendly new shareholder, beef up the company, and make it more expensive to acquire. The same day, Disney made a deal to purchase Gibson Greeting Cards for $315 million.

Steinberg didn't blink. He waited only two days to launch a hostile takeover attempt. He had more than a billion dollars in his arsenal from partners who were prepared to split up the company. In fact, Roy Disney had hoped to be one of them, offering to throw in his lot with Steinberg if he could get the studio, copyrights, and merchandising rights for $350 million after Steinberg took over. But Steinberg didn't need Roy and rebuffed him.

With that option closed, Gold and Wells went another way. Their only hope was to team up with the Walt forces and try to buy the company. The financing would require them to sell off some assets, but maybe not too many. The important thing, they agreed, was that Disney should not pay "greenmail" to Steinberg—in other words, the company should not buy back his shares at a premium just to get him to go away. That, they agreed, would invite a pack a jackals hoping for the same type of payoff to come at the company.

With this strategy in mind, Wells and Gold met with Watson and Miller

at Miller's home in Encino on a Sunday afternoon. Miller was not especially happy to see Wells, who was a friend but had never quite gotten
around to telling Miller that he was a key part of Roy's "brain trust." Wells
tried to smooth things over by saying that Roy's team wanted to keep the
company intact. Nobody mentioned that Roy's team had offered to help
Steinberg break up the company.

Even as the meeting was under way, Miller and Watson had dispatched
Disney's lawyers to negotiate with Steinberg. On Monday, Disney agreed
to exactly the type of greenmail deal that Gold so vehemently opposed.
Having pocketed a $32 million profit, Steinberg took his leave.

Wells and Gold were outraged on several fronts. They were incensed
over the greenmail. They had disapproved of the deal to buy the Gibson
greeting-card company. And Gold had angrily told *Business Week*: "Disney
needs those 20,000 acres of Arvida land like they need another asshole."
The Roy team decided to retaliate. They would demand several seats on
the board and a high-level job for Wells. If Disney didn't come across, they
would attack. They would sue to block the greenmail payment and the
Gibson acquisition. They would launch a proxy fight to unseat the board.

At first, Disney declined to meet their demands. But the day before the
Roy team was going to file a notice of its intentions with the SEC, financial
columnist Dan Dorfman reported that Roy was about to start a war against
Disney management. That prompted the company to call, wanting to make
a deal. Watson agreed to give Roy a bloc on the board—including seats for
Gold and Roy's brother-in law—but the company still refused to give Wells
a job. Wells said he would not let the settlement collapse over the issue.

Gold accepted the verdict but insisted on reshaping the board's executive
committee, which took the lead on key policy matters. Former Disney chairmen Don Tatum and Card Walker had to be dropped. This gesture would
humiliate the two Disney career men and Wells advised Gold not to insist
on it. But Gold was relentless. He thought it would establish that Roy was
back with real clout. Reluctantly, Watson gave in.

That evening, when the exhausted Roy team went to dinner to celebrate,
Roy fainted in a hallway outside the dining room. Moments later, Gold
fainted, too. Some said he keeled over at the thought that Roy Disney—
with whom he was making such a splendid career—was no longer among
the living. Both men, however, were apparently suffering only from exhaustion and recovered rapidly.

Soon after he was installed on the board, Gold got a call from Sid Bass.

"In thirty seconds, I knew it was going to be a natural alliance," Gold said later. Gold's colorful denunciation of the Arvida deal was quickly forgotten. Gold and Bass started to call the shots. Both agreed that the Gibson Greeting Cards deal should be scuttled. After putting up a brief fight, Watson went along. Before the Disney board even had a chance to ratify that decision at an August 17 meeting, Gold and Richard Rainwater, a key man at Bass Brothers Enterprises, began to install their own management.

Gold first had to convince Rainwater that his candidate, Wells, was right for a top job. Gold may have been defeated earlier in his attempt to put Wells in place, but he did not intend to let the matter rest. Wells flew to Nantucket to visit Rainwater at his vacation home there. Wells was on his way in, and Ron Miller, the weak chief executive, was going to be the first one out the door.

By now, Disney's board was prepared to accept that Miller could not survive. At the August 17 meeting, the Gibson deal was canceled and a committee was appointed to study options about the company's future. Miller was the only one who seemed not to understand that the committee was set up to search for his successor. After the meeting, board member Phil Hawley took Miller aside and told him that the study would probably result in a request for his resignation. As he absorbed the news, Miller began to weep.

THE FOLLOWING SUNDAY night, Gold and Wells invited Eisner to join them in Gold's study, where they were drinking grappa as they mulled over their next move. By now, it was August 19 — just about three weeks before Diller announced his departure from Paramount. Eisner knew an ill wind was blowing at Paramount. A few months earlier, he had asked Roy Disney if there was any opening at the company. Roy seemed responsive and Wells had subsequently assured Eisner that he might indeed find opportunity at Disney if Roy's plans worked out. In July, Roy kept Eisner warm by calling him in Vermont, where he was visiting his children at Camp Keewaydin. Despite Eisner's efforts to engineer his way into Diller's job at Paramount, Eisner knew Davis was unlikely to give it to him. So by the time Wells finally invited Eisner to join him in Gold's study, Eisner was seriously on the job market.

The meeting went well — Eisner spewed forth ideas for reviving the studio, making movies, getting into television production, putting cartoons on

Saturday morning. Gold told Eisner that the front-runner for the Disney job was Dennis Stanfill, a buttoned-down former head of Twentieth Century Fox who had won the favor of board member Phil Hawley. Like Wells, Stanfill had been a Rhodes scholar. Hawley was convinced that Stanfill, an investment banker, could command respect on Wall Street.

Gold was backing Wells and Eisner as a team, and he invited Watson to meet Eisner. Watson drove to Eisner's house in Bel Air and the two sat in the living room and talked. It is easy to imagine Eisner explaining that any of his hit shows at ABC or Paramount—*Happy Days, Laverne & Shirley, Taxi*—would be perfect for Disney. He also sang the praises of Walt. And he explained that Marty Davis was demanding a rate of growth at Paramount that simply could not be achieved. Disney, on the other hand, could only get better. "If I go somewhere, I want to go to a place that's on the mat and build it up," Eisner said. "That's how Paramount was when I came in. That's how ABC was when I went there." Eisner's intelligence, humor, and disarming candor worked like a charm on Watson.

Without even meeting Stanfill, Watson wrote a six-page memo to the board recommending Eisner as chief executive. He would recharge the studio while Watson stayed as chairman and focused on Disney's real estate holdings. Several board members, including Hawley, were unconvinced. They didn't believe Eisner had sufficient business experience. Many industry observers also believe that some of the old guard felt that as a Jew, Eisner would make an inappropriate choice to run the Walt Disney Company. The board members were willing, however, to consider him for a lesser job.

On September 5, Watson once again visited Eisner at home. Unbeknownst to Watson, Paramount was about to explode. Marty Davis was visiting Los Angeles that very week. But Eisner was not prepared to take what Watson offered now—the number-two position, chief operating officer. Eisner knew what he wanted: chief executive or nothing. He would be perfectly happy if Watson remained as chairman. Watson promised that he was going to get the board to approve exactly that arrangement.

Watson went into the next board meeting, on Friday, September 6, expecting Eisner to get the nod. Meanwhile, Eisner had an interesting day ahead of him. That evening, he was attending Diller's dinner party for Davis. But before then, he met with Davis, even as the Disney board convened, to say he was probably going to be offered the top job at Disney.

But Phil Hawley wasn't ready to give up on his choice, Dennis Stanfill. To Gold's dismay, he argued that the board should not act quickly. There should be no vote at the board meeting that day. The question should be studied by a committee, and the committee should pick someone with solid business experience. Gold was astonished when Watson, who had been Eisner's advocate, merely said, "Okay."

While this was going on, Eisner was sitting in his office nervously waiting for the phone to ring. It didn't—not until the middle of the afternoon, when Wells told him the result of the board meeting. Eisner now felt that he was a man who had crawled out on a limb that was unexpectedly slender. "What kind of an organization is this?" he demanded. "Don't you have any management? Stanley, I thought you were running the company."

"I've barely got my oar in the water, kid," Gold replied.

Quickly, before Diller's dinner, Eisner went back to Davis. Maybe he wasn't going to take this Disney job after all, he said. Davis didn't seem to care.

∞

WHEN DAVIS CALLED Eisner the following Tuesday and asked him to come to New York for their final showdown, Eisner said he couldn't leave at once because his children had their first day of school. The real reason was that on Wednesday, Eisner was supposed to meet at eight A.M. with Phil Hawley. Unlike Watson, Hawley was not bowled over. He kept returning to the question of corporate experience. It wasn't just Eisner. Hawley thought Wells, who had been an attorney before going to Warner, also lacked the kind of corporate stature that would impress Wall Street.

Meanwhile, Watson seemed to be taking Hawley's side. Wells told Gold that Watson had invited him over and asked him to take a relatively inconsequential business-affairs job at the film studio. "Schmucks," Wells said to Gold. "Can you believe it? . . . It's over."

But Gold wasn't ready to quit. When the screening committee met at the end of the week, Gold attacked Stanfill as a martinet. "You see guys like Eisner as a little crazy or off-the-wall," he told Hawley. "Every great studio in this business has been run by crazies. What do you think Walt Disney was? The guy was off the goddamned wall." Hawley countered that Eisner and Wells had "never run anything but a division." Gold replied that Paramount may be a "division" but it was a billion-dollar operation, as was the Warner studio.

The meeting ended inconclusively, but Roy's team was losing the battle. They floated the notion of putting Eisner, Wells, and Stanfill into an "office of the president." It was a short-lived idea. With about a week left before the board was to vote, Gold decided that Eisner and Wells needed to go on the attack. They had to campaign with board members and convince them that they were the best choice for the company. First, Gold had to get Eisner—who was by now out of the Paramount job and being courted heavily elsewhere—to throw himself into the effort after he had already been left dangling once.

On a Sunday night, Gold invited Wells and Eisner to his house. It was getting to be zero hour—exactly what were Eisner and Wells going after? The issue of titles had to be resolved. Eisner insisted on being chairman and chief executive. Wells—with his hope of claiming the chief-executive title fading—suggested that he and Eisner share the top job. Eisner declined. "I don't think you can have coheads," he said. "The buck has to stop somewhere. You have to have one person who is the head and I really don't want to go into this, Frank, unless I'm the head."

Finally, and with more than a passing pang, Wells gave in. "Okay, you're right," he said. "I'll go in as number two." He would be president. But he would report to the board, not to Eisner. It may have been that Wells suffered a failure of nerve—or perhaps he simply knew his own limitations. As much as he might want the top spot at Disney, he had tried it at Warner and the results weren't good. If there was one thing he didn't want, it was to fail publicly at Disney. He needed Eisner and was willing to let him have the top title if that's what it took to get him.

But this concession still was not enough for Eisner. Now he wanted to talk money. He had brought his lawyer, Irwin Russell, to negotiate for him. Gold interrupted: "Do you want to be chairman and CEO of Walt Disney Productions? It's the best job in the world. Give me a break."

Eisner agreed to campaign, for a time. "I'll give you one week," he said.

The two began an extraordinary effort to persuade board members to back them. They enlisted Steven Spielberg and George Lucas to help. These influential filmmakers were impressive, but Eisner knew he had to convince the board that he wasn't a lightweight. "What was most important was they saw that I did not come in a tutu, and that I was a serious person, and I understood a [profit-and-loss statement], and I knew the investment analysts, and I read *Fortune*," Eisner said obligingly—in an interview given to *Fortune* magazine after the dust had settled.

One key was for Eisner to win the support of Sid Bass, the influential shareholder. So far, Bass was in favor of Wells but doubted Eisner had the chops to run the whole company. His lieutenant, Richard Rainwater, apparently had been so impressed with Wells that he advised Bass to stick with him. In Rainwater's view, Eisner didn't have the depth to run the company.

When Eisner heard from Wells and Gold that Bass was against him, he phoned Bass—with Wells, Gold, and Jane Eisner present—to try selling himself one last time. "Would you like to know why I should be the chairman?" Eisner asked.

"Yeah, I'd love to know," Bass replied.

Eisner began to speak and didn't stop for several minutes. "I could not tell you what I said, but I said something like, 'The company should be run from a creative point of view rather than a financial point of view,'" Eisner said later. "I have no idea where I got the speech. Maybe I'd seen a bunch of movies like *Mr. Smith Goes to Washington*, but I made one of those speeches. And I stopped and I said, 'So that's why I think I should be chairman,' and there was silence for about three seconds and Sid said, 'Sounds good to me. Okay.'"

At first, Bass thought Eisner seemed "a little high-handed." But it was a rare day when Eisner couldn't make some inroads when he tried to persuade and charm. Wells took the phone to express his approval of the arrangement and Bass gave in.

Eisner subsequently cited another factor in Bass's decision. Bass had read Schwartz's *New York* magazine piece and saw a picture of Eisner with his wife and sons. Later, Eisner recalled, Bass told him he had seen that photo and said to himself, "Well, he looks like a family guy. . . . Maybe he can run a family company."

Now Gold could tell board members that the Eisner-Wells team had Bass's backing. In fact, Bass warned, if Eisner and Wells didn't win the board's approval, the Bass brothers would start a proxy fight and fire the board. By now, Bass and his allies, including corporate raider Irwin Jacobs, controlled about 40 percent of Disney's stock and the Basses were continuing to increase their stake.

With the board divided even in the face of Bass's threat, Gold concluded that Card Walker—the former Disney chairman whom Gold had thrown off Disney's executive committee—was the swing vote. Gold was persona non grata with him, so Wells would have to lobby him. Wells could promise a concession: Gold would resign from the board in favor of a Walt person— Ron Miller or one of Walt's daughters, Diane or Sharon. As it was, the

Walt side was unrepresented. What Gold proposed would bring the family together in backing the company.

Walker was fishing in Arizona when Wells flew on Roy's jet to meet him. It was a Friday afternoon; the board was to meet the next day. That evening, Wells called Gold to say he had won Walker over. The idea of placing a Walt person on the board had appealed strongly to Walker. He also foresaw continued warfare if the Wells-Eisner team lost. Eisner, who had been dispatched to two other board members, had been less successful. But the Roy team now had the votes it needed. Eisner was so relieved when the offer came through that he nearly wept. The next morning, he appeared at Gold's house at six o'clock to hammer out a contract so that Gold could take a proposal to the board.

On September 22, the board unanimously approved Eisner as chairman and chief executive and Wells as president and chief operating officer. Watson resigned, making room for Wells. And Gold resigned so that Walt's daughter, Sharon Disney Lund, could take a seat on the board. The arrangement now had the Walt seal of approval.

Eisner was given a six-year contract, and though the terms were not immediately disclosed, it was known that his deal was heavy on stock options. Once details became public, Eisner allowed, it would be perceived as "outrageous." One reason was that Eisner was getting a 50 percent raise over the $500,000 salary that had been paid to his predecessor, Ron Miller (and Miller had only been making that since May 1984, when the board gave him a 33 percent raise). And at the time that Eisner came aboard, the company was asking Disneyland workers to be good corporate "citizens" and help Disney survive by accepting slashed benefits and a 17 percent wage cut over the next three years.

Eisner would make $750,000 a year and receive a $750,000 signing bonus. He was promised an annual bonus tied to improving the company's net income. He would get 2 percent of any growth in net above 9 percent — roughly the company's average return in the previous five years. He also got options on more than two million shares of Disney stock at $14.359 each. The board amended company bylaws to permit Eisner to borrow money to exercise his options. Wells would receive $400,000 a year, a $250,000 signing bonus, an annual bonus equal to 50 percent of Eisner's, and options on 460,000 shares. Both men bet heavily on the Disney stock.

Two days after Eisner and Wells got their jobs, they visited Sid Bass at his black-tower headquarters in Fort Worth. The future of the Disney company still hung in the balance. Irwin Jacobs, the raider who had gobbled up a block of Disney shares, was also present and still thought he might ultimately take control of Disney and sell it off in pieces. Bass was uncommitted for the long term and warned Eisner and Wells that the company's ownership could change. "We intend to make it a great company no matter who owns it," Wells said. Eisner talked about the potential for growth through syndicated television, video, and cable. It was a vintage Eisner presentation — casual, with nothing but handwritten notes and a green felt-tipped marker.

Bass had some other items on the agenda, focusing on areas that were not Eisner and Wells's strong suit. He believed that the price for admission at the theme parks was a joke. And Disney's hotel business was a mess. Bass's chief financial officer, Al Checchi, had paid a visit to Orlando and concluded that Disney was sitting on its hands while the community around it was booming. Disney hadn't built a new hotel in more than ten years while others were growing them like weeds outside the Disney gates. And the prices for rooms in Disney's existing hotels were too low. Eisner and Wells agreed that future visitors would have to shell out more money to enjoy the Disney experience.

When the meeting broke for lunch, Sid Bass told a surprised Jacobs that he might not sell after all. Then he huddled briefly with his own men, including Rainwater and Checchi. When the group reconvened, Bass gave the word. "We're not selling," he said. "We're with you for the next five years." Bass quickly cut out Jacobs and continued to acquire Disney stock. In short order, the Bass stake was up past 24 percent.

Bass was a born-again owner. And with nearly a quarter of the company in his pocket, he could give Eisner and Wells all the power they needed as they attempted to breathe life into the comatose giant. In return, they would make the Disney purchase the single most lucrative deal of his life.

12

A RAVENOUS RAT?

SECRETARY WHO started working at Disney in the mid-eighties remembers attending an orientation class for new employees. Seated nearby was a craggy gentleman who introduced himself simply as "Frank." "Poor old guy," she thought. Starting a new job at his age seemed rough. Later, she found out that the poor old guy was the new president and chief operating officer of the company.

In many ways, the Disney headquarters in Burbank could have been a rather dull attraction at one of its theme parks: the land that time forgot. The company's forty-four-acre plot had at its center a cluster of low, unpretentious buildings surrounded by gardens and hedges. Mickey Mouse peered from mailboxes and signs on buildings. Tom Hanks, who had eaten at the commissary while making *Splash*, said the place was like "a Greyhound bus station in the fifties." There was also a moldering backlot with ersatz shopfronts and city streets. The set used for the *Zorro* television series still stood even though the show had been out of production for nearly thirty years.

The animation building looked like a hospital. According to legend, that had been deliberate. At the time of its construction, Walt was working on *Fantasia*. Concerned that the studio might go bust, the banks demanded that the buildings be designed so that they could be put to another use if the need arose. So Walt put in wide, linoleum-floored corridors and offices arranged on wardlike wings.

Disney didn't go bust, of course, but by 1984 the studio was all but off the map. Its distribution system was so creaky that the company had trouble getting *Splash* booked into decent theaters. Disney was no longer even counted among the majors. Ron Miller had tried to resuscitate animation with the expensive *Black Cauldron*, but the film was a failure. And the theme parks, which generated 70 percent of the company's profit, were faltering. The costly Epcot center in Florida wasn't drawing as well as Disney had hoped. Attendance at Disneyland in California had fallen from a peak of 11.5 million in 1980 to less than 9.5 million in 1984. Some blamed the Olympics, which had been held in Los Angeles that year. But Eisner acknowledged that his own kids favored Knotts Berry Farm—an attraction close by Disneyland that offered more exciting rides. Disney was losing its allure. All the arteries were clogged and the company was saddled with nearly a billion dollars of debt.

The old regime had spent heavily on the Disney Channel but the fledgling operation was not yet in the black. There was a network television department but it was producing no network programming. Disney had stopped making its regular Sunday-night *Wonderful World of Disney*—an hour that promoted the brand name and theme parks—a couple of years earlier to avoid competing with its new cable service. This was the kind of self-defeating blunder that Eisner would never have made. To him, any positive exposure of the Disney brand was a plus.

As soon as they arrived, Eisner and Wells addressed the troops from a gazebo built for the expensive 1983 flop *Something Wicked This Way Comes*. "There was a great sense of apprehension," says Dick Cook, who started as a theme-park-ride operator but had risen to vice-president of distribution. "Everyone was freaked out." But Eisner and Wells spoke in a seemingly extemporaneous manner. "They were a little awkward, so it wasn't too polished," Cook says. That soothed their audience—as did their obvious joy at finally having arrived. Their listeners walked away with a sense of relief. That wouldn't last long.

It was clear that the intersection of Mickey Avenue and Dopey Drive would never be the same. The *Zorro* set was to be replaced by temporary offices for new executives. Dozens would soon arrive, many from Paramount. Among the first was Jeffrey Katzenberg, who had rejected Martin Davis's blandishments to remain at Paramount and was now installed as chairman of the Disney studio. Despite his earlier frustrations with Eisner, Katzenberg remained bonded to his boss.

Soon to follow from Paramount were Rich Frank, the television chief; Bill Mechanic, head of pay television; Bob Jacquemin, head of syndicated television; Helene Hahn, a studio lawyer; and production executive Ricardo Mestres. Leaving Paramount was such a routine phenomenon that executives at Disney called it "going through the fence."

Eisner and Wells let it be known at once that they didn't want to lose any time dealing with disgruntled Disneyland workers who were striking to protest a pay freeze and a cut in benefits imposed by the old management. Unfazed by picketers outside the Anaheim park, management ordered the hiring of new workers. By October 15, the strike was over.

Within a year, more than a thousand employees were gone from Disney. Eisner hired Jeff Rochlis, the former head of Gulf + Western's Sega game unit, as an executive in the film division. He became a hatchet man for the whole company, known on the lot as the Terminator. Rochlis had plenty of firing to do. He was stunned to find an employee on the payroll as Walt's personal photographer even though Walt had been dead for almost twenty years.

New management also winnowed out projects it didn't want and Disney took a $166 million write-down. (That figure also included the costs incurred during the takeover fight as well as settlements for Ron Miller and Ray Watson.) Eisner didn't want to look bad because of the last regime's loser pictures.

But he needed new product to fill Disney's rusty pipelines, and not just movie ideas. Eisner wanted Saturday-morning programming with new characters — new ideas for toys and theme-park rides. "The days when Hanna-Barbera had 90 percent of Saturday-morning television will soon be over," Eisner declared, referring to the studio that was home to the Flintstones, Yogi Bear, and the Jetsons. And he wanted television animation to be done a lot more cheaply than traditional Disney animation.

About a month after he started, Eisner arranged for George Lucas to tour the company's "Imagineering" facility at Glendale, where theme-park rides were developed and designed. Eisner encouraged Lucas to create some new rides. The ill-fated Ron Miller had approached Lucas a couple of years earlier hoping to get him to work on a flight-simulator ride, but Lucas had passed. Lucas was more responsive to his old friend Eisner, who had stepped up on the *Raiders* deal. Now he immediately glommed onto the flight-simulator idea and began to work on the Star Tours ride.

Soon after Lucas made the rounds, Katzenberg took Michael Jackson around the facility and started discussing an attraction with the pop star, who was hot off the newly released *Thriller* album. Jackson went to work on *Captain EO*, a seventeen-minute film packed with effects. George Lucas would act as executive producer and he persuaded Disney to let Francis Coppola direct. (In the wake of *One from the Heart*, an expensive fiasco, the *Godfather* director had suffered a serious blow to his reputation.)

And Eisner and Wells soon heard presentations about another idea that had been brewing for years: building a theme park in Europe. The year before they arrived at Disney, construction had been completed on Tokyo Disney and now the company had begun to search for a site in Europe. Eisner and Wells decided to go forward with the Europe project, but they were determined that this time — unlike the situation in Tokyo — Disney would be the primary owner.

There were more efforts to invigorate the existing parks. The old regime had refused even to advertise. When the outgoing management was still on its last legs, theme-park chief Dick Nunis had tested the effect of advertising and found that the impact on admissions was demonstrable. Nunis and marketing executive Jack Lindquist wanted to do a television campaign promoting Disney World and proposed a promotional car giveaway. New management quickly embraced these ideas and amazed Nunis by offering to do more.

But there was one simple and key component to the Eisner-Wells strategy. The old guard had stubbornly resisted raising the cost of admission to the parks, concerned that higher prices would alienate the public. But even in the first meeting with Eisner and Wells, Bass had offered his opinion that ticket prices were "absurd." Just raising the fee by a dollar would bring about $30 million more into the company's coffers each year. Eisner and Wells concurred that prices should go up but worried about moving too fast. After some study, Wells proposed a dollar increase. Al Checchi, the Bass chief financial officer who had been dispatched to consult with (and keep an eye on) the new regime, lobbied vigorously for a stiffer $5 hike. Concerned about a backlash, Eisner decided against such an abrupt increase. The price would go up by $5, but in increments. The full increase would be in place within fifteen months at Orlando and two years at Disneyland — and the impact on Disney's bottom line would be dramatic.

❧

WHEN EISNER AND Wells arrived at Disney, perhaps the biggest financial morass at the company was Walt Disney Imagineering, the shop where the theme-park attractions were developed. The unit was always over budget, remembers Pete Clark, an executive in charge of Disney's corporate partnerships who worked at the company from 1957 to 1995. "Walt spoiled 'em badly," Clark says. "He was their hero. They would always overspend on things that only they would appreciate, like copper downspouts in Epcot."

"We were always the misunderstood child of the organization because [Imagineering] was pampered and protected and there were a lot of people who weren't part of it and didn't like the idea," says Pat Scanlon, who spent eighteen years in the unit and rose to senior vice-president.

According to former Imagineering executives, the upside was that the Disney parks were built to exacting standards. The downside was the cost. But several Imagineers argue that the unit was always in an awkward position because it never got credit for revenues generated by the rides it created. "The parks make money and hate Imagineering because it's expensive, when they should be paying Imagineering," one such executive says. Scanlon says facetiously, "We were a cost center. The guys who ran the cash registers at the parks—they were the income generators."

"It's been a battle since the beginning of time," says Dave Fink, a longtime Imagineer who was head of the research-and-development division.

At first, Eisner and Wells did not fully tackle Imagineering. It was unfamiliar turf—eccentric and insular. "The part of the organization in the best shape was the theme-park side," says Scanlon. "It was profitable. The movie business was in a shambles and the television business was nonexistent." Though most managers from other parts of the company were replaced within a year after Eisner and Wells took over, Imagineering remained virtually intact.

But Eisner was clearly eager to make his mark on the parks. "Michael was like a kid in a candy store," says Scanlon. "You could see he was itching to do one of his own projects." Soon he "was ordering new projects like they were new movies," says another executive who worked in the unit. There was a studio-based attraction that would become the Disney-MGM tour, Pleasure Island, and Splash Mountain. Eisner also moved forward with Typhoon Lagoon and the big one, Euro Disney. All of these projects would be profoundly troubled. "It was too much to do at once," says another former Imagineering executive. "That was Michael—push, push, push."

Scanlon says several Imagineers were happy that the unit would be reinvigorated after a frustrating lull under the old management. (In the wake of major cost overruns at Epcot, the unit shrank from more than 2,500 to about 500.) But he says the company got into trouble by attempting to build attractions using a voguish concept called "design-build." The idea—which

predated Eisner and Wells—was to save time and money by bringing contractors into the design process. Disney would have to produce fewer drawings and employ fewer people. Scanlon says such an approach works when
projects are built according to a standard pattern—like warehouses—but it
creates problems when each design is unique, as was the case with Disney.

"The construction world bought it hook, line, and sinker," Scanlon says.
"They saw it all as warehouses with a facade and then you'd dump in the
ride or show and you're done. These people underestimated the complexity
. . . in their excitement to do a Disney project." And Disney, in its eagerness
to save money, failed to realize that the results would not be up to its
standards and would require expensive second and third efforts. "You ended
up giving up a level of control that you weren't prepared to give up," Scanlon says. "You can't do unique, one-of-a-kind projects on a fast-track design-
build basis. Too bad it took so much hemorrhaging to realize it."

In 1985, Disney spent almost twice as much improving its theme parks
(more than $280 million) as it had the year before. And even though the
price of admission had been raised, crowds were swelling. In 1986, even
before Star Tours opened, theme-park profits were $548 million—nearly
triple the take in 1983.

But with new management lacking experience in this type of business,
Eisner and Wells would soon learn painfully that Imagineering could be a
black cauldron into which untold sums could vanish.

∞

AS WOULD HAPPEN so often when the new administration tackled
new theme-park attractions, Star Tours and *Captain EO* went substantially
over budget. Set to open in November 1986, Star Tours was beset with
problems and soon exceeded its projected $30 million cost. Disney had to
undertake unanticipated structural renovations to accommodate the ride,
which started out at a nausea-inducing twenty minutes and was reduced to
three minutes and then taken back up to four minutes so it wouldn't seem
too short. It didn't open until January 1987, having missed the profitable
holiday season. The budget for *Captain EO*, initially set at $11 million, rose
to $17 million.

In *Captain EO's* case, several executives on the Imagineering team were
hostile to the presence of outsiders from the start, says writer-producer Rusty
Lemorande. "Eisner's first take was they were these genuises," Lemorande
says. The mandate was to use them as much as possible. But when the

filmmakers tried to get Imagineering to perform tasks like set construction, the division stuck to the high hourly rate it routinely charged outsiders who hired the Imagineers as consultants.

Katzenberg, who was overseeing the making of the *Captain EO* film, tried to get the division to charge a lower rate but couldn't, so such jobs were routed to contractors instead. To Lemorande, it was clear that the Imagineering team could not understand why Lucas and his crew had been brought in to do theme-park work at all: "The attitude was, 'Just give us a movie and we'll know what to do with it.'" But *EO* was supposed to be a wild, three-dimensional show with fiber-optic illusions, lasers shooting across the theater, and smoke effects—a radical departure from the old Magic Journeys Theater that had occupied the same space.

The producers hired renowned designer John Napier, who had just had a stunning success with the musical *Cats*. He built an enchanting miniature theater in scale to demonstrate the effects that would be in the show. Most of the project was supervised by Katzenberg, but Eisner came to view the work in progress. Just as Eisner leaned down to peer into the miniature theater, Napier drew on a cigarette and blew in a puff of smoke to simulate the foggy, magical mood that the finished piece was intended to have.

"It was a fairyland in there," Lemorande remembers. "Eisner lifted his head. He had this glow, like a child. He said, 'Whatever you need, it's done.' . . . When he saw that theater was going to be like no other theater on the planet, he knew it was worth it." When Napier wanted to lift the ceiling in the existing theater to eliminate an interfering beam, Eisner approved the additional expense. He knew that this was one of his first creative moves at a Disney theme park, and it had to be good.

Nonetheless, *Captain EO* was nearly a disaster. Coppola's footage proved to be completely out of sync with Jackson's throbbing rock performance and lacked the energy of a high-speed space chase. (Meanwhile, Coppola had moved on to directing *Peggy Sue Got Married* and Lucas was mired in making the megaflop *Howard the Duck*.) Lucas hid the *EO* footage from Disney and made his associates take a vow of silence: no one was to breathe a syllable about the extent of the problem. And it was huge. The piece lacked structure and story line—a whole new dance number had to be added. Lemorande and Jackson labored to salvage the project with extensive recutting and reshooting. At one point they had to use a spray-painted ball cock from a toilet as a stand-in for the head of a puppet, Minor Domo. The original had vanished and they were out of money.

Though Disney had hoped to use Imagineering for special-effects work, Lucas got his own shop—Industrial Light and Magic—to fix the film. ILM rushed through the job. Lemorande told Katzenberg that the work was delayed because of Lucas's perfectionism. By the time Disney executives saw the footage, he says, "they loved it."

When *Captain EO* opened in September 1986, its premiere attracted Jack Nicholson, Jane Fonda, Whoopi Goldberg, and Debra Winger. Clearly, Disney was hipper than it had been in years. Only one major person was missing. Michael Jackson, miffed that his trademark crotch-grabbing shots had been cut (they were considered inappropriate for a Disney attraction), was a no-show. Eisner, however, didn't want to disappoint the crowd. The eccentric pop star was present, he told the audience. It was just a matter of penetrating his disguise for the evening.

Star Tours also instantly attracted huge lines when it opened a few months later, in January 1987. Lucas had gotten Disney off to a tremendous start. As it turned out, Frank Wells and Disney attorney Robin Russell had signed him to a killer deal. Lucas had given Disney the rights to his *Star Wars* and *Indiana Jones* characters in perpetuity for $1 million a year. At the time the theme parks had no characters other than Disney's. Lucas wanted a permanent home for his creations. But as it became clear that Disney had made a tremendous bargain for itself, Lucas began to feel resentful. "There was quite a bit of bad feeling that is still there today," says a source familiar with Lucas's thinking. "I think George still feels that Frank Wells and Michael Eisner took advantage of him."

∽

AL CHECCHI WAS the Bass brothers' man on campus. A Harvard business school graduate and former treasurer for Marriott Corp., Checchi was there to ease whatever residual anxiety the Basses had about Eisner and Wells as businessmen in general or as hotel operators in particular. He later acknowledged that Eisner may not have been happy to see him at first, but Eisner could hardly be inhospitable to a Bass emissary. Eventually, the two men formed a bond—helped by the fact that Checchi's ultimate ambitions clearly lay outside of Disney. But a top-level insider says Checchi never got close to Wells. "Al thought Frank was not up to the job," this observer says. "And at [the beginning], he probably wasn't. But as the team molded, he became an important cog."

Checchi soon introduced Eisner to his mentor, Gary Wilson, who was

Marriott's highly remunerated chief financial officer. Wilson was a Wharton-educated executive whose expertise was in the hotel business. Eisner was impressed with Wilson and gave him a deal that made him the best-paid chief financial officer in U.S. history. Unlike Checchi's, Wilson's ambitions could easily have included running Disney—and he acknowledged as much when he met with Eisner and Wells. At the time Wells said he intended to leave after five years to make another attempt on Everest. If all went well, it was implied that Wilson could step into Wells's position. Among his first duties, Wilson went to Europe to scout locations for a new theme park and the hotels that would surround it.

Checchi spearheaded another prong in the Eisner-Wells thrust: hotels. Disney had thousands of acres awaiting development in Florida. When Eisner and Wells had first met with the Basses, Checchi explained that Disney had to develop its real estate, adding hotel rooms that would be profitable themselves and would also feed tourists to the Orlando park. Checchi introduced Eisner and Wells to his old boss, Bill Marriott. Checchi's plan was for a partnership in which Marriott would build more than a dozen hotels with almost twenty thousand rooms. This decision eventually brought a $1.5 billion lawsuit from the Tischman Corp., which had a signed deal with Ray Watson granting it exclusive rights to build hotels on the Orlando property.

The Marriott deal collapsed when Eisner began to suspect that it was too generous to his prospective partner. Why shouldn't Disney build its own more imaginative hotels instead of letting Marriott keep the money? Eisner tested his theory by demanding that Marriott sweeten the deal by committing to build a $70 million pavilion at Epcot. "When they agreed so quickly, I knew it must have been a great deal for them," Eisner said later. That was enough for him.

Eisner and Wells dumped the deal and started building—with the plans that had been developed with Marriott. Tischman got to construct two hotels. Eisner, fascinated by architecture, stipulated that Disney would control the design. The commission went to postmodern architect Michael Graves, who came up with two fanciful plans: the 1,509-room Dolphin and the 758-room Swan, each topped with large renderings of the animals for which they were named.

Tischman was not the only company that had to fight to hang on with the new regime. Walt Disney had pioneered corporate sponsorships, getting companies to kick in funds toward the construction of Disneyland in exchange for the right to advertise themselves or shop their wares on the premises. Such deals were throwing off almost $100 million a year by the time Eisner and Wells arrived. Pete Clark, the executive who was responsible for negotiating these arrangements, said Wells was amazed that such deals existed: "He called Michael and said, 'Do you know that companies pay us to be part of the parks?'"

But Wells caught on fast and quickly decided that there was still plenty of juice in those lemons. Wells squeezed; for example, he got Kodak to ante up for *Captain EO* and for theater renovation at the parks. In a twist on corporate sponsorships, Disney came up with corporate partnerships; for example, in exchange for putting in money for *Captain EO*, Kodak's contract to run an exhibition at Epcot was extended and Disney agreed to consider using Kodak's new line of copiers.

Disney wasn't bashful about breaking up with some of its old friends. At Gary Wilson's prodding, a long-standing deal with Eastern Airlines ended when the struggling carrier couldn't meet Disney's demands for richer terms. Delta was promptly ushered in, paying $40 million over ten years and agreeing to shell out for future projects. That was good enough to make Delta the official airline of Disney World. By 1985, Disney was getting $193 million from its various corporate partners—about twice as much as the company had been getting before Eisner and Wells arrived.

From the start, Eisner and Wells were thrilled to find dozens of opportunities waiting to be exploited all over Disney. Hundreds of Mickey Mouse cartoons were in Disney's vaults and had never been syndicated to television. Eisner and Wells couldn't wait to release Disney's animated classic feature films on video, starting with *Pinocchio*. At the time no one suspected the vast potential of that market—especially for animated films that children would watch again and again. Rich Frank pushed for pricing the videos low enough so that they could be bought by consumers (rather than selling more expensive copies in limited numbers to video stores for rentals). Video would become a staggering source of revenue for the new regime.

Disney was like a deep mine whose mother lode was still untouched. "You could finance a new Disney World by the unused value of our film and television library," Eisner chortled to the *New York Times* soon after he arrived at the company. "Such a bounty has fallen into my lap. Every day a new asset falls out of the sky. The real estate is just the gravy. There are 40 unused acres next to Disneyland planted in strawberries."

Wells was similarly incredulous. "I can't believe it," he marveled to

Disney Channel chief Jim Jimirro. "Every time I open a door at this company, there's money behind it."

There were so many opportunities at Disney that Wells felt he could never tire of exploiting them. "No one should be this lucky," he said. "My only wish is that I was thirty instead of fifty-three, not for any other reason than that it would be fun to keep doing this for the rest of my life."

∞

EISNER AND WELLS may have been smiling, but over in MCA's famous black tower, Sid Sheinberg wasn't happy. It was July 1985 and Michael Eisner had just announced plans to build the Disney-MGM studio tour in Orlando. Sheinberg, the outspoken and cranky president of MCA, was getting angrier by the hour. Since 1981, MCA—owner of the prototypical Universal Studios Tour—had been developing plans for a working studio that would double as a tourist attraction in Orlando. But MCA had been slow off the mark. The company wanted a partner to help defray the expense, expected to exceed $200 million. Unfortunately, the quest had not gone well. Florida governor Bob Graham had asked the state legislature to support the project with a loan, but the proposal had died. Its demise was hastened by a Tallahassee lobbyist named Bernie Parrish, who denied that he was then working for Disney but nonetheless pressured one of the governor's aides to consider whether he shouldn't be considering Disney's interests in the matter.

Now, in 1985, Michael Eisner and Governor Graham stood together as Disney announced its own working studio and tourist attraction. Sheinberg felt that the resemblance to MCA's plan was too close to be coincidental. "Disney's ability to decimate you by acting in a predatory way is chilling," he said in a memorable interview with the *Orlando Sentinel*. "Do you really want a little mouse to become one large, ravenous rat?"

Sheinberg's anger stemmed partly from an incident a few years earlier, when MCA had turned to Paramount as a possible partner to help finance its studio tour in Florida. "MCA had a relationship with Paramount that was unique in business," Sheinberg says. It dated back to a bond between MCA chairman Lew Wasserman and Charlie Bluhdorn. Wasserman was Hollywood's powerful elder statesman, the "godfather" who mediated many aspects of Hollywood life, from negotiations with the unions to relationships with Washington. (After all, Wasserman was a former agent whose star client, Ronald Reagan, had done rather well in politics.)

"Bluhdorn loved Wasserman and respected him—worshiped him, literally," Sheinberg says. During Bluhdorn's day, Sheinberg saw himself and Barry Diller as "custodians of the relationship" between their bosses. Earlier, MCA and Paramount had joined to create the USA Network. So when MCA wanted a partner in the planned Florida theme park, Wasserman naturally turned to Bluhdorn. After a major presentation, Paramount passed. "But we had shared with them all kinds of information," Sheinberg says.

Then Eisner and Wells went to Disney. "Those guys have a hard road cut out for them," Wasserman told Sheinberg. "These are friends of ours. You ought to call them up." Wasserman suggested that something mutually beneficial could emerge. Sheinberg called and told Disney that MCA would love to be "helpful."

There was no response. Wasserman went back to Sheinberg. "Did you make the call?" he asked.

"Yes."

"Make it again."

Sheinberg tried again but Disney refused to meet. Wells told Sheinberg he didn't want to have any discussions because the talks might cover certain ideas that Disney wanted to pursue on its own.

Then came word that Disney was planning its own studio tour in Florida. Now it was clear which ideas Disney had been reluctant to discuss. To this day, Sheinberg insists he knows where Disney got those ideas in the first place. "Michael Eisner had been exposed to a lot of very confidential information and knew a lot about what our plans were," he says. "And Frank Wells was a friend of ours. What happens in life so often is you end up feeling foolish. And when they spit on you, you feel angry at them. Maybe we should be angry at ourselves."

Sheinberg called Eisner and Wells to protest. There were some discussions about Disney paying MCA a royalty to use the Universal name and film properties on its tour. After all, Disney didn't have a library full of films that would appeal to adults, and MCA could provide them. But the parties couldn't come to terms. "How we would be compensated was nearly impossible to define," Sheinberg says. "More importantly, their perception was that they were going to run it. . . . We didn't want to be a little adjunct off to the side getting what amounted to a royalty of some sort."

Sheinberg considered suing but concluded that it would be hard to win. Still, he remains convinced that Disney's attraction was "a rip-off of a concept that we worked hard to develop." Disney may have been in Orlando first, he concedes, but "they sure as hell weren't in the studio-based theme-park business."

Eisner argued that it was MCA who invaded Disney's "home turf" in Orlando. And he denied attending meetings in which MCA's plans were discussed while he was at Paramount. Sheinberg scoffs at that. "Basically, he's a liar," Sheinberg says.

In some ways, MCA had only itself to blame. The company was slow to launch its own project. And even if Eisner had made secret microfilms of MCA's plans while he was still at Paramount, any competitor could have cribbed the idea of a studio tour from the existing attraction at Universal City. But another MCA theme-park executive says Disney's plans were so close to MCA's that MCA had to redesign its own attraction. Sheinberg sees this episode, and some that followed, as evidence that Hollywood had changed. In the old days, people respected relationships. In the old days, people who were tempted to screw their competitors worried about facing them across the table when the moguls gathered for meetings of the Motion Picture Association of America.

"We were the last knights," he says wistfully. "We were trying to behave by a code of chivalry that I guess may have been out of date."

MCA retaliated in 1987 when Disney made a deal to build an attraction on a forty-acre site in Burbank. MCA filed suits against the city and sent out anonymous anti-Disney pamphlets to local residents. Eventually, Disney decided the project would cost too much and dropped it.

Meanwhile, Disney had found another supplier to provide a library of films to launch its Florida attraction. MGM, which owned such classics as *Gone With the Wind* and *Singin' in the Rain*, had fallen on hard times. For a ridiculously low price, Disney made a deal to use the studio's famous name as well as its library (for example, parts of *The Wizard of Oz* and *Singin' in the Rain* were used in the Great Movie Ride). That wasn't all. Disney got the right to use MGM's renowned Leo the Lion logo. MGM owner Kirk Kerkorian was furious when he found out that the studio had signed away the use of one of the world's most recognized trademarks. And when he heard the price, he was apoplectic.

When MGM executives tried to back out of the deal, Wells told them to forget it. Finally MGM sued, arguing that Disney had not disclosed exactly how it intended to use the logo. MGM lost the case in 1992.

Eisner also got permission from other studios to use images from their films. In this effort, he drove his employees to distraction by constantly

changing his mind about what he wanted to use. As soon as one deal was
done, says a former Disney attorney, Eisner began pursuing something else
instead. "And he never wanted to pay for [the rights]," this staffer continues.
"You would be amazed at the prices we got. Michael was very good at it.
He'd send his minions out there and we'd beg. We'd buy people off with
silver passes at the park. We got images of John Wayne and we never paid
any money to the Wayne family. We'd give 'em silver passes and fly 'em to
the opening."

Eisner did his best to open the Disney-MGM Tour before MCA got its
show off the ground. He pulled off a dazzling, heavily promoted kickoff on
May 1, 1989. MCA didn't open its gates until June 1990. While the MCA
tour would ultimately prove successful, the first day was filled with glitches.
And Disney did what it could to distract from MCA's attraction by hosting
a world premiere of Warren Beatty's *Dick Tracy*, costarring Madonna, on
its own Pleasure Island attraction just two days after MCA's opening. MCA
made its own silent comment: A boat ride that featured an attack from the
famous *Jaws* shark left the water bloodied, littered with severed limbs — and
a set of mouse ears.

IN 1987, MCA became the subject of intense takeover speculation. A
few weeks after watching Disney announce its Florida studio tour in May,
Lew Wasserman, then seventy-four, underwent surgery on his colon. For
three weeks, he lingered in the hospital. Rumors that he had died ripped
regularly through the industry. The morbid joke in the industry held that
when Wasserman's fever rose, the stock went up, too. The company he had
helped build since 1936 was underperforming and undervalued. The stock
jumped due to speculation that the company would be sold once Wasserman died. There were any number of rumored buyers — including Disney.
But Disney emphatically denied that it would acquire MCA.

Even as Disney was publicly denying its interest, Eisner was scribbling
a handwritten note suggesting that he and Sheinberg meet at the beach to
discuss a merger. It could have made sense. MCA had some things that
Disney lacked: a library of live-action films, a successful television operation,
a record company. The theme-park businesses could have been complementary. "Other than personalities, [a merger] would have been a damn
good idea," Sheinberg says.

When the two met, Eisner proposed that he would remain chairman of any combined company while Sheinberg could be chief operating officer. That raised the question of what role Frank Wells would play. Eisner brushed the question aside; Wells wouldn't be a problem, he said. But Wasserman wasn't ready to sell.

Sheinberg was shocked by Eisner's apparent disloyalty to Wells — although it can never be known whether Eisner would have followed through and kept Sheinberg as the number-two man. Sheinberg says he had already concluded that Eisner was not to be trusted. "I've never been surprised that Michael Eisner's been successful," Sheinberg says. "I've never questioned that he would be successful and do a good job in leading the company. But at what price?"

13

HITS AND MISSES

A S IMAGINEERING TOILED over its various theme-park projects, overages piled up virtually unchecked. The new management started to get nervous. "There were lethal letters written by
[chief financial officer] Gary Wilson to Frank Wells about Imagineering
and how stupid it was," says Dave Fink. "'Imagineering will be the
downfall of the Walt Disney Company.'" In 1987, Disney dispatched Jeff
Rochlis, then a trusted studio executive (and a known quantity to Eisner
and Katzenberg), to take control of the unit. Rochlis, who was already
known as the Terminator because he had fired so many employees elsewhere in the company, began to wield his scythe again. It seemed clear
almost immediately that the Imagineering managers had told staff to conceal the real cost estimates for ongoing projects from outsiders—including
Eisner and Wells.

Other Imagineers said there was no policy of keeping information secret.
"There would be an overall attitude—'Let's get this [attraction] open' and
probably some culture to spend money and get the thing open and deal
with money problems later," Fink says. "That may have seemed to Jeff
Rochlis like conspiracy. It wouldn't take much of a push to get someone to
spend more than they had to get a project open."

But the Imagineers believed that Rochlis's attempt to make the design
process more predictable simply imposed a crushing bureaucracy with
scores of forms to fill out. He formulated his approach in a tome called
"Achieving the Triangle of Success." It was a bomb with the rank and file,
who saw the program as unworkable in a creative setting. "He had no
appreciation for or understanding of the human component," says Pat Scanlon. "You can use an autocratic approach to exact immediate results but
you never build any esprit de corps. You never build any confidence in
people whose throats you're cutting. . . . Under the Rochlis era, if you were

going to acknowledge mistakes for the sake of creating a better tomorrow, you might be signing your own death warrant."

But the new guard at Disney perceived Imagineering as a problem that had to be solved. One former Disney executive said Imagineering was regarded at top levels of the company as "the sinkhole of the Western world." A project like Pleasure Island in Florida, a nighttime entertainment complex meant to lure young adults with discos and a roller rink, became a typical exercise. It was built and rebuilt three times before it finally worked properly, according to an Imagineering insider. It's original $30 million budget rose to about $90 million.

Pleasure Island was one of several projects — the others were the Norway Pavilion at Epcot, featuring a large wooden church and castle; Splash Mountain, a flume water ride at Disneyland; and Typhoon Lagoon, a fifty-six-acre water park at Walt Disney World in Florida — which even in-house were known as "disasters." Splash Mountain didn't function properly when first built and missed a scheduled opening that was to be tied in with a McDonald's promotional effort. Two top Imagineering executives, Rochlis and his deputy, Mickey Steinberg, had to call Wells and break the news. "It was a horrible afternoon," says a former employee. "They had to tell Frank that not only didn't the ride work, but they didn't have a clue as to when it would be open."

Rochlis's tenure in Imagineering was short and he was replaced by Mickey Steinberg, who promptly dropped most of the "Triangle of Success" approach. Meanwhile, Frank Wells commissioned a series of "black books" — analyses of each of the "disasters" — which pinned some blame for the problems on Disney's own staff. The company's lawyers were undoubtedly appalled that Wells had created written documentation of Disney's woes. Disclosure of such materials could prove extremely damaging in the event of litigation with various companies that contracted to provide services. In any event, the black books were systematically collected from the executives who had them.

The lawyers' concerns were hardly unfounded, because there were constant disputes with outside contractors. "The problem was, we would say, 'Do it this way,' " says an Imagineering veteran. "They'd say, 'Okay.' And then you'd say, 'It doesn't work.' And they'd say, 'It's your fault.' " In many cases, Disney changed design specifications and then got into disputes about paying the resulting costs. "They would start building and then make changes," this source says.

To some degree, the Imagineers' excesses were understandable and even justified. By definition, they were breaking ground all the time. And in the culture of Disney, the Imagineers had no bottom-line responsibility. Wells tried to make each business have profit-and-loss responsibility, but Imagineering got no credit for profit from the theme parks, so the model didn't work.

Under pressure to save money, Imagineering sometimes tried to control costs by ignoring pragmatic considerations that the operations side would face once the attractions were up and running. It was cheaper, for example, to build Pleasure Island with separate air-conditioning units instead of central air — even though the Imagineers knew it would have been less expensive over the lifetime of the project to go the other way. When Imagineering went over budget on the Mickey's Toontown attraction at Disneyland, the designers eliminated catwalks that would have aided park operators with routine maintenance.

But even with these attempts at control, the Imagineers simply had the ability to spend and not much could be done to rein them in. The operations executives felt that the design group in Imagineering were "artistic brats," says a former Imagineering executive, and in some ways it was true. "I've never seen an organization spend so much money doing ridiculous things in the name of art," he says. "You talk about no controls. I could go anyplace I wanted to go. You just sort of went."

Eisner was part of the problem, too, according to several Imagineering executives. "Every time he went somewhere, we got a whole new list of changes and ideas," one remembers. "The worst thing you could hear was that Michael was going to tour Pleasure Island or Splash Mountain." Eisner was aware of his own inexperience when it came to the theme parks; this observer concludes that he "had pretty weak instincts and was always second-guessing himself."

Scanlon remembers that early on, when Eisner was overseeing the creation of the Swan and Dolphin hotels in Florida, he resisted a Disney tradition of ensuring that any visitor inside the theme park should have a 360-degree view. Nothing was supposed to disrupt the fantasy world of the park. (When undertaking new construction, Disney traditionally conducted tests, floating a balloon to the height of a proposed project and then checking from the parks, whether in Anaheim or Orlando, to be sure that the balloon wasn't visible.)

The giant animal shapes on the new Disney hotels in Orlando were

visible from Walt Disney World. "You'd look behind the France Pavilion
and see this monstrous hotel behind it and it destroyed the whole illusion
that you could imagine yourself actually being in Paris," Scanlon says. The
Imagineers pointed that out when the project was still in model form. "Michael said, 'I know we're taking a risk but let's do it,' " Scanlon remembers.
"When Michael saw the result full-scale, he came back and said, 'What can
you do to hide this? Can you build a berm?' You couldn't build a berm
high enough."

This was the same Eisner who had come up with dozens of crazy ideas
at ABC. Only now he was in charge. To his credit, he learned a lesson.
"After that, he was really conscientious," Fink says. When it became clear
that the Tower of Terror attraction would be visible from the Florida studio
tour, Fink says, the project was expensively reconfigured.

THANKS IN LARGE part to frequent ticket-price hikes, cash continued
to pour in from the theme parks. But when it came to film, Eisner and
Katzenberg had to start from scratch to put their own slate together. That
required a good infusion of working capital. The old Disney board had
been against using tax shelters to finance movies, but that conservatism was
over. If there was anything Eisner was willing to share, it was risk. Paramount had hedged its bets on many pictures by teaming with outside investors; Eisner would do the same. With interest rates in the stratosphere,
bank loans were expensive. Besides, the new Disney had no track record
and no credit rating. Finding financing to build a vibrant full-fledged studio
would have been difficult. So Wells flew to New York to meet with Roland
Betts of Silver Screen Partners.

Betts knew Wells from the Warner days (Betts had financed the film
Gandhi, which Warner considered buying). Now he got in touch with
Wells to suggest a new approach to financing. The idea was to get ordinary
investors to buy shares in a package of movies. Betts had tried such a venture
and raised $83 million to fund an unsuccessful HBO venture into film-
making. Now he was hunting for a new partner at Disney. For the investors,
it was not an especially savvy deal. In effect, they provided Disney with five-
year interest-free loans in exchange for a share in the profits—but only after
everyone else was paid. If there was no profit after five years, Disney would
have to refund the investors' money. As it happened, Disney films performed
well and investors made a steady profit. But even Eisner had to acknowledge

that the investors would have made more money if they had bought Disney stock. Critics saw the Silver Screen partnerships as one of several examples of Disney using its good name and clean image to pass off lousy deals to investors.

The shares were to be sold through E. F. Hutton brokers. But Betts and his partner, Tom Bernstein, found that it wasn't easy to get the sellers worked up about offering shares in the Silver Screen partnership. "Hutton thought it was nuts," Betts says. "They said, 'Disney's not a film company.' " But Betts and Bernstein pitched Eisner and Wells as the two genuises behind whatever successes Paramount or Warner ever enjoyed. They arranged to present Eisner and Wells at a brokers' meeting at the Sheraton Yankee Clipper hotel in Fort Lauderdale. Betts instructed Eisner, Wells, and Katzenberg to speak for no more than fifteen minutes each. "Michael Eisner spoke, Frank Wells spoke," Betts remembers. "Jeffrey delivered a monologue describing each film he was even thinking about making. The brokers were like, 'I don't know about that little fucking guy. The two dull guys are okay.' "

That night there was a party, with Disney characters jollying up the crowd. Eisner and Wells worked the room, and by the time it was over, the two "dull" guys had gotten the Hutton brokers pretty excited. On May 1, 1985, the very first day that the shares went on sale, Hutton mopped up $14 million. But the next day brought bad news. Hutton had pleaded guilty to a massive check-kiting scheme and agreed to pay a $10 million fine. It was the last thing Eisner and Wells wanted to hear. Here they had splashed Mickey Mouse's precious face all over materials associated with this offering, which now associated him with admitted lawbreakers. But Disney was in too deep to back out. With sales at a virtual standstill, Eisner and Wells rallied the Hutton troops. Before the offering closed in September, Betts and Bernstein decided that the initial goal of raising $150 million was too modest. They went for $200 million and managed to raise $193 million.

The Silver Screen partnerships kept raising money: $300 million in 1987, and $400 million in 1988 (Disney got $600 million that year because some profits from that partnership were reinvested). At successive meetings of Hutton brokers, Bernstein says, "Michael would get up and say, 'I don't think you ought to invest in Silver Screen. I know last year we did great. We don't have any more good ideas. I don't know if we can do it again.' And they loved it." Wells charmed the crowd with slides from the seven-

summits expedition. "Both came across as larger-than-life and very accessible," says Bernstein. "They were a big hit in brokerland."

∽

IF ANYONE DOUBTED that the old stodgy Disney mold was smashed,
Katzenberg had reiterated that message soon after he arrived at the studio
by announcing what would be the company's first R-rated film—a comedy
with Bette Midler and Nick Nolte called *Down and Out in Beverly Hills*.
The film, based on the 1932 French farce *Boudu Saved from Drowning*, told
the story of a bum who moves in with a wealthy couple. The project had
been dropped by Universal. Every other studio wanted it, says director Paul
Mazursky, but his agents, Sam Cohn and Jeff Berg, pushed him toward
Disney. "Why there?" Mazursky asked. They explained that the film would
get extra-loving care because it would be one of the first released by the
new regime.

Down and Out was not really the first film green-lighted by the new
regime although Katzenberg wanted it to be remembered that way. The
real first picture, according to several executives who worked at the studio,
was a film called *OffBeat*, produced by Harry Ufland and a young man
named Joe Roth. *OffBeat* was going to star Robin Williams as a man who
masquerades as a cop to impress a woman. But Williams opted to make
the ill-fated *Club Paradise* instead, so Eisner and Katzenberg pushed for
Judge Reinhold, whom they knew from Paramount's *Beverly Hills Cop*.
They expected Reinhold to become a major star. But the picture wasn't
destined for greatness and Disney discreetly opened it a couple of months
after *Down and Out in Beverly Hills* made its debut in January 1986.

"[Jeffrey] didn't want to claim [*OffBeat*]," says Jane Rosenthal, part of
the executive team in those days. "So when do we say it's the beginning of
the new regime? The first successful movie." Hollywood business wasn't
covered as avidly in those days and the news media were less inclined to
cover moviemaking as a series of horse races. So *Down and Out in Beverly
Hills* was the first picture of the Eisner era—which was just as well for new
management.

For Disney, *Down and Out* was a template. The story of a neurotic,
wealthy family seduced by a drifter was not going to be a big-budget operation. Mazursky had made some modestly successful films—*An Unmarried
Woman* and *Bob & Carol & Ted & Alice*—but he wasn't so much of a

hotshot that his fees would break the bank. His proposal to cast the pricey Jack Nicholson as the rich husband was not met with enthusiasm. Instead, the studio went with Bette Midler and Richard Dreyfuss, who were not exactly A-list stars at the time. Midler, in fact, was almost untouchable coming off the 1982 bomb *Jinxed*. After Katzenberg pointed out to Midler's agent that her career was "in the fucking toilet," Midler accepted a $150,000 cut from her asking price of $750,000.

Dreyfuss, who had won an Oscar for his role in *The Goodbye Girl* in 1977, was a recovering cocaine addict whose career was in the commode right alongside Midler's. He wanted $1.2 million; he took half. Neither star got any profit participation. It was a strategy that Disney used very effectively: yesterday's stars today. If they got hot and more expensive, they could go elsewhere.

Keeping up the tradition begun at Paramount, Katzenberg was determined to keep the budget down. "Jeffrey was wonderfully ruthless on budget," says a former studio executive. "He was questioning the size of trucks carrying equipment to [some of the] shoots. Mazursky came out of that meeting and said, 'Nobody has ever talked to me that way.'"

The picture would be a $62 million hit, eclipsing *Splash*. But if the talent expected some sort of belated thank-you to make up for the company's cheapness going in, they were doomed to disappointment. "I thought a huge gift would be forthcoming," Mazursky acknowledges wistfully. "But I never got one." He also nursed some hope that the studio would reward him by backing *Enemies: A Love Story*, a tale about a Holocaust survivor with much less commercial appeal than a broad comedy. Once again, Disney didn't oblige. (Joe Roth, the producer who had made *OffBeat*, agreed to make Mazursky's film a few years later.)

Down and Out in Beverly Hills was a vulgar romp. If the Disney staffers who had held prayer meetings at the suggestiveness of *Splash* now suspected Disney was damned, all doubt must have been eliminated when Katzenberg pursued the vampy Madonna to star in the studio's next film, *Ruthless People*. In the end, Katzenberg was too much of a tightwad to cast the singer, who demanded a million-dollar fee. Instead, he signed Midler for a $600,000 encore. But the idea of hiring Madonna showed that life had changed forever at Disney. In one letter to the editor, some angry *Los Angeles Times* readers suggested that the notion of Madonna in a Disney movie was "a little like Fritz the Cat co-starring with Mickey."

Disney hired the Zucker brothers and their partner, Jim Abrahams—the team that had done *Airplane!* at Paramount—to direct. When the film was screened, executive David Hoberman laughed until he hurt. Early the next morning, he and Jerry Zucker excitedly showed the picture to Eisner and Katzenberg. Perhaps it was too early in the day for comedy, but the two greeted the film with painful silence. Zucker and Hoberman took a walk around the lot, utterly deflated. Their hopes were buoyed when the picture had a well-received test screening in Santa Barbara. In fact, *Ruthless People* would beat *Down and Out in Beverly Hills* with a $72 million gross.

Eisner was a great enthusiast but often he responded glumly to projects that would turn out to be hits. Just as Eisner hadn't much cared for *Grease* or *Flashdance* at first, he laughed only once during a preview of Arthur Hiller's *Outrageous Fortune*, a Shelley Long–Bette Midler comedy. He was silent until the film ended and then turned to Katzenberg. "Burn the negative," he said. Eisner was naturally a pessimist—and maybe he held back to drive his staff harder. But Hoberman felt that Eisner possessed a kind of "negative brilliance." If he raved about a project—as he did about Paramount's almost unreleasable *White Dog*—maybe it was time to worry.

Like so many Disney projects, *Ruthless People* ended with a successful film but a ruptured relationship. Just like Mazursky in the wake of *Down and Out in Beverly Hills*, the Zuckers were upset that the studio never showed its appreciation for their efforts. "We'll get no net profits from *Ruthless People*," Jerry Zucker said after the film was released. "We won't go on *60 Minutes* and complain that the big, bad studio didn't pay us. We signed that contract. But we didn't want to sign that contract again."

By the time *Ruthless People* opened, the new Disney was a hit—ruthless or not. Eisner, who had modestly or cautiously declared that his long-term goal was to bring Disney "into parity with our sister entertainment companies," was moving beyond parity with blinding speed. The stock that had traded below $60 per share when Eisner and Wells took over eighteen months earlier had climbed to $120. And the numbers would only get better.

∞

ONE AREA WHERE Eisner and Katzenberg were slow off the mark was television. At first, Eisner tried to apply the same principles of thrift that were working so well in the movie division. But television was different. Writer-producers wielded a lot of power. Eisner quickly passed on deals with Stephen Bochco, who was about to launch *L.A. Law*, and Jerry Perrenchio, whose Embassy Communications held the rights to *All in the Family, Maude,* and *The Jeffersons.* In both cases, Eisner thought their prices were too rich. Embassy was about to produce the lucrative *Who's the Boss?* and the company became an extremely reliable profit center for Columbia Pictures, which bought it in 1985.

Disney did make a deal with Paul Junger Witt, Tony Thomas, and Susan Harris. They brought the hit series *The Golden Girls* (Disney distributed the show but owned only a piece of it). Disney was so hungry for programming, Witt says, that he and his partners were able to cut an exceptionally favorable deal. But several years later, Disney felt the deal was simply too generous and Witt-Thomas left for Warner. Witt says the parties almost came to terms but the discussions soured when Disney wanted to lock up the contract for longer than Witt-Thomas did. This was a frequent Disney negotiating point, and it didn't ingratiate the studio with many television writers and producers.

In that first year, Eisner seemed to have forgotten whatever he had learned in his years at ABC. "Disney was a laughingstock in the television community, particularly since Michael had been so strong in television," says Dean Valentine, who spent nine years at Disney and eventually ran its television division. "Michael and Jeffrey would troop in [to network meetings] with great fanfare and make these terrible presentations."

While his top television staff brought in glossy binders to make their presentation, Eisner would unexpectedly offer his own ideas. In one meeting, a former network executive remembers, "Michael pulled some napkins out of his pocket from Arby's and he'd written down a bunch of his ideas — 'What if we do this?' It was incredible. It fundamentally didn't leave his employees anything to do."

Back at the studio, executives had other reasons to feel frustrated. "Michael believed very strongly that he could will television to happen the way he wanted it to happen — by using low-cost writers," Valentine says. Television chief Rich Frank thought the instant success of the *Golden Girls* series created a misconception in Eisner's mind. "Michael thought everything should be like that," he says. "We wouldn't go out and spend a lot of money on writers . . . and we would not be willing to [risk as much money on] a show as others would. So it discouraged people coming to us. It was very difficult."

When Disney got a show on the air, it tended to be a brief victory. Five of the company's first seven shows were instant failures. Efforts to use stars who were not in their first bloom—such as Ellen Burstyn and Alan Arkin—weren't as effective in television as they were in film. Only *The Golden Girls* and a spinoff, *Empty Nest*, stayed on the air.

Eventually, Disney loosened its purse strings considerably. Katzenberg and Frank convinced Eisner to go on a spending spree of $25 million a year for five years. That produced several deals—including one with Matt Williams, a writer who had helped create the hit sitcom *Roseanne*. Williams delivered Disney its one huge hit—*Home Improvement*. The studio began to perform better in television, with other moderately successful shows including *Ellen, Blossom, Dinosaurs*, and *Boy Meets World*. But the studio never became a juggernaut, and Eisner, after perusing the results of a ten-year study of Disney's performance, reportedly complained that the company could have made about as much money overall by investing in certificates of deposit.

Disney did revive its Sunday-night movie, though the show was a poor performer—decimated by the unstoppable *60 Minutes*. But getting the show on the air was a moral victory for Eisner. Eisner and Rich Frank cut the deal with Fred Pierce, Eisner's former boss at ABC. Frank remembers that Eisner had a bad back at the time. In the midst of one meeting, Pierce started offering advice about exercises that could help. Frank looked on with surprise as the two men stretched out on the floor for an impromptu training session.

There was a good deal of discussion about who should host the program, acting as the new voice of Disney. Should it be Cary Grant, Lowell Weicker, Walter Cronkite, Roy Disney, or Mickey Mouse? "Walter Cronkite made no sense," says Marty Katz, who ran physical production at Disney. "Cary Grant wasn't going to do it. Roy looked like Walt, but he couldn't talk."

One day Eisner returned from Orlando and called Katz into his office. "I want to show you something," he said. He showed Katz a tape that Eisner had made secretly of himself talking about the studio. "What do you think?" Eisner asked.

"It's out of focus, the lighting is horrible—it doesn't do you justice," Katz replied diplomatically. "Do you want me to do a better version?"

"Tell me what you think," Eisner persisted.

"Others do it," Katz said. "You could be brought to be as good as them."

"You think so?" Eisner replied. "What about my hair?" Eisner's hair—always troublesome—was abandoning him.

"We do this with movie stars all the time," Katz said.

"Keep pursuing other names," Eisner said at last. "I've been talking to Jane. . . . I don't want to do it but I guess I have to do it."

Eisner maintained that he took on hosting duties with great reluctance, but some studio executives had the distinct impression that he wanted to do it from the start. The taping of a test reel was to be secret, so Katz assembled a crew that included Jane Eisner as executive producer and one of his executive team as an assistant director. Jane sat in a trailer and watched as Eisner attempted take after take. She was not bashful with her criticisms. "We finally got Michael to stop moving his hands so much, to feel more relaxed," Katz says. The consensus was that Eisner could pull it off. He recruited Michael Kay, who had done political commercials for Senator Bill Bradley, on the theory that Kay knew how to make a nonprofessional look good on television. He also went on a diet, dropping about fifteen pounds.

Some were put off by Eisner's decision to step into Walt's role as host of the program. "Among a lot of Jews in my generation, there's a tremendous anti-Disney feeling," says *Star Trek* producer Harve Bennett. "How a New York Jew can say, 'I'm going to be Walt Disney incarnate' — that defines a kind of ego need." Though Bennett thought it took guts to try, he also found the exercise to be "like jerking off in public."

But others believed that Eisner saw the role as rightfully his. "Michael had dreams of being Walt Disney the Second," says one of his former colleagues. "That was what he saw for himself."

Television executive Valentine says Eisner may have expressed a wish to be the second Walt, but that wasn't exactly what he meant. "There were many things about Walt Disney that Michael wanted to replicate: his status, his creative-figurehead role," Valentine says. "But I don't think there's any room in Michael to want to be anything other than Michael. He wanted to be Michael Eisner the First — not the second of anything."

◦◦◦

IT DIDN'T TAKE Eisner long to get into serious bonus territory. In his first full year as chairman and chief executive, Disney reported a 15 percent return on shareholders' equity, almost double the previous year's performance. With his salary and bonus, Eisner cashed in that year to the tune of $2.12 million. The following year, his bonus alone was worth $2.6 million, bringing his total compensation to $3.4 million. And that wasn't counting the value of his stock options. The numbers continued to soar as the company's performance broke one record after another.

It took until 1988 to demonstrate the real magnitude of Eisner's deal. That year, he became the $40 million man—America's highest-paid corporate executive. Aside from his salary and $6.8 million bonus, he had realized $32.6 million from the company stock-options program—and he still had a paper profit of $50.5 million on his remaining options. Right behind him was Wells, who netted $32.13 million.

Eisner must have been deeply satisfied to see that his compensation put him on the best-paid list three spots ahead of Martin Davis, who cleared a paltry $16.25 million. And Barry Diller, who was still working for Rupert Murdoch at Fox, didn't make the list at all.

14

" A W H I F F O F T H E M O U S E "

T HROUGHOUT THE YEARS of Disney's astonishing resurgence, Wells was ubiquitous, yet relatively invisible to the public because he was so often in Eisner's shadow. From the beginning, he involved himself primarily in various corporate affairs while Eisner focused on the creative aspects of reinvigorating Disney's theme parks and film studio. "For Michael, I make life easier," he said in a 1991 interview with *Fortune*. "For me, he makes life more fun."

A Disney board member says Wells functioned more as Eisner's consigliere or chief of staff than as a hands-on manager running the company. And Wells frequently was involved in major negotiations across the board. He was responsible for the bargaining over executive contracts, including Katzenberg's. He attended important previews and showed up at studio retreats, exuding a bit of nostalgia for his days as a movie executive at Warner.

Employees like Pete Clark, the longtime executive who oversaw Disney's corporate partnerships, remember Wells with great affection. Clark thought Wells was an impressive emissary for the Disney company in meetings with the heads of global companies, such as Don Keough of Coca-Cola. Despite a manner that sometimes was aloof or even brusque, Wells could be a compassionate boss. Clark remembers him attending the funeral of a colleague's son. "Michael was less concerned about the staff—people, what they were doing," he says. Clark also remembers that Wells worked closely with the First AME Church in Los Angeles to set up a loan program for minority-owned businesses after the 1992 riots.

Wells was not great at setting priorities, so he had to put in exceptionally long hours. Eisner remembers that Wells was routinely so exhausted that he would doze off whenever he was required to sit still for more than a moment—in meetings, for example, or even when trying out a theme-park ride that went through a darkened structure.

Wells drove the company's general counsel, Joe Shapiro, to distraction by trying to outlawyer him. As a joke, Shapiro had a fake letterhead made up describing Wells as an "attorney-at-law" specializing in everything from patents and copyrights to personal injury and archaic forms of pleading. To his credit, Wells thought it was hilarious.

In the early days, when Paramount had complained about Disney's constant raiding of executives, Shapiro proposed a terse response stating that the company was acting within its rights. Wells drafted a four-page letter which stated, among other points, how much Eisner and Katzenberg cared for Paramount and how loath they would be to hurt the company. "Michael looked at this and said, 'We could never send this,'" remembers one executive. In several instances, this executive says, Wells would indulge in "flowery" and unlawyerlike language and "you could drive a truck through what he was trying to say."

And Wells allowed himself to get bogged down in the minutiae of running the company. Roland Betts of the Silver Screen partnership remembers that when the two men traveled to a meeting of stockbrokers, Wells's secretary delivered a duffel bag full of letters to the jet. During the flight, Wells began to dictate: "Dear Mrs. Armstrong, I'm sorry your son got sick on the roller coaster . . ."

Initially, Wells kept up his quest for exotic extracurricular adventure. In the late eighties, he teamed up with Betts and Tom Bernstein of the Silver Screen partnership to help finance the recovery of the *Whydah*, a pirate ship sailed by Black Sam Bellamy that had sunk off Cape Cod in 1717. Sometimes Wells showed up for weekend dives to explore the wreck. "We'd stay at a run-down house with a dank, disgusting basement and Frank would always volunteer to stay down there," Bernstein remembers. "Word would go out [to the crew] that Frank Wells was in town and dinner was on Frank Wells."

Eventually, Wells's appetite for more extreme experiences seemed to diminish. In the early nineties, he and his son took a trip to South America with the intention of climbing Aconcagua again. "He called me from Argentina [and] he had decided he didn't want to do it," says Clark. "I think he got down there and said, 'I don't have the passion for this.'"

In fact, chief financial officer Gary Wilson quit Disney in 1989 when he realized that Wells's plan to leave and take another run at Everest was no longer on the agenda. Having concluded that Wells would not be making way for him anytime soon, Wilson and Al Checchi pulled off a successful bid to take over Northwest Airlines. (Wilson was later moved out of the line of direct command after he was busted at an airport for possession of marijuana.)

But Wells still used his swashbuckling image to advantage at Disney. He donned scuba gear to cut the ribbon to the Living Seas exhibit at Epcot. On another occasion, he surprised an annual gathering of two thousand Disney employees on a soundstage at Burbank when he followed Tinker Bell down a two-hundred-foot wire to the stage.

Wells also remained an avid environmentalist and drove an electric car specially fitted with solar panels. Once, when he left the car at the Van Nuys airport, thoughtful Disney employees moved it inside a hangar, not realizing that it needed to be exposed to the sun to recharge itself. They pushed it back into the lot before Wells returned from his trip. When he found the car dead, he called in a troubleshooter from Disney Imagineering, and eventually contacted the manufacturer, trying to figure out what had gone wrong. Finally the staff confessed that their efforts to do Wells a favor had backfired.

As a matter of routine, Disney executives say, Wells and Eisner wandered in and out of each other's offices. "They completed each other," Clark says. And Clark is one of several executives who say Wells functioned as a governor on Eisner's engines.

"When we had a grievance list, going to Frank was like going to the Supreme Court," says Bernstein. "You felt you got a fair hearing and you got justice."

"Frank Wells was totally discreet," says a prominent industry figure who frequently quarreled with Eisner. "Whenever there would be a situation that involved Michael lying and I would confront Frank, he would say, 'Let me try and take care of this.' He was no Saint Frank [but] he was very conscious of Michael's foibles." Another former insider concurs: "He was a conscience but he never took [Eisner] on in public. It was always in that back room."

And many other observers in and out of the company believed that Wells was actually the one who kept the vaunted "Team Disney" operating as a team. Wells was one of the few people who could command Eisner's respect at all, said Don Simpson, who eventually became a producer on the Disney lot. "Frank Wells was a Rhodes scholar," Simpson said. "He was the highest of the high goyim. He represented everything Michael wanted to be."

Another critical factor was that Eisner never felt Wells's breath on his neck. Wells may have had dreams beyond his job; certainly he gave serious thought to running for governor of California, though he ultimately decided against it, possibly because it would have brought too much scrutiny to his private life. (Wells had been rumored for years to have strayed during his marriage.) But there was no ambiguity about his future at the Walt Disney Company. That issue had already been resolved before he and Eisner started working together. Wells was comfortable letting Eisner have the spotlight, and Eisner, in turn, was comfortable with Wells.

"When they were hired, Frank maybe had more status," says Betts. "From the beginning, Michael wanted the attention. He wanted to be the public figurehead. Frank said, 'Fine. I'll stay in the background.' Michael was never threatened by Frank."

This is confirmed by Eisner's recollection of his reaction when Wells agreed to take the number-two spot. As Eisner later explained, "I knew it was going to be a great partnership—not because I got to be number one, which I wanted to be, but because I was going to be with a person who was completely selfless. . . . It was kind of like a marriage where you completely trust your wife and you know that when everything else is bad, at least your wife is there." Later, he put the same feeling in different terms. "We had trust," Eisner said. "If you look at the difference between him and others, who I am not going to talk about . . . I could say anything to Frank about the way I felt." This was a rare sentiment for Eisner to express about anyone with whom he was in business.

"Frank definitely was the glue," says Pete Clark. "He was the one unselfish member of that group."

Another former executive who worked closely with Wells sees the equation a bit differently. For all his loyalty, that insider says, Wells did not necessarily perceive himself as doing Eisner's bidding. "Frank felt he could figure out a way to control Michael," he says. "Frank always felt he could pull the strings."

❧

ONE DIVISION OF Disney that particularly appreciated Wells was Imagineering. Wells was in much closer touch with the division than Eisner, who was greeted by some of the Imagineers with contempt. "When we presented [ideas] to Eisner," remembers one, "we were always shocked that this guy doesn't have a clue what was going on." One of Imagineering's top research-and-development executives boasted to staffers that he "had to walk Michael through operating his microwave oven" and claimed that Eisner once called him to find out how to load his camera. Wells seemed much more in touch and hands-on. At one budget review meeting, there was a proposal to replace an air-conditioning unit. "Frank said, 'Well, let's go take a look,' " remembers an executive. "They went and got a ladder and climbed on the roof."

Overall, says a former Imagineer, Disney often seemed split between "warring factions," with one side pushing for unbridled creativity and the other arguing for fiscal restraint. When it came to the theme parks, Eisner and Wells encapsulated this struggle. Eisner churned out ideas often without realizing the financial consequences and Wells applied the brakes. "I think Michael probably learned some pretty tough lessons waving his arms around and then realizing that people were trying to scurry around and do what he said," Scanlon remembers. "And then—where's the money for this? Michael kind of played a bit and caused some results he didn't expect."

But Scanlon says Wells often kept Eisner in line. "Michael had 100 percent confidence in Frank," he recalls. "In a certain way, Frank was Michael's keeper. Frank was the only guy who could ignore Michael or take issue on things . . . and Michael knew he was kind of flighty at times and he relied on Frank to make sure the ship steered a steady course."

Another former Imagineer shares the same impression. "Michael and Frank would walk the parks on a regular basis," he says. "Michael would say, 'I don't like the color of that bench. Change it.' . . . Frank would grab people and say, 'What did he ask you to do? Don't do that! Tell me how much that's going to cost.' . . . Michael would speak ideas out loud and people would write them down and think he meant for them to [follow through]. Frank would say, '[We] aren't doing that.' I think Michael knew this was going on. It probably made him more comfortable knowing he was going to have some base in reality. . . . With Frank Wells by his side, there was a governor there."

Sometimes, of course, Eisner's ideas worked beautifully. Someone once snapped a picture of him hitting the drop on the Splash Mountain ride. "I want every guest to have the opportunity to buy this," Eisner said. The Imagineers set up cameras that took high-resolution, Disney-quality photos of visitors on the ride (pictures were snapped every thirteen seconds). The pictures were processed and displayed for guests to buy on their way out— with enough time to censor unseemly shots (some riders mooned the camera or exposed their breasts, leading to the nickname "Flash Mountain"). The photos were wildly popular, low-cost, and extremely profitable.

The mantra inside Imagineering was to enhance the guest experience, and Eisner also pushed for bigger, faster rides. With the Typhoon Lagoon ride, remembers an Imagineering executive, "Michael wanted nine-foot waves, twelve-foot waves. We said, 'Michael—we'll drown people.' "

Wells enjoyed Imagineering's toys and liked to get reports on ski conditions in Asia in the days before the Internet was on every personal computer. And Imagineering had plenty of toys. The unit had an eccentric research-and-development division that toiled in secrecy on all manner of ideas, from the notion of developing a potato chip shaped like Mickey Mouse to figuring out how to launch a giant billboard into geosynchronous orbit with the earth. Another proposal was to project Mickey's image onto the moon—using a laser powerful enough and bright enough to do the job. A former scientist in the division says the Imagineers actually got access to secret military laser technology to see if it could do the trick. The idea was rejected as impracticable.

Getting access to military secrets wasn't especially unusual, though. Disney was the first non-NASA contractor to gain access to the agency's database. And an insider says Disney frequently made extravagant requests of other companies—asking them to develop technologies or loan machinery with no quid pro quo. "My boss would say, 'Tell them we're Disney.' [He] expected them to give us half a million dollars' worth of equipment. We just took advantage of them in any way we could. What they got in return was 'a whiff of the mouse,' " says the former employee.

"I was one of the best at that and I was always surprised at how easily I could pick up the phone and have [a company] bring over a $100,000 instrument that we had no intention of buying but just wanted to play with," acknowledges another former Imagineer. "It was Disney magic. . . . It was not that we were taking advantage of people outright. People wanted to be taken advantage of."

When the idea of beaming Mickey's image on the moon was dropped, another Imagineer proposed setting up huge mirrors in the desert that would reflect light from the sun. "They were picturing paving the Saudi desert," a former insider says incredulously. But another says the research unit was "a blue-sky think tank" that was supposed to explore seemingly far-fetched ideas.

The Imagineering researchers had a broad and rather formless mandate, from shooting (literally) for the moon to setting up computers and high-end stereo equipment in the homes of top executives. Eventually, they were also asked to come up with inexpensive attractions. Someone produced a huge magnifying glass, several feet across, that he hoisted on a forklift and used to burn holes in various objects. A favored trick was to heat a Coke can until it exploded. Visiting executives from Kodak were treated to this stunt and the employee proposed that guests at the theme parks could blow up their own Coke can, make a video of the explosion, and go home with a computer screensaver of the spectacle. Like many ideas tossed around within the division, this one never made it to the parks.

But there was also a mandate to create attractions with the broadest possible appeal. One insider says he left Disney after a colleague told him that his ideas for a particular exhibit were too sophisticated. "He said, 'Our guests are dumb as posts. They have to have the plots of [the Disney television show] *Blossom* explained to them.' I realized the best I could aspire to was creating things for an audience that was supposed to be 'dumb as posts.' . . . They really had zero respect for the guests. Guests are stupid. Guests are destructive. The only thing they liked about guests is they have pockets of money."

∽

TYPICALLY, WELLS KEPT up a hectic pace. Some years into his tenure at Disney, for example, his old climbing partner, Dick Bass, was getting married (for the third time). Rick Ridgeway, the climber who helped train Wells and cowrote the seven-summits book, decided he couldn't make the trip to Dallas for the nuptials. Late on the night before the wedding, his phone rang.

"We've got to go to Bass's wedding," Wells said.

Ridgeway protested but Wells persisted. "Meet me at the airport in six hours," he instructed. "I've got a jet lined up. We'll be back by the evening."

Wells, as usual, brought along a pile of paperwork and started plowing through it. But he also knew the plane would arrive in Dallas several hours before the reception. He had planned to drop by the Disney store (which perhaps would help explain the use of the company jet). He could do that in forty-five minutes, which left him with three or four hours to spare. He pondered what to do. Then he told Ridgeway, "We'll go see Ross."

"Ross" was Ross Perot, the irascible Texan then making a run for the presidency. He was invited to the Bass wedding, too, but Wells had never met him. As Ridgeway looked on in amazement, Wells picked up the phone and called Perot. The billionaire invited them right over and gave them a tour of his office — including a glance at his Remington originals.

"Frank was so charming and disarming," Ridgeway remembers. "He towered above Perot." Ridgeway couldn't believe Perot was devoting three hours to entertaining these drop-in visitors. He was even more surprised when Wells suddenly grabbed Perot's protruding ears and declared, "You gotta do something about your hair. With these ears sticking out like that — you're unelectable."

They moved on to the wedding. Just as the party was in full swing, Wells glanced at his watch. "Gotta go!" he told Ridgeway. By now, it was about ten P.M. "I've got to go to Disneyland and meet Michael," Wells told Ridgeway. "I need some company or I'm going to fall asleep."

The two flew back to Burbank, made the long drive to Anaheim, and pulled in at Disneyland around midnight. The park was open for another hour. Wells decided to check out various rides until Michael and Jane arrived at one A.M. The theme park was putting the finishing touches on a laser show and the work in progress had to be viewed at night. Ridgeway sat with Wells and the Eisners as they watched the demonstration. "Frank and Michael Eisner started taking the thing apart, piece by piece," Ridgeway says. "I couldn't believe the level of micromanagement." Finally they were done. Wells drove Ridgeway home; he dragged himself through his front door about twenty-four hours after he left. Wells went straight to the office. Ridgeway had been climbing with Wells before, but now, he reflected, a day in his corporate life could be pretty exhausting, too.

∽

AS EISNER AND Wells flourished at Disney, Michael Ovitz was creating his own legend in the industry. By the mid-eighties, Ovitz was no longer a guy who had to wangle a meeting with Eisner by courting his secretary with a bottle of cologne. In 1975, he and his colleague Ron Meyer, both junior television agents, had decided to leave the William Morris Agency. The two had scouted out cheap office space but they had little to go on: Meyer, a high-school dropout who had joined the marines at age seventeen, didn't have a great client list. Their biggest star was Sally Struthers, and Meyer figured he might have to pay the rent by hustling at pool—for which he was well equipped. Before they had to try their luck on their own, however, they were drawn into a group of more senior agents who had also decided to defect from William Morris. A longtime William Morris executive says Ovitz had a last-minute failure of nerve and asked to stay at the agency, but it was too late. His bosses had learned of his plans and there was no going back. Creative Artists Agency was born.

All of the founding partners had worked in television at William Morris, where they had grown increasingly restive under the controls imposed by their New York colleagues. The East Coast held on to power that lingered from the days when a single sponsor supported an entire program and the agency put the shows together. "The problem with William Morris is nobody ever died or retired," says CAA cofounder Michael Rosenfeld. "We knew these guys would live forever." (The eldest of the founding CAA partners, Rosenfeld was twelve years older than the twenty-six-year-old Ovitz when the new agency opened its doors.)

With all five of the defectors coming from television, the group naturally made one of its first stops at ABC. Eisner welcomed them with an extraordinary luncheon in the boardroom of the network's Century City offices. Later, he arranged for ABC executives to meet with Ovitz's team and ordered them not to leave until they had generated projects to do with CAA.

These gestures gave the new agency a recognition that it desperately needed. But it wasn't just generosity on Eisner's part. He was savvy enough to know that fragmented power among the agencies would increase leverage for buyers at the network. "He wanted to encourage us and show the town and probably show places like William Morris that we were being taken seriously," Rosenfeld says. "Part of his motive was to get other people antsy." Eisner also undoubtedly figured that if he was one of the first to extend a hand to a promising group, he'd get first crack at choice projects that might eventually come CAA's way.

Ovitz quickly formed other important alliances. Literary agent Mort Janklow in New York started funneling him best-selling books to package as miniseries. Gary Hendler, an attorney who had offices in CAA's building, guided several major clients—including director Sydney Pollack—toward Ovitz and CAA. "Getting into the movie business was a slow, arduous task," Rosenfeld remembers. "Ovitz decided the best way to get a client was to romance them, and their attorneys and business representatives. Ovitz was brilliant. When you met Mike Ovitz and shook hands with Mike Ovitz and talked to Mike Ovitz, you felt like you were in a fast car on the highway."

A sense of momentum developed as CAA slowly ate into the client lists of older, slower competitors—including William Morris. Ron Meyer, Ovitz's number-two man, liked to boast that CAA's team would parachute out of an airplane into a backyard to snag a client. Another one of Meyer's favorite lines was that CAA could sell anything to anybody. If he could get Barry Diller into a haberdashery, he contended, he could sell him a green suit.

Ovitz in particular was fearless. "There was nobody he wouldn't pick up the phone and call and court," says Rosenfeld. And though the stars were an important part of CAA's equation, Ovitz also had to work with the buyers who ran the studios. Here he found one of his greatest strengths. "Ovitz early on realized that courting that powerful group was something he was good at doing," Rosenfeld remembers.

Eisner remained friendly with Ovitz after he made the move to Paramount. He hired Ovitz's affable brother, Mark, as a television executive (though he subsequently put TV chief Rich Frank up to firing him). The two Michaels also socialized together, dining out or taking ski trips. Just as Eisner had refused to accept Ovitz's terms for director Ivan Reitman after his surprise hit *Meatballs*, he would resist Ovitz's deals over and over again. Eisner almost always opted for thrift, while Ovitz felt that Eisner would not reward those who had brought great profits to the studio.

But CAA, the small operation that started with card tables and wives answering the phone, grew into a juggernaut. The agency's primacy was established in 1980, when CAA snagged Robert Redford, Paul Newman, and Dustin Hoffman—a stunning hat trick. CAA became known for its lockstep discipline, its seamlessness. "We felt we had the best company in the entertainment business," says former agent Jack Rapke. "Was it a perfect place? No. Did we rock-'n'-roll? Damn right we did."

By the mid-eighties, as Eisner was performing astounding feats at Disney, Ovitz was well on his way toward establishing his image as the most powerful man in Hollywood. He created his myth by maintaining an aura of mystery and by promoting himself as virtually omniscient and omnipotent in industry affairs. The media was tantalized by his secretiveness. And the denizens of Hollywood played along; they seemed to need someone to scare them and to check the chaotic forces of the entertainment industry. Studio executives soon learned that fighting with Ovitz was costly and exhausting and many tried to accommodate him when they could. If, for instance, Ovitz wanted client Bill Murray to get a particular role in Universal's *Mad Dog and Glory*, Murray got the part. The fact that Universal preferred someone who would work for less money was beside the point.

Michael Eisner was not a man to be frightened by a Michael Ovitz. Eisner was conscious of pedigree and Ovitz's bourgeois San Fernando Valley upbringing didn't impress him. And with Eisner, business always came first. Eisner and Katzenberg modeled themselves on Paramount as it had been in the Bluhdorn days. The standard approach was to do things cheaply and to keep control. That meant resisting the growing influence of CAA and Ovitz.

Rather than cowering as many other studios did, Disney cheerfully went on the attack. Early on, remembers one former executive at the studio, Katzenberg called his staff together and declared that Disney was "at war" with CAA. No one was to return phone calls from CAA agents, make deals with CAA, or do anything to accommodate the enemy. A couple of days later, Katzenberg declared a truce. Presumably, he had made his point for the time being. But these battles would be repeated. "I did not buy into Mike's game," Katzenberg says. "I did not service his enterprise, his ego, and his ambitions at all. I made clear I was a buyer in a buyer's business and he could sell or not."

When Katzenberg fought, however, he was acting at Eisner's behest. "Michael was always candid about CAA being a business adversary," says Marty Kaplan, then a vice-president at Disney. "He thought what CAA was trying to do on behalf of its clients was a disaster. They were driving up prices. They didn't care about the health of the industry. Whatever friendship he had with Mike Ovitz didn't affect that view."

But if Eisner was candid within the company, he was not so direct with Ovitz. When there were conflicts, Ovitz called on Eisner for help. "Michael [Eisner] loved it," Katzenberg says. "He'd call me up and say, 'More. Be tougher on him.' " But somehow, Katzenberg says, he never perceived Eisner as pitting him against Ovitz to preserve his own relationship with the agent. "I always thought we had the same agenda, which shows what a naive schnook I was," he says. Ovitz also says Eisner had him convinced that Katzenberg was the one behind the problems.

The fights were frequent and the theme was often the same: Disney paid a below-market wage to a director. Then the studio would get a big hit out of the deal and the director's fee for the next project would rise accordingly. But Disney would still demand a discount. "We'd say, 'Everybody in town is offering $3 million,'" says a CAA insider. "They'd say, 'Yeah, but we were the ones who gave him his break.'" To CAA, the problem was what one agent called Disney's "feeling of entitlement." Disney saw CAA as a rapacious force bent on ruining the industry.

But Eisner made sure the relationship with CAA didn't degenerate too severely. "Michael was pretty clear that you could not just ignore Mike Ovitz," says Marty Katz, then a Disney executive. "Michael would often help in the CAA area. But don't think Michael was ever really, truly the good cop." If anybody was a good cop, it was Frank Wells. His natural counterpart at CAA was Ron Meyer, who often smoothed feathers ruffled by his intransigent partner. "Disney and CAA were sort of natural business enemies," Meyer says. "We wanted to get the very most for our clients and Disney wanted to pay the very least. Frank and I were sort of arbiters of these relationships."

So there was some friendly intercourse between Disney and CAA. Early on, Katzenberg offered a backhanded tribute to CAA during one of the agency's retreats. Katzenberg had his staff sift through the cartoon archives to stitch together a reel of clips depicting Mickey Mouse and other characters in various settings. The joke was that the reel supposedly showed that several hit films that had been big CAA packages—*Tootsie, Ghostbusters, The Natural*—were ripped off from old cartoons. Katzenberg appeared on the video, explaining the dark discovery, and his top attorney, Helene Hahn, declared that Disney was going to sue.

There were other friendly gestures. When Ovitz wanted to develop a vehicle for his martial-arts teacher, Eisner told his executives to give it a shot. No one particularly wanted to try. "Jeffrey wasn't too sure about the guy and neither was Eisner," says former Disney executive Jane Rosenthal, who found the instructor "engaging and seductive." The studio decided to let him do a scene from an upcoming movie—just as a test—with Burt Reynolds directing. "He wanted to do something from Shakespeare," Rosenthal remembers. "They just wanted to see if he could run and jump." The test never came together. Eventually, Warner took on the martial-arts teacher, and Steven Seagal became a star.

(Eisner was more helpful in launching the movie career of Arne Glimcher, an art dealer who sold to Ovitz as well as to Eisner. He allowed him to produce *The Good Mother*, a 1988 film starring Diane Keaton and a still-unknown Liam Neeson. The project, directed by Leonard Nimoy, was a box-office failure.)

Early on, Eisner and Katzenberg decided to make *The Color of Money*, a follow-up to *The Hustler*, the 1961 film starring Paul Newman as pool player Eddie Felson. Fox had made the original but Newman had fallen out with the studio when it was acquired by media magnate Rupert Murdoch, who also owned the tabloid *The Star*. After Murdoch's publication wrote about the suicide of Newman's son, the chances that Newman would reprise Eddie Felson at the studio were nonexistent. Ovitz, who represented Newman, got the studio to give up the sequel and directed it toward Disney.

Ovitz also represented director Martin Scorsese and author Walter Tevis, who had written the novels on which the films were based. Another CAA client was Newman's costar, Tom Cruise, who was coming off the very successful Don Simpson–Jerry Bruckheimer film *Top Gun*, at Paramount. Cruise was on the rise but not yet a megastar. Nonetheless, Disney had to give up back-end profits to get him and Newman. In this case, Eisner and Katzenberg were willing to make the sacrifice. They were looking to bring a little of the old Barry Diller class to their lineup. "Saying you have a Paul Newman, Marty Scorsese movie was better than saying you had Bette Midler and Richard Dreyfuss," observes Rosenthal, the executive assigned to shepherd the film.

Despite positive reviews, the picture lacked mass appeal. It grossed $52 million. At the time the company was minting money at the box office. Fifteen of its first seventeen films made money, from the modestly successful Barry Levinson film *Tin Men* to more profitable efforts like *Ruthless People* and *Outrageous Fortune*. It was an extraordinary run in a business where consistency is almost impossible to achieve. Even so, Eisner regularly reminded his troops that disaster might be just around the corner. "Don't get cocky," he told film executives at staff lunches. "It'll all come down. Stay humble."

15

WINNING UGLY

EISNER AND KATZENBERG still needed their first blockbuster. To get it, they broke their own rules again and plunged into a bidding war. Not surprisingly, CAA was in the middle. The agency was hoping to get Frank Price, then the head of Universal, to buy the rights to a French film comedy, *Trois Hommes et un Couffin*, as a vehicle for client Bill Murray. Price and Ovitz were strong allies and Ovitz was regularly shipping expensive CAA packages to Price—including several hits (*Tootsie* and *Out of Africa*) and a few dogs (*Legal Eagles*).

But producer Robert Cort, who had a deal at Disney and had just scored with *Outrageous Fortune*, wanted Disney to buy the rights. For this particular film, Eisner was willing to enter the fray. "It's a sitcom!" he exclaimed—which was high praise from him. How much more high-concept could a film get? The story was contained in the English title: *Three Men and a Baby*.

Eisner negotiated against Universal and his rival Frank Mancuso at Paramount. Even though rights for foreign films generally sold for less than $100,000, Eisner agreed to pay more than a million dollars. But key to the deal was the successful courtship of Coline Serreau, director of the French film, who had a great deal of influence over the sale. Eisner promised her a chunk of the profit plus the right to direct the American version.

Disney figured it could save money on *Three Men and a Baby* by casting three inexpensive stars—Ted Danson, Tom Selleck, and Steve Guttenberg—as the male leads. But Serreau resisted the idea of "Americanizing" the script. She simply translated her screenplay, laboring over each idiom. Disney had no intention of putting up with that. "They totally tortured her," says Rosenthal. "There was always an intent to let her go, though nobody will ever say that." She left, ostensibly for health reasons, and was replaced by Leonard Nimoy. James Orr and Jim Cruickshank were brought in to rework the script.

Though the original plan was to open the film at Christmas 1987, Disney could see that the field was getting too crowded. *Terms of Endearment* director James L. Brooks, now reunited with Barry Diller at Fox, had *Broadcast News* coming out. Orion was releasing *Throw Momma from the Train*, a comedy with Danny DeVito and Billy Crystal. Disney decided to gamble by opening *Three Men* at Thanksgiving, a time that had been considered something of a dead zone in the movie business. Katzenberg told his staff that if the picture sold more than $4 million worth of tickets on the Saturday morning after the holiday, he would dance on his conference-room table. That Monday morning, Katzenberg had something to dance about — and dance he did. *Three Men* became the blockbuster that Disney sought, racking up an astonishing $170 million in the U.S. alone. The picture had cost a paltry $11 million.

A few weeks later, Barry Levinson brought Disney its second smash, *Good Morning, Vietnam*. The picture starred Robin Williams in a manic performance as maverick army disc jockey Adrian Cronauer. Ovitz had steered Levinson toward Disney when the director wanted to make *Tin Men*, the tale of rival aluminum-siding salesmen in Baltimore that teamed Richard Dreyfuss with Danny DeVito. Released in 1987, it wasn't the kind of commercial fare that Disney favored, but Ovitz had convinced Eisner that the picture could be made for a modest price. It cost $11 million to make and grossed $25 million. The film brought Disney a modest profit and was one of the studio's few well-reviewed efforts.

Katzenberg found the script for *Good Morning, Vietnam* languishing at another studio and brought it to Disney. But Ovitz didn't want Levinson to make the film. He was concerned that Robin Williams (also a client) wasn't enough of a draw to give the movie a big opening. And he didn't think the script was magical, either. (The film would depend on Williams's improvisational style.) But Levinson's producer, Mark Johnson, believed in the project. He exhorted Levinson to make the film and sealed the deal by taking Levinson to Thailand, where the film would be shot. Levinson loved the trip and had such a good time that he was only too glad to make a movie there.

In fact, Williams was perfectly situated to become a Disney star: his career was faltering and he was willing to work comparatively cheaply ($1 million plus a percentage of the gross, as opposed to the $2 million he had

commanded before). Despite his success on television, his film career had
suffered from ill-chosen bombs like *Club Paradise*. Williams was also a
recovering addict. With stars like Dreyfuss and Williams, Disney was getting
to be known as Hollywood's answer to the Betty Ford Clinic.

Disney again defied conventional scheduling wisdom by opening the
film in wide release during January, when most studios dumped their losers.
Good Morning, Vietnam cost $14 million and became a $124 million hit.
When it became clear that the film was going to be a smash, Katzenberg
took Levinson and his producer, Mark Johnson, to dinner to celebrate. He
handed them envelopes. Both were thrilled: this was Levinson's first blockbuster and it would hardly be surprising for Disney to show its appreciation
by tossing him a huge bonus. But a peek inside the envelope showed that
Disney was not about to depart from its customary cheapness. There was a
check inside, all right, but it merely represented an advance against profits
that the studio was sure to owe anyway.

When it came time to negotiate Levinson's next deal, Ovitz sought more
money than Disney was willing to pay. The studio's counteroffer was hardly
satisfactory. "I was insulted," says Johnson. "I confronted [Katzenberg] with
it and his answer was, 'It's just business.' It was a 'this is my nature' speech."
Levinson's next film, done for United Artists, was *Rain Man* with Tom
Cruise and Dustin Hoffman. The film was not only an enormous commercial success, grossing $173 million, but Johnson was called to the po-
dium that year to accept the Oscar for Best Picture. It was an honor that
consistently eluded Disney.

∽

EISNER WAS MORE interested in the bottom line than making friends
or winning gleaming statuettes. And the studio was generating 16 percent
of the company's operating income—more than triple its contribution in
the year before new management had arrived. And it was part of a bigger
pie: in fiscal 1987, the company's operating income was $776.8 million, up
dramatically from $291 million in 1984.

"How does one present an 80 percent increase in net income and pre-
tend such an improvement is nothing special?" Eisner wondered in a folksy
December 8, 1987, letter to shareholders in the company's annual report.
He also noted that he had been tardy in writing that year's missive. "I'd like
to say that the only reason for delay in writing this letter is my difficulty in
communicating how well we have done without sounding too cocky, too

confident and certainly too proud! . . . But honestly, my delay has been caused by the numerous ice hockey games in which my 14-year-old son has played over the last two weeks in Southern California . . . plus college-interview time in four cities for my 17-year-old high school senior."

Eisner also noted that his mother—who, as he said, had probably wondered in 1955 how her son would ever earn a living—surely was proud of the company's record-breaking performance.

This would be a year remembered in part, Eisner said, because the company had signed an agreement with the French government to proceed with the development of Euro Disneyland. The park, he promised, "will be a great place to visit." He didn't mention the staggering cost overruns that Euro Disneyland had already incurred.

∽

KATZENBERG HAD ASSEMBLED an eclectic staff of executives. At first, Paramount veteran Ricardo Mestres—controlled and efficient—was the number-two man. Katzenberg filled out the team with David Hoberman, an agent from International Creative Management. A Southern California native, Hoberman had dropped out of UCLA and gotten a job in his father's office—which happened to be at ABC. When he started there as a mail boy, one of his duties was to get Barry Diller's yellow Porsche washed. Eventually, he became an agent. Mestres was one of his closest friends and helped him land a job as a vice-president of the Disney studio.

The baby-faced Hoberman was more emotional than the tidy, tightly wound Mestres—and not nearly as methodical. But he was good at wooing talent and affable enough to make Disney's toughness a little easier to take. "Ricardo's strength was story development and being to Jeffrey what Jeffrey had been to Michael: the best lieutenant," says Marty Kaplan, then a creative executive in Disney's Touchstone film division. "David was much more the guy for talent relations, out in the world, the guy who could schmooze." Together, the inside man and the outside man seemingly made a perfect match.

Katzenberg was as obsessive at Disney as he had been at Paramount. Jane Rosenthal, who joined the staff after working at Universal, thought Disney was like boot camp. She had just bought a new house, but she never had time to furnish it. "You'd go to work in the dark and come home in the dark," she recalls. Meetings were often scheduled at 6:30 A.M. and there were Sunday sessions, too. Now Robert De Niro's producing partner, Rosenthal remembers Eisner, dressed in sweats, dropping by an early Sunday session and remarking, "I'm glad it's you and not me." At one point, she says, "There was a bomb scare and Jeffrey didn't let us leave."

Katzenberg often hired newcomers to the business. For instance, Kaplan was a former White House speechwriter and deputy campaign manager for Walter Mondale's unsuccessful 1984 presidential bid. Pete McAlevey had been a *Newsweek* reporter. And there was Lou Kamer, the eighteen-year-old son of one of Hollywood's plastic surgeons to the stars. None had any experience in the movie business.

Katzenberg had blossomed from the put-upon production chief who cheerfully sat on the toilet during overcrowded flights on the compact Gulf + Western jet. Rosenthal had the impression that the relationship between Katzenberg and Eisner had become "a partnership." Kaplan concurs: "Michael gave Jeffrey lots of authority and Jeffrey used it. That didn't mean Michael stopped sticking his nose in Jeffrey's business. [But] Jeffrey ran that thing brilliantly. Michael saw it and appreciated it but was never disengaged from it." Kaplan thought the relationship was "usefully antagonistic," adding, "They were very up front about disagreements. . . . The tone was set by Jeffrey saying to Michael, 'You're full of shit,' and Michael saying to Jeffrey, 'No, you're full of shit.' It seemed healthy. I never thought that underneath there was a level of smoldering resentment. It was an ideal combative-buddy situation."

Even though he seemed to have gained more of Eisner's trust, it was never clear to what extent Katzenberg had the authority to green-light a picture. (As a practical matter, no chairman at any studio would pull the trigger on a big-budget film without winning the support of the company's chief executive.) But by 1988, as Eisner was spending more time on corporate matters and the theme parks, he expressed confidence in his studio chief. "At Paramount, Jeff brought home the bacon," Eisner told the *New York Times* magazine in February of that year. "Now he knows how to cook it." His old boss, Barry Diller, also chimed in: "Jeffrey is doing the only great job in the motion picture business today because he has defined the business for himself."

Hopped up on junk food and a few six-packs of diet Coke a day, Katzenberg networked furiously. (Katzenberg preferred diet Pepsi but switched when the Disney theme parks struck a deal with Coca-Cola.) He was developing a style, dressed in dark suits, and drove a black Mustang. He was also cultivating his own legend. In 1987, the *Wall Street Journal* described him as "the most brutal, the stingiest, most compulsive—and possibly the best—deal maker in town." Katzenberg was particularly appalled when the article illustrated the point by recounting a tale about a childhood watergun fight that ended when young Katzenberg pinned an opponent to the ground "and then squashed the other kid's hand into a pile of dog droppings." Katzenberg wanted to be seen as tough but this was going too far. He denied the story vehemently.

Katzenberg worked when he played, shepherding various members of the Hollywood establishment on annual camping trips. In August 1989, for example, he took a group that included Don Simpson and various agents from each of the top shops to the Grand Canyon. These friendly competitors spent their time in hot pursuit of Katzenberg's most special guest, Tom Cruise. "It was hysterical watching these producers and agents chasing him around," remembered one participant. "Then you had an agent from [CAA] making sure no one laid a hand on him. The poor guy could not go up in the woods and have a peaceful sit on the potty without somebody pursuing him."

At one point the raft carrying Cruise, Katzenberg, Simpson, and screenwriter Nat Mauldin flipped over as they were navigating the treacherous Lava Falls. Mauldin took in lungfuls of water and "looked like he'd seen God," said one observer. A fellow rafter said his first impulse was to find a phone. "When I saw Jeffrey flipping up in the air," he joked shortly after the mishap, "I wanted to sell my Disney stock short!"

Katzenberg had indeed positioned himself as a key man at Disney. His staff was supposed to function as a well-melded fighting machine. *Ruthless People* director Jerry Zucker wondered fancifully whether Katzenberg "was so driven because of a small sled with 'Katzenbud' written on it that was taken from him at an early age."

Under orders from Katzenberg, Mestres sent a memo to Hoberman and Rosenthal that included a list of agents. In order to help "parcel up the town," he said, each person was to mark an A or B next to the names to indicate the quality of the relationship. "We'll map out a complete strategy," Mestres wrote. "It is essential that you keep [Katzenberg's] list confidential." (It would hardly do to have the town know whom Katzenberg listed as a "B" relationship.) Each day, Katzenberg started with a list of names—from "Avildsen" to "Zucker"—and rolled through his "relationship" calls. Some days would be devoted to A-list, some to the B-list, some to "other."

In the early going, at least, Disney made a conscious effort to depart from the Paramount experience by fostering a greater degree of camaraderie and keeping the infighting to a minimum. "They were determined not to have it be the way it was at Paramount," Kaplan says. "They were very explicit." But executives were also expected to adopt the tone of outspoken challenge that Diller had demanded at Paramount. "Lou Kamer was encouraged to be Michael's equal at the table," Kaplan recalls. "That's what got you ahead." Eisner and Katzenberg held feisty staff meetings — called "gong shows" — in which people tried to run ideas up the flagpole before someone shot them down. Unpopular ideas were dismissed with a bluntness bordering on brutality. "I remember bringing up someone's name and Jeffrey barking," says Rosenthal. "You had to be really fast. If you were at all timid and didn't want to argue in a group, you weren't part of the team."

Staff meetings could be "vicious," she says, but they were also funny to those who could handle the rough humor. Once, when the studio executives had a meeting with the Imagineers, Katzenberg found himself repeatedly interrupted by the head of physical production, Marty Katz, who was correcting some detail or interjecting a point. Finally Katzenberg told the group, "In case you don't know this person, this is Marty Katz, otherwise known as my hemorrhoid." Later, Katz sent him a note: "Just remember — a hemorrhoid would be nothing without a big asshole to look up to . . ." Katzenberg returned the note with the inscription "Ain't that the truth!!!"

∽

KATZENBERG AND HIS crew had little inclination to make an expensive "event" movie. They weren't going to coddle the stars, as Warner famously did. They weren't going to give up big percentages of profit to Harrison Ford or Tom Cruise. Disney didn't develop an action franchise with expensive effects like the *Lethal Weapon* or *Batman* series. Katzenberg and his lieutenants were running a tight ship. "Jeffrey made you feel like you were working at the best studio in town," says one former executive. "Let the industry go in [a different] direction. We were not. It wasn't haughty — it was just, 'This is our point of view and it's going to work.'"

The studio had developed a "very polished system," says Katz, and succeeded while surpassing its rivals in holding films to their budgets. "It was scary," Katz says. "It was unbelievably superior to everyone else. If a filmmaker came in and wanted a certain cameraman or editor, and he thought he could demand a rate, we'd say to the filmmaker, 'If you want him, convince him to do it.' In the early days, that was okay." But it wouldn't be okay forever. The studio was building up a store of ill will that would eventually overflow.

The Disney team unleashed its ruthless impulses on agents and the talent they represented. The studio might go easy on a respected director like Martin Scorsese or Peter Weir, who directed *Dead Poets Society* for Disney, but the lesser talent recruited for the mass-appeal films had to knuckle under. "They would really intimidate the hell out of 'em," Rosenthal says. One producer remembers Katzenberg shrieking at him during a fight—just inches from his face, spraying saliva as he sputtered about some now-forgotten issue.

Every deal was negotiated to the last penny. "Within a year," Kaplan says, "Disney business affairs had the reputation of being a nightmare to deal with. I remember Michael saying, 'Every time I hear someone complain about Ricardo being a bastard in a negotiation, that means more money in Ricardo's bonus.' "

"Jeffrey once said, 'Marty, you're getting the reputation of being a real production Nazi,' " remembers Marty Katz. "I said, 'If I'm Goebbels, guess who's Hitler?' "

∽

AT FIRST, THE live-action slate absorbed most of Katzenberg's attention. But as time wore on, it became a side show, eclipsed by the original source of Disney magic.

Katzenberg's affair with animation began inauspiciously. Roy Disney and Michael Eisner were in the middle of a meeting when Roy received an urgent message. This was in the early days of the Eisner administration and the new regime was making its presence felt. *The Black Cauldron*, an animated film that had been in the works for more than ten years at a cost of nearly $40 million, had been snatched from its producer by Katzenberg, who decreed that it had to be recut. Katzenberg was right that *Black Cauldron* needed help: the animation was stunning but the picture was too dark to get a child-friendly G rating. Test audiences despised it. But producer Joe Hale protested that no one ever slapped an animated film into an editing machine and started chopping. Katzenberg refused to listen. Hale's appeal to Roy prompted Eisner to call the editing room. "What are you doing?" he asked.

"I'm trying to salvage this mess," Katzenberg replied.

Indeed, animation—Walt Disney's single greatest legacy—had become a sleeping beauty by 1984. And it wasn't something the Eisner-Katzenberg team particularly cared about. After all, their experience lay elsewhere. The chances that Katzenberg would turn out to be the man to salvage the mess seemed slim to none. But *Black Cauldron*'s problems were so apparent that neither Eisner nor Roy could really protest when Katzenberg started tampering with it. Even so, Roy chided Katzenberg to be "more sensitive." Thus began what Katzenberg later called "my sensitivity lessons from Roy."

Meanwhile, the animators were starting to panic. They had heard that Katzenberg had not only ordered the film to be put on the editing machine, but had also asked to see outtakes. In animation, there were no "outtakes," no finished sequences that had hit the cutting-room floor. Clearly, Katzenberg knew nothing about animation. The barbarian had entered the gates.

Eventually, Katzenberg had some scenes added to *Black Cauldron*, but he couldn't save the film. It was tagged with a PG rating and grossed only $21 million. It was not the kind of movie that would excite the new Disney regime by illustrating the potential value of animation. There were no *Black Cauldron* T-shirts or lunch boxes in the offing. In fact, the film wasn't even to be released on video until 1998 — almost fifteen years after Eisner and Katzenberg arrived.

After the *Black Cauldron* experience, the already nervous animation community began to buzz with rumors that Eisner and Katzenberg, eager to avoid another debacle, planned to shut down the division altogether. And the animation department was already demoralized. Things had been going downhill at Disney for years. In 1979, animator Don Bluth and a team of about sixteen others had defected, complaining that Disney quality was slipping. As Eisner arrived, nearly seventy animators were working on *Black Cauldron* but others were idle. The old administration had nothing else in production.

At first, the animators had been convinced that whoever took the helm at Disney would recognize their value. But then reality hit. "It was like, does anybody know we're here? What we're doing?" says Disney animator Ron Clements. Soon enough, they learned that they had been noticed: Katzenberg fired some of the staff and moved the rest off the studio's Burbank lot to a refurbished warehouse in nearby, unglamorous Glendale. Eisner and Katzenberg told the animators that live-action film was in so much trouble that they needed to keep a close watch on that division while animation didn't need such careful supervision. But the artists didn't buy that line. "The feeling was, they're putting us out to pasture," recalls one. In a memo, new management promised that the exile from the main Disney lot would last only a year or two. It lasted ten.

Even if Eisner and Katzenberg weren't especially interested in animation themselves, they knew that keeping the division alive was part of their mandate. Animation was close to Roy Disney's heart. In fact, as soon as Eisner took over in 1984, Roy had asked to be named head of the animation department. He had never worked in animation before, but of course Eisner said yes.

Animators weren't especially consoled by the arrival of fifty-four-year-old Roy, who was still known as Walt's feebleminded nephew. But he won some of them over when they saw that he was committed to preserving Walt's heritage. An avid sailor, he worked from an office in Burbank designed to look like a ship's interior—complete with nautical maps, timbered walls, and a compass. He had another office in Glendale. He didn't show up at either very regularly but he made his wishes clear. At his prodding, the new regime committed to release an animated film every eighteen months.

Roy stood by when Eisner and Katzenberg watched animators Ron Clements and John Musker prop up storyboards in the wide main corridor of the original animation building and pitch a project that had been in development for two years about mice living in Sherlock Holmes's apartment. "I'm not sure that Michael and Jeffrey knew what they were looking at," Roy told reporter Ron Grover in the book *The Disney Touch*. "But they said go ahead anyway." Katzenberg says the project had been around while a team of animators sat idle: "Our attitude was, we're paying them to do nothing and we might as well pay them to do something."

As animators labored over the film that would eventually be called *The Great Mouse Detective*, Eisner and Katzenberg ordered secret tests that played directly into the artists' worst fears. Television cartoons were far cheaper than animation for the big screen, so Eisner and Katzenberg wanted to know why movies were so expensive. "They said, 'How much money do you think this is going to cost?' " Clements remembers. "We said twenty-some million. They wanted it for half that. We said it would take two years. They said, 'We want it in one.' "

Eisner and Katzenberg were convinced they could beat the old Disney system. If they could get thirty minutes of television animation for $350,000 to $500,000, they wondered, why couldn't they get a movie that was less than an hour and a half long for $1.5 million? In fact, feature-length cartoons were costing far more. *The Great Mouse Detective* would have a $14 million price tag.

Obviously, Eisner and Katzenberg could see that television animation was of much poorer quality than Disney film animation. But what if television work was made twice as good? The film would still cost only $3 million. And if the quality were three times better than television, the film should cost $4.5 million. How bad could it be?

So during the making of *Great Mouse Detective*, different scenes were shipped overseas, where most of the inexpensive television work was performed, to see whether some parts of the animation process—background painting, layouts, effects—could be done on the cheap. But this was not a road Roy wanted Disney to take. He hadn't taken control of the company to see the quality of animation degraded. The experiments were dropped.

Roy says he told the animators that he wanted "to show these new guys that I'm part of the team." But Katzenberg says it wasn't in Roy's nature to get deeply involved. "He is not someone who sets out goals and goes out to achieve them," Katzenberg says. Indeed, an animator who worked on the picture says he didn't see Roy during production. Roy did, though, provide some feedback as the work moved toward completion.

"From the beginning, Roy and Jeffrey didn't get along," that animator says. "Roy is soft-spoken and Jeffrey will dominate a room. So when they set up a screening for notes, Roy would always cancel at the last minute. Then he would reschedule and give us his notes. And their [comments] were not the same, so the project was going nowhere."

In 1985, Disney hired Peter Schneider as vice-president of feature animation in part to resolve this conflict between Roy and Katzenberg. Schneider, whose background was in theater, had worked as theatrical coordinator for the Los Angeles Olympic Arts Festival in 1984. "It fundamentally [made] no difference who was hired," Schneider said years later. "They didn't care. Roy cared. But in retrospect, Jeffrey and Michael couldn't have cared less. Animation? Who cares? It wasn't making any money. As a matter of fact, it was losing money. I got lucky because they were not that picky."

A former Disney animator says that even though Schneider was recommended by Roy, he immediately and enthusiastically signed on to Katzenberg's team. "You'd hear Peter starting to use a phrase and realize it was part of Jeffrey's vocabulary," says the animator. He remembers that Roy continued to attend important screenings and offered notes on subsequent animated pictures, but that "we generally ignored them." *The Great Mouse Detective* wasn't a big hit but it managed to gross a decent $25 million.

Long before *The Great Mouse Detective* was in theaters, Eisner and Katzenberg had set up their first "gong-show meeting" with a group of animators to select projects that would follow it. "We want everybody to come up with five ideas," Eisner said. "You've got two weeks to find five really good ideas. If we don't like something, we're going to say it right away. Don't take it personally."

The first film put into motion was based on Katzenberg's own idea: an update of the Charles Dickens tale of an orphaned boy taken in by a gang of thieves. In *Oliver & Company*, the hero would be a kitten. In an attempt to add some hipness, the voices would come from Billy Joel, Bette Midler, and Cheech Marin. The songs were from Billy Joel, Barry Manilow, and the team of lyricist Howard Ashman and composer Alan Menken, who had worked on the 1986 musical version of *The Little Shop of Horrors* (a film produced by David Geffen).

As *Oliver & Company* got under way, Katzenberg still wasn't particularly enamored with animation. "It was just part of the territory," he says. "It came with the job. I didn't know anything about it." But he made waves by insisting that the animators change their old formula of developing a story by creating extensive "storyboards" outlining the plot. This was time-consuming and expensive, as animators created perhaps seventy boards, each covered with fifty or sixty individual drawings. Traditionally, the animators wrote much of the dialogue as they created the boards. Katzenberg insisted that they write a full script before they started storyboarding.

Animators, often wed to tradition, resisted vigorously. "It was revolutionary," said Glenn Keane, one of Disney's star animators. "There was a big battle." But the animators found that doing some advance script work made sense — and Katzenberg found that he had to be flexible and allow for changes as the work progressed.

Nothing went smoothly in the making of *Oliver & Company*. While Katzenberg was intent on getting the writers to come up with a script he liked, the animation team played Trivial Pursuit for weeks. As work got under way, the picture didn't really click. The animators were unhappy and Katzenberg didn't particularly like what he was seeing on the screen. The animation was rather heavy-handed; one of the animators later concluded that Katzenberg "trusted us a little too much" and didn't interfere enough.

It was quite a revolution in the perception of a man initially seen as the likely murderer of the medium.

Despite the film's shortcomings, Disney was determined to give it a big push. The previous summer, Steven Spielberg had released *An American Tail*, the saga of a Russian mouse who emigrates to the United States, under the Universal studio banner. Directed by Disney defector Don Bluth, the film pulled in $40 million at the box office. That made it the highest grossing animated film ever (not counting revenue that other pictures had generated in repeat releases). "We said, 'We've got to be able to top this,' " recalls Clements. With an expensive advertising campaign and a little pressure to get theater owners to keep the picture on the screen, *Oliver & Company* grossed $53 million.

16

TOONTOWN

B ACK WHEN MICHAEL Eisner was running Paramount, aspiring director Bob Zemeckis was chagrined to learn that Eisner thought he had no talent. True, the young filmmaker had two unsuccessful movies under his belt—*I Wanna Hold Your Hand*, about a group of teen-agers going to a Beatles concert, and *Used Cars*, a dark little comedy starring Kurt Russell. But some people—including Steven Spielberg—thought Zemeckis had tremendous promise. Eisner believed the opposite. Paramount executives passed the word to Zemeckis's agent, Jack Rapke, at CAA: Eisner had decreed that Paramount Pictures had nothing to discuss with Zemeckis.

If Eisner didn't want Zemeckis in those days, Disney did. In 1980, Ron Miller had bought a book called *Who Censored Roger Rabbit?* and studio chief Tom Wilhite asked Zemeckis to direct this tale of intrigue in a fictional Los Angeles bedroom community inhabited by cartoon characters. Disney had made up a sculpture of a proposed Roger Rabbit character with a big red nose; Pee-Wee Herman was to provide the voice. The rabbit character wasn't to Zemeckis's liking. At the time he was developing *Romancing the Stone*, but Disney wanted him to commit full-time to the rabbit project. Forced to choose, Zemeckis concluded Disney would never let him make the movie as he saw it. Roger Rabbit would have to wait for new management.

With 1984's *Romancing the Stone*, Zemeckis finally showed that he could fulfill the potential that Spielberg saw. The romantic adventure starring Michael Douglas and Kathleen Turner grossed $75 million. While other studios came calling, Zemeckis heard that Eisner thought the film was "a fluke." Over lunch at the Palm, Katzenberg told an incredulous Zemeckis that Eisner's low opinion hadn't changed and that the studio still wouldn't discuss any projects with him. "Those are the kinds of tasks Jeffrey had to do in those days—explain this inexcusable behavior," Zemeckis says.

Zemeckis followed *Romancing the Stone* with the clever and engaging *Back to the Future*, a Michael J. Fox film that became the number-one hit of 1985. At this point Eisner dashed off a note offering a self-deprecating apology. He described a college experience in which he had written a paper about the "picturesque novel" when the assignment was to write about the "picaresque" novel. Perhaps that helped explain why Eisner had been mistaken about Zemeckis—but the director took the gesture as belated and "cynical."

When Eisner and Katzenberg arrived at Disney, they concluded that the rabbit could become the first important new Disney character in years. Like *The Color of Money* or *Three Men and a Baby*, this project would require Disney to depart from its preferred way of doing business. To get the top-quality results it desired, the studio would have to pay for high-powered talent. Disney approached Spielberg about taking on the project. He agreed to produce and recruited Zemeckis to direct.

"There's a big problem," Zemeckis told Spielberg. "Michael Eisner doesn't think I can direct."

"You'll never have to speak to Michael Eisner," Spielberg promised.

Zemeckis signed on, though he expressed a wish that the project could be done at Warner. Roger was going to mingle with other "Toons" in the film and Zemeckis thought the Disney stable of characters seemed boring. On the other hand, he thought, the Warner cartoons invented by Tex Avery—Daffy Duck, Roadrunner, and Yosemite Sam—were funny. Even Spielberg didn't have the clout to get the project away from Disney, but he did manage something the old Disney regime had attempted but failed to achieve: he got permission for non-Disney characters to perform in a Disney film. He even got Warner to allow superstar Bugs Bunny to appear in an unprecedented cameo alongside Mickey Mouse.

But Eisner wasn't willing to be quarantined. Zemeckis had put in a year of preparation and was about to leave for London (where he and Spielberg had decided to make the film, in part to stay far away from Disney) when Eisner demanded a meeting. He was going to talk to Zemeckis, or he wasn't making the film. To Zemeckis's surprise, the conversation went on for hours and wasn't nearly as bad as he anticipated. He had to call his wife to say he would miss dinner. It was the first time he had ever encountered a studio executive who really wanted to know what he was doing. Eisner questioned him closely about the film's tone and even got down to some squeamish questions about the Eddie Valiant character, who was a down-on-his-luck drunk.

"How dirty will Eddie be?" Eisner asked. "Is he going to have dirty fingernails?"

"I never thought of that but I don't think so," Zemeckis replied.

The bemused Zemeckis went on his way. He had been enthusiastic, even passionate, but Eisner's anxiety still ran high.

∞

WHO FRAMED ROGER Rabbit was one of the most praiseworthy efforts of the Eisner-Katzenberg regime. Disney was doing what Disney ought to do—breaking the animation mold. The film offered a never-before-seen technique that blended animation and live action with a new realism. Instead of the flat cartoons seen in Mary Poppins more than twenty years earlier, the toons in Roger Rabbit were rounded and real. They cast shadows. They reached out and touched objects. They grabbed live actors by their lapels.

Spielberg and Disney concurred that the animation had to look great. To make it blend seamlessly with the live-action footage, the animation had to be drawn frame by frame, instead of drawing every other frame (as on other major animated features) or every sixth frame (out of twenty-four per second) as animators did for cheap television cartoons. But full animation—the old-fashioned way—meant that each minute of film took a team of about twenty animators a week to complete. And that cost money.

To develop the new blend of live action and animation, Disney brought in Richard Williams, an Oscar-winning Canadian expatriate living in London. His plan was to throw out "every rule that these stupid animators developed for working with live action." The past approach had been to lock down the live-action camera so the horizon line remained steady. That way, the animated characters were the same size in each frame. Live scenes were lit with a minimum of shadow so the contrast between live actors and the animated figures was less striking. But Williams and Zemeckis thought such techniques were for the faint of heart.

The Disney and Spielberg camps didn't agree on everything. Spielberg, for example, wanted a star like Harrison Ford or Bill Murray to play the live hero, detective Eddie Valiant, opposite Roger. Katzenberg argued that the spotlight should be on Roger; presumably, the cost of a major player factored into his thinking, too. The talented but comparatively inexpensive Bob Hoskins got the role.

Early in 1987, filming began on the live-action part of the film. The sets were built nearly ten feet off the ground so puppeteers could stand underneath, using robot arms and wires to move about guns and glasses and other props that would end up in the hands of Toons (who would be drawn in later). On the sidelines, comic Charles Fleischer read Roger Rabbit's lines while dressed in a rabbit costume. Hoskins found filming to be challenging and painful. "All kinds of wires were attached to me," he said. "I had to bounce off the walls, same as the cartoons." In the end, the role's requirement that he "see" still-invisible characters began to take its toll: he started to hallucinate.

Zemeckis moved the camera fast and furiously. The result would be more lifelike, but it also made it much harder for animators to achieve the desired effect as they adjusted the characters' size, lighting, and location to accommodate the camera's movement. This radical approach started tongues wagging in the animation community.

Zemeckis didn't really trust the Disney animators with the project. *The Black Cauldron* had been a disaster and he wasn't that impressed with *The Great Mouse Detective*. Disney allowed him to set up a temporary animation studio in a restored Edwardian factory in north London and he recruited a multinational animation army. The effort to lay in realistic-looking Toons was extremely labor-intensive: with special effects included, as many as eight thousand pieces of artwork might have to be assembled for a single thirty-second shot. From the beginning, Williams drove the Disney team crazy, starting when he took the animators out for a screening of his own work in progress, *The Thief and the Cobbler*, without first getting permission. "I'm not a corporation man," Williams acknowledged. "They do things through channels and I don't know how to do that." For him, it was astounding that Disney wanted the animators to sign in each morning.

Back in Los Angeles, word streaked through the animation community in the San Fernando Valley that Disney was undertaking a massive folly— "the *Ishtar* of animation," people were calling it. It wasn't a compliment. *Ishtar* has been eclipsed by so many other expensive losers that it has been virtually forgotten, but in the late eighties, the Warren Beatty–Dustin Hoffman film had become the emblem of Hollywood excess. It led to a situation that studios are desperate to avoid: a film better known for its price tag than its content.

For a time it seemed that the animators might be right. *Roger Rabbit* was running way over budget. If the film's cost had seemed high at its original $29.9 million, things only got worse—far worse. As the budget edged toward $40 million, Eisner became deeply concerned. Later, he said that Katzenberg hid the bad news from him. After he found out that the price tag was getting bigger, he cornered Spielberg at a Hollywood function and reproached him: "You promised me! You promised me I would never see a four!" Spielberg laughed and said, "Michael, you won't see a four." Those were the right words for the wrong reason. Eisner wouldn't see a four because the film would end up costing more than $50 million—one of the most expensive films ever made at the time and certainly the most expensive movie in Disney history.

∽

EVEN AS THE clouds gathered, Katzenberg maintained a game face. "I believe we are the only company that could and would do this," he said in an interview even while he was wrestling to get the film under control. "I don't know whether it's a hit or not. I know it's a wonderful, pioneering experiment. It is a quantum leap."

After finishing up his shooting in London, Zemeckis returned to Los Angeles to edit, leaving Williams to oversee the animators in London. But to Katzenberg, the film seemed so entirely out of control that he couldn't figure out when it would be done, much less what the final tab would be. One afternoon, Katzenberg called Zemeckis to his office. He also summoned Frank Marshall, Spielberg's producer, who was then at work on *Empire of the Sun*.

"We really have a problem," Katzenberg said. "None of the animation is getting done on time." It was four P.M. but Katzenberg told the group that they were going straight to London. Sure enough, they boarded a jet without even stopping to pack a toothbrush. But instead of going to London, the parties met in the middle. Katzenberg had awakened Williams and other key players in London and told them to jump on a plane to New York.

Before the meeting, the filmmakers had time for breakfast in a deli. No one was sure what Katzenberg would do. To Zemeckis's surprise, Williams spoke up. "I really like Jeffrey," he said.

The others looked at him in disbelief. "We're going to get our asses kicked," one said.

"If you're going to get your throat cut, wouldn't you rather have it done with a sharp razor instead of a blunt stick?" Williams replied.

In fact, Zemeckis says, Katzenberg stepped up and provided more production support. He told Williams to quit supervising and focus on animating two characters — Roger and Baby Herman. Marshall was assigned to ride herd on the project full-time along with producer Don Hahn.

Disney animation chief Peter Schneider was responsible for ensuring that the project stayed on schedule. Using a computer program to calculate the animators' productivity, he pushed relentlessly for more "pencil mileage." Some of the animators were disgusted with Disney's approach. "It's now an accountancy agency and it's scheduled very much in the conveyor-belt fashion," lamented one working on the project.

Williams also felt that Disney was putting too much emphasis on the number of frames produced without focusing on the special challenges that a particular artist may have faced in a given sequence. Those who appeared to have done less might in fact have accomplished more, he argued. Disney's attitude ultimately caused Phil Nibbelink, one of four supervising animators on the project and a ten-year Disney veteran, to depart after the project was finished. "It's just been a real sad situation at Disney," he said ruefully. Schneider countered that getting Disney animation out of its "tailspin" had been tough but the rewards were manifest: the studio was in "the most creative and most productive period in the last ten or twelve years."

Zemeckis faced the full brunt of the animators' sour mood. Producer Frank Marshall convinced him to attend their Christmas party, during which Zemeckis unwarily decided to give a rally-the-troops speech. Unluckily, the troops had just run out of liquor and they became outright surly. "We're really doing something special . . ." Zemeckis began.

"Fuck you!" someone shouted.

"Who's going to get the money?" came another voice.

Zemeckis beat a hasty retreat.

∽

JUST BEFORE CHRISTMAS, Zemeckis — now back in Los Angeles — had started shooting the last live-action sequence of Hoskins driving into Toontown, where the animated characters lived. He began with a $3 million budget. But it soon became clear that the real price would be $6 million.

Katzenberg—despite his good mood from the recent successful opening of *Three Men and a Baby*—flipped. This was a nightmare; as he saw it, talented people with the best of intentions had gone offtrack. They had underestimated the scope of what they were doing. He demanded that Zemeckis show him the film to prove that he really needed the sequence. Zemeckis complied. Katzenberg agreed to proceed but imposed a tight schedule. Zemeckis, working at Industrial Light and Magic in Northern California, was so pressed for time that the producers arranged for a police escort to the Oakland airport so he could get to his son's second birthday party in Los Angeles.

Meanwhile, the animation was progressing too slowly for the film to make its June 1988 summer prime-time release date. "We've got all these things in position, all this merchandise, all these tie-ins," Katzenberg said at the time. "We move the feature back two weeks and [we could lose] $40 million." (In fact, Roger Rabbit was not only set to appear on wristwatches and lunch boxes, but McDonald's had committed about $15 million to promoting the newest addition to the Disney family.) Disney was becoming desperate to make the deadline.

If *Roger Rabbit* was becoming a grinding ordeal for Zemeckis and everyone else working on it, Katzenberg never confided what he was going through. In fact, he and Eisner were in the midst of one of their biggest fights ever. Even after their earlier meeting, Eisner still disagreed with Zemeckis's vision of the film and had provided the director with copious notes. He had tried to talk Zemeckis into making extensive changes, including the elimination of Eddie Valiant's love interest, played by Joanna Cassidy. Zemeckis had refused, arguing that Valiant's character needed a happy ending.

Eisner had instructed Katzenberg to get the film under control or he would take over himself. Katzenberg believed that Eisner simply wanted him to run over Zemeckis and Spielberg with the same heavy-handed brutality that was usually reserved for lesser talents. He wasn't prepared to do it. "I said, 'I'm doing the best I can. If that's not satisfactory to you, then I'm not the person to do the job,' " Katzenberg says. The two men barely spoke for weeks.

When *Roger Rabbit* finally previewed for a test audience in late April, Katzenberg must have feared that Eisner would finally fire him. He later told Zemeckis that he saw his life flash before his eyes as the screening turned into an unmitigated debacle. Zemeckis and his crew had been feeling very upbeat about the movie. But when Disney loaded a San Fernando Valley theater full of fifteen-year-olds who thought they were going to see *Rambo III*, it quickly became clear that a mistake had been made. A good part of the movie wasn't fully animated and the teenagers weren't charmed by the line drawings that represented the cartoons. In the middle of the screening the film broke and half the audience walked out.

When the screening ended, Zemeckis and his associates stood with Katzenberg at the back of the theater. Katzenberg closed the door and turned to the group. "We have just had the greatest preview ever," he said solemnly. "The movie just previewed through the roof." He swore the filmmakers to secrecy and prevented the bad smell from escaping. Amazingly, he succeeded in keeping a lid on the screening.

The filmmakers retreated to L'Express restaurant in misery. They had invited their wives, anticipating a triumph; now it looked like the early rumors that the film was a disaster were dead-on. "Could we be this wrong?" they asked themselves. The next day the movie was to screen again in Pasadena for an audience of five-year-olds. "Jeffrey, don't make me go," Zemeckis pleaded. But he went, and to his surprise, the five-year-olds seemed to like the movie. He rallied and started massaging the film, brutally cutting several minutes' worth of expensive animation. With each preview, the test scores went up. It also seemed to Zemeckis that the film was growing on Eisner.

By now, Zemeckis had bonded with Katzenberg. They had been through two years of hell, and Katzenberg's spirit had never flagged. In every meeting, Katzenberg would say, "We're here to talk about what will be the number-one film of 1988." He had made encouraging calls to exhausted film editors who normally never heard from a studio chief. He had arranged for a cover story in *Newsweek*. He had been tough, but Zemeckis felt that he had never allowed the fights to become destructive.

And during the ordeal of making *Roger Rabbit*, something had started to happen to Katzenberg. "I saw Jeffrey transform before my eyes," Zemeckis says. Katzenberg, the management robot whose creativity had been a question mark at best, was falling in love — at least after his own fashion. He had started to have fun on *Oliver & Company* and Zemeckis believed that *Roger Rabbit* pushed him over the edge. So Zemeckis was starting to feel bad about a little joke he and Spielberg had decided to play.

When Zemeckis filmed the live-action part of the film in London, he had decided to let Joel Silver play a producer who makes a brief appearance with the rabbit at the beginning of the film. Zemeckis and Spielberg knew, as did almost everyone in Hollywood, that Katzenberg and Eisner had fought bitterly with Silver during the making of *48 Hrs.* and that Silver was anathema to both men. By now, Silver was producing the first in the *Lethal Weapon* series for Warner. He loved the idea of sticking himself into this big, expensive Disney baby and bought his own airline ticket so Disney would have no record that he was present on the *Roger Rabbit* set. His name was kept off the sheet of cast members. He also did something he had never done in anyone's memory. He shaved his black beard. Eisner and Katzenberg had actually seen the footage in which he appeared without recognizing him.

Then Katzenberg asked for a screening of the completed opening sequence—which included Silver directing Baby Herman in a cartoon. The footage was finally finished about three weeks before the film was to open. Zemeckis cringed as Katzenberg, sitting behind him in the theater, laughed at the scene. Then he said, "You know who this guy reminds me of? Joel Silver."

"Is this a setup?" Zemeckis asked. "Jeffrey—it *is* Joel Silver."

"Really?" Katzenberg replied. Zemeckis waited for the onslaught, but instead there was a more ominous silence. Katzenberg never mentioned it again.

Silver's old boss, Larry Gordon—now bitterly estranged from his former protégé—broke the news to Eisner. "Guess who's in *Roger Rabbit*?" he said.

"Who?"

"Who do you hate more than anybody in the world?"

Eisner immediately thought of *48 Hrs.* "Not Walter Hill!" he exclaimed.

"Worse than that," Gordon said.

"Not Joel Silver!" Eisner said. He reflected a moment. "You know," he mused, "he was pretty good."

∞

ROY DISNEY SAID he liked the completed *Roger Rabbit*, but he was appalled that Katzenberg wanted it released under the Disney family banner. He felt that Jessica Rabbit was too sexy and Baby Herman was too vulgar. (Little did he know then that mischievous animators had dropped in a few frames of Jessica topless—too fast to be perceived by viewers but nonetheless visible if the film was slowed down.) Katzenberg wanted Disney to start associating its brand name with more sophisticated fare, but Ze-

meckis secretly hoped for the more adult-oriented Touchstone label because he didn't want the movie to be written off as a kiddie film. After
Eisner and Roy watched the film together, the question was resolved. The
lights came up and Eisner declared, "It's a Touchstone movie."

"I agree," Roy said.

As it turned out, Katzenberg's prediction that *Roger Rabbit* would be the
number-one film of 1988 was wrong. It was the number-two film, behind
Barry Levinson's Oscar-winning *Rain Man*. *Roger Rabbit* was nominated
for six Oscars and won three, but they were all in technical categories
(Visual Effects Editing, Sound Effects Editing, and Film Editing). Still, this
was the Eisner regime's best performance ever at the Academy Awards.
More important to Disney, perhaps, the company made money. The picture
grossed $154 million and inspired Disney to create a Mickey's Toontown
attraction at Disneyland.

As for Zemeckis, he felt he had arrived when Eisner asked him to direct
a video for the new Disney-MGM tour that showed Eisner interacting with
Toons. But Eisner offered to pay only the minimum wage set by the Directors Guild. Zemeckis passed.

"Don't you want to be able to have that there for all time so your kids
can go?" Eisner asked. This was an argument that persuaded many other
major talents to work cheap. But not Zemeckis. To him, it was ridiculous
to act as though Disney were some kind of charity.

"It's a lot of hard work," he replied. "I'd rather do nothing."

∽

ZEMECKIS HAD BEEN right. Katzenberg had become increasingly enamored of animation. Ron Clements, director of Disney's next animated
release, *The Little Mermaid*, was a Disney veteran who saw it happen. Like
many animators, Clements had mixed feelings about Katzenberg's growing
involvement. "Jeffrey was right a good percentage of the time," he says.
"And sometimes he wasn't right at all. There was a fair amount of arguing.
He would always back down if you could convince him he was wrong. We
would back down and he would back down. I think it had a lot to do with
the success of the films. . . . But he could turn up the pressure. There's good
and bad in that. It got pretty stressful."

Roy Disney had made another important contribution to the health of
the division: he convinced Eisner to invest millions on the development of
a sophisticated computer system that revolutionized production of the ani-

mated films. Rather than degrade the quality of Disney animation, the new system — which would be first used on parts of *The Little Mermaid* — freed the artists to create previously unfeasible sequences.

Ron Clements had pitched the idea for *The Little Mermaid* in his first "gong-show meeting" with Eisner and Katzenberg. They were intrigued by the idea but wanted to bring in live-action writers to do the script. Clements convinced them to let him and colleague John Musker take a swing at it. Katzenberg liked their script. The project was a go, with Clements and Musker directing.

Perhaps Katzenberg's most important decision in animation came when he hired Howard Ashman and Alan Menken to write the music for *The Little Mermaid*. The Ashman-Menken collaboration would revitalize animation as a medium and bring back the musical as a popular form. The partnership also helped bring billions of dollars into the Disney coffers.

The first time Katzenberg heard Ashman and Menken's music for *The Little Mermaid*, Clements said, he was entranced. "He started to get more and more into it," he says. "But I think live action was [still] much more important to him. Animation was fun, but that didn't put it in the same category as live action."

Katzenberg's relationship with Ashman was sometimes tempestuous. "Howard and Jeffrey would fight like cats and dogs," remembers one animator. But Katzenberg managed to bring out some of the team's most brilliant work. "Jeffrey knew how to edit, how to get a key change, knew when it wasn't working," that animator says. With no musical training, Katzenberg learned to trust the gut that no one thought he had. If a moment didn't feel emotional enough, he pushed for something more.

As the film neared completion, Katzenberg told Clements that it would turn in a reasonable performance. But he warned that the movie probably wouldn't do as well as *Oliver & Company* because *The Little Mermaid* seemed likely to appeal primarily to little girls. Such films didn't perform as well as those that attracted boys.

Eisner took a few looks at the film as it progressed. In the first presentation, he heard some of the songs and listened to some of the voices. "Michael was really excited," Clements remembers. But the second presentation, which involved showing him "story reels" of drawings with little animation, was a nightmare. The film was very rough and there were a number of technical glitches. Eisner was obviously displeased. He had issues with certain plot points. For example, Sebastian the crab initially did not side with Ariel the mermaid; then he suddenly assists her in her plot to reach dry land. It was unclear what brought about the change of his crab's heart. "Why can't we solve these problems in the script stage?" Eisner demanded. Clements concedes that Eisner was right. "We wrote a new scene where Sebastian is on the beach with Ariel and he just sort of breaks down and gives in," Clements says. "It really helped a lot. He wasn't involved a lot but his contributions did make a difference. His overview helped strengthen the arc on the characters."

Roy Disney was not much more of a presence than Eisner, but, avid sailor that he was, he made sure that any nautical terms used in the film were correct. Harkening back to his early days working on Disney nature films, he also provided footage of an octopus that served as a model for Ursula the sea witch.

The first test screenings before recruited audiences were encouraging. Then the studio decided to do an all-adult screening with no children at all. "They had never actually done that before," Clements remembers. The preview in the suburb of Sherman Oaks got an enormously positive response. "Jeffrey was just glowing," Clements says. In the lobby, he told Clements, "We've got to rethink our marketing on this."

Menken and Ashman collected two Oscars for *Little Mermaid* in March 1990. The picture also showed the potential power of animation. It grossed a record-setting $85 million and made more than $40 million in pure profit—not counting the enormous additional revenues that it produced in merchandise and home video.

Disney had not really been prepared for the bonanza and didn't have nearly as much merchandise on hand as it could have sold. (The toy manufacturer complained that a red-haired doll wouldn't sell well, so the first Ariel dolls were strawberry blondes. But the public wanted Ariel as she appeared in the film. Later, when the film was rereleased in 1997, Disney was ready with battalions of red-haired dolls.) Disney began to appreciate the staggering amounts that could be wrung from a medium that allowed the studio ultimate control and didn't include any live actors who were in a position to demand a percentage of the gross. And for Katzenberg, there was no turning back. Animation claimed an ever-larger share of his time and passion.

17

STAR WARS

DISNEY'S SUCCESS ALONE would have been enough to earn it a good deal of enmity in the Hollywood community. But within a few years, the Eisner administration was fighting with virtually everyone in and out of town—even way out of town.

Some of the company's litigiousness sprang from its desire to protect its valuable rights to its characters. Frank Wells argued that these aggressive tactics were necessary. But Disney's unyielding stance began to take a toll from a public relations standpoint. Disney threatened to sue the tiny Canadian town of White River over its plan to erect a Winnie the Pooh statue and ordered three day-care centers in Florida to paint over Disney characters on their walls. MCA capitalized on the Florida case by painting Flintstones characters over the Disney figures and throwing a party for the kids. Lest anyone miss the point, the media were invited, too.

Disney also got embroiled in some lawsuits simply because its corporate culture was to play hardball. In 1988, Disney had negotiated with Rupert Murdoch, now the chairman of Fox, to team up on a satellite network in Europe. Disney wanted to use Murdoch's Sky Television to broadcast the Disney Channel overseas, with the aim of boosting merchandise sales abroad and paving the way for the Euro Disney theme park that was to open in 1992.

The two sides quickly started to feud over issues of control. The Fox side aggressively pursued deals to buy the rights to movies made by other studios; Disney complained that the Murdoch executives were overpaying. Disney felt it wasn't being consulted and the company wasn't comfortable that the Fox side would take adequate care to position the Disney brand properly, either. (News Corp's decision to flog the satellite service—including the Disney Channel—alongside a picture of a scantily clad young woman in one of Murdoch's British tabloids didn't strike Disney as the right

approach.) But Disney had never anted up the $75 million that it promised
to pay into the joint venture. In 1989, Murdoch sued and the case was
quickly settled. The joint venture was abandoned. It was an expensive decision. According to a former Fox executive, Disney's share in the service
would have been worth about a billion dollars by 1999.

That kind of fast resolution was relatively unusual. In 1990, Eisner tan-
gled with Murdoch again. This time he got into a self-defeating feud with
his former boss, Barry Diller, who was running the Fox studio. Disney had
created a series of half-hour animated shows that aired on weekdays. *The
Disney Afternoon*, as the shows were called, became the Disney television
division's best profit generator at the time. Diller had started running the
Disney shows on the seven Fox-owned television stations. Those stations
and many others that were affiliates of the new Fox television network
constituted more than 80 percent of the stations carrying the Disney afternoon package.

The fight started when Disney bought KHJ, a television station in Los
Angeles, and told Diller that it would stop supplying afternoon cartoons to
the local Fox-owned station, KTTV. Enraged, Diller said he would drop
the shows from all Fox-owned stations. And he would retaliate by having
Fox make its own cartoons and sell them to all 120 affiliates of the new Fox
network. There would be some small markets where Disney wouldn't even
have an alternative station that might buy its wares. Fox's first effort would
be based on *Peter Pan*—a move that Disney regarded as an encroachment
because it had made an animated version for the big screen. (In fact, *Peter
Pan* was in the public domain and didn't belong to Disney.) In time, Fox's
Power Rangers became the top children's show and Fox dominated afternoons. Within two years, Eisner had forfeited a major profit center to service
one, stand-alone television station. Still, he insisted, he "couldn't justify
depriving our . . . station of highly desirable Disney programming."

Disney not only sued but attacked Fox before the Federal Communications Commission. The fight grew so ugly that Diller reportedly refused
to remain in a room if Eisner was present, took his name off charity events
if Eisner was participating, and even began referring to the Walt Disney
Company as "the Evil Empire." In 1992, Disney dropped the case.

Disney also came to public blows over its attempt to acquire the Muppet
characters. The brilliant Muppet creator, Jim Henson, started discussing
the sale with Eisner in spring of 1989 and an agreement to consummate the
union was announced with great fanfare that August. Disney publicized the

deal as "a business association made in family entertainment heaven." But while Henson had wanted the sale to ensure a good, stable home for his characters, many of his creative staffers were nervous. "I was surprised about Disney because Disney is a corporate entity and Jim and the Muppets [had] a very fuzzy, Grateful Dead kind of sensibility," said Mark Saltzman, a writer who worked on *Sesame Street* and the short-lived but acclaimed show *The Jim Henson Hour*.

During the negotiations, Disney offended the Muppeteers by suggesting that they could quickly train personnel to operate the characters. "I don't think they understood that it took Jim years to get a single puppeteer up to speed," said Joan Ganz Cooney, head of the Children's Television Workshop (home of the *Sesame Street* characters, including Big Bird and Bert and Ernie).

But Henson "loved Michael and trusted him a lot," says Bernie Brillstein, Henson's manager for many years. So before the deal was final, Disney went ahead with a couple of theme-park projects, including a 3-D film and stage show.

Despite his rapport with Eisner, Henson was surprised to find that Disney was determined to negotiate to the last decimal point. "You'd have to call Michael Eisner and say, 'This is where it's gone with your zealous robots,'" one of Henson's representatives complained. "Every single issue was pushed as a deal point by Disney. As opposed to focusing on the big points, they focused on everything."

As he often did, Wells kept Eisner in line. "Wells consistently was the good guy," says David Lazer, then president of Henson's company. Eisner seemed to forget certain deal points that the Henson side thought had been resolved—and then would become petulant about his position. "He's like a spoiled child sometimes," Lazer says.

The negotiations stalled over such issues as Henson's reluctance to hand over the rights to the *Sesame Street* characters. Cooney said that Henson regarded *Sesame Street* as "a holy place" to be kept separate from Disney. "He told me not to worry about them trying to exert pressure on us," she said. "He said, 'Joan, that would never happen.' A few days later, he called back and said, 'Joan, I was wrong.'" Cooney said Henson had made it clear that the issue was a deal breaker. "Jim said, 'It is not discussable.' [But] it went on and on," Cooney said.

Henson prevailed on that point, but when he died suddenly in May 1990, the deal had not been signed. As it turned out, Henson's five children stood to incur huge tax losses on the estate. Henson had also promised substantial payments to some of his top employees. The children stood to make much less than anticipated from the sale. Meanwhile, Disney discovered that Henson had already licensed the Muppet characters to some stores outside the United States. The deal would not give Disney the exclusivity it wanted.

By December 1990, negotiations to rework the deal with the Henson children had collapsed. The rift would end up in court.

∽

WHILE DISNEY WAS fighting with outsiders, friction was growing within the studio as well. It didn't take long for the natural competition to take a nasty turn between Ricardo Mestres, the meticulous executive who had been with Jeffrey Katzenberg since the Paramount days, and David Hoberman, the newcomer agent. At meetings, former studio executive Marty Kaplan recalls a "barely concealed mutual contempt." Hoberman was more demonstrative and emotional than the carefully controlled Mestres, and nervously avoided flying and even elevators.

Despite Mestres's long history with Katzenberg, other film executives at Disney saw that Hoberman, who as an agent had been out in the world more and had developed his own network of relationships, was gaining favor with Katzenberg while Mestres fell behind. "David was more charming and smooth and adept at navigating the Hollywood waters," says a Disney executive. "He was a popular, handsome guy. He was a player."

Many of those who worked for Mestres thought he was a good boss. But he was widely judged to be too corporate and cerebral for the movie business, which retained more than a trace of lunacy despite ongoing efforts to impose more regular discipline. "He was into memos and positioning paper clips and having his pencils sharpened," says a former colleague. "He was a very decent guy. I just don't think he was someone who should have been deciding what movies should be made." Ultimately, however, neither Hoberman nor Mestres was responsible for picking movies. Those decisions rested with Katzenberg and Eisner.

For a time Katzenberg dealt with the Hoberman-Mestres rivalry "the way Bluhdorn and Barry Diller used to handle [internal conflict] — enjoying the creative tension," says Kaplan. But eventually Katzenberg elevated Hoberman to president of Touchstone and Walt Disney Pictures (the family label). After the announcement, Mestres barely emerged from his office for a week. He tried to get out of his contract. Finally he had to go back to work. "It was ugly because David didn't want Ricardo there," says a former staffer. "He publicly embarrassed him and countermanded him in meetings. Before, they used to sit in the middle of the conference room, next to each other. But now they sat at opposite ends of the table."

At the same time Mestres was lobbying Katzenberg and Eisner, and after some months, they came up with a solution. They dusted off the name they had registered a few years earlier when they were about to leave Paramount: Hollywood Pictures. In late 1988, Disney announced the creation of a new division that would be run by Mestres. He reported to Katzenberg.

The competition between Hoberman and Mestres continued unabated. One executive remembers that the two even started a sartorial war. The uniform for a Disney executive was a dark suit with a shirt. Only Katzenberg wore striped ties (and handmade shirts with extra-long cuffs). But when Mestres was given Hollywood Pictures, says a colleague, he started dressing more professionally. He asked producer Bob Cort, who had made *Three Men and a Baby*, to help him suit up at Versace. Mestres began to appear at work in full corporate regalia. Hoberman promptly began to wear suits and ties himself. "It was like, he who dresses best wins the prize," says Adam Leipzig, a bemused studio executive at the time.

Some Disney film executives thought from the start that adding another label made no sense. The creation of Hollywood Pictures did little more than increase overhead. Eisner would later insist that he went along so that Katzenberg could accommodate his two lieutenants. But the advent of the new division roughly coincided with Eisner's decision that Disney would start to crank up production to dominate market share. It was a move that he would later try to disavow, but at the time it was part of his strategy. While other entertainment companies were expanding, first by snapping up theaters and then buying a broadcasting outlet or cable systems, Eisner had for years maintained that he wanted to "stick to his knitting." Disney's rivals had concluded that they needed a pipeline to the public to ensure that their wares would win some shelf space in an increasingly crowded and competitive market. Katzenberg and Rich Frank argued strenuously that Disney should buy Capital Cities/ABC or NBC. But while Eisner window-shopped, Disney didn't act.

Eisner concluded that Disney would simply make so much entertainment that all the networks and cable operators would have to reckon with it. Thus Disney started on a slippery slope of trying to make a lot of movies cheaply, just at a time when its old methods were starting to fail. The bland formula that defined Disney "product"—usually high-concept comedies that were designed for mass appeal, that weren't too edgy, that made do with stars from television like Tom Selleck or recycled film talent like Bette Midler—no longer had mass appeal. Few executives or producers can tap into audience tastes for more than a fleeting moment, which explains why the industry puts up with so much excess from those who know what the public wants to see.

The Hollywood Pictures logo was, inexplicably, a sphinx. (Insiders joked that the sphinx bore a resemblance to Mestres.) Executives who worked for the new label found that Hollywood Pictures would mostly stick to making comedies for a price. "They kept saying, 'We'll make more interesting movies later, once we have success with our cookie cutters,'" says Michael Peyser, then an executive at the studio. Peyser soon learned that he would have a long wait.

∽

O N E   O F   T H E last successful films made according to the old Disney formula was *Pretty Woman*, a bright romantic comedy that sprang from a dark script about a prostitute hired for a week by a ruthless businessman.

There is some dispute over whether it was Disney science or just dumb luck that made *Pretty Woman* such a huge hit in March 1990. Screenwriter Jonathan Lawton contended that Disney executives "didn't have a clue what they were doing" and merely stumbled into the fortuitous chemistry between Julia Roberts and Richard Gere. "They're so desperate to try to justify this concept of managing ideas, and it has no basis in reality," he said.

But certainly, a theory informed Disney's decision making. "It was at the peak of studio executives believing that their imperative was correct," concurs an executive who worked at Disney during this period. "If they could fix a movie in postproduction, like *Cocktail*, or fix a movie that had sort of ignoble beginnings, like *Down and Out in Beverly Hills*, it proved that they were the ones who achieved [the success]."

Katzenberg made *Pretty Woman* over the objection of virtually all of his underlings. The script was mentioned in a meeting dismissively, but Katzenberg immediately glommed onto the idea. If it could be brightened up, he said, it would be a hit.

Laura Ziskin, the producer of *Pretty Woman*, says director Garry Marshall very deliberately set out to make it into a fairy tale, a popcorn version of *Pygmalion*. But the filmmakers had no idea that they were working on a film with the potential to become Disney's biggest hit ever.

Casting the film was such a nightmare that any other studio might well have given up. Julia Roberts, coming off the modest independent film *Mystic Pizza*, had been loosely attached to the project in an earlier incarnation at Vestron, a struggling company that had sold it to Disney. But once Disney acquired it, she had to win the part all over again. Her screen test wasn't outstanding. Disney wanted to cast the film with Sean Connery and Meg Ryan, but that pairing fell through. Katzenberg and Marshall also discussed using Madonna, who passed. Laura Dern, Diane Lane, and Valeria Golino were considered. Everyone was impressed with Golino but concerned about her Italian accent. Finally they concurred that Roberts had star potential and she was cast.

Finding a male lead was almost impossible. Dozens of actors, including Al Pacino and Robert Redford, passed. The producers wanted Sting but couldn't get him. They considered Charles Grodin and Donald Sutherland before turning to lesser stars like Christopher Lambert and Sam Neill. Disney even considered Pat Riley, then coach of the Los Angeles Lakers basketball team. Eventually, Katzenberg sent the script to Richard Gere, who had been rejected at first because his career was in a slump and he wasn't known for romantic comedy. After Katzenberg and Marshall took him to lunch, he signed on. (Gere still commanded a $2 million fee; Roberts was a $350,000 bargain in those days.)

There were still some sticking points. Katzenberg pushed Gere to dye his gray hair but the star refused. Meanwhile, Gere let Ziskin know that he wasn't happy with the script, which was going through numerous rewrites. "I promise you, we will get this right," she said.

With that pledge, Gere suited up for wardrobe tests. Word came back from Katzenberg that Gere's stylish suits were fine but the points on the shirt collars didn't look right. Ziskin had no idea what he was talking about but costume designer Marilyn Vance assured Ziskin that the collars would be changed. Just before shooting began, Gere came to do a read-through of the script. As he read, it was obvious that he wasn't happy. When the session broke up, Donald De Line, then vice-president of Touchstone, showed up with a Polaroid camera. "Jeffrey wants you to get Richard in wardrobe so he can see that you fixed the shirt-collar problem," he told the producer.

"I would not be surprised if the actor did not come to work Monday," Ziskin replied. "We have bigger problems than the fucking collars."

Sure enough, Gere called the next day. "You promised you were going to fix the script and it's not fixed," he said. "We can't start."

Ziskin and Gere holed up in his trailer, cutting and pasting the script together for three nights. The cameras finally started to roll after some dark moments had been replaced with lighter touches. When the prostitute played by Roberts first retreats into the bathroom at Gere's hotel room, for example, she flosses her teeth. In the original, she was using drugs. A drug overdose was entirely eliminated from the script.

Director Garry Marshall had his own problems. Like everyone who made movies at Disney, he had to watch every dime he spent. Marshall particularly wanted Hector Elizondo to play the manager at the hotel where Roberts and Gere stay. But Disney refused to pay his fee. "I got so mad that I paid half his salary myself," Marshall remembered later. That, of course, was fine with Disney. (Eventually, Disney gave him the money back.) Marshall was also particularly attached to the idea of filming Gere and Roberts on a big, glamorous date at the War Memorial Opera House in San Francisco. It was considered too expensive; he was advised to shoot them watching a video of an opera or maybe just taking in a movie. Finally Marshall had art director Albert Brenner build a clever set on a soundstage that allowed him to cheat and use only a handful of extras.

"At Disney," Marshall said later, "they'll harass you while you're shooting and drive you crazy and rush you and all these things, but finally when you put the picture together and you get it there, that's when Jeffrey Katzenberg looks and says, 'Oh, well! We had to have it right this minute, but this needs another week—you'd better go reshoot it like you wanted to.' Their last decision is always okay. The ones leading up to it could drive you insane, but that last one is always right."

Despite *Pretty Woman*'s wild success at the box office, even some high-level studio executives were uncomfortable with its premise that prostitution can lead to wealth and happiness. "This could be popular but I think it's sort of reprehensible," executive Michael Peyser (who did not work on the picture) told Katzenberg when he saw the finished film. "I hope you give some of the profits to AIDS centers and runaway shelters."

"It's just a fantasy," Katzenberg protested.

"That's one way of looking at popular culture," Peyser replied.

Meanwhile, Ziskin's three-year deal at Disney was winding down. Like *Good Morning, Vietnam*'s producer, she was extremely disappointed by the studio's offer to renew her contract. It wasn't that Disney didn't want to do business with her—she had two other projects in the works that the studio would make. But Disney wouldn't ante up to keep her, and like several others before and after, Ziskin made a better deal at another studio.

∽

BY THE TIME *Pretty Woman* was released in 1990, it provided very welcome relief at the studio. The only other live-action picture that would perform respectably that year was *Dick Tracy*—and that was just in terms of grosses, not profits. Only *Pretty Woman* would bring in serious money.

Dick Tracy was Katzenberg's most complete surrender to a big star yet. He and Eisner had considered making the film based on the cartoon detective when they were still at Paramount but Diller had concluded it was too expensive. The project languished in development hell for several years; eventually, Warren Beatty bought the rights. And in 1987, he brought the project to Disney.

No one had better reason to be wary of Beatty than Eisner. He had been at Paramount when Beatty made *Reds* there. And though Beatty had won an Oscar for Best Director for the film, it had been late and gone more than $12 million over its already substantial $23 million budget. All would have been forgiven if *Reds* had been a commercial success, but it wasn't. And Frank Wells had lived through his own bad experience with Beatty at Warner, when he and the star had fought over *Heaven Can Wait* and Beatty finally took the project to Paramount. Now Disney—the industry's most controlling studio—faced the proposition of working with one of Hollywood's most deliberate, perfectionistic, and manipulative talents.

But in *Dick Tracy*, Eisner saw a possible franchise—a fountain of money that could provide a series of sequels as well as a merchandising bonanza. Paramount was working on its third in the *Indiana Jones* series; Fox was making the second *Die Hard*; Warner was making the second *Lethal Weapon* and the first *Batman*; Universal was in production on a pair of *Back to the Future* sequels. Disney had avoided spending on the kind of effects that those films demanded but it wanted a piece of that kind of action. And Eisner realized that sometimes the studio would have to step up to the plate to compete.

After an arduous negotiation so high level that Eisner and Wells attended many meetings, the studio agreed to pay Beatty $9 million to star, direct, produce, and rewrite the film. Beatty would also be entitled to more than 15 percent of Disney's gross from the movie and the anticipated merchandise sales. Disney hoped to control Beatty by approving a budget of $23 million, with an agreement that he would pay overages out of his own salary.

Wells had been involved in the negotiation in part to mend the fences that had been damaged years earlier during their fight over *Heaven Can Wait*. Some late-night negotiations with Beatty took place at Wells's Beverly Hills house—the same one he had owned since his Warner days. Late one night, as the talks wore on, the star said he was hungry and asked Wells if he could get him an apple. Wells was as clumsy when it came to domestic matters as he had been during his mountain-climbing days, and Eisner knew it. "What are you going to do?" he asked. "Wake Luanne to find an apple?"

"No," Wells replied. "I can find an apple."

He disappeared and returned fifteen minutes later—with a banana. "Typical Disney!" Beatty protested. "You ask for an apple and you get a banana!"

⤸

DICK TRACY DRAINED the entire company," says an executive involved in the film. "You could feel the weight of the entire company pushing this thing forward. Everybody was completely exhausted on the other side of it."

One reason was that dealing with Beatty—even in the best of circumstances—was fatiguing. He pondered every decision at length. While other directors might quickly decide which poster was best to sell a movie, Beatty mulled over such matters endlessly. Beatty also shot fifteen or twenty takes of a given scene, recalls Dick Sylbert, the former Paramount executive and renowned production designer. As he ground out repeat after repeat of a scene, costar Madonna would call out, "War-ren. I'm losing my hard-on"—a line that became a standing joke on the set.

Colleagues say Katzenberg was entirely indulgent of Beatty and loved to spend time with the charismatic star. One crew member recalls Beatty literally genuflecting before Katzenberg in a display of mock surrender, and Katzenberg getting down on his knees and returning the gesture. The two met almost nightly at ten P.M., at the Hamburger Hamlet in West Hollywood or in an editing room. Beatty also liked to conduct meetings in his kitchen. "Jeffrey wanted on some level to be Warren Beatty," says a colleague. "Jeffrey just loved walking around with Warren. When he's talking to you, if he is playing the movie star, it's like there's no one else in the room." Meanwhile, Beatty soaked up Katzenberg's opinions like a sponge. If Katzenberg wanted to offer extensive comments on the dailies, Beatty was a willing listener.

Katzenberg was not the only one who found him mesmerizing. "Warren," says one of those who worked closely with him on the film, "can be an aphrodisiac. Over time, that had an effect. He just entices you." Beatty flirted with high-level women executives in various departments. One Disney executive remembers dropping by a soundstage one evening and finding Beatty there with one of the studio's top women executives. "There was this corporate executive dressed in these ass-tight blue jeans, red cowboy boots, and this white frilly blouse," this insider remembers. "You'd come into a room and these women — these ball-busters during the day — were actually sitting on his lap." Beatty also had visits from women who were not from the corporate suites. On some occasions, executives and the film editor had to wait outside an editing room while Beatty finished with some assignation. When it was over, says one who waited, "He'd come out as though nothing was happening."

At the same time Beatty was carrying on an affair with Madonna. Disney executives regarded the romance with skepticism. The singer had agreed to work for guild scale because she wanted the role so badly. "Everyone who knew Warren, and knew what a controlling force he was, figured he was boffing her to get her through the movie and the promotion, and then it would be over," says a Disney insider. "She kept him on a leash two inches long — or so she thought. That was the genius of Warren. She thought she had him under control."

Some observers believed that Madonna was quite serious about Beatty. On his birthday, she threw him a surprise party with a guest list that included *Dick Tracy* costars Dustin Hoffman and Al Pacino as well as political figures like Gary Hart. It was close to Easter, and the unsuspecting Beatty walked in carrying a big chocolate rabbit. Madonna presented him with a painting. "This was Madonna on the prowl for Warren," says one insider. "She bought him a red mesh shirt — silk with these solid circles. He looked ridiculous."

Three weeks into the shoot, Sean Young was fired from the part of Tess Trueheart, Dick Tracy's girlfriend. Though Beatty rarely went to see dailies, he expected his associates to report problems. They did: Young, who was notoriously difficult on other productions, was behaving like a professional but she didn't deliver as Tess. "It took a while to convince him to make the change because Warren was on the hook for overages," recalls a source on the set. "Disney didn't want to replace anyone because it would cost money to reshoot." But finally Beatty agreed that Young had to go. She was replaced with Glenne Headly.

Another problem arose when the prosthetics used to create the film's garish gangster faces looked too phony in early dailies. After a number of negative reports, Beatty finally came to look at dailies at the Technicolor facility. With his cinematographer Vittorio Storaro and editor Richard Marks present, Beatty looked at the disappointing footage and suddenly turned on producer Jon Landau, who had advised him that more work was needed. "Jon," Beatty said reproachfully, "don't you realize Vittorio has the toughest job on this movie? Don't you understand that?"

It was a deft move. Instead of being defensive, Storaro found himself springing to Landau's defense. "Maybe Jon is right," he said. "I can make it better."

"Okay," Beatty said. After he left, Marks turned to Landau and said, "That was his best performance yet."

As the movie's release date approached, Katzenberg received a taunt from his old boss Don Simpson, whose ego could scarcely be contained on the Paramount lot. Simpson was immersed in making *Days of Thunder*, a hopelessly clichéd race-car movie with Tom Cruise and Tony Scott, the star and director who had helped make *Top Gun* such a smash. The production was troubled and wound up destroying Simpson's relationship with the studio he had called home for years. In fact, it would nearly wreck his career. But before the film was released, Simpson's braggadocio raged unabated and—with *Days of Thunder* set to open that summer just a couple of weeks before *Dick Tracy*—he sent a fax to Katzenberg saying, "You can't escape the Thunder!"

Katzenberg promptly faxed back: "You won't believe how big my Dick is!"

∽

ACTUALLY, IT WAS Beatty who was causing more problems than competition from *Days of Thunder*. A split developed between Helene Hahn, who oversaw the studio's business and legal affairs, and one of her top executives and protégés, Robin Russell. In Hahn's view, Beatty had been end-running her by bonding with Russell and then exacting concessions that he could not get otherwise. Russell was at least as taken with Beatty as many other Disney executives, but in her view, she was being made into a scapegoat. She may have been a little infatuated with Beatty, but who at Disney wasn't? (Russell also put in a cameo as a prostitute in the film.) No one had the nerve to say no to Beatty, who was used to getting his way and who was, after all, an Oscar-winning director.

This strain between Hahn and Russell turned into an open rift when the studio allowed Beatty to give scriptwriter Bo Goldman a credit as a coproducer on the film. The Writers Guild has final say over which writers receive credit, and in this case, Jim Cash and Jack Epps got the nod. Goldman, who had reworked the script, was angry when Beatty failed to get him a writer's credit. Beatty gave him a producer's credit instead. The guild regarded this as a "consolation credit"—a sham intended to evade guild rules—and announced its intention to block screenings of any copy of the film that listed Goldman as a producer.

That bad news came just as Beatty and top Disney executives arrived in Orlando for the film's premiere—with a print that included the unscreenable credit. As they stood in the lobby of the Dolphin hotel, "Jeffrey and Robin Russell were just screaming at each other . . . and Warren was having a panic attack," says one eyewitness. The premiere went forward after Disney agreed that it would pay a fine and destroy the offending copies of the film as well as printed materials that included the Goldman credit. But Hahn blamed Russell for having indulged Beatty by approving the offending credit. After that, the relationship between Hahn and Russell was irreparable.

The cost of making *Dick Tracy* had soared to $47 million. Meanwhile, Disney rolled up its hype machine to its highest pitch ever, spending a shocking $54.7 million on marketing. As a condition of making the movie, Katzenberg had gotten Beatty to commit to promoting it. It was something the press-shy star had refused to do even for his own sweetheart project, *Reds*, but now he publicized the picture so relentlessly that *New York Times* columnist Anna Quindlen found "something sort of pathetic" about the sight of Beatty "shilling up a storm." He was interviewed on *David Letterman*, *20/20*, *Arsenio Hall*, and *Larry King Live*. He talked to *Time*, *Newsweek*, *Rolling Stone*, and *Premiere*.

It worked only after a fashion. Some critics warmed to the picture; Roger Ebert said the film was "original and visionary." The *Washington Post's*

Desson Howe, on the other hand, said the film was a celebration of "everything that's wrong with [Hollywood]: the hype, the agent-negotiated star system, the . . . copy-cat mediocrity, etc." It was an ironic broadside to level at Disney, which usually prided itself on shunning star-stuffed agent packages.

The picture opened better than the vaunted *Days of Thunder* ($22.5 million versus $15.4 million), and it managed to gross over $100 million. But Disney had to drag it across the finish line. With all of its stunning visuals, its carefully chosen color scheme, and an all-star cast, *Dick Tracy* was too cerebral of an exercise. It never connected emotionally with the audience. Given all the time and money Disney had spent, *Dick Tracy* was destined to be perceived as a failure. The extensive lines of *Dick Tracy* merchandise didn't leap off the shelves. (An attempt to sell T-shirts that served as a ticket to the film was an outright disaster.)

Despite the expense, Disney didn't satisfy the audience's appetite for action and effects. *Dick Tracy* couldn't compete with the big bangs in the first *Die Hard* sequel or the Arnold Schwarzenegger sci-fi fantasy *Total Recall*, both of which opened that year. And the live-action kids' movies that scored in 1990 were hipper than *Dick Tracy*. *Home Alone* and *Teenage Mutant Ninja Turtles* ran away with the box office.

Katzenberg says he remains proud of *Dick Tracy* and defends the process that went into getting it made. "It was not a movie that got out of control," he says. "*Roger Rabbit*, I couldn't control. *Star Trek*, I couldn't control. This doesn't fall into those categories." Even so, for Katzenberg, the whole experience had been draining and debilitating. He started to realize that aside from animation, he wasn't having fun anymore.

18

ONE FALSE MOVE

WHILE TOUCHSTONE STRUGGLED through *Dick Tracy*, Hollywood
Pictures had been expected to have a quick start with its first
film, which was released a month later. But *Arachnophobia*,
the spider-invasion movie directed by Steven Spielberg protégé Frank Marshall, wasn't a huge performer, grossing $53 million. The studio never fig-
ured out whether to sell the movie as fun or horror. Katzenberg decided to
call it a "thrillomedy," but audiences were not moved. Between the mid-
dling box office and the profit participation that went to producer Spielberg,
the picture didn't produce the windfall that had been anticipated.

The division fared even worse when Mestres picked up *Marrying Man*,
a comedy that had been in development at Touchstone. The Kim Basinger–
Alec Baldwin picture was based on a Neil Simon script about a millionaire
playboy who falls in love with a gangster's moll and ends up marrying her
four times. At the time Baldwin was on the rise—still awaiting the release
of *The Hunt for Red October* but not yet as hot as the industry expected
him to become. Basinger was a bigger name thanks to *9½ Weeks* and *Batman*, but she was slumping. She also had a reputation for being tardy to
work and hard to manage.

This was meant to be a typical Disney film, with a budget below $15
million and a tight shooting schedule. Katzenberg hoped that Jerry Rees,
an animator making his directing debut, would be as brilliant a gamble as
Joe Johnston, a special-effects man who scored a major hit when the studio
gave him a chance to direct *Honey, I Shrunk the Kids*.

Basinger started off by showing up late for rehearsal. Then she was five
hours late for her first makeup test. When she arrived, she worked for a
couple of hours and left. She demanded that the studio fire the director of
photography, Ian Baker, because she didn't like the way she looked in the
test. Disney gave in. So it went at first, until Basinger announced that she

had to fly to Brazil in the middle of the production to consult a psychic. Disney told her she would face charges of $85,000 a day to make up for time wasted. Basinger skipped the trip but her behavior didn't improve. She drove Simon, who had written the script, off the set. "This isn't funny," she reportedly told him at one point. "Whoever wrote this doesn't understand comedy." Simon walked off and was scarcely seen afterward. (Executives associated with the project say there were problems with the script, which lacked a workable ending, but Mestres could never get Simon to address them.)

A blossoming romance between Basinger and Baldwin seemed to inspire the stars to increasingly extravagant displays of temper. At one point Baldwin, apparently upset because the phones in his trailer didn't work, knocked over glasses and ashtrays, and then grabbed executive Jay Heit's cell phone and threw it to the ground. When he kicked over a case full of lenses, Disney had Panavision tally the costs and threatened to make Baldwin pay.

Eventually, Baldwin and Basinger—who later married in real life—essentially took over the film. They rushed through preparations, and some shots were out of focus and needed to be done over. That made Basinger "go crazy and start throwing stuff," a member of the crew reported. The stars banned producer David Streit from the set. From time to time Katzenberg demanded something from them; for example, he insisted that they reshoot a scene in a wedding chapel. When Baldwin refused, Katzenberg threatened to shut down the production. He prevailed.

Though Basinger and Baldwin steamrolled novice director Rees (who wound up in the hospital by the end of the production, stressed and exhausted), he actually laid some of the blame on Disney. "A primary source of Kim's and Alec's frustration was the pressures that come from working with a studio that presses so hard for money savings," he said. Despite those pressures, the savings didn't materialize. The movie wound up costing $23 million and it bombed at the box office when it was released in February 1991.

In fact, by 1990, Hollywood Pictures was looking at a string of films that would turn out to be losers. *Taking Care of Business* was an empty-headed James Belushi–Charles Grodin comedy that cost $15 million (not counting millions for prints and advertising) and only grossed about $20 million. Many more flops were in the works. Meanwhile, to his credit, Mestres tried to get the studio to make *In the Line of Fire*, a thriller starring Clint Eastwood. Katzenberg thought it was too expensive; the project was a major hit for Sony Pictures in 1993.

Within two years of Mestres's ascension, speculation about whether Katzenberg would fire him was beginning to percolate through the community. But those who knew Katzenberg said he wouldn't turn his back on his longtime lieutenant. And others said Mestres didn't deserve to take the fall because much of what he'd done was to execute Katzenberg's plans. Indeed, Hollywood Pictures' loser movies bore the fingerprints of Katzenberg and even Eisner. It was their idea to let Rees direct *Marrying Man*. Eisner was responsible for putting Patrick Dempsey in the ill-fated drama *Run*. Katzenberg not only went to every preview of every film, but acknowledged that he made decisions on every script and every pitch. The joke around town held that Hollywood Pictures was "Jeffrey Katzenberg unrestrained."

⤬

BACK AT TOUCHSTONE, Katzenberg was working on another project that brought with it a great deal of strife and anxiety. *Pretty Woman* producer Laura Ziskin had started to develop *What About Bob?* at the beginning of her three-year deal at Disney. The film was based on a story that Alvin Sargent and Ziskin had written hoping to get Bill Murray as the star. Initially, Katzenberg balked at paying Murray's fee and the producers looked at Robin Williams, among others. Williams passed and finally the studio turned back to Murray.

Disney wanted Garry Marshall to direct, but Murray said he wasn't interested in working with Marshall. (Marshall and Ziskin teamed up on *Pretty Woman* while *What About Bob?* was still in development.) The studio searched for a director willing to work with Murray, whose unpleasant reputation preceded him. Finally they settled on Frank Oz, whose credits included *Little Shop of Horrors*. Meanwhile, Murray's agent, Michael Ovitz (who also represented Oz), exacted Murray's biggest payday ever — $8 million.

In return, Murray was a nightmare throughout the production. He and costar Richard Dreyfuss got into arguments that once involved throwing ashtrays at one another. And Oz was not one to step into a confrontation.

Ziskin tried to pamper Murray, and when the cast was filming on location in Virginia even got a Richmond high-school marching band to surprise him with a rendition of "Happy Birthday" when the star turned forty. But when Murray found out that the producers planned to work on

Columbus Day, he was incensed. When Ziskin came on the set, he asked loudly, "So, Laura, are we getting the day off?"

Ziskin knew this was a sore point, so she stopped short of answering. "Were you expecting the day off?" she asked.

Murray jumped up and screamed, "Was I expecting the day off?" He picked up a light, threw it against the wall, and pulled down a piece of the set before walking out. Ziskin felt she had to follow him. In the parking lot, he turned on her, ripped off her glasses, broke them, and threw them at her. "I'm going to throw you across the fucking parking lot!" he yelled. She stood her ground and he stalked off. The rumor immediately sped through the industry that he had belted her.

After this treatment, Ziskin told Katzenberg that he had to back her up and make the star work on Columbus Day. Katzenberg didn't have the stomach for the fight. "What is that Kenny Rogers song?" he says with a laugh. " 'Know when to fold 'em.' It's not as though I didn't have more than my fair share of battles." With Ovitz's help, Murray got an expensive day off—along with the crew.

What About Bob? was about a psychiatrist (Dreyfuss) driven mad by a particularly irksome patient who follows him on vacation. The original ending had Dreyfuss's character trying to kill Bob and going insane. Once it was shot, it was clear it didn't work. Ziskin came up with a new ending in which Bob ends up marrying the psychiatrist's sister. Oz wanted an ending where everyone came together on a boat.

Katzenberg backed the director. Ziskin pleaded to be allowed to shoot both and see how audiences responded. After protracted begging, Katzenberg finally agreed. The two versions were screened with recruited audiences, back-to-back. Ziskin heard that Disney production executives had a wager over which version would fare better.

Oz's ending unspooled and the audience sat, unmoved. Then Ziskin's ending played to a much more enthusiastic reception. The audience scored Ziskin's version twenty points higher than Oz's. As Ziskin stood in the theater enjoying the applause for her ending, Katzenberg walked up the aisle and gave her a hug. After rejecting her proposed ending, he was only too happy to eat crow. "I couldn't lose," he said. "I bet on your ending."

∽

AS 1990 DREW to a close, the country was in a recession, the Gulf War was about to begin, and the entertainment industry was suffering through a terrible holiday season. Universal unwrapped an enormous bomb in the shape of *Havana*, an expensive Robert Redford film about the last days of Batista's Cuba. Warner had a staggering flop in *Bonfire of the Vanities*, with a star-loaded cast that included Bruce Willis, Tom Hanks, Morgan Freeman, and Melanie Griffith. Paramount suffered through *The Two Jakes*, Jack Nicholson's long-in-the-making sequel to *Chinatown*, and the doomed sequel *Another 48 Hrs.* It was a lean holiday all around. Disney wasn't doing much better with the disappointing *Three Men and a Little Lady*, a lackluster sequel, and *Green Card* (another comedy, matching Gerard Depardieu with Andie MacDowell). Even animation brought only *The Rescuers Down Under*, another wan sequel. After that, Katzenberg swore off animated movies that didn't have songs.

Compared with other studios, Disney was faring fairly well. The studio had *Pretty Woman* and *The Little Mermaid* — both major hits — to bolster its performance for the fiscal year (which ran from October 1, 1989, to September 30, 1990). But Disney was hardly performing like a well-oiled machine. In January, its stock had taken a thirty-point dip due to nervousness about bad movies in the pipeline and bad winter weather in Orlando. The price quickly rallied and by June it was trading over $136 a share — a stunning 750 percent increase since the advent of Eisner and Wells.

But even though profits were up, they weren't growing at the same astonishing level that Disney had taught the public to expect over previous years, when one record-breaking quarter had followed another. For the first time the Disney juggernaut seemed stoppable. "Disney is looking just a little fragilistic," *Business Week* had said in June. "How long can Eisner keep up the frantic '80s growth?"

In the movie division, profits for fiscal 1990 were the lowest they'd been in three years. On the live-action side, *Pretty Woman* had been the only really bright spot. All sorts of Touchstone pictures had disappeared — *Betsy's Wedding, Spaced Invaders, Firebirds, Mr. Destiny*. And compared with *Batman*, the 1989 megahit that Warner had enjoyed, *Dick Tracy* was an expensive mistake, emotionally and financially. There was no comfort to be found at Hollywood Pictures.

Disney's friends at Silver Screen, who had raised more than a billion dollars in three offerings that funded its film slates from 1984 to 1991, were starting to opt out of certain films that appeared to be too expensive or too generous to talent. In fact, Silver Screen partners Roland Betts and Tom Bernstein passed on *Three Men and a Little Lady* — which required more generous remuneration of the stars after the success of *Three Men and a Baby*. "We said *Three Men* could outperform the original and be a lousy investment," says Bernstein. "We started to get religion and realized it was time to move on."

"I said, 'Jeffrey, give me the hypothetical. Tell me what the film is going to gross,'" Betts says. "Jeffrey said, 'If I don't do this I won't get Selleck's next picture.'" But Betts and Bernstein weren't enraptured with Selleck and their concern proved to be justified. (They refused to back the 1991 films *Billy Bathgate* and *Scenes from a Mall*—both bombs—bringing an end to the Silver Screen relationship with Disney.)

Television was doing worse than film. The company had spent money to make deals with some television talent, and at first, the investment seemed to be working. The studio got six shows on network television for the season that began in September 1990. But within weeks, it was clear that most of the shows would fail, causing Disney to lose millions.

It wasn't just filmed entertainment that was hitting a rough patch. In the fourth quarter of 1990, the theme parks felt the effects of the recession. The company generated record revenue of $5.8 billion in 1990, but for the first time Disney fell short of Eisner's stated goal of achieving a 20 percent increase in earnings per share (by two percentage points).

Eisner dealt with darkening skies by going way over the top with his annual letter to shareholders—working in the family's Thanksgiving in Vermont, his eighty-eight-year-old father-in-law's illness, and his twelve-year-old son Eric's Pee Wee hockey tournament all in the first two paragraphs. Disney was a family-oriented business and Eisner had never been bashful about using his relatives to win over stockholders. Sometimes Eisner's flights of fancy were oddly revealing for a man who headed up one of the world's most influential entertainment companies. In the November 25, 1990, letter, he talked about visiting Russia and mentioned the company's efforts to open a Disney Store in Moscow. "How else would I answer my mother, who was with my wife Jane and me on that trip, as we looked at the four-hour line waiting to get into McDonald's on Gorky Street?" Eisner wrote. "Before she questioned me, in a motherly way, I said, 'We'll do one, too, Mother, soon, I promise.' I think I have said that to my parents before—the 'Soon, I promise' part."

He acknowledged that the company's performance hadn't been perfect. Eisner kept up a jolly tone. "Let's face it, we got lucky!" he wrote. "We didn't do too many stupid things in the '80s. We didn't overpay for anything. We didn't buy movie theaters, media conglomerates or Brooklyn bridges. We didn't leverage our company up to Goofy's neck. . . . We stayed scared. We stayed lean. We stayed financially conservative."

Eisner fudged on the studio's performance, which he described as "stellar." To support that, he cited the success of *Pretty Woman*, the release of the "widely acclaimed" *Dick Tracy* (no mention of profits here), and the record-setting performance of *The Little Mermaid*. And Eisner noted that 1990 was the launch of what would be "the Disney decade," which was to see the launch of new theme parks in Florida, Southern California, Japan — and Europe.

∽

WITH DISNEY IN a slump, Katzenberg, now forty years old, found himself restless and dissatisfied. What had happened to the good old days, when movies were cheap and tarnished stars were grateful to work? Just a couple of years earlier, Disney had been riding very high when Katzenberg had tried a bit of Eisnerian pessimism on a reporter. "We are going to run into a bad streak," he had told the *New York Times Magazine* in 1987 as the studio was poised to release *Three Men and a Baby*. "We are going to fail big. Just so the scales get properly balanced, we are going to have one of the all-time big flops." At the time it hardly seemed likely that Katzenberg had believed what he was saying. Now those words seemed almost prophetic with the wan grosses of *Three Men and a Little Lady*, *The Rescuers Down Under*, and *Green Card*. Disney hadn't had a megabomb, but the studio was hardly firing on all its pistons.

Katzenberg's old adversaries at CAA were flourishing. Mike Ovitz had triumphed — he had positioned himself as a key player in the recent sale of MCA, the entertainment company where Lew Wasserman and Sid Sheinberg had worked for decades, to Japanese electronics giant Matsushita. A year earlier, Ovitz had played a part in brokering Sony's purchase of Columbia Pictures. He had transcended the traditional role of the agent, but at the same time he had successfully steered CAA into a position of daunting power. Katzenberg's way of doing business was that much harder to sustain. "He was finding it harder and harder to make economic deals," remembers a former top executive at the studio. The average price of Disney movies ticked upward. Meanwhile, the executive says, Eisner undoubtedly kept pressuring Katzenberg to prevent CAA from running the studio over altogether. It was an increasingly wearying battle.

Colleagues noticed that Katzenberg was flagging and his friend, music mogul David Geffen, thought he might try psychiatry. (He didn't.) In this gloomy mood, Katzenberg took off for his usual Christmas holiday in Hawaii. That year, rain poured nonstop for days while the hyperactive Katzenberg sat inside at the Kahala Hilton, reading biographies of William S. Paley and Samuel Goldwyn, as well as a lengthy *New Yorker* article about the MCA sale.

Katzenberg had considered taking a leave of some kind. Instead, as he sat in Hawaii, he started writing a memo—a declaration of purpose that would get Disney back on track. It would be twenty-eight pages long, consisting of about eleven thousand words that Katzenberg would hone with a rewrite man upon his return to Los Angeles. It would be a manifesto.

As we begin the new year, I strongly believe we are entering a period of great danger and even greater uncertainty. Events are unfolding within and without the movie industry that are extremely threatening to our studio.

His thinking wasn't startlingly original. Movies cost too much. Disney had swerved from the path of making cheap pictures with "talent we believed in." There were more big stars, higher costs, greater risk, and less profitability.

If we remain on our present course, there will be the certainty of calamitous failure, as we will inevitably come to produce our own Havana *or* Two Jakes *or* Air America *or* Another 48 Hrs. *or* Bonfire of the Vanities . . . *and then have to dig ourselves out from under the rubble.*

Katzenberg recognized that a recession was under way, but that wasn't the only cause of the industry's woes. The problem was the blockbuster mentality that was gripping the industry. Every studio wanted the biggest opening weekend, the fastest $100 million gross. Thanks to this hunger for the blockbuster, movies had a shelf life "somewhat shorter than a supermarket tomato." Hadn't Hollywood been down this road before? Remember the colossal 1963 flop, *Cleopatra*?

Dick Tracy *is a case in point as to how the box-office mentality is affecting the moviegoing experience.... [We] knew that its success would be for the most part judged by its opening weekend box-office performance. So we did everything that we could in order to get the film [the] audience and recognition we felt it deserved.... It seems that, like lemmings, we are all racing faster and faster into the sea, each of us trying to outrun and outspend and outearn the other in a mad sprint toward the mirage of making the next blockbuster. In this atmosphere of near hysteria, I feel that we at Disney have been seriously distracted from doing what we do best.*

Dick Tracy, Katzenberg continued, "made demands on our time, talent and treasury that, upon reflection, may not have been worth it.... The number of hours it required, the amount of anxiety it generated and the amount of dollars that needed to be expended were disproportionate to the amount of success achieved." And, he wrote, if Warren Beatty showed up with another big period action film with expensive talent and a $40 million budget, Disney should "soberly conclude that it's not a project we should choose to get involved in." That one cost him, in a sense. Warren Beatty wouldn't speak to him for years. On the other hand, Beatty did have just such a project—*Bugsy*—which he made for Tri-Star. The picture would lose more than $30 million when it was released in 1991. Production designer Dick Sylbert recalls that after he was nominated for an Oscar for *Dick Tracy,* Katzenberg called. "Hope you're not upset about the memo," he said.

As soon as Sylbert hung up, he phoned Beatty. "Guess who just called," he said.

"Jeffrey Katzenberg," Beatty replied.

"Guess why," Sylbert said.

"He wants you to thank him if you win."

Sylbert did win—and he didn't mention Katzenberg when he picked up his statuette.

Katzenberg went on in his memo to concede that Disney was spending big on projects in the pipeline, including *What About Bob?* and *Billy Bathgate* (exactly the type of expensive period-piece movie that he was now warning against). And he acknowledged that these movies probably cost more time and money than they were worth. Once they were finished, Katzenberg said, "We'll have to do a better job of controlling our appetite."

Katzenberg wasn't done. He spoke nostalgically of *Pretty Woman*, "the kind of modest, story-driven movie we tended to make in our salad days." So there was the key—a good story, well executed. Those who thought they could guarantee a certain return by throwing together a big-star cast, big effects, and a lot of hype were deluding themselves. There was only one answer: passion.

> *Passion is the only word that can explain why one would choose to burrow through 10 to 15 scripts every weekend on the chance of uncovering something great. Passion is the only word that can explain why one would spend a 60-hour week at a studio and then, for fun, on the weekend go see three movies. . . . So let's go back to the drawing board and get back to basics. And, as we do, let's not be afraid to admit to others and to ourselves, up front and with passion, that we love what we do.*

Warren Beatty wasn't the only one who didn't like the Katzenberg memo. The response was hardly what Katzenberg might have anticipated. The memo was widely leaked—and most observers, including Eisner—concluded that he leaked it himself in an effort "to position himself as an industry statesman," as *Variety* put it. (Katzenberg denied leaking the memo and said he was "embarrassed" by all the attention.) At first, various executives—questioned by the media—said the memo made some worthwhile points. But then the press reported that others found it self-serving and hypocritical. (After all, Disney had just signed a deal with Don Simpson and Jerry Bruckheimer, who had departed from Paramount after breaking the bank on *Days of Thunder*.) Perhaps worse than the charge of hypocrisy, many concluded that the Katzenberg memo was pretty obvious stuff.

A lacerating spoof also made the rounds. It claimed that Eisner, having earned a mere $11.2 million in 1990, down from $50 million the year before (thanks to his stock options), was asking employees to take 78 percent pay cuts in sympathy.

But when Eisner read the real memo, he was far from amused. He scrawled some complimentary comments on a copy that he returned to Katzenberg, but warned that it should be kept under wraps. In fact, Eisner was livid. He thought much of the content had been cribbed from the memo he had written several years earlier at Paramount. Katzenberg had traded some of Eisner's basketball metaphors for baseball terminology—

talking about going for "singles and doubles"—but many of the fundamental concepts were the same. Eisner had even questioned Paramount's judgment in making *Reds* while Katzenberg, years later, focused on another Beatty effort, *Dick Tracy*. Katzenberg acknowledges that he was influenced by Eisner's work; he also says that many ideas in the memo were "stone-cold, dumb-butt obvious." His intention was simply to revisit the fundamentals of the business. "When you restate it, it gives you a clarity of thinking, which is why I did it," he says.

Eisner had also cautioned Katzenberg to keep the memo quiet and that hadn't happened. Eisner's outrage was not unreasonable. The industry did not hail Katzenberg as a statesman; instead, the entertainment community turned on him—and Disney—with fangs bared. It was, as journalist Peter Boyer observed in the November 1991 issue of *Vanity Fair*, as though the memo had "burst the dam on a reservoir of pent-up ill will too vast to be explained by mere success envy."

Just months after the memo leaked, Boyer could already see that Katzenberg—bored, depressed, and hotel-bound in a sodden Waikiki hotel over the previous Christmas holiday—had made "the biggest mistake of his career." And there was something else he noted as he wended his way through Hollywood, reporting his story about Katzenberg's "seven-year itch." As he talked to various industry executives and agents, he says, it became clear that there was "a Michael camp and a Jeffrey camp." It was a situation that paralleled the rift detected by Tony Schwartz's 1984 *New York* magazine article, when he reported on Eisner and Diller at Paramount. Yet this time, Boyer discerned a truth that had eluded Schwartz years before: this was a corporate situation that was fraught with peril.

19

MOUSCHWITZ

IN MAY 1991, Bill Murray put in an appearance on *Larry King Live* to promote the newly released *What About Bob?*

"What's it like working with the Disney people?" King asked.

"Well, you know, they have this terrible reputation," Murray replied.

"What?"

"Well, they have a reputation of being very difficult to work with and very tough with a buck and stuff like that."

"And?"

"It's all true."

Katzenberg and Disney's hard image had begun to take a toll in the entertainment community and even with the public at large. In another widely quoted bon mot, Alec Baldwin condemned the studio by maintaining that Katzenberg was the "eighth dwarf—Greedy." Of course, Warren Beatty wasn't speaking to Katzenberg at all after his state-of-the-industry memo. The anti-Disney faction was reaching critical mass. And even some on the lot began calling Disney by a new name: Mouschwitz.

The media was prompt in picking up on the problem. From spring until fall of 1991, there were why-everyone-hates-Disney stories in *New York* magazine, *Vanity Fair*, and the *Washington Post*. *Forbes* speculated that the company could not keep up its dazzling success and suggested that Disney was "overweight, arrogant and paranoid."

"They hate us, I guess," Eisner told *Vanity Fair* a couple of months after Murray's interview. "I don't know whether it's me, maybe Jeffrey, maybe the combination. It may just be a lot of history."

Of course, Eisner's bafflement seems disingenuous. The tone at Disney had been set from the top, though certainly there was never a more willing lieutenant than Katzenberg. But if Eisner tried to distance himself from decision making with a childlike charm, his dominance was still apparent to the more astute filmmakers who worked with him. "I admire Michael and his ability to be childlike and also very, very shrewd," says director Randal Kleiser, who directed *White Fang* and *Honey, I Blew Up the Kids* at Disney. "I've never met anyone who can flip back and forth like that, almost like a schizophrenic. I knew he was tough and I would see him suddenly ask a question like a four-year-old. I think he cultivates that because he knows it works."

Looking back, former studio executive Marty Katz believes that the studio reaped what it had sown. "The more success we had, the more we felt invited to give direction, unsolicited advice, to give voluminous, voluminous script notes," says Katz. "I feel the reason there was such a backlash was twofold. We weren't willing to pay the money that other studios were willing to pay. We held the line to the point of walking away from deals. That bugged agents, that bugged filmmakers. And for those who did [take] the deals, they felt they were besieged by creative direction. The endings were subject to countless debates."

Worst of all, it wasn't working anymore. It seemed as if Hoberman and Mestres were having a contest to see which of them could release more bombs. From January to the end of April, Hollywood Pictures and Touchstone took turns putting out flops. Hollywood Pictures, February: *Run*, a chase movie starring Patrick Dempsey as a student who inadvertently kills a mobster's son, grossed a pathetic $4 million. Touchstone, same month: *Scenes from a Mall*—a Paul Mazursky–directed film with Woody Allen and Bette Midler. (Allen was making a rare appearance in a film he didn't direct.) This was the shriveled fruit of Katzenberg's assiduous courtship of Allen, part of his quest to bring some prestige to the studio. Katzenberg's colleagues and Eisner tried to discourage Katzenberg from making the film, but he didn't listen. He was so devoted to Allen that he accommodated Allen's wish to remain in his beloved Manhattan. The film became the first major studio release in which a Los Angeles location was shot in New York; the Beverly Center mall was re-created for Allen's convenience.

In April, Hollywood Pictures released *The Marrying Man* and saw it bomb. That same month, Touchstone had *Oscar*, Sylvester Stallone's doomed attempt to partake of the comedy bonanza that Arnold Schwarzenegger was reaping at Universal with *Twins* and *Kindergarten Cop*. Hollywood Pictures in May had *One Good Cop*, a lackluster drama with Michael Keaton. The film sold only $10 million worth of tickets and cost $18 million to make. Touchstone, that month, got some rather limited relief. Despite

Murray's bitching, *What About Bob?* opened to a healthy $9.2 million and ultimately grossed $64 million.

But June brought a particularly painful blow: Touchstone released *The Rocketeer*, an expensive picture about a Nazi-fighting hero who flies with the help of a jet pack. Disney was hoping for a breakaway hit. The film cost nearly $46 million, having gone $10 million over its original budget, and it fizzled at the box office. Part of the problem, says Katz, was that director Joe Johnston, who had been so successful with *Honey, I Shrunk the Kids* in the summer of 1989, underestimated the amount of time and money he needed to get the movie done. As production progressed, the studio realized that it couldn't get the title character to fly convincingly just by suspending an actor with cable, as in the old *Superman* programs. The effects had to be enhanced by Industrial Light and Magic, which was expensive. Meanwhile, Katz says, Johnston wasn't especially cooperative about finding ways to save money.

But Johnston publicly blamed the studio and its penchant for pabulum for the film's problems. "You could screen five movies and pick out the Disney movie because it just had a feel to it," he said. "It wasn't going to make you cry too much or feel too strongly. You'd walk out and say, 'That was a nice movie,' and forget about it. . . . They don't like to take chances at all. That's really the heart of the problem. . . . It's the lack of textures, it's pulling back to make something more palatable to a larger number of people."

These losses were the worst that the Disney studio had ever incurred. Previously, the studio's biggest flop was 1989's *Blaze*, a disappointing film that cast Paul Newman as Louisiana governor Earl Long and Lolita Davidovitch as stripper Blaze Starr. But now the bombs were getting bigger. *Scenes from a Mall* and *Marrying Man* each lost about $18 million. Disney wasn't suffering the way other studios had the previous Christmas—*Havana* lost about $50 million and *Bonfire of the Vanities* tanked to the tune of about $40 million—but it needed some hits.

The combination of bad films, bad press, souring relationships, and the hostility engendered by the Katzenberg memo finally hit home. It was time for a new strategy. The Disney studio had to be mellower—a change that Katzenberg promptly signaled in off-the-record chats with reporters—and by switching his uniform from dark suits to a more casual look. In the ensuing months, Hoberman says, Katzenberg's clothing shifted with his moods. "He used to confuse the shit out of me," Hoberman says. "We started off wearing suits without ties. Then he started wearing blue jeans. Then khakis and tennis shirts. So we all started to wear khakis. I used to go home every weekend and put a hat on so I knew it was the weekend."

Of course, some must have found these changes unconvincing, particularly when Mestres had petite twenty-four-year-old executive Elizabeth Guber thrown off the lot that spring (escorted by no fewer than three security guards) for refusing to sign a five-year contract. Other studios routinely asked for two- or three-year commitments, but the ostensibly gentler Disney asked for more—and reacted badly when its wishes weren't granted. The friendlier Disney seemed to be "a public relations move but not an internal reality," says Adam Leipzig, a film executive who worked at the studio during this period.

That impression was underscored at a retreat on the lot. Touchstone executive Donald De Line stood up to express concern about Disney's aggressive business practices and about how the company was perceived in the community. One executive who attended recalls: "Michael stopped Donald in his tracks and said, 'If I can make an extra million dollars by fucking Donald De Line, then fuck Donald De Line.'" The comment made such an impression on that observer that he wrote it down and pasted it into a drawer in his desk—"to remind myself," he says, "of where I worked."

∽

IN APRIL, THE litigation with the Muppets exploded when the Henson heirs sued Disney over its use of the characters at Disney World in Florida. They accused Disney of "greed," "sheer corporate arrogance," and "outright theft of Jim Henson's legacy." Disney, which was so aggressive in protecting its own characters that it initiated some two hundred legal actions in that cause, had started selling Muppets merchandise (with a Disney logo) and advertised the characters as Disney property, all before there was a contract signed.

"I am emotionally outraged and slightly disgusted," said Henson's son Brian. "My father didn't make a mistake when he shook hands with Michael Eisner, but then he was misled and mistreated and disillusioned. Now . . . with the way we've been treated, I can say there is no space remaining for any relationship with Disney."

Disney tried to characterize the family as greedy. The company argued that it had put some $90 million into developing the film and stage show and had an implied right to use the characters. Disney also said it had increased the original price for the company to help the heirs deal with their tax issues, but the Henson children disputed that.

Within two weeks, the suit was settled. Disney had sought a twelve-year license for the Muppet characters in the stage show and 3-D movie and exclusive use of the Muppets in all its theme parks; instead, the company got an exclusive eighteen-month license for the Florida parks with an option to renew. (The deal excluded the *Sesame Street* characters, which remained in the control of the Children's Television Workshop.)

The Henson family also demanded that Disney issue a humiliating public apology for its bad behavior. In a joint statement, the parties said Disney had "requested" a license to use the Muppets at the Florida park with "deep regret for . . . a serious misunderstanding, and apologies to the Henson family and their company for any harm that may have been caused."

A source on the Henson side summed up the settlement succinctly: "Disney was being a bully, and they got it shoved up their nose."

The following month brought more bad press when a jury voted in favor of seventy-year-old, wheelchair-bound singer Peggy Lee, who had sued over Disney's refusal to give her a share of $32 million in profit from the video version of *Lady and the Tramp*. Lee had written six songs and recorded the voices of four characters. Even though taking the case to court meant that Disney would be the Goliath fighting Peggy Lee in her wheelchair, Eisner was adamant. If Disney settled, he said, it would set a precedent that would entitle other artists to sue. But the jury sided with Lee, who ended up with $2.3 million.

Katzenberg claims that in many cases—involving Peggy Lee, the day-care centers, the Muppets—he tried to convince Eisner that the company's image was being hurt. But Eisner always reverted to a "self-righteous" position—a sense that Disney was being wronged, that the law was on the company's side, and that the company's welfare was genuinely at stake. "He'd say, 'If we do this, it's the end of the world as we know it,' " Katzenberg says. "Michael never understood colossal collateral damage."

Journalist Peter Boyer, who interviewed Eisner for a November 1991 *Vanity Fair* article, got a glimpse of the intractable person who remained hidden from public view. Usually, Boyer noted, Eisner seemed to be the least imperious person in Hollywood moguldom. "There is something otherworldly, in a benign way, about Eisner's looks, his huge forehead, his tiny, close-set eyes, his Jagger lips, that suggests he is the creation of some animator's pen, just as surely as Mickey and Goofy, with whom he is forever posing," Boyer wrote. No one would say of Lew Wasserman or Mike Ovitz what producer Don Simpson had said of Eisner: "He's like a big Gummi Bear."

But when Boyer asked about the famously demanding workload placed on young executives, Eisner departed from his "real, but . . . very carefully cultivated" image. "I haven't not worked on a Saturday and Sunday since I left college," he began. "Now that doesn't mean I come in and work all day long. I'm pretty good with my children, I have a great relationship with my wife—look, there are ways to work and not to work. . . . I mean, you know what? I guess, you know what? I think we pay too much money. If we paid less, and if it was a little tougher to make money out here, maybe they'd work. . . . I feel as if I'm getting aggravated."

And so he was, as he flushed and his voice became hoarse. "You know," he went on, "they don't have to work! They can work for someone else! They should quit! You know how many people around America . . . I get thousands, thousands of letters a day: 'Can I be an intern?' "

These words did not go unnoticed within the company and Boyer drew his own conclusions. At that revealing moment in the interview, Eisner was "Gummi Bear no longer. More like the Big Bad Wolf."

∽

DESPITE KATZENBERG'S ASSERTION that he had written his memo to provide clarity, Disney's filmmaking strategy in the new era wasn't well defined. Was Disney doing cheap movies the old-fashioned way or opening its wallet to attract big stars? Was the studio putting controls on directors or giving them freedom? Looking back, Hoberman says, "It was a very schizophrenic time."

Perhaps feeling overexposed, Katzenberg let Hoberman do some of the talking. He gave an interview, pledging that Disney would loosen up controls on filmmakers—which was certainly his plan at that point. The old Disney wouldn't have hired director Randa Haines (*Children of a Lesser God*) to do a film like the summer of 1991's *The Doctor*, a drama with William Hurt, Hoberman said. But Haines was hired and permitted to make the film her way. Disney wanted a more comedic ending, while Haines preferred a more reflective finish. When both endings were tested, Disney's did better with audiences, but the studio still let Haines have her way. And though the picture didn't perform, Hoberman said, the studio had "never received more goodwill from a film."

Even so, Disney hardly sounded like a haven for artists. In many ways, the "new" Disney seemed a lot like the old Disney—only a bit less so. Hoberman said the studio would return to a strategy that it had never abandoned: casting fading stars in cheap movies. He cited, as a case in point, the upcoming thriller *Deceived*, which starred Goldie Hawn. But the studio was also spending big on pictures like *The Distinguished Gentleman* with Eddie Murphy, a film that Hollywood Pictures had in the works for release in December 1992. In the end, these movies had only one thing in common: they didn't work.

"Part of the problem is [Katzenberg's] taste," said a lower-level studio executive at the time. "People get all over him for these simple feel-good movies. That's who the guy is and that's not going to change. We are a big commercial company and we are not going to make *She's Gotta Have It*."

Katzenberg was—in theory, at least—delegating more authority. And Hoberman and Mestres were giving more freedom to their creative executives—or so they said. But Katzenberg still swooped in with his myriad opinions. Most of his attention was focused on Hollywood Pictures. In May, for example, Katzenberg pulled the plug on *Evita* in one of its incarnations because Mestres couldn't squeeze another $3 million out of the budget. He also cut back an ill-conceived remake of *Born Yesterday* by knocking out Tom Selleck and Nick Nolte, leaving Melanie Griffith as the only major player. And Katzenberg was so obsessed with Kurt Russell's seedy look in parts of the doomed comedy *Captain Ron* that he almost insisted on reshoots.

"Jeffrey read every single script, gave notes on every script," says a former Disney executive. "Jeffrey was involved on a micromanagement level in the movies. I remember sitting in a screening of *Straight Talk* with Dolly Parton and he was commenting that he didn't like James Woods's tie. This is the chairman of the motion picture division. There was a very, very short leash."

Other executives say Katzenberg's involvement may have seemed intense but that it wasn't nearly what it had been. In the past, he might attend eleven previews of a film. Now he showed up at only one—usually when it was too late to do much surgery. "In terms of his attention level and his passion, he was gone," says one former Disney insider who is close to Katzenberg. "The rap was that Jeffrey was too much in everybody's business, he didn't share. In an effort to show he could give power to everyone else, he gave too much power to David and Ricardo."

Katzenberg also had his eyes on other horizons—with Eisner's encouragement. "Jeffrey got involved not just in animation but in consumer products and the parks," says a former high-level studio executive. "Michael would have him fly down to look at a new hotel. Jeffrey was sort of shadowing Michael, reviewing park attractions, paying attention to [ongoing construction]. He was trying to show everyone, from Frank to the shareholders to the company at large, that he was more than a movie guy."

Meanwhile, Hoberman and Mestres wrested what control they could. "Each of those guys is a tremendously ambitious person," this executive says. "Jeffrey was constantly being pushed against the wall to give them a chance to pursue what they were interested in." But between Hoberman and Mestres, says another Disney film executive who worked with both, there was too much caution and not enough clarity about what moved them. "You couldn't get a handle," he says. "You couldn't figure out who anybody was, or what their opinion was, or what they wanted. . . . They were message carriers." This executive remembers that when he argued with Katzenberg in a meeting, insisting that a project needed a bigger budget, Hoberman chastised him later. "Let that be the filmmaker's fight," he advised. (Hoberman says he doesn't remember making the remark.)

Hoberman says the real problem was that the effort to ramp up production simply "stretched everybody to the limits." And despite the best intentions, he adds, the studio could not break its own habits of meddling. "We didn't know how to stop ourselves," he recalls. But most of all, he sees the studio's problems at the box office as the inevitable valley following the many years of Disney success. "You can't be lucky all the time," he says.

❧

PERHAPS IT WASN'T fair that *Billy Bathgate* became emblematic of what was wrong at Disney. It was far more expensive than most Disney films, and far more ambitious. *Billy Bathgate* was one of the highest-voltage packages the studio had ever put together. Katzenberg had been a fan of *Ragtime*, and when executive Adam Leipzig told him that E. L. Doctorow was finishing a novel about a young boy's relationship with gangster Dutch Schultz, Katzenberg remembers that "the old golden retriever's tail shot up in the air." Disney made a preemptive $1 million offer. "It had everything in it," Katzenberg says. "It was an adventure, a coming-of-age story, this incredible world of corruption as seen through the eyes of an innocent. It seemed so phenomenally cinematic."

Katzenberg got playwright Tom Stoppard to write the screenplay and hired Robert Benton, who had the Oscar-winning *Kramer vs. Kramer* in his credits, to direct. The star was the notoriously finicky Oscar winner Dustin Hoffman. The plan called for the entire film to be shot, expensively, in New York. Marty Katz, then the head of physical production, says it is axiomatic in the movie business to avoid New York because of expenses imposed by union rules. "There are three rules of production: you don't take a New York crew on location, you don't shoot in New York at night, and you don't build sets in New York," Katz says. "We did all three."

Hoffman, as deliberate as Warren Beatty any day, wasn't at all bashful about making his opinions known while the picture was being shot, remembers Katz. "Dustin was very particular—an absolute fanatic about everything being right," he says. "He was standing there at the camera while Benton directed. He would give input. Benton was an Academy Award–winning director and a smart man. I was a little surprised."

"I knew it was a disaster from the first day," says another executive who worked on the film. "Because from the first day's dailies, you could hear Dustin's voice yelling, 'Action.' "

Initially, Katzenberg told Katz to give Benton a lot of room to work even though the director had never dealt with a period film on this scale. But one day Katz strolled into a production office and noticed an enormous pile of unpaid bills sitting on someone's desk. Those expenses, he realized, probably hadn't even been tallied yet. The picture could be spiraling out of control.

"Unfortunately, it was true," he says. "We had to replace the entire production and accounting staff." Already, Disney was millions over budget on the film. But the studio didn't bring down the hammer. It continued to spend lavishly on sets, laying on a level of detail that, at least in Katz's opinion, wasn't necessary. "If you build a closet, and it's supposed to be a cedar closet and you build it out of real cedar so the actors can get the scent—that's a bit much," Katz says. But Hoffman wanted to smell cedar and he did. (The closet scene hit the cutting-room floor.) There was such attention to detail that matchbook covers and coasters were printed for scenes in a nightclub even though they weren't really visible in the film.

Eventually, Benton started to get fed up with Hoffman's help. The production moved to Saratoga, New York, to shoot scenes that didn't involve

Hoffman, and Benton let the actor know that he didn't need to come along. The production then moved to Brooklyn, where Hoffman showed up to offer advice. Benton took him aside and asked him not to do it again. Hoffman reportedly felt betrayed and said he would confine himself to acting only from that point forward.

But when Benton finally delivered his first cut to the studio, Katzenberg began to panic. The picture was what was sometimes called "a feathered fish"—a picture that lacks a cohesive concept. It was neither a love story nor a gangster movie. Hoffman told Katzenberg, "Jeffrey, you will not make your money back, you don't have a chance, if there isn't work done on this picture." Disney pushed back the film's release date and told Benton to go to work.

When the director returned with a revised cut, it was still so problematic that Katzenberg considered firing Benton, who offered to quit. Katzenberg declined but asked him to collaborate with Hoffman to improve the film. By now, Hoffman was working on *Hook* with Steven Spielberg and said he didn't have time, even when Katzenberg offered to move the entire operation from New York to Los Angeles, where *Hook* was shooting. At last Hoffman agreed to put in a weekend—far less than the six weeks Katzenberg had requested—with Benton, Katzenberg, and an editor.

By the time they met in May 1991, *Billy Bathgate* had been in production for a year and wasn't getting any cheaper. Hoffman wanted to do extensive reshoots but Katzenberg balked. Most of the changes would have to be made in the editing room.

Just as Benton was setting to work, his son was involved in a serious accident in Italy. He left the country on the very day that Tom Stoppard arrived to look in on the project. Stoppard made several suggestions that Benton ultimately adopted. As Benton reshaped the film, Hoffman once again felt excluded. He was particularly angry when he found out that a trailer for the film was playing in theaters even though he had been told that Disney had not yet set a release date. At that point Hoffman stopped speaking to Katzenberg. And he declined to do any publicity for the film.

By the time it was over, the film—originally budgeted at $38.5 million—cost nearly $60 million. "Jeffrey was so embarrassed by the amount it cost that the figure was not allowed to appear on even internal memos," says one executive. "It was whited out like a Pentagon budget."

When the film, unfocused and uninvolving, was released in November 1991, it was roundly trashed by critics. *Newsweek*'s David Ansen acknowledged that the novel "seemed to have all the right stuff for a blockbuster both popular and prestigious." But in the film, he concluded, "all the elements are in place . . . and nothing ignites." The supposed central character, played by the young Loren Dean, had become "an amiable cipher," while Hoffman played Dutch Schultz "as if he were Willy Loman's maniacal uncle." *The New Republic* was even less charitable, deriding the movie as banal and saying that Benton's attempt to do a gangster film "is to Martin Scorsese as a pickup truck is to a Ferrari."

Without the critics' support, Disney had an absolute debacle on its hands. The film lost more than $50 million—the biggest single failure of Katzenberg's career.

In Katz's analysis, Katzenberg had been burned by trusting the talent, just as he had done with *Dick Tracy*. "He respected the body of work that Benton had done and he respected Dustin Hoffman," says Katz. "He thought he had a group that would deliver the goods. . . . He did what everyone said he should do. He wasn't being passive. He picked up the phone and said, 'Don't you think . . . ?' and 'Maybe we should . . .' but he didn't say, 'You have to, or we will.' "

"There are films that you launch and they have their own guidance system," Katzenberg says. "There's nothing you're going to do along the way that can really change the course of where they're headed." In the case of *Billy Bathgate*, he says, "everything about it seemed great, and the soufflé never rose."

20

BEAUTY AND THE DEBACLE

A GRIM JOKE AT the Disney studio during the summer of '91 held that the July rerelease of the animated 101 *Dalmatians* was "an act of Walt" to help the studio through a long, cold summer. But in fact, Walt was merely tuning up for the real act of salvation, which would be the November debut of *Beauty and the Beast*. The picture would save the studio's year.

When they had picked up their Oscars for *The Little Mermaid*, Howard Ashman and Alan Menken were already at work on *Beauty and the Beast*. Katzenberg had imported a team of British animators, Richard Purdum and his wife, Jill, to develop and direct the film, but the Purdums wanted to animate in a style that would break the Disney mold. They were soon on their way back to London. Kirk Wise and Gary Trousdale, two young men who had worked on a short film at Epcot center, were brought in as acting directors and wound up staying. Don Hahn, the *Roger Rabbit* producer, was riding herd again.

By now, Katzenberg had landed in animation with both feet. "All directors working under Jeffrey on these things are in the same position," said story supervisor Roger Allers. As Brenda Chapman, a member of the storyboarding team explained, "They're in the second seat."

And Katzenberg acknowledged that his life had changed. "I have been seduced by this, completely and utterly," he said.

"He liked the people, for one thing," animator Ron Clements remembers. "He said the people he had to deal with most of the time in live action were different from the people in animation. Animators are more quiet, easygoing, introverted people. They like the art, the craft. They're not people whose egos are going rampant. And Jeffrey would comment that animation had a more fun, relaxed kind of atmosphere—and was sincere, I think, in a way."

In the early going on *Beauty and the Beast*, Katzenberg had a secret. The brilliant Howard Ashman had confided that he had AIDS. No one was to know; he wanted to continue his work. So when Katzenberg ordered a team of animators to camp out in a hotel in Fishkill, New York, to work with Ashman at his home, they all assumed that the songwriter was being a prima donna. Finally Ashman's illness became apparent.

There were times when he could only work confined to his bed. He listened to recording sessions through speakers. He became so weak that he could barely make himself heard. Eventually, Menken had to sing parts that Ashman normally vocalized.

In March 1991, Katzenberg and David Geffen — who had produced *Little Shop of Horrors* — paid a final visit to the dying Ashman. "David Geffen in that room with Howard Ashman is one of the real inspirational things I have seen," Katzenberg said later. "Things poured out of David in his love for Howard at that moment. He talked about miracles, told Howard he was a man who inspired people to believe in magical things, that he had to believe, that maybe it wasn't over, that he should never give up."

Days later, Ashman was dead. He had finished his work on *Beauty and the Beast*. "I don't think there has been anything more difficult, challenging, and ultimately more rewarding to me than having been a patron to Howard Ashman in the last year of his life," Katzenberg said as *Beauty and the Beast* was in its final stages of completion. "I was a patron to a genius." When Alan Menken climbed the steps to accept the Oscar for Best Original Song that year, he would be alone.

∽

KATZENBERG'S IDEAS DIDN'T always suit the animators. Some of the jokes he proposed struck them as tedious. But they came to realize that he cared about their projects and sometimes had a certain instinct for what worked. After a *Beauty and the Beast* preview, he urged them to improve the scene where Belle and the Beast first touch. "The moment they actually touch is the moment in which they are saying, 'I love you,'" he told the assembled group. "You have to milk the hell out of it. I know with every ounce of my being — we should have a tear in our eye."

Even the animators were having fun now. "People are kind of buzzed about this movie," said Tom Sito, an animator on the *Beast* team, a few months before the film opened. "You're actually kind of embarrassed to admit you like the footage. You've sold out. You're a company man."

In July, four months before the film opened, there was a test screening with a recruited audience. Eisner and Frank Wells both sat in. Afterward, Eisner joined the key filmmakers at a Burbank sidewalk café. Wearing a red Columbia Pictures baseball cap, he grilled the nervous group. "What was the general consensus?" he asked.

Peter Schneider, the head of animation, replied. "We feel it's there," he said. "By and large, it's there."

Eisner wasn't satisfied. "I am nervous about recruited audiences," he said. "Even in the biggest hit movies, kids get up and go to the bathroom." In fact, the kids sat transfixed through the film. But Eisner seemed to regard that as a bad sign.

"We like to think it's because they were interested," director Kirk Wise volunteered.

"Have you had any problems with the long narration?" Eisner persisted, referring to the film's opening sequence.

"You find it long?" Schneider asked quickly.

"I'm asking," Eisner said.

"None of the cards [completed by the audience] mention it," Schneider replied cautiously.

"So you don't think it would be any different with a paying audience?"

Schneider hedged. "We were deceived on *Rescuers*," he said, referring to *The Rescuers Down Under*, the unsuccessful sequel to *The Great Mouse Detective*. (In fact, Eisner was a proponent of making that film in the first place. "They wanted to do a sequel to something," Clements remembers. "They felt there was something safe about it.")

Finally Eisner relaxed a little. "I think this audience loved the film," he said. "I think they were unbelievably polite. I think the movie's fantastic. My children aren't as polite as those kids. I've never seen kids not go to the bathroom for that period of time."

No one knew what to say next. Finally Wise broke the silence with a proposed tag line for the film: "You'll laugh, you'll cry, you'll hold your water."

No one was sure whether *The Little Mermaid* had been a fluke. *Beauty and the Beast* demonstrated that Disney had reinvigorated the medium. After its release in November 1991, it became the number-three movie of the year and the highest-grossing animated film of all time, pulling in $146 million at the domestic box office alone. But that was hardly its only achievement. In *Beauty and the Beast*, Katzenberg would pull off an audacious goal that he had set for himself. The film would be the first animated feature ever to be nominated for the Best Picture award at the Oscars. In fact, it picked up six nominations and won for Best Original Song and Best Original Score. Whenever it released an animated film, it seemed, Disney could claim that pair of awards at will.

∾

EISNER LEANED ON the success of *Beauty and the Beast* in his message to shareholders prefacing the 1991 annual report. With attendance at the theme parks down because of an ongoing recession and a feature-film performance "best forgotten," Eisner said he didn't know quite how to write his yearly missive. "Somehow writing about my family, my kids' school or hockey, my sister Margot's job at a museum in New York, or my mother seemed inappropriate this year," he acknowledged.

Though revenues were up to $6.2 billion, the company's operating income had fallen by 18 percent to $1.2 billion from the previous year. Revenue from the theme parks was off by 5 percent and operating income had taken a 31 percent ($155 million) tumble. The film division had suffered through an abysmal year with profits flat. Overall, Disney's earnings were off by 23 percent.

Still, Eisner pointed to what bright spots he could. Among them was Disney's success in getting eleven programs on the networks, the highest total for any studio. "Aside from my middle son, Eric, getting into college this year and, as of this date, staying in college, our television success has been the highlight of the year for me," Eisner wrote. (So much for not slipping in a family reference.) Though he couldn't know it at the time, only one of this batch of shows would be a long-term survivor. *Home Improvement* would turn into the biggest television hit in the company's history—a veritable fountain of money.

But that was still in the future. For the moment all Eisner was left to rhapsodize about was the success of *Beauty and the Beast*. "It is amazing how a single creative act can change everything," he wrote. "[This film] has confirmed that your company still has it! It is that simple because *Beauty and the Beast* is one of the great movies of all time (he said shamelessly). And the products coming out of *Beauty* will be around forever. And the rides emanating from *Beauty* in our parks will be around forever. And someday, the home video of *Beauty and the Beast* will sell 20 million cassettes worldwide."

Eisner ended his 1991 letter to shareholders on an upbeat note — slipping entirely back into his usual aw-shucks voice. "I'll let last year fade away as a child's bad report card fades away and others come in good," he wrote, somewhat awkwardly. "I will simply remember that in 1991, my 21-year-old son Breck directed the three-hour stage play of Shakespeare's *Antony and Cleopatra* at his college and my 13-year-old son Anders sat still for the entire evening and told me it was 'not bad, kind of okay.' "

For his parting note, Eisner said he and Frank Wells were looking forward to a better 1992. "I am pretty sure it will be far superior to 1991; but one thing is certain, we will open Euro Disney on April 12 at 9:01 A.M." Eisner's upbeat tone concealed the anxiety that consumed him. As he knew, Disney was pouring ever-increasing sums into Euro Disney in the rush to get it open on time.

∽

KATZENBERG COULD NOT help being proud of *Beauty and the Beast*. But the cloud to this particular silver lining was Roy Disney, who resented Katzenberg's place in the spotlight. This was a problem that Eisner warned Katzenberg about repeatedly. "Don't forget to take care of Roy," he cautioned. Katzenberg says he tried to respond. But perhaps it was simply impossible to take care of Roy. When Katzenberg was working with *Premiere* magazine on an article about *Beauty and the Beast*, he implored the reporter to mention Roy Disney's contribution to the film. But the reporter, who had never seen Roy or heard any of the animators mention his name, refused.

And perhaps Katzenberg, who considered himself such an indispensable part of the company, didn't try hard enough to nurture this crucial relationship. One Disney board member says it was simply too late. "He had seven years of history of putting [Roy] down," this insider says. "Jeffrey's very good at giving you importance when you're important to him. . . . He doesn't see the big picture." To this observer, Katzenberg was reaping the fruits of his own disrespect. If Katzenberg expected a congratulatory call from Roy after the film opened, he was to be disappointed.

There were other disappointments. Eisner, who had been criticized for taking a $10.5 million bonus in 1990 while the company was cutting costs, earned a 1991 bonus of only $4.7 million (the amount was based on net income and return on shareholder equity). He also cut the studio's bonus pool in half, upsetting Katzenberg and some two hundred executives who were affected.

Certainly, the division had turned in lackluster results. But it was also the home of animation, which was now Disney's crown jewel. On the other hand, executives in live action had nothing to do with animation, and Eisner undoubtedly felt they should suffer the consequences of their bad year. But that message wasn't delivered gently. To justify Eisner's decision, Wells wrote a lengthy read-and-destroy memo "that was so nasty and so demeaning of all the executives," remembers a former high-level studio source. "We didn't expect that, but that was part of his role. That's what he did for Michael."

The blow was especially heavy because Disney generally paid less than other studios, which meant that its executives depended on bonuses to make up a substantial part of their compensation. Many were keenly aware that Eisner was racking up a fortune through his stock options. And with the mandate to produce more films, the executives felt that they had been pushed to—or perhaps beyond—their limits. "Morale was so low anyway— [the cuts] brought morale even lower," says Hoberman. "Everybody had worked so hard. It was a very tense time."

Katzenberg went to bat and, after some bruising meetings with Wells, managed to get some more money for his team, but many remained bitter. "For years, Michael always said the real test will be how we hold up when things are bad," a studio executive remembers. "Then we saw. When things were tough, he was terrible."

∽

THE OLD DISNEY formula still had some gasps left. In January 1992, Hollywood Pictures opened its standout hit *The Hand That Rocks the Cradle*. Touchstone would have a welcome smash from Whoopi Goldberg in May 1992 with *Sister Act*. Hollywood would at least make a profit with the sophomoric Pauly Shore film *Encino Man* in the same month. Disney's family label released *The Mighty Ducks*, the first in a franchise that Eisner said was inspired by his son Anders's adventures on the rink. These films wouldn't bring prestige to Disney, but they delivered at the box office.

Still, the string of flops was absolutely abysmal: *Medicine Man, Blame It on the Bellboy, Noises Off, Newsies, Passed Away*, and *The Gun in Betty Lou's Handbag*. Hollywood Pictures may have hit a low point with *A*

Stranger Among Us, which cast Melanie Griffith in the unlikely role of an undercover detective in a Hasidic Jewish neighborhood. The industry nick-named the project *Goyz N the Hood*, a takeoff of John Singleton's 1991 sleeper hit for Columbia Pictures.

Still, Eisner had been correct in predicting improved results for fiscal 1992. Thanks in part to the home-video release of the animated classics *101 Dalmatians* and *Fantasia*, the filmed entertainment division's revenues were up 20 percent to $3.1 billion and operating income increased a whop-ping 60 percent to $508.3 million. It was the most profitable year for any studio in the history of Hollywood. Overall, the company rallied with a record $7.5 billion in revenues, a 23 percent increase over 1991. Operating income increased 31 percent to $1.4 billion.

There was another factor in the film division's stellar performance. *Beauty and the Beast* had opened in November 1991, which meant that its gush of revenues began after the start of fiscal 1992. In his annual letter to stockholders that year, Eisner again acknowledged the importance of ani-mation in general and *Beauty* in particular to the company. "I have yet to find the adjective to suitably describe the success of this film," he said. He lavished praise on the artists. "Your company," he told shareholders, "has nothing less than the most talented, inventive, creative, original, resourceful and brilliant people working in animation."

And there was another animation blockbuster in the theaters, though it had opened in November 1992 and wouldn't show up on the books until fiscal 1993. *Aladdin* was the last film to feature lyrics from Howard Ashman, whose partially completed work was finished by Tim Rice. It not only claimed the two music Oscars but five Grammys (its big hit, "A Whole New World," was named Song of the Year). And *Aladdin* was the first animated feature to be number one at the box office since *The Jungle Book* had scored that coup in 1967.

Eisner also noted that June 1993 would mark the hundredth anniversary of Roy O. Disney's birth. And while he mentioned in one long paragraph that the elder Roy "virtually gave his life" to the company, he also took the opportunity to praise the contemporary Roy in the ensuing eight paragraphs.

"With all that Roy Sr. gave to this company, perhaps his number one legacy to our company is his son, our Roy, who did nothing less than save the company in 1984—with the help of Stanley Gold, Roy's partner and friend, from the outside, and Ray Watson, the chairman of the company, from the inside," Eisner wrote. Roy not only kept the company together, Eisner continued, but he knew that Disney had to recommit itself to animation. At the time, Eisner remembered, "the common wisdom was that drawing a movie frame by laborious frame was archaic and too expensive. But Roy bought none of that."

When Katzenberg was hired, Eisner said, "one of his major responsibilities was to work with Roy to restore Disney's lost luster in animation." He offered this history to show "how insightful and downright gutsy Roy was to insist way back in 1984 that we pour major resources into what most people thought was a moribund, money-losing enterprise that would only be relegated to kids' matinees." As the company broke box-office records and collected Oscars, Eisner said, "we should always remember that we have Roy to thank." In his entire paean, Eisner barely mentioned Katzenberg.

∽

EISNER HAD SOME other, personal business to take care of in his letter. His compensation had rallied—rather dramatically—in 1992. In December, he and Wells had exercised options on about 6.6 million Disney shares, selling nearly 5.1 million of them. That fiscal year, in a feat that the *Wall Street Journal* described as "one of the single most lucrative transactions in the annals of executive compensation," Eisner took home a breathtaking $197 million. (Wells netted $60.3 million before taxes.) With his salary and bonus, Eisner was taking home more than $200 million. Eisner's remuneration set a record for a chief executive of a public company. (Obviously, he was the highest-paid executive for that year. The first runner-up, Sanford Weill of Travelers Corp., earned $52.8 million.) As *Newsweek*'s Allan Sloan marveled, by pulling off "the most lucrative stock option since money was invented," Eisner at age fifty had actually propelled himself onto the *Forbes* 400 list of richest Americans. That was no mean feat considering how few executives managed to make their way onto that list simply by being employees rather than major shareholders, founders, or inheritors.

Eisner said he understood that the sale of what amounted to about 1 percent of the stock by its two top officers was a sensitive issue. (Disney stock actually dropped $1.875 a share the day of the sale but recovered later in the week.) But the options had to be exercised because of legislation— supported by newly elected President Bill Clinton—that would eliminate breaks for companies that lavished compensation in excess of $1 million to top executives. By selling now, he was actually saving the company money. Besides, he still held three million shares of the company's stock. He was not bailing out of Disney.

If Katzenberg was indeed jealous over Eisner's compensation, the news of Eisner's big payout must have been especially hard to take. His division had set a record for profit, and Eisner—who had steered the company into burgeoning losses at Euro Disney—nonetheless set a record for making the most money ever.

Eisner's rich compensation set off a round of public debate. *The New Republic* derided Eisner as a hypocrite for supporting Bill Clinton but dodging his anticipated tax reform. In the *Los Angeles Times*, columnist Peter H. King wrote, "I read somewhere that Walt Disney had a maxim: 'Pig, don't make a hog of yourself.' It no longer seems to apply." But James Flanagan, another *Times* columnist, took Eisner's side. He quoted a pension fund manager who said, "[Eisner] deserves every penny. He's the best thing that happened to the company since Mickey Mouse."

Allan Sloan, who acknowledged that he had complained in the past that Disney had used "its squeaky-clean image to stick investors with overpriced, trashy securities" (including a very successful sale of stock in Euro Disney), also came to Eisner's defense. Before Eisner and Wells, he pointed out, Disney's stock-market value was about $2 billion. Now it was $22 billion. "Who can begrudge Eisner a tad more than 1 percent of that increase?" Sloan asked. "Even I can't."

∽

ASIDE FROM ITS brilliant music, the key to *Aladdin*'s success was a star turn by Robin Williams as the Genie, whose rapid patter included jokes that appealed as much to adults as to children. In the course of the film, Williams whacked out about sixty impressions of everyone from Ed Sullivan to Arnold Schwarzenegger. Initially, Williams was reluctant to take the role, but after seeing a mock-up of the Genie, he agreed to work for the Screen Actors Guild minimum of $485 a day. He saw it as a chance to make a film that would delight his own children. But if he was going to work for so little money, Williams laid down some conditions. He insisted that Disney not use his voice or the Genie image (which he considered to be a caricature of himself) in any tie-in promotions (like Burger King's offering of *Aladdin* figurines). In trailers and television commercials, the Genie could appear but only in proportion to his role in the film (he was on-screen about 25 percent of the time).

Disney met his terms through the opening of the film. But when Disney created some new advertising for it, including a poster that showed the Genie's face, Williams felt that he had been exploited without his permission. At Williams's insistence, the poster was removed from bus shelters all over the country. He was also upset when the Disney Channel showed footage of him and his family attending the January 1993 opening of the Toontown attraction at Disneyland. The final straw came when Disney decided to give the film another burst by creating a coupon booklet that theater patrons could use for discounts on *Aladdin* merchandise. The studio didn't use the Genie's image in a television commercial advertising the promotion, but it showed the character of the merchant (an alter ego of the Genie) and used another actor to provide his voice. The studio argued that the voice was not a sound-alike, but Williams vehemently disagreed. He felt that Disney had violated the spirit, if not the letter, of its deal.

There was plenty of very heated conversation with Williams's agent, Michael Ovitz. Katzenberg also got into a loud dispute with Williams, or more precisely his wife. The fight could have been settled had Williams been paid—and his agents at CAA figured that his participation in the film, had it been a normal deal, could have been as great as $25 million. Katzenberg tried to appease the star by giving him a Picasso painting that he claimed was worth $8 million. (Ironically, Katzenberg enlisted producer Mark Johnson—who had felt so shortchanged by Disney when he made *Good Morning, Vietnam*—to plant the gift in Williams's hotel room in New York.)

Williams's agents (who probably got the real scoop from Ovitz's dealer, Arne Glimcher) believed that Disney had gotten the painting for less than $1 million. Besides, Williams thought it was ugly. "I've known Robin for ten years and I've never heard him so angry," says one business associate. "He was livid, just livid. He was so angry that they fucked him like that." Williams's wife—known as Lady Macbeth within the confines of his manager's office—was furious, too; she apparently thought the studio should have given the star a Learjet. In the end, Williams—who had starred in *Good Morning, Vietnam, Dead Poets Society*, and *Aladdin* for the studio—no longer had a working relationship with Disney.

❧

EVEN AS EISNER had reported to shareholders that the company's results from fiscal 1992 were "great," he knew that trouble loomed ahead.
Euro Disney, he asserted, was "one of the greatest man-made attractions in
the world"—"somewhat expensive but still fantastic." Calling Euro Disney
"somewhat expensive" was quite an understatement. And Eisner acknowledged in December 1992 that as winter approached, "[we] frankly do not
know what will happen."

Eisner must have known that the difficulties ahead went far beyond mere
dips in the mercury. In fact, Euro Disney was a burgeoning disaster that
would make the other so-called disasters in the domestic theme parks pale
in comparison. It would fall to Frank Wells, who had helped preside over
the company's slide into this morass, to find a way out.

Of all the challenges that Wells had faced in his working life, none
compared with trying to salvage Euro Disney. "To him, it was Waterloo,"
Katzenberg says. "He said it was the most horrible thing that happened
professionally to him in his career."

In building Euro Disney, Eisner was determined not to repeat the mistakes of Tokyo Disney, which was built and owned by an outside company.
Nor was Disney going to cede hotel development to others, as had been
done in Orlando (where Disney owned only 14 percent of the area hotels).
The Euro Disney plan called for six hotels with 5,200 rooms, a campground,
and a golf course.

But that wasn't all. Eventually, there was to be a second gate—another
studio-themed attraction like the Disney-MGM tour in Florida—and perhaps three times as many hotel rooms (notwithstanding the fact that the
initial plan created more rooms than could be found in the entire city of
Cannes) as well as offices and 570 new homes. Disney would design and
construct all these elements and then sell them.

What went wrong with this most ambitious part of Disney's dramatic
expansion? Executives who worked on the project disagree about where to
lay the blame. Was it a simple matter of a recession and bad timing? Was
Euro Disney overly ambitious and too expensive? Did Disney try to cut
itself too sweet a deal, draining too much profit from the park? Did the
plan rely too heavily on debt to finance the project? The answer is all of
the above, as well as what *Newsweek* called Disney's "blinding arrogance."
In Europe, the *Wall Street Journal* suggested, Disney reaped the consequences of its "brash, frequently insensitive and often overbearing style."
Certainly Eisner walked stubbornly into a multibillion-dollar mess.

Michael Eisner in 1960, his senior year at Lawrenceville, an elite boarding school in New Jersey. Eisner would later say that he suffered his first encounter with anti-Semitism at the school, where attendance at chapel was mandatory. Lawrenceville fed bright young men to Princeton, but Eisner was not destined for the Ivy League. (Seth Poppel Yearbook Archives)

Barry Diller in 1960, his senior year at Beverly Hills High School. Classmates called Diller "the old man." One remembers that he wore galoshes on rainy days and hated rock music. He later dropped out of UCLA and got Danny Thomas, whose children were his schoolmates, to help him get a job in the mailroom at the William Morris Agency. (Seth Poppel Yearbook Archives)

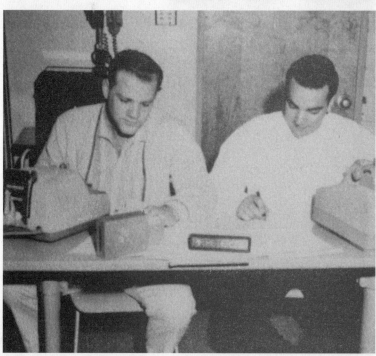

Jeffrey Katzenberg with his father. Katzenberg grew up not far from Eisner on Park Avenue, but his family was not nearly as wealthy. A close friend says Katzenberg's relationship with his father was competitive; Katzenberg sought out strong male mentors throughout his life. (Courtesy of Jeffrey Katzenberg)

Jeffrey Katzenberg in 1969, his senior year at Fieldston School in New York. Katzenberg was hardly an academic star. By age fourteen, he had already started to spend most of his time working in the administration of Mayor John Lindsay. Like Barry Diller, he never got a college education. (Courtesy of Jeffrey Katzenberg)

Michael Ovitz (seated on the left) with junk-bond king Michael Milken (standing on the right) in 1964, Ovitz's junior year at Birmingham High School in Van Nuys, California. The future superagent was a member of the school's Boys' League. (Seth Poppel Yearbook Archives)

Jeffrey Katzenberg with New York mayor John Lindsay. As a teen Katzenberg worked his way into a position of trust with the top men in Lindsay's administration. He also developed a reputation as a Lindsay "bag man" that would haunt him for years. He was investigated by a New York prosecutor but never charged with any misconduct. (Courtesy of Jeffrey Katzenberg)

Eisner in the seventies during his tenure at ABC. Eisner nearly lost his job after tangling with rising producer Aaron Spelling, who created *Mod Squad, Charlie's Angels, The Love Boat,* and other hits for the network. Eisner played a key role in putting such hits as *Happy Days* and *Laverne & Shirley* on the air. He left the network when his rival, Barry Diller, offered him a top job at Paramount Pictures. (Photofest)

Barry Diller in 1974 when he was vice-president in charge of prime-time television at ABC. Diller was a frightening boss who was locked in competition with another rising star at the network, Michael Eisner. "The fact that he was a son of a bitch to work for never really bothered me," said Dick Zimbert, a former Diller employee. (Corbis/Bettmann-UPI)

Paramount president Frank Yablans (left) with Charlie Bluhdorn, the "mad Austrian" who controlled Paramount's parent company, Gulf + Western. Bluhdorn was an erratic boss whose wild ideas for movies included one that involved a meeting between Sitting Bull and Adolf Hitler. (Peter C. Borsari)

Cindy Williams and Penny Marshall with Michael Eisner in a rare happy moment. The two *Laverne & Shirley* stars were at each other's throats from the beginning. Williams claimed that Marshall was getting more screen time and all the best lines. When forced to choose, Eisner sided with Marshall, whose brother, Garry, had created the series. (Peter C. Borsari)

Flamboyant producer Allan Carr brought the film version of *Grease* to Paramount. He insisted that Diller and Eisner didn't really support the film until it had a successful test screening in Hawaii. *Grease* was one of several hits greenlighted by Paramount executive David Picker, who later came to believe that Eisner took credit for his work. (Peter C. Borsari)

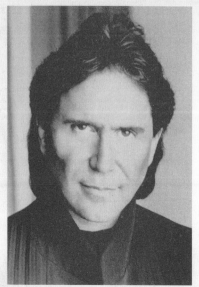

Don Simpson, the macho president of production at Paramount, apparently had trouble standing up to Eisner. He was moved out of his job at the studio after his substance abuse started to interfere with his work. Immersed in hookers and drugs, he nevertheless became part of the exceptionally successful producing team that made *Flashdance, Beverly Hills Cop,* and *Top Gun.* (Reuters/Archive Photos)

Jeffrey Katzenberg with John Travolta on the set of *Staying Alive,* the ill-fated 1983 sequel to *Saturday Night Fever.* Barry Diller says Paramount boss Charlie Bluhdorn talked Travolta into making the film. "Really, if his career had not been completely dead, it was buried on the heels of this movie," Diller says. (Courtesy of Jeffrey Katzenberg)

Eisner with Roy Disney. Dismissed by the old guard as Walt's feebleminded nephew, Roy came back with a vengeance in 1984 when he effectively won control of the company. He played a crucial role in keeping Disney animation alive but felt snubbed by studio chairman Jeffrey Katzenberg. (Reuters/Joe Skipper/Archive Photos)

Eisner with Muppet creator Jim Henson in August 1989. Disney's deal to acquire the Muppets went sour after Henson's sudden death the following year. Henson's heirs sued, and eventually the company issued a public apology for using Henson's characters without permission. (Corbis/Bettmann-UPI)

A Rhodes scholar, the charismatic Frank Wells
was one of the few who could command Eisner's
respect. "He was the highest of the high goyim,"
producer Don Simpson said of him. "He represented
everything Michael wanted to be." Retired Disney
executive Pete Clark remembers, "He was the moral
compass." (Peter C. Borsari)

Euro Disney, later to be renamed Disneyland Paris, opened in April 1992. With Eisner
insisting on meticulous attention to detail, the project ran wildly over budget. Frank
Wells told Jeffrey Katzenberg that mopping up the financial mess was the worst
nightmare of his career. (Reuters/Christine Grunnet/Archive Photos)

Warren Beatty at the 1990 premiere of *Dick Tracy*. During the making of the film, Beatty romanced Madonna and entranced top executives at Disney, including Katzenberg. "Jeffrey on some level wanted to be Warren Beatty," says a colleague. Later, Katzenberg infuriated the star by saying that the picture probably had not been worth the time and effort that Disney had put into it. (Corbis/Bettmann-UPI)

"The Final Merger"

Jeffrey Katzenberg (right), the chairman of the Disney studio, and superagent Michael Ovitz. For years, they did battle as Katzenberg tried to hold down costs and Ovitz tried to get the best deal for clients like Tom Cruise, Robin Williams, and director Barry Levinson. Outwardly, Eisner stayed out of the fray. Later, Katzenberg said he had been a "naive schnook" not to realize that Eisner pitted him against Ovitz to preserve his own relationship with the agent. (Peter C. Borsari)

Frank Wells (right) and his friend Dick Bass enjoy a heli-ski trip in Nevada over Easter weekend in 1994. In the early eighties, Bass had been Wells's partner in attempting to climb the tallest mountain on each continent. While Wells made it to six of the seven summits, he didn't make it to the top of Mount Everest. Bass did and became the first person to conquer the seven summits. This was their last outing together; Wells would not live through the weekend. (Mike Hoover)

The downed helicopter in which Frank Wells died in April 1994. Only Mike Hoover, a documentarian, survived. Hoover's wife was killed as was the pilot and a guide. Wells's death catalyzed a series of events that changed the face of Hollywood. Many in the industry believed that Eisner had lost the only governor on his engines. (Mike Hoover)

Longtime MCA chairman Lew Wasserman (right) and president Sid Sheinberg in 1994. Sheinberg accused Eisner of copying MCA's plans for a studio-tour attraction in Florida and warned that Disney was becoming a "ravenous rat." (Reuters/Fred Prouser/Archive Photos)

Michael Ovitz (left) with Eisner. The former superagent thought Eisner was his best friend and sat at his bedside after his emergency bypass operation in 1994. But after Eisner hired him as president of Disney in 1995, Ovitz felt betrayed. The relationship ended with a bitter rupture. (Reuters/Lee Celano/Archive Photos)

Jeffrey Katzenberg and his wife, Marilyn. She had been an attractive schoolteacher whose boyfriend sometimes let the younger Katzenberg tag along on dates. She knew Katzenberg only as "Squirt," as he was called during his years with the Lindsay administration. When he called to ask her out, at first she didn't recognize his real name.
(© Pacha/Corbis)

Katzenberg (left) with Steven Spielberg and David Geffen in 1994 as the three announced the ambitious formation of DreamWorks. Geffen was so anxious before the press conference that he reportedly spent the morning throwing up.
(Reuters/Sam Mircovitch/Archive Photos)

Michael Eisner and his mother, Margaret, arrive at the forty-eighth annual Tony Awards in June 1994. Eisner's mother was a formidable woman. Later in life, Eisner's secretary at Paramount referred to her as "the barracuda." (Jeff Christensen/Corbis/Reuters)

"Is Michael Eisner O.K.? I haven't seen his name in the papers for days."

Eisner with Capital Cities/ABC chairman Tom Murphy in 1995 as they announce the $19 billion merger of the two companies. Turning ABC around would prove an elusive goal, but Eisner said getting ESPN alone justified the deal. As a member of the Disney board, Murphy later made a futile attempt to get Disney to settle the costly lawsuit filed by Jeffrey Katzenberg.
(Reuters/Peter Morgan/Archive Photos)

Eisner with his wife, Jane, and sons Breck and Eric. When Sid Bass saw a photograph of Eisner and his family in *New York* magazine in 1984, he decided that Eisner might be the right man for the top job at Disney. Eisner frequently alluded to his sons (including the youngest, Anders) in folksy letters to Disney shareholders.
(Peter C. Borsari)

Robert Iger, the chairman of Disney's ABC Group and president of Walt Disney International, would become the first full-fledged number-two man since the death of Frank Wells, though no executive would report solely to him. Iger was precisely the type of smooth, presentable executive that appealed to Eisner, but critics said he was a bit too eager to ingratiate himself with his boss.
(Reuters/Mark Cardwell/Archive Photos)

An attorney who managed Roy Disney's affairs, Stanley Gold sought out his former law partner Frank Wells for a top job at the faltering Walt Disney Company in 1984. Later, he played a key role in ending the disastrous lawsuit brought against Disney by Jeffrey Katzenberg. (Shamrock Holdings)

Eisner attends the premiere of *Tarzan* in June 1999. While *Tarzan* performed strongly at the box office, Eisner was facing trouble on many fronts. Disney's stock was faltering, and Eisner's personal stock was taking a drubbing as he waged a futile court battle against his former studio chairman Jeffrey Katzenberg. (© Pacha/Corbis)

THE EUROPEAN DISNEY had been kicked off in March 1987 when Eisner signed an agreement with French premier Jacques Chirac. After a tough negotiation, the French government offered a generous incentive package to lure the project, including $750 million worth of loans, cheap real estate, and a promise to improve rail transit and highways leading to the site. Still, this was Disney's biggest gamble ever.

Chief financial officer Gary Wilson created a series of partnerships designed to insulate the Walt Disney Company from potential problems while also squeezing as much profit as possible out of the new theme park. Euro Disney was structured as a separate company, 49 percent of which would be owned by Disney. Disney also put up only $150 million in exchange for equity that soared to a value of $2.3 billion when stock rose before the park opened. Disney expected to make money from rich management fees and royalties, as well as a share in profits.

Aside from Disney's relatively tiny investment in the project, former Imagineer Dave Fink says that structurally the deal was inherently unfair to outside investors because Disney had total control over the design of the park and the shareholders paid the costs. And Imagineering was charging Euro Disney top dollar for its services. "If a single designer said he wanted to spend more time, they did it and billed the client," Fink says. "No one at the Walt Disney Company ever thought, 'Is this fair to the client?' because it's not about the client. . . . [It was], 'We will tell you when the design is done. We're going to spend your money on it until it's ready.' It's a very difficult situation. The justification for it is, that's how they would have done it for themselves."

Wilson's job was to come up with a plan to pay for the project—and he saddled it with debt. "The financing of Euro Disney was such a critical, critical issue for the company," says an executive who worked on it. "An enormous amount of capital was required. And how do you get partners to share the risk?" The answer was a public offering combined with about $3.5 billion in debt as well as the concessions that Disney had wrung from the French government.

The Disney name had such cachet that raising money wasn't a problem, although the company still had to fight hard to do it on Disney's terms. The French found the company's bare-knuckle style jarring. But even so, the government and bankers were determined to do business with Disney, so the project went ahead. One executive who worked on the financing remembers that Eisner was interested in the financing but didn't want to deal in specifics. "He'd [act] like I was the plague," that executive says. "He joked with people about me. He'd ask, 'Things going okay? Okay. Don't tell me [the details].' . . . His interest was in the [guest] experience, architecture, and design."

Eventually, however, Eisner had to confront the fact that a major problem was developing. Imagineering was literally hundreds of millions of dollars over budget on Euro Disney. The theme park alone (excluding the hotels that Disney intended to build and sell) had been budgeted at $1.3 billion. Five years before the project's planned opening in April 1992, this source says, the overage was already $850 million. The project was also about nine months behind schedule, which meant the company would have to pay premiums to finish construction on time.

Naturally, Eisner was appalled. "This is how our predecessors lost their jobs," he said, alluding to the overages that had plagued Epcot and weakened the company. As Euro Disney loomed nearer, it must have seemed as though the doom he had feared for so long was at hand. As he later acknowledged mournfully: "I've always been fearful . . . because in most of the corporations that I worked at before I came to Disney, I saw the one big mistake bring down companies or people. So I'm very conservative and try to stay away from the one devastating mistake where the risks are extremely high, as in building a multibillion-dollar park in an area where there's a massive recession and we don't really know the culture perfectly."

As it came time to secure financing from a consortium of European banks, says a source familiar with the situation, Eisner and Wells, along with Wilson, became convinced that they had to conceal the severity of the problems with the project. The banks, with Banque Nationale de Paris in the lead, had hired Coopers & Lybrand to audit the Imagineering organization. That meant Disney had to give the impression that its house was in order. Eisner, Wells, and Wilson considered postponing the financing to give them time to rework plans for the park but decided against it.

Disney did slash some costs by redesigning certain attractions and renegotiating contracts with vendors. But even though these measures saved more than $500 million, it wasn't enough.

Fearful of jeopardizing the financing of Euro Disney, Eisner and Wells were desperate to minimize the impact of the overages. If Eisner thought that the Euro Disney project endangered him, he certainly trusted Frank

Wells to stand with him. "I knew that if we were going to get in trouble," he said, "we were going to be in trouble together. I wasn't going to be in trouble and he wasn't going to take the rap. We would take the rap— together."

∞

DESPITE THE OVERRUNS, Disney remained optimistic. Paris was a big city and the French were the world's most avid consumers of all things Disney. More than 310 million people lived within a two-hour flight of the park. There were good airports and the French government had promised to build new roads and to improve the rail system. Europeans took long vacations. And the park would be even more "weatherized" than Tokyo Disney, which was open all year in conditions similar to those in France.

Eisner encouraged the park's designers to make a European version of Disneyland that was exquisitely crafted, more than just a rerun of the American parks. And the more he encouraged the designers, the more the costs went up. A French architect told a friend that he was astonished that Eisner thought nothing about flying him to the United States repeatedly to discuss what seemed rather minor points, such as his opinion of a door that might be used in one of the hotels. And one frequently repeated tale inside Imagineering was that after Eisner looked at an enormous, detailed model of Euro Disney, he said, "I think this building should be over here." With that, he nudged a model over a bit. No one contradicted him and the building was moved even though the new site posed logistical problems. "The story goes that the nudge cost $1.5 million," a former Imagineer says.

Another executive who worked closely on Euro Disney says Eisner made a conscious decision to upgrade everything to make a quality statement. This was Disney's debut in Europe and he wanted it to be dazzling. Eisner insisted on adding an entertainment complex called Disney Village to provide after-hours entertainment. Several members of his staff wanted to postpone the project but Eisner would not hear of it. He was offered a choice between a relatively modest plan based on a New England–style village or a daring series of oddly shaped buildings designed by architect Frank Gehry. Eisner's design team voted overwhelmingly for the more conservative village. Eisner commissioned the Gehry design.

Disney courted Italian architect Aldo Rossi to design one of five hotels for the property. But Rossi soon found himself frustrated. In a letter to Eisner, he compared himself with the great Bernini, who, invited to Paris for the Louvre project, found himself "tormented by a multitude of functionaries" to make changes in his plan. "It is clear that I am not the Cavalier Bernini," Rossi wrote to Eisner, "but it is also clear that you are not the King of France. . . . I do not intend to be the object of minuscule criticisms that any interior designer could handle." With that, Rossi quit.

Eisner fussed endlessly with the hotels. He wanted wood-burning fireplaces installed. The company imported hundreds of cedar, sweetgum, and pine trees for the Sequoia Lodge, an Antoine Grumbach–designed hotel. The costs rose. "There were occasional voices of caution," Eisner acknowledged later, "but none of them was loud or persistent. If anything, we grew more ambitious over time." (He also made it clear that he blamed Gary Wilson for the company's decision to build such an enormous number of hotel rooms.)

Even at the last minute, Eisner was ordering changes at the park. At great expense, two steel staircases in Discoveryland were moved because they blocked a view. Even the roller coaster on Thunder Mountain was redesigned. Between Eisner and the Imagineers, the costs kept going up. "We're not reinventing the wheel here—that's what I bitched about constantly," says a former high-level executive who worked on the project. "But [Imagineering] wanted to do this customized thing. Look at the detail there."

Meanwhile, some of the bankers and businesspeople were finding that Disney could actually beat the Parisians in an arrogance contest. One evening, when Eisner was visiting Jean-René Bernard, the chief negotiator for the French government, at Bernard's apartment in the western part of Paris, Eisner said, "You live in the west of Paris, as do your friends, but your children and grandchildren will live in the east of Paris" near Euro Disney.

There were other questions about how well Disney understood the European culture. In one strategy meeting, an executive wondered aloud whether Europeans would stand in line during winter. Disney remained convinced that Europeans would wait because the Japanese did. But Europeans were different in many ways from the Japanese. They had a lower per capita income and they tended to parse it out over long vacations instead of splurging on expensive four-day visits to a theme park. Disney was convinced its park could change those habits. And the company's plans stayed the same, including the ambitious program of hotel construction.

"We were arrogant," said one executive later. "It was like, 'We're building the Taj Mahal and people will come—on our terms.'"

∽

IN OCTOBER 1989, Michael Eisner and Robert Fitzpatrick, the head of Disney's nascent Euro Disney subsidiary, pulled up to the Paris Stock Exchange in cars chauffeured by drivers attired in Mickey Mouse and Pluto outfits. They were there to announce the sale of Euro Disney stock to the public. But others were wearing Disney masks as well — young Communists who had come to pelt Eisner with eggs and ketchup. It was hardly the warm demonstration Eisner had hoped to stage. But the protesters, with banners that read UNCLE SCROOGE GO HOME, thought the $6.4 billion that the French government was willing to spend to attract Disney's business should go to schools or unemployment relief.

Despite the protests, the stock offering for the new Euro Disney was a dazzling success. Not only did stock sell out at once but Disney's own stock ticked up six points based on all the excitement. The British investment banking firm S. G. Warburg, which arranged the sale of the stock in Britain, called the project "relatively low risk" and predicted that the new park could bring in more than a billion dollars in its first year and turn a profit of $400 million. That would pour more than $100 million into Disney's coffers. Those predictions were wildly optimistic, but the excitement was undeniable. In October 1990, Euro Disney raised another $770 million from a bond offering.

In fact, the banks were eager to participate and many accepted Disney's rosy revenue projections. But several European institutions, including Disney's own advisers at Lazard Frères, worried that Euro Disney was simply strapped with too much debt. Disney brushed those concerns aside. In 1990, Fitzpatrick told *Business Week*, "We're seeing Cartesian skepticism meeting American can-do-ism."

"Frank and Michael were yin and yang," says one executive intimately involved in structuring Euro Disney. "These guys were wowing them with these unbelievable presentations and there was nothing there but air. And then they'd go off and spend a lot of money."

∽

ONE OF THE many questions raised about Euro Disney involved its location outside Paris. Disney also considered Barcelona, which was attractive because of its relatively mild winters. But Eisner says he rejected the site because Spain used a different rail line from the rest of Europe, lacked a countrywide highway system, and had erratic phone service. The location also did not have a huge metropolitan area nearby that could feed the park during off-peak months (as Disneyland and the park in Tokyo do).

Besides, Disney contended that it got a fabulous deal on about 4,400 acres in Marne-la-Vallée in France. The French government agreed in December 1985 to sell the land on favorable terms. Eisner thought he could wrap up the deal in three months, but the negotiation was so complex and Disney was so relentless in its demands that the deal didn't close until March 1987. Eisner and Wells pushed for better terms by repeatedly telling general counsel Joe Shapiro, their lead negotiator, that "almost nothing his team got was enough," Eisner said later.

An executive closely involved says the great deal on the French land was more an excuse to select the location that Eisner wanted in the first place. Eisner never seriously considered Barcelona, that executive says. "Michael had never been to Barcelona," he continues. "They didn't do any due diligence." The acquisition of the French land, he says, was nothing more than "going to a shitty area and getting a great real estate deal. . . . Nothing grew out there but beans and even they suffered because of the wind and the cold and the microclimate."

And Disney failed to take into account an advancing European recession. Admission to Euro Disney cost more than Disneyland's or Disney World's. And the Disney hotels—many of which had been upgraded to three- and four-star quality as Disney's ambition swelled—cost a hefty $340 a night. But with the franc strong, a Disney board member points out, it turned out that a Briton could visit sunny Florida more cheaply than traveling to Euro Disney. Gary Wilson had been betting on higher inflation, which would allow the parks to keep prices high, and lower interest rates, which would have cut the burden of the company's debt service. On both counts he was wrong. Meanwhile, the real estate market fell on hard times, putting a crimp in Disney's plans to reduce its debt by selling its hotels. (Disney said it had buyers but didn't like the prices being offered.)

There were also troubles with the contractors that had been hired. In January 1992, sixteen subcontractors demanded that they be paid about $155 million because of cost overruns on construction. They alleged that Disney ordered up extra work without paying. (One painter reportedly was asked to apply twenty different shades of pink to a hotel before the company settled on its choice.) Other subcontractors sought about $20 million they said they were owed after a Euro Disney contractor, Gabo-Eremco, went bankrupt. Disney settled the claims.

Even before the park greeted its first visitors, Euro Disney executives were forecasting $35 million in losses for the company's first six months. Opening day on April 12, 1992, was a disappointment. Only about twenty thousand people—considerably short of the projected sixty thousand visitors—showed up. By June, Disney acknowledged that its earlier projections of a small profit by the end of the fiscal year in September were wrong. Attendance picked up, and by October, the park had entertained more than seven million guests. Eisner told the French newspaper *Le Monde* that the park was off to a "splendid" start. "We are happy with the . . . reception from the public," he said staunchly. "We cannot allow the idea to take root that we have in part failed."

But that impression was hard to escape. Not only did the profits predicted by Wilson fail to materialize, but the costs of building and servicing the debt were simply too high. In August, Richard Nanula, the company's chief financial officer, wrote a memo warning that the company should reduce its losses by making dramatic cutbacks at the park. Nonetheless, Eisner committed to spend an additional $200 million to add attractions.

The value of the Euro Disney stock, which had peaked at 165.2 francs in March, had tumbled to a low of 61.2 francs even as Eisner's interview was published. The following month, an unusually negative report from the influential Banque Paribas said the shares were still overvalued and should be sold at once by all but the most risk-tolerant investors. The report questioned every aspect of Euro Disney's operations and structure. Disney declined to comment.

"We have been [here] before," Eisner assured shareholders in his letter accompanying the 1992 annual report. "Disneyland was too expensive. Walt Disney World's Magic Kingdom opened and the company's stock fell by half (it recovered quickly, I might add). Tokyo Disneyland threatened the very existence of the Oriental Land Company. And Epcot Center was the mother of all expensive parks. But, like all good fairy tales, the company not only survived, but it is living happily ever after."

But Europe, as Disney continued to learn every day, presented daunting problems. The issue wasn't attendance. The visitors came but they didn't behave as Disney had hoped they would. Many of the hotel rooms were empty. Guests who checked in stayed for one night but moved on instead of staying a few days and returning to the park. There was so much turnover at the hotels that they had to install additional computer stations to handle the traffic. "Would you rather stay in a hotel that stops getting train service at midnight or go to the heart of Paris, which is open all night?" asks a former Imagineer. "There was an arrogance about the whole thing."

In the days before the park opened, French intellectuals became increasingly grumpy about it, and Euro Disney was variously described as a "cultural Vietnam" or a "cultural Chernobyl." The press piled on, happily chronicling every setback.

Disney was indeed showing a tone deafness to European culture. For example, the company refused to serve wine or beer, prompting press attacks over this assault on one of France's great traditions. "That was [more] arrogance on Eisner's part," this former employee says. "Thinking we were going to change European culture. I watched Eisner make decisions all the time and I'm a pretty ballsy guy. It took all my restraint not to walk up to him and say, 'You know, this is wrong.'"

But too many of Eisner's executives exercised that restraint, and mistakes were made. Disney believed that many European visitors wouldn't expect breakfast and were caught off guard when they showed up hungry in the morning. And Europeans weren't spending with the same abandon as visitors to the American parks, who shelled out almost as much on souvenirs and food as they did to enter in the first place. Disney also made a short-lived attempt to forbid employees to wear beards or mustaches.

"We had a cultural problem," Eisner acknowledged later. "We had a financial problem. We had a recession problem. We had the French problem. We had the facial hair problem. We had the deodorant problem. We had the beer and wine problem. We had all these problems. They all went away."

Euro Disney head Robert Fitzpatrick warned that the park would lose a billion dollars in its first year. But he had lost the company's confidence. Inside Disney, he was referred to as "le concierge"—a gibe suggesting that his primary skill was getting Eisner reservations at the finest French restaurants. In 1993, he was replaced with Philippe Bourguignon, a French executive who stood a better chance of gaining acceptance in his native land.

In the third quarter of fiscal 1993, the park lost $83 million. Disney confirmed that it was undertaking a "strategic reexamination" of the project. But Eisner said rumors that Euro Disney might close were "insane."

By this point Eisner was waging a public relations war. "We have planted a flag in the middle of Europe, which is among the most spectacular things any company has ever done," he told the *Los Angeles Times* in August 1993. "Do I wish it was profitable in the first week? Absolutely. But it will not bring down Walt Disney Co. or even dent it substantially." He blamed others for overreacting to the park's problems. "It's unbelievable," he said. "People approach me as if someone died when they talk about Euro Disney. . . . We have a creative smash. It's as good a piece of entertainment as we've ever delivered anywhere in the world. So I know this is like a movie that starts off slow. You just have to be a believer in better times."

But even as he spoke, Eisner was digesting a lengthy presentation at a company retreat in Aspen. Sid Bass had flown in for the occasion, and to Eisner's chagrin, the news was awful. "I think he was genuinely surprised about the depth of the problems . . . hearing it in an organized fashion for the first time," says a former top Euro Disney executive involved in the meeting. "It's one thing to hear the numbers are bad. It's another to go through two days of what the problem is—everything from A to Z." Eisner reportedly acknowledged that Euro Disney was a drag on earnings and a public relations nightmare.

Euro Disney was running out of money. The company swung into action to cut the losses. That fall, a thousand Euro Disney employees were laid off. Eisner and Wells also concluded that the planned second attraction, modeled on the Disney-MGM studio tour in Florida, would have to be put on hold. But they knew that these measures, without a major restructuring of the company's debt, would not prevent losses of several hundred million dollars in 1994 and 1995. It would fall to Wells to figure out how to get Disney's creditors to swallow a very bitter pill.

Eisner would later say that even at the Aspen meeting, he remained steadfastly optimistic about Euro Disney, which would be renamed Disneyland Paris. But the unfolding debacle seems to have marked a major turning point for him. This was the first real morass of his career, and it was a deep one. Eisner's anxiety was growing. Just as Katzenberg was coming into his own with animation, it seemed, Eisner became more distrustful than usual. And at least with respect to his studio chairman, Eisner did indeed feel exactly that way—more so than Katzenberg could have imagined at the time.

21

THE CRASH

L ATE IN AUGUST 1993, Jeffrey Katzenberg was taking what was, of course, a working vacation. As he hiked down the Grand Canyon with an all-male posse of Hollywood executives and agents that he had invited on one of his annual camping trips, he turned to Tom Pollock, then head of Universal Studios. "Last week, I blew Michael's mind," he boasted. In fact, he had; he had sent Eisner a letter exercising an option to terminate his contract in a year, at the end of September 1994.

At the time Katzenberg was finishing the third year of a six-year contract. But at the end of 1993, he had the right to give notice that he wanted to leave in 1994. He would forfeit a great deal of money in stock and other remuneration for 1995 and 1996—an amount that could easily have reached $100 million. Eisner "could not believe I would do it," Katzenberg told his hiking partner.

In fact, Eisner was incredulous. "You really want to give that up?" he had asked Katzenberg. To Frank Wells, Eisner predicted, "There is no chance he will do this." His skepticism was well placed. It just seemed impossible that Katzenberg, such a die-hard Disney man, would take the game of chicken to a conclusion. But if he did, Eisner knew what he intended the outcome to be—and he wasn't inclined to give Katzenberg a golden handshake.

∽

AS IT HAPPENED, Katzenberg's deal with Disney—created by Wells in 1984—had given him a certain leverage that he now intended to use to his advantage. When Wells and Eisner had taken the helm in 1984, they had sat down with Katzenberg and his attorney, Arthur Emil, at the Beverly Hills Hotel—the pink palace on Sunset Boulevard. Katzenberg had written out his wish list on a studio "buck slip"—an oblong piece of memo paper. Among the perks he considered requesting were "2 secy's, beach house . . . corporate jet, travel-family-etc., screening room, house maintenance? butler?"

He started by asking for a big stock-option package like the ones Eisner and Wells had designed for themselves. Wells replied that the Disney board would never go for that and instead promised Katzenberg 2 percent of the profit from "all forms of exploitation" of the projects he would put into production as Disney's studio chief. At the time the studio had no shows on television and hadn't ever released a picture on video, so it's doubtful that Wells or Eisner or Katzenberg could have begun to grasp the potential magnitude of such an arrangement.

Every year, Katzenberg was to receive a payment based on 2 percent of the company's profit based on anything he had put into production — including everything from live-action and animated films to television shows. And he was to get a piece of the income from video, merchandise, and theme-park attractions based on his movies and programs. When he left the studio, he would get a lump sum that would cover 2 percent of the future value of every project he'd put into development at Disney. It was shockingly open-ended. Wells described it as "an annuity" for Katzenberg's twins, who were eighteen months old at the time.

Four years later, Wells had approached Katzenberg about renewing his deal even though it didn't expire until 1990. He wanted to keep Katzenberg at the company through 1996. At the time Disney was flourishing. The company's operating income had shot from $242 million to more than $884 million.

But Disney's accounting was conservative. The company counted all its expenses but didn't count income from theaters, video, network deals, and other revenue streams until the money was in the bank. (If the studio had an obvious hit, Disney's books would still show it losing money until the cash was in its coffers.) Katzenberg had discovered at the end of each year that the envelope was consistently empty when he looked for his annual 2 percent bonus. In fact, he had been told that his division was still in the red — despite hits like *Ruthless People, Down and Out in Beverly Hills,* and *Three Men and a Baby,* and despite the fact that the Disney studio had gone from dormant to dominant.

Disney was obviously minting money. In 1988, Wells wrote to Katzenberg's lawyer addressing the studio chief's disappointment and assuring him that Katzenberg had been "perfectly reasonable" to have expected a bonus given "the enormous success" of the studio. Wells urged patience. "Many of these pictures still have substantial revenues forthcoming . . . and of course, will continue 'forever,' " he wrote. The company expected to reap at least $100 million from the television series *The Golden Girls* alone.

And Katzenberg could still look forward to the final 2 percent lump-sum payment that had been promised when he left the company. But as Wells set about renewing Katzenberg's contract, he tried to persuade Katzenberg to give that up. Katzenberg agreed, as long as he could get 75 percent of whatever Eisner would earn. Eisner's stock-option packages were paying off more handsomely than Katzenberg's 2 percent had thus far. Wells said the board would never tie one executive's compensation to another's.

Katzenberg tried to sweeten his deal, asking if Disney would include the library product—the animated classics like *Snow White* and *Sleeping Beauty*—in his annual 2 percent payment. After all, Disney was making a lot of money from rereleases and Katzenberg figured he had worked on those campaigns. Wells agreed—but only on condition that Katzenberg give up the final 2 percent lump-sum payment for profit in perpetuity that would be due when he left his job. Katzenberg said he'd rather keep the bonus—the so-called annuity for his twins.

The 1988 contract discussions dragged on for months. Katzenberg balked at committing to a six-year term. He insisted on being granted an option to leave in 1994. Wells ultimately agreed. Already, perhaps, Katzenberg had concluded that he either had to move up or out, and he had started counting his cards. During the negotiations, Katzenberg's lawyer had scrawled a note on a draft proposal from Wells: "If Frank leaves you replace him." Disney never made such a promise a part of the contract, but Katzenberg later said Wells assured him that if he or Eisner left Disney—"if the plane goes down," as Wells put it—Katzenberg would become the number-two man in the company. Katzenberg said Wells told his lawyer that the matter had been discussed with major shareholder Sid Bass, Roy Disney, and with Roy's point man, Stanley Gold.

As further incentive to sign the contract, the company agreed to pay $4 million toward Katzenberg's beach house and gave him a bundle of stock options. And Wells also promised Katzenberg the final 2 percent lump sum when he left. It was "a tremendous concept," Wells scrawled in his notes. The payout "should increase by a big amount" in the years ahead. Katzenberg was about to release *The Little Mermaid*; he had *Beauty and the*

Beast and *Aladdin* in the works. Still, Wells probably didn't begin to suspect how enormous the payout could become.

After the 1988 contract negotiation was behind him, Katzenberg was relieved and grateful—though not, perhaps, entirely satisfied. Nevertheless, he wrote a thank-you note to Eisner. His letter may have been a routine exercise in diplomacy but it also expressed his yearning for a bond with Eisner that he had doggedly sought for more than a decade. "Most importantly to me . . . way beyond the dollar and cents of it all, is the fact that in the end you came thru and delivered for me," Katzenberg wrote. "We've been together a very long time—in fact in terms of Hollywood timekeeping about 3 lifetimes so far. I not only hope but I'm counting on us staying together *forever*. You've been great. You've handled my crap with extraordinary patience and care and understanding. I'm deeply appreciative and do love you for it."

∽

BY THE TIME 1993 had rolled around, Wells was still in place and Katzenberg was still ablaze with the ambition that had prompted his ill-fated 1991 memo. In April, he asked to see how much his 2 percent lump sum would be if he elected to leave the company in 1994. It was a request calculated to scare Eisner. But a month later, Disney's lawyers sent Katzenberg a letter expressing the company's position that he could forget about a final 2 percent payout if he left in 1994. Katzenberg said later that he assumed this was an error. He went to Wells, who said he would look into the matter. Katzenberg recalls that the discussion was "calm." He says he was confident that Wells would put things right. At this point Katzenberg had no idea how much money was at stake. But Eisner and Wells, as would later be revealed, had secretly been monitoring the potential payout for some time.

In August 1993, a Disney lawyer wrote a letter asking Katzenberg to state his intentions. Katzenberg, who had never heard back from Wells, asked his lawyer, Arthur Emil, to get Disney to clarify its position on the 2 percent payment. No doubt Katzenberg expected Wells to reassure him that he would get his bonus if he left in 1994. But he was in for a big disappointment. Instead, Wells told Emil to "read the contract."

"I don't have to read the contract, Frank," Emil angrily replied.

"Listen, it's not going to be an issue. Jeffrey's going to stay these next two years," Wells said.

Katzenberg began calling Wells himself. According to him, he told Wells he didn't understand why Disney was playing games with him. At one point he said, Wells told him that Eisner had "a misunderstanding" about Katzenberg's deal and believed that Katzenberg would forfeit the money if he left early. Katzenberg offered to have his lawyer send Eisner a letter. But Wells urged him to hold off. "I will handle it with Michael," he told Katzenberg—or so Katzenberg says. And Katzenberg assumed that he did exactly that.

∽

AS HE PLOTTED his course, Katzenberg relied primarily on the advice and comfort provided by a strong-willed older male figure—another in a series that had peopled his life. Having sold his music company to MCA, David Geffen was beginning to measure his wealth in the billions. Katzenberg talked on the phone with him at the break of dawn every day, gossiping and strategizing. Like Katzenberg, Geffen had a long-standing antagonism to Michael Ovitz, dating back to a bitter fight that had occurred during the making of the 1982 film *Personal Best* with Mariel Hemingway. (Geffen, who produced the film, believed that Ovitz put the entire project at risk when he tried to get Paramount Pictures to give director Robert Towne a richer deal. In fact, Paramount dropped the picture, which could have cost Geffen millions of dollars. He got off the hook when Warner agreed to make the movie.)

Geffen's influence on Katzenberg had long been an irritant to Eisner, who had complained about it in a 1988 conversation with Katzenberg's lawyer. Geffen and Katzenberg had been on vacation together in Acapulco during Katzenberg's contract-renewal discussions and Eisner was convinced that Geffen had gotten Katzenberg riled up. Geffen, for his part, felt that he was looking out for his protégé's interests and he had no intention of being stared down by Eisner.

Both Geffen and Katzenberg figured that Katzenberg's value to Disney was high, notwithstanding the studio's continued failure in live action. Hollywood Pictures had recently released bombs like *Swing Kids*, the story of rebellious youths trying to dance the Third Reich to death (by defiantly listening to American music) and *Born Yesterday*, the pointless remake of a Judy Holliday classic, with Melanie Griffith as the lead. Things were barely better on the Touchstone side. The spring had seen the release of *The Cemetery Club*, which brought together Ellen Burstyn, Olympia Dukakis, and Diane Ladd in an attempt to mimic the 1991 success of Universal's female-audience-pleasing *Fried Green Tomatoes*. And summer hadn't improved with the dead-on-arrival *Life with Mikey*, a James Lapine–directed film with Michael J. Fox as a former child star turned talent agent. It had been a bleak season; the rerelease of *Snow White and the Seven Dwarfs* turned in the studio's best performance with a $37.6 million gross. "It was really depressing," says a studio executive. "A couple of years were very bleak and very humiliating."

"We could hardly get a movie to open to more than $6 million," says David Vogel, who headed Walt Disney Pictures (the Disney live-action family film label). "Jeffrey was always saying, 'Next. It'll turn around. It'll be fine. Hang in there.' Jeffrey's the greatest cheerleader in the world."

Katzenberg acknowledges that in live action the record was grim. "I never made a movie or caused a movie to be made in which I wasn't certain that people involved in the making were going to do something creative and successful," he says. "We can rattle off a list of stupendous stinkers. It's easy to say, 'What could you have been thinking?' *My Boyfriend's Back*—what could you have been thinking? *Cabin Boy* is the whipping boy of every Jeffrey joke—not even a movie I wanted to make. But somebody was passionate and believed in it and thought it was a great shot to take. And at that time I shared that belief, or believed in that belief. Who sets out to make a stinker? But we all get there."

There were a few glimmers. Hollywood Pictures had its best showings with the modestly successful *Joy Luck Club*, based on the Amy Tan novel, and *Tombstone*, a sleeper with Kurt Russell and Val Kilmer reprising the shootout at the O.K. Corral.

And Hoberman's Touchstone label had a well-reviewed summer performer with *What's Love Got to Do with It?*, with Angela Bassett doing an impressive star turn as singer Tina Turner. Later that year, Touchstone had *The Nightmare Before Christmas*, a unique animated creation from director Tim Burton. Burton had done a treatment for the film years earlier as an animator at the studio, and his agent, Mike Simpson, had called asking if he could buy it. Instead, Hoberman offered to finance it. It was a critical success and did well at the box office, grossing $50 million. While the film was in production, Hoberman told Katzenberg that he was depressed because Katzenberg would receive all the plaudits if it turned out to be a hit. It did, and Katzenberg stepped aside so that Hoberman could enjoy the limelight.

On the strategic level, Katzenberg had an enormous triumph. Having pretty much given up on his efforts to grow his own prestige product, he pulled off the 1993 acquisition of Miramax, the most rapacious and successful independent label in the business. Founded by brothers Harvey and Bob Weinstein, Miramax was behind sophisticated films, including *The Piano* with Holly Hunter, and *The Crying Game*, the brilliant film about an IRA terrorist who takes part in a botched kidnapping. (The profit margin on the latter film, which cost a couple of million and grossed about $63 million, helped convince Eisner to make the deal.)

The Weinsteins were among the industry's toughest and roughest customers. They fought with each other relentlessly and brutalized their staff. But they had great taste. Katzenberg got to know them when Disney agreed to help finance *Sarafina!* starring Whoopi Goldberg as a defiant schoolteacher in South Africa. Katzenberg loved the film and was impressed with the Weinsteins' passion for moviemaking. He was also struck by their skill in piecing together the financing for their films. They seemed to be "Scotch-taping" *Sarafina!* together, Katzenberg says, and he came to believe that with a real bankroll, the Weinsteins could be formidable.

The deal was barely signed when a script arrived on Katzenberg's desk for *Pulp Fiction*. The Weinsteins intended to make the film with Quentin Tarantino, the young director of *Reservoir Dogs*. Katzenberg had found that film so violent that he had literally covered his eyes when he saw it. *Pulp Fiction* promised to have plenty of violent content, too, not to mention stories involving drugs and sadomasochistic sex. This was a far cry from Disney fare, as the Weinsteins well knew. On top of that, they had set John Travolta, whose career was comatose at the time, to star. Katzenberg says that after Harvey Weinstein called to tell him about the project, "he must have hung up that phone and rolled over laughing for twenty minutes." But if this was a test, Katzenberg intended to pass. A day later, he called back and said, "I wish you well. I want to remind you that [under your deal], no NC-17."

The Weinsteins immediately justified Katzenberg's faith in them. Despite its quirky content, *Pulp Fiction* was a $100 million hit. They followed with the Italian charmer *Il Postino*. Miramax scored Oscar nominations for these films and in ensuing years became a daunting Academy Award contender.

The Miramax relationships hit rough patches on occasion. Notably, there were controversies over Miramax's decision to release such material as *Kids* and *Priest*, two challenging adult films that had the potential to embarrass the Disney company. (There was another problem some years later when Miramax was caught exceeding the bounds of good taste in exaggerating the opening-weekend tallies from its pictures. Other studios overstated their numbers but Miramax finally went too far with *Scream 2*, overestimating the real number by $9 million. Eisner made it clear that such "errors" had to stop.)

Katzenberg's biggest coup, however, was keeping the mighty engine of animation purring. The studio, which had generated pretax profits of about $2 million in 1984, would make $800 million in 1994. Eisner had all but credited *Beauty and the Beast* with saving the company in 1991, and the grosses from animated films just kept growing. The animation division was gushing profits that boosted results throughout the company and Katzenberg certainly deserved credit for some of that success.

But if Katzenberg thought these achievements made him indispensable, he seriously underrated the tensions that had begun to emerge with Eisner after the Katzenberg memo. In fact, Katzenberg showed signs that he enjoyed tweaking the boss. It wasn't just his pleasure in Eisner's incredulity over his contract decision. Around this time, he also gleefully told his staff that Eisner was annoyed about Katzenberg's involvement in Dive!, a restaurant in the Century City shopping mall on the west side of Los Angeles. Katzenberg had created Dive! in partnership with Steven Spielberg and reveled in the new project.

In fact, Eisner later said it showed "bad judgment" on Katzenberg's part to get so deeply involved in an extracurricular activity. But there was another element in the equation: Disney's attempt at a fast-food chain, Mickey's Kitchen, had died quickly after two prototypes withered. Meanwhile, the partners behind Dive! — a near-theme-park experience with flashing lights, sonar screens, deep-sea videos — were boasting about plans for expansion. (Those plans never materialized although a branch was opened in Las Vegas. By 1999, Dive! in Los Angeles was out of business, though the Las Vegas location was still open.)

Later, Spielberg defended Katzenberg. "I know for a fact that from the inception of Dive!, Jeffrey was concerned about any issues Michael and Frank would have," he said. "He made it clear that if they had any objections whatsoever, he would not have gone ahead. Not only did they approve Jeffrey's involvement, they told him they had gotten it cleared by the board of directors."

But another former studio chairman, observing the interplay of the parties, said Katzenberg had violated a law of corporate survival. "With people you care about in business," he said, "you've got to make sure that your self-interest is identical."

∽

AFTER THE AUGUST blowup over whether Katzenberg was entitled to his 2 percent payout if he left in 1994, Katzenberg thought his gambit had paid off. The critical conversation, in Katzenberg's mind, happened on an October day when he and Eisner had strolled the streets of Aspen. Both were in town for a meeting sponsored by the Aspen Institute, a nonprofit educational organization. As Marilyn Katzenberg and Jane Eisner shopped for sweaters across the street, Eisner and Katzenberg stood outside Boogies, a diner, and discussed the delicate topic of Katzenberg's future.

Katzenberg wanted a new challenge. One idea that he and Rich Frank had been pushing was the purchase of a network. Eisner said he didn't like the prices. What was there for Katzenberg to do? Eisner floated another idea.

"I am prepared to make you vice-chairman and put you on the board, if that's what you want," he told Katzenberg—according to Katzenberg's account. "I don't necessarily think that's what you want, but I'd be willing."

"I want to be involved in the reinvention of the Walt Disney Company," Katzenberg answered. And he made a bold suggestion. "Would it be inappropriate if I became president of the company?" he asked. In his scenario, Wells—who had just agreed to renew his contract with the company for another seven years—would become vice-chairman. Katzenberg insists that he did not mean to displace Wells. Nonetheless, Eisner said that such a change would be perceived as a demotion for Wells.

"I could never do that to Frank," Eisner told Katzenberg.

Katzenberg says he quickly insisted that he meant Wells no harm. "I would never want you to do that to Frank," he said.

"I believe Frank would accept it because he would do anything to keep you in the company," Eisner continued. "But in the quiet of his room, he would feel hurt."

"I would not want to take anything away from the guy," Katzenberg remembers saying. But Eisner insisted later that Katzenberg was deliberately trying to elbow Wells out of the way—perhaps because Eisner had done exactly that to Wells himself when the pair had sorted out their roles at the

Disney company back in 1984. "I think he was hopeful that Frank would step aside once again," Eisner said later. "But he backed off immediately. It was unreasonable and he realized it very quickly."

At that point in the conversation, in Katzenberg's account, Eisner said the words that Katzenberg took so much to heart: "If for any reason Frank is not here—if he decides to run for political office, if he goes off to climb the summit—you are the number-two person and I would want you to have the job."

At the time, of course, it seemed highly unlikely that Wells would not be around. So Katzenberg walked away gratified by the sentiment but not truly satisfied. He did not become vice-chairman or join the board. The Disney board was not particularly independent and he knew that becoming a member would require him to disclose financial information he preferred to keep private. But refusing the opportunity to carve out his own profile with the board was a decision he would later regret.

Eisner put him in charge of launching the company's New Amsterdam Theatre in New York and the stage production of *Beauty and the Beast*. He also offered him responsibility for Disney's failing record label and new interactive media. Katzenberg enjoyed working on the Broadway show and new video games, but none of this appeased him. Eisner would have to come up with a better offer if Katzenberg was to remain with Disney beyond 1994.

∽

AT THE SAME time that Katzenberg was threatening to opt out of his contract, Eisner was getting more and more bad news about Euro Disney— information that undoubtedly left him feeling deeply threatened. And several other projects failed to gel.

The nineties were meant to be "the Disney decade," and Eisner had ambitious plans to build more projects than had ever been constructed in the company's history—billions of dollars' worth of work. There was an oceanside park at Long Beach, near Disneyland; the addition of ambitious second gates in Europe and Tokyo; and the creation of an attraction in Burbank. With so much to do, the Imagineering staff had been dramatically expanded to some three thousand people.

But all these projects were dropped or put on hold. "They completely misjudged the timing, the level of investment, the requirements on all levels," says former Imagineering executive Dave Fink. "They were driving deals way too hard. Every one of those projects involved a relationship with a community or a partner. Disney could not do a deal. They went in too hard, too heavy. Either that or there were environmental problems." Meanwhile, he says, "Every one of the projects had a fairly high level of design completed—and the costs associated with that." Around Imagineering, he adds, the failed "Disney decade" became known as "the Disney minute" or, sometimes, "the Disney second."

Of all the projects that ran into trouble, one was a particularly painful public embarrassment. The plan got into trouble after Eisner made a political miscalculation that showed he had learned little from the company's experience at Euro Disney. Ironically, the problems at Euro Disney had been a major catalyst for Disney's plans to build a history-themed attraction called Disney's America. In the wake of its difficulties abroad, the company decided to develop some smaller and more manageable theme parks. In 1993, having homed in on the Washington, D.C., area, Disney bought an option on 2,400 acres in suburban Prince William County. The company wanted to buy several hundred more acres and was intent on keeping its plans for the attraction secret to prevent a surge in prices.

But by October 1993, word of Disney's interest in the area began to leak out. Eisner later acknowledged that Disney made several key errors, among them the failure to lay the groundwork for the project with local leaders and members of the community. He also lamented the decision to give the project the presumptuous-sounding title Disney's America. That almost ensured that Disney's take on history would be contested by some group, no matter what it was. And Eisner said Disney failed to understand that local residents wanted to keep their community as it was. This was an especially serious problem, because the land to the west of the project was owned by the rich and powerful—including *Washington Post* publisher Katharine Graham.

With rumors about the project beginning to circulate, the company felt compelled to announce its plans. Disney's America was to include an Indian village, an ersatz nineteenth-century development, and a World War II fighter aircraft. The $625 million plan eventually burgeoned to include Disney-built hotels, shopping, and houses. The Imagineers believed that these additions were a mistake and that Eisner's overly ambitious approach to Disney's America sparked hostility from wealthy locals who feared overdevelopment. Other protesters were concerned about the impact on the environment. (A *Washington Post* headline observed that some feared A

SMOGGY, CLOGGY TRANSPORTATION MESS.) And Disney had failed to consider how strongly Civil War historians felt about preserving the sanctity of a nearby battleground at Manassas.

From a public relations standpoint, Disney's America was a disaster. Overall, Eisner's dealings with the media had suffered since late in 1992, when he had lost Erwin Okun, his chief of corporate communications and a capable survivor from the old Disney regime. Okun had a shrewd yet avuncular style that worked well with the press; many reporters had made the unusual gesture of dropping by his office when on the Disney lot merely to say hello. He died at age fifty-eight in November, two months after being diagnosed with cancer.

Okun had always made sure that Eisner was up to speed on any journalist who was about to interview him, probing reporters about their interests so that Eisner was prepared with some engaging banter. After each meeting, Eisner sent a note (or in one case, dropped it by a reporter's home himself), offering some charming and humorous comment on the interview that had taken place. When Katie Harris, then a business-affairs reporter for the *Los Angeles Times*, had a baby, Okun dispatched Mickey Mouse to the hospital. "He somehow pushed that button in all of us that said Disney is an honest, good company that meant well," says journalist Peter Boyer. "He packaged [Eisner] well without seeming to do so."

Eisner said he relied on Okun "to counsel, review, berate, encourage, and protect me." After Okun's death, the press felt his absence keenly. His successor, John Dreyer, came from the theme parks. He lacked Okun's cordiality and treated the press with suspicion bordering on hostility. At the *Washington Post*, he quickly alienated the very reporters whose coverage of Disney's America would prove most influential.

The result was that Eisner was suffering through humiliating problems with Euro Disney and Disney's America — not to mention the loss of a trusted aide like Okun — and Katzenberg was agitating. And possibly Eisner started to scent betrayal. When the editorial staff of the *Wall Street Journal* invited Katzenberg to address them at a lunch, he accepted. Eisner ordered him to cancel.

❧

IN THE EARLY 1990s, Eisner had become increasingly enamored of Peter Rummell, the head of the company's real-estate-development unit. Rummell was the kind of smooth, presentable executive that Eisner was increasingly coming to favor; as a former Imagineer remembers, he "wore a suit very well." And through Rummell, Eisner met leading architects and indulged his passion for building. "Michael became a kind of modern-day Medici patron and he liked doing that," says Pat Scanlon, a former senior vice-president in Imagineering.

The Imagineers blamed Rummell, whom they inevitably nicknamed "Rommel," for promoting the shopping and housing developments that were supposed to sit adjacent to their theme parks. They held him partly responsible for the glut of overpriced hotels at Euro Disney and for con-vincing Eisner to expand the plans for Disney's America. They thought that building hotels, aligning roads, and putting utility lines in the right places — the jobs handled by Rummell's unit — were pretty simple propositions com-pared with designing thrilling new theme-park attractions. The Imagineers felt that the predictability of those processes not only appealed to Eisner after the struggles he had encountered within the parks, but made Rummell's operation look good compared with the more chaotic Imagi-neering.

In 1993, Eisner put Rummell in charge of Imagineering. He was already strongly disliked by many in the division, who joked that he seemed to hate theme parks, perhaps because of some unfortunate childhood incident. In 1994, he ordered major layoffs that were handled with little tenderness. "It was a bad sign when you came to a desk with empty cardboard boxes," one former Imagineer remembers. "Guards were hired to wait while you cleared out your desk."

Mickey Steinberg, the division chief, left for Sony, where a number of his colleagues followed him. Disney reacted to these departures with hos-tility. "There was literally a memo that forbade people from communicating with people at Sony," says an Imagineering insider. "If you bumped into somebody at a trade show, you had to fill out a report of the contact and what the conversation was about."

Dave Fink, who was among those who went to Sony, has the bitterest of feelings in the wake of what he considers the reckless expansion and subsequent demolition of the Imagineering unit. "I think Michael Eisner would shoot himself — literally — if he knew what his reputation was," he says. "He thinks he has remained above all the damage and harm he has done. The fact is, he has treated thousands of people like shit and he is the cause of almost all of it. . . . Do you know how many lives were absolutely screwed over? Those were all as a result of bad decisions at the highest level of that company.... People would say the guy's a maniac when it comes to thinking through what his decisions do."

∞

BY THE END of fiscal 1993, the problems at Euro Disney had hit Disney's bottom line. The Walt Disney Company's net income had dropped precipitously from $816.7 million to $299.8 million, mostly because of a $514.69 million loss on Euro Disney and a related $371.5 million accounting charge. For the first time since he had arrived at Disney in 1984, Eisner took no bonus. Euro Disney had dragged the company's return on equity to 6 percent—below the 11 percent minimum that contractually entitled him to a payment.

In October, Disney suggested that its European theme park's $3.75 billion debt had to be cut by $2 billion. Disney would kick in a billion dollars in cash and deferred fees but said the banks who had loaned money for the park would have to share the cost of restructuring the rest. "The banks were shocked," says a former top Euro Disney officer. But they shouldn't have been. A reporter asked one of the French bankers why Disney's revenue projections had been so readily accepted when the financing was arranged. "Disney was a magic name," he replied.

"They had a formidable image and convinced everyone that if we let them do it their way, we would all have a marvelous adventure," lamented a top French banker.

In December, Euro Disney reported that it had lost $1.03 billion in less than two years since it had opened.

That year, Eisner wrote the most levity-free letter to shareholders that he had ever devised. He acknowledged that Disney was confronting its "first real financial disappointment." Based only on financial criteria, he conceded, Euro Disney barely deserved a D on the company's report card. "Some would call it dreadful and, in a financial sense, I would be forced to agree," he wrote. But Eisner said the park and hotels were "great." There would have to be a restructuring in which Disney's partners would "bear their fair share" of the burden. Whatever happened, he concluded, Disney would "take no action to endanger the health of Disney itself."

In January 1994, Disney signaled that it was willing to play hardball when Eisner told a French magazine that if a deal wasn't cut by March 31, he would consider facing a bankruptcy or even shuttering the park. "If the engine of an airplane falls out in full flight, what are the options?" Eisner asked his interviewer. "Anything is possible today, including closure." Disney also moved up its deadline for resolving its differences with the banks to March 15, when Euro Disney was scheduled to have its annual meeting.

Negotiations with the banks got under way in February. In the first session, a lawyer for the banks stunned Disney by stating that the banks intended to prove "a detailed pattern of fraud" with respect to the park. Disney counsel Sandy Litvack, who was representing the company, was enraged. After demanding an apology, he walked out of the meeting. Within a couple of days, the banks asked him to return to the table.

As the park continued to lose a million dollars a day, the bankers insisted that they were fed up with Disney's overbearing style. "The Walt Disney group is making a major error in thinking it can impose its will once more," a leading French banker told the *Wall Street Journal*. But really, the banks had to do what they could to keep Euro Disney alive. If the park went bankrupt or closed, their losses would only deepen dramatically.

Wells oversaw the restructuring negotiations. "Frank was much more attuned than Michael to the issues that the Euro Disney executives had of legal liability and fiduciary responsibility," says a former Disney executive who played a key role in the negotiations. "He would be more sympathetic to us saying, 'We can't do that,' as opposed to Michael saying, 'Do it.'"

In the midst of this brutal exercise, Wells decided to tag along on a ski trip with his friends Roland Betts and Tom Bernstein from the Silver Screen partnerships. They stayed at Betts's house in Santa Fe. Betts remembers that Wells woke up each morning at five o'clock and talked on the phone to Europe for two or three hours. By eight, he would emerge from his room in his underwear and say, "Let's go." All day on the chairlifts, Wells mulled over the puzzles presented by Euro Disney. By four-thirty or five P.M., he returned to the house and started talking to Eisner for an hour or more. "Michael was much tougher to deal with and intransigent about settling," Betts remembers. Wells emerged from these conversations exhausted.

"He said he made a promise to Luanne that he would have only one glass of wine at dinner," Betts says. "I said, 'Okay.' I got a glass and he said, 'Not that one,' and pointed. I said, 'Frank—that's a vase.'"

On March 14, 1994, a deal was announced. Euro Disney and the bankers agreed to a restructuring of $1 billion in debt. The banks forgave all interest payments for sixteen months and deferred payment of principal for three years. Disney, which had cut itself in on annual management fees from the

European park, agreed to waive payment from 1992 to 1998. After that, it
agreed to cut those fees from 6 percent to 1 percent of net revenue (gradually building its rates back to 6 percent). Disney also forgave $210 million
that it was owed by the park for various services and made a low-interest
loan to Euro Disney.

Just as that deal was gelling, Saudi prince al-Waleed bin-Talal bin-
Abdulaziz al-Saud, a thirty-seven-year-old Disney fan, agreed to pay $247
million to buy shares in a billion-dollar rights offering that was part of the
bailout package. Disney negotiated by satellite with the prince. As the parties neared an agreement, Eisner popped in a last-minute demand: the
prince would also have to make a low-interest $100 million loan to Euro
Disney to construct a convention center that was planned but still not built.

Not only were the prince's advisers stunned by Eisner's audacity, but
even Richard Nanula, the chief financial officer, feared that Eisner had
blown the deal. But the prince agreed. When it was all done, Disney's stake
in the European park had been cut from 49 percent to 39 percent. The
park would continue to be hampered by its debt and the obligation to
resume payment of fees to the Disney company. But even though the picture would not brighten for shareholders, the immediate crisis was over for
Eisner and Wells.

A few weeks after his visit with Betts, Wells called to say that he was
sending a plaque reading "The Euro Disney debt was restructured in this
room" for Betts to hang at his house in Santa Fe. He also told Betts that
he was leaving for an Easter weekend helicopter-skiing trip to the Ruby
Mountains in Nevada. "Why don't you come along?" he asked.

Betts declined. "I don't like helicopters," he said.

∽

WELLS HAD GATHERED an eclectic group for this trip. His old buddy
Clint Eastwood was there, as was Wells's thirty-one-year-old son, Kevin. And
Wells had been especially pleased to see Dick Bass. Wells had invited dare-
devil documentary filmmakers Mike Hoover and Beverly Johnson, a married couple whose work often appeared on CBS News. Avid climbers,
Hoover and Johnson were part of a large circle that congregated every year
in Sun Valley, Idaho, for the Wells Cup, a downhill race that Wells organized with his wife. Given the thrill-seeking and even reckless nature of
some of Wells's friends, the race had become a pretty serious com-

petition. But it was followed by an evening of revelry, song, and skits, masterfully emceed by Wells. It was the kind of event that Wells loved, combining physical challenges with good fellowship.

Bass hardly ever made it to the Wells Cup ski competition, so it meant a lot to Wells that he had come along on this trip to Nevada. "It was fabulous," Hoover remembers. "The two of them together, joking around, Bass telling incredible stories, both of them laughing."

Typical for Wells, the trip included an element of adventure. There were no towlines or chairlifts for Wells and his friends. Helicopters transported them to the remote slopes of Thorpe Creek Canyon, where they would be able to cut trails on untouched powder.

The trip had started auspiciously with good weather and good skiing. The second day started out fine, too. As soon as the group reached the top, Wells took off downhill. Eastwood followed but he could see only the track that Wells had left. As he shussed down the snowy slope, Eastwood suddenly heard an alarming cry pierce the silence. Concerned, he picked up speed. As he caught up to Wells, he realized that the awful noise was merely his friend's fractured rendition of the Beatles classic "Hey, Jude."

After the first run, visibility worsened and the helicopters stopped flying. Instead, the skiers had to be hauled in groups on lumbering Sno-Cat vehicles. Several members of the party, including Eastwood, quit for the day. As the tractor made the long climb, Bass entertained the group with songs and poetry.

By the afternoon, the weather had cleared enough for the helicopters to be used to bring the skiers back from the slopes. The first carried away Dick Bass and several others. Mike Hoover and Beverly Johnson said they would stay for a while, suggesting that they might ski and hike back to the lodge if the weather turned again and a second helicopter couldn't pick them up. Wells liked the idea of the hike but the guide discouraged the group, explaining that they would face a long and difficult walk. In normal conditions, the helicopter could cover the same distance in less than five minutes. Hoover, Johnson, and Wells agreed to wait for the second helicopter. Kevin Wells wanted to stay, too, but Frank said no. "We shouldn't ride on the same helicopter, you know," he explained. Kevin left and the guide, Paul Scannell, stayed.

THE HELICOPTER ARRIVED shortly after three P.M. and Wells, Scannell, Mike Hoover, and his wife clambered aboard as the weather closed in. By the time pilot Dave Walton took off, visibility was so poor that the route the first helicopter had taken was no longer navigable. Walton chose a different course and flew over a ridge hoping to make his descent. But the canyon was shrouded in fog. "We're going to have to land and wait this out a little bit," Walton told the others. No one minded: they expected a brief stop. But about forty minutes dragged by and conditions didn't improve. Hoover felt crowded and got out of the helicopter for some air. The afternoon grew colder and Walton turned on the ignition to warm the engine and his passengers. They sat for about twenty more minutes.

Finally the visibility improved and they took off. A moment later, Hoover, seated in the back, looked over the pilot's shoulder and noticed that warning lights on the control panel were illuminated. He heard Walton radio that there was engine trouble. Everything seemed normal—no unusual sounds or frightening dips—but Hoover knew that Walton was going to attempt an emergency landing. He told his wife, seated in front of him on the opposite side of the craft, to brace herself. Johnson, herself a seasoned helicopter pilot who had flown rescues in Yosemite, glanced at the panel and saw that her husband was right. Then Hoover turned to Wells, who was beside him. "The engine went out on this thing," he yelled. "We're going to go in, so brace yourself."

Unlike Johnson, Wells didn't seem to take in the information. He gave Hoover a quizzical look. "Frank, the engine is out," Hoover repeated. "We're going to crash-land. Brace yourself." Wells still looked baffled.

Hoover leaned back. He was calm. He didn't think the emergency landing was especially dangerous; he just expected a sharp jolt. But the impact was much greater than he anticipated. Everything went black.

When he regained consciousness, Hoover was aware of a volcanic pain in his elbow. The helicopter had crashed and Hoover could hear the voices of rescue workers. From the hushed tones, the lack of urgency, he knew the situation was bad. "I didn't hear anybody saying those words that they always say, even when things are horrible," he says. "Those words—'You're all right, you'll be okay'—I didn't hear anybody saying that. Just very hushed, quiet, almost like they were in shock with what they were seeing."

The helicopter—its mechanisms clogged with snow—had hit a tree, then smashed into the hillside. Someone wrenched Hoover out of the wrecked chopper. "Take care of Beverly," Hoover pleaded. He was aware that she was being pulled from the mangled machine and laid on the ground. He could hear her moan. Hoover also heard other rescuers tending to Wells, Walton, and Scannell and he could tell that the situation was bleak. Then he heard someone murmur, "She's gone."

Hoover was literally smashed to bits. His skull was cracked, his neck was broken, his ribs were fractured, and at the elbow—the only place where he felt pain—bone protruded from the skin. As he was flown to the hospital, he asked no questions about the others. He already knew. He knew but he didn't want to hear the words. Only Scannell, the guide, lingered briefly. Hoover alone would survive.

22

CHEST PAINS

MICHAEL EISNER HAD been eating dinner at his son's home that Sunday night when he got a call from his secretary, who told him the terrible news about Wells. "There are no words to express my shock and sense of loss," Eisner said in a statement released that night. "Frank Wells has been the purest definition of a 'life force' that I have ever known. . . . The world has lost a great human being."

On the Monday after Wells's death, as Disney executives reeled from the shock, Katzenberg awaited Eisner's call. It was a suspenseful time. Katzenberg says he was devastated by Wells's death, that he had never fully expressed his affection and gratitude, though he had written him a note some months earlier acknowledging his patience and tolerance as Katzenberg agonized over his future at the company. Now Wells was gone. Though these were hardly the circumstances that Katzenberg might have wanted, it seemed that the uncertainty about his future at the company might evaporate. As things stood, Katzenberg was supposed to leave in October 1994. But Katzenberg was also convinced that he had been promised a promotion if Wells were not around.

Surely Eisner would turn to him now. Surely he would remember their conversation in Aspen. On Sunday, Katzenberg had told Eisner that he would arrive at work at six A.M. on Monday. But as he sat in his immaculate off-white office and the minutes ticked by, he heard nothing.

At midday, with the staff gathered for the usual staff lunch, Eisner passed out a press release. A glance told Katzenberg its contents: Eisner would assume Wells's responsibilities. No successor would be named. Katzenberg was paralyzed with shock. "I don't think I blinked for the entire lunch," he said later. If Eisner had said something to him in private about the move being only temporary, he would have been fine. But Eisner hadn't spoken to him at all.

Perhaps Katzenberg should not have been surprised. Nearly ten years earlier, when he was leaving Paramount to follow Eisner to Disney, a colleague had warned him, "Eisner doesn't want a partner. Michael will never accept you as a partner." But Katzenberg had replied with his usual determination: "He will if I'm good enough." After all the Walt Disney Company's success, Katzenberg surely felt he had been good enough.

That night at their weekly dinner at Locanda Veneta, Eisner and Katzenberg didn't touch on the topic. The next morning, Katzenberg demanded a lunch with Eisner. He vented his anger and disappointment and demanded that Eisner make good on his promise to give him the number-two job. Now it was Eisner's turn to be furious. How could Katzenberg hand him an ultimatum at a time like this? The company had just been through a trauma and Katzenberg's departure would only make things worse, both in terms of morale and media scrutiny. "Are you telling me that if I don't do this, you'll leave?" Eisner asked in amazement.

"I want you to do what you said you wanted to do," Katzenberg replied.

"You're putting a gun to my head," Eisner said. With that, he walked out.

Later that afternoon, Eisner sent his general counsel, Sandy Litvack, to talk to Katzenberg. "You can't do this to Michael," Litvack said. Katzenberg replied that he was very upset and would stay only until his contract expired in October 1994.

But by the end of the day, the two combatants had decided to put questions about Katzenberg's future on hold until passions could die down. True to his word, Katzenberg got back to business as usual. The Broadway version of *Beauty and the Beast* was about to open. *The Lion King* movie would premiere in a couple of months. "What impressed me is he was acting as though he had a full new contract," Eisner later conceded.

In the coming weeks, Eisner weighed hiring a variety of others for the Frank Wells slot, from Warner cochairman Bob Daly to George Mitchell, the retiring Senate majority leader. Certainly both men had a gravitas that Katzenberg lacked. It was difficult to imagine that Daly, rich and autocratic, would have any interest in working for Eisner. As for Mitchell, his experience seemed ill-suited to the task that Eisner had in mind. Neither deal came to be.

Katzenberg continued his campaign of mending fences with the creative community and others in the industry. Within a few weeks, even his old enemy Michael Ovitz told the *Los Angeles Times*: "Jeffrey is a pleasure to do business with."

JUST A COUPLE of weeks after Wells died, Katzenberg decided he could not continue protecting Ricardo Mestres. Even though he had spent ten years with Mestres at Disney and several more before that at Paramount, Katzenberg pushed the thirty-six-year-old Mestres out of his job as president of Hollywood Pictures. He was given an independent production deal at the studio. Mestres's old rival, David Hoberman, was promoted to run the division as well as Touchstone and the Disney family label.

The decision to put one man at the top of Hollywood Pictures and Touchstone was perceived as a ramping back—an admission that Disney had failed with its "product is king" strategy of releasing as many as sixty films a year while rival studios issued as few as fifteen. Ironically, other studios, including Warner and Sony, had also geared up production. But no Disney live-action film had grossed more than $100 million since *Sister Act* in 1992. Hollywood Pictures never had a film reach blockbuster status. (Its top grosser was *The Hand That Rocks the Cradle*, at $88 million.)

Disney was keeping up its volume thanks in part to a rich, five-picture-a-year deal with producer Joe Roth, the former chairman of the Fox studios. Roth, with his dark hair and sleepy eyes, was by far the best-looking of Hollywood's clutch of top executives. He had a deceptively casual style, smooth and charismatic. As the only top executive who had ever directed a film (the 1990 *Coupe de Ville*, a comedic road movie with Alan Arkin, Patrick Dempsey, and Daniel Stern), Roth had enjoyed a certain distinction among the suits even though the movie hadn't done much business.

His track record as a producer and executive was wildly mixed. At Fox, he had picked up the huge sleeper hit *Home Alone* when Warner, to its lasting sorrow, dropped it. He had also rushed a *Die Hard* sequel into production, giving Fox a needed hit for the summer of 1990. But he had been the champion of such expensive bombs as *Shining Through* and *For the Boys*. Eventually, he and Barry Diller, then chairman of Fox, had parted ways and Roth again became a producer.

Katzenberg had recruited Roth and his Caravan Pictures production company to Disney in 1992. The deal was discussed over a lunch at Ca'brea, a restaurant in Los Angeles, in the private upstairs dining room. Eisner and Katzenberg were there, of course, and Roth brought Michael Ovitz to represent him. At the time Roth was poised to make a deal at Sony and went into the discussion thinking that Ovitz was simply using Disney as a prod to close that deal. But as the meeting progressed, it seemed clear that Ovitz and Eisner were in serious deal-making mode. After the lunch, Roth pulled Katzenberg aside. "From the body language between these two guys, I've got the feeling they want to park me at your place, and I'm not sure that's good for you," Roth said.

"Don't worry about it," Katzenberg replied. "It was my idea."

From Katzenberg's point of view, Roth could succeed him at the studio when he ascended to the number-two job. But it was obvious to everyone inside the studio and in the industry at large that Roth could also succeed Katzenberg if something less positive happened to him. With Katzenberg's future in constant doubt, every move that Eisner made with respect to Roth was closely scrutinized by the staff.

And indeed, not long after Roth set up shop at the studio, Katzenberg arrived with his troops at the Mighty Ducks arena for a company outing to a hockey game. When the group arrived, they could see Eisner sitting in his box with Roth at his side. To one Katzenberg loyalist, the moment was unforgettable and its meaning was clear. Katzenberg was the one on thin ice.

EISNER MAY HAVE been impressed with Katzenberg's demeanor in the wake of their quarrel after Wells's death, but he also believed that Katzenberg was taking his case public, with articles in the *New York Times*, *Wall Street Journal*, and *Los Angeles Times*, among others, that proclaimed his importance to Disney. To Eisner, the articles seemed to be part of putting a gun to his head. "I said a couple of times, 'You're doing a massive lobbying job for a constituency that has one vote,'" Eisner said later.

The irony of Eisner's reaction was that years earlier, he had defied his own boss, Barry Diller, and pursued coverage in the media when things began to destabilize at Paramount. (The widely read *New York* magazine article hadn't helped Eisner with Martin Davis at Paramount, but Sid Bass had said it impressed him when he decided to back Eisner as chairman of Disney.)

But now it was Eisner's show to run. Annoyed as he may have been, however, he had no reason to fear that Katzenberg's good press coverage would prove influential with the Disney board. Roy Disney's feelings toward Katzenberg had not warmed, and as Roy went, so went Stanley Gold. No one else on the board was likely to challenge Eisner on any subject.

If anything, Katzenberg's relationship with Roy Disney was about to get worse thanks to the stunning triumph that Disney was about to achieve with *The Lion King*. The problem was typified in May 1994 when *Wall Street Journal* reporter Rich Turner was writing a story about the making of *The Lion King*. As he pursued his research, the article began to focus on Katzenberg and his contribution to Disney's flourishing animation division.

Eisner never believed it, but Turner had initiated the story on his own—without prompting from Katzenberg. In fact, Katzenberg asked Turner to shine some of the spotlight on Roy Disney—as he had asked *Premiere* magazine to do in an earlier article about *Beauty and the Beast*. But Turner saw that Roy was at best a "marginal figure," and refused. In fact, Roy was frequently out of the country at his refurbished castle in County Cork, Ireland. He wasn't available for consultation during the making of the film, or for the extensive publicity blitzes the studio planned around its opening. Katzenberg tried to keep him in the picture, making sure he was visible, for example, in an Elton John television special created to promote the project.

One can only imagine how infuriated Roy must have been by passages like the one in Turner's article that said: "Prominent in the Disney formula is Mr. Katzenberg . . . who, if not exactly the re-incarnation of Walt Disney, brings his own blend of passion and obsession to Disney's mission of creating Disney animated 'classics.' Unlike most studio chiefs, who typically confine creative input to a few suggestions at screenings, the 43-year-old Mr. Katzenberg has made Disney's animation efforts a deeply personal mission. Tweaking, tinkering, bullying, cheerleading, his frenetic presence looms over virtually every aspect of [*The Lion King*]."

This put Katzenberg in a peculiar situation. He was enjoying his biggest success ever, but his bosses were mad at him. The tension was obvious at a summer evening party thrown at the National Zoo after *The Lion King*'s premiere in Washington, D.C. (The site was chosen, according to a former Disney executive, to curry favor for the embattled Disney's America.) While members of Congress milled about enjoying food and games, Eisner and Katzenberg sat at a table together. "You flew all the way across the country to throw this party and you sit with each other?" one guest teased.

A studio publicist standing nearby spoke up. "It's to show that they still speak," she said loudly.

When the film's opening foretold huge grosses, Katzenberg dutifully phoned Roy to congratulate him. He was stunned when Roy simply replied,

"Thank you," and rang off without even a mention of Katzenberg's efforts. Katzenberg soldiered on, calling all six hundred people who worked on the film to thank them for their efforts. Grossing $313 million, *The Lion King* became the most successful animated film ever made, and the biggest hit in Disney history.

∽

IT WAS TWO A.M. on Friday, July 15, and Eisner was becoming alarmed. He was experiencing pains in his arms, and he wasn't within striking distance of a large, well-equipped Los Angeles hospital. He was in Sun Valley, Idaho, spending a couple of days at investment banker Herbert Allen's annual retreat. Now he was bolt awake in the quietly elegant Sun Valley Lodge—a magnet for the rich and famous since W. Averell Harriman had it built in 1936.

Herbert Allen was the leading investment banker in the entertainment community, and every summer he gathered a who's who of the media world to discuss business in the mornings and to broker deals over tennis and golf in the afternoons. Eisner had arrived for his first visit to the Allen retreat on Thursday afternoon; Katzenberg had been coming for years, as had Frank Wells. Eisner recognized that Wells enjoyed "the purposeful posturing, the subtle gamesmanship, the camaraderie of shared interests, and the fierce underlying competitiveness" of the event. With Wells gone, Eisner now felt compelled to go himself. He was reluctant, in part, because it was counter to his superstitious nature to talk about what Disney had accomplished or might accomplish in the future.

And he avoided events that he considered "clubby." He always felt like an outsider, even among these powerful men who were now his peers. "On a rational level, I had no reason to feel out of place, but I did," he said later. He noticed that guests at the very top of the pecking order got to use the condominiums on the property while he and Jane were assigned to one of the smaller rooms in the main lodge. Nonetheless, he and Jane were among those invited to take their meals at Herb Allen's condo.

Though Eisner later said that the others seemed to share "an easy connection," the tensions that hummed among those gathered were too myriad to be counted. In comparison, the strain between Eisner and Katzenberg was rather pale. The guests included tycoon Rupert Murdoch, TCI magnate John Malone, legendary investor Warren Buffett, and thirty-eight-year-old Bill Gates of Microsoft.

Viacom chief Sumner Redstone, who had recently prevailed over Barry Diller in a fight to buy Paramount Pictures, was there, as was Diller, who had also lost out on a subsequent bid for CBS and was left to run the QVC home-shopping network. Diller surely must have been asking himself how his former employee, Eisner, had managed to get so wealthy and powerful at Disney while he was running an outfit that sold cubic zirconium to the masses. Diller could also contemplate the success of another old friend and adversary in attendance: music mogul David Geffen was now a billionaire pondering his next move as his contract with MCA neared expiration. Also present was foundering Time Warner chairman Gerald Levin and the Warner studio cochairmen, Bob Daly and Terry Semel. Young Seagram's scion Edgar Bronfman Jr. was now part of the group, holding 15 percent of Warner stock and getting a none-too-friendly reception from Levin.

Michael Ovitz was in attendance, having effectively transcended the agent's role by helping broker Sony's 1989 purchase of Columbia Pictures and Matsushita's acquisition of MCA the following year. Neither deal had worked out well for the buyer, but billions had changed hands. Ovitz was perceived as a man who could make a very powerful phone call. And Ovitz had flown there with Eisner in his jet. According to Eisner, the purpose was to discuss a plan for Ovitz to join Disney. On the ride, however, Ovitz had sounded a sour note. "We should be co-CEOs," he'd said. In Ovitz's mind, an alliance would work only if he reported directly to the board, as Wells had done. There were models for such arrangements—Daly and Semel had made it work at Warner for years. But such a partnership was hardly what Eisner had in mind and the trip became awkward. As they parted, Eisner's wife—unaware of the turn the talks had taken—said something about how helpful it would be if Ovitz were to join the company. "Yeah," Ovitz replied. "I'm the one guy who can save [him] from having a heart attack." To Eisner, it didn't feel like a joke.

∽

AS HE MINGLED at Sun Valley, Eisner inadvertently amused some of the other studio chiefs by openly questioning the wisdom of Disney's high-volume film strategy. That year, Disney would release thirty pictures—twice the number in 1990 when the studio started to step up the pace of production. Disney was now distributing a third of all major studio films for the year even though it was only one of six players. Why, Eisner asked, was Katzenberg making so many movies? Some thought Eisner's complaining seemed disingenuous because they all knew that he himself had embraced the volume strategy. Some contended that Katzenberg still couldn't even green-light a big-budget film without Eisner's consent.

"Jeffrey works for you," one of the studio chairmen told Eisner. "Why don't you tell him what to do?" Eisner said he intended to do just that.

According to Katzenberg, the two talked privately that Thursday night. But instead of reproaching him for making too many movies, Eisner seemed to send an entirely different message. From about nine-thirty to eleven, Katzenberg says, the two men conferred in the presence of Jane Eisner beside a huge oblong ice rink that the lodge kept frozen even in the summer months. In the quiet darkness, they engaged in a broad-ranging talk about the future of Disney—including areas such as Euro Disney that were outside the scope of Katzenberg's authority. Katzenberg felt included at last. He rejoiced inwardly: it seemed to him that Eisner had decided to make him the number-two man after all.

Eisner did not mention to Katzenberg that he wasn't feeling well. But by two in the morning, Eisner was in pain. He went to a local clinic for an electrocardiogram—paying in cash to avoid setting off a round of anxious press reports about his health. The test showed no immediate cause for alarm.

The next day, Eisner attended a morning panel at the Allen & Co. conference as scheduled. Despite his conversation with Katzenberg the night before, he would later say that he thought Katzenberg told bad jokes and presented himself poorly. Afterward, he and Katzenberg went to lunch with Allen. Meanwhile, Eisner's secretary had called Michael Engelberg, his internist, to ask when Eisner had taken his last stress test and to schedule another. Engelberg, who also happened to be producing The Puppet Masters—a troubled science-fiction project—for Disney, told Eisner to return to Los Angeles at once and go directly to the hospital. Eisner took that advice. He flew home and went to Cedars-Sinai Medical Center, where he registered under an assumed name. After just minutes on a treadmill, he was scheduled for emergency quadruple-bypass surgery.

As he was about to be wheeled into the operating room, Eisner—drugged and, by his own later account, thinking that he might be "playing out a death scene"—had a conversation with his wife and two of his sons. As he later recounted the discussion, he made three requests.

"I want to be buried aboveground."

It was an odd wish, though perhaps understandable for a man with a strong dislike of dirt.

He also had a brief negotiation with his wife. He and Jane had bought a parcel of land and designed a house that Eisner had concluded would be "too big and . . . a pain in the neck." So just before surgery, Eisner made his move.

"Jane, if I get through this, let's sell it," he said. "I don't want to build a house." Naturally, she gave in. It meant that Eisner, the patron of architects, would not design and build his own home despite his enormous wealth.

Finally Eisner told Jane that if anything should happen to him, she should get herself a seat on the board and tell the directors to hire Barry Diller to succeed him. Having addressed the future of the company, Eisner was ready to go under the knife.

∽

THAT SATURDAY MORNING, Jeffrey Katzenberg—who had returned from Sun Valley separately—called Eisner's house as usual to brief him on the previous night's box-office report. The company had just opened *Angels in the Outfield*, the Joe Roth–produced kids' baseball film, and the $9.2 million in sales was better than expected. It was nice, for once, to have good news to deliver about a live-action film. *The Lion King* had also pulled in another $17 million. To Katzenberg's surprise Jane Eisner answered the phone, and it was obvious that she had been asleep. Normally the Eisners were awake by now. Something was wrong.

"Did I wake you?" Katzenberg asked.

"I—I meant to call you," Jane replied.

"About what?"

Jane told Katzenberg what had happened the previous day. "He came through the surgery," she said. Everything, she assured Katzenberg, was fine. The incident had not been made public—yet.

By his account, Katzenberg warned Jane that the secret of Eisner's hospitalization could not be kept for long. Better to be aggressive, he said, than have something leak that might make the situation sound more dire than it was. Take the initiative, he urged. Stress the positive. Then he asked, "Who knows about it?"

She rattled off a list that included Roy and Patty Disney; Stanley Gold;

Sid Bass; the general counsel, Sandy Litvack; Eisner's public relations man, John Dreyer, and his wife, who worked for Eisner as an assistant; and Eisner's secretary, Lucille. And there was one more: Katzenberg's old enemy Michael Ovitz.

Katzenberg was shocked that the list was so long yet didn't include him. He offered to help in any way he could and hung up. Then he turned to his wife, Marilyn.

"Wives don't lie," he said.

"What are you talking about?"

"Wives don't lie," he repeated.

"So what does that mean?"

"In a moment of Michael's greatest vulnerability and her greatest need, she has enlisted those whom he trusts," Katzenberg said, somewhere between anger and sorrow. "She's told us everything we need to know. It's over."

∞

BUT IT WASN'T. Even though Katzenberg later said that he knew beyond a doubt that matters between him and Eisner were resolved, some part of him didn't believe it yet. Disney was soon putting out the word that Eisner was walking around and asking about box-office receipts by Sunday, not even two full days after his surgery. (In fact, Katzenberg says he was amazed when Eisner called to ask about grosses.)

Eisner was also receiving visitors. Ovitz, who had rushed to the hospital on Saturday afternoon, was back on Sunday. And Roy Disney—who was in Ireland but quickly returned to California—also stopped by. A Disney spokesman said Roy would "mind the store" during Eisner's absence, which was projected to last as long as four weeks.

On Tuesday afternoon, Katzenberg arrived, having been told by Jane to confine himself to "happy news." Nonetheless, Eisner at this time had the impression that Katzenberg was primarily interested in his own advancement even while Eisner still lay in bed with a tube in his arm.

On Wednesday, July 20—the day after Katzenberg's visit—the *Wall Street Journal* and the *New York Times* published major stories suggesting that Katzenberg was unhappy with his prospects for promotion and might leave the company. Neither article included a comment from Katzenberg. But Eisner thought it was hardly a coincidence that the two newspapers that wielded the most influence on Wall Street—and accordingly on Disney's stock, which was always Eisner's primary focus—reported such similar stories on the same day. The *New York Times* reported that Katzenberg's friends had disclosed his chagrin that he had been excluded from the loop immediately after Eisner fell ill. And Eisner homed in on a quote from an unnamed source in the *Times*: "The question is, does Michael want to share power with Jeffrey? If he doesn't, Jeffrey will leave the company by the end of the year." Once again, Eisner felt that he was being handed an ultimatum—at an appalling time.

Katzenberg, who says he spoke to neither paper, contends that the stories appeared merely because his contract was up in less than ten weeks and Eisner was in the hospital, raising obvious questions about the future. But even if Katzenberg did not speak to the papers himself, there can be little doubt that when Eisner saw a quote from one of Katzenberg's closest friends, he immediately thought of David Geffen and resented, not for the first time, what he perceived as Geffen's bad influence on Katzenberg.

The outlook for Eisner's health was so positive that the stock remained unmoved during the episode (which conveniently happened on a weekend when the markets were closed) and even ticked up by twenty-five cents the next Monday, when Eisner was said to be dictating instructions to top executives from his bed.

Still, the press was awash with speculation about whether Eisner would be forced to name a number-two man who could be a successor. The *Los Angeles Times* observed that other entertainment-company chiefs, including News Corp.'s Rupert Murdoch and Time Warner's Gerald Levin, worked "without a net." The *Wall Street Journal* pointed out that the phenomenon was hardly confined to the entertainment industry. But *Newsweek* described Katzenberg as a contender for promotion, describing him as "widely considered to be Disney's most valuable human resource" and quoting financial analyst Larry Haverty as saying, "Katzenberg is probably 80 percent responsible" for the increased value of Disney's stock. *Newsweek* even had an anonymous Disney board member suggesting that Katzenberg might be a candidate for the number-two job. ("Obviously Jeffrey doesn't have the same background as Frank. But that doesn't mean you can't make adjustments if you want to," read the quote.) *Time* reported that Katzenberg's friends "were busy making Katzenberg's case [for promotion] to anyone who would listen." All these reports—coming while Eisner was still recuperating—undoubtedly pressed every button on Eisner's keypad.

As it happened, Eisner had already articulated his thoughts before his unplanned trip to the hospital. At the end of July, the *Los Angeles Times* published an article based on an interview Eisner had given before he made his ill-fated trip to Sun Valley. No matter what he might have said to Katzenberg at the skating rink in Sun Valley, Eisner had signaled strongly to the newspaper that Katzenberg was not going to advance. An associate of both men described their relationship as "a withholding father and a son looking for love and recognition from that father."

Eisner, at age fifty-two, started off with plenty of complimentary words for Katzenberg, now forty-three years old. He told the newspaper that there was no one in the industry whom he trusted more than Katzenberg. He talked about Katzenberg's loyalty and devotion. "He ... is very supportive of the whole company," Eisner said. "He is very much a team player." It would turn out to be a confusing statement considering that just a few weeks later, Stanley Gold would say that soon after Wells's death, the board had rejected Katzenberg's bid for advancement because he was "not collegial" and "not a guy who can foster the teamwork we need."

In the interview, Eisner told the reporters that he and Katzenberg had disagreed on occasion but added, "We've never had a fight!" Given their long history together, that statement was difficult to believe on its face. The *Times* reporters didn't know at the time that Eisner had walked out on a lunch with Katzenberg just a few weeks earlier, so they couldn't ask him whether that qualified as a fight.

Eisner also defended the very strategy that he would question, just days later, at Sun Valley — releasing lots of movies. "Our leverage is volume," he said. "As the industry becomes content-starved, our strength became being a volume company."

But Eisner groused about Katzenberg's efforts to mend fences with Ovitz and others in the film community. "My note to Jeffrey Katzenberg would have been to ignore all these people," he said. "As we become more user-friendly, I feel we've become less effective. I would encourage Jeffrey Katzenberg to be more detail-oriented. . . . When he was involved in the details and not caring what CAA, ICM or the *L.A. Times* thought, he did it great."

Waxing nostalgic, Eisner recalled the good old days at Paramount, when Katzenberg's role had been so clearly defined. "He is clearly the best golden retriever I ever met," he said. "He's the best person to follow through on a project, an idea or slate of ideas . . . that is his main attribute." (By 1997,

Eisner had apparently forgotten about this comment; he told interviewer Charlie Rose, "I never called [him] ever my 'golden retriever.' ")

Early in the relationship, Eisner continued, "I did 100 percent of the thinking and he was the one to get something done." That had changed over the years, Eisner said. Katzenberg and his allies, reading these comments, found them unbearably patronizing.

Eisner said he granted the *Times* interview reluctantly and turned to his corporate PR man, John Dreyer, no fewer than six times as he talked to the reporters, saying, "I know I'm going to regret having done this." He said his decision to keep Katzenberg in place as studio chief was in Katzenberg's best interest. "I don't want Jeffrey at the moment to worry about corporate insurance and that's what Frank Wells did. . . . He kept the machine running," Eisner said. "I want to keep my stars in star roles." The *Times* concluded that, clearly, "Eisner viewed himself as the sole king of the Disney jungle."

Before the story appeared in print, *Times* reporters Claudia Eller and Alan Citron had gone back to Disney to check whether Eisner's position had changed, now that his emergency surgery appeared to increase pressure to appoint a second-in-command. Eisner's illness didn't merely highlight his mortality—it raised questions about the burdens he was shouldering at the company. And these were stressful times for Eisner. Euro Disney was still an ongoing problem. Other plans for expansion were snarled. Disney's America was falling off the drawing board fast.

But Katzenberg was riding high. *The Lion King* had cruised to $175 million in just five weeks and looked like it might become the top-grossing movie of all time (it went to number two; *Jurassic Park* stayed in first place). *Beauty and the Beast* was the number-one show on Broadway. The Miramax deal was paying off. Even so, Eller and Citron were told that Eisner's views on Katzenberg were unchanged.

⁓

EISNER WENT HOME on Thursday, July 22—less than a week after his surgery. Within a week, an item ran in Army Archerd's column in *Variety* expressing his frustration at being unable to return to the office. Archerd reported that Eisner sounded "strong." He had watched a lot of television. He had made an excursion to Chasen's, the old-guard Hollywood eatery, and was reported to have eaten a salt-free fish dinner. Eisner said he had learned something during his convalescence: "They don't need me" at the company. Archerd asked if Eisner was going to appoint a successor, but the question was cheerfully deflected. "I haven't thought about business," said the man who supposedly had been issuing directions to key executives from his hospital bed. "I'm not allowed to do anything like making decisions right now."

Eisner's first visit to the office went unheralded in the press, but a former studio executive remembers that Eisner attended a meeting that day—and brought Jane with him. The purpose was to review ads designed to rebut the negative press about Disney's America. After Eisner looked at a couple of spots, he said he wanted others that showed Abraham Lincoln to give a flavor of America's past as it would be represented at the park. Executives protested that such an approach would play into the hands of critics who complained that Disney would distort history.

"They're wrong," Eisner said. But otherwise, says that executive, it was Jane who spoke up. "She would give her opinion but she wasn't speaking for him," he remembers. "He was so ashen and pale—but he wouldn't stop. He was actually quite frail but she was there to protect him."

Later, Eisner acknowledged that the cardiac episode changed him. It was more than a newfound obsession with diet and exercise. (Eisner transformed a conference room next to his office into a private gym, though there were already two workout facilities on the Disney campus. More than a dozen workers toiled overnight—at considerable extra expense—so that they wouldn't disrupt business during the day.) "The truth is, I went from being young to being old," he mused. "All of a sudden, I even looked my age. When you go through a period of screwing around with your heart, you realize that you not only aren't immortal, you could have been one of those people who drop dead on the tennis court or in the office at fifty-two. That realization has an impact on you."

AS EISNER RECUPERATED, Katzenberg retreated to his new, multimillion-dollar Charles Gwathmey–designed beach house in Malibu to brood and strategize. Finally, on a weekend afternoon in August, he headed over to the Eisners' house for a meeting. The two sat in the library, Eisner wearing his bathrobe. Katzenberg says he realized that Eisner was never going to make good on what Katzenberg regarded as his earlier promise, so he had decided once and for all to resign. Eisner started off by saying that he was upset with the numerous press reports that Katzenberg was lobbying for the job—and especially that he had threatened to quit. Katzenberg remembers interrupting to say, "I never told Frank Wells how much I liked working with him and how much I loved him. I realize I've never told you how much you've meant to me." He thanked Eisner for their years together and all he had learned. Then he said he planned to leave.

"Have you taken a job?" Eisner asked.

"No."

"Is it something we can discuss?"

"We can talk about it, Michael, but I suspect the decision has been carved in stone by other people," Katzenberg persisted. He pointed out that Roy Disney and the board were hostile, and said he didn't want to deal with that animosity. According to Katzenberg, Eisner said, "I can fix it. . . . I'm going to Ireland over Labor Day weekend and spend time with Roy and I'm going to make it work."

"I don't have a good feeling about it," Katzenberg replied.

Eisner asked for a few days to work things out. Katzenberg said whatever happened, he would stay until his contract was up in October. Before he left, Eisner asked if Katzenberg had thoughts on how the company might be reorganized.

Katzenberg spent most of the next ten days drafting a four-page plan for the company. Several days later, on August 23, he had dinner with Joe Roth. Roth had every reason to know how dire Katzenberg's situation was, but he didn't let on. He told Katzenberg that he had been too public in his quest for advancement and that pushing Eisner while he was still recuperating was a bad strategy. "The guy is [recovering]," Roth said. "You should go in and offer to take out the garbage."

"I've drawn a line in the sand," Katzenberg said that night. "It's either this way or nothing at all." Roth could see that Katzenberg had passed a point of no return. To Roth he didn't seem to care that Eisner was recovering from a traumatic episode.

"If it doesn't go down, they're going to come to me," Roth said. Katzenberg didn't seem to believe that would happen.

But in fact, they already had gone to Roth, who had spent that afternoon negotiating an extraordinarily rich deal to take over as chairman of the studio.

The next day was Eisner's first full day back at the office. Eisner called Katzenberg in. On his way to the meeting, Katzenberg ran into Bob Levin, the marketing chief. Levin was thinking about restructuring his department and said he needed answers on certain issues. "I'm going to see Michael, and I hope I can start finalizing some of the details," Katzenberg said.

But there was only one detail that mattered. When Katzenberg walked into the office, Eisner told him there was no way for the two to come to terms. "This is a day I've dreaded for a long time," Eisner said. "I wish it hadn't come to this and that we could have made it work." He handed Katzenberg a four-page press release and said it was going out to the media later that day. It announced a reorganization of the company, with Joe Roth as chairman of the film studio. Rich Frank, the television chief who had previously reported to Katzenberg, would run an expanded television and telecommunications division and report to Eisner. Animation would report to Eisner and Roy Disney. Almost as an afterthought, the release briefly mentioned the departure of Jeffrey Katzenberg as chairman of the studio.

Katzenberg, who had brought his plan to reshape Disney to the meeting, never got a chance to present it.

23

A BITTER DIVORCE

"T HERE ARE TWO kinds of divorces," Katzenberg told Eisner on the day of their ill-fated meeting. "There's one in which you're best friends and one in which you're enemies." Eisner quickly said he wanted to be friends. Katzenberg asked for a few concessions. He still had a few weeks on his contract, and in that period, he wanted to see through some events that were on his calendar: the release of *Pulp Fiction*, the upcoming Miramax sleeper hit, and the Robert Redford–directed *Quiz Show*. He wanted to attend the London premiere of *The Lion King*; composer Elton John was throwing a party in his honor.

And he wanted the money issues to be resolved quickly and fairly. He reminded Eisner of their last days at Paramount, when they had walked to the bank after Eisner demanded his cashier's check. "It's not that you weren't going to get your money—you just wanted your business cleared up," Katzenberg said. "I would like the same." Katzenberg said he was entitled to his lump-sum payment of 2 percent of future profits from projects he had put into development—and that would be a rather large check. Katzenberg wasn't sure exactly how big it would be, but he was convinced that he was owed at least an eight-figure sum.

According to Katzenberg, Eisner agreed to resolve things quickly but immediately started to break his promises. In fact, Katzenberg didn't even get a chance to review Eisner's press release; it had been sent to the media before he went into the meeting. As soon as he returned to his office from his meeting with Eisner, his secretary told him Steven Spielberg was on the line from Jamaica. Spielberg, who had worked with Katzenberg on *Roger Rabbit* and was now his partner in Dive!, was visiting at the vacation home of Bob Zemeckis, the director of *Roger Rabbit*, who was no particular fan of Eisner. Both men said they had already heard the news of Katzenberg's demise. As Spielberg offered his condolences to Katzenberg, Zemeckis yelled, "Why don't you guys do something together?"

Meanwhile, Spielberg quoted a line from *Back to the Future* — offering Christopher Lloyd's final remark: "Where you're going, you don't need roads."

"What do you mean, 'you'?" Katzenberg answered. "I'm thinking 'we.' "

∞

TOUCHSTONE PRODUCTION CHIEF Donald De Line was returning from a forty-eight-hour trip to Italy to recruit Bruce Beresford to direct a film. When his flight landed in Los Angeles, he was surprised to find a colleague waiting for him at the gate. "What are you doing here?" he asked. "Did someone die?"

"I have disturbing news," his coworker replied. "Jeffrey is gone." It almost was like a death. Separating Katzenberg from Disney was like ripping flesh from bone.

"This is not true," De Line protested. Before he would believe the news, he insisted on calling Hoberman. "I'm sorry to tell you it is true," Hoberman said.

The marketing staff heard the news from chief Bob Levin. "I have an announcement to make," he said. "At two o'clock today, Jeffrey was let go. He resigned or was let go but he's left the studio." His staff gasped — not surprised, perhaps, but stunned that it could come to this seemingly impossible conclusion.

On the Disney board, however, there apparently were few pangs of regret. While the directors had previously been convinced that keeping Katzenberg was important, Eisner had apparently rooted out that perception. Convincing board members to accept his view of the world "is Michael's particular corporate genius," says a high-level Disney executive. On the other hand, no one was likely to put up a fight as long as Roy Disney and Stanley Gold were on board. ("The board doesn't control Disney, and the investors don't control it," Barry Diller said in an interview a few months later. "Michael controls it.")

The day before Eisner handed Katzenberg his walking papers, he conducted a secret negotiation through general counsel Sandy Litvack and Irwin Russell, Eisner's own lawyer and a Disney board member, to sign up Joe Roth as head of the studio's live-action division. The negotiation had been awkward because Helene Hahn, the studio's business-affairs chief, was the person most familiar with Roth's deal as a producer—a deal that had to be eliminated so he could become chairman. But Hahn was deeply loyal to Katzenberg, so she was carefully excluded from the loop. Eisner must have been convinced that she would warn Katzenberg if she knew what was brewing.

Roth benefited from such a hastily conducted discussion. In fact, a former Disney lawyer says the company paid Roth about twice as much as he should have gotten. "They justify it to this day," this executive says, "because the stock didn't go down because they had a guy in the wings. Michael ordered Sandy and Irwin Russell to get Joe on board—committed that night before Michael spoke to Jeffrey the next day."

This put Roth in the catbird seat except for one problem. Three of his first four movies under his Caravan deal had been bombs—*Three Muske-teers*, *Angie* with Geena Davis, and the biggest flop, *I Love Trouble* with Julia Roberts and Nick Nolte. (Only the fourth, *Angels in the Outfield*, performed at all.) And Roth owed $15 million on *I Love Trouble*, having agreed to pay budget overages out of his pocket if the picture didn't make money. Eisner's first bit of generosity was to forgive the debt.

As head of Caravan, Roth was to receive a producer's fee and percentage of gross for each of his movies. The agreement called for five pictures a year over five years, which meant he still had twenty-one pictures left in the deal. In the negotiation, Roth contended that he would have received at least $42 million—or $2 million for each of those twenty-one pictures. But according to his deal, Roth was to receive only $1 million per picture; he only collected another million dollars if the picture earned its money back. Certainly, that hadn't happened on three of the first four movies he had made. But either Litvack wasn't familiar enough with the deal to make that argument or Roth simply had Disney over a barrel. Either way, in addition to forgiving the $15 million overage, Disney wrote Roth a check for about $40 million to take the studio job. It was a nice payday for Roth, who otherwise might have had to produce as many as fifteen movies over three years for free to make up the money he owed to Disney. Instead, he got a deal worth some $55 million—and that was before he negotiated the millions he would earn as studio chief. (Based on stock prices and an estimate of the number of options awarded to Roth, that package would be worth tens of millions of dollars more.)

SEVERAL HOURS AFTER Eisner had told Katzenberg that their sixteen-year relationship was over, he was on his way to spend the evening at Warner cochairman Bob Daly's house. Daly's future wife, songwriter Carole Bayer Sager, thought it would do Eisner good to explore the mind-body connection with one of Hollywood's favorite spiritual leaders, Deepak Chopra. Despite his fascination with health issues, Eisner was far too skeptical to be attracted by Chopra and came away unimpressed. Besides, as he observed later, he didn't need any help from Chopra. "Settling Jeffrey Katzenberg's future," he explained, "had provided enough stress reduction for the next several months."

✺

AS THE NEWS of Katzenberg's imminent departure spread throughout the entertainment community, there was a sense of utter shock. Of course some people inside and outside Disney thought Katzenberg deserved a comeuppance. "No one could do cold and callous better than Jeffrey," said one longtime Disney executive. "He was as tough and mean as anyone in the business." But others at the studio literally wept. Certainly Katzenberg had his flaws, but his zest for his job and his love of Disney could not be questioned. Over the Labor Day holiday, Katzenberg went, as he always did, to Disney World. It must have been a painful visit. The animation department in Florida surprised him with a keg of his favorite drink, diet Coke, and a picture of himself surrounded by Disney characters. As some 250 members of the department stood by, Katzenberg signed their *Lion King* books or drawings, while Marilyn Katzenberg watched and wiped away tears.

Back in Los Angeles, Don Hahn, who had produced *Roger Rabbit*, *Beauty and the Beast*, and *The Lion King*, likened Katzenberg's departure to the champion Dallas Cowboys losing their coach. "Jeffrey has seen animation as his passion, his baby, his life, and his breath. That's what's so sad," Hahn said. "I feel like I lost a friend just when I was having fun."

On the other hand, Peter Schneider ultimately grew tired of hearing the paeans to Katzenberg. "The story that's been written for the last ten years, which is that Jeffrey did everything, is a myth," he complained to *Premiere* magazine. "Time will show that this place will stand up very well for the next five, six, ten years without his ruling hand."

In fact, Disney's next three animated features—*Pocahontas*, *The Hunchback of Notre Dame*, and *Hercules*—all failed to meet the standard set by their predecessors. Katzenberg played a role in developing them but was gone for nearly a year when *Pocahontas* opened in June 1995. It grossed $141.6 million domestically. (Disney would start to hit the target again in 1998 and 1999 with *Mulan* and *Tarzan*, which grossed $121 million and $170 million, respectively. Some said Disney films simply weren't as good as they had been. Others thought the broad audience had wearied of the formula, leaving only the youngest children as Disney's market.)

But long before *Pocahontas* was in theaters, a serious spin war was under way. Although Katzenberg said he wanted a minimum of acrimony in the hope that Eisner would settle his contract quickly, he couldn't resist trying to justify himself. The press swarmed over the story. Soon, *The New Yorker* and *Vanity Fair* were working on major articles about the split-up. The daily papers had already dived in. "This is not a Shakespearean tragedy," Eisner told the *Los Angeles Times*. "This is people moving on with their lives and doing new and interesting things." But Steven Spielberg told the newspaper that Katzenberg's departure was Eisner's "Machiavellian loss." At the same time Disney board members portrayed Katzenberg as an egomaniac who wasn't up to getting Wells's job.

The day after the Spielberg quote appeared, Eisner called Katzenberg in a fury. He complained that Katzenberg was whipping up a maelstrom of bad press that exceeded whatever Eisner had expected. He was stunned to find that the story had merited the cover of *Newsweek*—and had portrayed Katzenberg's absence as a serious problem for Disney. The article even described Eisner as sobbing in the hospital after his surgery because he was so frightened about his condition. Eisner vehemently denied that this had ever happened.

Not all of the coverage had cut Katzenberg's way; the *Wall Street Journal* called him "creative but unpolished." (In a sense, this was still something of a triumph for Katzenberg, because some years earlier the *Journal* had questioned whether he had any taste at all.) But Katzenberg was scoring enough points that Eisner demanded a cease-fire. Katzenberg confided to a friend that this conversation with Eisner was their angriest ever and he quickly asked his supporters to decline further interviews. In the superheated environment, however, it was not easy to cool the rhetoric.

He also consulted litigator Bert Fields, who had handled several cases against Disney, about his severance package. Katzenberg told Fields he was owed 2 percent of the profit from projects he had put into production— and he wanted to collect.

Katzenberg set a September 9 deadline for Eisner to come up with a deal. If Eisner didn't resolve the matter, Geffen warned in an interview, "he's going to have to tell the truth under oath about everything. . . . Eisner's lack of kindness, lack of generosity, and inability to give credit were simply shameful." On the day before the deadline, a company attorney asked Katzenberg how quickly he could vacate his offices. Katzenberg pointed out that he had planned to stay until his contract expired at the beginning of October. Disney backed off.

On Saturday, September 10, Eisner visited Katzenberg at home. Once again, Eisner complained about the bad press. "You know how to stop it," Katzenberg said. "You have not fulfilled one single promise that you made to me in terms of how you were going to deal with this. You've done an assassination job on me. I've yet to be paid a nickel. Deal honestly with me."

"I can't go to the board right now," Eisner said. "They're too angry with you."

Katzenberg pointed out that the board's anger had nothing to do with Disney's contractual obligations. The matter was in Eisner's hands. Katzenberg told him he would wait for a settlement proposal, and if he didn't like it, Disney would have to work things out with Bert Fields.

On Friday, September 16, Katzenberg paid one last visit to Eisner in his office. The issue of money was still unresolved. Katzenberg left him with a copy of the July 1, 1988, deal memo that had been written by Frank Wells. Katzenberg underlined the relevant language. "My eleven-year-old would read this and understand what it means," he said. "It's that clear."

The meeting became "very short very quickly," Katzenberg said later. "He literally did not want to physically take the piece of paper. He stood up from his desk and literally backed away. . . . He took the piece of paper and said he would give it to Sandy Litvack." With that, Eisner showed Katzenberg the door.

∞

DESPITE THE ATTEMPT by both sides to impose a cease-fire in the press, the war continued. The *New York Times* reported that Katzenberg had been told he was unwelcome at *The Lion King*'s London premiere in September, which scotched the plans for the Elton John party. Katzenberg did get to attend the Washington premiere of *Quiz Show*. But the article said Disney animators had been prevented from throwing a party for Katzenberg on the lot.

The *Times* reported a jumble of reasons for Katzenberg's ouster — complaints that Eisner had shared with unnamed friends. Eisner reportedly said he had been mulling over a decentralization of Disney's management for the past two years and that Katzenberg's days had been numbered ever since. And he said he had ousted Katzenberg because of the weak live-action slate. Another report had him saying that Katzenberg's lack of a college degree and his ownership of Dive! worked against him.

It was true that the restaurant and the whole ongoing drama was stuck in Eisner's craw. Eisner reportedly told a staff meeting, "I don't want to hear any more about who is happy and who is unhappy and who is staying and who is leaving." As far as he was concerned, he added, Katzenberg could become head of a studio, a high-tech entertainment company, or "run his deli." Either way, he said, he was tired of discussing Jeffrey Katzenberg.

When stories in *The New Yorker* and *Vanity Fair* hit the stands in late September and early October, respectively, they included Katzenberg's first public recounting of the 1993 walk in Aspen and of Eisner's supposed assurance that he would advance if Wells were not in position. In *Vanity Fair*, Eisner didn't quite seem to deny it. "He says I said to him, 'If Frank wasn't there, it would be a different story.' In other words, that I gave him the body language to believe that," Eisner said. "I can't say whether I did and it's unfortunate if this became a misunderstanding. I wish I had made my message clearer."

(Perhaps neither of the two principals remembers exactly what was said in this pivotal conversation, but they do agree that Eisner had said that Wells "would feel hurt" if he was asked to step aside. But in a 1997 interview, Eisner seemed to contradict that assertion. Eisner told Charlie Rose that during Katzenberg's tenure as studio chief, he had considered bringing in Michael Ovitz as president and making Wells vice-chairman — exactly the arrangement that Katzenberg had proposed for himself. In the Rose interview, Eisner said Wells "had said he would step down and become vice-chairman," but the plan was dropped out of concern that Ovitz "would have been in conflict with Jeff Katzenberg." Katzenberg says if there were discussions about hiring Ovitz at any time during his tenure at the studio, he was unaware of them.)

When it came to retaliating against Katzenberg's press blitz, Eisner let Disney board members do the heavy swinging. Stanley Gold told *Vanity Fair*, "I thought Jeffrey was an extremely talented, hard-working, efficient executive for most of the 10 years he was [at Disney]. But there came a point in time where Jeffrey's ego and his almost pathological need to be important overtook his good judgment." Gold said some of Katzenberg's behavior had created considerable ill will on the part of the board. There was the Katzenberg memo, for example. Eisner had told Katzenberg to tear it up, Gold said, "but Katzenberg went to the Xerox machine and sent it out."

Then Gold cited a speech Katzenberg had given in July in which he attacked rival MCA (parent of Universal) at a video-industry conference in Las Vegas. Katzenberg urged his audience to fight MCA's decision to sell cheap copies of such videos as *An American Tail: Fievel Goes West* through McDonald's. He charged that such sales were "a Faustian bargain that threatens the future of the video business." Customers would be reluctant to pay regular prices for videos if they could "just walk across the street for a Big Mac with Fievel and fries."

Not surprisingly, MCA chief Lew Wasserman was said to be livid over these comments. Eisner had infuriated MCA before — notably when he embarked on the Disney studio tour in Orlando — but Gold said Katzenberg had not been authorized to fire this particular volley. "That is a huge policy statement by the Disney company that Jeffrey never cleared with Michael," Gold said. "And when questioned about it, Katzenberg says, 'From now on, when I speak publicly, I have to speak on important matters.' That's what got him in trouble. . . . He had this need to be the more important guy in Hollywood. At the end of the day, he is the tragedy here."

Katzenberg said he regretted offending MCA, but he argued that Eisner was in the hospital when this speech was drafted and was not available for consultation. (Considering that Eisner was already talking box office on Sunday after his surgery, this explanation may be less than persuasive. But Katzenberg said he was ordered to talk to Eisner only about light topics during this period.) His position, Katzenberg said, was meant to defend "the most vital, income-generating" part of the Disney studios. "I defy Stanley Gold or anyone else to tell me that what I did wasn't singularly in the interest of the Walt Disney Company," he said. "I guess Stanley is right — and it is a tragedy — that I was not sensitive enough to the issue of style in this case. But I only wanted what was best for the company."

But the Katzenberg camp was throwing its own hardballs. David Geffen, who many observers blamed for encouraging Katzenberg to fight too hard for advancement, went after Eisner with unrelenting energy. He came up with several different ways to call Eisner disingenuous and ungenerous, knowing that the press couldn't resist the sound bites. "Michael is not a guy who likes to share," he said in one typical interview. "He is not a generous person. Michael Eisner is a very tall little guy. And Jeffrey Katzenberg is a very short big guy."

Eisner responded: "I think Geffen is one of the most talented record entrepreneurs that I know. And I don't understand why he is so involved in our business."

Geffen wasn't the only one hurling bolts at Eisner. Veteran producer Ray Stark—who had long ago allied himself with Geffen and Katzenberg against Mike Ovitz—now rallied to Katzenberg's side. Katzenberg's success at Disney exceeded the visions of Walt himself, Stark said, adding archly, "I have a great deal of respect for Mike Eisner and I hope his next move is not to give the gate to Mickey Mouse."

It was the *New Yorker* article, in particular, that infuriated both sides. Eisner later said that Katzenberg inadvertently faxed him a note thanking Bert Fields for his help with the story. Eisner thought Katzenberg had agreed to cool the press coverage, but here was evidence that he had fanned the flames. Katzenberg was also incensed. In the article, Eisner made it clear that as far as he was concerned, he didn't owe Katzenberg a dime. "His contract is over," he said. "When people's contracts are over, they're over."

∽

IT WAS A tough time for Eisner. On the heels of ejecting Katzenberg, he finally had to announce a decision to jettison the Disney's America park. It was a stinging defeat. Spokesman John Dreyer still says the park will be built someplace, someday, but the company decided "not to roil the community" any further.

Former Imagineer Pat Scanlon—who observed the project's failure after leaving the company—thinks Wells as a strong second-in-command might have salvaged the situation. "There wasn't anybody at a high enough level to keep Michael in his box," he says. "Michael was making public remarks that weren't helpful. Michael sounded a bit like an abrasive Hollywood producer coming to town. Frank would have shaped public relations because he would have made Michael more aware. Frank was the consummate diplomat."

Disney's America wasn't Eisner's only problem. Disneyland Paris con-

tinued to sputter financially and plans to expand on the West Coast refused
to gel. Eisner would have had his hands full even if he had not decided to
reorganize the studio. No wonder he was sick of hearing about Katzenberg.

Roth had nothing to do but focus on live action. As rumors spun that
he was replacing everyone in the studio, he immediately signaled the advent
of a more openhanded era merely by taking out bigger ads for upcoming
films. Always known for spending lavishly on marketing, Roth kept up that
practice when he took over at Disney. Within relatively short order, he
announced that he would trim the number of films that the studio released
each year.

An exodus from the studio began that was inevitably compared with the
departures from Paramount when Eisner had gone to Disney in 1984. Bob
Levin read that he was out as marketing chief in the trades; eventually, he
wound up at Sony Pictures. Many others followed, and in less than a year,
several key executives who had followed Eisner to Disney from Paramount
years earlier were gone. David Geffen described Michael Eisner as "the
Marty Davis of his day"—an allusion to the too-tough boss who had dismissed Eisner years earlier at Paramount.

As soon as Katzenberg left, the newly promoted David Hoberman started
to worry about his future. He went to see Eisner, who spent about forty-five
minutes trying to explain the recent turn of events to him and to soothe
his anxieties. But soon after that, Hoberman started to feel a chill from
Eisner. He called and requested a meeting, but to his dismay, nearly a
month passed before he got in the door. Finally the phone rang late on a
Friday afternoon and Hoberman went dashing to Eisner's office. He told
Eisner he was concerned that he was too strongly linked with Katzenberg
in Eisner's mind to survive the change.

"I picked Joe Roth to run the studio," Eisner said. "If Joe loves you,
that's fine. If he doesn't support you, that's that." It was clear to Hoberman
that Eisner had nothing against him. He had simply turned the decision
over to Roth and didn't care what happened. Hoberman could respect that.
It wasn't personal; Eisner had simply moved on. Within a couple of months,
so had Hoberman. Roth wasn't inclined to keep him. Like many Hollywood
executives who are no longer wanted, Hoberman was given a production
deal at Disney and an office near the one where Mestres had taken up
residence. One executive on the lot called their home "the Dead Presidents
building."

24

BIG DREAMS

"Y OU GET THAT psycho to call me," Jeffrey Katzenberg said to Joe Roth in an early-morning phone call in October 1994. The "psycho" was Michael Eisner, and Katzenberg wanted to be congratulated on the founding of his new company, which would later be named DreamWorks. "This is about making things better," Katzenberg told Roth. "So when I stand in front of a hundred journalists, I can say, 'The first call I got was from Michael Eisner.' Which is what I'll do. I'll completely exaggerate what he said." (Katzenberg now says he can't remember whether Eisner made the call.)

When he left Disney at the end of September, Katzenberg moved into new offices on Maple Drive. But not even two weeks later, he was already packing. That day, Katzenberg was introducing a roomful of reporters to his new partners: David Geffen and Steven Spielberg. The three were announcing the founding of an unnamed entertainment company that lacked neither ambition nor hype. The goal was nothing less than establishing a new studio—something no one had achieved in more than sixty years. At the time there were only seven such companies: Warner, Sony Pictures, Fox, Universal, Paramount, MGM/United Artists, and of course, Disney. Each of them depended on a library of films and television shows to throw off cash. This new company would face a daunting challenge without that steady source of income.

The new company had its seeds in the call Katzenberg had received from Spielberg on the afternoon of Katzenberg's dismissal from Disney. A few days later, Katzenberg had visited Spielberg at home. Spielberg observed that he, too, had long been under the protection of older mentors—Steve Ross, the legendary chairman of Time Warner, and Sid Sheinberg, president of MCA. But now, at forty-six, he thought he might be ready to head his own business. Even so, the actual advent of the partnership came as a surprise to him. "Over the years I've had almost a religious fervor in not investing my own money in show business," he said. "Not in my wildest imagination would I have guessed that this trio would have come together."

In fact, Spielberg had to work hard to convince his wife, Kate Capshaw, that the new company was a good idea. "I love Jeffrey. But I never want you to become Jeffrey," she said wisely. "I don't want you to become involved in that lather of workaholism." Spielberg promised he would not allow the new company to become all-consuming—and put Katzenberg on notice that those were the terms of any deal. Spielberg also made it clear that he would not be exclusive to the new company; he would be open to directing projects at other studios. Clearly, the pressure would be on Katzenberg to prevent him from doing that.

Spielberg also sought the approval of his old friend, Sheinberg, who had discovered Spielberg when he saw the then-twenty-year-old director's short film *Amblin*. He signed him to a contract and the two had been close ever since. Spielberg had handsomely repaid Sheinberg's faith with the seminal hit *Jaws*, as well as *E.T.—The Extra-Terrestrial*, *Schindler's List*, and *Jurassic Park*.

"Why do you need this? How does this benefit you?" Sheinberg asked when Spielberg approached him about the new venture.

"It benefits me because the idea of building something from the ground up, where I could actually be a co-owner, where I don't rent, I don't lease, I don't option but actually own—that appeals to me," Spielberg replied. Finally he added, "Sid, if you don't want me to do this, I won't. You don't even have to explain yourself. You can just say, 'No.'" But Sheinberg gave his blessing. With that, Spielberg told Katzenberg the new company would have to have some relationship with Universal as long as Sheinberg was president of MCA.

That was beginning to seem like a situation that might not last forever. Sheinberg and MCA's chairman, Lew Wasserman, were chafing under the tight controls imposed by MCA's Japanese owners. In 1990, Wasserman and Sheinberg had sold the company to Matsushita for $6.1 billion (with Michael Ovitz acting as the marriage broker). At the time it was perceived as a means to cash out while keeping control of the company. Wasserman pocketed about $350 million of Matsushita preferred stock while Sheinberg made about $90 million in cash. (The same deal also vastly enriched David Geffen, who had sold his music company to MCA before the Matsushita transaction.)

Wasserman and Sheinberg had been hoping that Matsushita would provide the money to expand MCA, but it quickly became apparent that the
Japanese wouldn't finance the acquisitions that the two men wanted to
make. Instead, Matsushita imposed tight financial controls. The marriage
had quickly soured and now it was widely known that the parties were
almost desperately unhappy with each other. After more than twenty years
at MCA, Sheinberg's future with the company was in doubt. That certainly
had colored his thinking when Spielberg came to him for his blessing to
start a new company. "I'm in no position to stop you," Sheinberg said,
"when I'm unsure what I want to do with my life."

Meanwhile, Katzenberg was also laboring to bring Geffen into the new
venture. At first, the music mogul was reluctant. He and Spielberg were
not best friends; when the two had worked with Warner, they had competed
for the affections of Ross. It was a relationship that Geffen later character-
ized as sibling rivalry. "I was jealous of him but I respected him and wanted
his approval," said Geffen. "And we were thrown together a lot." In her
caustic tell-all, *You'll Never Eat Lunch in This Town Again,* producer Julia
Phillips had tattled that Geffen had once called Spielberg "selfish, self-
centered, egomaniacal and worst of all—greedy." Geffen denied ever
having made such a statement and clearly Spielberg now elected to believe
him. But the competition was still there. A knowledgeable source said that
one argument Katzenberg used to provoke Spielberg into joining the new
venture was, "If you're so successful, how come Geffen has more money
than you?"

And Geffen certainly had a lot of money. At age fifty-one, did he need
the problems of starting a new company? He was rich several times over.
His contract as chairman of MCA's Geffen Records division was going to
expire in about six months. "I hadn't been working to my capacity," he said
later. "I'm not sure I wanted to. I was comfortable." He was collecting art,
renovating the Jack Warner estate, hanging out with the president of the
United States, enjoying his role as mogul-at-large. "Why do you need me?"
he asked. In a meeting with Katzenberg and Spielberg—in which Katzenberg hoped to start forming a bond among the three—Geffen was told that
his financial acumen, talent relations, and skills in music were essential to
the new company.

At the end of September, hours after attending a White House dinner
for Russian president Boris Yeltsin, Spielberg and Katzenberg sat in Spielberg's suite at the Hay-Adams Hotel in Washington hashing over final plans

for the studio. It was 1:30 A.M. but they decided to phone Geffen, who was spending the night in the Lincoln Bedroom at the White House. "Come over here now," Katzenberg said.

"How do I get there?" Geffen asked.

"Call a taxi!" Katzenberg urged.

"You can't call a taxi to the White House," Geffen replied. He also felt that he couldn't stroll into the hall to ask a guard for directions (though the hotel was only a short distance away). But by 6:30 A.M., he had made his way to Spielberg's rooms with a White House car. "We all looked at each other and said, 'Let's do it,' " Spielberg said later.

Perhaps Geffen was finally convinced, at least in part, because of his painful awareness that many were blaming him for encouraging Katzenberg in his campaign for advancement at Disney. This would be a way of standing by his friend and getting back into the game in a more challenging way. As he later acknowledged, "The reason there's a [company] is because Michael Eisner wouldn't give Jeffrey the job. Jeffrey is the catalyst for all this. I mean . . . he said to me, 'Do you want to do this?' and I said, 'No. This is a lot of work and I am a very, very, very rich man. . . . But I got caught up in it, and I did not want to hand him a 'no' as he had gotten from Michael Eisner. I did not want to be another person that didn't want to give it to Jeffrey."

Katzenberg had achieved his immediate goal. "I felt like I'm driving the stagecoach and holding the reins of these two world-class stallions," Katzenberg said. All he had to do was keep two of the world's largest egos at peace. Characteristically, Katzenberg cast himself as the subordinate. "There's a piece of paper that says we're partners, but honestly, in my heart, these two guys are my superstars and I'm here to take care of them," he said at the time. "I feel like I work for them."

∞

THE NEW COMPANY would have everything: film, television, music, and an interactive unit. And in a shot that undoubtedly was heard at Disney, there were plans for a major animation operation headed by Katzenberg. This would be Katzenberg's chance to show whether he had overplayed his role at Disney or if he really had the goods when it came to animated product. In any case, it meant there would soon be a bidding contest for talent between Disney and the new studio.

On October 12, Katzenberg arrived early at a press conference at the

Peninsula Hotel in Beverly Hills to announce his new plans to the media. Geffen was so nervous that he spent the early hours of the day throwing up. Though Katzenberg had done everything in his power to keep the new company a secret, it was reported in that day's *New York Times* and *Wall Street Journal*. Spielberg was furious with Michael Ovitz—convinced that his own agent, and one of the few people in on the plan, had leaked the story.

Ovitz was said to have been angry because he had not been allowed to play some role in setting up the new company. (In fact, there was a certain logic to Ovitz having leaked the story, because the Ovitz camp had blamed Geffen in 1990 when MCA's negotiations with Matsushita seeped out to the press.) Ovitz vigorously denied that he was the source of the stories, but the episode did nothing to smooth his already-tense relations with the DreamWorks founders. There were also reports that Ovitz was privately questioning the viability of the new enterprise, which only made matters worse.

The company's name was not announced that day, though Katzenberg hinted at it by saying, "This has got to be a dream team." Indeed, the *New York Times* hailed the company as "the biggest merger of talent since Charlie Chaplin, Mary Pickford, Douglas Fairbanks and D. W. Griffith founded the United Artists movie empire in 1919." DreamWorks announced itself with an éclat that could satisfy even the outsized appetites of Jeffrey Katzenberg.

Of the trio, Katzenberg was by far the poorest. Spielberg's wealth was estimated at more than $600 million and Geffen said he was now worth $2 billion. Katzenberg was still struggling to get the money that he felt Disney owed him. He even let it be known that, much to his wife's consternation, he had mortgaged himself heavily to buy into his new company—including his new beach house in Malibu as well as his house in Deer Valley, Utah. Though financial information was not disclosed to the public, the three men reportedly put up $33 million each to start the company. "I am in hock up to my eyeballs," Katzenberg told the *New York Times Magazine* cheerfully.

The partners set out to raise more money and Katzenberg correctly predicted that this would not be a difficult feat. Microsoft cofounder Paul Allen quickly put up $500 million for slightly more than 18 percent of the company. Korean investor Mie Kyung "Miky" Lee pledged $300 million more. (In 1998, Lee's Cheil Jedang Corp. reduced its stake because of the Asian economic crisis while Allen upped his share to more than 24 percent.) DreamWorks quickly assembled $2 billion worth of operating capital. Other equity investors included Capital Cities/ABC, Microsoft, the Ziff Brothers investment partnership, and Chase Securities. There was an additional billion dollars in bank financing underwritten by Chase Manhattan.

Katzenberg and Spielberg started shopping for real estate. Though Geffen didn't see why the studio couldn't be "virtual," without going to the expense of creating a lot, Spielberg's vision was to "drive through his own studio gates," according to a DreamWorks insider.

With the launch of his new company, Katzenberg realized that he would have to open his fist and finally lay to rest his image as a cheap and controlling executive. It wouldn't be easy. A spoof of his ill-fated 1991 memo made the rounds — this one so full of rage that it pretty much forgot to be funny. *"This time it's all about me,"* the memo said. "Working for our company is going to be like enlisting in the Marines, minus the health benefits, the low-interest loans, the job security, the travel discounts and the life expectancy."

Katzenberg quickly set about making deals to show that the memo was out of date. Jeremy Zimmer, the agent who represented writer-producer Gary David Goldberg in one of the first television deals at DreamWorks, said the negotiation lasted a mere twenty minutes. "It wasn't like the old Jeffrey — 'I'm going to try and get it wholesale,' " Zimmer said at the time. "It was definitely a retail deal." The DreamWorkers also announced that everyone who worked at the company would receive shares in it. And they shunned the notion of assigning titles to anyone, including themselves.

∽

SOON AFTER KATZENBERG'S departure, Disney announced results for fiscal 1994, which ended on September 30. It had been a banner year, with record revenues of $10.06 billion. Operating income was up 14 percent to $1.97 billion, also a record. Eisner, having missed out on a bonus in 1993 because of Euro Disney's problems (though he'd netted $203 million thanks to his stock options), was back in the game with a $7.4 million reward. And largely, he had Katzenberg to thank. His bonus was due in great part to profits reaped from *Aladdin* and *The Lion King*. (His total compensation for the year was $10.6 million.) With hits like *The Lion King*, the Tim Allen sleeper film *The Santa Clause*, and Miramax's *Pulp Fiction*, Disney in 1994 became the first studio in history to gross more than $1 billion at the box office.

That year, Disney made 43 percent of its income from filmed entertainment and only 35 percent from theme parks. (In 1984, the company relied on theme parks for nearly 80 percent of its operating income and movies provided only 1 percent.) *The Lion King* had also provided the number-one record album of the year. Disney's sitcom, *Home Improvement*, was the year's top-rated show. As a reminder of the company's depth, Disney sold thirty million copies of *Snow White* on home video.

In his annual report, Eisner commented on the many changes that had taken place in 1994. The death of Wells "was a horrible exclamation point during a tragic year," he said. He added that Wells would have said that Eisner's surgery was a display of "excessive theatricality, showmanship, and risk taking." But Eisner reported that he had run three miles through the Vermont woods before he sat down to write his letter. His recovery was well under way.

As Eisner recounted the "shocks and distractions" that Disney had endured, he mentioned Los Angeles fires, an earthquake in January, the loss of Wells, his own heart surgery, the death of board member Sam Williams, and Katzenberg's "decision not to renew his contract." (The earthquake and fires, as well as a series of tourist murders in Florida, did nothing to help the theme-park business. Eisner didn't mention the demise of Disney's America among his woes.)

Eisner reflected that Disney was a company that attracted unusual scrutiny and "when we release a disappointing movie or make a decision some find questionable, we get criticized with . . . intensity." But the company's financials showed that "Disney is stronger than most have given us credit for, that we can withstand all kinds of adversities and still produce the financial results of a winner. . . . Our critics did not stop us. Frank's death did not stop us. My heart surgery did not stop us. Our studio reorganization did not stop us." Truly, Disney was a juggernaut. The stock market, which had valued the company at $1.8 billion in 1984, now reckoned its worth at more than $28 billion.

∞

THE EXODUS OF Eisner's old guard continued. Helene Hahn, the petite but tough-as-nails head of business affairs at the studio, had immediately followed Katzenberg to DreamWorks; so had Gary Kreisel, who ran tele-vision animation, and Ann Daly, the head of home video. Rich Frank, who had been with Eisner since the Paramount days, made it until April 1995.

In the wake of the studio reorganization, Frank ran television, cable, home video, and telecommunications. Over the years, Frank thought, he had also brought a valuable element to the mix at the studio. Katzenberg, always rushed, lacked the ability to connect with employees. But Frank made time to listen to his staff's anxieties and concerns, professional or otherwise. "If people came into Jeffrey's office, he would give them two minutes and take calls while they were there," Frank says. "I spent a good 30 percent of my time with people who worked for us, keeping it going from a personal standpoint. . . . It wasn't that Jeffrey didn't care. That's just the way he was." Frank joked with Katzenberg, "You work the morning shift, I'll work the night shift." He was the one who went for drinks after work, while Katzenberg was all business.

He was also ambitious and increasingly visible, lobbying the Federal Communications Commission, serving with Vice-President Al Gore as head of a summit on the information superhighway, and putting in his second term as president of the Academy of Television Arts and Sciences. But he had a provision in his contract stating that he would have a shot at Katz-enberg's job if it became vacant. If he didn't get it, he had the option to leave in six months with his retirement benefits and stock options—the latter valued at more than $30 million. (Also, when his title changed from president of the studio to chairman of the newly formed television and telecommunications group, his contract provided that he could leave the company with his benefits and options.)

When Katzenberg left, Frank expressed his sorrow. "Frank Wells died. Now Jeffrey's gone," he told the *New York Times* sadly. "The family's been broken up." But he vowed to soldier on. A former Disney executive says that despite Frank's long hours and increasing visibility, Eisner thought Frank had lost his fire. Dean Valentine, then Frank's deputy, says that was hardly the case. "The idea that Rich was lazy in any shape or manner is a disservice to the truth," he says.

Another theory held that Eisner actually was uncomfortable with Frank's ambition. "He was really lobbying for some [more] senior management position," an inside observer says. "It was never going to happen. Michael was fond of Rich but didn't feel a deep kinship with him—or with anybody." Frank concurs on the latter point: "I liked Michael. I wouldn't have stayed there for nineteen years if I didn't respect the guy and think he was terrific. . . . Overall, I think he's basically a good person. [But] I think Michael finds it a little difficult to truly open himself up."

Frank also clashed with strategic planning chief Larry Murphy. He wasn't the first to have problems with Murphy, who was another Marriott alumnus; Katzenberg had been so contemptuous of Murphy that he declined to work with him and refused to invite him to annual planning meetings. Eisner had a catchphrase that he frequently used when considering a proposal: "Tell me the parade of horribles." To Katzenberg and to Frank, providing the most pessimistic possible view of any proposal seemed to be Murphy's only job. Eisner was naturally risk averse, so it was difficult to get him to pursue new ventures as it was. Katzenberg thought Murphy and his people represented a kind of "strategic gestapo" that strangled many initiatives in their cradles.

Frank also believed that Eisner allowed Murphy to stifle ideas — especially the one that he and Katzenberg had pushed so passionately for so long: the acquisition of a network. Frank shared Katzenberg's hostility toward Murphy — and in nearly identical terms. "Michael used [strategic planning] as a police force — almost a gestapo group," he says. "That was the last straw for me. . . . Larry Murphy would say, 'You did twenty movies last year. Think how great we would have been if we didn't do these ten.' I would say, 'Here are the twenty for next year. Tell me the ten we shouldn't make.' "

The company became overanalyzed by strategic planning, Frank continues. And unfortunately, Murphy didn't have a clearly defined point of view. "Larry always switched his mind depending on where Michael was," Frank says. In one staff meeting, Frank tried to get Murphy to lead off with his opinion about a proposal under consideration. "He said, 'I don't want to go first,' " Frank remembers. "Michael said, 'Why are you doing this?' I said, 'Because whatever he said to me yesterday, he's going to switch when he finds out what you think.' . . . I used to say to [Murphy], 'I know you're not a yes-man. If Michael says no, you say no.' "

In Frank's opinion, "Larry Murphy [was] the single biggest negative factor in the Walt Disney Company." When Disney was working on a cruise line to launch in 1998, he adds, executives joked that they hoped Murphy would go out on the first ship and it would meet the fate of the *Titanic*.

Frustrated by Murphy's interference — as well as Eisner's ongoing refusal to buy a network — Frank started to remind Eisner about his deal. He hadn't gotten Katzenberg's job and his contract gave him the option to leave. If he were going to remain, Frank said, Murphy had to be kept out of his affairs. "We went through a number of times where I was told [he] wouldn't interfere, and at the end of the day, that just wasn't the case," Frank remembers.

On March 2, 1995, the *Los Angeles Times* reported that Frank was mulling over his departure from Disney. Frank denied that, as did a Disney spokesman. But in fact, Frank had confronted Eisner about his deal and the two men had a tense discussion. Finally Frank said he intended to leave. Eisner replied, "You can't. I won't let you."

"I can and I am," Frank replied. "And since you're not going to change, and I'm not going to change, there's nothing you can do about it."

"How about your stock options?" Eisner reportedly answered.

Frank protested that Eisner owed him that money.

"I'm not disputing that," Eisner is said to have shouted. "I'm just saying that if you walk out the door, you're going to have to sue me to get it."

Eventually, Eisner and Frank reached a settlement in which Frank collected his money but agreed not to work for Katzenberg for two years. Frank was stunned when he heard rumors that his replacement would be Dennis Hightower, an executive from the consumer-products division who had no television experience at all. Frank dismissed these reports as implausible. How could a person who had been selling plush toys in Europe take over the entire Disney television, video, cable, and telecommunications operation?

Frank buzzed Eisner. "There's a rumor that Hightower's taking my job," he said.

Eisner was evasive, but called Frank a few hours later and confirmed that Hightower was getting the position.

"He said we were going to go in a few minutes and announce it to the entire group, and he wanted me to be there," Frank says. "He basically wanted me to endorse it. I said obviously I would come to the meeting but I certainly wasn't endorsing it. He never asked me if I thought this would be a good choice or not." When Eisner made the announcement, Frank says, "to say there was shocked disbelief around the table would be one of the all-time understatements."

Eisner felt that with his own television experience, he could help Hightower learn the ropes. "Now at least we have an enthusiastic executive in the job," Eisner told the press at the time. "Dennis is excited to be running TV. He's not disappointed to not be running movies." Besides, he said, "Dennis Hightower is a very smart man." Though he lacked experience with the major networks, "he's very experienced sitting down with our partners in Luxembourg and Taiwan," Eisner said.

It quickly became apparent that Hightower, fifty-five, lacked the seasoning to run the $4 billion division. "There was just too much for him to learn too quick," Frank says. "He didn't know the people. How do you call [a network] and say, 'Can we talk about the schedule?'" Hightower lasted only a year and Eisner's reorganization of the company quickly broke down as Frank's responsibilities were divided up again. Roth took control of network television programming and home video, reassembling much of Katzenberg's old empire. Animation remained a very notable exception, though Roth was in charge of marketing the animated films.

Frank's departure did little to ease an increasingly nervous environment at Disney, and Eisner came under fire in the press for his autocratic management style. The *Wall Street Journal* commented that Eisner appeared to be "increasingly isolated." Eisner responded: "If all of a sudden people think I'm not the goofy little seventies executive with unkempt hair standing on a soundstage, that may be. But I have a different job today. My job is to keep the quality and the vision of our company intact." His most important mission, he added, was to "make sure the baton gets passed from one generation to another." This seemed an odd declaration from a man who had refused to install a second-in-command after Frank Wells's death and his own cardiac episode.

He also argued that the longevity of his relationships with Katzenberg and Frank proved that he was not a bad boss. "One of these men worked for me for eighteen years, the other for nineteen years," he said. "It's hard to say that nobody can work for me. I've had many close relationships with little turnover throughout my career. This is not an issue."

But the press kept up the drumbeat, with the naughty *New York Observer* reporting that Disney employees were suffering under "what has been alleged as [Eisner's] 'paranoia,' his seeming unwillingness to countenance dissent and what insiders term his 'erratic . . . removed-from-reality decision making.'" Some staffers insisted that their calls were being monitored. (When a staffer was suspended for sending a fax to someone who worked for Katzenberg, it seemed that they were.) There were some suggestions in print that the medication Eisner was taking after his heart surgery was interfering with his judgment. "Michael has lost it," one employee said. "He has become Captain Queeg."

Even Barry Diller seemed to concur in an April 1995 interview with *Fortune*. "Michael is competitive, but he's also paranoid," he said. "Eighty-five percent of his toughness is for good reasons; 15 percent is over the line. There is an excessiveness that has always bothered me."

Eisner acknowledged that his behavior might be more extreme than it was before his illness — though he also argued that Disney was perhaps not as tough a place to work as other, less visible companies. "I have less patience for betrayal than I had," he conceded. "I deal with a broad range of talent and if the talent is really there, I will put up with a lot. But there is a whole level of maybe not really talented people who really test you. I am less patient with that group now." Besides, he added, "If you're soft and fuzzy, like our little characters, you become the skinny kid on the beach, and people in this business don't mind kicking sand in your face."

25

THE DOMINOES FALL

S SOON AS DreamWorks sprang into existence, it became part of a chain reaction that would change the face of Hollywood. One domino fell after another, remaking the industry's power structure.

It all began with speculation about the role that the new company would play in shaping the fate of MCA, now in turmoil as Lew Wasserman and Sid Sheinberg joined in battle with Matsushita. By now Wasserman, eighty-one, had headed the company for forty-eight years; the fifty-nine-year-old Shein-berg had been president for twenty-two years. Their frustration with Mat-sushita's control had been exacerbated when the Japanese declined to back the purchase of Virgin Records in 1991 and, more recently, when they ve-toed plans to open a theme park in Japan and wouldn't even hear a proposal to acquire a stake in a television network. If Matsushita wouldn't go along with such moves, Wasserman and Sheinberg thought, MCA could not keep up with its rivals. For its part, Matsushita was worried about problems devel-oping in the Japanese economy. They also worried that purchasing a stake in a network would roil anti-Japanese sentiment in the United States.

As the new DreamWorks venture was being announced, Wasserman and Sheinberg were scheduled to meet with Matsushita executives the following week to discuss their future. They were adamant about winning more au-tonomy. There were rumors that if they were successful in wresting some control of MCA, they would form some kind of combination with Universal and with DreamWorks.

Spielberg had made it clear that if Wasserman and Sheinberg weren't happy, he would take his talents elsewhere. He had even asked Sheinberg if he would like to become the fourth DreamWorks partner, but Sheinberg declined. Undoubtedly, Katzenberg was greatly relieved; the older Shein-berg was even more used to being a hands-on executive than he was.

If the talks with Matsushita were unsuccessful, the clear threat was that

Wasserman and Sheinberg would quit, causing a rupture even more dramatic than the Katzenberg departure from Disney. It wasn't just the loss of Wasserman, a true Hollywood patriarch known as the "godfather" of the industry. The studio would also lose Spielberg, the man who had minted money for Universal that year with the top-grossing picture of all time to date, *Jurassic Park,* and brought it prestige and profit with *Schindler's List.* The prospect of so damaging a breach could hardly have appealed to the Japanese. At the same time it was clear that tradition-bound Matsushita did not relish being bullied by its managers in Hollywood—and with Sheinberg talking quite openly with the media, the company particularly resented the public nature of the fight.

By December, Matsushita hired the investment banking firm of Allen & Company, along with Goldman, Sachs and the New York law firm of Simpson Thacher & Bartlett, to provide advice. Herbert Allen insisted that Michael Ovitz should be brought in as a consultant. It was Allen & Company's job to place a valuation on MCA and offer a list of options for Matsushita, including a possible sale. Sheinberg and Wasserman saw some hope that Ovitz might help them smooth things over with Matsushita and explain to the Japanese that they were extremely valuable assets. Ovitz said he would do his best.

But in fact, Matsushita had decided not only to wash its hands of Wasserman and Sheinberg but to get rid of most of its holdings in MCA as well. In April 1995, rumors started to swirl that Edgar Bronfman Jr., the thirty-nine-year-old heir to the Seagram fortune, had made a preemptive offer to buy MCA. Tall, slender, soft-spoken, and studiously polite, the young Bronfman was a sometime songwriter and film producer who pursued a career in show business instead of going to college. Eventually, he joined the family business and emerged as his father's successor. But he wasn't satisfied with the company's extensive beverage-and-liquor empire and had started to cast about for opportunities in the entertainment world. His approach to Time Warner had been rebuffed. But buying MCA was as dramatic an entrance as anyone might want to make.

During the negotiation, Matsushita had insisted on strict secrecy. Once news reports of the talks appeared, Edgar Jr. sought Matsushita's permission to have a conversation with Wasserman and Sheinberg. He pleaded that the Bronfmans' silence was an embarrassment in light of the published accounts of the discussions. Matsushita relented and Edgar Sr. made a courtesy call to Wasserman. It was too late. Wasserman and Sheinberg already felt that they had been treated shabbily. Edgar Sr. knew Wasserman only vaguely but says he understands Wasserman's feeling. "Lew sort of looks at himself as the emperor of Hollywood and felt he was owed a call," Bronfman says. "And in that regard, he was." Bronfman promised in the Wednesday-afternoon call that he would phone Wasserman at once when an agreement with Matsushita was signed.

The deal was announced the following Sunday, and the next day, the Edgar Bronfmans junior and senior paid a visit to MCA's famous black tower to have lunch with Wasserman and Sheinberg. It was a difficult meeting. Both Wasserman and Sheinberg were agitated. "It was very rough," Edgar Sr. recalls. "They were screaming about the fact that nobody had told them anything." They were also worried about the future. Who would manage the company? Both were fearful that the Bronfmans would choose Ovitz, whom they now believed had betrayed them.

When Edgar Jr. said no decisions had been made, Wasserman replied, "I don't believe that. How can you buy a company without deciding what management is going to be?" Sheinberg was livid, accusing the Bronfmans of bad faith for not letting him and Wasserman know that they were seeking to buy the company. "In life, there's right and wrong," he said.

Sheinberg says he's not surprised that the Bronfmans—particularly the father—were affronted. "I don't think Edgar Sr. is used to people telling him what they think about his behavior," Sheinberg reflects. "I think he's used to people bowing. [But] I think it was a horrendous rudeness and simply unacceptable behavior, whether or not we owned the company at the time. Lew Wasserman was the founder of the company. There is only one Lew Wasserman in the United States. There isn't enough money in Swiss banks for Edgar Bronfman to ever be of the stature of Lew Wasserman and it was rude and I told them."

Edgar Sr., who had never met Sheinberg before, was thoroughly put off. "I wouldn't buy a toy store and hire Sid to run it," he says. "I think he's an idiot, an egocentric maniac. I finally said, 'Enough of this.' . . . I don't like being yelled at, especially by a piece of shit like Sid Sheinberg."

Edgar Jr. responded by laying out the options bluntly. "Look, there are two ways to deal with this," he said. "The first is to decide that you love the company you built and you'll help the new owners figure out how to keep the company going. Or you'll decide you're so angry you're going to leave. Either outcome is okay with me. I would prefer the first but I can live with the second."

Sheinberg says he agreed to help during the transition but said he wouldn't stay indefinitely. On that unsatisfactory note, the parties split up. The two elder men went to Wasserman's office while Edgar Jr. remained with Sheinberg. In the meeting with Edgar Sr., Wasserman relented. "I just want Sid to be okay," he said. After that, says Edgar Sr., "We played that game Lew loves to play called Presidents Lew Has Met. We went to the bathroom to wash our hands and I asked Lew to be on our board." Meanwhile, Sheinberg told Edgar Jr. about the horror of dealing with Matsushita. He talked about having written a letter to the management there and having not, as yet, received even the courtesy of a response. To which Edgar Jr. said, "I'm the response."

"I suppose you are," Sheinberg conceded. The two agreed that Sheinberg would leave the company with a rich production deal.

Bronfman turned to Michael Ovitz, the superagent. A deal for Ovitz to run MCA seemed so certain that the *New York Times* actually reported on June 5 that Ovitz along with his number-two man, Ron Meyer, and several other CAA agents, were taking the helm there in a move that would "profoundly alter the landscape of Hollywood." But the report was premature. Ovitz and Bronfman engaged in a protracted, high-profile negotiation that finally collapsed. *Newsweek* was chagrined to find that it had Ovitz on the cover of its June 5 issue but no deal to justify its coverage.

In early July, Hollywood was turned on its ear again. To the shock of everyone in the industry, Bronfman hired Ron Meyer for a lesser version of the job that would have been offered to Ovitz. Meyer was good-natured, often having smoothed the feathers ruffled by Ovitz. But Meyer was a high-school dropout who openly proclaimed his own lack of formal education. He was affable but not a man that the industry expected to see in such a high position at a studio—at least not without Ovitz. Now it turned out that Meyer was Cinderella, and Ovitz—having alienated many of his associates with his apparent willingness to leave CAA—was to be left behind.

Ovitz had flown to Herb Allen's annual Sun Valley retreat a day before Meyer's new job was announced. When he learned that Meyer and his new boss, Bronfman, were headed to Sun Valley, too, he packed his bags and went home. "I just don't feel comfortable," he told Eisner, "at someone else's coronation."

ON HIS SECOND visit to the Sun Valley retreat, Eisner was pleased to discover that he and Jane had been promoted to a condo instead of a room in the lodge. He charmed the crowd with a jovial, self-deprecating presentation even while he offered up impressive figures on Disney's performance. After his presentation, he quietly did what Katzenberg and Rich Frank had implored him to do for so long: quickly and secretly, he put in motion a deal to acquire a television network. It started in earnest when Eisner ran into Warren Buffett, the largest shareholder in Capital Cities/ABC Inc., and said, "Do you think our two companies could do something together?"

This was not an unrehearsed question. The day before he left for Sun Valley, Eisner had conducted an in-house session with his strategic planning team to discuss the idea of buying a network. Larry Murphy, the head of the division, had long opposed the plan, but there was an aggressive new player in the room. Stephen Bollenbach, the former chief executive of the Host Marriott Corp., had just joined Disney as its chief financial officer. (His predecessor, Richard Nanula, had been dispatched to run the Disney stores.) Bollenbach had engineered a major restructuring at Marriott. Before that, he served as chief financial officer to Donald Trump's company and helped the flashy developer escape from near bankruptcy.

Eisner knew that Bollenbach had an appetite for the top job at Disney, but was confident that he lacked the entertainment background to get it. Before Bollenbach figured that out, however, Eisner thought Disney could benefit from his strategic skills. And the time was right to make a deal. Eisner still believed that Disney stock was undervalued and Eisner's image wasn't what it had been, either. Both he and the company could use a boost. From the start, Bollenbach argued that Disney was perfectly situated to make a major acquisition. Interest rates were down. The company's debt was low and Disney would derive tax advantages from borrowing. So by the time Eisner appoached Buffett at Sun Valley, he was prepared to act.

Buffett responded positively to Eisner's question about selling Cap Cities/ABC. "You should go find Tom," he suggested. He was referring to Tom Murphy, the chairman of Cap Cities/ABC. The three had a short conversation, Eisner said later. He remembered asking, "We're buying. Are you selling?"

"I'll get back to you," Murphy replied.

Eisner was filled with excitement; he sensed that Disney was on the brink of making a deal. He confided in Barry Diller, also attending the Sun Valley retreat. Diller had been frustrated in his own attempts to buy ABC and CBS—just two months earlier, he had made an unsuccessful run at the latter network in partnership with Disney. Now Eisner couldn't resist asking Diller whether he'd be interested in running ABC. Diller looked at his former employee and smiled. He doubted that he would, he said.

By the end of the month, the second-largest acquisition in U.S. history to date was rapidly and quietly sewn up. Disney, so reticent for so long, briefly became the world's largest entertainment company (surpassing, but soon to be surpassed again by, Time Warner) with the $19 billion purchase of Capital Cities/ABC Inc.

On the night that the Disney board approved the deal, Eisner had dinner with his mother. From there, he went to the law offices of Dewey Ballantine to review the last details of the deal. The next morning, the news broke.

The move transformed Eisner's image from a somewhat paranoid, isolated cardiac patient to brilliant deal maker. "This rejuvenates him just when he needs it most," Viacom chairman Sumner Redstone told *Business Week*. With the acquisition, Disney bought the broadcast network, ten television stations, twenty-one radio stations, as well as significant ownership of Lifetime and the Arts and Entertainment Network. To Eisner, one of the crown jewels of the deal was the powerhouse ESPN sports channel, seen in 66.3 million American homes and 95 million around the world. Eisner called ESPN "a magic name," comparable with Coke or Kodak. Disney had also secured a guaranteed outlet for its programming at a time when federal regulators were permitting networks to own more of their own shows. Disney could sell its own shows to ABC and resell to its cable channels and television stations for reruns.

When the news came, Hollywood was once again stunned. After the drama of Wells's death, Eisner's cardiac episode, Katzenberg's departure, the advent of DreamWorks, the sale of MCA, the departure of Wasserman and Sheinberg, the suspense surrounding the failed Ovitz negotiation, and the ascension of Ron Meyer, it seemed as though astonishing news simply would not stop coming. Now Disney had remade itself with one bold stroke. Its market value was $40 billion and Disney became roughly the eleventh-largest company in the country. It was more than a Hollywood story—it was major national news. But still, Eisner asked a *Los Angeles Times* reporter, "Do you think this [story] will make page one?"

Eisner was celebrated universally, though he took a little ribbing. "[Eisner] was stating both publicly and privately how bad an idea [buying] a broadcast network was—until last Monday," noted NBC president Robert Wright.

"It's never been easy for Michael to buy anything," said Diller. "He's too cheap. But this merger says, more than anything, that he has graduated."

Despite those backhanded comments, the deal was well reviewed by almost everyone—Diller, Rupert Murdoch, and even David Geffen. Katzenberg was quoted, graciously calling the merged companies "the most prestigious, important, and powerful media enterprise on the planet in every respect." On Wall Street, shares in Capital Cities/ABC surged by $20.125; and defying the usual trend when a company makes a big acquisition, Disney ticked up $1.25. Not even the issuing of 155 million new shares as part of the purchase discouraged investors. The legendary Buffett, who had seen a $345 million investment in Cap Cities turn into a stake in the combined company worth $2.3 billion, helped matters by saying that he was only too happy to become one of Disney's largest shareholders. Buffett even boasted that he had won a $100 bet with a Disney executive that the company's shares would not drop when the acquisition was announced.

One of the few doubters was John Tinker, an analyst at Furman, Selz & Co., who wondered whether Capital Cities/ABC might slow Disney's growth. Some noted that ABC, the number-one network, had no place to go but downhill, making it a surprising choice for a man who described himself as "a bottom fisherman." A couple of years earlier, said sources close to the company, Eisner balked at buying ABC for $11 billion. He had defied his own wisdom—and been handsomely rewarded by rave reviews.

There was some editorializing over whether Eisner would show appropriate respect for ABC News, though Eisner vowed that the division "will be left alone to operate autonomously." The only other murmurs came from some politicians and consumer advocacy groups, who worried about increasing consolidation in the media world.

And there was DreamWorks, which had made a deal worth up to $200 million to produce television shows with ABC, and was now looking at the prospect of an unanticipated partnership with Disney. DreamWorks' plans for ABC's Saturday-morning cartoon schedule were doomed, because Disney would clearly take over the time slot. But flush with victory, Eisner was inclined to magnanimity. Just a few days after the deal was announced, he called Katzenberg—as well as Spielberg and Geffen—to express a desire that some peace be brokered. Katzenberg said he responded enthusiastically:

"Michael, we've had nineteen fabulous years and ten terrible months. Let's not make it eleven." But that call was as far as Eisner was prepared to go. Katzenberg's hopes that the door would open to resolution of his contract claims would be dashed again.

With the acquisition of Capital Cities/ABC, Eisner was now master of the domain where he had worked as a young man. But he still had some problems. Even as the ABC deal was announced, the issue of succession at Disney was still undecided—and it was perhaps even more important than before this dramatic expansion. Eisner had a concerned wife who wondered how he would handle his duties without a second-in-command. It was time to go looking for a partner—and Eisner had a candidate in mind.

26

SUPERMAN STUMBLES

MICHAEL OVITZ WAS the youngest of CAA's five founding partners who had defected from the William Morris Agency in 1975, but he rapidly asserted himself as the first among equals. In fact, the others soon became a bit less than equal. Mike Rosenfeld was forty years old at the time — thirteen years older than Ovitz — but he said it took him "about four days" to realize that Ovitz would dominate. By the mid-eighties, Ovitz controlled 55 percent of the agency, while the two remaining founders, Ron Meyer and Bill Haber, split what was left.

Ovitz had grown up in the San Fernando Valley, where people were very conscious of social status. His family was middle class but Ovitz quickly convinced his classmates that he was destined for big things. "We knew in the fifth grade," says boyhood friend Fred Fox. "From the beginning, you just felt he was going to be very successful."

He was a member of an exceptional class at Birmingham High School in Van Nuys, just a semester behind Sally Field and Michael Milken; one group shot from the 1964 yearbook shows the future junk-bond king standing behind the seated superagent-to-be. Another picture shows Ovitz, vice-president of the student body — stern, unsmiling, disconcertingly baby-faced in a cardigan and an inch-wide tie. Based on the photo, Ovitz had more natural gravitas than half the faculty.

A friend from the Zeta Beta Tau fraternity at UCLA remembers Ovitz as a strong-willed president who engineered the chapter's move into an abandoned hotel on Wilshire Boulevard while the house was being rebuilt. Before he joined the fraternity, Ovitz already had a job at the Universal Studio Tour and he subsequently helped other brothers get jobs. And his brothers helped him, too, by agreeing to name his girlfriend, blond Judy Reich, the official ZBT sweetheart. Ovitz argued that because she belonged to the Waspy Kappa Alpha Theta sorority, naming her would be a coup for the predominantly Jewish ZBTs. "Mike said, 'It's good, it's good. We need that image,' " says former ZBT brother Daniel Beck, now an attorney in Santa Rosa. "Mike knew he was going to be a star as far back as I can remember."

Ovitz wasn't the best-liked fellow in the house but the others looked up to him. "The word is respect," Beck says. "You respected him but there was always this sense that he was in charge and you weren't. . . . No one got too close to him."

After UCLA, Ovitz attended Loyola law school but quickly dropped out. Then, like Barry Diller and David Geffen before him, he went to work in the William Morris mailroom. Veteran writer and producer Bill Persky re-members that Ovitz seemed intimidating even as a delivery boy: "Ovitz, he was so mysterious. It was always like he knew more than he was telling. Michael, even as a junior executive, always convinced you there was some-thing he knew that was going to make a difference."

This was a tactic that Ovitz later honed to perfection at CAA. At weekly staff meetings he was prone to making cryptic announcements about major events he said would happen at a certain studio in "30 to 60 days" or sometimes "60 to 120 days." He was right often enough that everyone paid attention. "It gave the impression to the people staring at him that he was in control of everything in the entertainment business," remembers a CAA agent. "It was so funny. You got to wondering, 'Is it going to happen on Day thirty-one? Oh well, it doesn't matter because Mike knows.' Ninety-five percent of the people left CAA meetings feeling, 'He's got it wired.' "

At William Morris, Ovitz rose to be assistant to Howard West, a leading television agent who was impressed by Ovitz's long hours and "insatiable thirst to learn." After a year, however, Ovitz surprised West by leaving to take another crack at law school, only to change his mind again and beg for his job back. "Senior management said, 'No,' " remembers West, who went on to be an executive producer of *Seinfeld*. "The attitude of upper management was, 'You leave, you're dead.' " But West pleaded for Ovitz, who was permitted to return.

Ovitz was eventually promoted to agent and plunged into the minutiae of packaging television game shows. "I thought this young fellow must be one of the best young agents I'd ever seen," says Ray Kurtzman, Ovitz's office partner. "He was totally prepared. He was a great salesman. He was and is the most dedicated person I know when he gets his teeth into some-thing. . . . He just does not take no for an answer."

In 1975, Ovitz and Meyer joined three other agents who had already broken away from William Morris. At first, the agency was little more than a group of guys working on card tables. But it wasn't long before CAA became a force. In a business brimming with bluster and gimcrackery, Ovitz was a model of steamroller drive and iron discipline. "He was incredibly good at managing not only clients but his company and the talent he had working for him," says Rosenfeld. "He was able to instill courage and balls into his young agents and he gave responsibility out like it was chopped liver. He made them feel like they were really better than maybe they were."

But Ovitz remained aloof. At one point Rosenfeld and Ovitz shared a condo at the beach. Rosenfeld told his children they had to keep quiet whenever Ovitz was around. One afternoon, as Rosenfeld's teenage son strummed his guitar in his bedroom, Ovitz yelled, "Stop making that fucking noise!" Then he relented and told the boy to come out of his room and play so Ovitz could see if he was any good. After the boy played three bars, Ovitz interrupted. "That's enough," he said. "You suck."

Though the elder Rosenfeld and Ovitz shared some laughs—and Ovitz had a sharp, dry sense of humor—it wasn't exactly a friendship. "I wouldn't say he let his guard down much or relaxed much," Rosenfeld says. Most of their time at the beach was spent reading scripts.

In his professional life, Ovitz demanded loyalty even from those who didn't work for him. If he was crossed, he made it unpleasant. When Joe Roth was the head of the Fox studio, he made the mistake of asking CAA agent Rosalie Swedlin if she was interested in running a film division there. Swedlin met with Barry Diller, then chairman of the company. But when she approached Ovitz about the possibility of leaving, he was enraged that she had not consulted him earlier. He rebuked Swedlin and froze Roth out for months, even though Swedlin remained at CAA. (Later, when Katzenberg went through channels and asked for permission to court Swedlin, Ovitz still withheld his blessing.)

Of course, Swedlin had been known to participate in Ovitz's power plays. A former CAA screenwriter remembers complaining to another Ovitz client that the agency had promised him a network job that never materialized. "Forty-five minutes after saying that," the writer recalls, "I get a call from [Swedlin], and she threw me out of the agency. She said, 'Mike heard you were bad-mouthing the agency and we don't want you here anymore.' There are dozens of disparate stories like this that happened to people large and small all over the place. . . . It was typical of the thuggishness there."

On the phone, Ovitz spoke so softly that listeners strained to hear; his half whisper could turn soothing or menacing. " 'Do you want to keep your job?' — he would always say things like that," says a former studio chief who recalls other standards: " 'Have I offended you in some way?' The 'I'm confused' line is famous. 'I find it hard to understand your rudeness.' He starts conversations to bring everything into the intrigue of a world in which he is at the center pulling all the strings."

Within a few years of launching CAA, Ovitz made it clear that he intended to go beyond the role of agent. He wanted to be included in deals. In 1986, producer-manager Bernie Brillstein sold his firm to Lorimar without giving Ovitz a role in the deal. After Brillstein took over as head of the combined companies, he found that CAA would not be an ally. "Mike felt betrayed and blindsided," says a former CAA agent. "There was a kind of mandate to service Lorimar but do nothing to help it grow." Another executive then at Lorimar remembers a getting-to-know-you meeting with a group of CAA agents. Expecting a lively exchange of ideas about clients and projects, the Lorimar contingent was greeted with stony silence. CAA can't be blamed for Lorimar's ultimate failure (the company was sold to Warner in 1989), but agents who were with CAA at the time acknowledge that they might have done more to help.

CAA's most publicized blowout came in 1989, when screenwriter Joe Eszterhas claimed in a series of "leaked" letters that Ovitz had threatened him when Eszterhas told him he wanted to quit the agency. Ovitz allegedly told Eszterhas that his "foot soldiers" would "blow your brains out." The story created a sensation but with no serious repercussions. "It didn't hurt us at all," says a CAA veteran. "I would say it probably was helpful. The people in this business want to have tough representatives. They're not interested in having nice representatives. When that all happened, people said, 'Wow, this guy is really ready to stand up and fight.' It kind of gave Mike a cachet. It added to the aura he had."

At one time Ovitz had displayed an engaging side to his personality, but even his original partners concede that it had faded as he became more successful. "In the early days, he did have a sense of humor and knew how to be charming," says Rosenfeld. "As he got more powerful, that took too much time."

∽

OVITZ MADE A quantum leap in the late eighties when Sony set out to buy an American studio. This gave him a chance to reposition himself as a man who had moved beyond mere agent status by brokering a big, multinational deal. Ovitz introduced Sony executives around Hollywood and then took them to Columbia Pictures, then owned by Coca-Cola. As the ill-fated acquisition loomed, Sony decided that Ovitz was the first choice to manage the studio. Sony's legal team drew up a proposal—code-named Superman—for hiring him.

But Ovitz wanted to be more than Superman; he made a bold play to run not only the studio but Sony's record division, with earnings of $2.9 billion. He sought an expanded empire and a package worth about $200 million. For once, Sony—which seemed willing to overpay for anything related to Hollywood—balked over price. According to insiders, the Japanese felt betrayed by Ovitz's audacity. When his proposal was rejected, he tried to return to the bargaining table, scaling back his demands. Sony politely turned him down. Ovitz then asked some executives in the Sony camp to back him up as he spread the story that he had rejected Sony's advances.

Ovitz collected an $11 million fee for his role in the Sony deal. But unbeknownst to most of his CAA associates, funds from CAA's various consulting activities, including work for Coca-Cola and Nike, were part of a separate partnership. The CAA agents knew nothing about CAA's finances. They had no idea how much CAA was making or how it was allotted among them. And they didn't ask questions. As agent Tom Ross put it, "All of us made more money each year, so we felt we must be getting part of this." The agents were later stunned to learn that for some years Ovitz had been flying around on a CAA-owned private jet. With the exception of Haber and Meyer, none even knew that CAA owned a plane.

In the wake of the Sony transaction, Ovitz won a new client—Matsushita—and helped broker the purchase of MCA. He was on his way to superstardom, and left the day-to-day client work to Ron Meyer and the other agents. During this period, a string of high-profile assignments—ads for Coke, the creation of a joint short-lived programming venture for the Baby Bells, a public role in helping Crédit Lyonnais rid itself of MGM/UA—led to a swelling tide of fawning reviews for Ovitz in the press. His celebrity had already been confirmed by a 1991 *New Yorker* article that included an unnamed "friend" suggesting that Ovitz's ambitions might even include the White House. He was named to the

Council on Foreign Relations as well as the board of the Museum of Modern Art in New York.

But at the end of the day, he was only an agent, and even a superagent is still subject to the whims of a fickle roster of demanding and high-strung clients. He had not enjoyed the prestige on Wall Street and in the world that the chairman of a major company accrues. And though he was rich, his wealth was dwarfed by the millions that his friend Michael Eisner was mopping up at Disney. He was making tens of millions, but he was not making hundreds of millions.

∾

OVER THE YEARS the central dynamic in the Eisner and Ovitz relationship had been their ability to war during the day and still see each other socially in the evening. The same competitive spirit emerged even when Eisner was in the hospital and Ovitz appointed himself Eisner's unofficial gatekeeper, stationing himself at his friend's bedside and screening calls and guests. Eisner later reported that he "took my phone away from me and told me Disney had plenty of gifted employees who would be better served if I rested." But Eisner was never content to rest.

As Eisner lay in bed, Ovitz continued to do CAA business, speaking on a cell phone. At one point Eisner overheard him pounding out the final details of the deal that became Tele-TV—a doomed joint venture in which the Baby Bells were to create programming, theoretically for transmission over phone lines. (Hollywood was in hot pursuit of such linkups with regional phone companies in those days, though they ultimately produced nothing.) Eisner had been arranging Disney's own deal with another group of telephone companies. He waited until Ovitz visited the men's room and then phoned Katzenberg. "Ovitz is about to put Tele-TV together," Eisner whispered. "You have forty-eight hours to close our telco deals."

"This is how Eisner feels about his 'best friend,' " a former Disney executive chortled later. "He couldn't wait for his best friend to take a tinkle so he could screw him."

Over the years Eisner had talked intermittently to Ovitz about working for Disney. He had brought it up, abortively, when the two flew to Sun Valley in 1994. After Katzenberg left Disney, Ovitz dispatched Ron Meyer to represent him in a negotiation with Eisner. They had a five-hour lunch at the then-fashionable but now-defunct restaurant Cicada on Melrose Avenue. Meyer returned to CAA and urged Ovitz to join the Disney team. He felt that CAA was ready for a transition and Ovitz was clearly restless. Eisner pledged that he and Ovitz would be partners. "I will never disagree with Mike in front of people," Eisner had pledged, "but in a room alone, I have to be boss." On reflection, Ovitz demurred. "I can't work for Michael Eisner," he said.

But Ovitz was pushing fifty and ready to make a move. It appeared that Matsushita's decision to sell MCA in 1995 might provide an opportunity. Speculation began at once that if there were a change in management at MCA, Ovitz—long an ardent admirer of the company—would love to take over. Some still doubted that he would leave his entirely autonomous perch at CAA, where he wielded influence over all the studios. Even Eisner joked that he wielded only "one-eighth as much" power as Ovitz.

But after Edgar Bronfman emerged as the successful suitor in the MCA deal, all Hollywood assumed that the hiring of Ovitz was certain. Lew Wasserman and Sid Sheinberg made no secret that they were horrified. During their struggle with Matsushita, Ovitz had assured them that he was taking their part and promoting their interests with the Japanese. Now they had learned that Ovitz had at least known about Seagram's interest in buying MCA and might even have helped instigate the deal. "I had at least one, maybe two conversations where Mr. Ovitz purported not to know what was going on when he knew goddamn well what was going on," Sheinberg says.

While Ovitz sympathizers say he was awkwardly situated and couldn't reveal the truth, Sheinberg thought Ovitz should have dropped out of the discussions and given him and Wasserman some warning of an impending sale. "He would have had no problem with Matsushita, no problem with Seagram, and no problem with us," Sheinberg says. "He really doesn't know what it is to be honorable and a friend."

It was a particular humiliation for Sheinberg because David Geffen had warned him that Ovitz was not to be trusted. "I was the guy defending Ovitz in the councils of DreamWorks," Sheinberg remembers. "When he did what he did to us, they just turned to me and said, 'Putz!' . . . They were probably thinking to themselves, 'How can this guy be such a fool?' . . . And I guess I was. I really thought Mike Ovitz was a friend of mine."

Wasserman and Sheinberg's enmity toward Ovitz put Edgar Bronfman Jr. in a tricky situation. It would be unbecoming to show disrespect to Wasserman and Sheinberg—and impolitic. If there were any hope of a

DreamWorks deal — which would be a nice way for young Bronfman to announce himself in Hollywood — alienating Sheinberg was out of the question. At the same time Bronfman was as enamored of Ovitz as anyone who had ever bought into the "most powerful man in Hollywood" myth, and he wanted his own man in charge at MCA.

On April 20, 1995, Ovitz officially declared that there were "no talks and no negotiations" with Bronfman. But by the end of May, it became clear that Ovitz was, in fact, in heavy negotiations for the position. Bronfman knew Ovitz lacked corporate experience, but he felt the agent had a good feel for the industry and its future, and he was convinced that Ovitz would surround himself with a strong team.

Hollywood had always known that Ovitz would have to make the deal of deals. In fact, the elder Bronfmans (Edgar Jr.'s father and his uncle Charles) questioned whether Ovitz was worth the kind of rich package being discussed. The value of the package he sought was said to be as much as $250 million. "What he was asking was ridiculous," Edgar Sr. says. "I said to my son, 'He may be better than anybody else but he's not that much better.' My brother said [the same]. I said, 'Edgar, I've always backed you but not on this.' . . . Michael sells himself very well. If it had been a reasonable deal rather than an unbelievable, monstrous deal, he probably would have gotten the job — whether Sid and Lew liked it or not."

At first, the younger Bronfman figured that Ovitz was simply starting from a high number. Among friends, he compared Ovitz with a teenager who asks his parents for a Rolls-Royce expecting to get a Volvo. But Edgar Jr. came to realize that Ovitz was serious. At the same time his own concerns were growing. He began to see how little Ovitz knew about running a public company, and he was becoming weary of Ovitz's paranoia. He found it trying that Ovitz would initiate even a trivial phone conversation by asking, "Are you on a hard line?" Some at CAA later speculated that Ovitz overplayed his hand out of anxiety. An agent is "Teflon," said one former agent. He could put a client in a movie for $20 million, and if the film tanked, no one would blame him. But an executive would be judged on specific criteria. "He realized that he would be so exposed," Ovitz's former colleague said.

Finally Bronfman backed away — explaining to Ovitz that his father and brother vehemently objected to his terms. Edgar Sr. says his son later recounted the conversation to him: "Michael got terribly excited and said, 'But then you're not in charge! You're telling me your father and uncle won't go for it.' Edgar said, in a calm voice . . . 'That's not the point. My father and my uncle are very large shareholders in this company.' "

In the most public and humiliating fashion, the deal finally collapsed. "This may be the luckiest thing that ever happened to you," Edgar Sr. told his son. "You'd have been at each other's throats in six weeks."

And so Ovitz committed one of the most spectacular balks in the history of the industry. Whatever the reason, every concession he had exacted from Bronfman left him wanting more. "He said to me, 'Who are they going to get? It's only me,' " said a Hollywood executive involved in the talks. "And they left. . . . He makes people not want to be with him anymore. He had everything he wanted. It wasn't enough."

Ovitz tells the story differently. He dragged out the talks, he says, because, in his heart, he was reluctant to leave CAA. "I just didn't want to do it, and I carried the negotiations on too long," he concedes. "I overplayed it. It was a mistake to carry it out for so long when I knew I wasn't going to leave CAA." In the end, he claimed, it was he who called Edgar Jr. and backed out of the discussions.

∞

THE END OF the Seagram negotiation left Hollywood agog and it left Bronfman without management. There were reports that Ovitz had met with his colleagues in CAA's screening room and freshly committed to his life at CAA, whereupon his subordinates stood and cheered. But it wasn't quite that simple. Ovitz's associates at CAA had learned a lesson about their leader. Despite rumors in the past that Ovitz might leave, they had chosen to believe his pledges of eternal loyalty. Now they had seen him walk to the door and put a foot out.

It was an uneasy reunion, particularly for five young agents—Richard Lovett, "Doc" O'Connor, Kevin Huvane, Jay Moloney, and Brian Lourd—known around town as the Young Turks. These were hungry youths who had steeled themselves to the idea that they just might have to run things without Ovitz. At news of the likely departure, they had jetted off to a private island in the Caribbean for Memorial Day weekend to ponder their future (only Huvane participated from afar, since he had gone to San Diego instead of joining the others). They considered their options, including setting up a competing shop. They decided to stay and run CAA. Now they were not entirely pleased to learn that the majority shareholder was returning—especially because none of them owned any stake in the agency at all.

Then came the news that Meyer was leaving to work for Bronfman. Ovitz had set something in motion that he couldn't control—and he was the one who had been stranded. "After Ronnie left," said a former associate of Ovitz, "Mike was left with a coat and a tie and his underwear." Since the mid-1980s, Ovitz had gradually withdrawn from client hand-holding duties that most agents dread. Meyer had taken on most of the task of administering CAA. (He was fond of saying that he was like the Harvey Keitel character in *Pulp Fiction*, who mops up when the brains got splattered.) "Ronnie was Mike Ovitz," said one veteran producer. "It was *The Wizard of Oz*. Who's that behind the curtain? Ronnie."

A return to the direct supervision of CAA, dealing with the petty complaints of spoiled movie stars, was the last thing Ovitz wanted. There were rumors that he was offering the Turks stupendous sums to stick around. And for days, Ovitz applied a "full-court press" on Meyer to change his mind, as a former CAA executive put it. Meyer wouldn't budge. Instead, he urged Ovitz to rethink his own career path. "Quit," he said. "Go sit on a beach. . . . Somebody will come and get you." Soon after Meyer left, Sylvester Stallone—a longtime client—started to get agitated. Ovitz called a Hollywood veteran and said, "What do I do with this guy?"

"Mike, you gotta hold his hand," the friend replied.

"I can't do that," Ovitz said.

It was then, at his lowest moment, that his old friend Michael Eisner beckoned.

According to Ovitz, the pivotal conversation came on a Friday afternoon early in August 1995 as the two men and their wives hiked in Independence Pass near Aspen. This time, Ovitz recalled later, Eisner suggested that Ovitz would run the company on a day-to-day basis while Eisner became something of a figurehead. "We are going to be partners," Ovitz remembers Eisner telling him. "I'll handle the ceremonial parts and you will handle the operational side. You will make the strategic decisions for the company." And within a few years, Eisner supposedly continued, Ovitz would succeed him as chairman.

Perhaps Eisner actually said those words, or maybe Ovitz simply heard what he wanted to hear. Either way, Ovitz decided that the number-two job at Disney might be the right thing for him after all. True, he had to take the position for far less money than Bronfman had offered to pay. But there were lucrative stock options to be had. And he considered that Disney was a much bigger company than MCA—a huge company after the acquisition of Capital Cities/ABC. And that ABC deal ensured that there was more than enough work for two men. Eisner had been through quadruple-bypass surgery. Ovitz had seen him so weak that he could barely get out of his chair. There might be room for Ovitz to make his mark after all.

27

A PLATINUM PARACHUTE

T HE DISNEY EXECUTIVES arriving at Eisner's Bel-Air home on a Sunday afternoon in August 1995 were stunned, angry, and confused. That morning, Eisner had broken the news to his top aides — chief financial officer Stephen Bollenbach, general counsel Sanford Litvack, and board member (and Eisner's personal attorney) Irwin Russell — that he intended to hire Ovitz as president of Disney. When Eisner had phoned with the news, Bollenbach had expressed serious dismay. "Why are you doing this?" he kept asking Eisner. He didn't know Ovitz and he didn't want to; he worried aloud that introducing an outsider would damage the chemistry of the Disney group. "You'll take a really good management team and destroy it," Bollenbach warned.

If, as Eisner suspected, Bollenbach had imagined himself the heir at Disney, the arrival of Ovitz would be unwelcome news. There had been no great affection between Bollenbach and Sandy Litvack, now the chief of corporate operations and a rival for Eisner's ear. But Ovitz presented a problem to both men. Bollenbach and Litvack were united, for once, in their horror.

Eisner explained that the idea of hiring Ovitz had hit him during meetings at ABC. "You know," he said, "I always knew how complicated this [deal] was. But it's just come to me how much there is to do. I can't do it all myself." He needed someone to share creative responsibility for the combined Disney-ABC.

Bollenbach pointed out that Ovitz had no experience running a major public company.

"It's not like he doesn't know about business," Eisner said, mentioning Ovitz's twenty years running CAA. "He's run a big company."

"That's not a big company," Bollenbach shot back. "It's a tiny company."

Seeing that Eisner had made up his mind, Bollenbach changed course, suggesting that Disney form a three-man office of the president consisting of himself, Litvack, and Ovitz. Eisner said no; he had seen it tried at other companies—including the then-chaotic Sony Pictures—and it always looked like a "display of weakness," as if the CEO couldn't decide on a chain of command.

"Well, I won't report to him," said Bollenbach, whose contract explicitly stated that he would be supervised only by Eisner. Litvack—the fifty-nine-year-old chief of corporate operations who had emerged as Eisner's consigliere after Wells's death—said he wouldn't, either. He and Bollenbach would overcome their previous mutual antagonism to form a daunting welcoming committee.

During this awkward meeting, Ovitz arrived. "We're certainly prepared to work with you," Bollenbach told Ovitz. But it was clear that he and Litvack did not intend to work for him.

Ovitz was alarmed. "[Eisner] kept assuring me, 'Don't worry about it. You're going to be the boss,'" he says. When Bollenbach and Litvack refused to report to him, Ovitz expected Eisner to take his part. "I was under the impression that he'd already greased that wheel," he says. "I sat at the table and I kept looking at him, waiting for him to say, 'You guys are reporting to him.'" Ovitz and Eisner excused themselves and spoke privately. "We'll work this through," Eisner told him. "Let's just get through this meeting." Ovitz didn't challenge Bollenbach or Litvack.

The news that Ovitz was coming aboard did not go over much better with Joe Roth, the studio chief. Roth was on vacation in Martha's Vineyard when Eisner called to break the news. When Eisner told him that Ovitz was coming to the company, Roth was shaken. "We better go take a walk," he told his wife. "This is not going to work." Roth resolved to go to Aspen, where Eisner had now gone, to express his concerns about the new arrangement.

Roth thought he should have seen it coming. A few weeks earlier, after the MCA negotiation had collapsed, Ovitz had called Roth and surprised him by sounding depressed. It wasn't like Ovitz to show that side of himself. Offhandedly, Roth had said, "Why don't you come here and be president?" Ovitz had replied: "Nobody asked." Roth realized that he was being asked, in Ovitz's indirect way, to send a message to Eisner. So he had done so. Eisner didn't sound surprised to hear of Ovitz's call. Now, a month later, Eisner called Roth to say that Ovitz was on his way in.

Even though he had been forewarned, in a way, the whole arrangement seemed to Roth like a freak development, and one that could hardly bode well for him. When he got to Aspen, he told Eisner, "The area in which the guy has become famous is in my area. And we operate the business from a completely different point of view. At Fox, I never bought packages. I developed material and hired talent later. And I'm afraid he's going to try to change the business I'm running."

Eisner assured Roth that Ovitz's goal was to make it on the corporate side of the company. In the last several years, Ovitz hadn't even been that interested in the movie business, Eisner pointed out. At that point Ovitz joined the two for lunch and offered further assurances that he had no intention of meddling in Roth's affairs at the studio. Privately, Roth still told Eisner, "I'm concerned this isn't going to work."

"It has to work," Eisner replied. If Ovitz caused Roth problems, Eisner suggested, Ovitz would be the one to pay.

Roth returned to Martha's Vineyard, where he found a message from entertainment attorney Jake Bloom, calling from a boat in Italy. Roth, already annoyed that his vacation had been disrupted, reluctantly returned the call.

"I'm calling on behalf of Brad Grey," Bloom said when Roth reached him. "Mike [Ovitz] has called. He's going to buy [Grey's] company." Grey was a partner in the Brillstein-Grey television production company, with shows including the Garry Shandling program on HBO. Bloom said Grey wanted a film production deal just like Roth used to have before he ascended to studio chairman. That was asking a lot. Roth's deal had given him "puts," the right to make certain films without the studio's approval.

Roth called Ovitz. "What's going on?" he demanded.

"We can give him a Caravan deal, right?" Ovitz asked.

Roth blew up. "Nobody gets 'put' pictures!" he said. "[Grey] is a manager! He's a packager! You're going to give him the opportunity to make what he wants to make?"

Roth's next call was to Eisner. "Six hours," he said.

"What do you mean?" Eisner asked.

"It took six hours for my fears to come true."

∞

AS EISNER AND Ovitz met the press to announce that Ovitz was coming to Disney, many reporters thought Ovitz seemed uncomfortable. And Eisner couldn't resist tweaking the new number-two man at Disney. In one phone interview, a reporter whose relationship with Ovitz had never been good suggested that confusion could be avoided during the conversation if questions to Ovitz would be addressed to "Mike" while Eisner could be referred to as "Michael." Ever sensitive to his image, Ovitz said he didn't want to be called "Mike." But Eisner cheerfully chimed in. "That's a good idea," he said. "He's been trying to graduate to 'Michael,' but I think he should be 'Mike.'" Before the conversation ended, Ovitz had become so exasperated that he hung up. Eisner, remaining on the line, was obviously amused by his new number-two man's discomfort.

Asked in another interview if Ovitz was Eisner's successor, Eisner stopped short of the ringing endorsement that he might have offered a true partner. "We haven't discussed succession at the company," he said, "but he's the number-two man, and if something happens to me, he'd be a pretty good candidate." Of course, Ovitz didn't quite have the Frank Wells job. He was president of the company, but not its chief operating officer. And he didn't report to the board — he reported to Eisner.

Roth's fears were quickly justified. Within short order, he had deals with Sean Connery, Martin Scorsese, and the producing team of Frank Marshall and Kathleen Kennedy — all thanks to Ovitz's intervention. And those were just the ones that Roth decided to accept in the name of getting along. He managed to resist at least half a dozen others. To Roth, it seemed that Ovitz didn't understand that all these deals would simply pile on overhead without producing much. But he wasn't surprised. CAA was a business about taking a percentage of other people's earnings. Disney had a bottom line to worry about.

Ovitz remembers things differently. Roth was defensive in the beginning, he says, but Ovitz believed that Roth eventually recognized that he genuinely didn't want to be in the movie business. If Roth took deals with Scorsese and others, Ovitz says, that was his choice.

∞

AS OVITZ TRIED to settle into his new job, Roy Disney fired off a memo indicating that animation chief Peter Schneider would continue reporting to Eisner. Ovitz found himself almost immediately surrounded by entrenched and resentful coworkers, and he had no clearly defined responsibilities. "He struggled with just what he was supposed to do," Bollenbach said later. "He had a huge problem setting an agenda. He just showed up for work the first day trying to make things happen."

Ovitz also believed that he should keep in touch with his former clients, even though it became clear to him that his many conversations with the talent that he had represented irritated Eisner. "Eisner wanted me to cut them off," he said later. "Eisner hates talent. When I took Cruise or Seinfeld to dinner, he criticized me. He didn't care about me winding down relationships."

In those first months, Bollenbach claimed, he and Litvack looked on in dismay as Ovitz busied himself with a string of marginal projects. A scheme to buy the Los Angeles Lakers basketball team fizzled. An effort to buy the Seattle Seahawks football team blew up in Ovitz's face when other owners signaled that they might block the proposed move to Los Angeles. Ovitz's most ambitious project, a plan to consolidate Disney's far-flung operations in a single place where executives could mingle and exchange ideas, fell flat after staffers calculated that the lot would have to stretch across several miles. That would hardly foster the creative intimacy Ovitz envisioned.

"You can't suck up company resources doing things that are meaningless," Bollenbach finally told Ovitz. He suggested that his new colleague sit down with briefing books and familiarize himself with the details of company operations. "Let's you and I take a day, a day and a half, and I'll go through all this with you, go through a budget, and you'll understand this business," Bollenbach remembers telling Ovitz. "His response was, 'Great. I can't thank you enough, let's set up a meeting.' That conversation occurred twenty-five times. And we never had the meeting. The point was, Michael Ovitz didn't understand the duties of an executive at a public company and he didn't want to learn."

But perhaps Ovitz didn't think he would benefit much from a Bollenbach tutorial. Ovitz was being shoved into a corner and Eisner wasn't helping him to get out. "He had his minions go out and say I did a terrible job," Ovitz says. "I found it interesting because I had no job to do." So he searched for projects that would have an impact. And he felt he made some contributions. He worked hard at helping Disney put its stamp on ABC's Saturday-morning cartoon lineup, for example, and Eisner acknowledged his efforts in a handwritten note.

But such positive experiences were the exception. Roth wasn't the only manager who was resisting Ovitz's moves. Ovitz complained to Roth, in fact, that he wasn't being permitted to run anything. "This is a really unfriendly place," he would say. He had warmed up to the animators and Imagineers, expressing admiration for their creativity. To him, it seemed as though they were starved for recognition. He hoped to build a facility to house a warehouseful of cells and other animation artifacts; he didn't think the company's archives were being adequately cared for. But Eisner seemed disinterested and the plan faded away.

It wasn't long before Roth could see that the great partnership between Eisner and Ovitz wasn't working. "Why don't you give him a business to run?" he asked Eisner. But by now, Eisner's unhappiness was becoming manifest.

"If I thought that would work," Eisner replied, "I would do it."

✍

OVITZ WORKED DESPERATELY to seem as though he had Eisner's ear—literally. He often whispered to Eisner, both at meetings and public events. "That was Ovitz's little power trip," Bollenbach said later. "It was so clear Michael Eisner was uncomfortable with it. . . . I told Eisner, 'You gotta stop this. You look crazy.' He said, 'I know. Someone else told me that, too.'"

Bollenbach, one of several at Disney who found their path to advancement blocked, didn't dally long: he left in February 1996 to become chief executive of Hilton Hotels. But when he was still at Disney, he said, he saw that Eisner quickly realized he had not hired an equal. "He was disturbed that Ovitz didn't come in and relieve him of the burden. He came in and created a new one. He was also offended by the Ovitz style in terms of staff: having six or seven secretaries, whatever he had; having drivers sitting outside when it was clear he wasn't going to need them. Eisner was horrified. He would tell me, 'I've known [Ovitz] for twenty-five years, but after he came to the company, I don't know him at all.'"

But Ovitz's behavior was hardly surprising. He was just as mysterious and imperial as he had ever been. In many ways, Eisner's decision to hire Ovitz hadn't made much sense. He didn't seem to be in the market for a successor or even a close ally. One after another, managers had fallen out of favor and ultimately left as it became clear that there was no room for advancement. "[Eisner] is not looking for it to work," says a senior Disney manager. "He's not out canvassing for someone to be his confidant."

So why did Eisner hire Ovitz in the first place? It is a question that Ovitz has asked himself again and again without reaching a conclusion. Others also speculated on Eisner's motives. "Michael Eisner bought into the mystique of Michael Ovitz," says a former Disney executive. "What actually happened at the crux of it was that Eisner believed everything he came to read and hear about Ovitz—that he was really the biggest, bestest, smartest, most entrepreneurial person in Hollywood. That's what he thought he was buying. And he learned the truth within days."

Another view holds that even if Eisner didn't quite buy the Ovitz legend, he did relish the idea of being the boss of the person once known as the most powerful man in Hollywood. In truth, Eisner was probably not that impressed with Ovitz, the son of a liquor salesman from the San Fernando Valley—any more than he ultimately felt much respect for Katzenberg, who lacked a college education. Neither man could touch the credentials of Frank Wells, who was literally a Rhodes scholar. The marriage between Ovitz and Eisner had been a long shot from the start.

"It really was a lunar eclipse," says a high-level Disney executive. "If Frank doesn't die, if Michael doesn't have the heart thing, if he doesn't get alienated from Jeffrey, if he doesn't buy ABC, if the MCA negotiation doesn't fail, if Ronnie doesn't leave [CAA], and if the wives aren't best friends—if any one of those things doesn't happen, it doesn't go down. It was Jane trying to protect her husband. It was Michael Eisner taking five hundred calls a day from Ted Koppel and Diane Sawyer—and he's not that comfortable with talent. The *Wall Street Journal* is giving him a hard time about succession. If those things didn't line up, this doesn't happen."

Ovitz soon sank into a situation of prolonged and increasingly public humiliation. His enemies, who had waited for years for him to falter, pounced. "He's not Michael Ovitz anymore," gloated David Geffen. "He's a guy who has a job working for Michael Eisner."

During Ovitz's tenure, Bollenbach said that Eisner was sometimes plainly impatient with his number-two man. But at first, they always seemed to make up, as they had done before Ovitz came to the company. "Eisner can really get after him, you know: 'Mike, that's not it! You don't get it! Forget it!'" Bollenbach said at the time. "And Ovitz gives it right back: 'Bullshit! I get it!' Then, later in the evening, you'd see them practically holding hands."

⚭

EARLY ON, OVITZ tried to fix one of Disney's lingering problems. Immediately after he started at Disney, he approached Jeffrey Katzenberg at ABC chief Bob Iger's wedding on Long Island in October 7, 1995. He told Katzenberg that he would resolve Katzenberg's contract dispute within two weeks. This was the kind of matter that Ovitz was used to settling at CAA. But as the unpleasant months went by, it became clear that Ovitz lacked the clout to carry out his agenda. He and Katzenberg met on a couple of occasions. Seeking neutral turf and anonymity, they even met in the emergency waiting room at St. Joseph's Hospital across from the Disney headquarters. But it soon became obvious that the parties were miles apart. "I was at a trillion dollars and they were at forty-two cents," Katzenberg remembers. But in fact, the parties were closer than that. At one point, a knowledgeable source says, Geffen — who got involved on Katzenberg's be-half — said his side would come to terms for $100 million. Disney had been willing to offer $80 million, this source says. Ovitz told Eisner that Disney could settle for $90 million, but Eisner refused to make a deal.

Indeed, Eisner did not seem inclined to patch things up with Katzenberg. The two men had barely spoken since Katzenberg's departure from Disney. Their first meeting came at a wake. Don Simpson, the onetime Paramount executive who had so admired Eisner and befriended Katzenberg when he was in that studio's marketing department, had been found dead in his bathroom on January 19, 1996. Simpson's demise had long been predicted: he had died obese, reclusive, and with a veritable pharmacy of drugs in his system. Simpson's friends had been aware of his decline; indeed, Katzenberg had attempted an intervention. Turn over your life to me for six months, he had urged, and clean yourself up. It was a cold-turkey approach that other Simpson friends, including agents Jim Wiatt and Jim Berkus, thought was hopelessly naive. Neither Katzenberg's efforts nor Wiatt and Berkus's go-slow approach had prevented Simpson from drugging himself to death.

The industry came together to mourn Simpson at Morton's, a restaurant that Simpson had frequented in better times. There were stars — Warren Beatty, Will Smith, Michelle Pfeiffer. Several of the old Paramount guard were reunited — Dawn Steel, Barry Diller, and of course, Katzenberg and Eisner. In this very public setting, Katzenberg was the one who crossed the room and greeted Eisner. It was an awkward moment. "Well," Katzenberg said, gazing about at the throng that had gathered to see Simpson off, "he's happy tonight."

Eisner looked at Katzenberg as if he were talking gibberish. "Jeffrey," he said pointedly, "he's *dead*." With that, the conversation pretty much petered out.

A few months later, Eisner called Katzenberg and proposed a meeting to discuss the television deal between DreamWorks and ABC. The meeting, brokered by ABC chief Iger, was to take place at Eisner's Aspen home. Anticipating an opening to settle the brewing legal dispute, Katzenberg rearranged his schedule so he could make the trip. But the day before the meeting, Eisner's office canceled. Livid, Katzenberg called Ovitz to complain. "He can't do this to me anymore," he said.

Katzenberg decided it would be a cold day in hell before he would jump through hoops trying to make things straight with Eisner again. Eventually, inevitably, this matter was going to wind up in court.

∞

BY THE SPRING of 1996, Ovitz was already so concerned about his future at the company that he had written Eisner a memo proposing ways to salvage his position. It produced no effect. In August, when Eisner canceled plans to take off the month, Ovitz was even more downhearted than ever. It seemed that Eisner would never let go for a minute. Ovitz eventually came to believe that Eisner had instructed all his division chiefs not to follow any Ovitz directive without first clearing it with Eisner.

Ovitz felt strangely optimistic, however, at a Disney conference for senior executives in September. Believing that perhaps he could outlast his detractors and recalling some words of encouragement that he had heard from Eisner, Ovitz pleaded with his colleagues to stop leaking damaging information to the news media. His remarks were instantly reported in the press. "That's when I said this is stupid," he said later. "It was a stupid idea that I could come in and change this culture. The insanity of my thought process overwhelmed me."

He wrote a letter to Eisner, saying the job wasn't working for him and that the two of them needed to talk. But weeks passed and no conversation took place. Meanwhile, the press was having a field day at Ovitz's expense. Perhaps most painful for Ovitz, at least initially, was a broadside in the *New York Observer* headlined POOF! MIKE OVITZ, FROM SORCERER TO SCHMO. The piece not only took the *Wall Street Journal* to task for using the adjective "powerful" to describe Ovitz, but described him as being "Mr. Eisner's whipping boy" with nothing much to do. Worst of all, to Ovitz, the article ended with an anecdote about a sleep-over party for children from the Thomas Dye School, which Ovitz's young son Eric attended. According to the story, one of Eric's classmates surprised his parents by saying, "Eric's father used to be powerful but now he's the number-two guy over half of

Disney." To Ovitz, who frequently accused his adversaries of attacking his family even when no such thing had occurred, the mere mention of his son's name must have driven salt deep, deep into his wounds.

Worse yet, Eisner was doing nothing to defuse the media attention. "He could have stopped it in his tracks," Ovitz says. "All he had to do was give a definitive quote, which I asked him to do."

On September 30, about a year after he started at Disney, Ovitz and Eisner attempted a public appearance on *Larry King Live*. Eisner said the talk of problems at the company was "just all baloney. The fact of the matter is that we together have almost as many enemies as Saddam Hussein, and so it's very difficult not to have this kind of gossip." Ovitz said he and his new boss "talked about a two-year learning curve. . . . I probably know about 1 percent of what I need to know." The interview was a flop. Both men looked uncomfortable and out of sync. Despite Ovitz's request, at no point did Eisner give him a ringing vote of confidence. In fact, the two barely made eye contact.

As the drumbeat grew louder that Ovitz was on his way out, Eisner offered *Vanity Fair* another pallid defense of his number-two man. "There is always a period of learning the business, the lingo," Eisner said at one point. "He understands the entertainment business . . . and I am very satisfied with his performance." He also dismissed the idea that Ovitz was a roving president without a portfolio. "He had been extremely helpful outside the United States, specifically in Europe and Asia. And in corporate governance, in cheerleading, in strategy for the whole company." Asked who reported directly to Ovitz, Eisner said: "Every division reports to Michael Ovitz. Some of the heads of divisions report to both of us. It's completely clear inside the company. Michael Ovitz is the number-two guy."

But within the walls of Disney, few were buying that scenario. "It's what we sit around talking about all day," said a Disney staffer at the time. "The betting is it's like *The Godfather Part II*. You've got Hyman Roth, who says he's going to die and pass it all to Michael Corleone. But in fact it turns out that Hyman Roth thinks he's going to live forever; he isn't going to give Michael Corleone anything and in fact ends up trying to kill Michael Corleone."

ASIDE FROM THE sheer impossibility of his position, several blunders marked Ovitz's tenure. His attempt to bring producer-manager Brad Grey to Disney backfired. Grey had a number of television shows on the air, including *News Radio* and *Just Shoot Me*. ABC already owned half his production company under a deal that predated the merger with Disney. To make a deal with Grey, Disney would have to buy the other half.

Ovitz offered Grey a number of jobs at Disney, even suggesting he might be right to succeed Bob Iger at the helm of ABC. But to Grey's surprise, Ovitz wavered when it came time to follow through on his own suggestions, especially regarding the price that Disney might pay to buy the rest of the production company. "The clear sense was Michael was trying to get Eisner's approval on every beat of what he was trying to do," says an executive close to the negotiation. "Michael [Ovitz] didn't have the wherewithal to follow his instincts without having to double- and triple-check."

When Grey flew to Aspen to talk with Eisner at his home there, it was clear that Eisner had no interest in making a deal. This was just one example of a pattern that would frustrate Ovitz: Eisner would allow him to start exploring an idea and not express his disinterest until Ovitz had already gotten himself involved in a negotiation. In retrospect, it would seem to Ovitz that Eisner enjoyed embarrassing him.

The parties continued to talk through their lawyers, but the situation turned nasty when Grey refused to lower his price. At one point, when the *Wall Street Journal* published an article suggesting that Brillstein-Grey was having financial problems, Grey accused Ovitz of spreading the story. The two men, once the closest of friends in the Hollywood style, engaged in several heated phone conversations including one in which Ovitz allegedly threatened to destroy Grey. Brillstein-Grey subsequently struck an extremely lucrative deal with MCA, and ended up under Ron Meyer's corporate roof instead of Disney's.

The most visible of Ovitz's moves was his wooing of Jamie Tarses, NBC's then-thirty-one-year-old senior vice-president of prime-time programming, to run programming at ABC. In an effort to get free of her contract, Tarses was rumored to have threatened NBC's West Coast president, Don Ohlmeyer, with charges of sexual harassment. Though she denied ever making such a threat, Hollywood rallied to Ohlmeyer's defense. Many blamed Ovitz, though there was no proof that he had supported Tarses's alleged tactics.

Insiders said Eisner had serious reservations about hiring Tarses, a young woman whose flirtatious, sometimes erratic manner definitely did not appeal to him. But he failed in his own play to get producer Marcy Carsey, whom he had known since his own salad days at ABC, to take the job. Tarses finally got the position as president of the entertainment division in June 1996. From the start, Eisner made it clear that his support for her was lukewarm at best. She dangled for months amid unfounded rumors that she was about to be fired. And just as the episode was fading from memory, the fight got another charge from the media. Ohlmeyer referred to Ovitz as "the Antichrist" in a *Time* magazine interview.

Another problem arose from the deal with Martin Scorsese, which turned out to be something of a Trojan horse for Disney. Scorsese brought with him a project called *Kundun,* the story of the Dalai Lama. Universal had decided against making the film because of concerns about how the Chinese government would react. But Ovitz, whose loosely defined job included opening China to all things Disney, apparently did not anticipate what was to come. In 1997, the Chinese government said it would ban new Disney ventures in China if the film was released under the studio's banner. Disney could hardly be seen as buckling to the Chinese government and proceeded with the film. Eisner was concerned enough to hire Henry Kissinger to try to smooth things over. "We cannot be intimidated to not distribute this movie," Eisner said at the time. But he added that he hoped "the Chinese'll understand . . . in this country, you put out a movie, it gets a lot of momentum for six seconds, and is gone three weeks later." In the case of *Kundun*—a film with only limited, art-house appeal, that is precisely what happened.

∞

LIKE KATZENBERG, OVITZ slowly and painfully came to accept the fact that Eisner would never share with him. "[Eisner] was my best friend for 25 years," Ovitz said later in an interview with author Robert Slater. "To this day I don't know why he brought me in there. . . . He was supposed to be less hands-on. He says I didn't know what I was doing, but he didn't give me the opportunity to do anything. We were going to be partners. We were going to run the company together. He brought me in as his successor. I thought there would be a two- or three-year learning curve. But it didn't work from the day I started."

By the fall of 1996, there were reports that Disney had become so hostile to Ovitz that chief financial officer Richard Nanula was investigating who paid for an Ovitz family party—his daughter's bat mitzvah—at the House of Blues. A Disney executive said the company was merely checking to see if the club, partially owned by Disney, was giving improper discounts to company employees. (Nothing was found to be amiss.)

The Eisners and Ovitzes discussed the growing impossibility of the situation at a Saturday-night wedding reception for oilman Marvin Davis's daughter in December. The two men agreed that Ovitz would have to leave soon, but they hoped to postpone an announcement until after the holidays. But that week, Ovitz took a business trip to New York. He escorted director Penny Marshall to a premiere of *The Preacher's Wife*, spoke to the Council on Foreign Relations, and met with Viacom executives about the possible sale of the company's radio operations. But his presence in Manhattan set off another round of job rumors—this time that he was in discussions to take over Sony's entertainment operations or that he was seeking a job at Viacom. Eisner was said to be furious.

Certainly Eisner was fed up with the constant media scrutiny and the stream of negative stories. That Thursday night, Ovitz and Eisner met for four hours at Eisner's New York apartment. Eisner told Ovitz that his departure could not be delayed. And so a couple of days before Ovitz's fiftieth birthday on December 14, 1996, the news came that he and the Disney company were parting ways. He had been in the job a mere fourteen months.

"After ruling the movie industry as a super-agent for more than a decade," the *Los Angeles Times* reported on its front page, "Ovitz suddenly is not even a player." Long anticipated, Ovitz's fall had been so precipitous that it still had the power to shock.

Initially, Disney announced that Ovitz was departing "by mutual agreement." But Ovitz implied that he was acting on his own initiative. "I hope that my decision to leave will eliminate any unnecessary distraction for a great company," he said in a statement. Disney underscored Ovitz's superfluousness at the company by noting that no successor would be appointed and no changes in the company's operations were anticipated. But both Ovitz and Eisner vowed publicly that their friendship would survive this breach. "We have been doing business together while being friends for many years and I know that both our personal and professional relationships will continue," Eisner said. In fact, their friendship was ruptured and Ovitz would later describe his doomed tenure at Disney as one of the most traumatic events of his life.

Immediately, word leaked out that Ovitz was walking away with a stunning severance package worth at least $90 million, including cash to settle his contract and three million shares of stock options then worth $40 million. The sum was astonishing—and it turned out that those initial estimates were far lower than the real number. Even the man who helped design Ovitz's deal at Disney, executive compensation expert Graef Crystal, acknowledged: "It's a lot of money for what was apparently a mistake." At Disney, executives who were getting holiday bonuses—which in some cases were lower than the previous year's—began to feel that their stocking had been stuffed with lumps of coal.

The leaks about the payment appeared to come from the Ovitz camp, and Disney was blindsided. Initially, some company executives unofficially suggested that the number was far too high and that Ovitz's payoff was closer to $30 million. The inflated figures, they said, were just Ovitz being Ovitz. There were reports about a letter of understanding outlining the real deal, and studio chief Joe Roth implored Eisner to release it. After all, if Ovitz's take was really $90 million, it equaled 7.5 percent of the company's fiscal 1996 net income.

Finally, in a January filing with the Securities and Exchange Commission, Disney disclosed that the $90 million figure was, in fact, conservative. Upon his hiring, Ovitz had been promised $1 million per year in salary and options on three million shares of stock. He would receive options on another two million shares unless his deal was not renewed after five years. In that event, he would get $10 million in cash. His final settlement gave him a total cash payment of nearly $40 million: about $3.5 million in salary, $10 million for the options he would have been granted had his contract been renewed, and about $25 million in bonuses. He also kept the options on the three million shares, which most Disney executives had to give up when they left the company. The stock had a history of appreciating, so the final value of Ovitz's payoff was a moving target that quickly surged far north of $90 million.

Disney also disclosed that Ovitz had been terminated. Had he left voluntarily, he might have had to sacrifice some of the bounty. Board member Ray Watson answered queries about the package by saying that the deal was similar to the one offered to Frank Wells or any executive in a similar position. "The only circumstances that arose here is that it didn't last very long," he said. "It's like doing a movie with Sylvester Stallone where you pay him $20 million and the movie loses money. It's unfortunate."

For the analysts and investors who tracked Disney, Ovitz's departure in itself was not troubling. But it once again put the focus on Eisner's lack of a successor. Beyond that, the excess of it all had made national news. Under the headline BEAVIS AND BUTT-HEAD DO THE DISNEY SHAREHOLDERS, columnist Holman W. Jenkins Jr. deplored the agreement on the editorial pages of the *Wall Street Journal.* "Nobody in the real world, not even in the far-out precincts of Hollywood, gets that kind of money for flubbing up after a year on the job," he wrote. In the *New York Times*, A. M. Rosenthal inveighed: "Why should a board responsible to the stockholders allow its chairman to pay so much to push out [Ovitz]?" he asked. "Everybody knows that a board of directors is responsible for the well-being of the stockholders, not executives."

Eisner apparently was not abashed by the complaints. In fact, even as the details of the Ovitz payment were disclosed, Disney announced that Eisner had signed a record-breaking seven-year extension of his employment contract. Although its total value could not be determined because it depended on stock performance, the package was estimated to be worth at least a minimum of $300 million. Compensation experts believed that Eisner had received the largest options grant ever given to a chief executive — eight million options that could be exercised between the years 2003 and 2006. Disney assigned a hypothetical value of $196 million to the options. (Consultant Graef Crystal, who helped design Eisner's package, estimated the ultimate value of the options to be $770.9 million.) Eisner already had options he could exercise at once that were worth more than $300 million, and another batch exercisable in the future that were valued at more than $60 million. The board also altered the formula for calculating Eisner's bonuses in a manner that favored Eisner. (For fiscal 1996, he had received a bonus of $7.9 million.)

"We wouldn't have done this if we believed he wasn't going to live out this contract," said board member Watson in an effort to dispel concerns about Eisner's health. "I had lunch with him today and he ordered a fat-free salad and fat-free pasta."

Compensation expert Crystal acknowledged that Eisner had received "a monstrous contract," but pointed out that Eisner's base salary of $750,000 had remained unchanged since he was hired. "I don't know anyone who has gone that long without a raise," he said.

That observation evoked little sympathy from columnist Robert J. Samuelson, who suggested in the pages of the *Washington Post* that Eisner should pay Ovitz's severance package out of his own pocket. *Time's* Calvin Trillin seconded the proposal (in an essay accompanied by a most unflattering caricature), urging that Disney "could just subtract $90 million from Eisner's paycheck, with the notation, 'turkey hiring.' "

∽

IN HIS 1996 annual report, Eisner focused on all that Disney had accomplished, not only in the past year but since he took the helm. Sitting in the living room of his family's farmhouse in Saxtons River, Vermont, over the Thanksgiving holidays, he noted that he was constantly distracted from drafting his yearly letter. A football game was on Disney's ABC in the background, and every time a McDonald's ad came on promoting Disney's upcoming film 101 Dalmatians, Eisner said, he was distracted again. Then he heard a rave review for The English Patient, from Disney's Miramax unit. He got a call from Florida reporting excellent attendance at Walt Disney World. Europe called to say The Hunchback of Notre Dame had opened well in twelve foreign territories. He made some more calls and found out that Disney's summer film The Rock was on track to become the biggest home video rental of all time, while Toy Story was also selling briskly. Finally came the call that 101 Dalmatians had just had a record-breaking opening weekend. "Now," he wrote, "as soon as the Mighty Ducks hockey game . . . at the [Disney-owned] Pond in Anaheim on [Disney-owned] ESPN was over, I would finally begin to work."

It was indeed an impressive kingdom to survey. But Eisner went on. Only in passing did he mention the death of his mother that summer—an event that must have marked some sort of emotional watershed for him. He also noted that his mother-in-law had died. He acknowledged that these changes put him "in a more reflective mood than usual."

And he reflected about Disney's phenomenal growth since he and Frank Wells had taken over the company. Eisner could rattle off eighteen new businesses that the company had entered since 1984, including more than 550 Disney Stores in eleven countries, ownership of professional sports teams, broadcasting, television- and radio-station ownership, live theatrical shows such as the Broadway hit Beauty and the Beast. (The critically acclaimed stage version of The Lion King was in the works.)

When he joined the company, Eisner pointed out, Walt Disney World had two theme parks and 6,373 rooms on the property. By the end of 1996, there were three theme parks, 23,421 rooms, as well as two nighttime entertainment centers and two vacation-club complexes. There were also 234,000 square feet of convention space, compared with 26,000 square feet in 1984.

There were six championship golf courses and an Indy car racetrack. In the year to come, the company would add 2,000 new rooms, a 95,000-square-foot convention center, and a giant new sports complex. As if that weren't enough, 1998 would bring the opening of the company's largest theme park ever, Disney's Animal Kingdom, and the launch of the Disney cruise line.

But there were some dark patches. Disneyland Paris was drawing more visitors than the Eiffel Tower and was the most visited paid tourist site in France, but that didn't mean its financial problems were over. Eisner merely noted attendance figures without addressing the looming need for another restructuring. The animated films released since *The Lion King*—*Pocahontas* and *The Hunchback of Notre Dame*—were not disasters, but they had not performed as well as the studio might have hoped. Accentuating the positive, Eisner simply commented that "the specific success outside the United States of *Hunchback* is particularly gratifying."

And the ABC network, which had been number one when Eisner made the deal to acquire it, with such leading shows as *Roseanne*, *Home Improvement*, *Family Matters*, and *NYPD Blue*, had started slipping in the ratings in the months before the merger was completed. The network's strongest shows were aging and no new hits had come along to replace them. (Indeed, some thought ABC had not invested heavily enough to develop new programming before the sale. "Do plenty of people think Tom [Murphy] and Dan [Burke] were fattening up the company and making it look fabulous?" says one former network executive. "Sure.")

Disney's stock showed some weakness after the merger closed and the company had repurchased 8.2 million shares for $462 million. But Eisner reported that the company was "making slow but steady progress toward better ratings." The progress was certainly slow but hardly steady. In the months ahead, ABC would set record ratings lows for a major broadcast network.

Still, Eisner had an impressive list of accomplishments to discuss before he finally and briefly turned to the debacle that had tarnished the end of the year. In two short paragraphs, he said that "we and Michael Ovitz have come to an agreement that he will leave his position as president but continue in a role as an adviser to the company and its Board of Directors." He reiterated that no successor would be named.

DESPITE DISNEY'S DAZZLING accomplishments, a number of shareholders seemed to agree with Calvin Trillin when it came to the Ovitz payout. In fact, the Ovitz issue and Eisner's compensation package brought new scrutiny and harsh criticism to the Disney board. According to standards recommended by the Council of Institutional Investors, directors could not be considered independent if they were former employees or had any professional or consulting relationship with the company. Although Disney considered twelve of its sixteen directors to be independent, most of the twelve had ties to Eisner. Among them were Irwin Russell, his personal lawyer; Reveta Bowers, the principal of the elementary school that his children had attended; Reverend Leo J. O'Donovan, president of Georgetown University, where one of Eisner's children was enrolled; architect Robert A. M. Stern, who did extensive work for Disney and designed Eisner's Aspen home; former senator George Mitchell, who acted as a paid consultant to Disney; former chief financial officer Gary Wilson; former chairman Ray Watson; and the eighty-year-old Card Walker, also a former chairman and chief executive. (Eisner, Roy Disney, Sandy Litvack, and theme-park chief Dick Nunis were the insiders on the board.)

Contrary to custom, stock ownership among the directors was low (four owned none at all), though the board had recently passed guidelines saying that owning at least $15,000 worth of stock was "highly desirable." The same guidelines included a definition of "independence" broad enough that all twelve of Disney's outside directors met the standard. Nonetheless, the board did not hold a regular planning retreat. The outside directors did not meet apart from the company executives nor did the board give Eisner an annual written evaluation of his performance, as most major corporate boards do.

Eisner's contract negotiation underscored just how unusual Disney's arrangements were. Irwin Russell, Eisner's personal lawyer, was also chairman of the board's compensation committee. During the negotiation, he acted solely as Eisner's counsel. Watson temporarily took Russell's role and acted as compensation-committee chairman. "I agree that that's not a profile you would normally want to see," Watson conceded to the *Wall Street Journal*. "But you've got to go to the individuals." Sometimes, he added, Russell's sense of fairness made it "very difficult to tell . . . whom he did represent." Russell protested that he would "never do anything that I thought wasn't appropriate."

But that wasn't enough for many institutional shareholders. Twenty-four of 103 pension funds composing the Council of Institutional Investors, including the Wisconsin State Board of Investments and Calpers (the California Public Employees' Retirement System), decided to withhold votes for Eisner's new contract and for five Disney board members who were up for reelection at the company's upcoming annual meeting in February. Together these funds represented only about 22 million of Disney's 650 million outstanding shares, so their protest was only symbolic. But John Nash, president of the National Association of Corporate Directors, said the Disney board was "living in the Dark Ages," adding, "It's too beholden to Eisner. There are too many conflicts of interest. There are too many business relationships that could cloud independence."

The question was whether the company's success entitled it to overlook ordinary good-governance standards. Eisner countered critics by pointing out that the company's market capitalization had increased from $2 billion to $53 billion since he had taken over. "I didn't go to business school, so I didn't have the benefit of two years of intensive training in this area," Eisner said facetiously. "But what I read about what is expected, I find quite counterintuitive—for me and for this company." He referred dismissively to "the Wisconsin pension whatever," and said if Calpers wasn't satisfied, he would gladly buy back its stock.

He would rather have "a teacher who taught my kids telling me about our products" than "have an old-boy crony network of CEOs that just share the same old war stories," he continued. Most chief executives didn't understand the entertainment business, he said. "If they have so much time to spend on our company," he said, "what are they doing at their company?" (Eisner himself did not serve on other corporate boards or perform much community service—nor was he apologetic. "It's very worthy and I wish I had time to do it and someday I will do that," he said. "But it's not the job of the CEO in one of these kinds of companies.")

Addressing the lack of succession at Disney, Eisner said he regularly wrote memos to Watson offering his ideas of "who I think could go all the way and who I think is overrated." Such memos often began, "I know I can't dictate this from my grave. But in case anybody wanted to know what Michael Eisner thought, just after the funeral, here is a letter you can read to the board." Eisner predicted that his eventual successor would come from inside the company, adding, "There's a list of forty, and it could be any one of those forty depending on when I get hit by the truck."

Eisner said that in one of these memos written just a few months after Ovitz was hired, he had warned Watson that he had made a mistake. "I made it very clear to Ray and a few other people that if I should get hit by this truck, he should not expand my error and continue it. They should deal with it. I made it very clear I had made a mistake way before it became clear to the public and way before I acted."

So even though Eisner had told Larry King in September that the talk of trouble between him and Ovitz was "baloney," he now said he had already been preparing the board for the idea that it would be best to pay Ovitz to leave. "I can tell you that my main shareholders were very happy that I was doing it," Eisner said. "They recognized the economic benefits to the company, not the economic liability. That in the end, we were better off financially by biting the bullet."

This disclosure prompted the *Los Angeles Times* to reflect on the flagrant mendacity that was routine in Hollywood. "In an interview with the *Times* in September, Eisner used the word 'ludicrous' four times to describe rumors of a rift between [himself and Ovitz], blaming jealous competitors as the source of such speculation," the *Times* reported. He had made similar comments to *Newsday*, *Newsweek*, and the *New York Times*. "It now appears that Eisner was deceiving the news media, his shareholders, analysts and others," *Times* reporter Claudia Eller wrote. "Some say Eisner was between a rock and a hard place. After all, what could he say? How about a good old-fashioned 'no comment' for starters?"

∽

THE COLD WAS bone-chilling in the Pond ice rink in Anaheim. This was the home turf of Disney's hockey team, the Mighty Ducks. But on February 25, 1997, more than ten thousand shareholders gathered here for Disney's annual meeting. No one expected the normally cheerful mood to prevail this time.

Disney started out with the usual jovial display: spirited singers performing a tune from the upcoming animated feature *Hercules*; there were fireworks and then Mickey Mouse appeared to introduce "my pal, Michael Eisner."

Eisner spoke about the company's strong performance, which he said was "a direct result of the excellent stewardship of your board." After running through more figures to underscore the company's robust performance, Eisner jokingly asked, "Do I hear a motion to adjourn?"

It was a vain hope. But if Disney couldn't send shareholders home after a brief and upbeat presentation, it could make them wait—and wait—before they were given an opportunity to ask any questions. First, the heads of various divisions offered lengthy presentations which one shareholder later described as "one of the longest infomercials" ever staged at a Disney annual meeting. Studio chairman Joe Roth, wearing a Dalmatian tie, boasted about the previous Thanksgiving's box-office success of the live-action 101 *Dalmatians*—"$1 million for every puppy." (The film would gross more than $500 million from all sources.) ABC chief Robert Iger talked via satellite with Peter Jennings, who offered a preview of the evening news. The glossy display didn't impress *New York Times* columnist Maureen Dowd, who wrote, "The presentations conjured up a bright, scary world where Disney has no more conflicts of interest because it simply owns everything."

Then Eisner took the offensive on the Ovitz question, saying, "I'd like to think the mistake thing doesn't apply to me. And at home I make that clear to my children. But in the office, it happens, as in the Michael Ovitz situation. Not good. A mistake. Won't happen again."

But that was not enough for the crowd. Eisner stepped off the stage, leaving Sandy Litvack to field questions about the Ovitz and Eisner payments. As he tried to respond, he was occasionally booed by his listeners. One woman drew applause when she told Litvack, "I feel that you are being arrogant in your answers." When Litvack tried to explain that Eisner had a big job and was being rewarded for the company's overall performance, another shareholder chimed in: "He gets paid more than the president of the United States, and look what he runs!"

There was also applause when a shareholder complained that Disney had "a very inside-type board," and noted that *Business Week* magazine had named Disney's as one of the worst boards at a major corporation. Litvack countered that by any measure, the board was "exemplary."

Ray Watson rose to defend Eisner's contract: "We are not shy about the fact that we have awarded him a contract that says if you are successful and this company is successful, you will be rewarded well."

"I have nothing against Mr. Eisner," one shareholder said politely. "He's done a fine job here at Disney. But it's just a little too lucrative." Not everyone was as pleasant. Another man was applauded when he pressed the idea that Eisner should pay Ovitz's severance out of his own pocket. Litvack replied that Eisner was rewarded on the overall performance of the company. "While Mr. Eisner himself said a mistake was made, overall the record speaks for itself," he said.

Disney scored a lopsided victory when the votes were taken to reelect its board members, with slightly more than 12 percent opposing reappointment. That number was high enough, however, to be considered a significant protest — a shot across Disney's bow. After the voting, Eisner took some more questions from those who had the stamina to remain through the four-hour meeting. Once again, he was pressed about Ovitz. "Be angry, be annoyed," Eisner said. "God knows I am, but there's nothing I can do about it anymore." Another woman argued, "You certainly have high-powered attorneys. . . . Get our money back."

"We honor our commitments," Eisner said.

As to his own pay, he again pointed out that his compensation was tied to the company's performance. "I worked for ten years at ABC with stock options, and when I left, they were worth zero," he said. He and Frank Wells had agreed from the start that they would take lower salaries at Disney and that their reward would be tied to stock performance. "Frank Wells was paid one-fifth of what he would be paid at any other company," Eisner said. "I was paid about half."

No one should assume, he added, that the stock would continue to grow as it had over the past years. "This company may not grow at all," he said. "We've got some problems in prime time. You know what? I wouldn't assume it." It began to seem as though Eisner was getting testy at the ingratitude of those gathered in the arena. "Somehow people have as much trouble dealing with prosperity as they do with failure," he said.

Despite the debate, his pay package was approved by nearly 90 percent. And at the year's end, he exercised 7.3 million options that had been awarded to him in his 1989 contract, giving him a one-day pretax gain of $565 million. He then sold four million shares, netting a profit of $374 million (about $131 million after taxes). It was by far the biggest stock-option gain in corporate history. With the Ovitz debacle more than a year old, Eisner was taking advantage of a period of relative peace at the company — he wouldn't want to panic other shareholders by selling off a large block of stock at a turbulent time. Wall Street reacted calmly. But once again, the pot was stirred among some institutional shareholders. Considering the gains he was realizing from options Eisner had held before renewing his contract, "did he really need options for eight million more shares on top of that?" asked Ann Yerger, director of research services at the Council of Institutional Investors. "There probably is a point where it's past bad taste."

The next year, Disney would hold its annual meeting in Kansas City — far from the madding crowd in Anaheim. The company said it was celebrating the site where Walt began to draw cartoons and was not avoiding shareholders who were once again pressing their case to have a more independent board.

Only about fourteen hundred shareholders showed up for the meeting, compared with the thousands who came to Anaheim. But the discontent with the Disney board clearly had not dissipated. This time, about 35 percent of voting shareholders supported a resolution that called for a more independent board. It was a far higher number than anticipated and close to the record in terms of shareholder support for such a resolution at any company.

Nonetheless, Sandy Litvack said Disney would resist changes sought by unhappy institutional shareholders. He took a conciliatory tone. "We do understand," he said, "that in this area, perceptions are important."

28

SQUARING OFF

ON APRIL 9, 1996, Katzenberg finally sued Disney in California state court, demanding the lump-sum payment—2 percent of the future income from all projects he had put into production—that he said he had been promised. He estimated the number to be in excess of $250 million. His claim took into account more than just box-office and video receipts from films like *Aladdin, Beauty and the Beast,* and *The Lion King.* Katzenberg said the deal included everything from Disney's *Lion King* on Broadway to its Mickey's Toontown attraction to pajama and lunch-box sales from *Pocahontas* and *Toy Story* (which he had put into production) and even a contemplated *Toy Story* sequel.

Eisner had told the *Wall Street Journal* that Disney didn't grant executives a piece of the pie. "It is not the policy of our company that executives have participation" in movie and television projects, he said. It was a strange statement given that Katzenberg had been collecting steadily increasing amounts from his annual 2 percent participation for the past several years. In 1990, with profits stoked by *The Little Mermaid* and *Pretty Woman,* he got a $3.9 million bonus; in 1993, the company paid him another $4.9 million; and in 1994, $7.1 million.

None of this was public, but it seems unlikely that a bonus that had gone from nothing to more than $7 million could have escaped Eisner's notice. In fact, Disney had secretly been keeping a close eye on what Katzenberg's ultimate 2 percent payout might be. But even when he filed his lawsuit, Katzenberg knew nothing about the project to track his projected final bonus.

Katzenberg had agonized for months about whether to file suit. His attorney, Bert Fields, one of Hollywood's most aggressive litigators, had urged him on, but hoping for a breakthrough, Katzenberg kept postponing the final confrontation. (At one point, when Katzenberg was vacationing in

Africa, he took a satellite phone call from Ovitz, who pleaded with him not to file on the date that Disney was finalizing its merger with ABC in January 1996.) He held off. When he sued in April, Fields gave several interviews in which he put the blame squarely on Eisner. "If Frank Wells were alive, this would never have happened," he said.

But the court papers contained no provocative rhetoric. Eisner called Katzenberg and thanked him. If in the end Katzenberg won, he said, he would promptly write him a check—no matter how big. But Eisner took the position that Katzenberg had forfeited any payments when he opted out of his contract in 1994 rather than remaining for another two years.

The litigation soon became a game of leak and counterleak. Well before the suit had been filed, Katzenberg's camp had let it be known that there might be a memo written by Frank Wells assuring Katzenberg of his share in the profit even if he opted out of his contract in 1994. And in the weeks leading up to the trial, Fields conceded that Eisner may not have been aware that such a deal had been struck. "It's possible Michael didn't really understand the impact of Jeffrey's contract," he said. "Frank wanted things to function smoothly, and he probably didn't think Jeffrey would leave anyway. He may have done what agents sometimes do. He may have told both sides what they wanted to hear, using enough ambiguity to keep the operation working well. So each guy thinks his needs have been met. Because Frank managed Michael, and after all, Frank thought he'd always be there to make it come out all right."

As time went on, however, Fields abandoned this position. If someone had to be depicted as playing fast and loose with facts, it wasn't going to be Wells. It made a better story to say that Wells had negotiated with Katzenberg in good faith. Eisner—alive and defiant—made a much better villain.

⟡

ALONG THE WAY to trial, Disney lost some major legal skirmishes. In June, Katzenberg forced the company to disclose some financial data. But this turned out to be something of a Pyrrhic victory because Disney filed documents showing a dismal performance of its live-action slate under Katzenberg. Now the public was informed that *Billy Bathgate* had lost $55.9 million, while the musical *Newsies* lost $42.8 million. *Blame It on the Bellboy* lost $10.8 million and *Passed Away* went nearly $19 million into the hole. Katzenberg responded that those numbers were misleading because they didn't include money from foreign release or video.

The documents also purported to show that though Disney had profited hugely from rereleases of animated classics (a 1992 release of *Fantasia* brought in $184.4 million, for example), the new animated films, such as *Beauty and the Beast*, had barely kept the overall movie slate profitable.

Then in September, Disney made a bid to have the court oust Katzenberg's legal team. This relatively rare and hostile move was based on Disney's contention that Helene Hahn, the former Disney business-affairs executive and attorney who now worked at DreamWorks, had obtained a memo from another former Disney executive that was a "road map" to Disney's internal accounting practices. The memo purportedly outlined ways that Disney might have hidden profits to reduce the company's potential obligation to Katzenberg. Disney complained that this information was ill-gotten, and tainted all of Katzenberg's lawyers. Fields argued that the memo included no secret or stolen information, and revealed nothing that he didn't already know. The judge agreed.

Fields also revealed that Katzenberg's attorneys had logged nine thousand expensive hours on the case thus far. Considering that Katzenberg had mortgaged himself to start DreamWorks—and with Fields alone known to charge $750 an hour—the litigation was proving to be an especially big pain in the wallet.

Much of the material in the lawsuit was under seal, but a smattering of documents was made public in September 1997. Among them was an excerpt from a deposition of Eisner that had been taken by Katzenberg attorney Herbert Wachtell. The snippet indicated that Katzenberg's team was angling to confirm that Disney had tried to conceal some profits that might have been due to Katzenberg. Wachtell asked Eisner about a secret operation called "Project Snowball." Eisner replied that he had no knowledge of "some secret project called Project Snowball."

"Were you aware that there was a secret project going on under Frank Wells's aegis stimulated by the fact that Mr. Katzenberg's 2 percent in 1990 started to run at far higher levels than previously anticipated?" Wachtell asked.

"No," Eisner said, "because I would say that I doubt whether a project was put into work stimulated by the fact that his 2 percent was higher than anticipated."

Nothing further was revealed publicly about Project Snowball at the time. But there had been a "very confidential" project, according to former Disney employee Cheryl Fellows, who worked on it starting in January 1991 (Snowball was already under way at the time and its exact start date remains murky). Fellows was instructed to keep this aspect of her work, aimed at tallying the ultimate value of Katzenberg's final bonus, secret even from Katzenberg. And if Eisner had never heard of it, it was not because Frank Wells hadn't kept him in the loop. Wells had sent at least two memos to Eisner with "Project Snowball" written on every page. Fellows had also briefed Eisner on the project.

∽

AS KATZENBERG'S ATTORNEYS probed the fraud issue, they got some encouragement from a ruling in a separate case. In 1989, Eisner had fallen in love with a European cartoon character, Marsupilami, during a trip to Europe. Disney bought the rights to the character, which was unusual because the company preferred to develop its own cartoon figures. But the U.S. District Court for Central California found that Disney had broken its promises about making Marsupilami a star in the United States. (For example, the company made no effort to put him on television.)

The court ruled that Disney executives had engaged in "fraudulent concealment" of their plans to drop the European cartoon. According to Marsu attorney Patricia Glaser, there were memos "up the wazoo" proving that Disney deliberately broke its word. Eisner was copied on these memos, although he claimed in his testimony that he was all but ignorant of Marsupilami's fate. Finding that Disney had "knowingly and in bad faith failed to perform its contractual duties," the court socked the company with a $10.3 million judgment. "We made a valiant effort to settle this beforehand for less than [the judgment]," Glaser said. "Disney did not respond with a remotely respectable number."

And just a few weeks before the Katzenberg trial was to begin in November 1997, as a team of judges was scrambling to negotiate some kind of settlement, Fields was trying another suit against Disney. This one was brought by MGM, which was still trying to recover from the deal it made years earlier when it licensed its name to Disney for use at its theme parks in Florida and elsewhere. According to the deal, if Disney failed to develop an MGM attraction in any territory within nine years, the rights would revert to MGM. Now nine years were up and MGM said Disney had forfeited the right to use its name outside of Florida. MGM's attorneys were surprised that Disney had never asked for an extension of the nine-year deadline. When MGM approached Disney to resolve the matter, Sandy Litvack repeatedly rebuffed the company. When the issue went to court, Disney argued that it still retained its claim to use the MGM name in Western Europe because it had spent $100 million or more designing various MGM-related attractions for Disneyland Paris. MGM countered that preparing a plan wasn't the same as developing an attraction. On November 5, the jury rejected Disney's argument and MGM salvaged something from a bad piece of business.

∞

OVER THE COURSE of several months in 1997, Katzenberg scored a major blow. After a series of skirmishes, he forced Eisner to turn over notes for a book about his experiences in business. The book, written with the help of former journalist Tony Schwartz, had long been in the works. Now it was scheduled for publication in October, just a month before the start date in the Katzenberg case. (Eventually, Eisner delayed the book so that it wouldn't be published so close to the trial.) The project was dear to Eisner's heart. Just days after Katzenberg had filed his suit in April 1996, Eisner and his wife had attended a Random House sales conference in Scottsdale, Arizona, to give a pep talk to sales personnel. After his talk, he went from table to table, chatting up the crowd.

At first, Disney claimed the notes were irrelevant to the Katzenberg case. Eisner even testified in a deposition that the book only covered events through his heart surgery. (By the time it was published, however, it went further than that.) But under pressure from Katzenberg's legal team, the company started to produce some material. These disclosures provided Katzenberg with powerful ammunition against Eisner—material seemingly so damaging that Katzenberg and his attorneys might have expected Eisner to go to considerable lengths to prevent it from getting into the public record.

∞

DISNEY AND KATZENBERG had agreed that the case would be split in two parts. First, there would be a trial to determine whether Disney owed Katzenberg any money at all. If the answer was yes, then there would be an arbitration to determine the amount. The trial was set for November 17.

All over Hollywood, executives were praying that the suit would not be settled, as seemed inevitable in a situation like this. A courtroom brawl between Katzenberg and Eisner could be far more entertaining to Hollywood than any film that was in production. There was hope that Disney might be forced to open its books and that all manner of linen would be laundered. The Los Angeles Superior Court was being besieged with media requests for passes to the trial. Court TV requested permission to broadcast it live.

As the start date approached, the rhetoric got hotter. The *New York Observer* reported that Disney had taken depositions from Spielberg and Geffen. "Both Katzenberg and DreamWorks will go on trial," boasted a Disney source. "We're going to put David and Steven on the witness stand and conduct an examination of their company as well." It was unclear how relevant such an examination would be to Katzenberg's claim, but Disney was rattling its saber, threatening to prove that any of DreamWorks successes came from Geffen and Spielberg, and not from Katzenberg. Nor was Katzenberg making much money, the Disney camp hinted, because the principals had delayed taking profits out of the company for several years.

DreamWorks—or someone—struck back by leaking a report to *Variety* that two mock juries assembled by Katzenberg's legal team had ruled in his favor. The Wells memo was said to be a significant factor in their reasoning. The report came on the same day that attorneys returned to court for a mandatory settlement conference—the last step before trial was to begin. A DreamWorks insider maintained that the pretrial exercises showed that jurors were inclined to dislike Disney as a corporation and Eisner as an individual. "The only reason that they don't dislike Jeffrey," a Disney lawyer quipped in response, "is they don't know him well enough."

∽

JUDGE JOHN OUDERKIRK had been laboring mightily to bring the parties to a meeting of the minds. Two of his associates, Owen Kwong and Enrique Romero, had been working all along to effect a resolution. Sometimes, when Fields emerged from his then-ongoing MGM trial versus Disney, Judge Romero would be sitting outside his courtroom, encouraging him to be "flexible." The court ordered the parties to meet repeatedly but they made no progress.

On Halloween evening—a Friday night—the adversaries gathered in the Intercontinental Hotel in downtown Los Angeles. In a last-ditch effort to reach a settlement, the court insisted that Eisner and Katzenberg sit down together. They had barely spoken since their rupture in 1994. Both sides were clinging to their own analyses of how much the 2 percent payment was worth and they were about $200 million apart. Their respective positions still seemed irreconcilable.

Eisner and Katzenberg met late in the day, and within a few minutes, they started arguing about money. Eisner not only rejected Katzenberg's math but said he couldn't get the board—especially Roy Disney—to approve the type of payment that Katzenberg was demanding.

Katzenberg was enraged. Angry words poured from his mouth. He could not remember ever speaking to Eisner like this throughout their years together. If members of the board wouldn't approve the payment, he asked, who had poisoned their minds? Eisner was responsible. He didn't give a damn about Eisner's problems with the board. Katzenberg would see Eisner in court. With that, he walked out.

Katzenberg returned to the suite where his attorneys were waiting. The meeting with Eisner was a failure, he told them. They talked about the upcoming trial for about an hour and then adjourned for the night.

But as Katzenberg waited for the valet to bring his black Mustang, he noticed that Eisner's car and driver were still in front of the hotel. If Eisner was going to trial, Katzenberg reasoned, he would have been long gone.

Sure enough, before Katzenberg's lawyers had left, Sandy Litvack approached Bert Fields in the lobby. Finally it was time to talk.

On Monday, November 7, Hollywood learned the disappointing news. Ten days before the trial was to begin, the parties announced a "partial settlement." Without admitting that it owed Katzenberg anything, Disney agreed to pay him 72.5 percent of the 2 percent bonus. When it came to figuring that sum, however, the two parties were still oceans apart. They had agreed to a trial before a referee who would come up with the final tally.

Disney also agreed to pay Katzenberg $117 million. Of that sum, $77 million would be a down payment against the final figure. The remaining $40 million would buy out his claims to profits from the merchandise based on his film and television productions. It would not count against the lump sum to be designated by the referee.

At the time, these payments were kept confidential. Disney appeared to have caved on Katzenberg's claim that he was owed money. What no one knew yet was that the company had agreed to cough up a minimum of $117 million. Considering that Katzenberg at one time would have settled for as little as $90 million, Disney had already sustained a serious blow. But there wasn't so much as a rumor about the payment, and for Disney, the silence was almost as good as not having to pay at all.

Disney had every intention of keeping its secrets. Both sides agreed that the trial before the referee would not be open to the public. In the wake of the Ovitz debacle, no doubt, Eisner was not eager to write Katzenberg a big check and face the wrath of his shareholders. But if the matter could be decided in a closed chamber—with an agreement that the sum be kept quiet—he could tell the public that he had fought to the bitter end and finally paid the least amount that he could in the circumstances.

∾

WHILE KATZENBERG WAGED war, the seemingly unsinkable Disney moved into one of the roughest patches it had hit in years. Everything seemed to go awry.

In September 1996, Disney had announced that it was not only taking on the cruise business, but would improve it. The company had been so confident that it could sail easily into these waters that it had handed out countdown watches that ticked off the minutes until the first ship's scheduled launch in early 1998.

But the $350 million *Disney Magic* ran into expensive delays. Instead of launching that spring, the ship's first forty sailings had to be canceled. The company offered 50 percent discounts to travelers whose trips were postponed twice, and 25 percent discounts to those who had a trip pushed back only once. Those who canceled got refunds and the company had to pay the commissions for travel agents. Disney also had to pay the crew that had been hired for the original launch date.

Disney blamed the delays on the ship's Italian builder, Fincantieri Cantieri Navali Italiani SpA. Fincantieri acknowledged problems keeping up with demand in the burgeoning cruise-ship business, but Disney competitors at the Carnival cruise line scoffed at the idea that the builder really was to blame. The real problem, they suggested, was Disney, which constantly changed its specifications. After the second delay, some Italian workers began to criticize Disney. Gianni Alassio, chief of engineering for the Italian firm Demont Srl, said Disney had insisted on adding pipe supports and new welds, requiring some areas of the ship to be redone four or five times. "They are too meticulous about unimportant things," Alassio complained. "Maybe Disney is not ready to work on ships."

Though most companies sent half a dozen executives to monitor construction, Disney had sent more than a hundred people to Italy. "We've
probably driven them nuts," said Robert Collins, one of Disney's specialists.
But he said the goal was perfection, which takes time. Workers at the site
came up with a new name for the *Disney Magic*: the *Disney Tragic*. Its
sister ship, the *Disney Wonder*—set to launch in 1999—was dubbed the
Disney Blunder.

As usual, Eisner had been immersed in the design details. He wanted
the *Disney Magic* to be a ship in the tradition of the grand ocean liners.
There was to be a fifteen-foot Goofy hanging from the stern, and the company wanted the whole ship to be color-coordinated. Disney wanted the
lifeboats to be yellow, requiring the company to get a special exemption
from international rules requiring them to be orange. Disney's insistence
on a long, slender hull also meant twenty fewer passenger cabins than most
cruise ships hold.

There would be two smokestacks—one purely for looks—that would
weigh down the ship and possibly render it unstable. Fincantieri contracted
for special lightweight fiberglass shells for the smokestacks, upping the cost.
When Disney decided to scrap plans for a casino and instead install a
country-music dance area, the change required more than a hundred new
detailed drawings. Meanwhile, Visions In Scale, a Florida-based firm, sent
artists who put in ten-hour days for weeks hand-painting ceiling panels to
create the effect of wood branches for one of the ship's restaurants.

Travel expert Arthur Frommer noted that Disney's prices were higher
than its competitors' and questioned whether that would hurt business. Most
families of four traveling during vacation times would have to pay about
$5,600 for a Disney cruise, Frommer said, while a comparable trip on the
Carnival line would cost about $4,098.

The ship finally sailed on July 30, 1998, well after most families had
taken their vacations and the hurricane season was only weeks away.

∽

DISNEY HAD OPENED its new Animal Kingdom park in Orlando during the summer of 1998, but only after so many animals died that the federal
government launched an investigation (Disney was cleared of wrongdoing).
At first, the Animal Kingdom was cannibalizing other Disney attractions in
the area at a much higher rate than anticipated. Families weren't staying
longer so they could spend time at each attraction, but merely paid shorter

visits to each park. "They did not get the lift that they had anticipated," said PaineWebber analyst Christopher Dixon. Within a year, however, Disney added an Asian extension to the original African display. The theme parks became the most vibrant sector of a troubled company.

In September, Disney warned that its fourth-quarter profits would reflect a 31 percent drop over the previous year and that profit for fiscal 1998 would be up only slightly over 1997. The stock had dropped 43 percent from its high in April because most Wall Street analysts had cut their future profit estimates and downgraded their recommendations on the company.

One reason for the company's disappointing results was the film studio. Disney had released a string of losers like *Krippendorf's Tribe* and *Holy Man*, the Eddie Murphy bomb. Even its big summer movie, *Armageddon*, had been so expensive that it couldn't make up for the other flops. Now Disney was cutting back on the number of films it put out each year, and the Hollywood Pictures label was effectively folded.

ABC also presented an ongoing problem. Naturally, Eisner had plunged in when Disney acquired the network, undoubtedly expecting to replicate his earlier success in programming. "Here's a guy who left network television in 1977 but who had a strong love for it," says Ted Harbert, who was head of programming when Disney bought ABC. "So a certain exuberance would be expected. He certainly has passionate opinions on all sorts of subjects, from the quality of a program to a particular actor to the business deal. Michael can talk about a show all day, which is great. But we didn't always agree. His management style is to make you prove your case, not just once but two or three times, and to chip away at his resistance. Occasionally that was frustrating, but in hindsight, I understand it. Sometimes I wondered, 'How does the chairman of the board of the huge company get involved in this level of minutiae?' But that's what he did."

Eisner promptly reinstated Disney's Sunday-night movie even though it had never made money for the network. For Eisner, reinforcing Disney's brand name with a regular network show—and using the program to promote the theme parks—was too good an opportunity to pass up. Although Harbert vigorously resisted giving up valuable Sunday-night real estate to the Disney show, lobbying instead to put it on Saturday nights, Eisner wouldn't hear of it. More Americans were sitting in front of their televisions on Sunday nights and Eisner wanted the Disney show to occupy that space, even if it meant taking the slot away from the eroding but still viable *America's Funniest Home Videos*. The new Disney show performed erratically.

Overall, Eisner's frame of reference was some twenty years out of date. There was a lot of eyeball rolling among some at ABC as Eisner continually alluded to *Happy Days*, *The Mod Squad*, and *Charlie's Angels*—all of which had debuted in the seventies. Eisner clearly was unfamiliar with the current schedules of other networks. In fact, the entire business had changed considerably in ways that he did not seem to understand. "I had the rather difficult task of reeducating him—how ridiculous the deals had become, star salaries, license fees, terms of deals," says Harbert. "He was quite appropriately shocked and upset about it. He felt that we couldn't make the same mistakes everybody else did. He didn't want to play ball the same way other players do."

While the other networks had started to push for more ownership in programs that they put on the air, Eisner thought that was an unnecessary risk—that this was "spending money for failure," as Harbert put it. He was content to let outside production companies spend their money developing new material, even though they would reap the bulk of the profit if there was any. But within a couple of years, Disney would start to see the wisdom of the other networks' strategy. It began to negotiate with producers for a stake in some shows.

Eisner also vetoed the idea of doing a costly program with *Cheers* star Ted Danson—which may have been a good call. DreamWorks subsequently failed expensively with the short-lived *Ink*. Eisner declined to do a show with another *Cheers* veteran, Kirstie Alley. She went on to do *Veronica's Closet* for NBC, a show that performed disappointingly even though it was given the desirable spot behind *Seinfeld*.

Eisner's level of involvement was a huge contrast from the management style of former Capital Cities/ABC chiefs Dan Burke and Tom Murphy, who gave their programming executives considerable autonomy. Eisner was hands-on and still sticking to his old credo, insisting that the network find new talent rather than pay top dollar for established names. "He said, 'Go make your own stars,' " remembers Harbert.

Harbert says Eisner's opinions were "valid and credible." But nothing seemed to pull ABC out of its doldrums as ratings dipped to historic lows. Even *Good Morning America*, the network's most profitable news show, wasn't having such good mornings anymore. The program, which had dominated from 1985 through 1995, had lost more than 25 percent of its viewers. Estimates showed that for the first half of 1998, the rival *Today* show—with the engaging team of Katie Couric and Matt Lauer—pulled in about $117 million for NBC, while the once stronger *Good Morning America* earned only about $77 million in the same period.

Eisner often argued that ESPN threw off such great profits that the cable service alone, with its famous brand name, made the Capital Cities/ABC acquisition worthwhile. But some questioned whether ESPN could sustain its momentum considering the staggering sums Disney had paid for contracts with the National Football League and National Hockey League.

Disney agreed in January 1998 to pay a record $9.2 billion for the eight-year rights to television football games. And in August 1998, even with the NHL's television ratings dropping, Disney anted up $600 million for a five-year contract. The amount was more than two and a half times what Fox Sports and ESPN had previously paid. Steven Bornstein, then president of ESPN and ABC Sports, predicted that Disney could boost ratings and increase ad rates. But this seemed like a tough promise to keep.

Even if ABC broadcast the maximum number of hockey games allowed by the contract, the network would have to charge $50,000 for each commercial just to break even. But advertising sources said Fox had been able to get $45,000 for commercials only once, for a Stanley Cup finals game, and had accepted much less for regular-season matches. "Maybe Disney knows something we don't know," said Ron Frederick, a media buyer at the J. Walter Thompson advertising agency. "On the face of it, it looks like too much money." In football, 1998 brought a ratings slump and *Monday Night Football* limped to an embarrassing finish of the season with the lowest ratings in the show's twenty-nine-year history.

Other problems included the Asian economic slump, which hurt sales of Disney merchandise abroad. And there were fears—groundless, at least for the near term—that the U.S. economy could falter, hurting business at the theme parks. Not only could attendance slip, but a tough economy could make it difficult for Disney to raise ticket prices—the very tactic that had helped its profits reach such dazzling heights after Eisner took over in 1984.

∞

THE REVOLVING DOOR at Disney seemed to be spinning all the time. Peter Rummell, the head of the real estate division who had taken over Imagineering, had left in January 1997 after an eleven-year run, to run

St. Joe Corp., a real estate concern. He was just one of many. Eisner increasingly surrounded himself with a certain type of employee and often style seemed as important as substance. "Michael has what he thinks of as the image of a successful executive," says one former Disney insider. "Six feet tall, guys that look great in suits, that are well read, calm, eloquent. That's what fits his image."

Eisner also became more isolated than ever. On one hand, he had devoted himself to building the company. He had merged his identity with Disney's, so that what was good for the company was good for him, and vice versa. But like many powerful men, he didn't want to look seriously at the company's well-being beyond his own presence there. And Disney was, with the possible exception of Rupert Murdoch's News Corp., the major media company most identified with its chairman and chief executive. Michael Eisner was one of the most famous CEOs in the world.

In a couple of years, Disney lost chief financial officer Steve Bollenbach as well as his successor, Richard Nanula; head of strategic planning Larry Murphy, who had been at such bitter odds with Katzenberg; and Geraldine Laybourne, head of cable programming. ABC executive Steve Burke—who had been seen as a particular favorite of Eisner's—left for the cable company Comcast. Burke, the son of former Capital Cities/ABC owner Dan Burke, had turned down the opportunity to be president of ABC, and his resignation was perceived as an especially severe blow—seen by some television veterans as a no-confidence vote in the future of ABC and the network business generally, as well as a sign of doubt about his own future at Disney.

"The brain drain is pretty serious," commented one of the many who left in recent years. "This is a huge, global brand that has to come to grips with the concept that this guy's not going to live forever. In concept, it's such a great company that they attract very talented executives quite easily. The difficulty comes with keeping them. Because for Michael Eisner, it's all about being able to stay there forever."

∞

IN SEPTEMBER 1998, Eisner's autobiography, *Work in Progress*, was published. It was an ill-timed and ill-starred endeavor. Not only was the company having its most serious problems in years, but the nation was obsessed with the Monica Lewinsky scandal. (The book was to have been excerpted as the cover story of *Newsweek*, but the magazine changed its plans when the House of Representatives rushed to vote for an impeachment inquiry.)

Why the usually pessimistic Eisner even considered writing his own biography while still sitting as the chairman of Disney almost defied explanation. It was completely out of character—or it showed how much the Disney chief had changed over the years.

Although a friend said the final version of the book was "sanitized," the Katzenberg camp was furious. Katzenberg's allies had been assured by Eisner that Katzenberg was not mentioned, but a glance at the index showed more than twenty-five references to him. He was portrayed as jealous of Eisner, and increasingly secretive and uncooperative.

The book received lukewarm reviews from critics who found its lack of introspection unsatisfying. The *Los Angeles Times* said those looking for tantalizing morsels would "undoubtedly find the book a yawn." The *New York Times* said some of Eisner's descriptions of events were "so calculatingly self-serving that they lack[ed] both credibility and nuance." His ego, the *Times* concluded, "leaves little room for perspective."

The book didn't sell well. Within a few months, it was clear that the book had been a grotesque miscalculation for Eisner. It was an expensive mistake in every sense of the word.

∽

WHILE DISNEY WAS suffering, DreamWorks wasn't exactly flourishing. With much hoopla, the company had announced its plans to be the anchor in a partnership that would build a 1,087-acre, ultra-high-tech, $8 billion community in Playa Vista, near the Los Angeles airport. DreamWorks intended to construct fifteen soundstages on the barren site where Howard Hughes had built his *Spruce Goose* seaplane. But the project bogged down in battles with the developer and warfare with environmentalists. It became an ongoing distraction for the DreamWorks partners.

While the struggle over Playa Vista dragged on, the company continued to be based on the Universal lot, where Spielberg's Amblin offices were located. Set on a shady corner redolent of eucalyptus, Amblin was housed in low-slung adobe buildings. (Some in the industry had been known to call the complex "the Taco Bell stand.") But Amblin couldn't hold all the DreamWorks employees, who at one point were working in nine separate locations in Southern California, from Beverly Hills to the suburb of Glendale. By 1998, the company completed a large animation complex in Glendale, across the street from Disney's Imagineering facilities. Still, DreamWorkers were scattered in four different sites. This was hardly the studio that Spielberg had envisioned.

DreamWorks didn't exactly blast out of the box with big hits. Its first television comedy, *Champs*, was short-lived. The drama *High Incident* failed to catch fire and *Ink* flopped. Only *Spin City*, a comedy starring Michael J. Fox, performed well in the company's first five years.

Katzenberg had been confident that he could sweep into DreamWorks and take over live-action film from Walter Parkes and Laurie MacDonald, the married couple who had been running Spielberg's Amblin. But Katzenberg underestimated Spielberg's loyalty to the pair. It soon became clear that initially, at least, Katzenberg's primary roles would be in television and animation.

The fledgling company's first live-action film, *The Peacemaker*, was a thriller starring George Clooney and Nicole Kidman. Its director, Mimi Leder, was a Spielberg protégée who had directed several episodes of *E.R.*, the hit television show that Spielberg coproduced. *The Peacemaker* was Leder's debut in feature films. But the project—bogged down with production difficulties in Eastern Europe—turned out to be a rather routine thriller. It turned in a lackluster box-office performance. *Mouse Hunt*, a comedy starring Nathan Lane and a menacing rodent, did better but was hardly a breakaway hit.

DreamWorks finally hit pay dirt in 1997 with *Deep Impact*, the second effort from Mimi Leder. The tale of the earth imperiled by asteroids grossed $141 million, but DreamWorks had to split the pot with Paramount, which cofinanced the movie. DreamWorks' other summer film, *Small Soldiers*, disappointed. Its domestic gross of $53 million failed to cover even the estimated marketing cost of $60 million, not to mention the $60 million budget.

Spielberg's first directing effort under the DreamWorks banner seemed to suffer from some kind of curse. Spielberg wanted to make a seminal film about the Middle Passage, but *Amistad* became embroiled in an ugly battle with novelist Barbara Chase-Riboud. Just before the film opened, she sued claiming that material from one of her books, *Echo of Lions*, had been appropriated.

Screenwriter David Franzoni—who claimed he had never read her book—had pitched a project based on the novel to Warner several years earlier. Many industry observers thought that DreamWorks handled the case badly, charging through attorney Bert Fields that Chase-Riboud was simply out to "grab money for herself." It seemed a ham-fisted approach at best, particularly given the awkwardness of Franzoni's position.

The case was settled the day before the Oscar nominations were announced in 1998. Chase-Riboud proclaimed Spielberg's innocence in the matter but some in Hollywood felt that the damage had been done. Others argued that *Amistad* simply didn't work, either artistically or as entertainment. The film lost money, grossing only $44 million, and failed to garner the major Oscar nominations that the DreamWorks partners had hoped to receive. Spielberg returned his director's fee to the company.

Spielberg, who took the film's failure hard, was rumored to have blamed Katzenberg for failing to resolve the litigation before it damaged the film. Katzenberg said he was willing "to be the focal point of whatever second-guessing might go on." But talk of a rift between Spielberg and Katzenberg continued to drift through the entertainment community. And DreamWorks seemed increasingly to be a conflicted committee of three men with varying agendas. Spielberg seemed primarily interested in making movies, not struggling with the difficulties of starting a big business. Geffen, many in the industry assumed, would have been happy to sell the company and call it a day. Only Katzenberg had everything to lose if DreamWorks didn't live up to its initial promise.

Finally, in the summer of 1998, DreamWorks got some good news in the form of Spielberg's summer film, *Saving Private Ryan*. The company had to share the project with Paramount, which owned the script. As part of the deal, DreamWorks had also agreed to share *Deep Impact*, another Paramount property that had intrigued Spielberg. The deal was that one of the films would be issued in the U.S. under the Paramount label and distributed internationally by DreamWorks; the other would bear the DreamWorks label domestically. The question of which studio would release which film was resolved by a high-level coin toss. Sumner Redstone, the cagey septuagenarian chairman of Paramount's parent company, Viacom, met with Spielberg at the Beverly Hills Hotel, the pink palace on Sunset Boulevard.

DreamWorks was desperate to get domestic handling of *Saving Private Ryan*, because Spielberg would direct the film himself. Not only were there commercial considerations, but there was the embarrassment of having

Spielberg directing under Paramount's banner when he had done only one film for DreamWorks—and an unsuccessful one, at that.

Spielberg had a premonition that tails would win. He hoped Redstone would toss the coin so he could make the call. But Redstone, perhaps sensing something about Spielberg's premonition, wouldn't allow it. He insisted that Spielberg toss the coin while he called. To Spielberg's relief, Redstone called heads. It was tails. DreamWorks ended up with *Private Ryan* under its banner in the U.S.

Saving Private Ryan was a gritty World War II film that nearly earned an NC-17 rating. (Spielberg personally appealed to the Motion Picture Association's ratings board for an R, which would make *Private Ryan* commercially viable. He pledged that he would personally campaign to make the public aware of the film's realistic violence.) Though the studio defied conventional wisdom by opening a film with extremely serious subject matter in the summer popcorn season, *Saving Private Ryan* was a major hit. It brought DreamWorks the kind of commercial and critical success that Katzenberg had craved for years. The film grossed $216 million domestically, eclipsing Disney's costly *Armageddon* as the top box-office contender of 1998. Foreign box office added another $262.8 million. Now all DreamWorks had to do was sweep the Oscars.

∞

IT WAS UP to Katzenberg to prove that he could contribute to DreamWorks with his first animated production. *The Prince of Egypt*, the story of Moses, was an idea that had arisen in early conversations with Geffen and Spielberg about the new company. Spielberg had talked about doing a film with the majesty of *The Ten Commandments* and the three locked onto the idea of the Moses story.

If they had understood what a challenge the project would be, they might have made a different choice. Early on, it became apparent that typical animation gags would not fit into a story as significant as the Moses tale. The film would have to be entertaining yet serious enough to deal with subject matter like the slaying of the firstborn.

Katzenberg went into a frenzy of consultation with scholars and clergymen from the Jewish, Christian, and Muslim communities, ostensibly to gain their advice but also to win their support. He even visited the Vatican. The last thing DreamWorks needed was to have *Prince of Egypt* turn into a lightning rod for controversy.

Val Kilmer supplied the voice of Moses and Ralph Fiennes was Ramses. Sandra Bullock, Michelle Pfeiffer, Jeff Goldblum, Steve Martin, Martin Short, Danny Glover, and Patrick Stewart also starred. The songs were composed by Stephen Schwartz and the score was provided by Hans Zimmer — both Oscar winners.

The nature of the film also meant that DreamWorks could forget about lucrative tie-ins and merchandising opportunities. After extensive discussions with Burger King, the parties concluded that Moses-related meals were out — as were burning-bush nightlights.

Katzenberg toiled relentlessly to make *The Prince of Egypt* into a major creative and commercial contribution to DreamWorks. Perhaps more importantly, this was his chance to answer Disney. No studio had ever succeeded in touching Disney when it came to releasing a major family-oriented animated feature. Many had tried. Fox had released the expensively hyped *Anastasia*, which had grossed $58.4 million. The film had cost far more than that to make and market. Warner had failed entirely with films like *Cats Don't Dance* and *Quest for Camelot*.

Meanwhile, Katzenberg became convinced that Eisner was trying to thwart *Prince of Egypt* any way he knew how. Originally, the film was to be released in November 1998, but Disney scheduled its *A Bug's Life* against it. *A Bug's Life* was the second effort from Disney's co-venture with Pixar, which had created *Toy Story*.

Disney had completely underestimated what a hit it would have in *Toy Story*. At one point animation chief Peter Schneider was said to have asked Katzenberg to pull the plug on the movie. But Disney was $7 million into the film at the time, and Katzenberg declined. (It ultimately cost $22 million.) Schneider appealed to Roy Disney, who asked Eisner to look into the matter. Eisner bounced the issue back to Katzenberg, suggesting again that he cancel the film. But *Toy Story* turned into a $192 million hit. Disney reaped huge profits, though the company was caught off guard without toys and other merchandise to sell. Now Disney was expecting great things from *A Bug's Life* and its merchandising deals and McDonald's meals were all in place. Apparently, Katzenberg was nervous about the competition. He moved *Prince of Egypt* into December 1998.

Disney promptly moved *Mighty Joe Young*, the story of a giant ape on the loose in New York, from summer of 1998 to December — putting the big beast head-to-head with Moses. While the studio insisted that the move

had been contemplated well before DreamWorks changed the date for
Prince of Egypt, Katzenberg didn't buy it.

Katzenberg had another card to play. Steve Jobs, who headed Pixar, had
accused him of stealing the idea for *Antz*—a DreamWorks film scheduled
for release after *Prince of Egypt*, in March 1999. Like Disney's *A Bug's Life*,
set for release months earlier in November 1998, *Antz* was the computer-
animated story of life in an ant colony. The film featured the voices of
Woody Allen and Sharon Stone. Pixar had presented the idea for *A Bug's
Life* to Disney just as Katzenberg was leaving the studio. But Katzenberg
insisted that he hadn't heard of it then and that the idea for *Antz* came
later from Nina Jacobson, a DreamWorks executive, who said she was inspired by watching a documentary about ants. (Jacobs, who had left
DreamWorks for Disney by the time *Antz* was completed, confirmed Katzenberg's account.)

Katzenberg made a schedule change. *Prince of Egypt* was to have been
DreamWorks' first animated release. But he decided to leapfrog *Antz* over
A Bug's Life. Instead of opening in March 1999, *Antz* now debuted in
October 1998—just a few weeks before Disney's similarly themed film. It
required some sacrifice: DreamWorks lost out on the chance to have a
Burger King tie-in by moving up the film, because such efforts must be
planned many months in advance.

Katzenberg denied that he moved up *Antz* to take business away from
A Bug's Life. Publicly at least, Disney said it was unfazed by the
DreamWorks change in scheduling. Both statements were equally credible.

The tough question for Katzenberg was how to sell *Antz*. The film—
with its Woody Allen brand of humor—seemed more likely to appeal to
adults than to children. But few adults were likely to go to a cartoon. If
DreamWorks could pull off the opening of *Antz*, Katzenberg hoped, it
might pave the way for *Prince of Egypt*, which was also not exactly kiddie
fare.

On its first weekend, *Antz* was number one at the box office with an
$18 million gross—the highest-ever opening number for the first weekend
in October. The following weekend, *Antz* held on to the top spot, deci-
mating Disney's new comedy, *Holy Man*, starring Eddie Murphy. Debuting
in fifth place at $5.3 million, *Holy Man* was one of the worst openings of
Murphy's career. DreamWorks basked in the number-one spot with its first
animated film—a movie that would briefly break the record for an ani-

mation effort from any studio other than Disney. Taking in $91 million, the film even passed the grosses of *The Little Mermaid*.

Despite his brief victory, Katzenberg would have to settle for half a loaf. *The Prince of Egypt* simply failed to catch fire the way he had hoped it would. (Not that Disney's *Mighty Joe Young* turned out to be much of a threat; the ape didn't perform at the box office.) *Prince of Egypt* wasn't a failure: it finally crawled to a domestic gross of $101 million, edging out Paramount's *Rugrats* to become the top non-Disney animated feature of all time. (Internationally, *Prince of Egypt* grossed another $125 million.) But it was hardly the blockbuster event Katzenberg had hoped it would be. The movie lacked sparkle and the heartland filmgoers whom he had hoped to capture didn't show up.

Despite *Prince of Egypt*'s respectable gross, *Rugrats* was far more profitable. No one, with the exception of a handful of insiders, knew what *Prince of Egypt* had really cost. But certainly no one believed the $75 million figure that the company floated.

Even so, DreamWorks had managed to make a mark. *Private Ryan* was the top film of the year; *Antz* and *Deep Impact* were hits. But no studio could survive on the profits from live-action features. The company's television division wasn't performing especially well. And the company's animation-dependent business plan seemed to be in trouble. An insider predicted with confidence in early 1999 that the company would have to make drastic changes to stay alive.

∽

CONTRARY TO EXPECTATIONS, *A Bug's Life* did not suffer because of the earlier release of *Antz*. The picture soared to an international gross of more than $300 million. Disney scored more hits at the end of 1998 with Will Smith in *Enemy of the State* and Adam Sandler's *The Waterboy*. But these successes came too late to save the company's performance for the fiscal year. In his annual letter to shareholders, Eisner took the unusual step of singling out the live-action unit for criticism. "We're glad fiscal '98 is over in this area," he said.

The end of the year was indeed a sobering time for Disney and its leader. While the market was down overall, Disney's stock continued to slump and many analysts didn't see a quick turnaround. Not since the Euro Disney debacle had the company faced such a difficult time. The options held by top executives had literally lost tens of millions of dollars in value. Michael

Ovitz's famous settlement, once valued at about $200 million, had dropped in value to about $50 million.

In November, the New York Times reported that because of internal concerns and worries about the global economy, "disillusionment" with Disney was such that the longtime favorite had actually been supplanted by Time Warner as the darling of Wall Street. At the time, perhaps, Eisner could not have imagined any more painful comparison. Only a few years earlier, Time Warner had been perceived as debt-laden, ungainly, and deeply committed to a bad bet in cable. Its ugly-duckling chairman, Gerald Levin, seemed doomed. Now the world had turned in such a way that Levin looked prescient while the once-formidable Eisner was mired in difficulty and sinking deeper.

∞

AS THE YEAR was ending, Eisner made another personnel move. In mid-December, he promoted veteran Judson Green, the forty-six-year-old president of the theme parks, to chairman of Walt Disney Attractions. He became the first executive to run all aspects of Disney's recreation and travel businesses: parks, resorts, Imagineering, and regional entertainment. The promotion came at a time when some workers at theme parks were com-plaining that the company had cut back dangerously on maintenance.

Soon after Green's appointment, on Christmas Eve, a Disneyland worker made a fatal error while trying to lash the sailing ship Columbia to a dock. The boat, which had just completed a slow circuit of the Rivers of America attraction, had overshot its mark. Rather than let it pass, the worker tried to dock the ship. A rope crushed the worker's foot and an eight-pound metal cleat came loose. Swinging fifteen feet into the waiting crowd, it struck thirty-three-year-old tourist Luan Phi Dawson in the face, ripping off his jaw and killing him. His wife was seriously injured.

Despite the gravity of the accident, the police were slow to respond. Disney was an important player in Anaheim. Authorities waited in a con-ference room while Disney workers cleaned up the scene. When the police arrived, they did not interview witnesses or collect evidence. Subsequently, there were reports that the injured dockworker, Christine Carpenter, was a manager filling in for another employee so that the ride could open on time. She had never been trained to operate it. Workers at the park said managers were filling in for ride operators far more frequently than they had in the past.

Just weeks later, Disney was fined $7,050 for stonewalling the efforts to obtain documents in a case filed by a woman who claimed she had suffered a brain hemorrhage while riding the park's Indiana Jones Adventure. Still, such serious accidents at the park were a rarity. "We had the first death in fifteen years," Eisner said later when asked about the death. "It was a freak accident. We can't do anything without getting a lot of publicity." Meanwhile, the state legislature passed a vaguely worded law requiring theme-park inspections. Disney had battled the bill unsuccessfully, and then belatedly embraced it.

∽

IN JANUARY 1999, Disney stock got a brief but sharp bump up with the launch of the Go Network, a new portal to cyberspace. The new site was operated by Infoseek, an Internet firm based in Sunnyvale, California. (Disney had bought 43 percent of Infoseek in June 1998 as it launched its Internet exploration.) Disney was making a substantial investment in the Internet. With Wall Street in a fever over anything net related, Eisner didn't want to miss the boom. He still remembered telling his unforgiving father not to invest in cable ("Dad, I know cable is not going to work") and he didn't want to repeat that mistake himself. He was hoping to make money from advertisers or site users or both. The Web could also be a way for consumers to click their way to buying more Disney products.

But Eisner conceded that he couldn't say when or how the company's thrust into cyberspace would turn a profit. "I really don't know," he said when asked where the new technologies would lead Disney. "And I think that's really an asset. Because if I knew and I demanded we go in a certain direction and was wrong, it would be pretty arrogant and stupid. I think we have to be open to change."

Change was in fact the order of the day. On the feature-film side, Eisner installed animation chief Schneider as president of the Walt Disney Studios—a move that some considered a promotion for chairman Joe Roth, because it enlarged his empire by adding animation. But Eisner's moves were fraught with ambiguity. He had been complaining about the studio's performance for months and some saw Schneider's arrival in live action as a slap at Roth, who was not known to be particularly fond of the sometimes abrasive Schneider. (Several months after his promotion, Schneider was asked to take an anger-management course.) Was Schneider in the on-deck circle to replace Roth? Certainly Schneider seemed to consolidate power quickly. By April, he had bumped off ten-year veteran David Vogel, who ran the Disney family label and had received a well-publicized promotion to chief of the Touchstone and Hollywood Pictures divisions not even a year earlier.

Eisner and Roth also announced that the studio would increase the percentage of family movies in its mix—hoping for more cash machines like 101 *Dalmatians* (ironically, a project that Vogel had shepherded through the system). Roth's mission was to slash the company's overall investment in film by about $600 million. Roth was inclined to be more extravagant than Katzenberg, particularly when it came to marketing. But now Eisner decreed, "We're going to be more cautious and conservative." In short order, Disney slashed eighteen production deals, cutting such famous players as Spike Lee, Tim Allen, Whitney Houston, Michelle Pfeiffer, and Robert Redford.

The year ahead included less expensive films like *Ten Things I Hate About You* and the quirky *Rushmore*, each of which cost less than $15 million. There were more child-friendly movies, including *My Favorite Martian* and *Inspector Gadget*. Even though such movies could be expensive (*Mighty Joe Young* didn't begin to recoup its nearly $90 million cost at the box office), Disney had many ways to exploit them through videos, merchandise, and theme parks.

Roth said the average cost of a Disney film would be $32 million, far lower than the industry average of $52 million. And following a growing trend among studios, Disney would look for financial partners to share the risk (and potential profit) on many of its films. It was a strategy that could prevent or inflict pain. Certainly Disney was glad to lay off some of the movie *Instinct*, a nonperformer starring Anthony Hopkins and Cuba Gooding Jr. But the studio was sorry it had decided to share the wealth of *The Sixth Sense*, its summer-of-'99 sleeper blockbuster.

∽

ON FEBRUARY 23, 1999, Disney held another peaceful annual meeting—this time at a restored vaudeville house in Seattle. Eisner demonstrated the Go Network. As he clicked from Web site to Web site, he wasn't risking any technological glitches: the computer wasn't actually hooked to the Internet in real time.

A couple of days later, Eisner announced another series of ambiguous changes at the company. ABC chief Bob Iger was named chairman of the ABC Group and president of Walt Disney International. Some in the media speculated that the succession question was now resolved. The forty-eight-year-old Iger was now at least nominally in charge of ABC as well as Disney's international divisions, including film, video, consumer products, and theme parks. Disney was about to make a major thrust into China and other foreign countries, so it seemed that Iger had a lot of important turf.

But other reports—notably the account in the *New York Times*—suggested that Iger was being kicked upstairs. Why would Eisner reward Iger for failing to turn ABC around? Eisner simultaneously promoted ESPN/ABC sports chief Steve Bornstein to take over the troubled network and some saw him as the real winner in the reorganization. Bornstein, forty-six, had started at ESPN in 1980 and taken over ABC Sports in 1996. He was a relentlessly tough deal maker in the Eisner mode.

Eisner denied that anyone had been anointed at all. Meanwhile, observers wondered who was really in charge at ABC. "I will meddle, Bob will meddle, others will meddle," Eisner said when asked about this issue.

Perhaps the situation was perfect. Iger was an extremely presentable if not a strong-willed executive. He certainly looked like a prospective successor, though there was no danger that he would trample on Eisner's prerogatives. Someone else would get a shot at fixing ABC. And Eisner could continue to rule, and rule alone.

∞

IN MARCH, JUST days before the second phase of Katzenberg's trial was about to begin, Disney and DreamWorks went head-to-head over the industry's most important creative report card—the Oscars. Disney's Miramax unit had two films—*Life Is Beautiful* and *Shakespeare in Love*—contending for the Best Picture award. At DreamWorks and Paramount, there was deep anxiety that the latter film could upset *Saving Private Ryan*, which had appeared to be a sure thing.

There was a swirl of rumors that Miramax was trying to "buy" the Oscar by violating the Academy's restrictive rules against running elaborate campaigns. Miramax did take out expensive ads but that was defensible because *Shakespeare in Love* was still in the theaters. There were also reports that Miramax had hired a "planter" whose job was to place negative items about *Saving Private Ryan* in the media. DreamWorks and its partner, Paramount, tried to counter, both by rereleasing *Private Ryan* and complaining bitterly about Miramax's alleged tactics.

Whether an Oscar can be "bought" is doubtful. Certainly *Saving Private Ryan* seemed like the sort of serious fare the Academy usually embraced, but maybe *Shakespeare in Love*, which had been released later in the year, was fresher in the voters' minds. Or maybe it simply seemed to be fresher material. In the end, Spielberg had to settle for Best Director's honors. It wasn't the ending that he or his partners at DreamWorks would have written.

∽

THE SECOND PHASE of the Katzenberg trial was scheduled for April 1999. Months ahead of that date, a dogged *Variety* reporter named Janet Shprintz started trying to rally members of the press behind an effort to have the court proceedings opened to the public. The case was being heard by a referee or rent-a-judge, so it was assumed that the trial would be closed. That was part of the deal between Katzenberg and Disney. But Sphrintz thought the case should be open to the public, as are most cases tried in court. At first, she had difficulty finding any other media organization to join her—and she couldn't find a lawyer who would take the case.

She made her first approach to the *New York Times*. In Los Angeles, the *Times* was represented in such matters by Kelli Sager, who also happened to represent ABC. This presented an obvious conflict for Sager. She offered an informal opinion, however, that the media was fighting a losing battle. Sager also represented the *Los Angeles Times* and the *Wall Street Journal*, both of which were unresponsive when Sphrintz tried to get them involved. Several other lawyers concurred with Sager's opinion that opening the trial was hopeless.

About a month before the trial's start date in April, Garry Abrams from the *Los Angeles Daily Journal*—a legal publication—joined Sphrintz's effort. They wrote a letter to the court asking to be admitted to the proceedings. To their surprise, Judge Ouderkirk responded with an encouraging letter suggesting that they file a formal motion.

In the few weeks before the opening arguments were set to begin, everything fell into place. Attorney Pierce O'Donnell—who had represented Barbara Chase-Riboud in her suit against Spielberg over *Amistad*—took the case (with some behind-the-scenes prompting from Katzenberg attorney Bert Fields, who reasoned that his hand would be strengthened if Disney knew it was facing a public proceeding). Shprintz sent a copy of Ouderkirk's letter to the *Wall Street Journal,* and in response got a call saying the paper would join in after all. Then came *Time* magazine and finally—belatedly— the *Los Angeles Times.* The effort to open the proceedings prevailed over Disney's resistance. The new turn of events made it seem even more certain that the Katzenberg case would once again be settled. But Disney was knee-deep in the Big Muddy and kept moving on.

29

K A T Z   V .   M O U S E

I N J A N U A R Y 1 9 9 9 , a few months before his trial's April start date, Katzenberg bumped into former Capital Cities/ABC chairman Tom Murphy at a fund-raising event for Save the Children. After his company's sale to Disney, Murphy sat on the Disney board. The two spent some time talking about Katzenberg's case. Murphy clearly believed it should be settled. Later, Katzenberg called Murphy, tracking him down on a golf course in Savannah. "Can't you please talk to Michael?" he asked.

Disney was hewing to the position that it might owe Katzenberg between $25 million and $50 million. "I think the number is closer to $300 million," Katzenberg told Murphy earnestly. "I'm not expecting to get what I'm asking for, but I'm very confident that this number is going to have a two, or be very close to having a two, in front of it. I think Michael is being very badly advised as to what the liability is."

A few hours later, Murphy called back. "I talked to Michael and they'd like to get together and meet," he said. But before Disney lawyer Lou Meisinger went further, he tried to impose a condition. The Disney team didn't want Helene Hahn, the rock-ribbed lawyer who had served as Katzenberg's top business-affairs executive at Disney and who was now in that role at DreamWorks, to attend the meeting. Katzenberg refused to exclude her. He and Hahn were a team and both thought Disney wanted her out of the room because she had too much insight into Disney's modus operandi.

Finally, the parties—including Hahn—gathered at Bert Fields's offices. As usual, they were kept apart, and the settlement judges shuttled back and forth. Katzenberg's team thought the judges had led them to believe that Disney had moved into a new range of settlement numbers. But Disney wasn't increasing its figures at all. The meeting was a failure; when it broke up, all the parties were incensed.

Fields began to complain to Katzenberg that the repeated, fruitless meetings were hampering his ability to prepare for trial. Attempts to cut a deal were dropped.

∞

AFTER THE PARTIAL settlement of his case, Katzenberg's suit against Disney slipped off Hollywood's radar. But behind the scenes, the battle over how to determine Katzenberg's payout raged on, as bitterly as ever. There were endless fights over which Disney documents could be admitted as evidence. And Disney resisted answering countless questions that were raised in depositions. After several frustrated efforts, Judge Campbell Lucas had to sit in on these sessions so he could make on-the-spot decisions about which questions Katzenberg's attorneys were permitted to ask the witnesses. He attended nearly 160 depositions and was flown to New York and London as part of the process.

The trial was to start on April 1 but it was delayed when Disney's Meisinger suffered an outbreak of shingles. Things finally got under way on April 16. The first day was to be devoted to dry procedural matters, but Katzenberg was there with his wife, Marilyn, at his side. "I've been waiting five years for this," he said grimly. As it turned out, once Meisinger recovered from his shingles, Fields developed laryngitis. After one day of proceedings, the trial was put off until April 26.

Katzenberg was in the courtroom throughout most of the trial, which continued on and off for the better part of thirty-three days. He was flanked by Helene Hahn and his wife, making up a diminutive trio. Marilyn Katzenberg, an attractive fifty-one, was one of the more understated Hollywood wives. Her dark hair was cut short and she was simply dressed, wearing little jewelry. On the first day, as the judge somewhat awkwardly entered the "chambers" without the benefit of a magistrate, Marilyn glanced at the team of lawyers seated at Disney's table. "They should all be wearing ears," she murmured disdainfully.

The case was being heard by a referee—the grandfatherly, bespectacled retired judge Paul Breckenridge—so it was not held at the downtown courthouse. Instead, the parties convened in the lawyers' offices. The two teams of attorneys worked in buildings that were mere blocks apart in Century City, a cluster of towering high-rises on the west side of Los Angeles. One week, the trial took place in the mock courtroom at Fields's firm, Greenberg, Glusker, Fields, Claman & Machtinger; the following week in the more spacious offices of Disney's attorneys, Troop Steuber Pasich Reddick & Tobey.

Both sides hired small armies of security guards to monitor who came and went. At the beginning of the trial, about two dozen reporters showed up, including a clutch of television cameras outside the building that taped the parties coming and going. There was even a skirmish when it came to attending to the creature comforts of the press. When the trial opened at the Fields firm, no concessions were made to reporters, even though Katzenberg's team was the one that had wanted the press to be present. The next week, Disney's firm put out a buffet of coffee, bagels, and fruit. The week after that, when the trial returned to the Fields offices, not only were there coffee and bagels, but Hahn had baked cookies.

In every sense, Katzenberg's team was smaller than Disney's. Katzenberg had fewer lawyers in the room; by now, he was represented by Fields and his partners, Bonnie Eskenazi and Brian Edwards. Disney began with general counsel Lou Meisinger in the lead role, but he was almost always surrounded by eight or more colleagues.

The two lead lawyers were a study in contrasts. Fields, a graying seventy, was thin to the point of gauntness while fifty-six-year-old Meisinger, though hardly obese, was heard to complain that he looked fat on television. In his free time, the Harvard-educated Fields amused himself by writing racy thrillers under a pen name, although his most recent book had been a serious study of the true character of Richard III. He was an accomplished cook. In court, he was polite to the brink of sarcasm.

Meisinger was much more of a regular guy. A UCLA graduate, he was an avid golfer and bowler. Having made a name for himself as an entertainment attorney, he left his firm in July 1998 to become Disney's general counsel. In court, however, he had a rather hectoring style—so much so that during the trial's first phase, a *Newsweek* reporter who was having lunch with a Disney executive in the studio's corporate dining room stopped by the table where Eisner and Litvack were eating to pose a question. "Is having a sweaty, clumsy lawyer supposed to work for you?" she asked with a smile.

"Sweaty and clumsy. That's our strategy," Eisner replied promptly.

∽

PERVERSELY, THE TRIAL'S first phase focused on the very issues Disney had seemingly laid to rest in 1997 when it had agreed to give Katzenberg his bonus. Having yielded on that critical issue, Disney now balked at paying interest on whatever Katzenberg ultimately would receive. Katzenberg argued that he was entitled to interest starting from 1996, when the lump sum had been due to him. Disney said it had never admitted breaching his contract and therefore did not owe him any interest.

This meant that Katzenberg's lawyers would have to prove that his contract had been breached. Also at issue was whether Disney had to pay Katzenberg for all the merchandise based on his projects. Disney said it would remunerate Katzenberg for toys and other products that had been licensed to other companies such as Mattel, but not for items it had manufactured and sold under its own label. Katzenberg said he had never been told that merchandise would be split into categories and that he wouldn't receive income from any subset of Disney products. Wells had assured him to the contrary, his attorneys argued.

If Katzenberg's side was going to tackle the breach-of-contract question, things were going to get personal quickly. When Fields began his opening argument, he took just minutes to home in on Eisner. Under Katzenberg's leadership, he said, Disney had sprung from being "a moribund place" to being first among studios, with income that had increased by four hundred times. And yet Katzenberg was still fighting to get his money. "Why did [Disney] treat Mr. Katzenberg in such a harsh manner?" Fields asked. "The evidence will show that it is the personal animus of one man."

Fields continued to hammer this point, referring to "Mr. Eisner's position" and "Mr. Eisner's claim" that Katzenberg was not entitled to be paid. Whenever he might normally have said "Disney," he generally focused instead on the chief executive. How could Eisner be believed, Fields asked, when he denied knowing about Project Snowball? Fields had copies of memos on the secret project that had been copied to Eisner. And Eisner had been briefed on Snowball. "It's not the kind of word you'd forget about, your honor," Fields told the court. "We have got a real credibility problem with this fellow."

Fields had a quiverful of documents that seemed to support his central argument that Wells had promised Katzenberg his payment even if he left in 1994. He propped up blowups of two sets of "strikingly similar" handwritten notes taken by Wells and Katzenberg's attorney, Arthur Emil, covering a June 1988 phone discussion of Katzenberg's contract. (Wells's notes were all but indecipherable; his scrawl was so atrocious that Katzenberg's team relied on a former assistant—subsequently employed by Dream-Works—to make sense of them.)

At the time the notes were made, the two negotiators apparently were starting afresh after earlier talks had stalled. Emil had written "Blank Slate" at the top of his notes. Wells had put down, with a flourish of erudition that fell short, "Tabula Erasa." (The correct Latin term is *tabula rasa*—blank slate.) Wells and Emil had each noted to themselves that Katzenberg had a right to leave the company in 1994. Each had also written that the 2 percent bonus remained in place. If Katzenberg opted out of his contract in 1994, he would lose a portion of the $4 million that Disney had offered to pay toward the building of his beach house. He also stood to lose out on some stock options. But neither set of notes said anything about Katzenberg forfeiting his 2 percent payment. Wells had also noted that the final bonus was "a tremendous concept" and that the payout—which as of 1988 had been nothing—"should increase by a big amount" in the coming years—as in fact it did. Emil's notes also said the bonus was a "big point."

Fields produced notes from a June 27, 1988, briefing that Wells had given to Irwin Russell, Eisner's longtime lawyer, who had also served on the Disney board and the compensation committee. Those notes, too, seemed to reflect that the 2 percent bonus was in place.

As a centerpiece of his case, Fields displayed an enlargement of a deal memo that Wells had sent to Emil on July 1, 1988. Having spoken to the board, Wells had wanted to bring the negotiation to an end. "It is with no little joy that I write to confirm the terms of the agreement," Wells had written. Among those terms was an "ongoing participation in the 2 percent bonus," even if Katzenberg opted out early.

Fields returned to his attack on Eisner, pointing to notes from a conversation between Eisner and his coauthor, Tony Schwartz. "Frank wrote them a deal memo which is completely on [Katzenberg's] side," Eisner had told Schwartz. "I went in to Frank and said I won't make this deal." If Eisner had ordered Wells to change the deal, Fields contended, then Wells had defied him on August 26, 1988, when Wells sent Katzenberg's lawyer a draft of a final contract. The contents, Wells had written, followed his own July 1 deal memo—the same memo that Eisner insisted he had refused to approve. Wells even highlighted the "most important changes" to Katzenberg's existing 1984 deal. There was no mention of a forfeiture of the 2 percent bonus, which clearly Katzenberg would have considered important.

Fields addressed another claim that Eisner had made in depositions: that Wells had assured him repeatedly that Katzenberg's bonus would never be worth anything. Wells's notes of his conversation with Emil showed that Wells had called the bonus "a tremendous concept" that should increase dramatically. Fields also had an October 1988 letter in which Wells had addressed Katzenberg's disappointment at receiving no significant payment from his annual 2 percent participation. Wells assured Katzenberg that his expectations had been "perfectly reasonable" given the studio's performance and urged Katzenberg to wait, adding that the final payout was likely to be big.

"Many of [the] pictures still have substantial revenues forthcoming," he wrote, "and of course, will continue 'forever.' " The company would collect at least $100 million from *The Golden Girls* alone, he added. The letter was copied to Eisner with the notation, "Probably worth a quick read."

Wells had told Katzenberg that the bonus would have great value, which Eisner must have known if he had read the memo that had been copied to him by his second-in-command. And Eisner had steadily maintained in depositions that he was in extremely close touch with Wells during Katzenberg's contract negotiations: "He kept me constantly informed," Eisner had said. "We spoke twenty times a day. I knew everything Mr. Wells was doing." If Eisner actually believed, based on Wells's assurance, that the bonus would always be worthless, then he must also have thought that Wells was deliberately misleading Katzenberg. But Fields suggested that Eisner never believed that the bonus was worthless.

And, Fields argued, if Eisner really thought the bonus had no value, then his refusal to approve any payment to Katzenberg if he left in 1994 put him in an odd position. He supposedly had demanded that Katzenberg be stripped of a worthless bonus. Fields raised the specter of Project Snowball to suggest that, far from thinking Katzenberg's bonus would always be worthless, the company was in fact deeply concerned.

Disney's only evidence to support its contention that Katzenberg had forfeited the bonus was the final 1988 contract. It contained a provision that Fields conceded was "ambiguous." While setting out a schedule for paying Katzenberg the money, the contract stated that if he left in 1994, Disney was obligated to pay him any bonus due "in respect of years prior to September 30, 1994, which is payable after such date by company." Disney would argue that this language restricted the bonus to profits realized before 1994 and effectively eliminated the lump-sum payment based on future income. But Fields described the provision as murky to the point of meaninglessness. The memos and notes from Wells made it clear that Katzenberg was not meant to forfeit his money if he left in 1994, he said.

Fields had another potentially awkward point to address. In 1993, when Katzenberg had stated his intention to leave the following year, Wells had sent him a letter stating that he would be forfeiting $97.6 million, including his final lump-sum payment (estimated by Disney at that time to be $23.7 million).

In conversations around that time, as Katzenberg had boasted that he was "blowing Michael's mind" with his threatened departure, he had seemingly conceded in conversations with Eisner and others that he was walking away from $100 million. As Fields knew, Disney could argue that those conversations demonstrated Katzenberg's awareness that he was giving up his bonus by leaving in 1994. (After all, Disney had taken the position that he would be giving up $97.6 million if he left—a number very close to $100 million—and Disney's figure had included his final bonus.) But Fields said Katzenberg's comments referred to other money—a fuzzy estimate of what Katzenberg would make from a new contract, from stock options that he would have collected in 1995 and 1996, and from salary for those years. Katzenberg never intended to walk away from his 2 percent payment, Fields said. It was an odd coincidence that he had talked of giving up $100 million, Fields conceded, but it was only a coincidence.

∽

LOU MEISINGER TOOK off his jacket as he stood to respond. Fields's version of events was "fiction," he said. Fields's allegation that the case was about Eisner's personal animus was simply untrue. Meisinger had some choice words for Katzenberg, who, he suggested, was not only "greedy" but had also been a credit grabber when it came to the animated hits. He had not treated Roy Disney "with the respect he was entitled to," Meisinger complained. "He was not allowing Mr. Eisner to have the role that Mr. Eisner wanted for himself." And Meisinger attacked the notion that Disney had tried to dupe Katzenberg by slipping an "ambiguous" provision into the final version of his contract that stripped him of his bonus. How, Meisinger asked, could Katzenberg—"the smart, dogged negotiator who fancied himself capable of being president of the entire Walt Disney Company"— fall victim to such a ploy?

During his tenure at Disney, Katzenberg had received more than $100 million in compensation, Meisinger observed. "Let's not get too sorry about Mr. Katzenberg," he said. His demands set "a new standard for arrogance in an industry which already has a rather high mark in that area."

But whoever deserved credit, the animated hits were an established fact and Disney was going to have to cut Katzenberg in—possibly with interest. And Meisinger had nothing to illustrate the negative: he had no memos or materials to rebut the documents and handwritten notes that seemed to say that Wells had assured Katzenberg of the bonus even if he left in 1994. "Mr. Eisner's book notes suggest, 'I wouldn't make that deal,'" Meisinger said. "According to us, he didn't."

The centerpiece of Meisinger's case was the contract. The forfeiture of the bonus wasn't "some last-minute contrivance on the part of Disney," he said. The deal memo and notes that seemed to show a different intent on Wells's part were irrelevancies, now being used for legal gamesmanship. "Mr. Katzenberg [is] cherry-picking from among any number of negotiations" while "ignoring the actual deal," Meisinger argued.

And Meisinger touched on the fact that Frank Wells, a key witness, was not able to speak for himself—to speak for Disney. "Conveniently, Katzenberg's case now focuses on the acts and the words of a man who is no longer here to defend himself," Meisinger said.

He questioned Katzenberg's claim that when a Disney lawyer sent word in May 1993 that he would not receive his bonus if he left the following year, he calmly went to Wells and walked away believing that Wells would correct Eisner's misunderstanding about the deal. "How convenient," Meisinger observed, "that Mr. Wells is not here." But if Katzenberg had really been told that the bonus was gone, he asked, one would have expected him to go to Wells in "some kind of rage" rather than have the friendly encounter that Katzenberg had described.

In Katzenberg's scenario, he added, it was hard to tell who was "the heavy"—Eisner or Wells. But it would have been unseemly for Meisinger to attack Wells—the late patron saint of Disney. The furthest he could go was to assure the court that "in no circumstances can Mr. Eisner be claimed to have engaged in any type of deceptive conduct."

Meisinger also tried to undermine the implications raised by Project Snowball. "There is nothing sinister about a company having a project to calculate a very complicated bonus," he said. The name "Snowball" itself was innocent, coined by employee Cheryl Fellows to describe the burgeoning amount of work that she would have to do. The Katzenberg view of

Project Snowball revealed "a conspiracy mentality that would make Oliver Stone proud," Meisinger contended.

"I hate to mix metaphors," he said in an ungainly conclusion, "but it's a red herring."

And Meisinger prepared the spin for the inevitable outcome of the trial. Thanks to the settlement, Disney would pay Katzenberg an "enormous" sum. But Meisinger said it would not be as much as Katzenberg was seeking. "The fact that Mr. Katzenberg receives a check is not going to make Mr. Katzenberg the prevailing party," he said. Katzenberg's real aim in this part of the trial was "to embarrass people," Meisinger said. But Meisinger predicted confidently, "We don't think there will be any Disney folks embarrassed here."

∞

KATZENBERG WAS THE first to take the witness stand. He gave a seemingly straightforward account of his contract negotiation with Wells and Eisner in 1984 and 1988. His children, those infants who were to be the beneficiaries of the "annuity" that Wells had supposedly promised Katzenberg all those years ago, were recently in possession of driver's licenses. Katzenberg also testified that Michael Ovitz, during his brief tenure at Disney, had tried to settle his case for something between $50 million and $100 million. "He is the one specifically who said Michael Eisner ultimately forbid him to do it," Katzenberg said.

On cross-examination, Meisinger tried to hammer home his point that Katzenberg was too smart and too ably assisted to have been duped by Disney.

"You have a reputation, sir, as being a very tough guy, a tough negotiator," Meisinger said. "Is that the way you consider yourself?"

"No," Katzenberg replied tersely.

Meisinger then asked if Katzenberg considered himself "a patsy." Katzenberg again said no.

Meisinger focused on the implication that Wells had slipped a provision into Katzenberg's contract stripping him of his bonus if he opted out of his job in 1994. Didn't Katzenberg have qualified lawyers? he asked. Did he believe that Wells tried to slip a change into Katzenberg's contract? On this point Katzenberg tried to have it both ways. "I don't want to characterize what Mr. Wells was doing," Katzenberg replied. "I think he was putting forward the [deal] and doing it fairly and honorably."

Meisinger seized on the thank-you note that Katzenberg had sent to Eisner following the 1988 negotiation, in which Katzenberg had written, "You've handled my crap with extraordinary patience."

"Did you cause him to incur a lot of your crap?" Meisinger asked ominously.

"Some, yes," Katzenberg conceded.

Meisinger asked about the meeting in which Katzenberg, having been told that he would lose his bonus if he left in 1994, went to Wells and — by Katzenberg's account — was assured by Wells that he would handle the problem. "The only person left who had knowledge of the conversation in which he told you that he would take care of it . . . [is] you?" he asked.

"Yes," Katzenberg replied.

If Wells did tell him that there was a misunderstanding with Eisner about Katzenberg's deal, Meisinger persisted, did Katzenberg ever bring that up with Eisner? Even after Wells had died? "Have you ever told anybody in the world about the conversation with Frank Wells, other than your wife and counsel?"

"No," Katzenberg said. But he insisted that once Wells told him that he would take care of the matter, "I assumed he did." Later, he said, Eisner never gave him a chance to explain the substance of his conversations with Wells.

As the testimony continued, Disney made good on its threat to attack Katzenberg's weakness in live-action film. Meisinger produced company documents purporting to show that after his ten-year run at the studio, the live-action film business had lost a staggering $231 million. Katzenberg tried to counter by saying that the company was not counting substantial income from his movies that was collected after his departure. "You're saying from the end of '94 until today, a $231 million deficit has been eliminated?" Meisinger asked.

"That is my opinion, yes," Katzenberg replied. The films were profitable by "hundreds of millions of dollars," he said. Despite an admitted lack of documentation, he insisted, "I know that to be a fact."

It quickly became clear how damaging Katzenberg found this line of questioning to be. The next day, Fields fought to introduce a document from a Disney expert showing that the live-action films in question had actually turned a profit of $400 million at the time of Katzenberg's departure. Leaping to his feet, Meisinger objected vigorously. But in one of the bitterest exchanges in the trial, Fields counterattacked. "It's been broadcast all over the world that this poor guy cost Disney millions," he argued. "It's just wrong to let them do this to this guy, broadcast it, spin it all over the world, and not bring out the truth. It's vintage Disney." Judge Breckenridge allowed Fields to introduce the document into evidence.

Next on the witness stand was Katzenberg's longtime attorney, Arthur Emil, whose story tracked Katzenberg's in most respects. Meisinger homed in once again on the alleged conversation in which Wells had supposedly told Katzenberg that Eisner misunderstood his deal. "Did Wells tell you that Mr. Eisner had a misunderstanding?" he asked. "Did he ever tell you he would handle it?"

"I don't believe he ever told that to me in so many words," Emil said.

Meisinger persisted: Was there any documentation of this important conversation between Katzenberg and Wells? Did Emil tell Katzenberg to make a note of it for his files? Did Emil make a note himself? "Not that I remember," Emil replied. Even after Wells died, Emil testified, he did not discuss with Katzenberg any need to follow up on Wells's promise to "take care" of Eisner's "misunderstanding" of Katzenberg's contract.

⌇

IRWIN RUSSELL, A portly, elderly man, was the first witness from Disney to take the stand. Russell was Eisner's personal attorney as well as a board member and a member of the compensation committee in 1988, when Wells was ironing out Katzenberg's deal. Fields asked Russell about notes that Wells had taken in June 1988 when he briefed Russell on the proposed new contract with Katzenberg. The notes reflected that Wells had said Katzenberg would lose stock if he left in 1994 but that his bonus would "continue." Russell's own handwritten notes appeared to match the ones taken by Wells—and included the provision that Katzenberg's bonus would continue even if he left in 1994.

But Russell insisted this was simple error. Nervously chewing his glasses, he said that he had forgotten to write the word "loses" before the word "bonus."

Fields questioned how Russell could have forgotten to write such an important word. "These were very quick notes strictly for my own purposes," Russell said.

"You had enough time to write the word 'loses,' " Fields pursued.

"Maybe, maybe not," Russell replied.

Next up was Sandy Litvack, the burly, gray-haired chief of corporate operations who now had the office—if not the titles—that once belonged to Wells. A former antitrust lawyer, the sixty-three-year-old Litvack had emerged as Eisner's privy counselor. He was particularly disliked by a number of top Disney executives who viewed him as a negative influence who constantly denigrated their ideas and played to Eisner's worst instincts. His apparent encouragement of Eisner's refusal to settle, his enemies said, was a prime example.

Fields turned to a series of letters Litvack had written to Katzenberg's lawyers from 1994 to 1996 as they pressed his case. The theme was always the same: Disney had not yet decided whether to pay Katzenberg the final 2 percent payment. In October 1994, for example, Litvack had written that it was "premature and unnecessary to take a position or reach a conclusion . . . as to whether Jeffrey is entitled to the additional payment under the contract." On November 4, he wrote again that it was "premature and unnecessary" for the company to take a position. On November 14, another letter said that Disney had made "no determination" about Katzenberg's claim because it was "premature and unnecessary." Disney had "not repudiated Jeffrey's right to a bonus," the letter continued. In a letter to Fields, Litvack wrote, "We have not yet made any judgment about whether Jeffrey is owed any additional money under his contract."

In his opening argument, Fields had referred to these letters as "the Litvack stall" and "the Litvack dodge." Fields had said that when Litvack took the stand, he would say those letters actually did not mean that Disney had not taken a position on the dispute. In fact, Fields had said, Litvack would swear that Disney had already concluded that Katzenberg wasn't entitled to the money. But the company was deciding whether to pay Katzenberg anyway. Fields had observed that it was "a bizarre concept for a public company" to pay Katzenberg money that he wasn't owed. "[Litvack] must think we're children to think we would buy that construction," Fields had said.

But now on the stand, Litvack stuck to his story. Confronted with his own seemingly unequivocal letters stating that Disney had not taken a position, Litvack said, "If that's what I wrote, that's what I wrote. It sounds familiar." But he insisted, "We had determined that he was not entitled to [payment] under the contract but we were considering paying him."

"I knew I had a dead witness on my hands," Litvack continued with an astonishing lack of delicacy. "I wasn't sure a trier of fact would agree with me because I knew I had a dead witness on my hands."

Fields hammered away at the specifics of the letters. In one of them, Litvack had written: "No one, not me and not Michael, has repudiated Jeffrey's right to his contractual incentive bonus." How could Litvack have written that if, as he now swore, the company had decided that Katzenberg wasn't entitled to the money?

"You repudiate someone's right in my lexicon when you say, 'I am not paying you. Go sue me,'" Litvack said.

⁂

IT WAS A little past ten on a Tuesday morning when Eisner finally appeared. *Forbes* had just anointed him the highest-paid chief executive in America. By reaping $589 million in fiscal 1998, Eisner had handily beat out the runner-up, CBS president and chief officer Mel Karmazin, by almost $400 million. It perhaps wasn't the right crown to be wearing, because Disney's stock was still dragging and its earnings had been down 41 percent in the second quarter.

On the day of the trial, Eisner was having his perennial sartorial difficulties. One of the courtroom artists poised to make a sketch gazed upon him with a look of horror. "He's wearing a new jacket," she whispered, "and he hasn't removed the stitching from his vents!" But with the usual pink tinge to his complexion, Eisner looked healthy and rested. He glanced at the reporters arrayed to watch this long-anticipated confrontation unfold. He and Katzenberg did not acknowledge each other.

Fields began by trying to force Eisner to acknowledge Katzenberg's contribution to Disney. He read from Eisner's 1988 letter to shareholders: "I can think of nothing but superlatives to describe [the] stunning performance of the entire Walt Disney Studio team starting with Chairman Jeff Katzenberg, and President Richard Frank." Turning to Eisner, Fields asked, "You did say that, sir?" Eisner acknowledged that he did. "And you believed it at the time?" Again, Eisner answered yes.

Fields focused on what Eisner knew about Katzenberg's contract and when he knew it. Eisner was vague and unresponsive. When asked whether he stuck by his claim that Katzenberg had agreed to forfeit his bonus if he left in 1994, Eisner replied, "I don't think I claim that. I think it's true but I don't think—as a matter of fact, I'm pretty sure—I can't remember. We may have discussed it; we may not have discussed it. I can't remember now." Pressed with his own testimony from depositions, Eisner said, "Now I'm confused as to what I knew when." It appeared that either Eisner had

THE KEYS TO THE KINGDOM

not allowed his lawyers to prepare him properly or they had done a poor job of it.

Eisner said he didn't talk to Katzenberg much about the deal when Katzenberg was renegotiating his contract in 1988. But Eisner testified that he had talked "many times" with Katzenberg about the notion that if he left in 1994, he would give up his bonus. "I never had a conversation with him, by the way, that was contentious," Eisner volunteered. "In our entire relationship, I think we've had two. . . . We had a couple of quite emotional and intense conversations when he asked to be president." Eisner also maintained that Wells had told him the 2 percent payment would be worthless.

Was it possible, Fields asked, that Wells could have ignored or misunderstood Eisner's orders in making the deal? "In my mind," Eisner said, "it would be impossible."

Fields tried to pin Eisner down on when he had told Wells that Katzenberg would lose the bonus if he opted out early. "I don't recall what specific proposal I objected to or didn't object to," Eisner responded. Had he given Wells his orders before June 1988? Eisner seemed to concede that he had. If that was true, then how did he explain the many subsequent conversations in which Wells had told Katzenberg's lawyers and the board that the 2 percent bonus would continue? (There was also the July 1, 1988, deal memo which Eisner later told Tony Schwartz supported Katzenberg's position.) "If you put your foot down . . . then Wells was making an [unauthorized] offer?" Fields asked.

"You're trying to make me impugn a man not here to defend himself," Eisner replied. "I'm not going to sit here and say Frank Wells disobeyed instructions or was insubordinate."

Eisner said he thought Katzenberg's insistence on a four-year deal was "greedy." Fields countered that if Katzenberg had signed the deal in 1988 and stayed through 1994, that would have kept him at the company for six years. "That's what you're labeling greedy?" he asked. "That was the length of your own contract."

After some more back-and-forth, Judge Breckenridge made a rare interjection: "I think we're getting a little argumentative here."

Fields continued to confront Eisner with examples of Wells memoranda that included Katzenberg's bonus. "I don't know when this was done," Eisner insisted. "I don't know what it means."

"We have four notes—June 6, June 13, June 20, and June 21—that you would have found unacceptable," Fields continued. How did that fit with Eisner's position that Wells kept him informed about everything he had done? Eisner dodged Fields's questions, prompting the judge to ask whether Eisner would have objected to what Wells had written in the memoranda. "I just don't recall," Eisner said at last. But he said he objected generally to a four-year deal with the 2 percent payment in place. "I don't know the timing of the objection," he said. "I may have been in Europe. . . . I don't even know if I was in town."

Fields turned to Project Snowball. Eisner admitted he was aware of a project to track Katzenberg's compensation but had never heard that name. Fields presented him with a memo — copied to Eisner by Wells — labeled "Project Snowball."

"I don't think I ever saw this memo," Eisner said. "I don't think that it came to me. . . . Maybe it was a draft. I never saw it."

Fields produced another memo addressed to Eisner. "I don't recall seeing it," Eisner said.

Why, Fields asked, would Wells tell Katzenberg's lawyer that the 2 percent was "a tremendous concept" if he'd told Eisner the bonus was worthless? "I would have allowed him to say whatever he thought was appropriate," Eisner said. "He was obviously encouraging Arthur Emil to accept this deal."

"While Wells was telling you the 2 percent was meaningless, he was trying to get it back from Mr. Katzenberg. Is that correct?" Fields continued.

"Yes," Eisner replied.

"Did you say to Mr. Wells, 'If it's meaningless, why do we want to make him give it back?' "

"No."

Whatever Eisner's credibility was when he took the stand, it suffered a direct hit when Fields asked about his autobiography. Eisner testified that he didn't know whether coauthor Tony Schwartz, who had been toiling on the project for almost ten years, had been working for him or for the Walt Disney Company. He wasn't sure whether he or Disney had paid what had to be hundreds of thousands of dollars.

Fields turned to the notes that Schwartz had taken. Now it was time to examine the issue of animus. All this time Fields had maintained his contemptuously polite tone, even when asking questions like "Has your memory slipped?" or, when asking about Katzenberg's share of merchandise, "Did you think zero would be a fair allocation?"

But suddenly Fields closed in. "Did you say you consider yourself to be the cheerleader and Mr. Katzenberg merely the tip of your pom-pom?"

Eisner seemed unfazed, at first. "If I said it, I'm quite sure it was in humor," he replied.

"Did you say, 'I think I hate the little midget'?"

Eisner stiffened. "You're getting into an area that I think is ill-advised," he said ominously. If he said it, he continued, it was "about a series of things that Mr. Katzenberg had done to me. . . . It was completely private." Then Eisner warned, "If you pursue this line of questioning, it will put into the public record those things that [should not] be in the public record."

"Didn't you say more than once that you hated Mr. Katzenberg to Mr. Schwartz?" Fields persisted.

"I do not hate Mr. Katzenberg," Eisner said. "We had a long and fruitful relationship." Then he said again: "You're going in a direction that I think is not in your client's best interest or mine, but particularly your client's."

What he meant by that, Eisner never said.

∞

MEISINGER GAVE EISNER a chance to explain some of his comments to Schwartz, including his remark that he didn't care what Katzenberg thought, he wasn't going to pay him any money. Eisner cited what he said was a misdirected fax from Katzenberg to Fields in 1994, just after he and Katzenberg parted ways. According to Eisner, the fax thanked Fields for helping him spin a story by Ken Auletta in *The New Yorker*. "I now said to Tony Schwartz, 'Screw that. If he's going to play this . . . disingenuous game' . . . I simply was not going to pay him his money. . . . I could have been more generous after this final, final confirmation of bad behavior — I just wasn't going to do it."

Eisner said he never intended to put his comments in his book. "I don't deal that way," he protested. "But occasionally somebody does something that goes toward the dark side, that makes you so aggravated that you get annoyed."

Under Meisinger's questioning, Eisner tried to reinforce the image of Katzenberg as a credit grabber. He said that when Katzenberg arrived at Disney, he had sent the animators "off the lot . . . into never-never land." (Of course, Eisner had been fully on board when the animators were moved to the suburb of Glendale.) And Eisner denied that he had thrown Katzenberg out of his office when he tried to plead for his bonus. The meeting, he said, seemed "quite pleasant" to him. After Katzenberg left Disney and started DreamWorks, he added, Eisner had approved a final $400,000 discretionary bonus for the year. "I thought it was fair based on what he had done," he said. "I couldn't remember the anger that I had before, I guess."

∽

IN THE FINAL analysis, Fields told the court, someone had to be lying. Either Wells had tried to pull a fast one by slipping unfavorable language into Katzenberg's contract—which would be "garden-variety, half-truth fraud"—or the provision was never meant to strip Katzenberg of his bonus. Fields concluded that Eisner was the one who had fabricated his story.

"Can Mr. Eisner really have gone into Mr. Wells's office and said, 'I won't make this deal?' No, he can't," Fields said in his closing argument. "Mr. Wells didn't make proposals without clearing them. It didn't happen." Fields referred to "the many stories of Michael Eisner" on the bonus. He invited the court to contrast Katzenberg's testimony with Eisner's. "Mr. Katzenberg answered the questions," he said. "He didn't try . . . and duck and bob and weave. . . . Can we say that about Mr. Eisner? No." He displayed a poster titled "The Circle of Animus." A photo of a smiling Eisner was encircled by examples of his alleged hostility. The "I hate the little midget" quote and the pom-pom remark were prominently featured.

But the Fields version was clearly a bit too simple. Was Eisner making up his entire story? It seemed more plausible that Wells had convinced Eisner that he had the situation under control. With or without explaining his thinking to Eisner, Wells might well have put the contested language into Katzenberg's contract to cover himself and Disney if the relationship blew up. He must have assumed that in the near term, at least, he could handle things. Katzenberg would be persuaded to stay, the question of his bonus could be postponed for years, and Wells could be satisfied that he had kept things running as smoothly as could be expected at a burgeoning corporation filled with egos and ambitions and relentless desires for more.

Did he do what Eisner had always feared most: mislead him—betray him, to Eisner's way of thinking—for what he might have considered the greater good? Or did he collude with Eisner to placate Katzenberg, planning all the while to whittle at the money Katzenberg had been promised? This was a central mystery of the case and one that the triers of fact would fail to illuminate despite all the enormous volumes of testimony and documents that had accumulated by the time Fields rested his case.

✐

OTHER NOTES THAT Schwartz had taken based on conversations with Eisner were introduced into evidence but never discussed during the trial. Though meandering and sometimes murky, they gave broad hints as to why Eisner might have said he hated "the little midget."

Eisner complained about "the fact that he comes to dinners and leaves after first course." Eisner alluded to "underlying insufferability," adding, "only i know how good and bad Jeff is." And another time: "pathological beyond belief; Jeff . . . sicker than sick."

And perhaps the hatred had begun in earnest in 1991, when Katzenberg wrote his ill-considered memo on the state of the industry. Eisner vented his anger over the memo—which he felt had been "plagiarized" from his own similar effort years before, when he was at Paramount. Of course Eisner knew what his own memo had been—an attempt to carve his own profile with the board, to step out of Barry Diller's shadow, to wrest distribution from Frank Mancuso, "the Sicilian." But if Eisner was disturbed that Katzenberg might have borrowed his technique in an attempt to establish himself—not just with the board but in the entertainment industry generally—he didn't cast his objections quite in those terms. Instead, he expressed disgust with Katzenberg's apparent self-satisfaction, his lack of originality, and most of all, his defiance. Perhaps Eisner's memo hadn't had the intended effect but at least he had been graceful about it.

"He didn't write anyway," Schwartz's notes read. "He was so proud of it . . . he wanted me to read it, thought it was so brilliant. . . . [I said] you should use it in your head, don't show to anyone; i wrote on the memo . . . DO NOT XEROX OR SEND THIS TO ANYONE. . . . i hear after that, some got it with that written on it; he completely disobeyed me; frank and i discussed throwing him out; i told him not to do it; from that moment on i knew it was over. it wasn't the memo, fact i told him not to show it and faxed it and lied about it. . . . i just let him have it; just sits there and stares at you and walked out; everyone knew i was pissed off . . . from that memo on never made a decent movie."

In an interview that apparently took place in New York not even six months before the final rupture with Katzenberg, Eisner gave Schwartz a detailed analysis of Katzenberg's performance in live-action film. From 1984 to 1989, he said, Disney released thirty-five films, thirty-one of which were profitable. The studio made an average of about $200 million a year. Then came the increase in volume, "through the same overburdened executives," Eisner noted. It was, he told Schwartz, "a recipe for disaster." Particularly, it seemed, because Eisner said he "stopped being a partner in the development process." In the next four years, Eisner said, the studio released seventy-six pictures of which only thirty-three were profitable. The average profit per year: about $62 million—most of it "eaten away by distribution, marketing, executive overhead of at least $100 million per year." Eisner concluded: "not worth being in the business at anything like this profile."

Katzenberg kept the three labels—Hollywood Pictures, Touchstone, and Disney—" 'cause embarrassing to fold one up," Eisner complained. Eisner seemed to feel that he had let Katzenberg have his way, and these costly examples of ego run amok were the result.

After having written his memo, Eisner resumed, "[Katzenberg] decided was genius and loving person, he excluded me . . . every time i talked to him it got worse." Apparently, Katzenberg asked Eisner not to sit in on his meetings. This seemed like chutzpah from someone who, Eisner told Schwartz, was "the end of my pom-pom." At one point, he said, "JEFFREY WAS MY RETRIEVER."

Schwartz's notes are a window into Eisner's doubts over his fateful discussions with Katzenberg over his future at Disney. Eisner recalled the talks they had in Aspen in 1993, when Katzenberg had asked if he could have Frank Wells's job. Katzenberg had always insisted that Eisner had promised to advance him if Wells was gone. In Eisner's recollection, Katzenberg had been pushy, reminding Eisner how Wells had made room for him to be the top man at Disney in 1984. "He stepped aside for you," Katzenberg said, in Eisner's recollection. "I'm more important than you were then."

He remembered telling Katzenberg, "It's over. You are not getting that."

But Schwartz's notes continue in Eisner's voice: "DON'T KNOW WHETHER I DID SAY HE COULD HAVE FRANK'S JOB." Eisner remembered telling Katzenberg that Disney was signing Wells to a new deal: "[I] had talked him out of climbing Mount Everest; got too old to do it; he loved the action at disney, frank." But Eisner could not or would not quite remember whether he had made a promise to Katzenberg. "I MAY HAVE . . ." he said to Schwartz, "what i clearly did [say] is frank has signed a new seven-year deal; and frank wouldn't climb mountains and health was perfect . . . only thing i MAY HAVE SAID IS: if he hadn't signed a perfect, seven-year deal, if he wasn't here . . . if i didn't have this wife, you'd be great, you would be right."

Immediately after Katzenberg first broached the subject in Aspen, Eisner apparently told Wells that Katzenberg wanted the president's job. And perhaps surprisingly, Eisner's notes suggest that Wells was willing to let him have it: "i had called frank; would you believe this . . . i am not giving him that job; frank was kind of heart. FRANK WOULD BECOME VICE CHAIRMAN; i said roy will like that; sharing vice chairman." When Eisner told Katzenberg that he wasn't getting the Wells job, however, Eisner remembers Katzenberg saying that he only needed "a new mountain to climb."

Eisner told Schwartz about Katzenberg exercising his option to leave in 1994. He had then gone through "a year of prima donna hell," he said.

Apparently, Katzenberg became increasingly upset over what he perceived as interference with his prerogatives. Eisner told Schwartz that Katzenberg wrote a letter complaining that Eisner was talking to animation chief Peter Schneider about *Pocahontas*, then still in production. Katzenberg set up a seven A.M. screening knowing that Eisner wouldn't make it. Katzenberg was "secretive," Eisner said.

Eisner recounted the final rupture with Katzenberg and how incensed Katzenberg had been when Disney refused to take a position on whether he would receive his bonus: ". . . called me a liar. . . . He HEARS WHAT HE SAYS not what OTHER PEOPLE RESPOND, that is jeffrey k."

And Eisner fumed: "I can't talk any more to jeffrey katzenberg . . . everything i ever said to him, he tells geffen, or media, now bringing up whole financial thing in media. . . . i said to jeffrey . . . i would suggest you don't negotiate with me in the newspapers, like you did your last situation."

And Eisner offered this bitter reflection — a comment that, with all his complaints about "bad behavior" and disobedience, might have come straight from his own self-righteous father:

"i spend my life keeping this company on an ethical course."

∽

ON MAY 19, the court ruled on the issue of whether Disney owed Katzenberg interest. The decision was a mere seven pages long. Without explanation of his reasoning, Judge Breckenridge simply reached "the inescapable conclusion" that Katzenberg had never forfeited his bonus. He found that Disney had breached Katzenberg's contract but made no comment on the credibility of the witnesses, on the alleged animus of Eisner, or on Project Snowball (though he found no evidence that Disney had committed fraud).

With this simple finding, the court made clear what so many in the media had already known: Disney's decision to fight over the interest, to expose Eisner to a disastrous turn on the witness stand, to put the phrase "I hate the little midget" into the public lexicon, had been an enormous miscalculation. The judge held that not only would Disney have to pay interest, but Katzenberg would also get the profits from all the merchandise.

Even before the ruling, veteran journalist Kathryn Harris had written the first review of Eisner's courtroom performance in a column on the Bloomberg Web site. Under the headline EISNER LOSES HIS COOL (OR WAS IT THE CASE?), Harris wrote, "The verdict is in: Michael Eisner is a charming, intelligent and facile executive who shouldn't be allowed near a witness stand." Eisner had lost his composure, she said, but "far worse . . . was the ebbing of Eisner's credibility—that most precious commodity in a witness, and certainly in a chief executive who has fused his likeness to a company."

Harris's critique was just the first in a barrage of negative media reports. The day of the ruling, the *Wall Street Journal* weighed in with a devastating commentary by Holman W. Jenkins Jr. Why, Jenkins wondered, would "the only media conglomerate with a brand name worth protecting" expose itself to such a spectacle? Frank Wells's absence was taking its toll. Eisner was rolling the dice on bigger wagers than ever before—ABC, the cruise-ship business, theme-park expansion—but to Jenkins it seemed that Disney was "placing billion-dollar bets all over the table with a gaping hole in its line-up." If Wells had been around, Jenkins continued, Katzenberg might never have left.

The article was something that Eisner might have seen in a nightmare—and it appeared in an especially influential publication. This was not history as Eisner wanted to see it recorded. The awful conclusion: "an appropriate check on Mr. Eisner's gifts has not been put in place, and his Melvillian pursuit of Moby Jeff may be evidence of impulses to come." Things had come to a dreadful pass. The *Wall Street Journal* was questioning Eisner's judgment on the same day that the court dismissed Disney's expensively wrought arguments in a few paragraphs.

∞

THOSE WHO HAD a major stake in Disney had been watching these developments with growing concern. Among them was Stanley Gold, who had gotten in touch with David Geffen during the first part of the trial. The two men had a passing acquaintance and now Gold had determined that the way to approach Katzenberg was through Geffen. In fact, Geffen had made earlier attempts to settle with Disney. When the dispute first erupted, that might have been accomplished for $90 million. Now it was going to cost Disney much, much more.

In early May, Geffen had invited Gold to come over. They met at Geffen's tranquil beach house, with bookshelves lining the walls and large windows opening onto the ocean. Geffen was slight and immaculate in his usual T-shirt and shorts when he greeted the now portly, bespectacled Gold.

Geffen had told Gold that Disney was making a terrible mistake pursuing the interest issue, opening everything that had been resolved by the earlier settlement of the liability question. The two sides were going to piss all over each other, he had said, and in the end, Katzenberg would receive a big lump sum and the interest question would be academic. Gold had told Geffen that Eisner's lawyers—Litvack and Meisinger—had told Eisner the case was worth no more than another $30 million. Based on that, it was clear that the men were poles apart and there were no grounds for settlement.

But after the ruling, Geffen called Gold. "I told you so," he said. The two men decided to meet again. On May 20, the day after the decision was rendered and less than a week before the second phase of Katzenberg's trial was to begin (in which the court would tote up the amount to be paid), Geffen again played host to Gold, this time at Geffen's beautifully restored estate in Beverly Hills—the former home of Jack Warner. Gold was stunned by Geffen's magnificent twentieth-century art collection. A canvas by David Hockney hung in the entryway while a Jackson Pollock glowed above the stairs—and that was only the beginning of Geffen's collection.

The visit was cordial but again fruitless. Two days later, Katzenberg called Gold and asked to meet. That Saturday, May 22—the weekend before the parties were to return to the courtroom—Gold met with Katzenberg and a clutch of his representatives in a room at the Four Seasons Hotel in Beverly Hills. Gold was treated to a detailed presentation of Katzenberg's case on the value of his 2 percent bonus, complete with an appearance by expert witness Dennis Soter, an analyst with Stern Stewart & Co., who had flown in from New York.

On Sunday evening, Gold went to Katzenberg's house in Beverly Hills and the two met for several hours. Gold was conciliatory. He agreed that

Katzenberg was owed something but he also said that he had reviewed the numbers with Disney's team. Disney's math didn't match Katzenberg's. "Stanley, I understand but they've been wrong," Katzenberg said. "I think they have a set of numbers that they've put together to serve Michael's agenda, which was to pay me nothing."

After he left Katzenberg, Gold went to visit Eisner. His mission was unsuccessful. Katzenberg sent Gold a box of Dunhill cigars. And he used his influence at Cedars-Sinai Hospital, where he was a generous donor and a board member, to ensure that Gold's father—who was just being admitted—would receive the best possible care while he was there in what would be his last illness. The second phase of the trial started as scheduled.

∞

LOU MEISINGER WAS shifted out of first position for Disney as the second phase of the trial got under way. Litvack now took the lead. The number-two man at Disney was in court day after day—doing a more effective job than Meisinger had done. Katzenberg's team hoped that his advocacy would be tempered in the judge's mind by his earlier lack of credibility as a witness.

Katzenberg had suggested that Gold come and sit in on the trial. It would be clear, Katzenberg said, that the judge was completely disenchanted with Disney and its attorneys. Gold did come, but to him, the judge seemed exceptionally polite and meticulously evenhanded.

But after the session ended, Gold approached Bert Fields. "Let's sit down and talk," he said. The two huddled on a sofa in the reception area of Fields's firm. Again, Gold offered his analysis of Katzenberg's case. The two men parted without resolving anything, but Fields was not displeased that Gold was still in there swinging.

Still, the parties appeared to be further apart than ever. Katzenberg's lawyers had adjusted their figures. After initially seeking something north of $250 million, they now said Katzenberg's 2 percent might be worth as much as $578 million. (After subtracting the $117 million that he had been paid and applying the agreed-upon discount, they said Katzenberg was due another $330.8 million.)

The math was based on Disney's 1995 buyout of the Silver Screen Partnership for $500 million. (Silver Screen had an interest in sixty-six films; all but three were to be counted toward Katzenberg's bonus.) Katzenberg charged that Disney had deliberately destroyed documents that had been generated during the Silver Screen transaction because they might have helped Katzenberg's case. Disney angrily denied it. The company argued that Katzenberg's top number was "a throwaway highball" to get the judge into a higher range. Disney said it owed Katzenberg a total of $140 million — or $20 million more than it had already paid.

Katzenberg's first witness was his friend Nathan Myhrvold, the cherub-faced technology expert from Microsoft Corp. He offered a bright prediction of the future moneymaking opportunities for Katzenberg's films and programs. He spoke about video-on-demand, the elusive technology that would enable viewers to beam the films of their choice into their homes, and "smart" toys that interacted with a television or computer. (A demonstration featuring Arthur, a talking non-Disney mouse, seemed to enchant the judge.) But Judge Breckenridge seemed disinclined to speculate much on technologies that didn't yet exist. Katzenberg's case began to seem less compelling in the second phase of the trial than it had been in the first.

But Disney was also facing a distressing prospect. Already, the company had been forced to attack Myhrvold's rosy projections about how much money it stood to make in China and India. A huge publicly held corporation hardly wanted to tell the world and its shareholders that the future wasn't that wonderful after all. And Eisner had made it clear that he hoped for great things from China in the future, so the two positions would be hard to reconcile.

When it came to debunking Katzenberg's witnesses, however, Disney scored some points. (Katzenberg had considerable difficulty finding experts willing to take his case; Fields had made repeated trips to New York only to be turned down by the leading investment-banking houses. Some said the case would be too time-consuming; others said they did business with Disney and didn't want to get involved.)

Under questioning from Brian Edwards, one of Fields's partners, expert Dennis Soter painstakingly detailed how he had reached the $578 million figure. The next day, Disney lawyer Harry Olivar said Soter had used the wrong multiplier when extrapolating from the figures used in the Silver Screen transaction. That alone would cut Katzenberg's award in half. Olivar attacked other aspects of Soter's math and pointed out that Soter had no experience valuing film libraries.

Michael Wolf from Booz Allen & Co. had an even rougher outing. He testified that ABC had gotten sweetheart deals when it bought Disney films for broadcast. This was a potentially explosive issue, because an array of profit participants from Disney films could go to court if they thought they could show that Disney had shortchanged them when selling their movies to its own network.

But Litvack got Wolf to concede that his analysis had been based on the broadcast dates of the films in question—not the dates that the sales had been concluded. Wolf was forced to concede that nine of the eleven films cited in his analysis had been sold to ABC before Disney acquired the network and should not have been counted at all. Wolf countered that eliminating those films would not reduce Katzenberg's award substantially.

But Litvack hammered at Wolf, asking if his projections were based on fact or "just your judgment." Judge Breckenridge admonished Litvack for being argumentative when Litvack suggested that Wolf had "not the foggiest idea" what the market was for certain technologies. He jumped on Wolf's prediction that Disney would derive profits from videos of its stage plays— which Disney said it had no plans to sell in the first place. Even though *Cats*, the most successful video of a play ever, sold only three million units, Wolf had reckoned that a tape of *The Lion King* on Broadway would sell thirty-seven million copies.

Litvack asked why Wolf had used *Cinderella* and *Snow White* to forecast profits from animated films made during Katzenberg's tenure. They were the two most successful films in Disney history, he said. Why not use *Dumbo* or *Lady and the Tramp*, which also had turned profits? Wolf maintained that Katzenberg's films were closer in quality to the two greatest Disney classics.

Litvack also homed in on Wolf's projections that *Beauty and the Beast* and *Aladdin* would each sell seventeen million units when they were released in home video for the second time, while *The Lion King* would sell twenty-two million tapes. "Is it correct that no rerelease has ever sold fifteen million units?" Litvack asked. Wolf conceded the point.

Fields tried to rehabilitate Wolf, who had acknowledged under questioning from Litvack that he had been paid $4 million for his services to that point. Wolf defended using *Cinderella* as a model, and said his calculations were accurate to within 10 percent. He also tried to establish that, despite his error, ABC did in fact underpay for Disney films. Using the price that NBC had paid DreamWorks for the rights to *Antz* and *The Prince of Egypt*, Wolf insisted that Disney—which sold *The Lion King* to ABC for $8.5 million—could have collected as much as $27.9 million more.

∽

AS JUDGE BRECKENRIDGE sifted the often-tedious testimony of the expert witnesses, Gold was still trying to end the spectacle. On June 15, he bumped into Arthur Greenberg, a senior partner in Bert Fields's law firm, at a party for the Israeli consul general. As Greenberg teased Gold about the drubbing Disney had taken in the first part of the trial, Gold held out a tantalizing possibility. He might, he said, be able to talk Disney into "a more realistic number."

Two days later, Gold was in Fields's office in Century City. The outlines of a possible agreement had started to emerge. Gold had worked on Eisner; Fields had consulted with Katzenberg. The gap between the parties narrowed but did not close. "Do you mind if I continue to involve David?" Gold asked, referring to Geffen. Fields said he did not.

Gold arranged to see Geffen over the July Fourth weekend at Geffen's beach house. The timing was right. Disney had attacked Katzenberg's experts but the company had not yet been forced to downplay its future profits. Eisner was poised to take the stand again—surely a development the company would want to avoid. At last Gold had managed to talk Disney into a higher number. Disney had said in court that it owed Katzenberg another $20 million. But the new number exceeded that by more than $100 million.

Gold and Geffen shook hands on a deal on Monday, July 5. On Tuesday evening, Judge Breckenridge got a call informing him that the details were in place. The next day, July 7, the parties surprised the industry with news of the settlement. Fields liked to say, "When you're a winner, go to dinner." That night, Katzenberg and Fields did exactly that at the Ivy in Beverly Hills.

The number was to remain secret, but sources close to the situation say Katzenberg walked away with a net of nearly $270 million. It was a tremendous payday. The controversial Ovitz payout paled in comparison. Yet Katzenberg found it hard to accept. In his heart, he had wanted a number that began with a three. But Geffen and his lawyers convinced him to put the ordeal behind him.

Katzenberg threw a victory party at the Palm in West Hollywood. But he was not overjoyed. "It's a little like being in a car accident and the insurance company paid you off," he explained. "Unfortunately, it doesn't take away from the trauma."

30

" T H A T   D A R K   P E R S O N "

EISNER HADN'T LET the trial slow him down during what had
been a busy summer. Disney continued its pursuit of cyberspace,
rushing its plans to buy out the balance of Infoseek, the Internet-
search firm. The company announced that all its Internet assets would be
combined. Eisner remained committed to establishing Disney as a presence
in cyberspace even though the Go Network was off to a bumpy start. The
portal had recorded a 36 percent increase in traffic during its first quarter
of existence but its revenues were flat, suggesting that advertisers weren't
rushing to embrace it. And it had been plagued by technical problems.

Disney stock was also not getting the kind of bang out of its Web operations that Eisner might have hoped. Internet investors were clearly concerned that traditional media companies would stifle innovation with their
bureaucracies. In fact, Infoseek employees complained that Disney was doing exactly that, holding up deals and requiring layers of review for designs.
Eisner also had been peppering executives there with e-mails about problems with Go. (At one point he complained that the portal's personal stock
tracker put the wrong value on his own holdings. It turned out that the
system couldn't handle the commas that Eisner had used when entering
the numbers. As an Infoseek executive pointed out, Eisner's figures had a
lot of commas.)

Disney ultimately put the Go portal and its various online services
(ABCNews.com, ESPN.com, and so on) into a separate entity and announced plans to issue a separate tracking stock that could be used to
compensate executives. They hoped this would address an ongoing brain-
drain problem. In fact, Disney had been losing Internet talent in droves as
executives left to mint money in this most entrepreneurial of businesses.
For example, Toby Lenk had been a business-development executive until

1998, when he left to help start eToys Inc. By the following year, his stock in that venture had a market value of $573 million.

In a similar vein, Patrick Naughton, the chief technology officer at a Web-site design firm that Disney had acquired, once told Jake Winebaum, the head of Disney's Internet group, that his team wasn't demanding big salaries but eventually they expected "to live in Michael Eisner's house." Disney coughed up substantial pay raises and even stock-option awards but still couldn't touch the kind of money that others were making in the field. And with Disney's stock faltering, the options weren't as appealing as they used to be.

The losses continued. Winebaum had toiled at Disney while others at start-up companies had grown very rich. On June 7, 1999—the very day Disney announced its plans to acquire the balance of Infoseek—Winebaum said he was leaving to start eCompanies, a firm that would nurture other Internet start-ups.

∽

IT MIGHT HAVE been one thing to have waged a painful losing battle against Katzenberg if the company was performing well. But by July 1999, Disney was in the second year of a deepening slump. Disney announced its third-quarter results and the trend had not reversed itself. Earnings were down 12 percent—or up less than 1 percent if the cost of investing in the Internet venture was factored out. While operating income at the theme parks and resorts was up 12 percent, sales at the stores remained sluggish. The studio's income was down 33 percent to $74 million despite the strong performance of the summer's animated hit *Tarzan* and the video release of *A Bug's Life*. And ABC was a continuing problem.

New York magazine took the dimmest view in July, stating baldly that "Michael Eisner's extraordinary reign at the Walt Disney Company is coming to an end."

But Eisner must have considered the views of *New York* magazine to be a fleabite compared with the opinions that were being aired in influential financial publications. Disney got a contrarian, positive cover story in the July 26 issue of *Barron's*. There was, to be sure, "a parade of horribles," as Eisner might have said. Disney's stock had been the worst performer in the Dow Jones Industrial Average over the previous twelve months. The stock was down 37 percent from the previous year. Disney was a favorite target of short sellers. Standard & Poor's had warned that it might downgrade the company's debt. But while there was no quick fix for the company's problems, *Barron's* said, Disney was simply too valuable not to recover in the end.

Eisner concurred. "Our problems are momentary, fashion-oriented, and limited," he said. He was going to pare down costs and simultaneously spend on new initiatives like his Internet venture.

But *Barron's* stopped short of fully endorsing Eisner. Instead, the report noted that some observers thought the solution for Disney "begins with Eisner—or better yet, without him." *Barron's* acquitted Eisner of causing the company's most serious problems, instead blaming factors like the on-going Asian economic crisis. "Our bet is Mickey and Michael remain a tight team, not least because the Eisner magic has worked like a charm for most of the past 15 years," *Barron's* noted, adding wryly, "Besides, the board is packed with Disney insiders."

Barron's optimism was tempered by *Fortune's* less sanguine appraisal. "After all," wrote reporter Marc Gunther, "earnings are dropping, top executives are defecting, and Disney stock is plunging like a ride down Splash Mountain." Gunther contended that Eisner presided "over an insular—some say arrogant—corporate culture where decision-making is hierarchical, centralized and slow"—and that Disney's style was "an utter mismatch for the Internet age."

In an interview, Eisner countered that Disney was the most profitable media company in the world. "We're being buried a little prematurely here," he complained. *Fortune* granted that point but noted that other key indicators were down—operating income for the first nine months had tumbled by 17 percent; return on equity, which had consistently been 20 percent in previous years, had slipped ever since the 1996 acquisition of Capital Cities/ABC and was below 10 percent. Some financial analysts had cut earnings estimates for fiscal 1999 as many as five times since the previous summer. "The company has simply stopped growing," Gunther wrote, "and it isn't a momentary dip either."

Eisner also expressed his regret that Disney hadn't settled the Katzenberg case sooner. Only when Wells's handwritten notes emerged at the trial did he accept that Katzenberg had a legitimate claim. Reading these remarks, Katzenberg's legal team was astonished. Surely Eisner must have known about the Wells notes, which Disney itself had turned over from its own

files during the litigation. Eisner had been asked about some of these materials in depositions. His comment that he knew nothing about the Wells
material was ridiculous on its face.

∽

AS *FORTUNE* HAD pointed out, the market had grown wary of Disney.
Some big investors had gotten out altogether. Gordon Crawford, who had
long controlled a major stake in the company through the Capital Research
& Management Group investment firm, had sold a position that had been
as great as forty-one million shares, his faith in Eisner in tatters. Brian
Stansky of the T. Rowe Price Media & Telecommunications Fund had also
sold the bulk of his stock.

There were so many problems. Disney was a unique brand but there
was a sense that the company had overexploited its most valuable asset—
the magic of its name. Its marketing had been too relentless. And Disney's
zeal to walk away from every deal the winner had strained relations with
licensees and retailers as well.

Disney insisted that its brand appeal was as strong as ever, citing the
vigor of the theme parks as proof. But Disney simply wasn't as cool as it
needed to be. Kids had not rushed out to buy *Tarzan* products and Disney
did not wield the clout that might be expected in video games for children.
In cable, it was third behind Nickelodeon and the Cartoon Network. The
company's products appealed mostly to the very young, and even among
that group, it faced tough competition from Tele-tubbies on PBS and Po-
kémon on the WB Network. Eisner held brainstorming sessions to figure
out ways to make Mickey hip (one idea: have the mouse on a skateboard).

Eisner later addressed the issue of "age compression" in a November
1999 e-mail he sent to staffers throughout the company. (He had taken to
sending regular messages to "fellow cast members" the previous summer,
presumably as part of Disney's embracing of the Internet.)

Under the heading "Age Decompression," Eisner insisted that "those
who think Disney is only for kids are dead wrong." The company was
actively finding ways to expand the appeal of the brand, he continued. "The
Rock 'n' Roller Coaster at Disney-MGM Studios integrates the music of
Aerosmith with three inverted loops for an entertainment experience that
is truly on the edge (I rode that three nights ago. WOW!!!)."

The company retrenched. It decided to prolong the gap between the
rerelease of animated classics from seven to ten years. It cooled its pursuit

of new opportunities to license its products. But that would also mean less short-term income from video sales, and less income from associated merchandise as well.

Disney would keep slashing to save money. There would be fewer movies. The film division was carving $550 million out of its budget. On the television side, the company engaged in a bruising but successful battle to get its 225 affiliate stations to cough up some money toward Disney's $5.5 billion, eight-year deal with the National Football League.

The company's plans to spend as much as a billion dollars to open as many as thirty Disney Quest arcades — sites that were to combine video games and small theme-park attractions — were dropped after only two had been opened. And the idea of building the cruise-ship fleet to as many as a dozen ships within ten years seemed to have fallen off the boards after the launch of the second in the series, the *Disney Wonder*.

Eisner continued his reorganization and belt tightening. Disney sold off publishing assets, including Fairchild Publishing. He looked for a buyer for the Mighty Ducks hockey franchise and the Angels baseball team.

In a major consolidation of television operations, he melded Disney's production operation with ABC's, hoping to achieve the elusive goal of synergy. Disney had developed only one show, *Once and Again* with Sela Ward, that would find a spot on ABC's fall schedule. (After a bright debut, it began to falter in the ratings. Nonetheless, ABC announced that the show would remain in the coveted Tuesday ten P.M. slot, displacing the long-running hit *NYPD Blue*. The series cocreator, Steven Bochco, said the network's decision was an "egregious and inevitable consequence of vertical integration.")

The lack of Disney prime-time programming on ABC was a major frustration for Eisner — especially since the network was quietly exploring a replacement for the underperforming Sunday-night show *The Wonderful World of Disney*. While Fox owned the top shows on its own network (*Ally McBeal, The Simpsons, The X-Files*) as well as strong shows on ABC (*The Practice* and *Dharma & Greg*) and the other webs, Disney had not had a prime-time hit on ABC or elsewhere since *Home Improvement*, which had finally concluded its long run. By having ABC take over production, Eisner hoped that ABC would develop and own more of its programming. Some in the industry were dubious about Disney's strategy. They wondered whether other networks would be wary of Disney's program ideas because they would assume that anything Disney pitched would be a leftover deemed unworthy of a slot on ABC's schedule. (Some of these concerns were allayed in November, when Disney sold a sitcom pilot to NBC.)

The short-term result of the merger was management chaos at the network. The shuffling of personnel produced a dramatic bloodletting at ABC. Among the most prominent victims: Jamie Tarses, the young executive lured from NBC by Ovitz. Tarses had continued to provide occasional color for the press. (She publicly denied, for example, that she was dating *Friends* star Matthew Perry and then the two were caught making out.) More importantly, she clashed with Lloyd Braun, the head of Disney's television-production operation — almost all of whose pilots had not been picked up at ABC. When his unit was merged into the network, Tarses tried to cut him out of the loop. In the end, she was the loser. After ABC abruptly dismissed her deputy, Steve Tao, without consulting her, she resigned.

In September, Eisner made a surprise move by naming Steve Bornstein to run the Internet venture. Just the previous February, Bornstein had been put in charge of day-to-day operations at ABC. This move was perceived as a sign of Bornstein's strength and the Internet venture's weakness. Eisner clearly hoped that Bornstein, having previously helped build ESPN into a force, could do the same for Disney's Go.com portal site. (Though consistently rated the fifth-most-popular Web site, the percentage of online users who visited had slipped from 24.2 percent in April to 22.8 percent in July, according to Nielsen NetRatings. The time spent on the site also shrank from 32.5 minutes in April to 22.7 minutes in May.) Like other companies, Disney was still groping for a formula to attract users.

Eisner wasn't done. At the end of the month, he promoted Sandy Litvack to vice-chairman of the company. "Sandy has been my key adviser over the past five years and has been invaluable in providing me with guidance and counsel," Eisner said in a statement. It seemed odd that Eisner, constantly anticipating betrayal, now embraced a man who had led Disney's failed battle against Katzenberg — an episode that had proved so damaging to Eisner.

A company spokesman promptly pointed out that the promotion was not a sign that Litvack was in line for further advancement. "It is not a designation of an heir," the spokesman said. There were reports that Eisner was under pressure to hire a strong lieutenant who had the potential to run the company, and some speculated that Litvack's promotion was meant to clear the way. Others thought that Litvack's advancement was merely a reflection of Eisner's stubbornness.

∽

NOTHING SEEMED TO go right for Disney in the fall of 1999. At the end of September, Patrick Naughton—the Infoseek executive who was overseeing Disney's online operation—was arrested for soliciting sex from a minor. Naughton had been communicating on the net with an FBI officer posing as a thirteen-year-old girl, and he had arranged to meet with his quarry. Of course, there was no way Disney could have anticipated this development, but the nature of the alleged crime made it particularly embarrassing for a family-oriented company.

At the same time Disney was drawn into a political storm over an exhibit in Orlando. The Israeli display in Disney's Millennium Village—one of twenty-three exhibits meant to celebrate the world's cultures—was to include a description of Jerusalem as Israel's capital. That offended several Arab organizations and a group of Arab foreign ministers threatened to call for a boycott. Disney assured the protesters that there would be no reference to Jerusalem as the capital of Israel. (Instead, the exhibit described the city as "the heart of the Israeli people.") An Israeli spokesman would not say whether the exhibit had been changed in response to the pressure. Eisner tried to minimize the damage. "It was never our intent to offer a political point of view," he wrote in a letter to the Arab League. "We are an entertainment company." While Arab foreign ministers decided not to support a boycott, other groups, including the American Muslims for Jerusalem, pressed ahead.

Eisner fared poorly with another attempt to celebrate the millennium. After attending a performance of Mahler's Eighth Symphony, he had come up with a plan to commission the Disney Millennium Symphonies. Two young composers, Aaron Jay Kernis and Michael Torke, were picked for the job. Eisner had created elaborate storyboards setting out a dramatic narrative that he hoped would be the inspiration for the music. His treatment covered the history of an American family, including references to the Korean War and life on a farm. But when the symphonies had their debut at New York's Lincoln Center in October, the critics pounced. The *Washington Post* called the performance "sublimely freakish," while the *New York Times* jokingly suggested that the composers might as well have been asked to sign contracts that stipulated "Think big. Be happy." Surely Eisner had hoped at least to get credit for good intentions.

WHETHER EISNER'S INITIATIVES would pay off over the long term remained to be seen. In the short term, he needed to win back the faith of Wall Street and his major investors. He had to overcome more than the company's poor results. The damage inflicted by the Katzenberg case was not to be underestimated. It was one thing for a company to go through a rough patch—even a protracted turn in the barrel. But Katzenberg had raised questions that went to the very core of Eisner's personality and judgment.

Eisner launched himself on a publicity blitz: *New York Times, Wall Street Journal, Los Angeles Times*. Even as a very young boy, Eisner had learned how to work his charm. But at age fifty-seven, Eisner found the media—once so willing to be seduced—looking at him with eyes that would not be dazzled. "Meet the new Michael Eisner," the *New York Times* invited with a subtextual sneer. The once-aloof Eisner was "now suddenly accessible," "suddenly . . . playing Mr. Nice Guy," seemingly "almost desperate to restore the company's mystique—and his own image."

In interview after interview, Eisner stuck to his script. Disney's problems were temporary. The company was still more profitable than its rivals, wasn't it? The results from 1984 to 1998 had been great, hadn't they? The Katzenberg litigation, like the Ovitz payout, had been "a mistake." But even as Eisner talked, he was wading into unknown difficulties. Implicitly acknowledging that he could ill afford to lose another high-level executive, Eisner boasted of Joe Roth, "I think I have him for his career." But Roth—seething with resentment at being disparaged by Eisner in meetings with outside producers—had long been telling friends in the industry that he was planning his exit.

In fact, Roth resigned in January to become an independent producer, maintaining that his departure had nothing to do with any strains with his boss. Eisner insisted he was saddened but unfazed: "I don't consider him a great loss to this company given the totally fabulous people we have," he said.

To the surprise of some in the entertainment community, Roth was replaced with the sometimes volatile Peter Schneider, a relative stranger to the world of live-action films. Eisner expressed confidence that Schneider would soon overcome his lack of relationships with agents and talent. "It's about material," he said, "not about friendships."

∽

IN EARLY NOVEMBER, Disney announced with great hoopla that it had at last achieved a toehold in China in the form of an agreement to build a theme park in Hong Kong. The plan called for the Hong Kong government to invest $1.5 billion, plus another $1.7 billion to install roads, a rail link, and other services. Disney was to kick in only $316 million for a 43 percent stake in the new venture. Many observers immediately concluded that Hong Kong had been taken to the cleaners by the hard-driving deal makers from Disney. The project required the approval of local legislators, several of whom criticized its high cost to Hong Kong taxpayers.

The splashy announcement was followed a couple of days later by troubling financial news. Disney had ended fiscal 1999 on another sour note. Its net income for the full year was $1.4 billion, down 27 percent. Fourth-quarter profits dropped 37 percent to $212 million, not counting costs associated with the purchase of Infoseek. Filmed entertainment lost $94 million in the last quarter despite a good showing by *Inspector Gadget*, which had been expensive, and a phenomenal performance by *The Sixth Sense*. (Disney had missed out on some of the profit because it had sold off a piece of that film.)

Sales of home videos and merchandise continued to be soft. Disney also warned that it expected problems in those areas to continue into the year 2000, though Eisner held out hope that the digital video disc might provide an opportunity to sell its films in a new format.

On the day the results were announced, Eisner conducted an unprecedented conference call with analysts. This was a practice that other companies sometimes followed, particularly when their stock was showing signs of weakness, but Disney had never taken such a step before. "We are a growth company," he said. "It's impossible to predict the exact day when growth will return. But we are hoping to get back to growth."

Eisner also sent an e-mail to his "fellow cast members." The company had enjoyed a good year creatively, he said, but "this kind of bottom line performance is unacceptable." Disney was devising new strategies to bring consumer products and home video back on track, he said, adding—more ominously—"we are focusing on internal measures to increase cash flow and operate our businesses more efficiently."

The message certainly lacked the sparkle of some of his earlier missives, though he expressed the hope that the next *Lion King* or *Home Improvement* might be waiting in the wings. On a conciliatory note, he added, "[Y]ou, indeed, are the future of our company." Some might have wondered if that were true, considering the promised "internal measures" to improve performance.

Finally, the end of November brought some relief from the seemingly endless parade of horribles. The surprise success of *Who Wants to Be a Millionaire?* gave ABC its first sweeps victory in five years. There were doubts among some in television about how long the quiz-show boom would last, but, for now, ABC was the number-one network. Then *Toy Story 2* brought in more than $80 million over Thanksgiving weekend. The Disney stock didn't soar on the strength of these developments, but Eisner was nonetheless said to be ecstatic. There was some good news at last. If Disney's fortunes would turn, so would Eisner's.

But the central question was the one that was so difficult to address: was the issue at Disney really a problem with the increasingly isolated and Nixonian executive whom Michael Eisner had become? The ingratiating young man who had begged ABC to put *Happy Days* on the air and gone bravely into battle to make *Raiders of the Lost Ark* at Paramount had been on his own for five years now. There was no Barry Diller, no Frank Wells, to act as a backstop. Was Eisner the man to lead Disney into the twenty-first century or was he too controlling, too arrogant, and simply too unedited to work the old magic? Weren't the clamors for a strong number two in part a way of saying that Eisner was not a man whose judgment was to be trusted?

As Eisner observed, none of his rivals was asked about succession as often as he was — not even the seventy-six-year-old chief executive of Viacom, Sumner Redstone, who had just wowed Wall Street with a deal to acquire CBS.

But Eisner could not seem to look seriously at questions about his leadership. He was not at fault; he was not "that dark person that people write about," he protested. He knew who his friends were. (Who were they?) He was the victim, wronged by forces that eventually would be vanquished.

"Maybe this is like a Disney fairy tale," Eisner ventured. "All's well that ends well. The truth will win out."

EPILOGUE TO THE PAPERBACK EDITION

AS BOOK WATCHERS might notice, the subtitle of this paperback edition is different from the hardcover version. The original, "How Michael Eisner Lost His Grip," turned out to be a distraction for many readers. The subtitle was meant to be figurative, suggesting that Eisner's increasing isolation had led him to make several costly and not completely rational decisions (such as his unsuccessful entanglement in the expensive lawsuit brought by former Disney studio chairman Jeffrey Katzenberg).

But it quickly became clear from questions that readers posed that many were confused. Those who did not follow the company closely asked when Eisner had been fired, which of course had not happened. Accordingly, the subtitle was changed because Eisner remains chairman of the Walt Disney Company and is, in fact, the last chief executive of a major entertainment company to have risen through the Hollywood ranks.

As the hardcover edition was being released in April 2000, Disney—which had suffered from a long spell of trouble in such businesses as home video and consumer products—was enjoying the type of extraordinary break that reverses fortunes at entertainment companies. *Who Wants to Be a Millionaire?* was proving to be more than just a hit. It was a phenomenon—the kind of lifeline that Eisner had hoped for when he had told analysts in November 1999 that the picture at Disney was bound to improve.

Millionaire not only jolted Disney out of its slump, it boosted the stock of Bob Iger. In February, host Regis Philbin joked—but only partly—that the reason Iger had been promoted to the number-two job at Disney was "because he was lucky enough to be president of ABC when *Millionaire* was put on the air."

In March, Disney stock surged from a fifty-two-week low of about twenty-three dollars a share into the low forties as analysts became encouraged by

ABC's resurgence as well as the company's prospects in DVD sales and theme-park attendance. It became known that Capital Research and Management Group's portfolio manager, Gordon Crawford, had a change of heart. After dumping a block of Disney stock early in 1999, Crawford bought more than 26 million shares by year's end. And Crawford was still accumulating the stock. What was not yet known—and what wouldn't be disclosed until early 2001—was that while Crawford started to re-accumulate his position, legendary investor Warren Buffett was selling. He got rid of more than 80 percent of his company's stake in Disney in the last quarter of 1999 and the first quarter of 2000. Nonetheless, when analyst Jessica Reif Cohen offered a favorable rating of Disney's prospects in April, the stock jumped nearly 5 percent to $43.63. Cohen said she expected the stock to climb a dazzling 20 percent in the year ahead.

And by the time third-quarter profits were announced in August, Disney showed a 48-percent rise in new income, excluding the impact of its struggling Internet unit, Go.com. Even though analysts were doubtful about Disney's ability to rebuild in the important areas of video and consumer-product sales, they nonetheless turned bullish on the company. Aside from the strength of the *Millionaire* show, which was lasting much longer than many had predicted, the company's theme parks remained strong. The company had new attractions on the boards, including Disney's California Adventure in Anaheim. And Disney was coming up with ways to make the parks more profitable. One approach was the "Fastpass" system, which enabled customers to avoid waiting in long lines for rides. Another was a decision in April to charge ten-year-olds the full adult price for admission to Disneyland.

∾

AS HE WAS trying to steer Disney toward a lasting recovery, Eisner waged a war on the political front. With Time Warner's merger with AOL looming, he set out to do what he could to undermine the deal in Washington. In an atmosphere of enmity, Time Warner unwittingly offered Disney the chance to score a highly publicized victory. The two companies had gotten into a skirmish over the fees that Time Warner would pay to carry Disney-owned channels on its cable systems. In December 1999, Time Warner insisted, Disney had agreed to a fee structure. Disney subsequently claimed there was no final deal. Whatever had happened, after the AOL deal was announced in January, Disney upped its asking price by $300 million, bringing its fee for supplying the programming to $1.3 billion over ten years.

In an astonishing public-relations blunder, Time Warner retaliated by pulling the plug on Disney-owned ABC at the beginning of the May "sweeps" period, when ad rates are set. Time Warner hoped that outraged viewers would blame Disney, but the opposite happened. The *New York Times* reversed its editorial position, offering the opinion that given Time Warner's behavior, its deal with AOL deserved greater scrutiny from the federal government. Time Warner had achieved the unthinkable: making Disney look like an underdog. The dispute was quickly settled, with Disney winning several concessions.

Disney pressed ahead with an aggressive lobbying campaign to get the Federal Communications Commission to impose conditions on the proposed merger. The government seemed to take a closer look at the deal than it otherwise might have done, but ultimately Disney failed to block the deal or even to get Washington to impose stringent conditions.

∽

BY THE TIME Disney announced what seemed like continuing good financial news in November, the story was overwhelmed by looming weakness in the advertising market. Disney acknowledged that *Millionaire*'s ratings had started to slip and that its audience was aging. The change in demographics meant that rates charged to advertisers would have to drop. Disney warned that results for the fiscal quarter ahead would probably be flat. Despite the company's report that operating income doubled in the fourth quarter, the stock dropped about 15 percent, closing at $31.50 by the close of trading that day. (Other media companies, including Fox, Viacom, and Time Warner, also dropped, but not as sharply.)

Analyst Jessica Reif Cohen, among others, cut her rating on the stock and trimmed her formerly optimistic earnings forecast. Certainly, the stock showed no signs of getting back into the low forties, which is where it had been trading six months earlier when she predicted that it would climb by another 20 percent in the year ahead.

Eisner wasn't buying the grim predictions, insisting that the economy remained strong and the advertising market would recover. "We don't see this dismal-looking future that people are talking about beyond this momentary softness," he told analysts.

In December, Eisner told analysts in London that the company was like a race car, "accelerating nicely but firing on only half its cylinders." By March 2001, Disney acknowledged that bad times were going to take a toll. The company said it was cutting 4,000 jobs. Continued softness in the economy required Disney to eliminate 3 percent of its 120,000 employees — the first time the company had ever undertaken a worldwide reduction in its workforce. Eisner and Iger offered voluntary buyouts, giving staffers three months to make up their minds about whether to take the severance packages. If the company's goals weren't reached, layoffs would follow with lower benefits to workers. Disney was hardly the first entertainment company to announce cuts: NBC, Viacom, and Time Warner had already gone down the same path.

∾

AT THE LONDON analysts' meeting, Eisner had singled out the consumer-product division and the studio as weak performers in fiscal 2000. The studio had suffered through a less than spectacular summer, falling short of expectations with the Nicolas Cage action picture *Gone in Sixty Seconds* as well as *102 Dalmatians*. In animation, *Dinosaur* was an especially vexing disappointment. The film had been a venture into computer-generated imagery, representing Disney's expensive attempt to build a unit to make the kind of innovative hits produced by its partners at Pixar, the maker of *Toy Story* and *A Bug's Life*.

The follow-up to *Dinosaur* was supposed to be a picture called *Wild Life*, but in a development that stunned some members of the animation community, the plug was pulled in September. A number of animators with knowledge of events said *Wild Life* was dumped at the behest of Roy Disney, and not simply because he was disheartened by the weak performance of *Dinosaur*. Instead, several animators said the project had an inappropriate adult sensibility — including sexual innuendo and what one insider called a "gay-friendly" tone. For example, there were reports that there was a risqué wordplay on characters descending into a "manhole."

Such material apparently led Roy Disney to declare, after viewing an early version of the picture, that *Wild Life* was "not a Disney movie." The central mystery was how a picture that one Disney insider called "a massive train wreck" got as far along as it did — and at a cost rumored to be about $20 million. Disney animation chief Tom Schumacher said in an interview that he — not Roy Disney — made the decision to pull the plug on *Wild*

Life, and that he did so simply because the story "just wasn't strong enough." Schumacher said the project was set "in a high-style urban setting," and acknowledged that "there were things in it that might have gone beyond the wink" that is accepted in other Disney movies. But Schumacher said the film was a work in progress, and material that crossed the line could have been excised. For that matter, the film could have been released under the Touchstone banner (as were *The Nightmare Before Christmas* and *Who Framed Roger Rabbit*) if it was deemed too adult for the Disney label.

In the wake of the debacle, Disney shut down the computer-animation unit. Eisner was said to have asked to review every project in the pipeline, even in live-action. Now Eisner said the company would also cut its budget in the live-action film division by $500 million a year.

Interestingly, many observers believed that Disney would have a hit with an uncharacteristically expensive live-action project, *Pearl Harbor*, set to premiere on Memorial Day weekend in 2001. Produced by action veteran Jerry Bruckheimer, with a cast led by Ben Affleck, *Pearl Harbor* was assembled primarily by production chief Todd Garner and approved by Joe Roth before both men left the studio (Garner joined Roth in his new company). The original budget was whittled from $200 million to $145 million.

Bruckheimer believed that Eisner had given his approval to start the film. But after Roth's departure, Eisner told the *Wall Street Journal* that *Pearl Harbor* had not yet been given a green light. According to an individual close to the situation, Eisner met with Bruckheimer and said, "I don't care what you've heard. We're not green-lighting the biggest movie of all time." He insisted on trimming the budget by $10 million—a decision that proved difficult to implement, especially because the sets had already been built. "Disney was under enormous scrutiny," says this insider. "Joe had left. The studio had just had [two box-office flops], *The Insider* and *Beloved*, and they were hemorrhaging red ink. . . . Eisner was showing the community and his board that he was taking charge. He was making a statement that there's a new sheriff in town."

In fact, *Pearl Harbor* still had one of the highest budgets ever approved at any studio. Unlike *Titanic*, however, the picture did not go wildly over budget and attract reams of negative publicity. While director Michael Bay was not thought to be the storyteller that *Titanic* auteur Jim Cameron had proved himself to be, *Pearl Harbor* was considered to be such a formidable contender that no studio wanted to schedule a major release against it. Once Eisner saw the movie, said a source close to the filmmakers, "he was proud of everything about it: the fact that they were tough and that they made this huge movie that was going to be a hit."

The buzz was less positive about the summer's animated film *Atlantis*. The picture lacked music and was said to be visually impressive but perhaps too sophisticated to engage young audiences. Meanwhile, Dream Works was poised to release the broadly comic *Shrek* with the voices of Mike Myers, Eddie Murphy, and Cameron Diaz. It seemed likely that in the animation wars, Dream Works—which had scored its second best-picture Oscar in two years with *Gladiator*—might prevail in summer 2001. (The previous year, Dream Works had *Chicken Run*, which grossed $106.8 million, while Disney's *Dinosaur* pulled in $137.7 million. But *Chicken Run* cost less than half of the more than $100 million budget that Disney had spent on *Dinosaur* and therefore was much more profitable.) Disney had another project that held hope for the year ahead. In the animation world, there was talk that *Lilo and Stitch*, the story of a little Hawaiian girl and a visitor from space, might be turning into a real hit. The picture was scheduled for a 2002 release.

∽

AFTER PASSING UP a bonus in 1999, Eisner collected $11.5 million (in addition to his salary of $813,000) for 2000. He wasn't granted any new stock options in Disney, but he got 2 million options in the company's struggling Internet group. That brought his total compensation for what had been a roller-coaster year to $14.3 million.

January 2001 brought a major defeat. Eisner, who had seemed to remain confident in Go.com even as the portal struggled, was forced to fold the Go.com portal that had been at the center of Disney's Internet strategy. A year earlier, Disney had announced that it would retool the portal to focus on entertainment and leisure. Meanwhile, Go.com had been plagued with another problem. The company behind a fledgling Web search engine called GoTo.com had sued, arguing that Disney had infringed its trademark. GoTo.com argued that Disney's Internet logo—a green traffic light— was too similar to its own. A federal judge agreed and Disney's appeal failed. Arguing that changing its logo would cost more than $40 million, Disney still balked at making things square with GoTo.com. In March, the court said it might hold the company in criminal contempt if it didn't get down to business. In June, Disney finally agreed to pay $21.5 million and change its Go.com logo.

Analysts were becoming increasingly skeptical about the business, but in April 2000, Eisner seemed to show his continued confidence by buying $1 million worth of the company's stock even as the price dropped. In September, Disney unveiled the redesign but the portal's fortunes did not improve. At year's end, the company's Internet group reported a loss of $249.4 million. Finally, Disney threw in the towel.

With the decision to fold Go.com, Disney took $790 million in noncash writeoffs and said it would incur as much as $50 million in expenses associated with closing the portal. Eisner said the company would focus on Web sites with powerful brands, such as ESPN.com and ABC.com, rather than trying to build a portal. "We were waiting for something at the end of the rainbow that was looking less and less worth waiting for," he said.

With other companies like AOL Time Warner, Viacom, and Vivendi Universal on the playing field, some industry observers began to question the wisdom of Eisner's long-standing conservatism. To cite just one example, Disney had passed up a chance to buy Yahoo a few years earlier, when it was valued at $8 billion, because Eisner insisted on being given a discount to the market price. By 2001, Yahoo was valued at about $25 billion, while Eisner had pursued a fruitless strategy trying to home-grow an Internet unit.

And there were other areas in which Disney had decided against expansion through acquisitions. "Disney has to recognize that it's becoming a niche player," analyst Christopher Dixon told the *Los Angeles Times*.

Eisner answered his critics in the company's annual report. "Companies often pay too much for other companies in search of a headline in the *Wall Street Journal* or because they are afraid to let cash burn a hole in their pockets," he said. "We didn't want to fall into this trap." Eisner also made it clear that expansion might not be worth pursuing if it were to be achieved the way Time Warner had done it when it had agreed to be acquired by the far smaller America Online for what seemed like rather overvalued stock. And as the new behemoths like AOL Time Warner and Vivendi Universal struggled to merge their cultures, it remained to be seen whether Eisner would stay on the sidelines and if so, whether that would turn out to have been the wiser course.

∽

The Door Did Not Stop Revolving at Disney

Joe Roth quickly assembled significant financing for Revolution Studios, one of the few truly powerful independent companies to be founded in a time when money was becoming increasingly hard to find in the entertainment business. Eisner had predicted that he would vanish off the Hollywood radar as soon as he left Disney. It was with no small satisfaction, therefore, that Roth announced in February 2000 that the world's biggest female star, Julia Roberts, was abandoning an expiring deal with Disney to follow him to his new company. "Basically, wherever Joe goes, I go," Roberts declared. Not only did she sign a multiyear deal with Roth, she asked him to direct her in a film. While Roth stepped behind the camera to direct *America's Sweethearts*, speculation continued that he would eventually become chairman of Sony's film studio. Roth also made a deal with Bruce Willis, who had starred in Disney's megahit *The Sixth Sense*.

Patrick Naughton, the Internet executive who was downloading images of child pornography on his computer and who arranged a rendezvous with an FBI agent masquerading as a thirteen-year-old girl, was convicted in March 2000 of crossing state lines to have sex with a minor. In an extraordinary arrangement with prosecutors, he escaped serving jail time because he developed several computer programs to help the FBI track down other sex offenders prowling the Internet. He was sentenced to nine months of home detention, five years of probation, and a $20,000 fine. He continued to deny that he was a sexual predator, but said, "[The] evidene being what it was, this is where we ended up."

Judson Green, the chairman of the theme parks and a nineteen-year veteran at the company, resigned in April 2000. Green's division had shown the most consistent success during Disney's difficult years. But he had been eclipsed by rising executive Paul Pressler, who was named president of the theme-park division in 1998. And he was said to have become frustrated with Eisner, whom he considered to be impulsive and manipulative.

Sandy Litvack resigned in October 2000. Litvack had suffered some more high-profile losses in court before he departed. There was the litigation involving GoTo.com, and more. In April, a jury ruled that Disney had no right to deny $2.8 million in benefits to executive Robert Jahn, an executive then dying of AIDS. Litvack testified in the trial that Jahn had admitted taking payoffs from vendors who made movie trailers and television ads for the studio. But the jury said Litvack should have gotten a signed confession. Jahn had died in May 1994.

And in August, a Florida jury socked Disney for $240 million, finding that the company stole the idea for Disney's Wide World of Sports complex near Orlando from a former baseball umpire and his partner, an architect. The two had shown Disney plans and a model of such an attraction in 1987. Disney had denied the allegation. Louis Meisinger, Disney's executive vice president and general counsel, said the sports complex was "independently created by Walt Disney employees" and that the verdict "was driven by [an] appeal to the jury's prejudices against corporations and business in general." Disney is appealing the decision.

When Litvack resigned, it was not perceived to be as a result of any loss of confidence relating to these court cases. Rather, Litvack was said to have been restless for some time, while Eisner was believed to have prevailed on Litvack to stay until the company started showing some better results (as it did by October)—when the departure of yet another high-level executive might not alarm investors. Given Iger's ascent, there was no hope that Litvack might ever rise to second in command. And a Disney executive said Litvack had grown tired of the game. "Bob is the future; he's not," that executive said. "Why fight it? It's a tough business and a tough company and you've got to be on your game every minute."

In an interview at the time, Litvack reflected on his relationship with Eisner. "Michael can sit and create and react to creative thoughts in a nanosecond," he said. "He's also charismatic—very charismatic. . . . Those are his skills. I am definitely more deliberative than Michael. . . . I brought a deliberate approach and I would restrain, at times, his impulses."

Litvack also indulged in some musings over the Katzenberg trial. "I wish [that] had come out differently," he said. "We all—certainly Disney and Michael, and Jeffrey to a lesser extent—sustained a lot of pain in that one. . . . I wish that damn thing had been handled by both sides quicker and easier and without the cost to everybody."

But Litvack still didn't think Disney could have done anything different. "In my judgment—and I think it was a failure on both sides—the thing could not have been reasonably resolved . . . until we were able to make some headway in the trial," he said. (In the second phase of a two-part trial,

Disney was able to chip away at some of Katzenberg's projections about the company's future profits. Those estimates were key to the amount of money that the former studio chief was owed.)

Pressed on the company's decision to go through a public and sometimes embarrassing trial despite an earlier agreement to pay Katzenberg a minimum of $117 million, Litvack said the decision was justified by circumstances that he declined to discuss in depth. "You can either believe that we are total fools, that the collective IQ is forty, or you can believe that there's something more that you're not seeing," he insisted.

He declined to elaborate.

SOURCE NOTES

MICHAEL EISNER DECLINED to cooperate in the reporting of this book, but the author has interviewed him numerous times since 1986 and discussed with him many of the developments described herein. Those conversations, as well as his many public statements and his autobiography, *Work in Progress*, have helped provide his perspective on events. Many others—notably Jeffrey Katzenberg—agreed to be interviewed but in no way authorized this book. And some sources who insisted on anonymity are, of course, identified neither in the text nor below.

Otherwise, *The Keys to the Kingdom* is based on hundreds of interviews. Several books were extremely helpful, including Ron Grover's *The Disney Touch*, John Taylor's *Storming the Magic Kingdom*, and Charles Fleming's *High Concept*. *The Hollywood Reporter Book of Box Office Hits* was the source of annual box-office rankings. AC Nielsen EDI provided many of the box-office grosses. It should be noted that Bert Fields briefly represented the author in 1999. The following list includes principal sources on a chapter-by-chapter basis. AI indicates material from author interviews.

PROLOGUE

AI: Michael Hoover, Bob Daly.
Corie Brown, "The Third Man," *Premiere*, November 1994.

1: POOR LITTLE RICH BOY

AI: Alfred Hare, Terry Eakin, Susan Baerwald, Patrick Hart, William Brasmer, Barbara Eberhardt, Alan Shevlo, Al Bonney, Fred Silverman.
"Their Silver Wedding," *Red Bank Register*, January 18, 1911.
"Thousands at Funeral," *Red Bank Register*, January 14, 1925.
"Sigmund Eisner's Will," *Red Bank Register*, January 28, 1925.
Helen C. Phillips, *Red Bank on the Navesink* (Caesarea Press, 1977).

2: ENTER THE DRAGON

AI: Leonard Goldberg, Barry Diller, Terry Melcher, Martin Starger, Dick Zimbert, Brandon Stoddard, Gary Pudney, Roy Huggins, Frank Yablans, Fred Silverman, Martin Davis.
Andrew Tobias, "The Apprenticeship of Frank Yablans," *New York*, September 23, 1974.
Tony Schwartz, "Hollywood's Hottest Stars," *New York*, July 30, 1984.
Kevin Sessums, "Barry Diller Interview," *Playboy*, July 1989.
Huntington Williams, *Beyond Control—ABC and the Fate of the Networks* (Atheneum, 1989).

Leonard Goldenson with Marvin Wolf, *Beating the Odds—The Untold Story Behind the Rise of ABC: The Stars, Struggles, and Egos That Transformed Network Television* (Charles Scribner's Sons, 1991).

George Mair, *The Barry Diller Story: The Life and Times of America's Greatest Entertainment Mogul* (John Wiley & Sons, 1997).

John Huey, Joe McGowan, and Therese Eiben, "Eisner Explains Everything," *Fortune*, April 17, 1995.

3: HAPPY DAYS

AI: Lee Wedemeyer, Martin Starger, Fred Pierce, Tom Miller, Garry Marshall, Leonard Goldberg, Marcy Carsey, David Geffen.

Sterling Quinlan, *Inside ABC: American Broadcasting Company's Rise to Power* (Hastings House, 1979).

Goldenson and Wolf, *Beating the Odds*, op. cit.

Joe Flower, *Prince of the Magic Kingdom* (John Wiley & Sons, 1991).

4: REVERSAL OF FORTUNE

AI: Barry Diller, Lee Wedemeyer, Leonard Goldberg, Pat McQueeny, Garry Marshall, Richard Sylbert, Allan Carr, John Avildsen, Art Linson, Warren Beatty, Frank Mancuso, Jeff Berg.

Garry Marshall, *Wake Me When It's Funny* (Adams Media Corp., 1995).

Mair, *The Barry Diller Story*, op cit.

John Douglas Eames, *The Paramount Story* (Crown Publishers, 1985).

David Blum, "Odd Man In," *Vanity Fair*, July 1983.

Lee Margulies, "The *Laverne & Shirley* Feud," *TV Guide*, August 28, 1982.

Charles Champlain, "What to Do for an Encore," *Los Angeles Times*, July 7, 1978.

5: SQUIRT

AI: Barry Diller, Jeffrey Katzenberg, Sid Davidoff, Craig Baumgarten, Richard Aurelio, Donny Evans.

6: THE GOLDEN RETRIEVER

AI: Barry Diller, Jeffrey Katzenberg, Martin Starger, Rich Frank, Leonard Nimoy, Harve Bennett.

William Shatner with Chris Kreski, *Star Trek Movie Memories* (HarperCollins, 1994).

Leonard Nimoy, *I Am Spock* (Hyperion, 1995).

Dawn Steel, *They Can Kill You but They Can't Eat You* (Pocket Books, 1993).

Aljean Harmetz, "Who Makes Disney Run?," *New York Times Magazine*, February 7, 1988.

7: THE KILLER DILLERS

AI: Tom Pollock, Charlie Webber, Barry Diller, Dick Zimbert, Frank Marshall, Lee Wedemeyer, Jim Zucker, Susan Baerwald, Garry Marshall, Richard Fischoff, Rich Frank, Dick Sylbert, David Kirkpatrick, Warren Beatty.

Steel, *They Can Kill You*, op. cit.

Aljean Harmetz, "Diller: Taking Risks Is What I Do for a Living," *Los Angeles Herald Examiner*, June 10, 1982.

Variety, June 9, 1982.

8: HIGH CONCEPT

AI: Don Simpson, Dick Zimbert, Leonard Nimoy, Craig Baumgarten, Lee Wedemeyer, Larry Mark, David Kirkpatrick, Walter Hill, Jeff Berg.
Steel, *They Can Kill You*, op. cit.
Charles Fleming, *High Concept* (Doubleday, 1998).
John Gregory Dunne, "Bully Boy," *New Yorker*, February 5, 1996.
Ellen Farley, "A New Kind of Family Connection," *Los Angeles Times*, August 19, 1979.
Peter Biskind, "Good Night, Dark Prince," *Premiere*, April 1996.
David Ansen, "Extraordinary People," *Newsweek*, November 21, 1983.

9: DEATH OF A MOGUL

AI: Martin Davis, Barry Diller, Jeffrey Katzenberg, Rich Frank, Don Simpson.
Tony Schwartz, "Hollywood's Hottest Stars," *New York*, July 30, 1984.
Jesse Kornbluth, "Why Hollywood Hates Martin Davis," *Vanity Fair*, May 1991.
Bryan Burrough, "The Siege of Paramount," *Vanity Fair*, February 1994.
Judith Miller, "G. & W. and SEC Sign Agreement Settling Suit," *New York Times*, October 29, 1981.
"G & W's Charges over SEC Investigation of Company Are Thrown Out by Judge," *Wall Street Journal*, July 24, 1981.
Sandra Salmans, "Barry Diller's Latest Starring Role," *New York Times*, August 28, 1983.

10: RISKY BUSINESS

AI: Vince Jones, Terry Semel, James Garner, Tom Pollock, John Calley, Herbert Allen, Roland Betts, Rick Ridgeway.
Dick Bass and Frank Wells with Rick Ridgeway, *Seven Summits* (Warner Books, 1986).
John Taylor, *Storming the Magic Kingdom* (Knopf, 1987).
Allison Moir, "The 6⅞ Summits of Frank Wells," *Forbes FYI*, September 30, 1991.
Marilyn Wellemeyer, "Executives on the Mountaintop," *Fortune*, May 16, 1983.
John Huey, "Secrets of Great Second Bananas," *Fortune*, May 6, 1991.
Corie Brown, "The Third Man," *Premiere*, November 1994.
Connie Bruck, *Master of the Game* (Simon & Schuster, 1994).

11: THE EIGHTH SUMMIT

Taylor, *Storming the Magic Kingdom*, op. cit.
Flower, *Prince of the Magic Kingdom*, op. cit.
Variety, April 11–17, 1994.
Myron Magnet, "No More Mickey Mouse at Disney," *Fortune*, December 10, 1984.
Michael Eisner, interview by Charlie Rose, *Charlie Rose*, September 24, 1997.
"The Hottest Game in Hollywood," *Los Angeles Times*, September 25, 1984.

12: A RAVENOUS RAT?

AI: Dick Cook, Pete Clark, Dave Fink, Pat Scanlon, Rusty Lemorande, Sid Sheinberg.
Tom Nicholson with Peter MacAlevey, "Saving the Magic Kingdom," *Newsweek*, October 8, 1984.
Aljean Harmetz, "Disney Hopes Eisner Can Wake Sleeping Beauty," *New York Times*, October 17, 1984.

13: HITS AND MISSES

AI: Dave Fink, Pat Scanlon, Roland Betts, Tom Bernstein, Jane Rosenthal, David Hoberman, Paul Mazursky, David Zucker, Dean Valentine, Paul Junger Witt, Rich Frank, Marty Katz, Harve Bennett.
Laura Jereski, "So You Want to Be in Pictures," *Forbes*, March 21, 1988.
New York Times Magazine, February 7, 1988, op. cit.
Julie Salamon, "Jeffrey Katzenberg: Disney's New Mogul," *Wall Street Journal*, May 12, 1987.

14: "A WHIFF OF THE MOUSE"

AI: Pete Clark, Roland Betts, Tom Bernstein, Don Simpson, Pat Scanlon, Dave Fink, Rick Ridgeway, Michael Rosenfeld, Jack Rapke, Jeffrey Katzenberg, Marty Katz, Jane Rosenthal.

15: WINNING UGLY

AI: Robert Cort, Jane Rosenthal, Mark Johnson, Marty Kaplan, Marty Katz, Ron Clements.
Aljean Harmetz, "Who Makes Disney Run?" *New York Times Magazine*, February 7, 1988.
Salamon, "Jeffrey Katzenberg: Disney's New Mogul."
Barry Singer, "Just Two Animated Characters Indeed," *New York Times*, October 4, 1998.

16: TOONTOWN

AI: Robert Zemeckis.
Kim Masters, "Bunny Hop," *Premiere*, July 1988.

17: STAR WARS

AI: Bernie Brillstein, Marty Kaplan, Laura Ziskin, Dick Sylbert.
Ron Grover, *The Disney Touch* (Irwin Professional Publishing, 1997).

18: ONE FALSE MOVE

AI: Laura Ziskin, Jeffrey Katzenberg, Roland Betts, Dick Sylbert.
Peter Boyer, "Katzenberg's Seven-Year Itch," *Vanity Fair*, November 1991.
John H. Richardson, "Star-Crossed by Love," *Premiere*, February 1991.
John H. Richardson, "California Suite," *Premiere*, August 1991.
Kim Masters, "The Mermaid and the Mandrill," *Premiere*, November 1991.

19: MOUSCHWITZ

AI: Jeffrey Katzenberg, Randall Kleiser, David Hoberman, Marty Katz.
Judy Brennan, "My Two Sons," *Premiere*, April 1994.
Boyer, "Katzenberg's Seven-Year Itch."
Victor Zonana, "Disney Apologizes, Receives Limited Rights to Muppets," *Wall Street Journal*, May 1, 1991.
Charles Fleming and Jennifer Pendleton, "Henson Charges Disney with Muppet-Mugging," *Variety*, April 22, 1991.
Rita Koselka, "Mickey's Midlife Crisis," *Forbes*, May 13, 1991.

Alan Citron and Nina Easton, "Disney Adjusts to Fallibility," *Los Angeles Times*, May 24, 1991.

Alan Citron and Nina Easton, "Magic Kingdom Battens Down the Budget Amid Recession," *Los Angeles Times*, May 28, 1991.

Joe Nocera, "For Every Bruce Willis, There Is Always Another Bruce Willis," *GQ*, October 1991.

20: BEAUTY AND THE DEBACLE

AI: Ron Clements, Jeffrey Katzenberg, Dave Fink.

Peter H. King, "Michael Spells It M-o-n-e-y," *Los Angeles Times*, December 9, 1992.

James Flanigan, "Who Cheers Eisner's Payout? Disney Shareholders," *Los Angeles Times*, December 8, 1992.

Allan Sloan, "Eisner Joins Select Group with $197-Million Option," *Los Angeles Times*, December 6, 1992.

New Republic, December 28, 1992.

21: THE CRASH

AI: David Vogel, Jeffrey Katzenberg, Dave Fink, Pat Scanlon, Roland Betts, Michael Hoover.

Jolie Solomon, "Mickey's Trip to Trouble," *Newsweek*, February 14, 1994.

Kurt Eichenwald, "Euro Disney Faces More Bad News," *New York Times*, November 16, 1992.

Bill Echikson, "Disney's Rough Ride in France," *Fortune*, March 23, 1992.

Peter Gumbel and Richard Turner, "Fans Like Euro Disney but Its Parent's Goofs Weigh the Park Down," *Wall Street Journal*, March 10, 1994.

James Bates, "No Magic Fix for Huge Losses at Euro Disney," *Los Angeles Times*, July 9, 1993.

Alan Citron, "Mighty Disney Learns to Duck," *Los Angeles Times*, August 24, 1993.

22: CHEST PAINS

AI: Jeffrey Katzenberg, Rich Turner.

Michael Eisner, interview by Charlie Rose, op. cit.

James Bates, "Eisner Earns $203 Million but No Bonus," *Los Angeles Times*, January 4, 1994.

Ken Auletta, "The Human Factor," *New Yorker*, September 26, 1994.

Elise O'Shaughnessy, "The New Establishment," *Vanity Fair*, October 1994.

Claudia Eller and Alan Citron, "Angst at Disney's World," *Los Angeles Times*, July 24, 1994.

Richard Turner, "Disney's 'Volume' Strategy Takes Toll as Mestres Leaves Hollywood Pictures," *Wall Street Journal*, May 16, 1994.

Richard Turner, "Disney, Using Cash and Claw, Stays King of Animated Movies," *Wall Street Journal*, May 16, 1994.

"Looking for Mr. Right," *Newsweek*, August 1, 1994.

Kevin Fedarko, "Mirror, Mirror, on the Wall . . ." *Time*, August 1, 1994.

Bernard Weinraub, "Pressure Growing at Disney," *New York Times*, July 18, 1994.

Alan Citron, "Eisner Situation Raises Questions of Firm's No. 2s," *Los Angeles Times*, July 19, 1994.

Joann S. Lublin, "Eisner's Surgery Underscores the Lack of Succession Planning at Many Firms," *Wall Street Journal*, July 19, 1994.

Army Archerd, "Just for Variety," *Variety*, July 29, 1994.

23: A BITTER DIVORCE

AI: Pat Scanlon, John Dryer.

Auletter, "The Human Factor," op. cit.

Bernard Weinraub with Geraldine Fabrikant, "Now Playing: Disney in Turmoil," *New York Times*, September 23, 1994.

24: BIG DREAMS

AI: Rich Frank, Dean Valentine.

Robert Sam Anson, "Heave-ho, Heave-ho! Mike Eisner Drives TV Head Out of His Grumpy Kingdom," *New York Observer*, March 27, 1995.

Thomas R. King and John Lippman, "Stalwart Disney Is Roiled by Defections," *Wall Street Journal*, March 13, 1995.

Bernard Weinraub, "Clouds over Disneyland," *New York Times*, April 9, 1995.

Huey, McGowan, and Eiben, "Eisner Explains Everything."

Katy Harris, "The Loneliest Man in the Kingdom," *Los Angeles Times Magazine*, March 26, 1995.

Peter Biskind, "Win, Lose—but Draw," *Premiere*, July 1995.

Lisa Gubernick, "We Will Not Dilute," *Forbes*, February 27, 1995.

Bernard Weinraub, "Attack of the Killer Mogul," *Playboy*, 1995.

Bernard Weinraub, "Three Hollywood Giants Team Up to Create Major Movie Studio," *New York Times*, October 13, 1994.

Bernard Weinraub and Geraldine Fabrikant, "A Hollywood Recipe: Vision, Wealth, Ego," *New York Times*, October 16, 1994.

25: THE DOMINOES FALL

AI: Sid Sheinberg, Edgar Bronfman.

Geraldine Fabrikant with Andrew Pollack, "MCA's Impatience with Wary Parent," *New York Times*, November 4, 1994.

Richard Turner, "Matsushita Appears to Tackle Dispute with MCA Officials by Hiring Advisors," *Wall Street Journal*, November 18, 1994.

Geraldine Fabrikant, "Wasserman May Leave If Ovitz Joins MCA," *New York Times*, May 30, 1995.

Geraldine Fabrikant, "Walt Disney to Acquire ABC in $19 Billion Deal to Build a Giant for Entertainment," *New York Times*, August 1, 1995.

Floyd Norris, "Disney's Stock Defies Usual Rules of the Game," *New York Times*, August 1, 1995.

Bernard Weinraub, "Don't Say No to Jeffrey," *New York Times Magazine*, June 30, 1996.

Thomas King, "Eisner, Katzenberg May End Feud, Saving DreamWorks, Cap Cities Venture," *Wall Street Journal*, August 7, 1995.

Claudia Eller, "Time for Eisner to Make Nicey-Nice," *Los Angeles Times*, August 8, 1995.

Ken Auletta, "Awesome," *New Yorker*, August 14, 1995.

Nancy Gibbs, "Easy As ABC," *Time*, August 14, 1995.

Richard Turner, "Hi-Ya!," *New York*, August 14, 1995.

26: SUPERMAN STUMBLES

AI: Sid Sheinberg, Edgar Bronfman.

Robert Slater, *Ovitz* (McGraw-Hill, 1997).

27: A PLATINUM PARACHUTE

AI: Michael Ovitz, Jeffrey Katzenberg.
Slater, *Ovitz.*
Bryan Burrough and Kim Mooter, "The Mouse Trap," *Vanity Fair,* December 1996.
A. M. Rosenthal, "Hardtack for the Journey," *New York Times,* December 17, 1997.
James Bates and Claudia Eller, "Ovitz to Leave Disney After Rocky Year as President," *Los Angeles Times,* December 13, 1996.
Holman W. Jenkins Jr., "Beavis and Butt-head Do the Disney Shareholders," *Wall Street Journal,* January 7, 1997.
Nikki Finke, "Poof! Mike Ovitz, from Sorcerer to Schmo," *New York Observer,* September 23, 1996.
James Bates, "Disney's Eisner Gets Contract Extension Fit for a Lion King," *Los Angeles Times,* January 10, 1997.
Bruce Orwall and Joann S. Lublin, "If a Company Prospers, Should Its Directors Behave by the Book?," *Wall Street Journal,* February 24, 1997.
Bruce Orwall and Joann S. Lublin, "Disney Chief's Stock Options Exercise Irks Some, but Street Remains Calm," *Wall Street Journal,* December 5, 1997.
Maureen Dowd, "Stocks and Socks," *New York Times,* February 27, 1997.
Claudia Eller, "Awful Truth," *Los Angeles Times,* February 28, 1997.

28: SQUARING OFF

AI: Patricia Glaser, Jeffrey Katzenberg, Bert Fields, Ted Harbert, Janet Sphrintz.
Nikki Finke, "Curtain Up on Dirty Disney Trial: Geffen, Spielberg May Take Stand," *New York Observer,* November 10, 1997.
Associated Press, "Disney Sees Profit from $600 Million TV Deal with National Hockey League." Published by the *Wall Street Journal,* August 25, 1998.
Bruce Orwall, "After Several Years of Good Times, Theme Parks Find Troubleland," *Wall Street Journal,* September 21, 1998.
Lawrie Mifflin, "A Hit from the 70s Is Fading in the 90s," *Wall Street Journal,* September 21, 1998.
Daniel Machcalaba and Bruce Orwall, "Slow Boat: Disney's Perfectionism Frustrates Cruise-Ship Contractors," *Wall Street Journal,* June 22, 1998.
Paul Lieberman, "Disney Opens Portal to Internet," *Los Angeles Times,* January 13, 1999.
Claudia Eller, "Disney Shifting Its Movie Focus to Family Fare," *Los Angeles Times,* February 2, 1999.
Leslie Helm and James Bates, "'Full Power' of Disney on Net Project, Eisner Says," *Los Angeles Times,* February 24, 1999.
Chris Petrikin, "In Nomads Land," *Variety,* June 29, 1999.

29: *KATZ V. MOUSE*

Holman W. Jenkins Jr., "Mouse Gets a Whiff of Waterloo," *Wall Street Journal,* May 19, 1999.

30: "THAT DARK PERSON"

Martin Peers, "Net Setbacks Put Media Companies in a Spin," *Variety,* April 13, 1999.
Michael Hiltzik, "Disney Picks ABC Chief to Lead Internet Group," *Los Angeles Times,* September 9, 1999.
"Disney Becomes Poacher's Paradise for Soaring Internet Start-up Firms," *Wall Street Journal,* June 9, 1999.
Marc Gunther, "Eisner's Mouse Trap," *Fortune,* September 6, 1999.

Brian Lowry, "'NYPD Blue' Likely to Lose Its Tuesday Night ABC Slot," *Los Angeles Times*, October 14, 1999.

Brian Lowry, "Disney Wondering If It's a 'Wonderful World' After All," *Los Angeles Times*, October 13, 1999.

Jim Rutenberg, "Eisner Squeezes ABC—Adds Commercials to Prime-time Lineup," *New York Observer*, September 9, 1999.

Michael Wolff, "Eisner Un-Moused," *New York*, July 12, 1999.

Geraldine Fabrikant, "Hey There! Hi There! It's a New Michael Eisner," *New York Times*, August 14, 1999.

Mark Landler, "Mickey and Minnie Go to Hong Kong," *New York Times*, November 3, 1999.

ACKNOWLEDGMENTS

I WOULD LIKE to thank the many people who made themselves available for interviews—some of whom asked not to be identified by name—and acknowledge the wonderful work of the journalists mentioned in the source notes. Others whose contributions have been invaluable include: Henry Ferris, a devoted editor; Kris Dahl, a great agent who worked it all out; and Graydon Carter, who offered inspiration and the opportunity to cover many of the events depicted in this book. My gratitude also to Kristine Kwon for her excellent research.

Most of all, I want to thank the wonderful Wine family—Nancy, Brian, Devin, and Tiffany—who gave me the best possible reason to write a book. Special thanks also to my long-suffering husband, Gary Simson, and to my family, friends, and colleagues—Karen Spar, Vicky Stamas, Sarah Connick, Bruce Bibby, Elaine Lafferty, Deborah Graham, Nancy Griffin, and Rachel Abramowitz—all of whom kindly listened to a lot of complaining.

INDEX